THE ELEMENTS OF EVIDENCE

OF EVIDENCE

Fourth Edition

■ ■ ■

Richard D. Friedman

Alene and Allan F. Smith Professor of Law
University of Michigan Law School

AMERICAN CASEBOOK SERIES®

WEST
ACADEMIC
PUBLISHING

PREFACE

I am delighted to present the fourth edition of *The Elements of Evidence*. As with the prior editions, my aim has been to present a relatively compact explanation of basic evidentiary principles together with a set of problems designed to facilitate class discussion. The book retains the basic format of prior editions, and though it has grown somewhat it remains relatively slender as law textbooks go. This should make it relatively easy for students to prepare for class. I have included references to the McCormick and Mueller & Kirkpatrick treatises for students who want to do some additional background reading. I believe, however, that most students should be able to prepare for class by reading the assigned pages in this book and, where appropriate, in a Federal Rules of Evidence pamphlet, without the need to consult a treatise, hornbook, or commercial outline on a regular basis. With respect to the Federal Rules: Joshua Deahl and I have prepared a rulebook, *Federal Rules of Evidence: Text and History* (2015), that presents the Rules and the history behind them in a way that is easy to follow.

The relative brevity of this book reflects my belief that the basic principles of evidence law can be learned in a four-credit course. At the same time, activity in this field for more than three decade has persuaded me that the law of evidence can continue to be challenging for a lifetime. I have learned a great deal writing this edition, as I did with the first three, but I continue to be deeply impressed with how much I still have to learn.

I have, of course, updated the book throughout to reflect developments over the dozen years since the third edition was published. In addition, I have made two significant organizational changes.

The larger of these concerns the unit on hearsay and confrontation. The third edition was near publication when the Supreme Court issued its momentous decision in *Crawford v. Washington*, 541 U.S. 36 (2004), transforming the law governing the Confrontation Clause of the Sixth Amendment to the United States Constitution. I was able to make some changes to take the decision into account, but the basic framework of the materials on hearsay and confrontation largely followed traditional lines—first working through the definition of hearsay, then spending most of the time marching through the principal hearsay exceptions, and working in references to the confrontation right along the way. *Crawford* and the developments since it have solidified my view that this approach is far from optimal. Much of hearsay law appears bewildering and even bizarre to students, and the many exceptions to the exclusionary rule seem to come in a flood of one unconnected thing after another.

And so in this edition, I have taken a far different approach, organizing the presentation by concepts underlying what I call the confrontation principle—the principle that a witness should testify face to face with an adverse party, at trial if reasonably possible, under oath and subject to cross-examination. Students understand this principle and the force behind it. It leads to several basic questions that frame the discussion: Is the statement being offered for the truth of what it asserts? Is it testimonial in nature? Is the witness who made the statement subject to the possibility of cross-examination at trial? If not, is the witness unavailable, and was there an earlier opportunity for adverse examination? Did the adverse party forfeit the objection by engaging in wrongful conduct that rendered the witness unavailable? Discussion of these questions gives students a good grounding in the doctrine of the Confrontation Clause, but more broadly it naturally leads to examination, and helps make sense, of much of hearsay doctrine. I have included in the unit a rather comprehensive examination of the doctrine of admissions (a term I still prefer for several reasons to "statements by a party"), and then a relatively brief run-through of the most significant hearsay exceptions. The latter can be done efficiently, because much of the ground has already been covered in the main presentation. All told, the unit is somewhat shorter than its predecessor in the third edition.

The second significant organizational is the creation of a new chapter on child observers. This brings together material on several questions— when a child is a competent witness, how child testimony should be taken, and whether very young children should have to testify in formal proceedings or be deemed to be witnesses at all. This new Chapter 20, coming near the end of the book, can offer a chance to bring to bear much of the material that students have learned throughout the course and apply it to a set of problems that is particularly important and difficult.

I will incorporate by reference the many expressions of gratitude I made in the prefaces to prior editions and will add a few. During virtually the entirety of the time that I have been working on this edition, I have had the capable and cheerful assistance of Margaret Klocinski. She has saved me from many errors, large and small. Andrew Mackie-Mason did a wonderful and thorough job helping me update what is now Chapter 21. Avery Johnson and Dorian Geisler pitched in ably near the end and helped me update other spots as well.

Life remains exciting for my wife Joanna and me. The number of editions now exceeds the number of our children, but all three of the latter—Rebecca, Daniel, and Julia—are a source of love, joy, and pride to us.

I dedicated the first two editions of this book to my parents, with love, admiration, and gratitude. A more complex dedication was necessary for the third edition, because my father died on the verge of press time. My mother, too, has since passed away. And so a simpler dedication is once again possible. I dedicate this edition to the blessed memory of both my parents. Both lived remarkably long and full lives that in many ways exemplified the American dream. My siblings and I, and our children, are the constant and enduring beneficiaries of their love, wisdom, and values.

RICHARD D. FRIEDMAN

Ann Arbor, Michigan
September 2016

SUMMARY OF CONTENTS

TABLE OF CONTENTS

PART III. OTHER EXCLUSIONARY RULES

PART IV. FURTHER STRUCTURAL AND
PROCEDURAL CONSIDERATIONS

TABLE OF CASES

TABLE OF RULES

TABLE OF AUTHORITIES

THE ELEMENTS OF EVIDENCE

OF EVIDENCE

Fourth Edition

CHAPTER 1

INTRODUCTION

■ ■ ■

A. SOME PRELIMINARY QUESTIONS

1. WHAT IS THIS COURSE ALL ABOUT?

You may not have thought about it this way, but your Civil Procedure course probably resembled a donut, with trial as the hole in the middle: You studied a good deal about what happened before trial, and what the courts do about the results of the trial, but relatively little about what actually happens at trial. This course fills in the hole in the donut—or, if you prefer a meteorological metaphor to a confectionery one, it focuses on the eye of the litigation storm. The course is traditionally called Evidence, but perhaps it should be called more broadly Trial Procedure. This book will survey the procedural rules and practices by which trials are conducted, from the selection of the jury to the issuance of a verdict. We will discuss how evidence gets created and preserved before trial, and how it gets evaluated after trial, but our focus will be on the trial itself.

The heart of the course, as its name suggests, is the law of evidence. That does not mean only the rules concerning whether a given piece of information is admissible or not, but also such questions as: What happens if there is no evidence on a given point? How much evidence, if any, must a party introduce to prevent a court from ruling against it on a factual proposition? What are the roles of the judge and the jury in evaluating the evidence?

2. WHAT DOES THE COURSE AIM TO ACHIEVE?

That seems pretty obvious: The course aims to give you a better understanding of how trials are conducted and, in particular, a good grasp of the law of evidence. What may be less obvious are two things that the course will *not* try to do:

The course will not try to prepare you for the bar exam. This book does not focus on the law of any particular state. It does concentrate to a great extent on the Federal Rules of Evidence, which have been adopted more or less closely by most of the states. Nevertheless, this is not a book on the Federal Rules. The Rules are not applicable in every type of

1

proceeding or in every jurisdiction. Nor, where applicable, do the Rules address every evidentiary question, nor are they completely dispositive even when they do. Nor are they uniformly commendable or assuredly enduring. Indeed, the law of evidence has shown constant growth and evolution, and you may be sure that change will continue unabated during your professional lifetime. Hence, as in most law school courses, this one will explore not only what the law is at present, but why it is that way, and what it should or is likely to become. Taking this course may incidentally make it a little easier to prepare for the bar, but that's not a good enough reason to take the course. To get really ready for the bar exam, it's a good idea to take a bar review course, or at least study books designed to prepare you for the exam

The course will not try to teach you what you can better learn in practice or in a clinical program. If you participate in a clinical program after you complete this course, you will probably report to your friends that you "learned more about evidence in two weeks in the clinic than in a whole semester in class." And in a sense that will be true. Although this course has more of the feel of the courtroom than most law school classes, and it offers the opportunity for some courtroom-type exercises, it cannot hope to duplicate the reality of the courtroom. In this class, you will not have to deal with an irascible or an irrational judge; you will not have to worry about how your objections will make you appear before the jury; you will not, except occasionally, be expected to phrase a well-considered objection to a question that has not even been completed; you will not have to spend money to procure witnesses; you will not have to spend weeks or months preparing the presentation of a single case; and you will not have to worry about the stakes of the game—you have no client to represent in this course, and it is highly unlikely that your professional standing will soar or crash based on your performance in class.

Practical factors such as these will not be ignored; they will be a significant part of our consideration of many problems. But, in keeping with the doctrine of comparative advantage, our focus will be on what can best be done in a classroom course, and not as easily in a clinic or in practice: gaining a broad, structural understanding of the law of evidence (understanding not only particular rules but how they fit together), and intensively examining the underlying theory. Some of this may sometimes seem to you to be divorced from reality. But, as in so many areas of the law, having a feel for the underlying theory will give you a useful perspective on, and help you deal with, the mundane questions that are likely to arise in practice. It is not surprising that clinical professors often require that their students take, or have taken, a basic course in Evidence.

3. WHO SHOULD TAKE THIS COURSE?

This is certainly a good course for anybody who intends to be a litigator; indeed, if you decide that you don't like the subject matter of this course, you may want to reconsider that intention.

But even if you have no desire ever to enter a courtroom, this may be a good course for you to take, for at least three reasons. First, it is a classic law school course, offering a chance to develop and hone, in a wide variety of problems, the analytic skills that any good lawyer needs. Indeed, it is one of the best law school courses for this purpose, for at times it concentrates almost totally on developing reasoning skills that you will always find useful whatever you do, without the distraction of doctrinal details that you will forget within a week after the exam. Second, evidentiary issues concern a wide variety of social issues—such as racial attitudes, domestic violence, and child sexual abuse—that should be of importance to everyone. Third, even if your professional aim is to keep your clients out of court, it is helpful, and sometimes crucial, for you to have some idea of what goes on there. Consider this problem:

> ¶ 1.1: You have a general law practice with a concentration in commercial law. Your spouse practiced law for three years but now works for a foundation. Ted, a successful playwright and a good friend of your spouse, calls up one Saturday morning and asks to come visit you. As he sits down in your living room, he tells you and your spouse how, ten years ago, when he was hard up for cash, he agreed with his publisher, Splashy Publishing Co., to waive all his future royalties on his previous works in return for an immediate cash payment. Ted now believes the deal was one-sided in favor of Splashy and seeks to renegotiate it. Do you ask your spouse to leave the room?

4. WHAT KINDS OF MATERIALS WILL WE STUDY?

To answer this question requires a rather broad discussion of structural factors underlying the law of evidence and distinguishing it from courses in substantive law. Many law school courses are taught primarily with the use of appellate cases. There are advantages and disadvantages to this method. The disadvantages of the case method are comparatively greater with respect to evidence. Appellate cases have an important role in the law of evidence, as do the Constitution, statutes, and court-adopted rules. More than with many other subjects, however, the law of evidence is determined on the spot by trial judges. Why is this so? Consider the following hypothetical.

> Ted, from ¶ 1.1, has decided to sue his publisher, seeking a declaration that the royalty waiver deal is invalid and claiming that the publisher breached a fiduciary duty to him by

encouraging him to enter into it. To prove that the seventeen-year relationship between him and the publisher was a fiduciary one, he intends to rely on his own testimony narrating the history of the relationship, including various episodes and conversations, and on the testimony of other witnesses concerning the usual relationships between playwrights and publishers.

Now, compare the questions of substantive law—contract, agency, and the like—with those of evidence.

First, there are likely to be far *more* evidentiary questions. There may be several substantive questions—such as whether, given the facts as presented by Ted and by the publisher, respectively, the relationship was a fiduciary one and the contract was valid. But these will be few in comparison to the number of evidentiary questions. Every piece of evidence presented by either party poses a potential evidentiary question: Is it admissible? That might be especially so in a case like this, in which the parties will be disputing some long-ago events and will be offering proof about the relationships of persons who are not parties to this action. In most cases, the trial judge will get the relatively few substantive questions right, or at least close enough to right, the first time around—and if not, almost certainly the second time around. But it is rarely true that a trial judge decides all the evidentiary questions in the same way that an appellate court would. If an appellate court had to reverse whenever it disagreed with an evidentiary ruling, reversals would threaten to become almost automatic—and perpetual as well, because there would be new evidentiary questions arising on the retrial.

Second, the evidentiary questions usually must be answered much *faster* than the substantive ones. There is almost always time for the judge to reflect on the substantive questions. Suppose, for example, such questions arise in the context of a pretrial motion to dismiss the complaint for failure to state a claim on which relief may be granted or a motion for summary judgment. If the matter seems at all difficult, the court will usually reserve decision and do whatever research it thinks is necessary. Even if the issues arise at trial in the context of a motion for a directed verdict (or more formally, judgment as a matter of law granted before verdict), the court has the option of deferring decision until after the verdict and then, after due reflection, determining whether to grant judgment notwithstanding the verdict. With respect to evidentiary questions, by contrast, there is usually a far greater premium on speed. Some evidentiary questions are posed before trial—often, the court must decide whether evidence offered in opposition to a summary judgment motion would be admissible at trial, and sometimes a party anticipating that his adversary will offer a given item of evidence makes what is known as an *in limine* motion to exclude the evidence. But very frequently, the first time an evidentiary issue is raised is when the party resisting evidence stands up at trial, with a witness on the stand and right after a question has been posed, and says, "Objection!" Indeed, in many cases the objecting lawyer could not have raised the objection earlier, because the posing of the question was the first event giving notice of the problem. (Sometimes, indeed, it is the witness's answer that presents the problem; then, to be technically correct, the proper response of the opposing party is not to object but to move to strike the evidence.) Usually, it is necessary for the court to rule on the objection promptly. Sometimes, the court can reserve decision or take a recess to consider the issue. But, especially with a jury waiting, this is not usually practical. And once the judge makes up her mind, there usually isn't a very good chance for reconsideration. She might tell the jury, "I made a mistake in admitting that evidence, so please ignore it." But, rather obviously, that is not a very satisfactory solution.

Third, there may be more *useful precedent* on the substantive issues than on the evidentiary ones. Many writers and composers have litigated against agents and publishers, and so one might expect to find guidance on questions such as whether there is a fiduciary relationship between an author and a publisher.[1] Sometimes courts even articulate *per se* rules with respect to such questions. It is less likely that there will be such a rule for an evidentiary question, because such questions tend to be very fact-dependent, requiring a balancing of the costs and benefits of admitting the particular evidence in the context of the particular case. Moreover, even if a judge in a previous case faced a substantially identical evidentiary decision, the press of time likely prevented her from writing an opinion on it—and the same factor may well prevent the judge and the parties in this case from looking hard for such precedent.[2]

Fourth, assuming that there is a "right" answer to each type of question, a wrong decision on an evidentiary question is likely to be *less damaging* than a wrong decision on a substantive question. If the trial court makes a wrong decision on the substantive law, it will likely be, or appear plausibly to be, outcome-determinative. Thus, if the trial judge sent the case to the jury on instructions that were too generous to the plaintiff and the jury came back with a verdict for the plaintiff, presumably a judgment on that verdict should not stand. Accordingly, the

---

[1] *See, e.g.,* Van Valkenburgh, Nooger & Neville, Inc., v. Hayden Publishing Co., Inc., 33 A.D.2d 766, 766, 306 N.Y.S.2d 599, 600 (1st Dep't 1969), *aff'd,* 30 N.Y.2d 34, 330 N.Y.S.2d 329, 281 N.E.2d 142 (1972) (holding that trial court erred in finding fiduciary relationship between author and publisher), *cited approvingly in, e.g.,* Spinelli v. National Football League, 96 F.Supp.3d 81, 134 (S.D.N.Y. 2015).

[2] At the same time, we should recognize that the very difficulty of retrieving law and deciding evidentiary questions in a timely manner sometimes leads judges to adopt shorthand rules of thumb; in deciding a substantive law question, they may be more willing to adopt and apply more complex rules.

appellate court is going to be very careful. If the trial judge errs on one of the multitude of evidentiary questions presented by the case, however, it will probably not be outcome-determinative. Moreover, the importance of consistency across cases, which we hope appellate courts will preserve, is greater with respect to substantive issues than with respect to evidentiary issues. It is unacceptable if before one judge the rule of law is that the author-publisher relationship is *per se* a fiduciary one, and before another judge the same relationship is *per se* non-fiduciary. It is somewhat more tolerable, even though not ideal, if one judge tends to be tougher on evidentiary questions than another. A baseball analogy: Though baseball administrators may wish that whether a pitch was called a ball or strike did not depend on who was the umpire, we expect different umpires to have somewhat different strike zones, one's more generous to the pitcher than another's. But we expect them both to adhere to the same rules on what constitutes an out and what constitutes a run.

As this discussion suggests, trial judges are generally given wide discretion in making evidentiary decisions because it would be impractical to deny them that discretion. Thus, although losing parties frequently appeal on evidentiary grounds, it is very difficult in many contexts to get a reversal on such grounds. *See* FRE 103(a) (providing that "[a] party may claim error in a ruling to admit or exclude evidence only if the error affects a substantial right of the party" and (except in the case of "plain error") the issue was properly preserved).[3]

In short, a concentration on appellate opinions gives the wrong emphasis, and does not point the spotlight where the law is really made. The focus of this book will be on the trial setting. The actual texts of appellate opinions, even opinions of the United States Supreme Court, will have relatively little importance.

In this book you will find only occasional passages from judicial opinions, none of them more than a sentence or two long. Instead of appellate opinions, you will find many problems and questions, set principally in the context of preparation for trial or of the trial itself. The problems will probably form the basis of most of the discussion in class.

---

[3]   *See also* Margaret A. Berger, *When, If Ever, Does Evidentiary Error Constitute Reversible Error?*, 25 Loy. L.A. L. Rev. 893, 895 (1992) (concluding after an extensive review of federal appellate cases from 1988 to 1990 that "an evidentiary error alone is not very likely to induce an appellate court to term the error 'reversible' on the ground that the error affected a substantial right of a party"); David P. Leonard, *Appellate Review of Evidentiary Rulings*, 70 N.C. L. Rev. 1155 (1992) (reviewing all published federal appellate decisions from a 10–year period that addressed a party's assertion of error by the trial judge in applying FRE 608(b) or 611, and concluding that appellate courts give trial courts free rein in areas where they should not (such as Rule 608(b), which governs the use of specific acts to impeach a witness's credibility) as well as in areas where they should (such as Rule 611, governing the mode and order of interrogation of witnesses)).

Many of the problems are taken from actual cases, and many of those cases did reach an appellate court. Thus, after many of the problems, you will note a citation to a case or some other outside source. Many of the case citations include a brief description of how the court decided that particular case. If occasionally a problem piques your interest sufficiently to make you look the source up, that is all to the good. For the most part, however, your concern should not be with the logic of a particular court. Do not think that the citation of a case is meant to reflect an endorsement of the result reached by that particular court or the reasoning by which it got there. Indeed, many of the cases cited seem erroneous or wrong-headed. Your principal effort should be to explore the possible approaches that you might take to the problem posed if you were the trial judge or one of the trial lawyers.

You should not get the impression from this discussion that the trial judge's discretion on evidentiary matters is unbounded, or that evidentiary decisions are decided in a legal vacuum. There is a recognizable body of evidentiary doctrine to which *most* trial judges *usually* attempt to adhere *more or less* closely. One purpose of this book is to set out the basics—the elements—of this doctrine. It aims to give you a grasp on the overall structure of evidentiary law and in that context to explain and clarify various important issues and to give you a sense of their interrelation.

Evidentiary doctrine has several different sources. First, the considerations sketched above do not make appellate courts willing to give trial judges unlimited discretion on evidentiary questions. Many thousands of published appellate decisions have considered evidentiary questions, and some of those—enough to warrant attention from the trial judge—have in fact reversed trial courts on evidentiary grounds. The appellate courts are bound not only by precedent but by other sources of law, including the Constitution; as a general matter, evidentiary reversal is perhaps most plausible, and most justifiable, when the constitutional rights of a criminal defendant may be at stake. Trial courts also sometimes write opinions on evidentiary issues, and these, too, may have some precedential force.

Second, a considerable amount of structure has been given to the decisions by the treatise writers. Wigmore's treatise, first published in 1904, has historically been the most influential.[4] Recently, the Weinstein treatise has probably received the most attention in the federal courts. The McCormick book, first published in 1954 and revised six times since

---

[4] A successor treatise, *The New Wigmore: A Treatise on Evidence* is now in preparation, under my general editorship. Five volumes of the new treatise have been published—one by David P. Leonard on selected rules of limited admissibility, two by Edward Imwinkelried on privilege, one by David Kaye, David Bernstein, and Jennifer Mnookin on expert evidence, and one by Roger C. Park and Tom Lininger on impeachment and rehabilitation.

then, is an excellent briefer treatment; although it was written in part for students, it carries a good deal of authority in the courts. And there are other fine treatises as well. The one by Christopher B. Mueller & Laird C. Kirkpatrick, first published in 1995, is more closely oriented to the Federal Rules of Evidence than is the McCormick book, and it has also gained a substantial degree of recognition by the courts. Although this coursebook is designed to provide you (in conjunction with a rulebook containing the Federal Rules of Evidence and background material on them) with as much doctrinal explanation as you need for a good basic understanding of evidentiary law, you may feel a need to do some outside reading. Thus, this book will make frequent reference to, and suggest readings in, two of the treatises mentioned above, which are now commonly used by students, *McCormick on Evidence* (7th ed. 2013) and Mueller & Kirkpatrick's *Evidence* (5th ed. 2012).

Third, in recent years, evidentiary law has been further structured and clarified in many jurisdictions by codification. In 1942, the American Law Institute published a Model Code of Evidence, but it was never adopted by any state. The Uniform Rules of Evidence, proposed in 1953 and endorsed by the American Bar Association, fared slightly better. They were adopted in Kansas, as well as the Panama Canal Zone and the American Virgin Islands, and formed the basis for codifications, with substantial revisions, in New Jersey, Utah, and most importantly, California. In 1965, the same year that California adopted its Evidence Code, the codification movement received an even greater boost when an Advisory Committee was created, pursuant to the Rules Enabling Act, to draft Federal Rules of Evidence (FRE). After a lengthy and sometimes contentious drafting process, the Supreme Court promulgated a set of rules in 1972.[5] Congress, however, passed a statute preventing the Rules from taking effect, so that it could review and amend them. After making some important revisions, Congress incorporated the Rules in a statute enacted in 1975. The FRE have been revised from time to time.[6]

---

[5] A 1969 preliminary draft was released to the public for comment. A revised draft was submitted to the Court in 1970, but the Court returned it for further public comment. The draft was released to the public in 1971 and, after further revision, submitted to the Court the next year.

[6] The Federal Rules of Evidence, like the Federal Rules of Civil Procedure and other codifications of federal procedural rules, are revised under a procedure partially prescribed by, and set up pursuant to, 28 U.S.C. §§ 2072–2074. As the procedure now stands, an Advisory Committee on the Federal Rules of Evidence proposes changes to the Committee on Rules of Practice and Procedure (the "Standing Committee") of the Judicial Conference of the United States; similar committees propose changes to the other codifications. The Standing Committee may revise the proposals and, if it approves them, pass them on to the Judicial Conference, which in turn may pass them on, with or without revisions, to the Supreme Court. The Court usually (but not always!) submits the proposals to Congress without change. Assuming it is submitted no later than May 1 of a given year, a proposed revision takes effect on December 1 of that year unless Congress prescribes otherwise. Any Rule "creating, abolishing, or modifying an evidentiary privilege," however, is not effective unless affirmatively approved by Congress. § 2074(b).

Codifications based more or less closely, and directly or indirectly, on the FRE have now been adopted in 46 states,[7] and presumably more will follow. Even before the FRE became effective, the Uniform Rules were revised to conform closely to their format, and for the most part to their substance.[8]

To some extent, the codified rules have become the law of evidence, and the FRE in particular provide structure for much evidentiary discourse and the language in which it is conducted. (The FRE were, however, completely restyled in 2011; though the structure and most of the key phrases remained intact, the restyling thoroughly altered the wording of the Rules, and most of the states that adopted codes based on the FRE adhere to the old phrasings.) Furthermore, even if the FRE were not applicable in any court, they would be a valuable teaching tool. Whatever criticisms may be offered of the FRE, their structure is clear, and for many evidentiary problems they do provide clear-cut rules, or at least guideposts to decision. Moreover, the legislative history, especially the Advisory Committee's Notes, provides a thoughtful, intelligent exploration of many evidentiary issues. Therefore, you should become familiar as the course goes along with your Federal Rules book.

Rules that the Court "prescribe[s]" pursuant to § 2072 may come back before it for interpretation, or even for a judgment as to constitutional validity. The Court has reflected awareness of the oddity of its position. *See* United States v. Abel, 469 U.S. 45, 49 (1984) ("Although we are nominally the promulgators of the Rules, and should in theory need only to consult our collective memories to analyze the situation properly, we are in truth merely a conduit when we deal with an undertaking as substantial as the preparation of the Federal Rules of Evidence."). Some members of the Court have found the "conduit" role chafing, and would rather be taken out of the procedure altogether. *See, e.g.,* the statement by Justice White on Amendments to the Federal Rules of Civil Procedure, Apr. 22, 1993, 507 U.S. 1091. Others have taken the view that, so long as the revisions must pass through the Court, the Justices should exercise genuine review, at least when the proposals touch on principle and purpose rather than merely on matters of expert detail. *See, e.g.,* the dissenting statement of Justice Scalia (joined by Justice Thomas and, in part, by Justice Souter) on Amendments to the Federal Rules of Civil Procedure, Apr. 22, 1993, 507 U.S. 1096. Occasionally the Court does decline to transmit proposed amendments to it. *See* Letter of Transmittal, Apr. 30, 1991, *reprinted at* 500 U.S. at 964 (noting that the Court, though transmitting various proposed Rules amendments, is not transmitting amendments proposed by the Judicial Conference to seven of the Federal Rules of Civil Procedure "pending further consideration by the Court"). In 1994, the Court made substantive changes to a proposed revision to FRE 412, the federal rape shield law, before submitting it to Congress. Interestingly, Congress affirmatively enacted the provision as it was presented to the Court by the Judicial Conference. The matter is discussed in Chapter 18. In 2002, the Court, by a 7–2 vote, refused to transmit to Congress a proposed amendment to Federal Rule of Criminal Procedure 26 that would have authorized taking of testimony from a remote location in certain circumstances. *See* Richard D. Friedman, *Remote Testimony,* 35 U. MICH. J. L. REF. 695, 695–96 (2002); H. Doc. 107–203, 107th Cong., 2d Sess.

[7] I am counting Massachusetts, because the Supreme Judicial Court "recommends the use of the Massachusetts Guide to Evidence," which is closely based on the FRE, thought the Court says that this does not represent "an adoption of a set of rules of evidence, nor a predictive guide to the development of the common law of evidence."

[8] An extensive set of revisions to the Uniform Rules was made in 1999. *See Symposium: The Uniform Rules of Evidence (1999),* 54 Okl. L. Rev. 443 (2001). For a thoughtful brief history of the codification movement, see Michael Ariens, *Progress Is Our Only Product: Legal Reform and the Codification of Evidence,* 17 Law & Soc. Inquiry 213 (1992).

But, as already suggested, the Federal Rules do not always provide answers. For one thing, the jurisdictions that have *not* adopted codifications based on the Rules—California, New York, Missouri, Kansas, and also the District of Columbia—have in the aggregate more than 21% of the nation's population and substantially more litigation than do the federal courts. Even states that have adopted such codifications have often made very substantial changes,[9] and when the Rules are amended the states do not follow as a matter of course. Furthermore, the Rules do not always provide answers even where they are applicable. For example, the important area of privilege is for the most part untouched by the FRE. It was particularly the proposed privilege provisions, Rules 501–513, that aroused Congressional opposition to the Rules as promulgated by the Court in 1972. Congress deleted these detailed proposed provisions (which still get some attention and may be reproduced in your Rules book). It replaced them with a brief Rule 501, which defers to state law on matters of privilege when state law provides the rule of decision on a civil claim or defense and otherwise leaves matters of privilege to the common law. The rulemakers have since added a procedural provision, FRE 502, but nothing resembling a codification of the law of privilege. Another obvious example is FRE 403:

> The court may exclude relevant evidence if its probative value is substantially outweighed by a danger of one or more of the following: unfair prejudice, confusing the issues, misleading the jury, undue delay, wasting time, or needlessly presenting cumulative evidence.

Clearly, this is not a self-enforcing rule; it demands discretion in application. And, for the reasons suggested before, the discretion will most often be that of the trial judge acting on the spot, without a written opinion. Thus, although the Federal Rules are critical, always bear in mind that they are only one set of solutions to evidentiary problems, and an incomplete set at that.

This book reflects my own perspective on evidentiary issues—hence, where it seems appropriate I will use the first-person singular. Naturally, this perspective differs on some issues from those that you will find in treatises, hornbooks, cases, or in your Rules book. One of the fascinating aspects of the law of evidence is that, although many of the problems are quite old, the law is still quite open-textured in many respects. Judges, lawyers, and scholars debate not only about what the rules should be but also about what underlying structure they should have and what policies they should reflect. This book will offer speculative discussions on many

---

[9]   And, on the other hand, jurisdictions that have not adopted such codifications sometimes do effectively adopt particular aspects of the Federal Rules by decisional law. *See, e.g.,* Jenkins v. United States, 80 A.3d 978, 991–92 (D.C. 2013).

evidentiary issues. Take these discussions for what they are worth: Give them a chance to persuade you, but be willing to challenge them and to develop your own perspective.

B. A SAMPLE EXAM QUESTION

The following is part of an old Evidence exam. Students were expected to complete this Part in 2 1/2 hours. Presenting it here is not meant to breed excessive or premature exam anxiety. Rather, it is offered to introduce you to several of the concepts that will be explored throughout this book, and to give you a sense of how they fit together; some of these concepts, you will be pleased to learn, are not all that complicated, and you may already have a basic sense of some of the issues. Just what type of exam you will have to take will, of course, depend on your instructor, but this one is rather typical of many exams. You may find it a useful study device, later in the course, to try writing an answer to this question.

For now, it is premature to try a formal written answer. But do come to class ready to discuss the question. Again, your answers must be quite suppositious, given your present knowledge of the law of evidence, but do the best you can with what you know and your common sense; you may be surprised how far you can get.

The question is set in the State of Fatigue, a new state that has not yet adopted an evidence code and that treats all sources of American evidentiary law as persuasive authority. By the way, the question has been adopted, with rather liberal amendments and elaborations, from a real case, *State v. Gold*, 180 Conn. 619, 431 A.2d 501, *cert. denied*, 449 U.S. 920 (1980).[10]

STATE v. SILVER

Murray Silver is about to stand trial for the third time for the murder of his former in-laws. The first trial ended in a hung jury, and a conviction in the second trial was reversed on appeal because of prejudicial comments by the prosecutor.

It is undisputed that Irving Pushkin, a prominent lawyer in the medium-sized city of Cadbury, and his wife, Rhoda, were savagely stabbed to death in their home shortly after 9 p.m. on September 26, 1974. Silver had been married to the Pushkins' daughter Barbara for 20 months before they separated in May 1964. Mr. Pushkin handled the legal affairs relating to the divorce, which was completed promptly. It is

---

[10] For an account of the extended litigation in this case, which did not end until 1995, more than twenty years after the murders, see Bernard Ryan, Jr., *Murray R. Gold Trials: 1976–92*, http://www.encyclopedia.com/doc/1G2-3498200255.html.

also undisputed that the Pushkins, who were Reform Jews, had been to synagogue earlier that evening, which was Yom Kippur, the Jewish Day of Atonement, and then had dined (no one said they were very observant Reform Jews) at the home of their other daughter, Myrna Levine, before returning home. Ms. Levine died of natural causes six months after her parents were murdered.

A. You are an assistant to the District Attorney, who tells you that he is contemplating offering the following items of evidence. He asks you to write a memo discussing what he must do to get each one into evidence. Where appropriate, tell him what theories of relevance he may offer; what foundation he must lay, and how he should do it; and what objections he should anticipate, and how, if at all, he might meet them. Also, if you believe that it would be counterproductive to offer any of these items, tell him why. Where appropriate and convenient, you may discuss more than one of these items together.

(1) A Police Department tape, which the D.A. tells you has been in the hands of various policemen and prosecutors since the night of the murder. The tape contains two brief conversations. In the first, a woman's voice, noticeably agitated, is heard to say:

> "Police? This is Myrna Levine. I was just on the phone with my mother, Rhoda Pushkin. My father just opened the door and I heard him yell, 'Get away from me!' I know something is terribly wrong. Please go over there quickly—225 Fern Street."

In the second conversation, which appears to have occurred seconds later, another woman's voice, apparently older and equally agitated, is heard to say:

> "Police? Please get over here quick, 225 Fern Street. There's a crazy man up here."

A pencil-written mark on the tape says, "Sept. 26, 1974, 2108."

(2) The testimony of Officer Monday of the Cadbury police that he arrived at the Pushkin house on Fern Street at 9:12 p.m. and found the following:

> (a) Mrs. Pushkin's body, with 24 stab wounds, in the upstairs bedroom near the telephone, which was off the hook.

> (b) Not far from Mrs. Pushkin's body, a bloody six-inch hunting knife (which failed to reveal any fingerprints).

> (c) Mr. Pushkin, dressed in his slacks and a bathrobe, dead on the kitchen floor, with 29 stab wounds and several more superficial cuts on his hands.

> (d) In Mr. Pushkin's pants pocket, $1174 in cash.

(e) Several bloody footprints with the "Cat's Paw" brand name clearly visible on the heels.

(f) A dark button and two white plastic button fasteners.

(3) The testimony of a neighbor of the Pushkins, Helen Hershey, who told Officer Tuesday of the Cadbury Police she had seen a "big blue" automobile parked near the Pushkins' house three days before the murders. Because there had been a rash of burglaries in the neighborhood, she told her brother Lew to write the number down. Lew has a slip of paper with "833–QED" marked on it. Officer Tuesday checked with the Department of Motor Vehicles and found that a 1973 Oldsmobile with that number was owned by Silver. He then traveled to Silver's home in Marsden, about fifty miles away from Cadbury, and found a dark blue 1973 Oldsmobile with that number parked outside.

(4) Officer Tuesday's testimony of a conversation he had with Ms. Levine, five days after the murders. She told Tuesday that, ten days before the murders, Silver visited her for the first time in a decade, asking the whereabouts of her sister Barbara, his former wife, and also asking whether her parents still lived on Fern Street.

(5) Five pairs of shoes with Cat's Paw heels and a "Buttoneer" button-fastening kit, containing dark buttons of the type found in the Pushkin home, all confiscated from Silver's home in Marsden after he consented to a search, seven days after the murders. Red Robins, who owns a local men's clothing store, has told Tuesday that he has never seen buttons of this type except in Buttoneer kits, of which he sells about 200 a year. A local cobbler, Giapetto Ghiardelli, has told Tuesday that he believes about 40% of all heels put on new or repaired shoes in the neighborhood have the Cat's Paw mark on them.

(6) Tuesday's testimony of a conversation he had with Silver at the time of the search. Silver told Tuesday that at 9 p.m. on September 26 he was dining with his parents (also Jewish; also not observant). He explained a bandage on his finger by saying that he had cut it severely while slicing carrots that evening. He also said that he had cut off his moustache (which he had worn for the previous five years) on September 27 in preparation for a singles weekend at a resort in the Catskill Mountains. He said that he had been in Cadbury briefly ten days before the murders but denied returning afterward.

(7) The testimony of Dr. Marcia Medic, who treated Silver for the cut finger, that Silver explained that he had cut it on glass, and the testimony of Nan Nabors, a neighbor of Silver, that Silver told her he had cut it peeling potatoes in preparation for his Yom Kippur feast.

B. Now assume that you are an assistant to the defense attorney, Kirsten Kearse. Based on the prior trials, Kearse anticipates that the prosecution will offer all the above items of evidence. Because she wants to be prepared for the worst, she tells you to operate on the assumption that all of them will be admitted. Kearse tells you that she is contemplating offering the following items of evidence. Your assignment is similar to that in Part A: Write a memo discussing what she must do to get each one into evidence. Where appropriate, tell her what theories of relevance she may offer; what foundation she must lay, and how she should do it; and what objections she should anticipate, and how, if at all, she might meet them. Also, if you believe that it would be counterproductive to offer any of these items, tell her why. Where appropriate and convenient, you may discuss more than one of these items together.

(1) The testimony of Patricia Rossiter, who says that she was a friend of Bruce Foxx, concerning two telephone conversations she says she had with Foxx. In the first, two nights before the murders, Foxx told Rossiter that he believed that Pushkin was advising Foxx's wife, Gloriana, about a possible divorce, and vowed that he would "get even with that Jew bastard one way or the other." The second conversation, according to Rossiter, was late on the night of September 26. Rossiter says that Foxx told her he was in a phone booth "covered with blood" and said, "I have just done something terrible that I am never going to get out of."

(2) The testimony of Dr. Thomas J. Rimini of Cadbury Hospital, who treated Foxx on the night of September 26 for a neck wound. Rimini is prepared to say that Foxx's clothes and shoes were covered with a large amount of blood, so much that it was unlikely that it all came from the neck wound. Gloriana Foxx has told Kearse that her husband cut his neck while drunk that night.

(3) Proof that Foxx was a former mental patient and a member of the Peddlers of Evil motorcycle club, and that six weeks after the murders he committed suicide.

(4) A transcript of the testimony at Silver's first trial of Craig Gorky, who has since died. Gorky testified that Foxx called him just before committing suicide and said, "I'm sorry I had to kill the Pushkins."

(5) The testimony of Jack Gellhorn, a friend of Silver, that Silver is a survivor of the Auschwitz concentration camp who, by hard work and ability, became a stockbroker with a leading brokerage firm in Marsden, and that in Gellhorn's opinion Silver is a truthful and gentle person.

C. Now assume once more that you are an Assistant District Attorney. Your boss anticipates that the defense will offer all the evidentiary items listed in Part B and wants you to proceed on the assumption that they will all be admitted. He now wants you to tell him how, if at all, the admission of the evidence offered by the defense will aid or hinder his arguments for the admission of the items of evidence listed in Part A. In particular, he wonders whether, if any of the evidence listed in Part A is excluded from the prosecution's case-in-chief, it may be admitted as part of the prosecution's rebuttal. You may, if you wish, integrate your response to this part into your response to Part A.

PART I

STRUCTURAL AND PROCEDURAL CONSIDERATIONS

■ ■ ■

CHAPTER 2

THE TRIAL—PREPARATION
AND STRUCTURE

■ ■ ■

A. PRETRIAL PREPARATION

Additional Reading: McCormick, ch. 1, §§ 1–3; Mueller & Kirkpatrick, § 1.6

It is important to emphasize at the outset that evidence does not come to you pre-packaged. A lawyer may have to exercise a good deal of discretion in deciding what evidence to use, and even what witnesses to put on the stand and what theories to pursue. But your task is not merely to choose between readily apparent alternatives. Often perceiving a useful strategy requires a good deal of imagination; much evidence is, in a sense, created by the lawyer preparing the case. And the first part of that creation is learning the facts yourself. You cannot do this on the eve of trial. The most important aspect of being a good trial lawyer is not the ability to "wing it" but the willingness to prepare intensively. You need to investigate the facts.

Much of your investigative work requires no involvement of the judicial system. Some people with useful information (including your client!) will be willing to talk with you, and you may have access to significant documents or other tangible items or to a location—the place of an accident, for example—that is important to the case. At some point, though, you are likely to want to invoke the power of the judicial system to compel the provision of information by persons who might otherwise be unwilling to provide it. You are presumably familiar with the discovery system from your Civil Procedure course. In most jurisdictions, discovery in criminal cases is much more limited; in others, it closely resembles civil discovery, but with the limitation provided by the defendant's constitutional right under the Fifth Amendment, made applicable to the states by the Fourteenth, not to "be compelled . . . to be a witness against himself." Even apart from devices designed principally for discovery, criminal lawyers find other means by which judicial procedures may be used for discovery. For example, in jurisdictions that depend on indictment by grand jury to begin a criminal case, the prosecutor may use the grand jury's ability to compel testimony as a method of learning what a recalcitrant witness would likely testify in court. Or, where the prosecution is commenced by a preliminary hearing before a judge, defense counsel may—if the court will allow—examine the witnesses rather thoroughly, not so much in the hope of persuading the judge to refuse to bind the defendant over for trial but in the hope of gaining the functional equivalent of a deposition.

¶ **2.1:** Remember your client Ted the playwright. Assume that he has given you only the information about his case summarized in ¶ 1.1. Be prepared to conduct the rest of your initial interview. What will you want to know about the substantive law to help you in the interview or in subsequent interviews?

¶ **2.2:** If you bring an action on Ted's behalf, whose depositions will you want to take? What do you hope to achieve by taking the depositions? What other discovery will you take, and what other investigations will you make? Why?

While one of the purposes of taking discovery is to create evidence that might be helpful to you, one of your goals in responding to discovery requests is to prevent the creation of evidence that might harm you, to the extent you can do so legitimately.

¶ **2.3:** The publisher has given notice of (or, as lawyers often say, "noticed") Ted's deposition. As Ted's lawyer, what is your goal for the deposition? What advice or instructions will you give Ted before the deposition? What else will you do to prepare Ted for the deposition?

Of course, determining the facts yourself and creating or trying to prevent the creation of evidence are only parts of your job. The bottom line is that you must be able to prove your case in court. This requires, first, that you decide what facts you have to prove. To do this, you must, even more than in the investigative aspect of your job, understand the substantive law that governs, or that you hope will govern; sometimes you will have to develop a creative theory of the case. Second, you must decide how you can prove the desired facts. Most proof requires witnesses. Even if you are relying on documents or other "real" proof, you will generally need a witness to explain what the physical evidence is. It is not always obvious who are the best witnesses to put on the stand, nor what they should say once they are there. Once you decide what witnesses you *wish* to call, you must decide whether you can feasibly do so. With respect to a lay witness, you must determine whether she is willing to testify voluntarily, and if not whether you can compel her to do so by subpoena. With respect to an expert witness, you cannot compel her to testify, and the fees she charges may make you think twice about whether it is worthwhile to present her testimony. With respect to both lay and expert witnesses, you must make arrangements to ensure that they will actually be in court when the time comes for them to testify—or if this is not feasible, that their testimony has been preserved in an admissible form.

¶ 2.4: In Ted's trial, what witnesses will you prepare to call? What testimony will you seek from each of them?

Looking at the case from the other side, if you know that your adversary is likely to offer some evidence that you believe might be inadmissible, you might consider making a motion *in limine*—an advance motion seeking a ruling before the evidence is introduced that it is inadmissible. The motion *in limine* has some great advantages: It gives the judge some time to reflect on the objection to evidence; it is made without the jury present and does not extend the period of the jury's service; if the motion definitively resolves the evidentiary issue, then the parties can prepare for trial, including their opening statements, with one contingency removed. On the other hand, the judge might find that before trial the matter is too contingent to be resolved. She may, for example, decide that the question depends on a balancing of probative value and likely prejudicial impact, and that she cannot make that balance sensibly—or definitively—until the evidence is actually offered at trial. Sometimes the judge will make a ruling but explicitly say that it is subject to re-evaluation depending on how things appear at trial.

¶ 2.5: Delotte, being prosecuted for illegal possession of crack cocaine, makes an *in limine* motion to exclude the following items of evidence:

(a) proof that a packet containing 50 grams of crack was found at Delotte's home. Delotte moves to suppress this evidence on the grounds that it was the product of an illegal search.

(b) proof that Delotte was previously convicted on a felony firearms possession charge. The prosecution concedes that this conviction would be inadmissible if Delotte does not testify, but contends that it would be admissible under FRE 609 to impeach the defendant if he does take the stand.

(c) a videotape, taken by a friend of Delotte's at a party three weeks before the date of the alleged possession, on which Delotte announces that he is going to use baby powder to demonstrate how to smoke crack, and thereupon does so.

As to which, if any, of these should the judge be willing to rule before trial? *See, e.g., Dallas v. State*, 993 A.2d 655, 664–65 (Md. 2010). As to each, if the court does rule, should it emphasize that its ruling is tentative?[1]

---

[1]   Note FRE 103(b), the substance of which was added in 2000 and which is discussed in Chapter 22. Under this rule, if the court "rules definitively" on the admissibility of evidence in

B. STRUCTURE OF THE TRIAL

Discovery is complete; motions to dismiss or for summary judgment have been denied; other pretrial motions have been decided; settlement efforts have failed. It is time for trial. What happens now? We will examine jury trials first, and then briefly note the differences for bench trials—i.e., trials without a jury.

1. JURY SELECTION

The first step is the selection of the jury. In some jurisdictions, jury selection is conducted by the lawyers, without the judge even being present for the most part. In others, the questioning (sometimes called "*voir dire*") of the potential jurors is done by the lawyers, but with the judge present. In others, the *voir dire* is conducted all or in part by the judge, perhaps based in part on questions submitted to her beforehand by the lawyers. *Cf. Carino v. Muenzen*, 2010 WL 3448071 (N.J. App. 2010) (holding that trial court acted unreasonably in preventing lawyer from searching on-line in courtroom for information concerning prospective jurors).

Why not simply take the first twelve people in the box? Obviously, some may not be qualified. For example, occasionally a juror is unable to understand the evidence well enough, even with accommodations that the courts deem reasonable,[2] and often, if a trial is expected to be protracted,

---

response to an *in limine* motion, or at any other time before the evidence is offered, the party against whom the court rules need not bring the issue up again in order to preserve a challenge to the ruling.

[2] Traditionally, courts were disposed to excuse a potential juror who was blind or so hard of hearing that she could not understand the oral testimony. In light of the Americans with Disabilities Act, though, courts now usually make accommodations for sight- and hearing-impaired jurors, sometimes including Braille transcripts of documents and a team of sign language interpreters. *See, e.g.,* Administrative Office of the Courts [New Jersey], *Guidelines for Trials Involving Deaf Jurors Who Serve with the Assistance of Sign Language Interpreters,* https://www.judiciary.state.nj.us/interpreters/wrkgdeafjur.pdf; Arthur Santana, *For Deaf Defendant, Special Precautions; To Ensure Fair Trial, 3 Interpreters Enlisted,* WASH. POST, May 9, 2002, p. B4. But satisfactory accommodations are not always possible. Note, for example, State v. Speer, 925 N.E.2d 584 (Ohio 2010), which held that "[t]he right to a fair trial requires that all members of the jury have the ability to understand all of the evidence presented, to evaluate that evidence in a rational manner, to communicate effectively with other jurors during deliberations, and to comprehend the applicable legal principles as instructed by the court." *Speer* was a homicide case; the victim had either fallen or been pushed out of the accused's boat. Crucial evidence was the recording of a 911 call made by the accused, and the court held that his right to a fair trial was denied by including a hearing-impaired juror who could not evaluate "whether there was urgency in Speer's voice, whether he slurred his speech, or whether he sounded deceptive or hesitant." *See also* Fendrick v. PPL Services Corp., 193 Fed. Appx. 138 (3d Cir. 2006) (no abuse of discretion in excusing deaf juror who was unwilling to use a hearing aid, amplification system being "of limited usefulness").

In federal court—including in Puerto Rico—a potential juror is ineligible to serve if she "is unable to read, write, and understand the English language with a degree of proficiency sufficient to fill out satisfactorily the juror qualification form." 28 U.S.C. § 1865(b). In New Mexico, "inability to speak, read or write the English or Spanish languages" cannot in itself be a ground for disqualifying a juror. N.M. Const., Art. VII, § 3. In State v. Rico, 52 P.3d 942 (N.M.

some jurors are unable without undue hardship to take the necessary time off from work or other responsibilities. Perhaps the most common disqualification is for bias. It will not do to have the plaintiff's brother-in-law on the jury, or an employee of the defendant corporation. Some arguable grounds of bias are less clear-cut.[3]

¶ **2.6:** Shane is on trial for rape and related charges. Juror 138 says on *voir dire* that, while "police are just like everybody else," he would find it more likely that a police officer was telling the truth than a lay witness because police officers take the oath more seriously. He also says that he knows the two officers involved in the investigation, but his associations and views would not affect his ability to be an impartial juror. Should Juror 138 be excused for cause? What if, in addition to the above, he is a police officer who works for the same department as the officers involved in the agency, though he was not an officer at the time of the crime? *See Shane v. Commonwealth*, 243 S.W.3d 336 (Ky. 2007).

¶ **2.7:** Bernie, a 37-year-old white electrical engineer, is accused of shooting four young black men who he says were about to rob him on the New York City subway. On the *voir dire*, Norton Green, a potential juror, who is a white man, has said that he is a 43-year-old accountant, and that he was once mugged while leaving a New York subway station. Should Green be disqualified for cause?[4]

2002), the court held that this right is not absolute and "must be balanced against practical considerations"—but the court vacated the convictions of two defendants because the trial courts had failed to provide Navajo interpreters for prospective jurors, which in the circumstances would have caused some delay.

   See generally Jasmine B. Gonzales Rose, *The Exclusion of Non-English-Speaking Jurors: Remedying a Century of Denial of the Sixth Amendment in the Federal Courts of Puerto Rico*, 46 Harv. Civ. R.–Civ. L. L. Rev. 497 (2011); Cynthia L. Brown, Note, *A Challenge to the English-language Requirement of the Juror Qualification Provision of New York's Judiciary Law*, N.Y.L.S.L. Rev. 479 (1994); Nancy Lawler Dickhute, *Jury Duty for the Blind in the Time of Reasonable Accommodations: the Ada's Interface with a Litigant's Right to a Fair Trial*, 32 Creighton L. Rev. 849 (1999).

   [3]   The need to determine potential grounds of bias is one reason why, as a general matter, the identity of potential jurors is disclosed to the parties. But in occasional cases, a court may decide that it is imperative to keep the identities of the venire members confidential. *See, e.g.*, United States v. Dinkins, 691 F.3d 358 (4th Cir. 2012), *cert. denied*, 133 S.Ct. 1278 (2013). A leading case, laying out criteria for the decision, is United States v. Ross, 33 F.3d 1507 (11th Cir. 1994), *cert. denied*, 515 U.S. 1132 (1995). *See also* 28 U.S.C. § 1863(b)(7) (allowing names to be kept confidential "in any case where the interests of justice so require"); 18 U.S.C. § 3432 (providing for confidentiality upon a finding by a preponderance of the evidence that disclosure "may jeopardize the life or safety of any person").

   [4]   *Cf.* Wainwright v. Witt, 469 U.S. 412 (1985)(discretion of trial court in "death qualifying" a jury); United States v. Godfrey, 787 F.3d 72 (1st Cir. 2015) (no abuse of discretion in denying cause challenge to juror in wire fraud case who had received a mailing similar to the one that defendants were accused of sending); United States v. Jones, 608 F.2d 1004, 1008 (4th Cir.1979), *cert. denied*, 444 U.S. 1086 (1980)(approving decision not to disqualify juror whose daughter-in-

¶ 2.8: Doris Reed, another member of the jury panel (sometimes called the "venire") in Bernie's trial, says that she has read newspaper reports of the case and that her "impression" is that Bernie was guilty of assault with intent to kill. Should she be disqualified for cause? What if she is asked if Bernie committed the crime, and she responds, "I wouldn't know"? *Cf.* Scott Turow, *Presumed Innocent* 234–35 (1987).

If a member of the venire is not qualified to sit on the case, it does not matter how many previous members have also been disqualified; thus, each side is allowed an unlimited number of challenges for cause. It is for the judge, however, to decide, as in the above problems, whether or not the asserted ground is a sufficient basis for disqualification.

In addition to challenges for cause, the parties are generally allowed a given number of peremptory challenges; these allow a party to bar a juror without stating a reason. For example, in federal civil and misdemeanor cases, each party is generally allowed three peremptories, while in federal felony cases the Government is entitled to six peremptories and the defense to ten, except that in capital cases each side is entitled to twenty peremptories. 28 U.S.C. § 1870; Fed. R. Crim. P. 24(b). Courts differ, but it is preferable to allow each party to exercise its peremptories, like its challenges for cause, outside the hearing of the jury, and not to inform either the struck juror or the remaining ones why that one has been excused from serving on that jury.

Traditionally, the parties are allowed to, and often do, indulge their hunches, whims, prejudices, and stereotypes in exercising their peremptories. Note the following passages from Scott Turow's novel *Presumed Innocent*, in which a former chief deputy prosecutor is on trial for murdering an associate with whom he had had an affair:

> [My lawyer wants younger jurors because they] might believe that co-workers adjourn to a woman's apartment for reasons other than sexual intercourse. On the other hand, he has said, older people will have more immediate respect for my past attainments, my position, and my reputation. . . . In general, [the prosecuting attorney] seems to be looking for his voters, older ethnic types, generally Roman Catholics. For that reason, without having planned to do it earlier, we strike all the Italians. (pp. 237, 238)

¶ 2.9: Suppose you are representing the defendant in an auto negligence case. The plaintiff's claim is that your client ran a red light; your client says that she had the green light and that

---

law had been a teller in a bank robbery similar to the one charged but who assured trial judge of impartiality).

the plaintiff moved into the intersection without looking. What information do you want to know about potential jurors? Will this information enable you to challenge for cause, or simply give you a reason to exercise peremptories? Be prepared to conduct the *voir dire* of a member of the venire.

The term "peremptory challenges" seems oxymoronic in a way. If, as they were applied traditionally, they are truly peremptory, they are not really "challenges" but rather, as they are sometimes also called, strikes: The party who wishes to see a member of the venire excused from the jury simply tells the court that it is exercising one of its peremptories. Traditionally, because they were indeed peremptory, these strikes were— whatever might be said against them—swift, simple, and uncomplicated to administer. That has all changed as a result of *Batson v. Kentucky*, 476 U.S. 79 (1986), and cases building on it.

Batson, a black man, was tried on theft charges. The prosecutor used peremptories against the four blacks on the venire, and an all-white jury was empaneled and found Batson guilty. He contended that the striking of the black members of the venire violated his right to equal protection, but the trial court flatly rejected the objection, without requiring the prosecutor to explain the challenges; peremptory means peremptory, the judge ruled in effect. The United States Supreme Court held this ruling to be a constitutional error. The Equal Protection Clause, wrote the Court, "forbids the prosecutor to challenge potential jurors solely on account of their race or on the assumption that black jurors as a group will be unable impartially to consider the State's case against a black defendant." *Id.* at 89.

¶ 2.10: What do you think of this logic? Was the prosecutor seeking "impartial" jurors? Was he necessarily proceeding on the basis that black jurors were less able to act impartially—or simply on the basis that black jurors were less likely to find in his favor than white jurors, so that as a matter of "comparison shopping" he would prefer having an unknown, randomly selected juror to the black venire member before him? *See* William T. Pizzi, Batson v. Kentucky: *Curing the Disease but Killing the Patient*, 1987 S. Ct. Rev. 97, 126. Note the wide disparities along racial lines in experience and in attitudes toward such matters as police behavior. This was exemplified in the decade after *Batson* by the huge disparity in opinions on the question of O.J. Simpson's guilt, and there remains a huge disparity between whites and blacks on the question of whether the criminal justice system treats the races equally. So was the prosecutor irrational in believing that he would rather have white jurors than black ones? On the other hand, in the modern age, can we tolerate a system in which a prosecutor prevents a qualified person from sitting on a jury because of the juror's race?

Batson was rapidly extended in several dimensions—what parties it governs, who has standing to invoke it, and what characteristics it applies to. First, the Court held that parties other than prosecutors are also governed by *Batson*. In *Edmonson v. Leesville Concrete Co., Inc.*, 500 U.S. 614 (1991), the Court held that *Batson* applies to private civil litigants— that is, like prosecutors, they are forbidden from exercising their peremptories on racial grounds. And in *Georgia v. McCollum*, 505 U.S. 42 (1992), the Court held that *Batson* also applies to criminal defendants. McCollum was a white defendant charged with racially motivated violence; the Court held that he could not constitutionally use his peremptories to keep blacks off the jury.

¶ **2.11:** Suppose instead that McCollum was black, that his alleged victims, and the jurors he wished to strike, were white, and that he is tried in an area of considerable racial tension. Should the result change? Note that in *McCollum*, the NAACP Legal Defense and Education Fund, Inc., submitted an amicus brief arguing that "whether white defendants can use peremptory challenges to purge minority jurors presents quite different issues from whether a minority defendant can strike majority group jurors." *See McCollum*, 505 U.S. at 62 n.2 (Thomas, J., concurring in the judgment, noting this argument and apparently finding it hard to fathom).

Second, the Court took an expansive view of standing to object to improper use of peremptories. In *Powers v. Ohio*, 499 U.S. 400 (1991), Powers, a white man, was tried for the murder of another white person. The prosecution used peremptory challenges to remove seven black venire members from the jury. Powers objected, and the prosecution contended that he did not have standing to do so. The Supreme Court disagreed.

¶ **2.12:** Why would Powers object to the peremptories? Whose rights were violated? Should Powers have standing to object?

¶ **2.13:** The Supreme Court decided *McCollum* against the defendant on the ground that his racially based exercise of peremptories was a violation of the Equal Protection Clause of the Fourteenth Amendment. Whose constitutional rights were violated? The Equal Protection Clause only prohibits denials of equal protection by the state. How was there state action here, given that the state was not the party exercising the peremptories, but rather the prosecutor of the party who exercised them? Does it make sense to allow the state to have standing to object to that exercise?

Third, the Court extended *Batson* beyond race. *J.E.B. v. Alabama ex rel. T.B.*, 511 U.S. 127 (1994), involved a state action for paternity and child support. Under Alabama procedure, this case was tried to a jury, and the state used nine of its ten peremptory strikes to exclude men from the jury. The Supreme Court extended *Batson* to cover gender discrimination.

Note the rather odd situation in which matters now stand. A party can now use peremptories, without explanation, on *nearly any* basis, no matter how whimsical or irrational, to excuse jurors whom the party believes to be less preferable than the unknown person "behind the curtain"—but race and gender are forbidden grounds of preference. Suppose you knew relatively little about a person and you had to pick factors that gave some hint of the person's likely attitudes on matters coming before a jury. Wouldn't race and gender rank rather high?

Naturally, the question arises how far, if at all, beyond race and gender the *Batson* rule extends. *Batson* itself, concentrating on the racial context, spoke of its scope extending to jurors who are members of a "cognizable racial group". Clearly, then, *Batson* applies to peremptories made on the basis that the venire member is, for example, Hispanic or Native American. *See Hernandez v. New York*, 500 U.S. 352 (1991); *United States v. Chalan*, 812 F.2d 1302 (10th Cir.1987). But the ethnic reach of *Batson* is not clear.

¶ **2.14:** In the *Presumed Innocent* passage quoted above, did the defense act improperly in "strik[ing] all the Italians"? If, in a trial of an Italian-American for Mafia-related racketeering, or of a prominent Italian-American politician for corruption, it is the prosecutor who "strike[s] all the Italians"—or more precisely, those whose surnames appear to be Italian—would that be proper? If the struck jurors are in fact of Italian heritage, do the strikes constitute a *Batson* violation? Are surnames in themselves a sufficient basis on which to determine ethnicity? *See generally Rico v. Leftridge-Byrd*, 340 F.3d 178, 184 (3d Cir. 2003); *United States v. Campione*, 942 F.2d 429 (7th Cir.1991) (reviewing cases); *People v. Snow*, 44 Cal.3d 216, 242 Cal.Rptr. 477, 746 P.2d 452 (1987) (applying California's broader counterpart to *Batson*, which applies to peremptories exercised on "racial, religious, ethnic, or similar grounds").

¶ **2.15:** To what extent should *Batson* apply to peremptories based on religion? Consider the following questions.

(a) Should a party be allowed to inquire into a potential juror's religion? *See, e.g., State v. Davis*, 504 N.W.2d 767, 772 (Minn.1993), *cert. denied*, 511 U.S. 1115 (1994) ("Ordinarily . . . , inquiry on *voir dire* into a juror's religious affiliation and beliefs is irrelevant and prejudicial, and to ask such questions is improper.").

(b) In *Davis*, the prosecutor struck a venire member who, she had learned, was a Jehovah's Witness. The prosecutor said she believed that the religion of Jehovah's Witnesses makes them extremely reluctant to exercise the power of the state over individuals. Was this proper? The *Davis* court held yes, and the Supreme Court denied *certiorari*; Justice Thomas wrote an opinion, joined by Justice Scalia, dissenting from the denial. *See also, e.g., Casarez v. State*, 913 S.W.2d 468 (Tex. 1994) (initially holding practice improper, but on rehearing holding it proper.) In contrast to *Davis*, see, *e.g., United States v. Brown*, 352 F.3d 654 (2d Cir. 2003).

(c) What if the prosecutor in *Davis* had said, "It has nothing to do with the particulars of the juror's religion. It's just that I've found that people who are religiously demonstrative, as this juror is, tend to favor criminal defendants more than those who are not"? *See State v. Fuller*, 862 A.2d 1130 (N.J. 2004) (collecting cases and disagreeing with *Davis*); *United States v. DeJesus*, 347 F.3d 500 (3d Cir.2003) (distinguishing "between a strike motivated by religious beliefs and one motivated by religious affiliation," and concluding that strikes based on concern that the "heightened religiosity" of potential jurors would prevent them from voting to convict was not improper).

(d) Rosen and Weissman, two former employees of the American Israel Public Affairs Committee, an influential lobby, are charged with trafficking in classified information. Would it violate *Batson* if the prosecutor struck jurors with identifiably Jewish surnames? If the defense struck jurors with identifiably Muslim names? Josh Gerstein, *Secret Case Eyes Jurors' Religion*, N.Y. Sun, Dec. 5, 2007, nysun.com/article/67422.

Batson and subsequent cases have set up a procedure by which, in effect, a mini-discrimination hearing may be appended to a trial. Let's focus on the most typical case, in which the party objecting to his adversary's use of peremptories is a criminal defendant. First, the defendant must raise a "prima facie case" of purposeful discrimination against a group covered by *Batson*. That prima facie case may be based on numbers—if the prosecutor used most of her peremptories to eliminate blacks from the venire, for example—but it need not be. The accused might base his *Batson* contention on a single peremptory challenge if the particular venire member seems—putting aside the forbidden consideration—to be one the prosecutor would want on the jury. *See*

People v. Bolling, 79 N.Y.2d 317, 323–24, 582 N.Y.S.2d 950, 955, 591 N.E.2d 1136, 1141 (1992).

If the defendant makes a prima facie case, the prosecutor must state a permissible ground for exercising the peremptories. But the Supreme Court has said that the bottom-line question is not whether or not the explanation offered by the prosecutor is a convincing one, but whether or not the court is persuaded that the prosecutor has engaged in "purposeful discrimination." *Miller-El v. Cockrell*, 537 U.S. 322, 328–29 (2003); *Purkett v. Elem*, 514 U.S. 765, 838 (1995) (per curiam). In other words, the Court has said that the trial judge may disbelieve the reason cited by the prosecutor and yet decline to conclude that the defendant has carried his burden of persuading the judge that the prosecutor has discriminated in violation of *Batson. Cf. St. Mary's Honor Ctr. v. Hicks*, 509 U.S. 502 (1993) (drawing a similar distinction in the context of employment discrimination).

Nevertheless, the justification articulated by the prosecutor is critical. First of all, it must be neutral with respect to the prohibited consideration—whatever that means.

¶ **2.16:** (a) Suppose Dominick, a black defendant, is charged with armed robbery. The prosecutor has used four of her first five peremptories to challenge the first four black members of the venire. Should these explanations with respect to a given venire member be regarded as race-neutral?

(i) "It's not that he's black, Your Honor. It's that he's got long, unkempt hair, a mustache, and a beard. People meeting that description are less likely to regard deference to legal authority as important." *See Purkett*, 514 U.S. at 766.

(ii) "It's not that she's black, Your Honor. I asked the members of the venire what they believed about the death of A.B. [a local black youngster who was recently shot to by police], and she did not believe the police officers' accounts. A juror who didn't believe the officers accounts of that case is less likely to believe the testimony of the officers here, and so much of my case depends on police testimony."

(b) Now suppose that the defendant is Dominguez, a Latino. Should this explanation be accepted as race-neutral? "It's not that this juror is Hispanic, Your Honor. A lot of the evidence in this case is going to be testimony in Spanish, and she speaks Spanish, but it isn't just that she speaks Spanish. Her demeanor when we talked about that during *voir dire* suggested to me that she would have trouble treating the translation, as opposed to her own understanding of the testimony, as the evidence." *See Hernandez v. New York*, 500 U.S. 352 (1991).

(c) Now suppose that in a civil employment-discrimination case the defendant corporation challenges the only black member of the panel and says, "It's not that she's black, your Honor. It's that her sister filed an employment discrimination claim." Should this explanation be regarded as race neutral? *See Tinner v. United Insurance Co. of America*, 308 F.3d 697 (7th Cir. 2002).

Second, if the trial judge concludes that the articulated justification is a pretext, then the judge may conclude (though she need not) that the peremptory was exercised invalidly. But recall that any ground at all is a permissible one, so long as it does not involve one of the forbidden considerations. The courts have been rather generous in accepting explanations offered by prosecutors; indeed, it has been said that only an incompetent lawyer would fail to come up with an explanation that a court would be willing to accept. In *People v. Randall*, 283 Ill.App.3d 1019, 1025–26, 219 Ill.Dec. 395, 401, 671 N.E.2d 60, 65–66 (1996), the court said, with well-placed sarcasm (and ample citations):

> Surely new prosecutors are given a manual, probably entitled, "Handy Race-Neutral Explanations" or "20 Time-Tested Race-Neutral Explanations." It might include: too old, too young, divorced, long, unkempt hair, free-lance writer, religion, social worker, renter, lack of family contact, attempting to make eye contact with defendant, "lived in an area consisting predominantly of apartment complexes," single, over-educated, lack of maturity, improper demeanor, unemployed, improper attire, juror lived alone, misspelled place of employment, living with girlfriend, unemployed spouse, spouse employed as school teacher, employment as part-time barber, friendship with city council member, failure to remove hat, lack of community ties, children same "age bracket" as defendant, deceased father and prospective juror's aunt receiving psychiatric care.[5]

Moreover, the courts have been generous to striking parties in "mixed motive" cases—when the strike appears to have been motivated both by permissible and impermissible factors. The most common rule seems to be that there is no violation if the court concludes that, were the impermissible factors not present, the party still would have exercised the strike because of the neutral factors. *See, e.g., Guzman v. State*, 85 S.W.3d 242 (Tex. Crim. Apps. 2002) (reviewing cases); *Snyder v. Louisiana*, 552 U.S. 472, 485 (2008) (suggesting without deciding that courts should apply the usual rule that "once it is shown that a discriminatory intent

---

[5] *See also, e.g.,* Rice v. Collins, 546 U.S. 333 (2006) (youth and lack of community ties).

was a substantial or motivating factor in an action taken by a state actor, the burden shifts to the party defending the action to show that this factor was not determinative").

¶ 2.17: Suppose that you are the trial judge in Dominick's case, from ¶ 2.16. Take a random sample of the "handy race-neutral explanations" listed by the *Randall* court, to which, with some imagination, we may add an unlimited number of entries. *See, e.g., United States v. Jones*, 245 F.3d 990 (8th Cir. 2001) ("restless" and "tired"); *Simmons v. Luebbers*, 299 F.3d 929 (8th Cir. 2002) ("seemed to dislike [me]"). If the prosecutor offers one of these explanations for one of her peremptories, should you be inclined to find that she has acted discriminatorily? Should you ask more questions? If you do conclude that she has violated *Batson*, what should you do?

Now suppose that you are an appellate judge, considering an appeal from a criminal conviction. What standard should you use in determining whether the prosecutor committed a *Batson* violation? *See Rice v. Collins*, 546 U.S. 333, 338–39 (2006). Suppose you conclude that in fact the prosecutor did commit a violation. Should that automatically be grounds for a new trial?

Note the North Carolina Racial Justice Act of 2009, N.C.G.S. §§ 15A–2010 to–2012. That statute provided that evidence of various types, including that "[r]ace was a significant factor in decisions to exercise peremptory challenges during jury selection," was "relevant to establish a finding that race was a significant factor in decisions to seek or impose the sentence of death" in the jurisdiction, and it gave a criminal defendant who was able to establish that finding a right to have his death sentence commuted to life without parole. The Act, passed by a Democratic legislature, was repealed by a Republican one in 2013. So far as it bore on the *Batson* problem, did the statute go too far? Not far enough?

It would be going too far to say that *Batson* is completely toothless. Presumably it inhibits some discriminatory use of peremptories. And it is not impossible to win a *Batson* claim—just very difficult. Consider, for example, *Miller-El v. Dretke*, 545 U.S. 231 (2005), in which the defendant ultimately prevailed on his *Batson* claim, but only after bringing a federal *habeas corpus* petition and making two trips to the U.S. Supreme Court. *See also Miller-El v. Cockrell*, 537 U.S. 322 (2003). This was a capital murder case. The prosecutor used peremptories against 10 of the 11 black members of the venire who had not been excused by agreement or for cause. Even more important than the statistics, Justice Souter wrote for the majority, were "side-by-side comparisons of some black venire panelists who were struck and white panelists allowed to serve." The Court pointed to the peremptory used against Billy Jean Fields, who, it seemed, would have been someone the prosecution would be eager to keep on the jury—he had "expressed unwavering support for the death penalty"—except for the fact that he was black. Defending the use of the peremptory, the prosecutor contended that Fields had said that he could vote for death only if the juror could not be rehabilitated. That contention was simply untrue and, in the Court's view, suggested an ulterior motive. Besides, said the Court, if that really were a concern of the prosecutor, it would be hard to explain the failure to strike three other jurors, two white and one Latino, who had clearly expressed reservations about imposing the death penalty if rehabilitation appeared possible. About two decades after the original trial, the Court held 6–3 that the prosecution had used peremptories improperly.[6]

This is all a terrible mess, a product of a system in which peremptory challenges are no longer quite peremptory, and in which the grounds that make them not quite peremptory continue to be very tempting ones for some parties on which to strike a juror. What should be done? Presumably there is no going back on *Batson*, at least not openly on *Batson* itself; the idea of prosecutors explicitly excluding black jurors because of their race, especially when the defendant is black, is a most unappealing one. But some of the developments described above severely undercut the effectiveness of the doctrine.[7] As two scholars noted in writing about the "stubborn legacy" of race in jury selection, "Among those who laud its mission, it seems that the only people not disappointed

---

[6] Note also *Snyder*, in which the Supreme Court rejected a prosecutor's asserted reason for striking a black juror, that the juror, afraid of missing student-teaching hours, would hesitate to vote for a first-degree murder conviction, because that would entail sitting in a penalty-phase trial. The Court concluded that "this scenario was highly speculative"—depending on what the other jurors thought, voting to convict might move the proceedings along quickly. Moreover, the trial was brief, and was anticipated from the start to be; the juror's dean had said that the missed time could be made up easily enough, and after hearing that, the juror expressed no concern about missed time; and the prosecutor accepted white jurors who appeared to have conflicting obligations at least as pressing. So that was a win for a *Batson* claimant—but it required a 7–2 decision by the U.S. Supreme Court to get the win. And a more recent win for a *Batson* claimant is Foster v. Chatman, 2016 WL 2945233 (U.S.S.C. 2016), in which a majority of the Supreme Court held, nearly three decades after the original trial, that the strikes of two black jurors were motivated by race. The Court engaged in an intensely fact-based inquiry, concluding that each of the explanations offered by the state lacked credibility, in some instances because the state had not objected to a white juror who bore the same trait that the state had cited as a basis for striking a black one.

[7] *See* Jeffrey Bellin & Junichi P. Semitsu, *Widening Batson's Net to Ensnare More Than the Unapologetically Bigoted or Painfully Unimaginative Attorney*, 96 Corn. L. Rev. 1075 (2011) (concluding that *Batson* is not achieving its objective and is unlikely ever to do so as the doctrine stands; arguing that findings regarding striking attorney's subjective intent should not be required and that procedures should enable seating of improperly stricken juror without her realizing she was ever made the subject of a strike); Leonard L. Cavise, *The* Batson *Doctrine: The Supreme Court's Utter Failure to Meet the Challenge of Discrimination in Jury Selection*, 1999 Wisc. L. Rev. 501 (showing that *Purkett* has almost rendered *Batson* meaningless, and presenting various alternatives).

in *Batson* are those who never expected it to work in the first place." Catherine M. Grosso & Barbara O'Brien, *A Stubborn Legacy: The Overwhelming Importance of Race in Jury Selection in 173 Post*-Batson *North Carolina Capital Trials*, 97 Iowa L. Rev. 1531, 1533 (2012).

If *Batson* and its progeny are not rendered an utter charade, then it may be that their complexity—not only the procedural complications they cause but also the fact that they confront courts and litigators with so many uncomfortable questions—will create pressure for the elimination of peremptories. Would that be a good thing? Compare the attitudes of Justice Marshall and of his successor, Justice Thomas. First, Justice Marshall, concurring in *Batson* itself, 476 U.S. at 102–03: "[E]nd[ing] the racial discrimination that peremptories inject into the jury-selection process ... can be accomplished only by eliminating peremptory challenges entirely." And Justice Thomas, concurring in the judgment (on the basis of *stare decisis*) in *McCollum*, 505 U.S. at 60: "I am certain that black criminal defendants will rue the day that this Court ventured down this road that inexorably will lead to the elimination of peremptory strikes."

My own feelings are rather glaringly mixed. On the one hand, I think that peremptories for a criminal defendant serve a valuable, and long-standing role, in offering, as Blackstone put it, "tenderness and humanity" to a criminal defendant. 4 *Commentaries on the Laws of England*, vol. 4, at *353. Assuming the venire has been fairly chosen, peremptories say to the defendant, in effect,

> If we punish you criminally, you will have no complaint about the composition of your jury. You will, of course, have an opportunity to persuade the judge that a given venire member is biased against you. And even if you can't do that, we'll still let you strike a few venire members just because you have a feeling that that venire member will be more disposed than the run of jurors to vote against you, even if that feeling is based on nothing more than gut instinct and stereotype.

Prosecutors, I believe, stand on a much different footing. They represent the power of the state, not the party the state is seeking to punish; there is not the same need for "tenderness and mercy." True, occasionally a juror may be so disposed against the prosecution that even the most overwhelming evidence will not be sufficient to persuade him or her to vote for a guilty verdict. But, if it is that clear that the juror is biased, a challenge for cause should succeed; it is unclear why the prosecutor needs the bludgeon of peremptorily striking jurors it doesn't like rather than having to convince the court of likely bias. Furthermore, though one or two committed anti-prosecution jurors may occasionally be enough to cause a jury to hang, they will almost certainly not have enough strength to turn a verdict of guilty to not guilty. Finally, lawyers seem to be considerably less successful than they think they are in affecting outcomes by their use of peremptories, even when they are aided by purportedly scientific selection methods. Reid Hastie, *Is Attorney-Conducted Voir Dire an Effective Procedure for the Selection of Impartial Juries?*, 40 Am. U.L. Rev. 703, 717–19 (1991). Appearance may be significantly more at stake than result in this area.

Many systems, including the federal courts with respect to noncapital felonies, treat peremptories asymmetrically, granting more peremptories for the defense than for the prosecution. I am inclined to the view that this asymmetry should be extended: Peremptories should be allowed for criminal defendants but not for prosecutors.[8] Not surprisingly, this is a suggestion that drives some prosecutors almost apoplectic.[9] For better or worse, I stick to my view.[10]

2. PRELIMINARY INSTRUCTIONS TO THE JURY AND OPENING STATEMENTS

After the jurors are selected and sworn, the judge gives them preliminary instructions about their responsibilities as jurors—to be fair, to keep an open mind, not to talk about the case with each other or anybody else until they begin deliberations, not to visit the scene of the events, and so forth. The lawyers may then make their opening statements. The defendant may, if she wishes, postpone her opening statement until the presentation of her evidence.

The opening gives each lawyer a chance to introduce herself to the jury, to explain the nature of the case, and to give the jury a preview of the evidence. Of course, if you do not know just what will be admitted into evidence, this can be a problem.

¶ **2.18:** Assume that you are the prosecutor in *State v. Silver*, the exam question from Chapter 1. You would like to refer during your opening statement to Officer Tuesday's conversation with Ms. Levine five days after the murders (Part

---

[8] *An Asymmetrical Approach to the Problem of Peremptories?*, 28 Crim. L. Bull 507 (1992).

I am inclined also to say that the defendant's peremptories ought to be truly peremptory— that is, *McCollum* should be overruled. As to civil litigants, I am inclined to say that either peremptories ought to be eliminated or they ought to be truly peremptory. In other words, I tend to favor a solution eliminating the need for *Batson*-type inquiries, in part by restricting the scope of *Batson* and in part by limiting the opportunity for *Batson* violations.

[9] Lynn A. Helland et al., *An Asymmetrical Approach to the Problem of Peremptories: A Rebuttal*, 30 Crim. L. Bull. 242 (1994).

[10] *Asymmetrical Peremptories Defended: A Reply*, 31 Crim. L. Bull. 337 (1995). On the general issue of asymmetry in the law, see Robert Laurence, *The Bothersome Need for Asymmetry . . .*, 27 Conn. L. Rev. 979 (1995).

A(4) of the exam question). May you? If you are unsure, what may you do?

Another limitation articulated by the black-letter law is that the lawyer may not argue during the opening. Sometimes the line between previewing the evidence and making an argument is difficult to draw. Some courts try to prevent advocates from drawing inferences during the opening statement, but that seems unrealistic. Some say that an advocate may discuss only the evidence she will present, not her impeachment of the other side—a rule that is chafing for a defense lawyer whose job at trial may be principally to challenge the case presented by the prosecution. Not surprisingly, the rule against argument in the opening statement is pervasively violated, and one scholar who has studied the matter with care has concluded that it is rare to find an opening that does not argue. L. Timothy Perrin, *From O.J. to McVeigh: The Use of Argument in the Opening Statement*, 48 Emory L.J. 107 (1999). Indeed, often opposing counsel do not object to assertions in opening statements that sound an awful lot like argument—such as a prosecutor's declaration in the O.J. Simpson murder case that Simpson killed his ex-wife out of jealousy, that "if he couldn't have her, then nobody could," and defense counsel's repeated assertion that the case was "about a rush to judgment, an obsession to win at any cost and by any means necessary." *Id.* at 150.

¶ 2.19: Consider the following passages from opening statements made in Ted's case. First, by Ted's attorney:

> And why did Splashy Publishing Co. offer such a one-sided deal? After you hear the evidence in this case you'll know why. Because they knew my client was in terrible cash trouble. Because they knew he trusted them. Because they knew he was naïve in financial affairs. And because they didn't care how much they took advantage of him.

And now by Splashy's lawyer:

> And why did Ted accept Splashy's offer? After you hear the evidence in this case, you'll know why. Because he had gotten himself into a position where he needed cash instantly, and because his credit was so poor he couldn't get a better loan anywhere else. Ted was a terrible credit risk, and only Splashy, in an act of extreme loyalty and good will, was willing to lend him the money.

Is either of these passages improper, in whole or in part? If you were the opposing party in each case, would you object? If you believe that your adversary will hesitate to object to your opening, should that belief affect the opening?

3.   PRESENTATION OF EVIDENCE

Additional Suggested Reading: McCormick, ch. 1, § 4; Mueller & Kirkpatrick, § 6.54

After the opening statements comes the main event, the presentation of evidence. The ordinary order of presentation is reasonably straightforward. For simplicity, let's focus on a civil case; a criminal case is pretty much the same in this respect. The plaintiff goes first because he has the burden of producing evidence on all the elements of his claim. There is actually a significant amount of ambiguity in this statement, which we will explore in Chapter 21: What is an element of the claim? What does it take to satisfy the burden? For now, though, it is enough to say that the plaintiff has to go first because if everybody went home immediately, without any evidence being presented at all, the defendant would win: It is, after all, the plaintiff who is seeking relief from the court, and who therefore has to prove his case.[11]

"Plaintiff first" is the usual rule. Be aware, however, that it may be subject to variation.

> **¶ 2.20:** Windsor Suppliers, a liquor importer, has told Discount Distributors Co., one of its wholesalers in the State of Confusion, that in two months it will stop supplying DDC with product. Windsor has stated to DDC that DDC was doing a poor job of marketing Windsor's brands. DDC has responded that the termination was the result of a price-fixing conspiracy with Windsor's other wholesaler, Upscale Liquor Co., and has threatened to bring an antitrust action. Before DDC brought suit, Windsor brought a declaratory judgment action. Which side should present its evidence first?

When the plaintiff has presented all his evidence—his *case-in-chief*—he rests. The defendant may then make a motion for judgment as a matter of law, contending that the plaintiff has not presented enough evidence to warrant further proceedings. (In some jurisdictions a criminal defendant may be deemed to have waived a motion to dismiss for insufficient evidence if the motion is not made at the close of the prosecution's case.) Assuming this motion is denied, the defendant then presents its case-in-chief. After the defendant rests, the plaintiff has an opportunity to present a *rebuttal* case, responding to the evidence the defendant has presented, and then the defendant gets a corresponding chance. In theory, the ball could keep bouncing back from one side to another, but it rarely does.

---

[11] The court may give the plaintiff some leeway in introducing evidence that does not bear strictly on elements of the plaintiff's claim but rather bears on affirmative defenses that the plaintiff anticipates the defendant will try to prove.

When both sides have finally rested, either side in a civil case, or the defendant in a criminal case, may make a motion for judgment as a matter of law, contending that it should win judgment on all or part of the case without the need to send it to the jury. This motion is sometimes known by other names, such as a motion for directed verdict or, in criminal cases, for judgment of acquittal. Again, timing is critical. For example, in federal civil litigation the motion must be made before the case is submitted to the jury or it will be waived. *See* Fed. R. Civ. P. 50(a); *Baker v. Advanced Mixer, Inc.*, 1994 WL 178106, at 8, Prod. Liab. Rep. (CCH) ¶ 13,920, at 44,304–05 (E.D. Pa. May 6, 1994).

Virtually all evidence is presented through the testimony of witnesses. Usually witnesses testify live in court, under oath. In some circumstances, where it is difficult or impossible for the witness to testify at trial, testimony taken and recorded at an earlier time may be presented at trial, either through the reading of a transcript or, in recent years, by video presentation. And occasionally child witnesses are allowed to testify in a separate room, in the presence of very few people, with the testimony shown in the trial courtroom by closed-circuit television. These methods of presenting testimony raise significant problems, which we will address in Chapter 20.

Much evidence is tangible stuff—documents and physical items that are either themselves significant to the case or demonstrative of what some significant item is like. Most tangible evidence is admitted through the testimony of a witness, who must explain what the evidence is. Similarly, if some sort of demonstration—an in-court experiment, for example—is presented, it will ordinarily be through the testimony of an explaining witness. A limited category of "self-authenticating" physical evidence is admissible without the need for a sponsoring witness. *See* FRE 902.

If the witness is a child, an adult may accompany her to the witness stand to help make her more comfortable. As we have seen, a witness who does not speak English well may be accompanied by an interpreter. In an earlier period, when trial practice was not quite so lawyer-dominated as it has become, sometimes two opposing witnesses would give their testimony at the same time, so that they could dispute each other; the 17th century judge Sir Matthew Hale, writing in support of the open English way of taking testimony, in contrast to the practice that dominated in Continental courts, said that it gave the "Opportunity of confronting the adverse Witnesses." But in a modern American courtroom, unlike congressional hearings, witnesses almost always testify alone, one by one. Indeed, courts often exclude prospective witnesses from the courtroom, so that they do not hear the testimony of other witnesses.

FRE 615 authorizes the court to do this on its own motion, and requires it to do so on request of a party. This Rule has limited exceptions, such as for a party who is a natural person and for a designated representative of an entity-party.

The usual procedure for taking testimony mimics that for the trial as a whole. The party who put the witness on the stand—the *proponent*— asks questions on direct examination. The opponent then has an opportunity for cross examination. The proponent may then take up issues raised by the opponent by conducting redirect. The opponent may have questions for re-cross; there could be re-redirect, and so forth, but usually the ball stops bouncing after a few trips across the net.

4.   CLOSING ARGUMENT AND FINAL INSTRUCTIONS

After both sides have rested, they each have an opportunity to sum up the evidence for the trier of fact. Here, unlike the opening, they may, and are expected to, make arguments. Moreover, courts will indulge some arguments that are not strictly appeals to cold reasoning from the evidence. The most effective arguments seems to be ones that connect to jurors' emotions and use explanatory devices like analogies and demonstrative aids but also reason through the evidence with the jury and are clear, organized, and (usually) brief. H. Mitchell Caldwell, L. Timothy Perrin & Christopher L. Frost, *The Art and Architecture of Closing Argument*, 76 Tul. L. Rev. 961 (2002).

There are limitations on argument, of course. Consider whether each of the following four arguments is proper. Would you make the argument? If your adversary made the argument, would you object?

¶ 2.21: Gerald Larson is on trial for possession of a deadly weapon with intent to use it. The prosecution has presented the testimony of Officer Betsy Fleck that, in the course of a chase, Larson pulled out a pistol and aimed it at Fleck. In explaining how the chase occurred, Fleck has given the following testimony:

Q: Now, at about 8 p.m. on the evening of July 3, while you were patrolling, did you have a conversation with one Diana Mears?

A: Yes, I did.

Q: And what happened as a result of that conversation?

A: I asked Ms. Mears to enter my patrol car. I then proceeded north on Eighth Avenue and then west on 63d Street.

Q: Did you then have a further conversation with Ms. Mears?

A: Yes, I did.

Q: And as a result of that conversation what happened?

A: I used the patrol car's mike to instruct a male who was running down the street to halt.

Q: Do you see that man here in the courtroom?

A: Yes, over there.

Q: Let the record reflect that the witness is pointing to the defendant.

In closing, the prosecutor makes the following statement:

It doesn't take a lot of imagination or common sense to realize that Ms. Mears had been the victim of a robbery, or at least had witnessed a robbery, and was directing the officer to find the perpetrator.

¶ **2.22:** Barry Walker is accused of burglarizing Clement and Anna Friday's apartment. The only evidence linking him to the crime is his fingerprint, found in the bathroom of the apartment. Walker has testified that he painted the apartment the previous August. Ms. Friday has testified, without objection, that to her knowledge the apartment was not painted then, and that her husband, who was home ill during that month, had not mentioned any painting. Mr. Friday did not testify. During closing, Walker's attorney argues:

So where is Clement Friday to testify? He's not here, and I think you can infer that his testimony would have been unfavorable to the prosecution. That's why he's not here.

See *People v. Walker,* 119 A.D.2d 521, 500 N.Y.S.2d 704 (1st Dept.1986). In evaluating whether the defense should be allowed to make this argument, should it matter that the defense made no attempt to subpoena Clement Friday to testify?

¶ **2.23:** Lorenzo Colston, a young black man, was stopped by two white police officers in what began as a routine traffic stop. The event turned into an altercation in which Colston was shot in the backside and seriously injured while running from the officers. He is now on trial for assaulting an officer of the peace. The prosecutor argues in closing: "The question is whether you 12 jurors will band together and send a message to our community that we support our law enforcement officers. Or will we send a message that it is O.K. to violently attack those officers?" Prof. Stephen Gillers, one of the nation's leading experts on legal ethics, wrote about this passage:

American juries are not asked to send messages, let alone messages about whether "it is O.K." to assault the police. The job of the American jury is to decide cases by resolving factual disputes. The only questions for the jury in Mr. Colston's trial were what the defendant and others did or did not do on a particular occasion.

See Letter to the Editor of the New York Times, Mar. 2, 1994, p. 14. Do you agree?

¶ 2.24: One adapted from the old TV show *L.A. Law*: Rattan, the son of a diplomat, meets Danvers at a party and later rapes her. After learning that diplomatic immunity precludes Rattan from being prosecuted, Danvers invites him to her house, purportedly to renew their acquaintance. She lures him to the bedroom and then shoots him to death. At her trial for murder she pleads insanity. Her lawyer presents no psychiatric evidence, but argues to the jury, "You have to find that she was insane, because that's the only way you can find her not guilty."

In some jurisdictions, the defendant gives the first argument and then the plaintiff (or prosecution) argues; in others, the plaintiff gets both the first and last words in argument. Occasionally—very occasionally—something happens at argument that makes it appropriate to re-open the evidence. Consider, for example, *Bangs v. Maple Hills, Ltd.*, 585 N.W.2d 262 (Iowa 1998). The plaintiff brought an action for injuries she suffered when she tripped and fell on a sidewalk grate that allegedly tipped forward when she stepped on it. After the accident, the defendant welded the grate shut, but under the rule for "subsequent remedial measures" evidence of that fact was not admissible to show that the defendant was negligent for not having done so earlier. *Cf.* FRE 407. In closing argument, the plaintiff's counsel said that defendant should have welded the grate shut. Defense counsel responded in her argument that this "wouldn't work." Bad move, as it turns out. To prove that it would have been feasible to take a remedial measure that would have prevented the accident, the plaintiff *may* prove that the defendant took that measure afterwards *if* the defendant controverts feasibility. The defendant's argument controverted the feasibility contention, and the court allowed the plaintiff to introduce photographs showing the grate welded shut. The plaintiff won a verdict, and the state supreme court held it was within the trial court's discretion to re-open the evidence.

Sooner or later, the real last word before the jury begins its deliberations usually belongs to the judge, who instructs the jury. There are two basic parts to the final instructions. First, the judge gives the jury general instructions as to its responsibilities in deliberations and the procedures it should follow. Second, the judge instructs the jury as to the applicable law, and in some jurisdictions discusses, with reference to the evidence presented at trial, the factual questions that the jurors must resolve.

This tradition may seem rather odd to you. The substantive instructions to the jurors tell them the issues they must decide and so give them the framework for evaluating the evidence and the arguments. And yet the instructions come only at the very end of the case, after the arguments as well as the evidence. This oddity was apparently not lost on the rulemakers. In 1987, Fed.R.Civ.P. 51 was amended to allow the court to instruct the jury before or after argument, or both. (Rule 51(b)(3) now provides that the court "may instruct the jury at any time before the jury is discharged.") Similar language has been added to Fed.R.Crim.P. 30.

¶ 2.25: (a) Recall ¶ 2.20, the Windsor-DDC liquor distribution case. Before trial, Windsor's attorney believes that she can prove that Windsor terminated DDC because DDC's price-cutting was destroying the image of Windsor's brands. The difficulty is that she does not know whether under the antitrust laws this should be considered a permissible reason to terminate; in particular, she does not know how the trial judge will rule on the issue. What can she do to gain some comfort? What does this suggest about when the court should hold the "charging conference," at which the court hears and rules on requests to charge? Assuming that the judge has not ruled on this issue before the closing arguments, may Windsor's attorney refer in her argument to how she thinks the judge will instruct the jury? What problems are created if she is allowed to do this? If she is not?

(b) If you were the judge in this case, would you give your instructions before argument, after argument, or some before and some after? If you were to split the instructions, how would you do it?

5. JURY DELIBERATIONS AND VERDICT

FRE 606(b)

The jurors of the early common law were not expected to be passive recipients of party-provided information. On the contrary, they were expected to be people of the community who would know the facts of the case or, if they did not, would go out and make inquiries. Over the course of several centuries, this model of the self-informing jury gave way to a model in which the jurors are generally expected to know nothing about the facts of the particular controversy being tried except the information provided to them at trial by the parties. The model of the passive jury has been carried to extremes at times. For example, traditionally courts forbade jurors to take notes—apparently out of fear that the literate jurors would then dominate deliberations. Most courts no longer adhere to this restriction; some judges, indeed, go so far as to provide jurors with pads and pens, actively encouraging them to take notes. The model of the passive jury still prevails, but in some ways it may be under assault.

¶ 2.26: Suppose you are the trial judge in a complicated criminal securities fraud case, which will likely take several weeks to try. Consider the pros and cons of instructing the jurors that

(a) they may not talk about the evidence among themselves until the case is submitted to them.

(b) any time a juror wants to ask a question of a witness, the lawyer, or the judge, she should raise her hand and at a convenient time she will be recognized, though if the judge deems the question an inappropriate one it will not be answered.

(c) any time a juror wants to ask a question, she should submit it to the judge in writing, and if the judge deems the question appropriate it will be answered.

(d) the law is as the judge is explaining it, but if the jury believes, notwithstanding these instructions, that the defendant should not be convicted, it may acquit him.[12]

During the course of the jury's deliberations, it may ask to view certain exhibits again or to hear certain testimony reread. These requests may be significant, because if the losing side claims on appeal that admission of that evidence was erroneous, the jury's manifestation of interest helps counter an argument that any error was harmless. Indeed, the amount of time that the jury takes to deliberate may have significance; other things being equal, the more time the jurors deliberated, the closer the case probably appeared to them, and the less likely that an evidentiary error, or some other problem that occurred during trial, will be deemed harmless.

After the jury foreman or forewoman reads the verdict, the jurors are usually polled individually—just to make sure that the verdict as read is correct. *See, e.g.,* Fed.R.Crim.P. 31(d). After the verdict is rendered, the parties and their attorneys are free to speak to the jurors, if the jurors want to speak with them. Suppose the attorneys learn that the jury

---

[12] See Nancy J. King, *Juror Delinquency in Criminal Trials in America, 1796–1996*, 94 Mich. L. Rev. 2673, 2736–37, 2742–44 (1996), and sources cited there. *Cf.* Paul Butler, *Racially Based Jury Nullification: Black Power in the Criminal Justice System*, 105 Yale L.J. 677, 679 (1995) (arguing that because of racism in the criminal justice system "it is the moral responsibility of black jurors to emancipate some guilty black outlaws"). On the history of "jury nullification," see Thomas A. Green, *Verdict According to Conscience* (1985).

reached its decision by lot, or by taking an average of the sums that each juror would award the plaintiff, or by reading newspaper accounts of the trial, or otherwise in violation of the judge's instructions. This is misconduct, and it seemingly should warrant the grant of a new trial. But if a new trial were granted every time the jury disregarded the judge's instructions, litigation could go on indefinitely. Accordingly, many courts are unwilling to be painfully honest, and instead treat the jury as something of a "black box," into whose machinations they do not want to look too closely. Note the rather strange resolution offered by FRE 606(b). That Rule provides in essence that, in an inquiry into the validity of a verdict, the court may not consider the testimony or any other statement of a juror about any occurrence during the jury's deliberations or any influence on the juror's mental processes—except that the court may consider what the juror says about any "extraneous prejudicial information" or "outside influence" that may have improperly affected the deliberations. According to the Advisory Committee's notes, that Rule does not govern the grounds on which a new trial may be granted, but only the circumstances in which a juror may testify, or an out-of-court statement by her may be considered, to impeach the verdict. But obviously if the testimony of the jurors is precluded, it may be impossible—absent a cooperative eavesdropper—to prove the irregularity.

The Supreme Court has treated Rule 606(b) quite stringently. Consider the remarkable case of *Tanner v. United States*, 483 U.S. 107 (1987). Tanner and Conover were convicted after an extensive trial of fraud charges arising from conduct related to a federally supported construction project. After the trial, juror Vera Asbul told Tanner's lawyer that several of the jurors had consumed alcohol during the lunch breaks at various times throughout the trial, causing them to sleep through the afternoons. Another juror, Daniel Hardy, gave the defense a sworn statement that he "felt like . . . the jury was on one big party." In addition to alcohol use by seven jurors, including himself, Hardy asserted that during the trial he and three other jurors smoked marijuana regularly, he observed two jurors ingest cocaine repeatedly, and one juror sold another a quarter pound of marijuana. By a 5–4 vote, the Court held that the trial judge was not required to hold a hearing inquiring into these assertions. It did not find such a requirement either in Rule 606(b) or in the Sixth Amendment's guarantee of "a tribunal both impartial and mentally competent to afford a hearing," *Jordan v. Massachusetts*, 225 U.S. 167, 176 (1912). The Court stressed the importance of finality, the danger of intruding into juror deliberations, and the availability of other methods of protecting the defendant's rights, such as jury selection and observation of the jury during the trial by the judge, other court personnel, and counsel. The Court left open the possibility of a post-verdict inquiry "when an extremely strong showing of [juror] incompetency has been made," 483 U.S. at 126. In this case, though the two jurors had testified to misconduct, there was meager evidence of incompetence. The Court said,

> There is little doubt that postverdict investigation into juror misconduct would in some instances lead to the invalidation of verdicts reached after irresponsible or improper juror behavior. It is not at all clear, however, that the jury system could survive such efforts to perfect it.

Id. at 120.

¶ **2.27:** Are you persuaded? Should the Court have held, as the dissent argued, that the prohibition of Rule 606(b) was inapplicable to this case? If you believe *Tanner* was rightly decided, do you think the result should be the same if it were a capital case? What should the result be if several jurors held a consultation with a ouija board to try to determine the facts in the case? *See R. v. Young,* [1995] QB 324, [1995] 2 WLR 430, [1995] 2 Cr App Rep 379 (Ct. App. (Crim. Div. 1994). What if two jurors made derogatory comments and jokes reflecting bias towards the defendant's racial group? *See Sander v. United Kingdom,* 8 BHRC 279 (Eur. Ct. Hum. Rts. 2000); *Pena-Rodriguez v. Colorado,* 350 P.3d 287 (Col. 2015), *cert. granted,* Apr. 4, 2016, No. 15–606.

¶ **2.28:** In ¶ 2.9, an auto negligence case, juror Jubal, who knows the area well, reports to the rest of the jury, "The way the sun is shining at that intersection at that time of day, I don't think the plaintiff could have seen the light, even if it was red." Should a verdict for the plaintiff be set aside for juror misconduct? What if Jubal's report was based on a visit he made to the intersection shortly before deliberations began, rather than on his prior knowledge of it? What if he did not report to his co-jurors what he had learned on his visit? *Cf. In re Beverly Hills Farm Litigation,* 695 F.2d 207 (6th Cir. 1982) (in case arising from fire caused by allegedly faulty wiring, witness experiments on wiring at home and reports to jurors).

¶ **2.29:** Kelly has been convicted of having sexually molested several children at a day care center. In a TV documentary about the case, one of the jurors says that in its deliberations the jury discussed an article from Redbook Magazine about pedophilia. Should the court inquire into whether this is true? If the court does make the inquiry, and it concludes that the juror was telling the truth, what should it do? Does it matter whether a juror actually brought the article into the jury room or simply described the article to the rest of the jury? In the latter case, should it matter whether she read the article before or after beginning to serve on the jury for this case? See Sheila Turnage, *Now It's the Jurors' Turn to Take the Stand*, Reuters World Service dispatch, Jan. 19, 1994.

¶ **2.30:** After the jurors have spent a day in deliberations without reaching a verdict, the bailiff tells them that the trial judge is prepared to keep them deliberating for a week if necessary. Shortly after hearing this statement, the jurors do reach a verdict. Is this misconduct? Is it ground for a mistrial? May a juror testify on the mistrial motion?

¶ **2.31:** Shauers, driving a truck, rammed into Warger, who was on a motorcycle; Warger lost a leg as a result of the accident. Claiming that he was stopped at the time of the collision, Warger sues Shauers in federal court. The jury returns a verdict for Shauers. Warger then makes a timely motion for a new trial on the basis of an affidavit given by one of the jurors. The affidavit says that Regina Whipple, the jury foreperson, revealed during deliberations that her daughter had been at fault in a fatal motor vehicle accident, and that a lawsuit would have ruined the daughter's life. Warger contends that Whipple had deliberately lied during *voir dire* when she said she would be able to award damages for pain and suffering and future medical expenses and that she would be an impartial juror. In support of the motion, Warger argues that Rule 606(b) does not apply because the affidavit reveals misconduct at *voir dire*, not in deliberations. And he says that this case satisfies the standards of *McDonough Power Equipment, Inc. v. Greenwood*, 464 U.S. 548 (1984), under which a party may obtain a new trial if he "demonstrate[s] that a juror failed to answer honestly a material question on *voir dire*, and . . . that a correct response would have provided a valid basis for a challenge for cause." (The *McDonough* Court held that the standards were not met in that case because the inaccuracy of the juror's answer—about which the party learned from a non-juror—was not dishonest.) What should the court do? See *Warger v. Shauers*, 135 S.Ct. 521 (2014).

There is one pocket of flexibility in Rule 606(b) that sometimes comes into play. Rule 606(b)(2)(C), the substance of which was added in 2006, allows a juror to testify about whether "a mistake was made in entering the verdict onto the verdict form." This amendment confirmed the holdings of some prior courts that determining whether the verdict reported to the court is actually the verdict to which the jury agreed is distinguishable from probing into the jury's deliberative process. Consider, for example, one of those cases, *TeeVee Toons, Inc. v. MP3.Com, Inc.*, 148 F.Supp.2d 276 (S.D.N.Y. 2001). There, the jurors had to make awards for 145 copyright infringements. They agreed on the overall structure of the verdict and left it to one of the jurors to calculate and enter the individual entries on the verdict sheet. Only when the total of the awards was mentioned in the news reports did they realize that she had goofed big-time; the awards announced in court amounted to only about one-tenth of the approximately $3,000,000 they had agreed on. The court was able to reconstruct what had happened—the jurors were unanimous—and correct the error.

¶ **2.32:** What should the court do in a case like *TeeVee Toons* if the jurors are *not* unanimous?

6.   A NOTE ON BENCH TRIALS

The same basic procedures are followed for bench trials, but obviously they can be simplified: There is no jury selection, no instructions to the jury, and no charging conference. Instead, once the evidence is in, the judge will generally hear arguments on the facts and the law. Often the parties will submit post-trial briefs explaining their side of the case and making references to the transcript, if the trial has been transcribed. The judge may decide the case immediately, or she may put decision off for some time to allow her to write an opinion. In jurisdictions following the Federal Rules of Civil Procedure, the court must "find the facts specially and state its conclusions of law separately," Rule 52(a)(1), but the judge may, if she wishes, state these findings and conclusions orally for the record. *See also* Fed.R.Crim.P. 23(c) (providing that in a bench trial the court shall make a general finding, guilty or not guilty, and also, upon timely request, "state its specific findings of fact," and permitting oral findings).

Rules excluding evidence generally apply to bench trials as well as to jury trials, though judges tend to give some exclusionary rules little force in bench trials. In part this tendency reflects the difficulty imposed on the judge of considering evidence for admissibility purposes and then putting it out of mind if she decides that it is inadmissible. And the tendency may also reflect the idea that, to the extent that the exclusionary rules are based on distrust of the jury, it is anomalous to apply them to a trial judge as factfinder. Indeed, in Britain, where there are now hardly any civil jury trials, the rule against hearsay has been eliminated in civil cases, and one of the principal reasons offered for the change is that the judge rather than a jury is the factfinder. But this book will suggest that distrust of the jury is a less persuasive basis for exclusionary rules than is often thought. Some applications of exclusionary rules are justified whether the factfinder is a judge or the jury. In such a case, it would be unfortunate if the conduct of a bench trial resulted in disregard of the rule. Thus, the continued persistence even in bench trials of some exclusionary rules, such as rules of privilege, is not anomalous but may reflect recognition that their value is not based on the presence of a jury.

Other applications of exclusionary rules are not well justified, and if the conduct of a bench trial provides a fortuitous basis for declining to make such an application, the result is a good one even if the reason given for it is unpersuasive.

CHAPTER 3

RELEVANCE

■ ■ ■

FRE 401–403

Additional Reading: McCormick, ch. 16; Mueller & Kirkpatrick, §§ 4.1–4.10

Chapter 2 dealt primarily with the big picture, with the structure of a trial and the procedures governing it. Now we will begin to narrow our focus to individual items of evidence. The law of evidence provides a gatekeeping role: Although jurors are expected to come to trial with a fundamental knowledge of the world—a topic we will explore more thoroughly in Chapter 21—their knowledge of the facts of the particular case is supposed to be based entirely on the information that is presented to them at trial. Only if the court *admits* an item of evidence will the jury learn of it and be able to consider it. Most of the rest of the course will examine what items are admissible and the procedure under which they are admitted.

Perhaps the most fundamental principle of the law of evidence is this: Evidence that is not relevant is not admissible. The second sentence of FRE 402 states this principle explicitly. In an oft-quoted passage, the great nineteenth-century scholar James Bradley Thayer said that this principle is "not so much a rule of evidence as a presupposition involved in the very conception of a rational scheme of evidence." *Preliminary Treatise on Evidence* 264 (1898). Unless evidence is relevant to some fact of consequence to determination of the action, there is no reason to admit it.

A companion principle expressed by the first sentence of Rule 402 is that if evidence is relevant to such a fact, then ordinarily it ought to be admitted—unless there is some reason not to. Rule 402 sets up a presumption that relevant evidence is admissible unless otherwise provided by the rules or by some other governing source of law. Whether or not this approach makes sense depends, of course, on the definition of relevant evidence and on the breadth of the grounds for exclusion. In this chapter, we will explore the definition of relevance and some of the general principles governing exclusion.

The Federal Rules take a fairly standard approach, providing a generous definition of relevance but also broad and discretionary grounds of exclusion. Rule 401 states the basic definition of "relevant evidence":

Evidence is relevant if:

(a) it has any tendency to make a fact more or less probable than it would be without the evidence; and

(b) the fact is of consequence in determining the action.

This definition makes perfect sense.[1] Certain factual propositions that are of consequence to the determination of the action will be in dispute; that is what a trial is all about. The trial will not ordinarily prove or disprove these propositions absolutely, and indeed such absolute proof is rare, if it exists at all. Rather, the proof will leave the proposition somewhere in the range between totally implausible and totally certain—in other words, somewhere between 0% and 100% probability. To be relevant, evidence must have a role in that determination. That is, it must either raise or lower the probability that would be assigned to the proposition in the absence of the evidence.

Lurking in or near this straightforward definition, however, are several important and frequently difficult problems. For now, we will focus on three. First is the determination of the category of material factual propositions; evidence is not relevant in the abstract but rather *to* some proposition, and for the evidence to be admissible it must be relevant to a material proposition. Second is the differentiation among three separate concepts—relevance, sufficiency, and conclusiveness. For an item of evidence to be deemed relevant, it need not prove a material proposition conclusively; indeed, even if such absolute proof were possible on the basis of an entire body of evidence, a single evidentiary item would not provide it. Neither need the evidentiary item be sufficient in itself to prove the material proposition. It is only necessary that the evidence alter the probability of the proposition. Third is the distinction between the relevance of evidence and its weight or probative value. Relevance does not guarantee admissibility, for countervailing factors may weigh in favor of exclusion. The more probative it is, the more weight will line up on the proponent's side of the scale, and the more likely will be admissibility.

---

[1] It might, however, be criticized for speaking of the probability of a proposition as if it were a quantity that can be objectively determined. The better view of probability, at least for the purposes of assessing evidence in litigation, is as a measure of an observer's subjective confidence in the truth of a proposition. This idea is further explored in part C.2(a) of this chapter.

A. WHAT PROPOSITIONS ARE MATERIAL?

The law of evidence does not tell us what facts are "of consequence in determining the action." At base, that is a matter of the substantive law that governs the case. Sometimes it is convenient to break a claim or defense down into a set of propositions called *elements*. For example, in a fraud action, the substantive law of the jurisdiction may provide that for the plaintiff to prevail he must prove that (1) the defendant made a representation, (2) it was false, (3) the defendant knew it was false or acted with reckless disregard to its truth, (4) the plaintiff relied on the representation, and (5) the reliance was detrimental.[2] Each of these propositions is, by definition, of consequence to the determination of the action—or, to use the term that the drafters of the Federal Rules avoided, "material." Thus, any evidence tending to increase or decrease the probability of any one of these propositions is therefore relevant.

But now we can extend the circle of material propositions more broadly. A subsidiary proposition may bear so closely, as a matter of logic or just plain common sense, on one of the elemental propositions, or on its negation, that the subsidiary proposition may itself be considered a material proposition. For example, suppose that in the fraud case the plaintiff contends that the defendant misrepresented the fertility of her cow in an oral statement made to a group of bystanders. It would then be a material proposition that the plaintiff was not within earshot of the defendant when she made the statement; if that subsidiary proposition is true, it is clearly less likely (though not impossible) that the plaintiff relied on the misrepresentation. Evidence of the plaintiff's location at the time of the statement would therefore be considered relevant to an issue in the case. And if a witness testifies that the plaintiff was standing next to Judith Jones at the time, then Judith's location is also a material proposition. There is no inherent limit to the length of such logical chains.

[handwritten margin note: close enough to count!]

[handwritten margin note: "proximity" not on issue for relevance (see "ingenuity of counsel" in FRE 401 note)]

Notice that relevance is always a relative term; that is, in saying that evidence is relevant we must cite a material proposition *to which* it is relevant. All evidence is relevant to *some* propositions. For example, if a witness testifies that Judith was wearing a blue blouse at the key time, that is certainly relevant evidence to show her color preferences. On its

---

[2] Sometimes this approach, breaking a claim down into elemental propositions each of which must be proven, does not accurately reflect the nature of the law. In some cases, the plaintiff's task is not so much to prove that each of several propositions is true as to prove that a combination of factors supports his claim. For example, the Supreme Court has said that under the "rule of reason," which applies to claims under § 1 of the Sherman Antitrust Act when the defendant's conduct is not *per se* unlawful, "the factfinder weighs all of the facts of a case in deciding whether a restrictive practice should be prohibited as imposing an unreasonable restraint on competition." Continental T.V., Inc. v. GTE Sylvania, Inc., 433 U.S. 36, 49 (1977). In such a case, any factor that the court deemed appropriate for the factfinder to weigh in that balance would be considered a material factor.

face, however, it does not seem to give us much information about where Judith was standing at the time.

¶ **3.1:** Should the objection to evidence of the color of Judith's blouse be "Irrelevant!", "Immaterial!", or some combination of the two? *– maybe connect to credibility of witness – corroborate they were there – w/ ev from someone else who saw blue blouse*

Much of the discussion in this chapter so far—and, indeed, much of *or establish* the structure of the law of evidence—may be summarized in the following *that witness* illustration, which is represented in Figure 3.a. Suppose that Donald is on *has good* trial for the murder of Victor. Donald admits killing Victor, and also that *memory* the two had a nasty argument one week before the killing. Donald pleads *of the* self-defense, however. He testifies, "When I saw Victor again, he said, 'I'm *events* going to kill you now, you pig,' and reached inside his pocket. Luckily, I *OR* beat him to the draw." Donald also offers the testimony of Wendy that, *condition)* after the argument but before the killing, Donald told Wendy, "I'm going *relevance –* to buy more life insurance for my wife and kids and dear old mother, *will prove* because Victor has a violent streak." In Figure 3.a, Wendy's testimony is *relevant* represented by the node marked **EVIDENCE**. This testimony is *after someone* admissible if it is relevant to a material proposition and no exclusionary *else testified)* rule bars it with respect to that proposition. Several propositions as to *other evidence* which Donald might try to offer **EVIDENCE** are represented by their *later links into* own nodes. If a proposition is material, its node is represented in the box. *the fact of consequence*

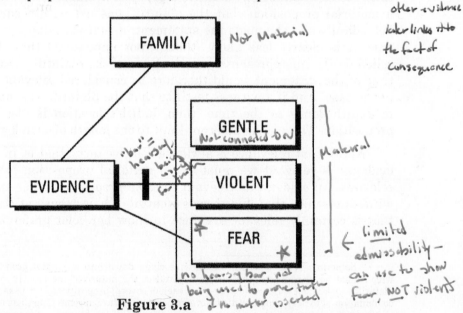

Figure 3.a

First, Donald might offer **EVIDENCE** to prove **FAMILY**, the proposition that he is a good family man. **EVIDENCE** probably is relevant to **FAMILY**—hence the line linking the two—but unfortunately for Donald **FAMILY** is not a material proposition.

b/c family good family man still needs c/o self defense

Next, Donald might offer **EVIDENCE** to prove **GENTLE,** the proposition that he is a person of gentle disposition. This is a material proposition, for if it is true **GENTLE** diminishes the probability that *buying life* Donald would be the aggressor in a fatal fight. But the relevance of *insurance* **EVIDENCE** to **GENTLE** is dubious; hence, no line is drawn connecting *≠ gentle* the two.

Donald's third theory is that **EVIDENCE** proves **VIOLENT**, that Victor is a person of violent tendencies. This, too, is a material proposition, for if it is true Victor is more likely to have been the aggressor. And **EVIDENCE** is clearly relevant to **VIOLENT**; indeed, that very proposition is part of what Donald asserted, according to Wendy. But now an exclusionary rule—represented in the diagram as a bar across the **EVIDENCE-VIOLENT** link—keeps the evidence out: As offered to prove **VIOLENT**, **EVIDENCE** is hearsay because, as you will more fully understand after Chapter 9, it is offered to prove the truth of something Donald purportedly asserted out of court. Perhaps Donald can find a hole in that bar—a hearsay exception—to allow the **EVIDENCE-VIOLENT** link to be made. If he does, then presumably **EVIDENCE** may be admitted to prove **VIOLENT**. But note that the hearsay exception would only help on this theory; it punches a hole in the bar across the link between **EVIDENCE** and **VIOLENT**, but that does nothing about the problems that rendered **EVIDENCE** inadmissible to prove **FAMILY** or **GENTLE**.

Donald's fourth theory is that **EVIDENCE** is relevant to **FEAR,** the proposition that Donald feared Victor. This proposition is material, because if Donald feared Victor he was arguably less likely to be the aggressor.[3] No exclusionary rule blocks the use of **EVIDENCE** for this purpose; there is no bar across the arrow from **EVIDENCE** to **FEAR**. (The hearsay rule is not a problem, as you will see in Chapter 9, because the evidence is being offered to prove the state of Donald's mind, not the truth of his statement.) Hence, **EVIDENCE** can probably be admitted to prove **FEAR**.

In short, to be admissible, evidence has to be relevant to a material proposition, without any exclusionary rule preventing admissibility. Here, **EVIDENCE** is relevant to **FAMILY**, but **FAMILY** is not material; **GENTLE** is material but **EVIDENCE** is not relevant to it; **EVIDENCE** is relevant to **VIOLENT**, which is material, but an exclusionary rule, the rule against hearsay, appears to block admissibility; and all conditions of admissibility are satisfied with respect to **FEAR**. So this appears to be a

---

[3] Note that one might also argue that the evidence points the other way—that if Donald feared Victor Donald might have been more likely to be trigger-happy, to kill Victor pre-emptively. But the prosecution would address this argument primarily to the factfinder; it would not likely cause the evidence to be excluded, because the factfinder could view the evidence in the way that Donald, the proponent, argues it should be viewed.

don't have to show which way evidence goes

case of *limited admissibility*—the evidence is admitted, but under restrictions as to what propositions it may be used to prove.

¶ 3.2: Two women give birth at approximately the same time, but one of the babies dies. For reasons unknown, it is unclear whose baby is the survivor. The two are unable to resolve the matter by mediation and conciliation, and they ask Solomon to arbitrate. Solomon suggests that the living baby be divided in half. One woman says, "That's a good solution." The second says, "No, better give her the baby rather than divide it." Solomon awards the baby to the second woman. *See* 1 Kings 3:16–28; *cf.* Bertolt Brecht, *The Caucasian Chalk Circle* (1944–45) (two women claiming one child pull; the biological mother, who hangs on, loses, and was a worse mother than the servant girl who raised the child).

What factual proposition or propositions were material? What is the source of authority for determining such materiality? To what proposition or propositions was the evidence relevant? How great was its probative value with respect to each such proposition?

B. RELEVANCE, SUFFICIENCY, AND CONCLUSIVENESS

In its Note to FRE 401, the Advisory Committee repeated a famous statement by Dean McCormick: "A brick is not a wall." A party's entire case is the wall; each evidentiary item is a single brick, with a limited function. Relevant evidence need only *alter the probability* of a material proposition. It is not necessary that the evidence be *conclusive* of the case.

Indeed, as suggested at the beginning of this chapter, rarely, if ever, can a disputed factual proposition be proven conclusively, either by a single piece of evidence or by an entire body of evidence. Part of the problem is that absolute certainty is virtually impossible to achieve. One leading decision theorist, Ward Edwards, put the point pungently. If you say that a given proposition is certain, he said, then you should be willing to accept a bet in which you lose your life and everything that is dear to you if you are wrong and you win a penny if you are right—and you should conclude that you got infinitely the better of the deal.

Moreover, however close an entire body of evidence can lead to certainty, the effect of a single piece of evidence is more limited. Suppose that in a criminal assault case the prosecution contends that defendant Dennis was the source of blood found at the crime scene. A DNA test indicating that Dennis's blood has a different profile from that of the blood found at the crime scene might appear conclusive in his favor. But there is some chance of error in the testing, and also a chance—more difficult to evaluate—that, either intentionally or not, the testers worked on the wrong blood.

Sometimes the law may give conclusive effect to a piece or a body of evidence; in Chapter 21, we will discuss conclusive presumptions, which treat one fact as irrefutable proof of another. But such presumptions, which are quite rare, are a matter of policy and not of logic.

Suppose now that the prosecution introduces DNA evidence strongly indicating that Dennis *is* the source of the crime scene blood, and that Dennis argues,

> This evidence doesn't prove that I'm the source of the crime scene blood. It could have arisen through various other courses of events. Perhaps the testers conducted the test wrongly, in any of various different ways, or perhaps they worked on the wrong blood, or perhaps the true source is somebody whose DNA happens to be quite similar to mine.

To this argument, the appropriate response would be,

> Fine. You'll have your chance to explain the evidence away to the jury. But the jurors are entitled to hear the evidence and accept the prosecution's view if they find it more persuasive. We don't demand that the evidence be conclusive as a condition of admissibility. And this evidence clearly has enough probative value to warrant admissibility.

[handwritten margin note: don't have to show conclusiveness of evidence]

Put another way, conclusiveness—which even a whole body of evidence can rarely, if ever, attain—cannot be the test of admissibility for a single item of evidence.

While conclusiveness is too much to demand even of a body of evidence, we can demand that a body of evidence be *sufficient* to prove a given proposition. The prosecution has the burden of producing sufficient evidence to support the elements of a crime; a civil plaintiff has the burden of producing sufficient evidence to support the elements of his claim; and a defendant, civil or criminal, has the burden of producing sufficient evidence to support the elements of any affirmative defense that he wishes to present to the factfinder. If the party bearing such a burden with respect to a given proposition fails to meet it, he loses as a matter of law with respect to that proposition, without the opportunity to persuade the factfinder. Sufficiency of a body of evidence to prove a proposition thus does not mean that the court is persuaded that the given proposition is probably true. Rather, it means that the evidence is sufficient to carry the proponent's burden of producing evidence with respect to that proposition, so that the factfinder could reasonably conclude, to the degree of confidence required by the law, that the proposition is true.

Though a body of evidence can be sufficient to prove a proposition, a single item of evidence need not, as a prerequisite to admissibility, bear the burden of sufficiency. Suppose the prosecutor wants to prove that Dennis was seen in the vicinity of the assault shortly before it occurred. We have just seen that it is not a valid objection to say, "This evidence doesn't prove Dennis's guilt conclusively." Nor is it a valid objection to the admissibility of that item of evidence to say, "This evidence is insufficient to prove Dennis's guilt beyond a reasonable doubt," or even, "This evidence is insufficient to make Dennis's guilt more probable than not." A sound ruling in response to this objection would be:

> Now we're just determining admissibility. At the end of the prosecution's case you will have your opportunity to move to dismiss on the ground that there is insufficient evidence to present to the jury. And if you lose that motion, you will have your opportunity to argue to the jurors that they should not conclude beyond a reasonable doubt that your client committed the crime charged.

(motion for directed judgment of acquittal)

In short, for an item of evidence to be admissible it does not have to be sufficient in itself to prove the party's contention. And for a body of evidence to satisfy the sufficiency standard, where the case is tried to a jury, the proponent need not persuade the judge that her factual contention is correct; she need only persuade the judge that a jury could so find, to the degree of certainty required by law in the particular case.

¶ **3.3:** Larry loves Fern from afar, 123 miles to be exact. Fern is uninterested because she is happily married to Mike, a traveling salesman. Larry writes Fern: "I love you. I am going to kill Mike when he comes to my city on Wednesday." Fern receives this letter Thursday, and she hasn't heard from Mike since Wednesday morning. Fern sues Larry Thursday afternoon for wrongful death and, under the state's rather unusual expedited procedure, the case is tried the same day.

(a) On the facts above, should the case go to the jury?

No. Insufficient evidence of element: death.

(b) Now assume that Mike has been found dead. Is there sufficient evidence for the jury?

Sure. Plan to kill ... ev of all elements. But ... it's homicide ... to cause ... death ... Show ...

(c) Assume again that Mike is dead but that Larry's letter read, "I love you and I wish your husband were dead." Is the letter sufficient? Relevant? What if Larry simply wrote, "I love you"?

'10k seems like a stretch. That's thought crime'. Sure! More likely mens rea *\ 10k ... that but to establish L knows F... subsidiary proposition to mens rea*

¶ **3.4:** Smith is suing the Blue Bus Company (BBC), claiming that one of its buses negligently drove her off the road in the very wee hours one morning. She did not get a chance to see the bus, and she presents no eyewitnesses to the incident other than herself. In its answer to Smith's complaint, BBC conceded that it owned all the buses bearing its logo, and that Smith was driven off the road by a bus, but it denied that it owned the bus that was involved in the incident. Ben Blue, the sole owner and bus driver of BBC at the time of the accident, died shortly afterwards, without having spoken about it. Smith presents results of a month-long observation that 72 of the 90 buses passing the point of the accident between 12:30 and 1:30 a.m. belong to BBC. The accident occurred about 1:08 a.m. Is this evidence relevant in determining whether the bus belonged to BBC? Sufficient to support a verdict for Smith? So strong that Smith should win judgment as a matter of law? *Cf. Smith v. Rapid Transit, Inc.*, 58 N.E.2d 754 (Mass. 1945), discussed in Chapter 21.

C. RELEVANCE AND WEIGHT

1. PROBATIVE VALUE AND COUNTERVAILING CONSIDERATIONS

Taken by itself, FRE 401 is not sensitive to matters of degree. It refers to "any tendency" to alter the probability of a factual proposition. In many cases, evidence may alter the probability of a material proposition in a minuscule degree. For example, suppose that David is on trial for a robbery that, it appears, must have been committed by someone from a given area with a population of one million adults. Suppose also that the prosecution offers evidence that Steve, a resident of that area with no apparent connection to the crime, was out of town at the time of the robbery. A reasonable juror might find that this evidence increases the probability that David was the robber, as assessed before any evidence linking him to the crime, from about one in 1,000,000 to about one in 999,999. Technically, then, the evidence is relevant. *See generally* David Crump, *On the Uses of Irrelevant Evidence*, 34 Houston L. Rev. 1 (1997), and succeeding commentary. And yet the evidence clearly should not be admissible on this theory.

¶ **3.5:** Now consider evidence that slightly *increases* the probability that somebody else committed the crime. Suppose that Nicole was stabbed to death outside her home and that her ex-husband is being charged with the murder. Should the defense be allowed to introduce evidence that Faye had stayed with Nicole, and that Faye was an active drug user—on the theory that perhaps drug dealers to whom Faye owed money murdered Nicole by mistake, or to send Faye a message?[4] *See Holmes v. South Carolina*, 547 U.S. 319 (2006) (approving rules that exclude evidence that a person other than the accused committed the crime where such evidence "does not sufficiently connect the other person to the crime, as, for example, where the evidence is speculative or remote . . .," quoting 40A Am.Jur.2d, Homicide § 286 (1999), but holding unconstitutional a rule that "where there is strong evidence of [a defendant's] guilt, especially where there is strong forensic evidence, the proffered evidence about a third party's alleged guilt does not raise a reasonable inference as to the [defendant]'s own innocence").

It seems only common sense, then, that we should be concerned not only with the binary (i.e., yes-or-no) question of whether a given piece of evidence is relevant but also with the question of degree. That is, *how much* does the evidence alter the probability of the material proposition for which it is offered? Put in other terms, we might ask how much *probative value*, or how much *weight*, the evidence has. And indeed, FRE 403, reflecting the common law, makes clear that the probative value of the evidence must be weighed against countervailing factors to determine its admissibility.

Among those factors are "wasting time" and, what is really a type of time wastage, "needlessly presenting cumulative evidence." Clearly, for example, the evidence regarding Steve's absence at the time of the robbery would consume far more time than it is worth. And if, shortly after the time of the robbery and near the scene, thirty people saw David run into a bar and immediately head to the men's room, it would be silly to have all thirty testify to that. Often, we may rely on the self-interest of the parties or of counsel to guard against undue waste of time; if presenting a body of evidence does the party little good and consumes a lot of time, we may hope that the party will not bother. But this is not a surefire protection. Counsel may be overly enthusiastic about the value of the evidence, or, if she is paid by the hour, she may be willing to run up a bill; even if she is paid by a flat salary or on contingency, she will not likely take into account the costs imposed on the court system and on her adversary.

This last point bears on another, closely related factor identified by Rule 403, "undue delay." This factor addresses not so much how long it will take to present the evidence but how long the trial must await the evidence; for example, if in the middle of the trial a party decides that he wants to add a witness whom he had not previously designated but the

---

[4]   *See* David McCord, *"But Perry Mason Made It Look So* EASY*!" The Admissibility of Evidence Offered by a Criminal Defendant to Suggest That Someone Else is Guilty*, 63 Tenn. L. Rev. 917, 972–73 n.251 (1996) (analyzing the more complex facts of the O.J. Simpson case).

witness is not immediately available, the court may decide—depending on all the circumstances—that the extra wait, involving cost and inconvenience to the court, the jury, and the other parties, is not worthwhile.

Another of the factors is "unfair prejudice." We may break this danger down into two types. First, some evidence may *bias* the factfinder, effectively distorting the burden of persuasion that it applies. For example, proof that an accused has a long criminal record might encourage some jurors to convict him even though they are not persuaded beyond a reasonable doubt about his guilt of the crime charged in this case; the jurors might decide that it would not be such a terrible thing to convict him even if he did not commit the crime, because he is a bad person who does not deserve to be free.

Second, some evidence might be *overvalued* by the factfinder. This consideration seems to be closely related to the concerns about "confusing the issues" and "misleading the jury". A great deal of the rhetoric of evidence law concerns the danger of jury overvaluation of the evidence. For example, in some cases jurors might be inclined to give some evidence with an appearance of scientific complexity far more weight than it merits. Nevertheless, we may well wonder to what extent the danger of jury overvaluation really provides a sound justification for exclusionary rules of evidence. For one thing, even if the jury overvalues evidence to some degree, that does not mean that the truth-determination process is better advanced by excluding the evidence than by including it. After all, excluding the evidence means that in effect the jury is prevented from giving the evidence any weight at all, and that may be a very substantial loss to truth determination. Furthermore, it is not a simple matter to determine how great a valuation is too much; if the jury, in deciding whether an accused committed robbery on the occasion in question, gives a great deal of weight to the fact that he committed robbery before, is it overvaluing the evidence or simply acting rationally? Finally, in at least some circumstances jurors seem less vulnerable than might be supposed to overvaluing evidence. Thus, contrary to the commonly stated concern that jurors will fail to take into account the weakness of hearsay evidence, some research suggests that juries tend to over-*discount* hearsay.[5]

Rule 403 does not state all the considerations that might weigh against the admissibility of probative evidence—such as intrusions on the personal life of witnesses and hopes of inducing the proponent to produce better evidence, to take two drastically different examples. The Rule may perhaps best be taken as a guidepost, a reminder to courts that they have

---

[5] We will examine this matter further in Chapter 15.

to weigh the probative value of evidence against countervailing considerations. In most cases, performing that balance is, as Peter Mirfield, an English scholar, has put it, like comparing apples to Tuesdays. That is, probative value and such concerns as waste of time and danger of biasing the jury are considerations on totally different planes, having nothing to do with one another. (Overvaluation may be different; it may be possible to compare along the same dimension the "proper" value that a juror could accord to the evidence with the "excessive" value that the juror might accord to it.) But weighing considerations of totally different types is something we do all the time, as when we decide whether to spend our money on travel or furniture or clothing. These decisions call for value judgments, and that is what the balance of probative value against countervailing considerations calls for: Is it worthwhile, for example, to gain the probative value that a given piece of potentially inflammatory evidence offers at the expense of a likely biasing effect and some loss of time?

¶ **3.6:** Suppose you are prosecuting a case of gruesome knifing murders, like the *Silver* case from Chapter 1. You are contemplating offering photos of the victims' horribly bloodied bodies, taken at the crime scene. Why do you want these admitted? In preparing to argue for their admissibility, what theories might you want to consider and explore? What arguments against admissibility might you expect? Should the evidence be admitted?

For some types of recurrent cases, the balance of probative value and such countervailing factors has been drawn in general, and a general rule of exclusion has been enunciated. Several of the rules that we will study in Chapters 17 and 18, part of Article IV (the 400 series) of the Federal Rules, are to some extent this type of rule of exclusion. But these rules, or even the rest of the specific Federal Rules, do not exhaust the possible grounds of exclusion. Virtually always the court must weigh the particular piece of evidence in a general balance as prescribed by FRE 403.[6]

¶ **3.7:** When Rule 403 speaks of the probative value of evidence, whose assessment of that value does it mean to be incorporating—the court's? the jury's? a hypothetical juror likely

---

[6] The "virtually always" qualifier is in deference to FRE 609(a)(2). That Rule concerns evidence that the witness has been convicted of a crime that involved dishonesty or false statement. The rule prescribes that this evidence "must be admitted," subject to a predicate finding, for the purpose of attacking the witness' credibility. FRE 609(a)(1), dealing with crimes punishable by death or imprisonment in excess of one year, also includes "shall be admitted" language, but admission is explicitly made subject to the court's discretion, the standard depending on whether the witness is a criminal defendant.

to be swayed by the evidence but still within the bounds of reasonableness? someone else's?

2. THINKING ANALYTICALLY ABOUT PROBATIVE VALUE

We have seen that an assessment of the probative value of evidence is important for determining whether the evidence should be admitted, because that value must be weighed against countervailing considerations. There are other reasons as well why it is important to be able to assess the probative value of evidence. In arguing a motion that one party's evidence is insufficient to reach the jury, you will be arguing about the probative value that can reasonably be accorded to that evidence taken as a whole. And, of course, in arguing your case to the jury, you will be trying to maximize or minimize the probative value that the jury accords to various items of evidence.

The following discussion presents one way of thinking about the probative value of evidence. It may appeal to you, or it may not—indeed, this style of thinking about evidentiary problems is controversial in scholarly circles—but give it a try![7] Although the analysis uses some numbers, don't let them throw you. For one thing, they are fairly simple. For another, they are used for expository purposes only. Although factfinders may assess probabilities intuitively ("highly likely," "very improbable," and so forth), they do not usually attach numbers to those assessments, and this discussion does not suggest that they should.

a. Prospective Reasoning

Juries must sometimes make predictions of the future, such as the probability in a personal injury case that the plaintiff will be permanently disabled, given certain injuries that she has suffered. Sometimes the jury must make what we may call a conditional prediction—that is, a determination of what would happen if a given factual assumption were true. Thus, in the personal injury case, a second part of the jury's task may be to determine what the plaintiff's future income would be had she not been injured. A conditional prediction may be made about a time period that has already passed. For example, the jury may have to make

---

[7] This presentation is adapted from Richard D. Friedman, *A Diagrammatic Approach to Evidence*, 66 B.U.L.Rev. 571 (1986). At least four symposia have included extensive discussion of the appropriateness of using conventional probability theory to model the factfinding process. *See Probability and Inference in the Law of Evidence*, 66 B.U. L. Rev. 377 (1986); *Decision and Inference in Litigation*, 13 Cardozo L. Rev. 253 (1991); *Bayesianism and Juridical Proof*, 1 Intl J. of Evidence & Proof 253 (1997); *New Perspectives on Evidence*, 87 Va. L. Rev. 1491 (2001). See also the more informal discussion in Ronald J. Allen, et al., *Probability and Proof in* State v. Skipper*: An Internet Exchange*, 35 Jurimetrics J. 277, 285 (1995).

a conditional prediction of what the plaintiff's income would have been in the period to date had she not been injured.

Whether the jury must make an ordinary prediction, or a conditional prediction as to a future period or as to a period already elapsed, its task is much the same: to determine, given a set of actual or assumed factual premises, how likely is any given outcome. That is, to introduce a spatial metaphor, the jury must place itself at a given point and predict what route events would be likely to follow from that point. In short, the jury must reason prospectively from the evidence.

Figure 3.b helps make this metaphor apparent. This is a map showing the roads connecting five towns with the unusual names **O**, **CLOUDY**, **NOT-CLOUDY**, **RAINY**, and **NOT-RAINY**.

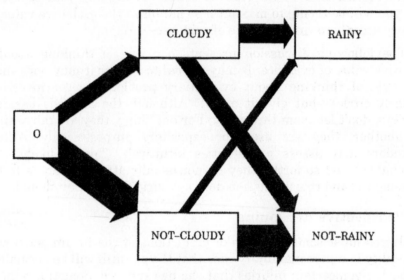

Figure 3.b

Traffic moves only from left to right. Traffic patterns are indicated by the width of the arrows; the wider a given arrow leaving a town is, the greater is the proportion of the traffic leaving the town that goes along that link.

Suppose that an observer, after watching the traffic leave **O** for some time, assesses the probability that a given car at **O** will go to **CLOUDY** to be .3 on a scale of 0 to 1, with 1 representing certainty. Because a car leaving **O** and not going to **CLOUDY** must be going to **NOT-CLOUDY**, it follows that the probability that the car will go to **NOT-CLOUDY** is .7. We can express this first probability assessment formally:

$$P(\textbf{CLOUDY}\,|\,\textbf{O}) = .3,$$

or, "The probability of **CLOUDY** given **O** is .3.", and the corollary

$$P(\text{NOT-CLOUDY} \mid O) = .7.$$

Now our observer moves to **CLOUDY** and watches the cars traveling to **RAINY** and **NOT-RAINY**. Six of ten go to **RAINY** and the rest to **NOT-RAINY**. On the basis of this data, she makes a probability assessment that

$$P(\text{RAINY} \mid O, \text{CLOUDY}) = .6,$$

with the corollary that

$$P(\text{NOT-RAINY} \mid O, \text{CLOUDY}) = .4.[8]$$

Finally, the observer moves to **NOT-CLOUDY** and watches the cars traveling from there to **RAINY** and **NOT-RAINY**. Only two of ten go to **RAINY** and the rest to **NOT-RAINY**. On the basis of this information, she assesses

$$P(\text{RAINY} \mid O, \text{NOT-CLOUDY}) = .2,$$

from which it follows that

$$P(\text{NOT-RAINY} \mid O, \text{NOT-CLOUDY}) = .8.$$

If we know only that a car is leaving **O**, what is the probability that it will reach **RAINY**? There are two possible, mutually exclusive routes to **RAINY**, one through **CLOUDY** and the other through **NOT-CLOUDY**. The probability that a car will follow the **CLOUDY** route to **RAINY** is .18: if the car is leaving **O**, there is a 30% chance that it will go to **CLOUDY**, and if the car is at **CLOUDY** there is a 60% chance that it will go on to **RAINY**. Similarly, the probability that a car will follow the **NOT-CLOUDY** route to **RAINY** is .14: the 70% chance that a given car will go to **NOT-CLOUDY** multiplied by the 20% chance that a car at **NOT-CLOUDY** will go on to **RAINY**. Thus, the probability that a car at **O** will go to **RAINY** by one route or the other is .32—i.e., .18 plus .14.

Now let's tie this discussion back to the law of evidence. Suppose that an issue in dispute is whether a given car went to **RAINY**. If we learn a piece of evidence, that the car went to **CLOUDY**, does that evidence have substantial probative value? The discussion shows that it does. If all we knew about this particular car is that it left **O**, then we would assess the probability that it would go to **RAINY** as .32. But when we learn that the car went to **CLOUDY**, we must reassess the probability of **RAINY** as .6. That is a considerable difference; the evidence of **CLOUDY** has

---

[8]   Notice that the observation that six of ten cars go from **CLOUDY** to **RAINY** is not in itself a probability; rather, it is just a datum, a bit of information. The observer may assess the probability that another car will go from **CLOUDY** to **RAINY** as higher than, lower than, or equal to .6, depending on what considerations she believes govern the course of that other car. But if she has no reason to believe that the new car is atypical of the cars she has already observed, she may well assign a probability equal to, or very close to, .6.

substantial probative value with reference to the disputed proposition
RAINY.

As you might have guessed from the town's names, Figure 3.b need
not be used only for spatial problems. Let **O** represent all the knowledge
the factfinder has about the world before the new evidence is introduced;
CLOUDY represent the proposition that the morning in a given city is
cloudy; and **RAINY** the proposition that the afternoon in the city is rainy.
If our observer assigns the same probabilities as the ones we have just
supposed for the spatial problem, then we can say that evidence that the
morning is cloudy has substantial probative value in determining the
likelihood that the afternoon is rainy. It is easy enough to see why: A
rainy afternoon is far more likely to follow if the morning is cloudy than if
the morning is clear, and so a rainy afternoon is substantially more likely
when we know that the morning was cloudy than it was before we knew
whether the morning was cloudy or not.

Now, in litigation, most events do not have the same recurrent
quality as these problems. We cannot usefully say, "In most cases in
which a person in Victor's position and with all his characteristics
threatens a person in Donald's position and bearing all his characteristics
in just the way that Donald threatened Victor here, the Donald-type
would fear for his life." Nevertheless, a juror *can* usefully say, "Given all
the information I know about Donald and Victor, Victor's threat probably
made Donald fear for his life." A probability assessment in this sense is
not a statement of how frequently a recurrent event will turn out one way
or the other, but rather a statement of the observer's subjective
confidence in the truth of a proposition. Though these assessments are
subjective, if we are thinking clearly they will be reasonably consistent, in
just the way that probability statements about the frequency of recurrent
events should be. For example, it would not make sense to say, "I don't
think it is probable that Donald feared Victor, and if Donald did fear
Victor I don't think he would kill him, but I do think it is probable that
Donald feared Victor and killed him."

As this example suggests, we don't usually assign numerical
probabilities to most propositions (though that is precisely what
meteorologists do for us when they say "60% chance of rain this
afternoon"). All the time, however, we do make probability assessments in
rougher, nonnumerical terms, as when we characterize a given
proposition in such terms as "extremely unlikely," "reasonably probable,"
or "almost certain." And even though we do not numerify, we are sensitive
to matters of degree: You may run across the street, even though a car is
rushing towards you, if the probability that the car would hit you is very,
very, very low, but take away a very or two and you will stay put until the
car passes. Indeed, if we did not generally make reasonably consistent

and reasonably sensible assessments of the probabilities of risks and benefits facing us, we would be either paralytic or dead.[9]

The following problems concern prospective reasoning from evidence to a disputed proposition. They do not involve numbers. But try to think about them as rigorously as you can: Does the evidence alter the probability of the disputed proposition, and if so in which direction and how?

¶ **3.8:** Knapp is on trial for the murder of Broderick, a marshal. Knapp admits the killing but pleads self-defense.

(a) To show that he had a legitimate fear of Broderick, Knapp testifies that he had heard before the killing that Broderick had killed an old man, McMahon, in another town. The prosecution offers evidence that McMahon is in fact still alive. Is that evidence relevant? *Cf. Knapp v. State*, 168 Ind. 153, 79 N.E. 1076 (1907); *Sherrod v. Berry*, 856 F.2d 802 (7th Cir. 1988) (holding irrelevant to objective reasonableness of police officer's conduct evidence that shooting victim, decedent of civil rights plaintiff, was unarmed).

(b) There is evidence that rumors spread quickly in McMahon's town, and from there to Knapp's town, and that Knapp works at the bus station connecting the two. Does this evidence help or hurt Knapp?

(c) Assume now that it is Knapp who wants to offer evidence of what really happened in the other town. His witness will testify that Broderick threatened to kill McMahon, though he never actually harmed McMahon. Is this evidence admissible?

¶ **3.9:** Jack Ruby killed Lee Harvey Oswald, and claimed that he was provoked because Oswald assassinated President

---

[9] Note the qualifiers: Clear thinking requires "reasonably consistent" probability assessments, and we usually make "reasonably sensible" assessments. Rigorously applied, probability theory can entail enormous computational complexity. *See, e.g,* Craig R. Callen, *Hearsay and Informal Reasoning*, 47 Vand. L. Rev. 43, 57, 76 n.150 (1994). And there is certainly reason to believe that often people make logical errors in thinking probabilistically. *See, e.g.,* Amos Tversky & Daniel Kahneman, *Extensional Versus Intuitive Reasoning: The Conjunction Fallacy in Probability Judgment*, 90 Psych. Rev. 293, 300 (1983). But we muddle through, with the aid of useful approximating devices. *See* Peter Donnelly, *Approximation, comparison, and Bayesian reasoning in juridical proof*, 1 Int'l J. Evidence & Proof 304 (1997). The argument being made here is not that people usually go through a probabilistic calculation in thinking about uncertain propositions, nor that they should do so. Rather, the argument is only that if people are thinking well they will reach assessments of probability that are roughly consistent with each other in accordance with the principles of probability theory. Without applying, or even being aware of, principles of physics, a good outfielder determines rather well where a batted ball will fall; similarly, a clear-thinking person need not know probability theory to reach results roughly in accordance with it.

Kennedy. Could the Government introduce evidence tending to show that Oswald had not killed Kennedy?

¶ **3.10:** In *Barefoot v. Estelle*, 463 U.S. 880 (1983), the majority held that the Constitution did not prohibit admissibility of psychiatric evidence regarding the future dangerousness of the defendant in determining whether the death penalty should be imposed. Dissenting, Justice Blackmun pointed to studies indicating that "psychiatrists and psychologists are accurate in no more than one out of three predictions of violent behavior, even among populations of individuals who are mentally ill and have committed violence in the past." *Id.* at 920.[10] He therefore argued that expert judgments of this type are less accurate than a coin flip. *Id.* at 930–31. Are you persuaded? What more information would you need to know to evaluate this argument? Consider this hypothetical: You are considering drilling for oil in an area in which a preliminary survey indicates that any given well will have a one in ten chance of striking oil. An inventor offers to sell you an instrument that, with minimal expense, makes a prediction as to whether oil can be found underneath a given spot on the ground. If there is oil, the instrument will hardly ever fail to report it. Two times out of three that the instrument does predict oil, there is in fact nothing underneath; the third time there is a gusher. Should you reject the instrument on the ground that it is worthless? Would you rather flip a coin?

b. **Retrospective Reasoning**

Now let's look at a *retrospective*, or backwards-looking, style of reasoning. Often, a jury has to determine whether a given event occurred on the basis of trace evidence—that is, evidence that arguably was left as a result of that event. We can see this by turning our **RAINY-CLOUDY** problem around. Suppose the material issue is whether a car that left **O** went to **CLOUDY** and that the new piece of evidence we have is that the car has arrived at **RAINY**. Alternatively, we may suppose that the material proposition is that the morning was cloudy and that the evidence we have just learned is that the afternoon was rainy; the analysis of each case is the same. How great, if at all, is the probative value of this new piece of information? That is, what is *P*(**CLOUDY** | **RAINY**, **O**), the probability of **CLOUDY** given **RAINY** and **O**, and to what extent does it differ from the "prior" probability—*P*(**CLOUDY** | **O**), the probability of **CLOUDY** assessed without learning of **RAINY**?

---

[10]   *Quoting* the first edition of John Monahan, *The Clinical Prediction of Violent Behavior* 47–49 (new ed. 1995).

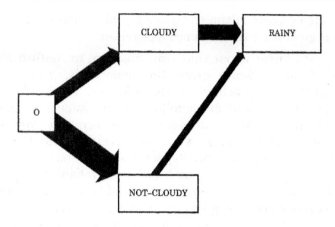

Figure 3.c

Figure 3.c can help us answer that question. This is essentially a simplified version of Figure 3.b—simplified by dropping out the routes to **NOT-RAINY**, which we can now ignore because we know that in fact **RAINY** is true. Now we know not only the beginning point of events, **O**, but also the end point, **RAINY**. Thus, we can focus on routes linking those two points together, and ask, "By which of those courses did events likely lead from there to here?" Recall that our observer's data showed that 32 of 100 cars leaving **O** reach **RAINY**, by one route or the other, and that, of those 32, 18 will have gone via the **CLOUDY** route and the remaining 14 via the **NOT-CLOUDY** route. From this data, the observer might assess the probability of **CLOUDY** given **O** and **RAINY** to be 18/32, or .5625. This probability differs very substantially from the probability of **CLOUDY** assessed without learning of **RAINY**, which was assessed at the outset as .3. In other words, the evidence of **RAINY** has significant probative value in determining the probability of **CLOUDY**.

We have begun with forward-looking probabilities—including those expressing how likely it is to rain given clouds and given the absence of clouds—and have used them to assess a backward-looking probability, the probability of earlier clouds given later rain. In doing so, we have performed a simple operation of Bayes' Theorem, named after Thomas Bayes, an eighteenth-century English cleric who explained this type of transposition.

This transposition is crucial. Much evidence appears to be *trace* evidence, which allegedly was created by the events in question—blood smears, a smoking pistol, running people, tire tracks, witnesses' memories, whatever. We may have some sense of the probability that the evidence would be created if the litigated hypothesis were true and the probability that it would be created if that hypothesis were false. But what we want to know is the transposed probability—how probable the hypothesis is given that the evidence has arisen.

It is easy to forget about that transposition, to confuse $P(E|H)$, the probability of the evidence given the hypothesis, with $P(H|E)$, the probability of the hypothesis given the evidence. Try hard to avoid this error. It might help to think of the following case, suggested in I.W. Evett, *Avoiding the Transposed Conditional*, 35 *Science and Justice* 127, 129 (1995).[11] Suppose that to start we know nothing about Gertrude other than that she is an animal. Our hypothesis is, "Gertrude is a cow," and the evidence is, "Gertrude has four legs." The probability of the evidence given the hypothesis is very high, presumably very close to one. The probability of the hypothesis given the evidence, though, is rather small.

Figure 3.d may also help understand the relationship between $P(E|H)$ and $P(H|E)$. Assume that this box has area equal to 1. Then the top rectangle represents $P(H)$, the probability of H assessed without the evidence E. An overlapping portion of the rectangle, between the diagonal line and the right border, represents $P(E)$, and the area of the overlap represents $P(E\&H)$, the probability that both E and H are true. $P(E|H)$ is represented by the area of the overlap divided by the area of the H rectangle; $P(H|E)$, on the other hand, is represented by the area of the overlap divided by the E area. In this case, though E is less than 50% probable given H, E tends to prove H: Because of the direction of the diagonal line, the overlap area is larger in proportion to the E area than the H rectangle is to the entire square.[12]

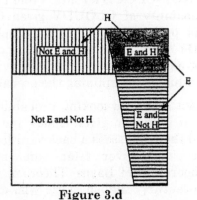

Figure 3.d

[11] *See also* Bernard Robertson, G.A. Vignaux & Chares E.H. Berger, *Interpreting Evidence: Evaluating Forensic Science in the Courtroom* §§ 2.2.5, 9.1(2d ed. 2016).

[12] This diagram, reprinted from Richard D. Friedman, *Assessing Evidence*, 94 Mich. L. Rev. 1810, 1813 (1996), also suggests one possible source of the confusion between $P(E|H)$ and $P(H|E)$: They are equal in the fortuitous case that $P(E)$ equals $P(H)$. And it can be shown rather easily that this happens in a particularly seductive case, when $P(H)$ equals .5—even probability—and E appears to be as good an indicator of H as **Not-E** is of **Not-H**. *See id.* at 1837 & n.66.

Bayesian analysis can yield further insights if we look at the problem in terms of the *odds*, rather than the probability, of the hypothesis in question. The odds of a proposition are simply the ratio of the probability of that proposition to the probability of the negation of that proposition. Thus, odds range from zero to infinitely high; a probability of .5 corresponds to even odds, which we will write in fraction form as 1/1 (though they are often written as 1:1), and a probability of .75 corresponds to odds of 3/1. So, before learning that **RAINY** was true, we assessed the odds of **CLOUDY** as being 3/7. We call this number, the odds of the uncertain proposition as assessed without the evidence in question, the *prior odds*. After learning of **RAINY**, we reassess the odds to be 18/14, or 9/7. These are the *posterior odds*, the odds of the uncertain proposition as assessed after receiving the evidence. Notice that in this case the posterior odds are three times as much as the prior odds. Now notice also that this 3:1 ratio is just the same as the ratio of $P(\textbf{RAINY}\,|\,\textbf{CLOUDY, O})$, which equals .6, to $P(\textbf{RAINY}\,|\,\textbf{NOT-CLOUDY, O})$, which equals .2. That is, the evidence—rain in the afternoon—is three times as likely to occur given the hypothesis in question, that it was cloudy in the morning, as given the negation of that hypothesis. This ratio is called the *likelihood ratio* of the evidence with respect to the hypothesis. In general, the likelihood ratio of a given piece of evidence with respect to a particular hypothesis is the probability that the evidence would arise given that the hypothesis is true divided by the probability that the evidence would arise given that the hypothesis is not true. That is, $L_H E$ equals $P(\textbf{E}\,|\,\textbf{H})/P(\textbf{E}\,|\,\textbf{Not-H})$. It is not hard to show that in general

$$O(\textbf{H}\,|\,\textbf{E}) = O(\textbf{H}) \cdot L_H \textbf{E}.$$

In other words, the posterior odds of the hypothesis, the odds assessed given the evidence, equal the prior odds multiplied by the likelihood ratio.[13] This is the *odds form* of Bayes' Theorem.

Examining this simple equation, we can see that, all other things being equal:

- The higher $O(\textbf{H})$ is, the higher $O(\textbf{H}\,|\,\textbf{E})$ will be; the more probable the proposition is before receiving the evidence, the more probable it appears after receiving the evidence. If we

---

[13] Just in case you want to see a derivation, here one is: Begin with the general propositions that $P(\textbf{X,Y}) = P(\textbf{Y,X})$ and that $P(\textbf{X,Y}) = P(\textbf{X}) \cdot P(\textbf{Y}\,|\,\textbf{X})$; this latter equation means that the probability of **X** and **Y** equals the probability of **X** times the probability that, if **X** is true, **Y** is also true. It follows that

$P(\textbf{E}) \cdot P(\textbf{H}\,|\,\textbf{E}) = P(\textbf{H}) \cdot P(\textbf{E}\,|\,\textbf{H})$,

and that

$P(\textbf{E}) \cdot P(\textbf{Not-H}\,|\,\textbf{E}) = P(\textbf{Not-H}) \cdot P(\textbf{E}\,|\,\textbf{Not-H})$.

Dividing the first of these two equations by the second yields the equation in the text: the $P(\textbf{E})$ terms cancel out; $P(\textbf{H}\,|\,\textbf{E})/P(\textbf{Not-H}\,|\,\textbf{E}) = O(\textbf{H}\,|\,\textbf{E})$, the posterior odds; $P(\textbf{H})/P(\textbf{Not-H}) = O(\textbf{H})$, the prior odds; and $P(\textbf{E}\,|\,\textbf{H})/P(\textbf{E}\,|\,\textbf{Not-H}) = L_H \textbf{E}$, the likelihood ratio.

believed it highly improbable, before hearing eyewitness testimony, that Daniel committed a robbery, that testimony might make us think the proposition is probable; we will think it is all the more probable in light of the testimony if beforehand we thought the hypothesis was rather likely.

• The higher $L_H E$ is, the higher $O(H \mid E)$ will be. If the likelihood ratio is 1, it leaves the prior odds unchanged; the evidence is irrelevant. If the likelihood ratio is less than 1, it diminishes the odds, if it is greater than 1 it increases them, and the further it is away from 1 the more it will alter them. Notice that if $P(E \mid H)$ is very low—that is, if the evidence is very unlikely to arise given the hypothesis—that does not necessarily mean that **E** diminishes the probability of **H**; what matters is the ratio, and if **E** is even *more* unlikely to arise given **Not-H**, then **E** will make **H** more likely than it was before the evidence was received. For example, most rapes do not leave physical evidence of trauma in the vaginal region. But such evidence tends to support the hypothesis of rape, because the evidence is many times more likely to arise given that the woman has been raped than given that she has not been raped.

¶ 3.11: Sharon, a six-year-old girl, was allegedly abducted on the street by a man who drove her some distance (how far is not clear), took her to an apartment, and molested her. Bridges is charged as the molester. Sharon testifies but is unable to identify him.

(a) Consider whether each of the following variations of Sharon's testimony would be admissible. Independent evidence shows that Bridges' apartment meets Sharon's description, and that Sharon probably wasn't in Bridges' apartment on any other occasion.

(i) Sharon testifies that she was molested in a bedroom that had a television near the door, a large bed, and a reclining chair.

(ii) Sharon testifies that she was molested in a bedroom that had a stuffed hammerhead shark on the wall, a mangy ficus tree in one corner, a large mirror on the ceiling, and a poster of Donald Trump in a basketball uniform on another wall.

(b) With respect to each variation in (a), is the description sufficient to send the case to the jury if there is no other evidence against Bridges? If a neighbor testifies that on the evening of the incident she saw from a distance a man who, from the rear, looked like Bridges, and that he was holding the hand of a young girl and walking into his apartment building? *Cf. Bridges v. State*, 247 Wis. 350, 19 N.W.2d 529 (1945).

Bearing the above analysis in mind will help you avoid some basic fallacies in assessing evidence.[14] One group of fallacies is the tendency to equate $P(E \mid H)$ with $P(H \mid E)$. We have just touched on a manifestation of this fallacy likely to be committed on behalf of a criminal defendant, when $P(E \mid H)$ appears to be low.

> **¶ 3.12:** As in ¶ 3.3, Larry is accused of killing Mike. Larry has written no letters, but his fingerprints have been found on a pistol that was found smoking by the side of Mike's body. Larry's lawyer argues: "This evidence proves my client is innocent. Very few people who have their fingerprints on pistols murder people, and very few murderers are dumb enough to leave their fingerprints on pistols." Are you persuaded? Why or why not?

When $P(E \mid H)$ appears to be high, it is more likely the prosecutor who will commit the fallacy of equating $P(E \mid H)$ with $P(H \mid E)$.

> **¶ 3.13:** In a terrorism case, an expert carries out a test under which, if the defendants had handled explosives, a positive result would be 99% likely. The result is positive, and the expert declares that he is "99% certain that the men had handled explosive." Bernard Robertson & G.A. Vignaux, *Interpreting Scientific Evidence* 92 (1st ed. 1995). What is wrong with that conclusion?

A second group of fallacies—also reflecting a failure to recognize transposition of the conditional—confuses $P(E \mid \text{Not-H})$ and $P(\text{Not-H} \mid E)$. If $P(E \mid \text{Not-H})$ is rather high, the defendant might argue that the evidence cannot provide significant support for the conclusion that **H** is true. Thus, if the evidence is a characteristic that the perpetrator of a crime was known to have, and the accused has that characteristic, the accused might argue that the evidence does not point towards his guilt if the characteristic is shared by a large number of people, so that there is a substantial probability that the evidence of a match would arise even if someone else had committed the crime. The accused is correct in trying to persuade the jury that $P(E \mid \text{Not-H})$ is high. But taken in isolation this probability has limited significance; if the likelihood ratio, the ratio of $P(E \mid H)$ to $P(E \mid \text{Not-H})$, is significantly greater than 1, then the evidence will tend to support **H**.

---

[14] *See generally* William C. Thompson & Edward L. Schumann, *Interpretation of Statistical Evidence in Criminal Trials: The Prosecutor's Fallacy and the Defense Attorney's Fallacy*, 11 L. & Hum. Behavior 167 (1987); David J. Balding & Peter Donnelly, *The Prosecutor's Fallacy and DNA Evidence*, 1994 Crim. L. Rev. 711; Robertson, Vignaux & Berger, *Interpreting Evidence, supra* note 11, § 9.1.

¶ 3.14: Here is a type of case that arose frequently before DNA testing became common. Mountain, a police officer, is accused of raping a young woman who was held for arraignment at the police station where Mountain worked. The victim has testified against Mountain, describing the incident and identifying Mountain.

(a) The prosecution also offers evidence that Mountain has type A-positive blood and now offers to prove, based on tests performed on semen traces retrieved from the victim, that the assailant had type A blood. Mountain objects that, because about 40% of the general population has type A-positive blood, the evidence has no probative value against him. Should the evidence be admitted?[15]

(b) Now suppose the blood-type evidence is admitted against Mountain. The defense lawyer argues, "There are millions of men in the world with type A blood. This evidence is worthless. All it shows is that Mountain is one of the millions of men who could have committed the crime." Are you persuaded by this argument? If you are, suppose that instead of blood type the key feature is that Mountain has only one arm and the victim testifies that the rapist was one-armed. Would that evidence be worthless?

(c) In evaluating these problems, it might help to think not of two but of three competing hypotheses: (i) the assailant was the defendant; (ii) the assailant was not the defendant but someone who shared with him the feature in the question; and (iii) the assailant was not the defendant but someone who did not share that feature with him. Which of these hypotheses does the evidence tend to support and which does it tend to disprove? What is the net effect on Hypothesis (i)?

Finally, and perhaps most perniciously, if $P(\mathbf{E} \mid \mathbf{Not\text{-}H})$ appears to be very small, it may be the prosecutor—or the prosecutor's expert witness, who should know better—who tends to equate it with $P(\mathbf{Not\text{-}H} \mid \mathbf{E})$.

¶ 3.15: Troy Brown is charged with rape. The prosecution's expert, Renee Romero, tested DNA taken from the victim's underwear, and determined that it matched Troy's, as determined from a blood sample, and that the probability that another person from the general population would share the same DNA (the "random match probability") was only 1 in

---

[15] *See People v. Mountain*, 66 N.Y.2d 197, 495 N.Y.S.2d 944, 486 N.E.2d 802 (1985) (holding in the affirmative).

3,000,000. At trial, the prosecutor asks whether "it [would] be fair to say . . . that the chances that the DNA found in the panties—the semen in the panties—and the blood sample, the likelihood that it is not Troy Brown would be .000033," and Romero ultimately agrees that it was "not inaccurate" to state it that way. And in closing, the prosecutor argues that the jury can be "99.999967 percent sure" of Brown's guilt. If Brown makes timely objection to the prosecutor's question and to the argument, what should the court do? *See McDaniel v. Brown*, 558 U.S. 120 (2010) (*per curiam*, explaining prosecutor's fallacy).

c. Combining Prospective and Retrospective Reasoning

Sometimes the prospective and retrospective forms of reasoning are combined in various ways. For example, the jury may reason backward from a piece of evidence to conclude that some proposition is probable, and then forward from that proposition to the issue that is material. Suppose that a group planning an afternoon picnic had to decide in the morning whether or not to go ahead as planned. A friend arriving in town on a rainy afternoon might conclude that the picnic was canceled by reasoning along these lines: "Given the rain now, it was probably threatening in the morning, and if that was so my friends probably canceled the picnic." Or, to adapt a famous case that we shall consider later, suppose that Walters' fiancée receives a letter from Walters saying that he intends to go to Colorado with Hillmon. The jury might take Walters at his word, concluding that in all probability Walters' statement resulted from the fact that he had indeed previously formed the intention to go to Colorado with Hillmon. And it might conclude that if he did form that intention this substantially increases the probability that in fact Walters subsequently went to Colorado with Hillmon.

¶ **3.16:** There are 3 disks in a bag. Each side of each disk is identical to all the others except that Disk 1 is red on both sides, Disk 2 is red on one side and white on the other, and Disk 3 is white on both sides. You reach into the bag without looking and pick out one disk. You look at one side only. It is red. What are the odds that the other side is red?

Hint 1: Before we look at the disk, how probable was it that the disk selected was Disk 1? Disk 2? Disk 3? Now consider the new evidence received—that the one side of the disk you have picked is red. How likely would you have gotten this evidence if the Disk selected was Disk 1? Disk 2? Disk 3?

Hint 2: If you play this game 600 times, how many times would you expect to see a red side when you first look? In how many of those times would you expect the other side to be white?

¶ **3.17:** Here are the facts of life: Every female has two X chromosomes in each ordinary cell and every male (with some strange exceptions) has one X and one Y. The child receives one of the mother's X chromosomes—which particular one is random—and either an X or a Y from the father, again at random. If the father donates an X, the baby is a girl, and if Y it's a boy.

Some women carry the gene for the dread Wigmore's Syndrome in one of their X chromosomes. This syndrome invariably causes pre-pubescent death. An ordinary X chromosome from the father will overcome the Wigmore gene, and the baby girl, though a carrier herself, will not suffer the symptoms. A Y chromosome does not counteract the Wigmore gene, however, so a boy receiving the gene from his mother will have the disease. (Scientists theorize that a woman with Wigmore genes in both chromosomes would have the disease, but they have never found such a case. Can you figure out why?)

One of Wanda's brothers died of Wigmore's Syndrome. Wanda is now married to Henry, and they have had two healthy boys. They are considering risking a third pregnancy and want to know how probable it is, given all the information they know, that their next child will have the disease. What is the answer?

Hint: First figure out the chance that Wanda is a carrier. To do this, it might help to imagine that Wanda has 799 sisters, and that each of the 800 women has given birth to two boys.

3.   PRESENTATION OF STATISTICAL EVIDENCE

Our principal concern in the preceding pages has been how to reason about evidence and assess its probative value. But, because some of the evidence discussed in these pages has been overtly statistical in nature, this is a good place to discuss some of the problems raised especially by statistically-based evidence and arguments, which have become pervasive in litigation.[16]

Many arguments, perhaps most, ask a factfinder to reason in a quantitative way, such as by determining that some body of evidence is *more* likely to have arisen given one hypothesis than given another. In itself, this is perfectly appropriate. Statistical evidence and arguments are attempts, sometimes spurious, sometimes not, to put precision on the quantification. See *United States v. Shonubi*, 895 F.Supp. 460, 514

---

[16] *See* United States v. Shonubi, 895 F.Supp. 460, 514 (E.D.N.Y.1995) (Weinstein, J.), *vacated,* 103 F.3d 1085 (2d Cir.1997) (endorsing a statement in David W. Barnes & John M. Conley, *Statistical Evidence in Litigation* 13 (1986) that "[t]here is at present virtually no area of the law in which properly conceived and executed statistical proof cannot be admitted.").

(E.D.N.Y.1995) (Weinstein, J.), *vacated,* 103 F.3d 1085 (2d Cir.1997) ("all evidence is probabilistic").

Consider first the famous case of *People v. Collins,* 68 Cal.2d 319, 66 Cal.Rptr. 497, 438 P.2d 33 (1968).[17] A woman named Juanita Brooks was mugged and robbed on a street in the San Pedro area of Los Angeles. Eventually Janet and Malcolm Collins were arrested and tried for the crime. The evidence against them included some ambiguous but suggestive statements they had made during interrogations and testimony by one John Bass rather uncertainly identifying Malcolm as the driver of the car involved in the crime. Eyewitness testimony also indicated that the assailants were a Caucasian woman with a blond ponytail accompanied by a black man with a beard and mustache, driving a predominantly yellow automobile. This description bore a close resemblance to the Collinses, though there was doubt as to whether Malcolm had a beard on the day of the crime, and descriptions of their car—which had a yellow body and a white top—varied somewhat. Another consideration against them was that Janet worked in San Pedro and her employer testified that Malcolm had picked her up that day at just around the time of the crime.

Trying to secure convictions with less than rock-solid proof, the prosecutor tried to be clever. Having introduced some testimony on probability by a college mathematics instructor, he presented to the jury the following table; the language as well as the probability assignments are his.

	Characteristic	*Individual Probability*
A.	Partly yellow automobile	1/10
B.	Man with mustache	1/4
C.	Girl with ponytail	1/10
D.	Girl with blond hair	1/3
E.	Negro man with beard	1/10
F.	Interracial couple in car	1/1000

The prosecutor multiplied these estimates together, reaching a probability of one in 12 million, and concluded from this that there could be only one chance in 12 million that defendants were innocent and that another couple meeting the descriptions committed the crime.

---

[17] The case has generated a great deal of academic discussion. For a critical commentary of the debate, see Mark L. Huffman, Comment, *When the Blue Bus Crashes into the Gate: The Problem with* People v. Collins *in the Probabilistic Evidence Debate,* 46 U. Miami L. Rev. 975 (1992).

This argument is so buffoonish it makes an easy target, and the California Supreme Court, reversing Malcolm's conviction, blasted away. Even assuming the individual probabilities he had assigned, the prosecutor had no business multiplying them together. That can be done only when the probabilities are *independent*—that is, when knowing one proposition in question does not alter the probability of another. That is plainly not true here. Knowing "Negro man with beard," for example, significantly increases the probability of "Man with mustache."[18]

Even more fundamentally, at best the prosecutor only calculated the probability that a given couple other than the Collinses would match the description of the assailants; this is *not* the probability that the Collinses were not the guilty couple. The *Collins* prosecutor appears to have committed one of the "prosecutor's fallacies" discussed above, equating $P(E \mid Not\text{-}H)$ with $P(Not\text{-}H \mid E)$.[19] Indeed, the court showed that, even accepting the prosecution's estimate of 1 in 12 million for $P(E \mid Not\text{-}H)$, in a metropolitan area of several million people there was a substantial chance—perhaps around 40%—that at least one other couple met the description.

¶ **3:18:** Here is a more modern manifestation of these problems: Wilson is charged with the murder of his two infant children, Brandi and Garrett, in separate incidents six years apart. Initially, both deaths were attributed to Sudden Infant Death Syndrome (SIDS). One expert, Dr. Kokes, uses an estimate of one SIDS death for every 1,000 live births, and notes that Garret had cerebral swelling, a condition that affects less than 1% of children who die from SIDS. He then concludes that the probability that Garrett died from SIDS was 1 in 100,000,000 (1 in 1,000 times 1 in 1,000 times 1 in 100). Another expert, Dr. Norton, uses a different set of statistics that indicates

---

[18] *Conditional* probabilities may be multiplied together. For example, if we assume a probability that a given man will have a mustache to be .1 and the probability that *if* he has a mustache he also has a beard to be .5, then the probability that the given man has a beard *and* a mustache is .1 x .5 = .05.

[19] Recall that $P(E \mid Not\text{-}H)$ is one of the components of the likelihood ratio, and so it does have a significant bearing on the probability of innocence—but it is not the same thing as $P(Not\text{-}H \mid E)$.

The court also pointed out that the prosecution's theory rested on the assumption that its witnesses had "conclusively established that the guilty couple possessed the precise characteristics relied upon by the prosecution." That is true enough, but a reasonable argument by the prosecution would not require such precision or conclusiveness, and would be compatible with slight errors in the description. Consider the court's hypothetical that the guilty couple "included a light-skinned Negress with bleached hair rather than Caucasian blonde." A juror might still reasonably conclude that the description was more likely to be given under the hypothesis that the Collinses were the perpetrators than under most of the alternative hypotheses that seemed significant before the description was offered. The point is comparable to that made by Knapp in ¶ 3.8(c), where he argued that although a report of murder would not be accurate if there was only a threat of murder and not murder itself, the threat makes the report more likely than it would have been otherwise.

that SIDS occurs in 1 infant out of every 2,000 live births, and concludes that the probability of two SIDS deaths occurring in one family is 1 in 2,000 multiplied by 1 in 2,000, or 1 in 4,000,000. Is Kokes's testimony proper? Norton's? *See Wilson v. State,* 803 A.2d 1034 (Md. 2002). Note also the sad English case of Sally Clark, convicted, apparently wrongly, after the second of two children died suddenly. *See, e.g.,* Ray Hill, *Multiple sudden infant deaths—coincidence or beyond coincidence?,* 18 Paediatric & Perinatal Epidemiology 320 (2004).

One must not take the *Collins* court's point too far, however. The court spoke of a 40% chance that the Collinses "could be 'duplicated' by at least *one other couple who might equally have committed the San Pedro robbery.*" But "equally" does not belong in that sentence: Even if another such couple were found, the Collinses—who, after all, had some other evidence against them and who were in San Pedro at the time of the crime, not anywhere else in the huge Angeleno sprawl—presumably would have been the more likely candidates.

The court also took the prosecutor to task for supplying probability assessments without any supporting evidence. And, though the prosecutor said he was providing these assessments for illustrative purposes only—he invited the jurors, as well as defense counsel, to supply their own estimates—it is easy enough to agree. By introducing numbers, the prosecutor was attempting to suggest unjustified precision.

Suppose, however, that the prosecutor had argued as follows:

Mr. Bass has identified Malcolm as the driver, and the Collinses' statements suggest they knew they were guilty. But you don't have to rely just on that. From the testimony of Mrs. Brooks and that of Mr. Bass, we have a good description of the assailants, and this description matches the Collinses very well. This is an extraordinarily rare combination: A black man with a beard and mustache driving in a predominantly yellow car with a blond Caucasian woman with a pony tail. This description matches the Collinses, who we know were in their car in the vicinity of the crime at the time of the crime. And so the evidence is just the type you might expect if the Collinses committed the crime. If they didn't commit the crime, the chance of getting evidence that coincidentally matches them so closely is vanishingly small.

Such an argument would presumably have been unexceptionable. Note that this argument invites probabilistic analysis, but it does not do so through artificial numerification.

In various settings, however, putting numbers on quantities as a way of gathering and transmitting information and showing its significance has proven very tempting, whether for good or ill. Consider first the following case.

¶ **3.19:** Father John, a Roman Catholic priest, wrote a rock opera called, Virgin, one of the singles from which was a song called "Fear No Evil." This song was promoted by Famous Music Corporation and achieved some success, reaching No. 61 on the "Hot Soul Singles" chart before falling back. Father John sues Famous, contending that it failed to promote the song with sufficient vigor. He presents a statistical analysis of every song that reached No. 61 (or higher) on the Hot Soul Singles chart during that year. This analysis showed that, of all 324 songs that reached No. 61, 98% reached No. 60; 76% reached No. 40; 51% reached No. 20, and 10% reached No. 1.

(a) Is this evidence relevant with respect to liability? With respect to damages?

(b) One argument made by Famous in resisting admission of the evidence is that the analysis takes no account of numerous factors that relate to the success of a song, such as the speed of its rise, the size and capacity of the company promoting it, the reputations of the various artists connected with it, and the overall quality of the song, however that may be judged. Does this argument persuade you? *Cf. Contemporary Mission, Inc. v. Famous Music Corp.*, 557 F.2d 918 (2d Cir.1977).

Now consider a particularly important setting in which most courts have found quantification to be almost irresistible—DNA evidence used to prove identity. *Cf. State v. Bloom*, 516 N.W.2d 159 (Minn.1994) (establishing "a DNA exception" to what it called, perhaps with some exaggeration, the state's "rule against admission of quantitative, statistical probability evidence in criminal prosecutions to prove identity").

DNA is a nucleic acid that determines the genetic information for living organisms. Within any organism, the DNA is constant across almost all cells. Accordingly, in recent years, DNA tests have become a tremendously important source of identification evidence—useful in attempting to determine, for example, whether the defendant in a rape case was the source of semen found in the victim's clothes. If we had a definitive way of comparing two samples and concluding that they must come from the same person—as has been the common belief in the case of fingerprints[20]—the inferential task in considering this evidence would be

---

[20] This belief has come under challenge recently. It is clear that a given person's fingerprints are unique and permanent. What is less clear is that a fingerprint expert can reliably determine that the print of a defendant taken in a controlled setting matches a partial fingerprint left at a crime scene. See the discussion of United States v. Llera Plaza, 179

quite simple. Advances in the science continue to bring us closer to that point, but it is not clear that we are there yet.

Most human DNA is identical for all or virtually all people; it contains the essential information that makes us humans rather than brown bears or grapes. Differentiation among humans in appearance and function is determined by a relatively small set of "loci" on the DNA molecule. DNA tests, though, are performed for the most part on portions of the DNA molecule that have no "coding" significance—that is, they do not affect how the person will turn out—but that vary greatly within the human population. Modern DNA tests examine several different loci and for each one measure how many times a given sequence of components (known as base pairs) is repeated. A substantial share of the human population may have the same number of repeats at a given locus. But the loci are believed to be nearly independent. That is, if two samples taken from different sources match at one locus, this barely alters the probability that they will match at another. Consequently, if we are trying to make a cautious estimate of the probability that a randomly chosen DNA profile would match a given profile at both of two loci, we can multiply the probability of a match at one locus by the probability of a match at the other, and make a very slight correction to account for any dependence that does exist between the two. DNA tests gain their power by testing several loci—13 particular loci have become standard in American jurisdictions. If two samples match at each locus, then the hypothesis that the two samples do not have a common origin depends on a coincidence that is not merely notable but altogether extraordinary. Indeed, if a laboratory reports that two samples match, it is far more plausible that the lab made an error—perhaps testing the same sample twice, or misreading the data—than that the two samples come from two separate people who happen to have identical profiles at the loci tested.[21]

Thus, a DNA test might justify a forensic scientist in making a conclusion in this form: "The crime scene sample and the suspect sample match, and if the crime scene sample were taken from a randomly chosen member of the United States Caucasian population, the chance of a match would be 1 in **X**." We must be careful; such a statement does not account for such possibilities as the ones just mentioned, contamination of samples or lab error in reading the test results. But, focusing just on the possibility of a coincidental match, there is no limit on how high **X** can be,

F.Supp.2d 492 (E.D.Pa.2002) (Pollak, J.), *vacated*, 188 F. Supp. 549 (E.D., Pa. 2002), below in chapter 5, n. 47. Whether fingerprint evidence is more appropriate for such an opinion than is DNA evidence, or whether opinions about fingerprint evidence have simply been "grandfathered" in from a time when there was less attention to the bases of expert opinion, is an interesting question. *See generally* Simon Cole, *Suspect Identities: A History of Fingerprinting and Criminal Identification* (2001).

[21] Erin Murphy, *Inside the Cell: The Dark Side of Forensic DNA* (2015); Richard Lempert, *Comment: Theory and Practice in DNA Fingerprinting*, 9 Stat. Sci. 255, 257 (1994).

with sufficiently precise and extensive testing and sufficiently large data bases. It can be larger than the Caucasian population of the United States, or even larger than the population of the entire world. The more information we have about the crime scene sample, the smaller the chance of a random match; 1 in **X** can be very, very close to zero, which makes **X** astronomically high. It has become rather routine for forensic scientists to assert random match probabilities of one in a quintillion or less.

Note that testimony in this form does *not* mean that the chance is only 1 in a quintillion that the defendant is not the source of the DNA. That is one of the fallacies that the prosecutor committed in the *Collins* case—but forensic scientists continue to commit it with distressing frequency.[22] Nor does it even mean that there is only a 1 in 1 quintillion chance that there is someone else in the world with matching DNA. Rather, it means that there is only a 1 in 1 quintillion chance that any *single* randomly selected person would share the DNA profile.

Thus, if the prior probability—that is, the probability as assessed without the DNA evidence—that the accused is the source of the crime scene sample is very low, even a DNA match might not make the posterior probability very high. In recent years, investigative authorities have maintained databases of DNA profiles of persons who, by virtue of some past involvement in the criminal justice system, have had their DNA analyzed. The British got a fast start on the process, but now there are databases in every American state, coordinated through the FBI to form what is essentially a national database. These databases offer a powerful tool for law enforcement, because they offer the possibility that if the police are otherwise unable to identify the perpetrator of a crime, but he left a DNA sample behind, a database search will point to the right person. There have in fact been many such "cold hits" already, and we can expect that as the databases grow there will be many more. This is a wonderful thing. But consider the strange case of Raymond Easton, a man from the west of England who was in the British database because of a history of domestic violence and who was arrested for a break-in because of a cold hit on that database—despite the facts that the break-in occurred 200 miles from his home and that he had advanced Parkinson's Disease and could barely dress himself. The arrest was based on a six-locus match; the authorities did a retest, using ten loci, and Easton matched the original six but not the additional four.[23] There are two basic

---

[22] *See* Jonathan J. Koehler, *Error and Exaggeration in the Presentation of DNA Evidence at Trial*, 34 Jurimetrics J. 21 (1993).

[23] *See* James Chapman, *DNA: After an innocent man is wrongly matched to a crime, could thousands in jail now appeal?*, Daily Mail, Feb. 9, 2000, 2000 WL 2434878, James Chapman & Julie Moult, *DNA test blunder nearly landed me in jail: branded a burglar by 'foolproof' database*, Daily Mail, Feb. 11, 2000, 2000 WL 14012932.

morals to the story. The first is that six loci is too few, except perhaps as an initial screening. The second is that we must avoid transposing the conditional. The probability that Easton's DNA profile would match that of the crime scene stain if he did not commit the break-in was very small. That does not mean that the probability that he did not commit the crime given that his DNA profile did match was also very small. The prior probability that he committed the crime was infinitesimal, and the oddity of the six-locus DNA match left the probability very small. Using enough loci should avoid a repeat of this problem.

Fears that jurors would be overwhelmed by statistical evidence, tending to give it excessive weight in comparison to evidence not expressed in numerical terms,[24] seem unfounded for the most part. Indeed, it seems that the more common problem is that jurors tend to give too little weight to evidence that entails numbers so extreme (high or low, depending on how you look at them) that they are beyond the ordinary experience of most people.[25] In any event, the problem of how DNA evidence should be presented, countered, and explained is a difficult one.[26]

¶ 3.20: Skipper is accused of criminal sexual conduct with a young girl, resulting in a pregnancy that was aborted. DNA tests show that Skipper, who is African-American, could have been the father, and that the chance of a randomly selected African-American male having DNA compatible with his being the father is 1 in 3,497. (This was an old DNA test!) A prosecution expert testifies that it is 99.97% probable that the defendant fathered the fetus; he explains that he did this by applying Bayes' Theorem and using prior odds—the odds assessed before receipt of the DNA evidence—of 50–50, which he contends "is a neutral starting point because it is just as likely that the defendant is not the father as that he is the father." *See State v. Skipper*, 228 Conn. 610, 637 A.2d 1101 (1994).

---

[24] *See* Laurence H. Tribe, *Trial by Mathematics: Precision and Ritual in the Legal Process*, 84 Harv. L. Rev. 1329 (1971).

[25] *See* Bruce C. Smith et al., *Jurors' Use of Probabilistic Evidence*, 20 Law & Hum. Behavior 49 (1996).

[26] For thoughtful considerations, see, e.g., Jonathan J. Koehler, *The Psychology of Numbers in the Courtroom: How to Make DNA—Match Statistics Seem Impressive or Insufficient*, 74 S. Cal. L. Rev. 1275 (2001); Mike Redmayne, *Presenting probabilities in court: the DNA experience*, 1 Int'l J. of Evidence & Proof 187 (1997); Jonathan J. Koehler, *On Conveying the Probative Value of DNA Evidence*, 67 U. Colorado L. Rev. 859 (1996); D.H. Kaye & Jonathan J. Koehler, *Can Jurors Understand Probabilistic Evidence?*, 154 J. R. Stat. Soc., Series A 75 (1991).

A committee appointed by the National Research Council (NRC) issued a report, *DNA Technology in Forensic Science* (1992), that was widely criticized as unduly hostile to DNA evidence. The NRC soon appointed a new committee, the report of which, *The Evaluation of Forensic DNA Evidence* (1996), was considerably—some would say excessively—more receptive.

(a) Should this evidence be allowed? *Compare* Richard A. Posner, *An Economic Approach to the Law of Evidence*, 51 Stan. L.Rev. 1477, 1514 (1999) (advocating use of prior odds of 1:1), *with* Richard D. Friedman, *A Presumption of Innocence, Not of Even Odds*, 52 Stan. L. Rev. 873 (2000) (completely persuasive demonstration of why this is wrong).

(b) The *Skipper* court held the evidence inadmissible in this form and declared that use of Bayes' Theorem in this way was improper, even if the jury was invited to supply its own prior probability of paternity, because a prior probability other than 0 is inconsistent with the presumption of innocence. Do you agree? Note the extensive academic exchange inspired by this case, cited in note 7 *supra*.

¶ 3.21: Adams is accused of raping a woman on the street within several miles of his home. The victim said she had an opportunity to observe the rapist, and the description she gave does not match Adams; she failed to pick him (or anyone else) out of a police lineup, and at another time she said that he did not resemble the rapist. Adams testifies that he spent the night of the rape with his girlfriend, and the girlfriend confirms this. The prosecution, however, has offered evidence that the DNA of a semen sample retrieved from the victim matches Adams's DNA, and that the chance that a randomly chosen person would have matching DNA is only one in 200 million. The prosecution expert has testified that the chance of a match in a randomly selected member of the population was approximately 1 in 200 million. The defense has countered this evidence on technical terms, contending that the random match probability may have been as low as 1 in 2 million. *See R. v. Adams*, [1997] 2 Cr. App. Rep. 467. Beyond this, how should the defense be allowed to counter the DNA evidence? Should it be allowed, for example, to present expert testimony that whatever odds a juror assessed for the defendant's guilt before hearing the DNA evidence, she should, according to Bayes' Theorem, multiply those prior odds by 2 million (using the lower figure) to take the DNA evidence into account? If so, should the expert be allowed testify as to how prior odds of 1 in 5 million would be reasonable, taking into account the population of the vicinity of the crime and the defense evidence?

¶ 3.22: In *R. v. Doheny & Adams*, [1997] 1 Cr. App. R.369, 375, involving two rape cases, the Court of Appeal of England suggested an instruction to the jury in the following form:

Members of the jury, if you accept the scientific evidence called by the Crown, this indicates that there are probably only four or five white males in the United Kingdom from whom that semen stain could have come. The defendant is one of them. If that is the position, the decision you have to reach, on all the evidence, is whether you are sure that it was the defendant who left that stain or whether it is possible that it was one of that other small group of men who share the same DNA characteristics.

(a) Allowing for the tradition of fuller summarization of the evidence in British courts than in American courts, is this an appropriate instruction? Why is the United Kingdom the (or an) appropriate domain? Would it be better to use instead (or in addition) the fifteen mile radius around the site of the rape? The entire world?

(b) Now suppose the DNA evidence is so strong that it is probable that there are *no* other people in the United Kingdom— or even the world—who could have been the source of the crime scene sample. Could the above instruction be amended to make it sensible and plausible for such a case?

¶ 3.23: (a) Should we do away with numbers altogether in presenting probabilistic evidence to the jury? Some observers have suggested a lexicon in which expert witnesses would translate likelihood ratios into pre-established verbal equivalents of how much support the evidence provides for the proposition in question; thus, the jury would not have to hear the numbers. For example, according to one proposal, if the likelihood ratio is equal to 1, the witness says that the evidence provides no support either way. Further:

If the likelihood ratio is	*then the witness says that the evidence provides*
between 1 and 10,	weak
between 10 and 100,	moderate
100 and 1,000,	moderately strong
1,000 and 10,000,	strong
10,000 and 1,000,000,	very strong
greater than 1,000,000,	extremely strong

support for the proposition.[27]

---

[27] Robertson, Vignaux & Berger, *supra* note 11, § 5.3.1; European Network of Forensic Science Institutes, *ENFSI guideline for evaluative reporting in forensic science* 16–17 (2015),

What advantages and disadvantages do you perceive in such a system?

(b) Robertson, Vignaux, and Berger suggest that experts testify in a form like this:

Whatever the odds of the hypothesis versus the alternative based on the other evidence (which I have not heard), my evidence makes them R times higher,

where R is the likelihood ratio. Robertson &Vignaux & Berger, *Interpreting Scientific Evidence, supra* note 11, § 5.1.1. What advantages and disadvantages are there to this style of testimony?

---

available at http://enfsi.eu/sites/default/files/documents/external_publications/m1_guideline.pdf. Note also the somewhat different table presented, without endorsement, in I.W. Evett, *Bayesian inference and forensic science: problems and perspectives*, 36 The Statistician 99, 103 (1987).

CHAPTER 4

COMPETENCE

■ ■ ■

Most evidence is admitted through questioning of witnesses. Even documents or other items of physical evidence are usually explained by a testifying witness. Traditionally, there have been many rules prescribing who may testify at all or as to a particular matter. Most of these rules of competence (or competency) have been eliminated, but some important ones remain.

A. COMPETENCE IN GENERAL

FRE 601, 603, 604, 610

Additional Reading: McCormick, ch. 7, §§ 61–64, 66, 70, 71; ch. 20, § 206(C); Mueller & Kirkpatrick, §§ 6.1–.2

We are heavily dependent on the testimony of witnesses. For the most part, testimony is helpful only if the witness is telling the truth, and truth-telling depends on the proper operation of several capacities. Consider this simple case. Fell is suing Grocer, claiming that he slipped and hurt himself on Grocer's floor because Grocer had negligently failed to clean up spilled ketchup that had spread over the floor. Grocer denies that there was any ketchup on the floor. Fell introduces the testimony of Witness, who says that she saw ketchup on the floor shortly before the accident.

This situation is represented in stylized form in Figure 4.a. The node labeled **O** represents everything the jury knows about the world, including the evidence it has heard, before hearing Witness's testimony. Now the jury has learned one additional fact, represented by the node at the right of the diagram, **TESTIMONY(SPILL)**—it knows that Witness has testified to **SPILL**. But how did events get to that point?

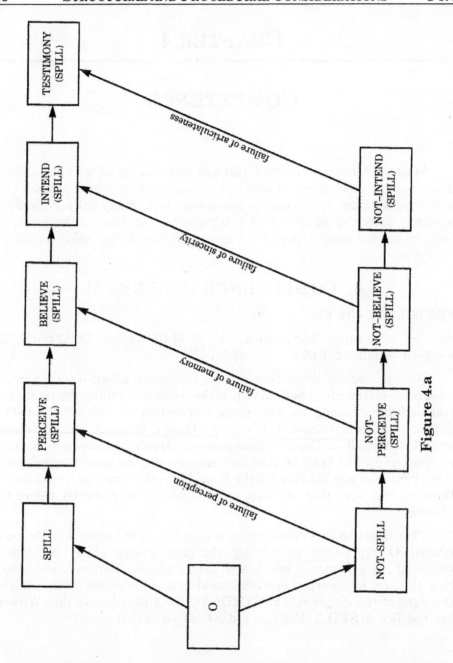

Figure 4.a

One possibility, represented by the top row of nodes, is what we might call the truth path. According to this account, **SPILL** is accurate. Witness accurately *perceived* **SPILL** to be true (so that proposition **PERCEIVE(SPILL)** is true). She accurately *remembered* what she perceived—both *retaining* what she had perceived and *retrieving* it from storage—so that at the time of her declaration she *believed* **SPILL** to be true (and so proposition **BELIEVE(SPILL)** is true). Furthermore, she sincerely *intended* to convey the information that **SPILL** was true (so that proposition **INTEND(SPILL)** is true) and she *articulated* this information at trial in a manner that her listeners could understand (so that proposition **TESTIMONY(SPILL)** is true).

There are other routes from **O** to **TESTIMONY(SPILL)**, however, that lead not through **SPILL,** but through **NOT-SPILL,** the negation of **SPILL**—meaning there was not in fact ketchup all over the floor. Figure 4.a represents the most important ones. In one of them, **NOT-SPILL** is true, but Witness *inaccurately perceived* that there was ketchup on the floor. According to another alternative route, Witness did not perceive ketchup to be on the floor but *inaccurately remembered*, and so at the time of her statement believed, that ketchup was on the floor. Another possibility is that Witness was *insincere* in that she attempted to communicate that ketchup was on the floor even though she did not believe that to be true. It might also be that, even though Witness was not attempting to communicate that ketchup was on the floor, she did so because she was *inarticulate.*

Thus, it may be that Witness's testimony is accounted for not by the event that she described but by one or more *testimonial incapacities.* How should the law respond to this possibility?

The common law, focusing on the incapacity of insincerity, developed numerous rules rendering incompetent—that is, barring the testimony of—various categories of witnesses whose credibility was, for one reason or another, deemed suspect. Felons, some children, the mentally disabled, atheists and agnostics, and even, in early days, spouses of parties and the parties themselves fell into these categories. Indeed, rather surprisingly, it was not until 1864 that any jurisdiction in the common law world allowed criminal defendants to testify under oath in their own behalf. Maine, under the influence of its notable Chief Justice, John Appleton, was the first, and other American states soon followed; England did not do so until 1898.[1]

In general, the incompetence rules began gradually to dissolve, for several reasons. First, it became clear that these rules sacrificed much valuable information and so hurt, rather than helped, the quest for truth. If the only witness able to tell about a crime was himself a felon, so be it; the jury would just have to do as best it could with this imperfect evidence.

---

[1]   See C.J.W. Allen, *The Law of Evidence in Victorian England* 10–11, 123, 177 (1997). In an earlier time, criminal defendants spoke informally at trial, not under oath, but this practice seems to have died out with the rise of defense counsel. *See* John H. Langbein, *The Historical Origins of the Privilege Against Self-Incrimination at Common Law*, 92 Mich. L. Rev. 1047 (1994).

Second, nobody's perfect. The credibility of many witnesses may be suspect even if they do not fit into one of the prescribed pigeonholes. Witnesses may have a financial stake in the outcome, or may be friendly with one of the parties, or may have an ax to grind, and so forth. Certainly we cannot tolerate the disqualification of all these potential witnesses. Moreover, it may well be that insincerity is not even the incapacity that accounts for most false testimony; it may be that misperception or failed memory is more significant. Nor can we really have confidence that we can prescribe categories that will sort out credible witnesses from the untrustworthy. It is better to judge the strength or weakness of each witness individually.

Third, courts have gained greater confidence in juries' ability to make that kind of evaluation, especially given that the testimony is subject to cross-examination. This is a trend that is manifest throughout the law of evidence. And fourth, a related point, one may perceive throughout evidentiary law, at least outside the constitutional context, a general intellectual trend resistant to categorical rules, a preference instead for dealing in matters of degree. Thus, much evidence that formerly would have been inadmissible because of fear that the jury would overvalue it is now admitted with the admonition that the defects "go to the weight." Instead of the testimony being barred, it is admitted and the opponent has an opportunity to show why it should not be heeded. For example, rather than holding that the wife of a party may not testify, the courts hold that she may and that the opponent can attempt through cross-examination and argument to persuade the jury—if persuasion is even needed—that she is biased and so her testimony should be discounted. We do not regard the jury as being so gullible as to be unable to deal with this factor.

Thus, the common law disqualifications have been nearly eliminated, and instead the grounds of suspicion may be presented and argued to the jury. As to one of the former disqualifications, lack of religious belief, not even this is so—FRE 610 expresses the universal rule in making this an unacceptable ground for challenging (or, for that matter, bolstering) the witness' credibility.

But does the near-elimination of the incompetence rules mean that anybody is competent to be a witness, or just that the judge should make the evaluation on a case-by-case basis? The first sentence of FRE 601 seems to adopt the former view, though subject to qualification, by providing: "Every person is competent to be a witness unless these rules provide otherwise." And the Advisory Committee Note to Rule 601 seems to confirm that the Rule means just what it says, "eliminat[ing] all grounds of incompetency not specifically recognized" in the succeeding provisions of Article VI of the Rules. The second sentence of Rule 601, however, by providing that when state law provides the substantive rule of decision in a civil case it also governs competence questions, recognizes that the states may adopt the latter view. And some states have done so. Several states, for example, have standards similar to those of Vermont's Rule 601(b):

> A person is disqualified to be a witness if the court determines that (1) the proposed witness is incapable of expressing himself concerning the matter so as to be understood by the judge and jury either directly or through interpretation by anyone who can understand him, or (2) the proposed witness is incapable of understanding the duty of a witness to tell the truth.

Furthermore, even under the Federal Rules much the same result can be reached via Rule 603. This Rule provides that every witness, before testifying, "must give an oath or affirmation to testify truthfully"[2] and that this "must be in a form designed to impress that duty on the witness's conscience." The Rule summarizes well the idea behind the oath requirement, which is very ancient. Most people today probably do not believe that lying under oath will condemn them to eternal punishment. But the oath still makes it somewhat more likely, at least in the case of some witnesses, that the witness will take extra care with the truth, because it is a clear reminder of the solemnity of the occasion and because lying under oath is criminally punishable. A party has a right to have testimony against him given under oath or some similar protection. And the fact that the witness has sworn to the testimony tends to lend it some additional weight.

¶ 4.1: In some countries of Continental Europe, one practice is much as it was in the older common law: A criminal defendant is expected to speak at his trial, but his statements are not taken under oath. Is there anything to be said for this practice?

The requirement of an oath or equivalent does not keep very many people off the witness stand. But it does mean that occasionally the court will conduct a preliminary inquiry that will look very much like a competency hearing to determine whether the prospective witness ought to testify. This happens especially when a party presents a young child as

---

[2] The source of some Christians' resistance to taking oaths may be found in Matthew 5:33–37, containing a portion of Jesus's Sermon on the Mount:

> Again, you have heard that it was said to the people long ago, "Do not break your oath, but fulfill to the Lord the vows you have made." But I tell you, do not swear an oath at all: either by heaven, for it is God's throne; or by the earth, for it is his footstool; or by Jerusalem, for it is the city of the Great King. And do not swear by your head, for you cannot make even one hair white or black. All you need to say is simply "Yes" or "No"; anything beyond this comes from the evil one.

And James 5:12 instructs more concisely:

> Above all, my brothers and sisters, do not swear—not by heaven or by earth or by anything else. All you need to say is a simple "Yes" or "No." Otherwise you will be condemned.

a witness. We will postpone to Chapter 20 consideration of the array of issues presented by child witnesses.

B. WITNESSES SUBJECTED TO SUGGESTION

Additional Reading: Mueller & Kirkpatrick, § 6.3

One of the problems with child witnesses that we shall take up in Chapter 20 is that they are particularly subject to suggestion. But adults as well as children are subject to suggestion. Sometimes suggestion can be useful, a way of prompting a person to retrieve memories; indeed, in Chapter 6 we will study techniques approved by evidentiary rules for refreshing the recollection of witnesses in court. But suggestion can also be harmful, creating evidence of dubious value; this is one reason why evidence law restricts the use of leading questions. Over the last few decades, "hundreds of studies . . . have demonstrated the ease with which memory can be distorted by suggestion, misinformation and leading questions."[3]

Concerns about suggestion are particularly pressing when a witness's testimony concerns a matter that has been the subject of inquiry while the witness was under hypnosis. Notwithstanding the general rule of competency of witnesses, some modern courts have balked at allowing the witness to testify after hypnosis. Unlike the situation with respect to children, the competency question with respect to previously hypnotized witnesses is not whether they are competent to testify at all but whether they may give a certain type of testimony.

In considering the following problems, it will be helpful to bear in mind what is often called the best-evidence principle. This is the idea that, even if a given item of evidence is more probative than prejudicial, it still might be appropriate to exclude it because doing so will likely induce the proponent, or future proponents in a similar situation, to produce better evidence—most frequently, evidence that doesn't have a flaw that the proffered item does. (An important article emphasizing this principle is Dale A. Nance, *The Best Evidence Principle*, 73 Iowa L. Rev. 227 (1988).) And this principle is particularly powerful when the proponent is a *repeat player*—that is, one who is regularly in the same litigation position. A prosecutor is a classical repeat player.

¶ **4.2:** Jane Sell was stabbed while sleeping at home. Immediately after the attack she was unable or unwilling to describe her assailant. Suspicion centered on her husband David, and on her former husband, Paul Hurd. At the prosecutor's initiative, she was hypnotized. While under the

---

[3]   Elizabeth F. Loftus & Laura A. Rosenwald, *Buried Memories, Shattered Lives*, 79 A.B.A. J., Nov. 1993, at 70, 73.

trance she relived the attack. She denied that the attacker was David, and in response to the question "Is it Paul?" emotionally responded, "Yes." Six days later Jane made a statement to the police identifying Hurd as the attacker.

(a) May Jane testify at trial, identifying Hurd?

(b) May the prosecution show the jury a videotape of the hypnosis session or repeat the session in front of the jury?

(c) If your answers to (a) or (b) were negative, what might the prosecution have done differently to improve the chances of admissibility?[4]

¶ 4.3: Vicky Rock is charged with manslaughter in state court for the shooting death of her husband Frank. Vicky tells police that she picked up a handgun after Frank, in the middle of an argument, choked her and threw her against the wall, and that after he hit her again she shot him. After two hypnotic sessions, however, Vicky recalls that she did not have her finger on the trigger and that the gun discharged after Frank grabbed her by the arm. A gun expert is prepared to testify that the particular gun is prone to discharge when hit or dropped.

State law categorically excludes testimony of hypnotically enhanced memories. Should the court adhere to this law and exclude Vicky's testimony? *See Rock v. Arkansas*, 483 U.S. 44 (1987)(holding that the state's *per se* rule "infringes impermissibly on the right of a defendant to testify on his or her own behalf," *id.* at 62).

Hypnosis is just one of several suggestive techniques that some psychotherapists use when they suspect that a patient is suffering from long-repressed memories of child sexual abuse. There seems now to be little doubt that child sexual abuse occurs with far greater frequency than

---

[4] *See* State v. Hurd, 86 N.J. 525, 432 A.2d 86 (1981) (imposing procedural requirements for admissibility of hypnotically refreshed testimony), *overruled by* State v. Moore, 902 A.2d 1212 (N.J. 2006) (holding hypnotically refreshed testimony generally inadmissible in criminal trials; emphasizing dangers of false confidence, confabulation, gap-filling, and suggestibility, and lack of empirical evidence supporting usefulness); *see also, e.g.,* U.S. v. D.W.B., 74 M.J. 630 (NMCCCA 2015)(collecting cases; concluding that most jurisdictions either treat hypnotically refreshed testimony as *per se* inadmissible or require case-by-case determinations, either by applying procedural requirements such as those in *Hurd* or examining the totality of the circumstances, and that a few jurisdictions admit such testimony and prescribe that doubts about it go to weight rather than admissibility); 2 David. L. Faigman, et al., *Mod. Sci. Evidence* §§ 18.1–.7 (2015–16 ed.); Earl F. Martin, *A* Daubert *Test of Hypnotically Refreshed Testimony in the Criminal Courts,* 9 Tex. Wes. L. Rev. 151 (2003); Daniel R. Webert, *Are the Courts in a Trance? Approaches to the Admissibility of Hypnotically Enhanced Witness Testimony in Light of Empirical Evidence,* 40 Am. Crim. L. Rev. 1301 (2003); Richard G. Montevideo, *Hypnosis— Should the Courts Snap Out of It? A Closer Look at the Critical Issues,* 44 Ohio St.L.J. 1053 (1983).

has generally been recognized, often with debilitating consequences for its victims. Some clinicians have taken the view that as a defense mechanism children often repress memories of this abuse, and that, with proper therapeutic guidance, the memory can be recovered in adulthood, with potentially cathartic effects. But these claims have raised bitter controversy as to whether long-buried memories—repression itself is a controversial term—can effectively be recovered, and how reliable purportedly recovered memories are.[5]

Part of the problem is that the techniques used by some therapists are so highly suggestive that, if indeed they do recover accurate memories, they seem almost designed to induce some false memories as well. One commentator has listed the following techniques among those commonly used:

> (a) telling clients who report no history of CSA [child sexual abuse] that their symptoms are indicative of repressed memories of CSA, that many survivors do not remember their abuse, and that psychological healing depends upon recovering memories of abuse; (b) using memory recovery techniques such as hypnosis, age regression, guided imagery, sodium amytal, and instructions to work at remembering CSA . . . ; (c) interpreting dreams and physical symptoms as memories of CSA; (d) recommending that clients who do not remember abuse join survivors' groups and/or read popular books on remembering CSA; and (e) uniformly endorsing all reports related to abuse as accurate memories, and countering clients' expressions of doubt.[6]

---

[5] *Compare, e.g.*, Ross E. Cheit, *Recovered Memory Project*, http://blogs.brown.edu/recovered memory/tag/ncrj/; Jim Hopper, *Recovered Memories of Sexual Abuse: Scientific Research & Scholarly Resources*, http://www.jimhopper.com/memory/#pref; Judith Lewis Herman, *Trauma and Recovery* (1992), *with* Moheb Costandi, *Evidence-based justice: Corrupted memory*, http://www.nature.com/news/evidence-based-justice-corrupted-memory-1.13543 (2013); Robert Timothy Reagan, *Scientific Consensus on Memory Repression and Recovery*, 51 Rutgers L. Rev. 275 (1999) ("The scientific principle of repression is not generally accepted among memory scientists. . . . Until purported recovered repressed memories are shown to be reliable evidence of historical fact, they fail to be the sort of proof on which courts should rely."); Elizabeth F. Loftus & Katherine Ketcham, *The Myth of Repressed Memory: False Memories and Allegations of Sexual Abuse* (1994); Gary M. Ernsdorff & Elizabeth F. Loftus, *Let Sleeping Memories Lie? Words of Caution About Tolling the Statute of Limitations in Cases of Memory Repression*, 84 J. Crim. L. & Criminology 129 (1993). *See* United States v. D.W.B., 74 M.J. 630, 642 (NMCCA. 2015) (adopting "totality of circumstances" test and noting that "memory recovered by means of a formal psychological process is the product of a scientific process and therefore subject to a baseline reliability determination as a precondition to admissibility"; applying test to uphold exclusion of testimony allegedly recovered after Eye Movement Desensitization and Reprocessing (EMDR) procedure); State v. Hungerford, 697 A.2d 916, 923, 927 (N.H.1997) ("A review of the psychological literature on the subject of memory repression and recovery convinces us that a case-by-case approach, tempered with skepticism, is most appropriate in this context. . . . The scientific community is completely divided, at best, on the issue of recovery of completely repressed memories."); 2 David. L. Faigman, et al., *Mod. Sci. Evidence* §§ 19.1–.7 (2015–16 ed.).

[6] Stephen Lindsay, *Contextualizing and Clarifying Criticisms of Memory Work in Psychotherapy*, 3 Consciousness & Cognition 426, 430 (1994), *quoted in* Sheila Taub, *The Legal*

¶ **4.4:** Melissa Merkel, a 38-year-old woman, has brought suit against her father, Jack, contending that between the time she was six and eight years old he regularly molested her sexually. At deposition, Melissa describes the molestation in vivid detail. Asked why she did not bring suit before, Melissa testifies that she had repressed memory of it; only after placing herself in the care of Dr. Timothy Turner, a psychotherapist, did she begin to recover the memories. Melissa began to visit Dr. Turner for a variety of complaints, including depression, bulimia, anxiety and panic attacks, and difficulty sleeping.

You are clerking for the trial judge. Assume tentatively that the governing statute of limitations does not bar the action; if Melissa only recently recovered memory of the abuse, and was not to blame for the delay in doing so, the action is timely.

(a) Is Melissa competent to testify as to the abuse? Are there any predicate issues you must resolve before deciding this?

(b) Suppose you have qualms about the entire phenomenon of plaintiffs bringing actions on the basis of purportedly recovered memories of abuse committed long ago. Is the issue of witness competence an appropriate one to use in implementing restraint?[7]

C. THE DEAD MAN STATUTES

Additional Reading: McCormick, ch. 7, § 65; Mueller & Kirkpatrick, § 6.2, at 440-41

The so-called Dead Man Statutes are a lingering remnant of the common law disqualifications. The idea behind them is that if death (or, in some statutes, insanity or infancy) prevents one party from testifying as to a certain event, then fairness demands that an adverse party not be allowed to testify to that event either. Most modern observers agree that this is a deeply flawed notion—otherwise known as a really stupid idea.

Treatment of Recovered Memories of Child Sexual Abuse, 17 J. Legal Med. 183, 191 (1996), a helpful review of the field.

    [7]   *Cf.* McCollum v. D'Arcy, 138 N.H. 285, 638 A.2d 797, 800 (N.H. 1994) ("[P]laintiff still carries the burden . . . if challenged, to validate the phenomenon of memory repression itself and the admissibility of evidence flowing therefrom."); State v. Hungerford, 1995 WL 378571 (N.H. Super.Ct.1995) ("Testimony that is dependent upon recovery of a repressed memory through therapy cannot be logically disassociated from the underlying scientific technique."), *aff'd,* 697 A.2d 916 (N.H.1997), *discussed in* Taub, *supra,* at 205–06. In *Hungerford,* the state supreme court said that allegedly recovered memories "may be actual recollections of actual traumatic events, manufactured narratives of events that never occurred, or some combination of these." 697 A.2d at 920. Hence, while recognizing that "treating the testimony of a percipient witness to a crime as scientific evidence is novel in our law," it agreed with the trial court that "a recovered memory that previously had been completely absent from a witness's conscious recollection cannot be separated from the process, if any, that facilitated the recovery."

Many claims are lost if the survivor is not allowed to testify. It does not advance fairness to hold that, because two views of the event are not available, the one that is available will be disregarded. As with the traditional grounds of incompetence, this is a situation that the jury can easily evaluate, especially if prompted by counsel for the successor to the dead person. There is no reason to suppose that arguments of the following sort cannot be digested by the jury:

> You have heard what Patrick testified about this conversation. And what evidence is there to corroborate his version? Nothing. There was only one other person present, and that was Dennis, of whose estate my client is the executor. Dennis is dead, so we do not have his version of events. Now, isn't that convenient for Patrick? And isn't it remarkable that Patrick's story just so happens to coincide perfectly with his own interests?

Under the Federal Rules, there is no Dead Man provision. *See* Advisory Committee Note to Rule 601. And in states that have adopted codifications based on the Federal Rules, the Dead Man statutes are generally held to have been abrogated by the general rule of competency of FRE 601.[8] Nevertheless, Dead Man's rules remain and continue to work mischief in a number of states, some of them large ones. New York, which has not yet adopted a codification, continues to adhere to its old statute.[9] And some other states, including Texas, Illinois, and North Carolina, that have adopted FRE-based codifications decided to incorporate a Dead Man's rule into them or retain the old statute separately. Thus, it is important to be aware of the existence of these rules and of the types of issues they raise. The rules, and the exceptions to them, vary from state to state, and tend to involve some very technical issues. Below are a hypothetical statute, drawn from some of the most common provisions of the statutes, and Texas's Rule 601(b):

Hypothetical Statute

A party to an action, or other person interested in the outcome of the action, may not testify concerning a transaction or communication with a person since deceased if the action is prosecuted or defended by the executor or administrator of the decedent; provided, however, that the surviving party or interested person may testify if called by the executor or administrator.

---

[8] *See, e.g.,* Johnson v. Porter, 14 Ohio St.3d 58, 471 N.E.2d 484 (1984), *reprinted in* 50 A.L.R.4th 1231 (1984).

[9] N.Y. CPLR § 4519. *See, e.g.,* Five Corners Car Wash, Inc. v. Minrod Realty Corp., 20 N.Y.S.3d 578 (2d Dept. 2015).

Texas R. Evid. 601(b)

(b) The "Dead Man's Rule."

(1) Applicability. The "Dead Man's Rule" applies only in a civil case:

> (A) by or against a party in the party's capacity as an executor, administrator, or guardian; or

> (B) by or against a decedent's heirs or legal representatives and based in whole or in part on the decedent's oral statement.

(2) General Rule. In cases described in subparagraph (b)(1)(A), a party may not testify against another party about an oral statement by the testator, intestate, or ward. In cases described in subparagraph (b)(1)(B), a party may not testify against another party about an oral statement by the decedent.

(3) Exceptions. A party may testify against another party about an oral statement by the testator, intestate, ward, or decedent if:

> (A) the party's testimony about the statement is corroborated; or

> (B) the opposing party calls the party to testify at trial about the statement.[10]

¶ **4.5:** Fred Docking, who owned a large farm, put one plot up for sale. When Alan and Ellen Pickering, potential purchasers, visited Docking, he said, "Rex, my hand, will show you around. He knows the property as well as I do." Rex, an overeager salesman, told the Pickerings that the plot included a wooded knoll that actually was part of the adjoining property. The next day Docking wrote the Pickerings a letter saying, "Glad you liked the property. Rex tells me you're thinking of putting a little hideaway on the wooded knoll. Great idea!" Eventually, the Pickerings bought the property as tenants in common.

The next year, the Pickerings divorced. As part of the settlement, Alan pays Ellen alimony and child support. The settlement also called for them to sell the plot of land, which they had not yet improved, and to split the proceeds. When they sold the land, they were chagrined to discover that the wooded

---

[10] *See also* 735 Il. Comp. Stat. 5/8–201; N.C. R. Evid. 601(c).

knoll was not in fact part of the plot they had bought; as a result, they received much less than their purchase price for the land. Alan and Ellen have each brought suit against Docking, claiming fraud. Docking promptly died, for if he had not there would be no dead person in this problem. The suit continued against his estate. Under the hypothetical statute presented above, what evidence may each plaintiff present? Under the Texas rule?

D. JUDGES, JURORS, AND LAWYERS

FRE 605, 606(a)

Additional Reading: McCormick, ch. 7, § 68; Mueller & Kirkpatrick, §§ 6.8–.9

It seems fairly self-evident that neither judge nor juror should testify at a trial in which she is sitting, and this is what FRE 605 and 606(a) respectively provide.[11] There is some fuzziness around the edges, however. Often the judge does give the jury factual information concerning the case; we will see this in Chapter 21 in discussing judicial notice.

It may also happen that events relevant to the litigated matter continue to develop even as the trial proceeds, and that the judge or a juror witnesses some of these.

> ¶ 4.6: You are clerking for a judge who is sitting in the trial of David Dane on bank robbery charges. Juror Jiminez approaches your boss, the judge, and says, "Your Honor, I thought I'd better tell you. I happened to be in the men's room at the same time as Mr. Dane during a recess, and he told me, 'If I like what you do to me, you'll like what I'll do for you.'" The judge calls in counsel and asks them what she should do. The prosecutor argues, on the basis of copious authority, that evidence tending to show the defendant is conscious of his own guilt is highly relevant and admissible to show guilt; therefore, she asks the judge to excuse Jiminez from the jury and allow him to testify. Defense counsel argues that the judge should declare a mistrial. The judge turns to you. Evaluate the arguments of the two sides and advise the judge what to do.

A related problem is that of a juror's testimony to impeach the jury's verdict. Recall Section B.5 of Chapter 2, which discusses FRE 606(b).

The Federal Rules say nothing about an attorney's testifying in a case in which she is also representing one of the parties. Lawyers' ethical

---

[11] Interestingly, though, in its earliest form the jury was a testimonial body that was expected to know the facts of a dispute submitted to it.

codes do, however. Rule 3.7 of the ABA's Model Rules of Professional Conduct provides:

(a) A lawyer shall not act as advocate at a trial in which the lawyer is likely to be a necessary witness unless:

(1) the testimony relates to an uncontested issue;

(2) the testimony relates to the nature and value of legal services rendered in the case; or

(3) disqualification of the lawyer would work substantial hardship on the client.

(b) A lawyer may act as advocate in a trial in which another lawyer in the lawyer's firm is likely to be called as a witness unless precluded from doing so by Rule 1.7 ["Conflict of Interest: Current Clients"] or Rule 1.9 ["Duties to Former Clients"].

This Rule is based largely on the possibility of a conflict in the roles of lawyer and witness. The lawyer's personal interest as a potential or actual witness—not to take the stand, perhaps, or to come out of it well if she does—may be in conflict with the needs of the client. Also, if the lawyer acts as a witness, her personal credibility may influence her ability to plead the client's case, and that is a situation we generally wish to avoid.

¶ 4.7: How strong are these arguments? Do they justify prohibitions as broad as those of the Model Rules? Note two important changes made by Rule 3.7 as compared to Disciplinary Rule 5–101(B) of the ABA's Model Code of Professional Responsibility, a predecessor to the Model Rules:

(1) D.R. 5–101(b) came into play from the beginning of representation, while Rule 3.7, at least by its own terms, operates only at trial.

(2) Rule 3.7 is considerably more generous than D.R. 5–101(b) with respect to testimony by lawyers in the firm not actually conducting the litigation; the earlier provision drew no distinction between the situation in which the lawyer considering the representation anticipated being called as a witness and the one in which she anticipated a lawyer in her firm being called.

Is Rule 3.7 an improvement in these respects?

FRE 605 and 606(a) say that a person fulfilling certain functions (judge or juror) cannot be a witness. Rule 3.7 says that a person who should be, or is likely to be, a witness cannot fulfill a certain function (lawyer). There is not necessarily a big difference between these approaches. If the testimony of a judge or juror would be important to a given case, she can give up that function, or be made to give it up, so that she can testify.

¶ 4.8: The purchasers of apartments in Shaky Towers, a condominium project, have decided to sue the sponsor, Greasy Neil, for fraud. Their claim is that the condition of the building is not as he represented it to be, and that he failed to do some promised landscaping work. Most of the alleged misrepresentations were in the prospectus for the condominium, but some of them were oral statements by Neil to eight purchasers. The claim is for about $150,000, and the residents have been unable to get any lawyer to take the case on a contingency. They are afraid that any hourly fees to a lawyer are likely to eat up a large percentage of any award they receive and leave them in debt if they lose. Some of the residents ask Folger, a lawyer who lives in the building, to take the case as a public service for a reduced fee. Some of Neil's conversations were with Folger, who not only is one of the more articulate residents of the building but, lawyer that he is, also has notes of the conversations. Folger is aware that before the case ever reaches trial it would probably be consumed for many months by discovery and by motions to dismiss and for summary judgment, and that a pretrial settlement is not only likely but very desirable. Is Folger free to take on the representation?

E. THE PERSONAL KNOWLEDGE REQUIREMENT

FRE 602

Additional Reading: McCormick, ch. 3, § 10; ch. 7, § 69; Mueller & Kirkpatrick, § 6.5

The requirement that witnesses speak from firsthand knowledge is fundamental to our trial system. But it is important to recognize what we mean by "knowledge" in this context. For Witness to testify, "The red car reached the intersection before the green car," it is not necessary that she *know* this to be true, in the sense of absolute certainty; indeed, truly complete certainty about such an event is probably unattainable. What we really mean is that the witness should report to the jury what she has perceived herself through the operation of her own senses, not information that she has assimilated from other sources. Thus, it is a sufficient basis for Witness's testimony that she was standing near the intersection and saw the events.

By contrast, Witness cannot testify about the red car's having reached the intersection first if the basis of her knowledge is, "It must have happened that way, given the positions of the cars after the accident." The evaluative function is for the jury; from the witness what we want is the facts. The problem is not simply that Witness has given an evaluation that we do not need. More important, perhaps, is that giving this evaluation might obscure what we *do* need from her, her rendition of what she actually perceived. Thus, Witness may testify, "Right after I heard a loud and sudden noise I went up to the intersection, and I saw the front left fender of the green car embedded in the left rear of the red car." Then it is up to the jury to determine what inferences it should draw from this and other evidence.

Now suppose instead the basis for Witness's testimony as to which car reached the intersection first is, "That's what everyone told me who saw the accident." The judicial response may be, "Well, then let's hear them testify." Sometimes that is practical, and sometimes not. Even if it is not, Witness's testimony as to the inferences she has drawn from what she has heard will not usually be the best method for her to transmit information to the jury; the same preference for her perceptions over her evaluations applies. Thus, it may be appropriate for the witness to testify, "Right after I heard the loud and sudden noise I came to the intersection and a man told me, 'Wow! The red car was about to make a turn when the green car blind-sided him!'"

Note that here Witness is testifying only about what she herself perceived—the sound and the man's making of the statement. You have probably noticed that part of what she heard is what someone else said. This testimony is hearsay, and there is a large body of law, which we will study in great depth, governing whether or not it is admissible; some hearsay is admissible and some is not. But whether or not this hearsay is admissible, it is not objectionable on grounds of lack of personal knowledge—because Witness is testifying as to what she perceived. Indeed, one of the purposes served by the personal knowledge requirement is that it flushes out what might be called hearsay coverups—in which the witness is really reporting only the substance of what she heard, but reporting it as her own conclusion. The personal knowledge requirement brings into the open that the witness is really relaying into trial the report of an out-of-court observer; the admissibility of that out-of-court observation can then be determined without a superfluous overlay cast on it by the witness.

And what, you may ask, if the out-of-court statement appears to be admissible under an exemption to the hearsay rule—does the declarant of that statement have to be shown to have personal knowledge? The Advisory Committee, in its Note to FRE 803, stated the usual black-letter rule: The declarant is treated as a witness in this respect, and so the hearsay exemptions do not "dispense with the requirement of firsthand knowledge."[12] But the requirement should be applied with some restraint in this setting. If it appears that the declarant was simply speculating, so that if she had been an in-court witness she would have had no valid testimony to offer, then there is probably no good reason to admit her out-of-court declaration. On the other hand, suppose that her statement appears to have been based principally on her personal observations—so that if she had been a witness at trial she could have given valid testimony reporting those observations—but she added an overlay of inference. For example, the declarant might have said, "I heard a crash from a couple of blocks away." If she were testifying in court, the judge might say, "Well, you didn't know it was a crash, so please just describe what you heard." But if the statement has already been made, before trial, then it cannot be shaped in the way that testimony can; the judge has to decide to admit it as it is or exclude it. In such a case, if the declarant is now unavailable, the judge might well reason, "There's nothing terribly wrong with this statement; it's apparently based on the declarant's personal observations, and just adds in a little bit of plausible inference. I'm not in a position where, by excluding this statement, I can induce the production of a statement in better form. So I may as well admit it." And even if the declarant is available, the court might decide that the benefit of bringing her in to court is not worth the trouble.

Notice again the operation of the best-evidence principle in this area. Though testimony not based on personal knowledge may be more probative than prejudicial, exclusion of it will often induce the proponent to produce better evidence—that is, the witness's testimony of what she actually knows, without the overlay of unspoken inferences drawn by the witness. The court can then decide whether that testimony, based on the witness's knowledge should be admitted. But if the evidence reports the statement of an out-of-court declarant, it may be that excluding the offered evidence would not induce the presentation of better evidence—or that the incremental improvement in the quality of the evidence would not be worth the cost of producing it.

Sometimes there is doubt about whether in fact the witness (or out-of-court declarant) does have personal knowledge of the matter that she is describing. For example, the witness may say that she was at the scene and others may deny this; in the case of an out-of-court statement, the statement itself may assert that the declarant was speaking from first-hand observation, but this may be ambiguous and there may not be other witnesses who can shed light on the matter. FRE 602 states the usually accepted rule: "A witness may testify to a matter only if evidence is introduced *sufficient to support a finding* that the witness has personal

---

[12] *See, e.g.*, United States v. Owens, 789 F.2d 750 (9th Cir.1986), *rev'd on other grounds*, 484 U.S. 554 (1988).

knowledge of the matter." (Emphasis added.) In other words, the personal knowledge question is a preliminary, or predicate, issue on which the admissibility of the testimony depends, and the proponent of the testimony has the burden of *laying a foundation* for the testimony, which in this case means producing sufficient evidence for a reasonable jury to find that the witness did have personal knowledge. In Chapter 8, we shall study the matter of preliminary issues. We shall explore why under the prevailing view the proponent need persuade the judge only that a reasonable jury could conclude that the witness had personal knowledge—and why even that standard is arguably too stringent.

¶ **4.9:** A witness wants to testify, "Nick Nelson is my uncle." Is a foundation necessary? *See, e.g., Brown v. Mitchell*, 88 Tex. 350, 31 S.W. 621 (1895) (allowing testimony by plaintiff in a will case that he was the son of the decedent). Now assume the court is being particularly persnickety in demanding a foundation. What questions would you ask to lay that foundation?

¶ **4.10:** You want a witness to testify, "The moon is made of green cheese." Prepare a line of questioning that will enable you to elicit this testimony.

F. LAY OPINIONS

FRE 701

Additional Reading: McCormick, ch. 3, §§ 11, 18; Mueller & Kirkpatrick, §§ 7.2–.4

Closely associated with the personal knowledge requirement, and to some extent the other side of the same coin, is the body of rules limiting the opinions to which witnesses may testify. Some testimony, we have seen, is based on the witness's personal observations but mixes in with them the witness's own inferences and evaluations—or, perhaps synonymously, her opinions. Like the personal knowledge requirement, the opinion rules reflect the law's preference for testimony in the form of factual perceptions, not evaluations, and its recognition that sometimes this preference may give way.

It is customary to think of the opinion rules in terms of a lay/expert dichotomy. We will adhere to the distinction here—dealing with lay opinions here and with expert opinions in the next chapter, as part of our general exploration of expert evidence—but with a qualification: The rules for the two types of witnesses may be substantially different, but to a very large extent they reflect the application of a common set of principles to different contexts. Indeed, the line between lay opinion and expert opinion is often blurry, and we should perhaps think more of a continuum than of a sharp separation.

We have seen that the basic demand on the witness is like that made by Sergeant Friday on the old TV show *Dragnet*: "Just the facts." Ideally, the witness should be a source of data that the jury evaluates in drawing its conclusions; the witness is called to the stand not as a factfinder or decisionmaker but only as a source of potentially useful information not in the jury's possession. But much—indeed, arguably all—testimony involves evaluations by the witness: Witnesses cannot, or at any rate ordinarily do not, transmit their undigested sense perceptions.

¶ 4.11: A witness testifies, "The tall blond woman was wearing a red dress." What opinions or evaluations has the witness offered in giving this testimony? If it is held improper for the witness to give these evaluations, in what terms should she testify?

This problem suggests that it is impossible to eliminate the evaluative aspects of a witness's testimony. There are two basic reasons for this. First is the witness's limited ability to gather and report information. People naturally assess, aggregate, and reassemble data in their own minds before reporting them. Think how many facts go into the recognition of a person. We might say, "I saw Barry," or even "I saw a person looking like Barry," quite naturally. It would be much harder for us to break down the data and our implicit assumptions into bits: "I saw what appeared to be a black male figure in his 50s, about 6 feet tall, skinny, with big ears and close-cropped graying hair." And even so elaborate a statement would not eliminate all assessments by the witness—how tall was the person really? Was the hair real?

Second is the limited capacity of the jury—or any factfinder, for that matter—to understand information presented in unfamiliar ways. Even if a witness could disaggregate the data into their elements, the jury would not likely be able to do much with them. Trials would not get very far if a witness could not say, "The dress was red," and instead were required to testify as to the apparent wavelength of the electromagnetic radiation emanating from different parts of the shape perceived as a dress. Or suppose that the witness testified to something like, "The coefficient of friction between the tires and the roadbed was .307." Surely the jury is likely to gain more information it can use if the witness says, "The pavement was slippery."

These difficulties mean that we must tolerate a certain amount of evaluation in testimony. Rather than testify purely in terms of hard data, a witness must often place the phenomena she perceives into categories, which may have uncertain limits. Thus, when a witness testifies that she has perceived a woman, she may be considered to have performed simultaneously two evaluative tasks:

(1) *Choice of standard.* At least implicitly, the witness must have some concept of what she means by "woman." What is her standard, for instance, in distinguishing between a woman and a girl?

(2) *Evaluation of the phenomenon.* The witness must assemble the information provided by her sensory perceptions and determine whether taken together it leads to the conclusion that she perceived a woman, as she understands the term.

Plainly, the witness must be allowed some leeway to testify in evaluative terms. But there are limits. To the extent feasible, we want the jury to evaluate the data, not simply accept evaluations offered by witnesses. Indeed, to the extent the witness can present the information to the jurors in a way that they can evaluate it, the witness's own evaluation is extraneous and distracting. Thus, if the witness can testify, "She was going 60 miles per hour down Main Street," we do not need her to testify, "She was going way too fast," and in fact we do not want her to. But perhaps the witness can't be so precise. Consider again the testimony about "slippery" pavement. Testimony focusing on an evaluative adjective like "slippery" invites further evaluation, for it leaves open an important question, of the type that Jimmy Fallon might invite: *"How* slippery was it?" If the witness is able to give a Fallon-type answer—"It was so slippery that limousines were doing donuts in the parking lot"—that might solve the problem, but if not the witness is probably going to be reduced to using an adverb. Would "very" be acceptable? How about "dangerously"? How else might you ask the witness to characterize how slippery the pavement was?

From all this, it follows that the question is not simply whether a witness should be allowed to testify in the form of an opinion or be required to give data, but rather where on the continuum between pure data and pure evaluation the witness's testimony should lie. In making this decision, the judge should assess, on the one hand, the necessity of allowing the witness to testify in a way that will be meaningful and helpful to the jury. On the other hand, the judge should ensure to the extent feasible that the jury's decision is made on the basis of its own evaluations of the data rather than on those of a witness. The two goals must be balanced, and so inevitably some evaluation will enter into the testimony. As a distinguished panel of the Second Circuit once put it,

> The question ought always to be whether it is more convenient to insist that the witness disentangle in his own mind—which, much more often than not, he is quite unable to do—those constituent factors on which his opinion is based; or to let him

state his opinion and leave to cross examination a searching inquisition to uncover its foundations.[13]

¶ 4.12: The parents of Scott Brewster, a high school football player who died of a heart attack during a team practice, have sued the coach for negligence in holding the practice on an excessively hot day. The plaintiffs want to put on the stand Will Windheim, a teammate of Brewster who was present at the practice. Which of the following would be appropriate testimony by Windheim? For any that are appropriate, what preliminary questions are necessary?

(a) "It was too hot to allow the team to practice." *No! opinion*

(b) "It was 95° and the relative humidity was 80%." *Sure... could have looked at phone*

(c) "It was really hot and humid." *Relative to... how did you feel*

(d) "It was so hot and humid, I felt faint after five minutes." *Sure?*

(e) "It was so hot and humid, guys were dropping like flies practically from the start of practice." *Another reason dropping? 602 objective - don't have personal knowledge why, just that they were*

(f) "It was the hottest, stickiest day we'd ever had practice." *Yes! could also get by hearsay exception if other ppl said it was hot*

could have observed the instruments w phone app is a form of hearsay

might try to object under 701, need medical testimony, but probably getting overruled

Note how FRE 701 approaches the problem of the lay witness. First, under subsection (a), a lay witness's opinion is admissible only if it is "rationally based on the witness's perception." The Advisory Committee's Note suggests that this is simply a confirmation of the personal knowledge requirement, but the "based on" language suggests a loosening of that requirement: The witness must have perceived information concerning the particular event or condition, and the connection between that information and the opinion she offers must be a rational one, not sheer speculation on the basis of unfounded premises, but the opinion may be more than a simple report *of* the witness's perceptions.

Second, and more comprehensively, a lay witness's opinion is admissible only if it satisfies subsection (b)'s requirement that it be "helpful to clearly understanding the witness's testimony or to determining a fact in issue." In a sense, this "helpfulness" requirement can be regarded as a basic requisite for the admissibility of all evidence. We can break down "helpfulness" into two aspects: Does the evidence give the jury information it would not otherwise have? And is that information useful to the jury in performing its factfinding function?

A witness, we have said, is called to the stand only because she purportedly has some useful information that the jury does not; thus the

---

[13] United States v. Petrone, 185 F.2d 334, 336 (2d Cir.1950) (per curiam; L. Hand, Swan, Frank, JJ.), *cert. denied*, 340 U.S. 931 (1951).

"rationally based on the witness's perception" requirement of FRE 701. Often, the source of the witness's information is that she was there, at the scene of an event. Sometimes, the source of information is longstanding familiarity with something with which the jury is not familiar. For example, a witness may be able to identify a person's handwriting, even though she has no particular skill in distinguishing different penmanship styles, simply because she has frequently seen the person's writing.

In either event, the witness's function is to put the jury, to the extent feasible, in as good a position as the witness herself to evaluate the data necessary for factfinding. This, we have seen, may require that the witness be allowed to give evaluations of the sort that the jury could not sensibly make without having had the benefits of the witness's own out-of-court perceptions. But the witness should not make evaluations that the jurors can make as well as she can, assuming the jurors have the benefit of whatever data the witness is able to communicate in a form they can understand.[14]

The other side of the coin is that the witness should not offer evaluations that she can make no better than the jury because she has no better basis, in information or qualifications, to make the evaluation than does the jury. If a lay witness says, "I'll suffer all my life from these broken toes," we may very well ask, "Who are you to say?" If the witness has no better basis for drawing the conclusion than the jury has, then the testimony is not likely to be useful. But of course there are potential witnesses who could offer a useful opinion on the subject—physicians and others with medical expertise.[15]

This naturally brings us to the subject of expert witnesses, the topic of the next chapter. The question of what the appropriate bounds of lay opinions are has recently drawn the attention of rulemakers. In 2000, Rule 701 was amended to add a third requirement, in subsection (c), that a lay opinion must "not [be] based on scientific, technical, or other specialized knowledge within the scope of Rule 702 [the Rule providing for expert opinion based on such specialized knowledge]." One may well doubt the need for and wisdom of this amendment. The Advisory Committee said that it would "eliminate the risk that the reliability requirements set forth in Rule 702 will be evaded through the simple expedient of proffering an expert in lay witness clothing." But if the court takes care to ensure that a lay opinion satisfies the requirements of subdivisions (a) and (b)—that the opinion be "rationally based on the

---

[14] *See* 7 John Henry Wigmore, *Evidence* § 1917.8, at 10 (Chadbourn rev. 1978) ("*[W]herever inference and conclusion can be drawn by the jury as well as by the witness*, the witness is superfluous; . . . a lay opinion is received because and whenever his facts cannot be so told as to make the jury as able as he to draw the inference.").

[15] See, e.g., Danny R. Veilleux, Annotation, *Necessity of Expert Testimony on Issue of Permanence of Injury and Future Pain and Suffering*, 20 A.L.R.5th 1 (1994).

witness's perception" and that it be "helpful to clearly understanding the witness's testimony or to determining a fact in issue"—then it would appear that the opinion is perfectly valid evidence. The discussion above has suggested that lay opinions are pervasive, and it may be a mistake to require, as a precondition for the admissibility of one, that expertise is *not* required. If the new requirement does not clog up the presentation of testimony, the reason may be that courts tend to ignore it.

The distinction between lay and expert opinion is an interesting and significant matter that warrants further attention. But we will postpone it to the end of the next chapter, after we have examined systematically the subject of expert testimony.

CHAPTER 5

EXPERT EVIDENCE

■ ■ ■

FRE 702–706

Additional Reading: McCormick, ch. 3, §§ 12–17; ch. 20; Mueller & Kirkpatrick, §§ 7.5–.22

A. INTRODUCTION

Recall that a witness must have some information that is of help to the jury. Lay witnesses offer the type of information that the jurors themselves might have known had they been in a particular place at a given time, or had they undergone one particular set of experiences of a type common to most people, such as repeatedly hearing the voice of a given person. But some witnesses can offer information of a type that most people do not have.

For example, even given an extended opportunity to observe a patient and examine her test results, most witnesses would not be able to testify from their own personal knowledge that she had cancer of the pancreas. An oncologist—a cancer specialist—should be able to do so, however. But one need not necessarily have advanced degrees to be an expert; this depends on the subject. Thus, a barely literate auto mechanic may well be able to testify as an expert on the durability of the transmission in a particular car model. Note the breadth of FRE 702(a), which makes opinion testimony potentially appropriate where "scientific, technical, or other specialized knowledge" of any type "will help the trier of fact to understand the evidence or to determine a fact in issue." This is a clear echo of the "helpful" language of Rule 701, which we have already seen in connection with lay opinions. Once it is determined that the subject is suitable for expert opinion, the question remains whether the particular witness is a qualified expert, and as it has been amended Rule 702 imposes additional requirements aimed at ensuring that the evidence is reliable. But Rule 702 does not impose technical limits on the source of an expert's "specialized knowledge"; indeed, the introductory part of the rule appears—somewhat incongruously—even broader than subsection (a), providing that "knowledge, skill, experience, training, or education" will do.

Section B of this chapter examines the question of whether there is a need for expertise on a given subject—that is, whether the subject is so much outside the jury's competence that expert testimony may be useful or even required to prove a point. It also considers the standards for determining whether the particular witness is qualified to give expert testimony. Section C addresses the question of whether, or the extent to which, a testifying expert should be foreclosed from stating an opinion on a proposition that is one of the issues the factfinder must determine. Section D then considers approaches to the frequently litigated issue of whether the particular evidence in a given case is sufficiently reputable to warrant admissibility; this discussion addresses concerns regarding "junk science" that have reached the Supreme Court most notably in *Daubert v. Merrell Dow Pharmaceuticals, Inc.*, 509 U.S. 579 (1993), and that were then reflected in a 2001 amendment to Rule 702. Section E takes up procedural issues—how experts are chosen, how discovery is taken from them, how they are questioned, and whether and how courts should make more extensive use of their powers to call "neutral" experts as witnesses or otherwise seek expert guidance outside the adversarial mold. Section F addresses the dividing line between lay and expert testimony, attempting to discern what the criteria are for distinguishing between the two and what consequences flow from the distinction, and considering the possibility that there really is a continuum rather than a binary distinction.

B. THE NEED FOR EXPERT ASSISTANCE; QUALIFICATIONS OF THE EXPERT

Suppose a construction worker falls to his death from an eight-story scaffold, and his estate brings suits against his employer and various other parties. If the plaintiff estate offers to put on an expert witness to testify as to whether and how much the decedent suffered physical and psychic pain on the way down, that would probably be admissible; these are questions involving physics and physiology that lie outside ordinary human experience.

If, however, the expert's testimony would be an explanation of how and why the impact inflicted on the decedent the particular injuries that it did, and not others, a closer question is created. This testimony would still tell the jurors something they presumably did not know before, but that something might be of too little value to the action to warrant admissibility. Even if a court would hold the testimony admissible, the plaintiff might decide that the value is too insignificant to be worth the time and expense that presenting it would require. Indeed, the first filters against expert evidence are a sense of self-restraint and limitations on the pocketbook of the potential proponent. A great deal of expert evidence that courts could probably be persuaded to admit is not even presented to them.

And if the expert's testimony was merely that an eight-story fall onto pavement is capable of causing death to a human being, the court would probably say, "Save your money and everybody's time. The jurors can figure that out on their own." Put in terms of FRE 702, the evidence is not necessary "to help the trier of fact to understand the evidence or to determine a fact in issue."

Sometimes the issue of whether expert testimony is necessary to assist the jury arises with respect to witness credibility. Courts are used to saying that the determination of credibility is a task lying within the competence of the jury and so is entirely in their province. That is a fair enough statement of the legal doctrine—which you probably studied at length in Civil Procedure—that the court should not impose its view of credibility and grant judgment as a matter of law when the testimony of a witness, if believed, would support a finding for the nonmoving party. But to say that the *court* should not *impose* its views of credibility does not really answer the question of whether in some circumstances an *expert* might be able to *assist* the jury. An expert might plausibly be able to offer such assistance if she is able to point the jurors to significant factors that they did not notice. Perhaps more importantly, for the very reason that judging credibility is so much a part of ordinary life, the expert might plausibly be able to inform the jurors that some of what they believe about credibility is in fact false.

¶ **5.1:** In Alger Hiss's second trial for perjury, he sought to impeach the credibility of Whittaker Chambers, his accuser, by putting on the stand a psychiatrist who had observed Chambers' testimony. The psychiatrist testified that some of Chambers' personal habits and mannerisms—such as slovenliness and gazing at the ceiling rather than meeting the eyes of his questioner—collectively supported the conclusion that he was a pathological liar. Should this testimony have been allowed?[1]

¶ **5.2:** In an assault case, the prosecution is relying heavily on eyewitness testimony. The defendant wants a qualified psychologist to testify to the following propositions: (1) Eyewitnesses to an event tend to conflate what they actually perceive with misinformation received shortly after the event. (2) There is not a strong correlation between a witness's accuracy

---

[1] *See* Allan Weinstein, *Perjury: The Hiss-Chambers Case* 437, 485–92 (1978) ; N.Y.Times, Jan. 11, 1950, p. 11, col. 4; United States v. Hiss, 88 F.Supp. 559 (S.D.N.Y.1950). The evidence in the *Hiss* case was admitted, but it was a disaster—the prosecutor was able to show that lots of famous and successful people were slovenly, and the analyst himself often looked up at the ceiling during his testimony.

and the confidence with which she delivers her testimony. (3) Cross-racial identifications are particularly prone to error. (4) Eyewitnesses tend to focus on unusual characteristics of people they observe, a phenomenon known as "detail salience." (5) Witnesses' memories are altered by talking about the event with each other after it occurs, a phenomenon known as the "conformity effect." (6) Accuracy of recollection diminishes rapidly after an event. (7) When one person both prepares and administers a photo spread, the probability of misidentification increases significantly. Should this testimony be allowed?[2]

Yes'. Helps jury give appropriate weight to testimony outside what an average juror would be aware of.

e.g. unconscious cuing

The more counterintuitive expert evidence is, the more justification there is for concluding that it will "help the trier of fact," because it provides a perspective that is different from, and even contrary to, the one that laypeople would likely have on their own.[3] Consider, for example, the "Stockholm syndrome," a psychological phenomenon by which a hostage develops positive feelings for his or her captor. Most of us would probably believe that if we were kidnaped, confined, molested physically and perhaps sexually, and generally mistreated, our feelings towards our captors would tend to be on the negative side. And it often is so—but often, too, the captive tends to develop a sense of identification with the aggressor. This is a well established phenomenon, and courts have admitted evidence concerning it to help a party explain conduct of a person that might otherwise appear incompatible with the party's theory of the case.[4]

Similarly, consider rape trauma syndrome, a constellation of symptoms frequently experienced by a rape victim. Some decisions hold that, because rape trauma syndrome is not a narrow set of criteria the presence of which demonstrates that the woman has been raped, it cannot be used to prove that a rape occurred. On the other hand, the syndrome may "play a particularly useful role by disabusing the jury of some widely held misconceptions about rape and rape victims."[5] For example, if the defendant tries to suggest that there is an inconsistency between the charge of rape and the fact that the complainant delayed in reporting the rape, or that she did not show outward signs of emotional distress, or that

---

[2] *See, e.g.,* United States v. Smithers, 212 F.3d 306 (6th Cir. 2000) (reviewing precedents and holding over dissent that without holding a hearing trial judge should not have excluded expert witness's testimony as to several of these propositions); Bomas v. State, 987 A.2d 98 (Md. 2010) (reviewing range of judicial views on admissibility of expert testimony on eyewitness identification); *cf.* Young v. Conway, 698 F.3d 69, 81 (2d Cir. 2012) (presenting academic findings on cross-race identification).

[3] On the other hand, the more counterintuitive the evidence is, the more difficult it may be to persuade the court that the evidence is sufficiently reputable to warrant admission.

[4] *E.g.,* United States v. Peralta, 941 F.2d 1003, 1009–10 (9th Cir.1991); Allen v. U.S., 2014 WL 2882495 (E.D. Mo. 2014).

[5] People v. Bledsoe, 36 Cal.3d 236, 248, 203 Cal.Rptr. 450, 458, 681 P.2d 291, 299 (1984).

she was not bruised, proof that a similar pattern frequently occurs in rape cases can be highly probative.[6]

In some circumstances, expert evidence is not only allowed but required. For example, in professional malpractice cases, courts demand expert testimony to support the claim that the defendant's conduct fell short of professional standards, though if the deficiency strikes the court as sufficiently obvious the plaintiff will be allowed to do without.[7] As part of the "tort reform" movement that swept through much of the nation towards the close of the twentieth century, some legislatures, too, have required expert testimony to show this point in medical malpractice cases; these statutes do not always have a safety valve for obvious derelictions.[8] Similarly, where a plaintiff is asking for damages to cover future pain and suffering from an injury, a court might demand— depending in part on the nature of the injury—that he present the testimony of an expert to show that an injury is indeed likely to have a long-term impact.[9] The issue of whether expert testimony should be required is significant because it is often expensive and difficult, and requires planning, to procure. In many cases, a party would rather take his chances without presenting expert evidence—if the court will let him.

---

[6] For discussions of the various possible uses of syndrome evidence—evidence that a person is a member of a class of persons who share a common physical, emotional, or mental condition that is widely recognized by experts—see, e.g., Nina Gupta, *Disillusioning the Prosecution: The Unfulfilled Promise of Syndrome Evidence*, 76 Law & Contemp. Probs. 413 (2013) (arguing that the law lags behind science in treatment of Post-Traumatic Stress Disorder (PTSD) and Rape Trauma Syndrome (RTS) and that courts are more willing to allow "defensive" use of PTSD and RTS evidence, to rebut contentions by the accused, than "offensive" use, as part of prosecution's case-in-chief); Paula Finley Mangum, Note, *Reconceptualizing Battered Woman Syndrome Evidence: Prosecution Use of Expert Testimony on Battering*, 19 B.C. Third World L.J. 593 (1999) (concluding that the rubric of "battered woman syndrome" should not be used, but that expert evidence on battering and its effects may be useful to explain recantation of accusation or other behavior by the victim that jurors might find puzzling); Larry J. Cohen, *Battered Woman Syndrome Evidence in Arizona*, 35 Arizona Attorney (Oct. 1998); Kathryn M. Davis, Note, *Rape, Resurrection, and the Quest for Truth: the Law and Science of Rape Trauma Syndrome in Constitutional Balance with the Rights of the Accused*, 49 Hastings L.J. 1511 (1998); Robert P. Mosteller, *Syndromes and Politics in Criminal Trials and Evidence Law*, 46 Duke L.J. 461 (1996); Myrna S. Raeder, *The Double-Edged Sword: Admissibility of Battered Woman Syndrome By and Against Batterers in Cases Implicating Domestic Violence*, 67 U. Col. L. Rev. 789 (1996); David L. Faigman, *The Syndromic Lawyer Syndrome: A Psychological Theory of Evidentiary Munificence*, 67 U. Col. L. Rev. 817 (1996).

[7] *See, e.g.*, In re Air Crash Disaster, 86 F.3d 498, 523–25 (6th Cir.1996) (holding that jury did not need expert assistance on question of whether airline followed maintenance regulations); Beattie v. Firnschild, 152 Mich.App. 785, 394 N.W.2d 107, 109–11 (1986) (holding that expert testimony was needed on question of whether attorney violated conflict-of-interest rule).

[8] *See, e.g.*, Idaho St. § 6–1013; NH St. § 507–C:2.

[9] *See, e.g.*, Danny R. Veilleux, Annotation, *Necessity of Expert Testimony on Issue of Provenance of Injury and Future Pain and Suffering*, 20 A.L.R.5th 1 (1991).

¶ 5.3: In *United States v. Hall*, 93 F.3d 1337, 1343 (7th Cir.1996), the court said:

> Suppose, for example, it were relevant for a jury to decide whether a person's use of foul or abusive language was intended to harm another person. Most of the time, the jury would be able to assess the circumstances without the need for expert testimony, since foul language is an unfortunate part of everyday life. In some cases, however, the individual might be suffering from Gilles de la Tourette's syndrome, which is a rare disorder manifested by grimaces, grunts, and, in about half of all cases, episodes of the use of foul language. AMA Encyclopedia of Medicine at 487 (1989). See also the Encyclopedia of Mental Health, Ada P. Kahn & Jan Fawcett, eds., at 375–76 (1993). A defendant wishing to explain his behavior by showing that he had Tourette's syndrome would need expert testimony both on the condition itself and his own affliction.

Do you agree? Why (assuming any problems of authentication and hearsay can be resolved) shouldn't the alleged Tourette sufferer be allowed to prove material facts about the condition by doing just what the *Hall* court itself did, relying on published sources? Why shouldn't he be able to prove his own affliction by introducing his own testimony, or that of someone else familiar with his condition?

Assuming a party will present expert testimony, whether by choice or because of a legal requirement, the particular witness must be *qualified* or *certified* as an expert on the subject in issue. That is, the court must be satisfied that she has the necessary qualifications to offer an expert opinion. Note that this is a matter for the court to determine under FRE 104(a), which refers to "whether a witness is qualified." Nevertheless, courts often are rather lenient in this respect. They recognize that it is not always practical for a party to produce the ideal expert. Moreover, if a party presents the testimony of a weak expert, it is probably that party who will suffer. But again, as part of the "tort reform" movement, legislatures have sometimes imposed more stringent qualifications on who may testify as an expert in medical malpractice cases. A common type of statute provides that if the defendant is a specialist then any expert testifying on the standard of care must have been a specialist, actively engaged in practice or education, in the same field at the time of the occurrence that is the basis for the action; moreover, if the defendant is a board-certified specialist then the testifying expert must be board-certified as well. *E.g.*, Mich. Comp. L. Ann. § 600.2169.

¶ **5.4:** You are representing the plaintiff, Barbara Blair, in an obstetrics malpractice case. Your claim is that the defendant, Dr. Edward Cutt, a board-certified obstetrician, performed an unnecessary Cesarean operation on Blair; Cutt's defense is that he had to perform the Cesarean because the fetus was in breach position. You have available as an expert witness Dr. Leslie Rosberg, who is prepared to testify that ordinarily a Cesarean is not necessary for a breach birth and that sound medical practice requires that other alternatives be exhausted before performing a Cesarean. No governing statute provides requirements for experts in medical malpractice cases beyond those applicable to experts in other cases.

(a) Dr. Rosberg is a board-certified obstetrician, but without any particular expertise in Cesareans. Should she be allowed to testify as an expert? *[handwritten: might book - but still on cross about it]*

[handwritten margin: sure - need gen expertise, speak to breach - has education in it even if no experience]

(b) What if she is not board-certified? *[handwritten: Er no]*

[handwritten: Some states require experts as well qualified as π/Δ - not FRE]

(c) What if the judge finds, on the basis of the evidence presented to him, that five complaints have been brought against her before the Obstetrics Peer Review Committee of her County Medical Society, that in two of them the Committee issued confidential reports concluding that she had used poor medical judgment, and that in both of those cases she had made payments in settlement of malpractice claims? *[handwritten: No. Still an expert, but credibility issues, will come out on cross.]*

(d) What if she is a general practitioner?[10] *[handwritten: No.]*

(e) Should Dr. Cutt be able to testify in his own behalf that, in his expert view as an obstetrician, the Cesarean was proper?[11] *[handwritten: Yes - obvi biased, but still qualified under 702 to give an expert opinion]*

---

[10] *See, e.g.,* Vearrier v. Karl, 2009 WL 2524581 (D. S. Dak. 2009) (allowing two physicians, one a pediatric neurologist, the other board certified in pediatrics and in neonatal-perinatal medicine, to testify to malpractice by an anesthesiologist; "it is a well-established principle that the testimony of a qualified medical doctor cannot be excluded simply because he is not a specialist in a particular school of medical practice" (citation omitted)); Wick v. Henderson, 485 N.W.2d 645, 648 (Iowa 1992) (holding that neurologist should have been allowed to give opinions with respect to responsibility of anesthetist to monitor position, location, and pressure against patient's arm during surgery: "We are committed to a liberal rule on admissibility of opinion testimony. A physician need not be a specialist in a particular field of medicine to give an expert opinion. An expert witness must be not only generally qualified in a field of expertise; but must also be qualified to answer the particular question propounded." (Citations omitted)).

[11] Most courts seem to allow a party to testify as an expert in his own case, assuming he is qualified. *See, e.g.,* James River Ins. Co. v. Rapid Funding, LLC, 2009 WL 481688 (D. Col. 2009); Rodriguez v. Pacificare of Texas, Inc., 980 F.2d 1014, 1019–20 (5th Cir. 1993);Tagatz v. Marquette University, 861 F.2d 1040, 1042–43 (7th Cir.1988). Doing so may, however, open himself up to embarrassing impeachment with respect to his credentials. *See* McCray v. Shams, 224 Ill. App.3d 999, 587 N.E.2d 66, 167 Ill. Dec. 184 (1992) (physician who explained his conduct in testimony deemed to have been testifying as an expert and subject to impeachment by proof that he had failed board-certification examination).

C. THE ULTIMATE ISSUE RULE

Sometimes, a party wants an expert to give an opinion on an issue that is identical or nearly identical to one that a decisionmaker—judge or jury—has to make. Traditionally, courts regarded that as a problem, and provided that an expert could not express an opinion on an "ultimate issue" in the case, such as an element of a claim.

The problem traditionally perceived was that for the expert to express an opinion on an ultimate issue would usurp the province of the jury. This is not persuasive, however. The expert's opinion is merely the expert's opinion, an item of evidence; expressing it does not take decisionmaking power away from anybody. (Note, however, Justice Thomas' statement, for a four-justice group in *United States v. Scheffer*, 523 U.S. 303(1998), that "polygraph evidence may diminish the jury's role in making credibility determinations," and Justice Kennedy's response, for another four-justice group, that this argument improperly relied on the now-rejected theory of the "ultimate issue" rule.)

A more valid concern is that the expert's opinion might have too great an impact on the jury. We will examine that concern more fully in the next section. However serious it may be, preventing a statement of opinion on the ultimate issue does not seem the right way to address it. Suppose for argument's sake that the jury is likely to be overwhelmed by an expert who testifies, "The machinery was being operated negligently," negligence being an element of the plaintiff's claim and so an ultimate issue. Is the jury substantially less likely to be overwhelmed if the expert's testimony takes the form, "The machinery was being operated at an excessive speed," or "The machinery was being operated at a speed greater than reasonably necessary"? The old-fashioned rule required courts to attempt to draw wafer-thin distinctions between ultimate and other issues, and often prevented experts from communicating in the most effective way they could.

Another concern may be that it is not particularly helpful to the jury if all the expert does is give a conclusory opinion on an ultimate issue. However true that may be, it does not justify preventing the expert from giving the conclusion, in terms of the ultimate issue being tried; rather, it weighs in favor of calling on her *also* to give the reasons for her conclusion. Together, the reasons and a crisply stated conclusion may be far more informative than either without the other.

Thus, FRE 704—with the qualification later added as Rule 704(b)— abrogates the ultimate issue rule with respect to issues of fact. The Rule purports to leave untouched the ban against opinions that, in the words of the Advisory Committee, are "phrased in terms of inadequately explored legal criteria." Opinions cannot be offered unless they are helpful to the trier of fact, emphasized the Committee. Thus, the Committee said that

"Did T have capacity to make a will?" would be excluded, but "Did T have sufficient capacity to know the nature and extent of his property and the natural objects of his bounty and to formulate a rational scheme of distribution?" would be allowed.

¶ **5.5:** What is the basis of this distinction? What good, if any, does it do to insist on the longer form? Is it that the first form asks for a legal conclusion and the second one does not? Or is it simply that the first one violates the "best evidence" principle in that it is so broad and vague that inadmissibility is warranted to induce the proponent to ask a question that will produce better information, like the first? Are "inadequately explored legal criteria" any different in this sense from any other conclusory terms?

In 1984, Congress drew back somewhat from the broad receptivity of Rule 704 by enacting FRE 704(b). This amendment was a reaction to the trial of John Hinckley, who had attempted to assassinate President Reagan and claimed insanity on grounds that seemed spurious to many. Rule 704(b) is rather odd. It applies to the question of a person's mental state, but only when the person is a criminal defendant and the question is raised as an element of a criminal charge or defense. Within that context, it restores the ultimate issue rule, providing that the expert may not offer "an opinion about whether the defendant did or did not have a mental state or condition that constitutes an element of the crime charged or of a defense." "Such ultimate issues," the Rule adds for good measure, "are matters for the trier of fact alone." That is a curious sentence, given the fundamentally different roles of juror and witness. As might be expected, many states have not amended their codifications to incorporate the exception expressed in FRE 704(b), which partially restores the problems of the ultimate issue rule along with the rule itself.[12]

¶ **5.6:** Your client Jack Hackney is on trial for attempting to assassinate the President. He admits to you that he did it and says that he was trying to impress Jim Carrey. You decide, wisely no doubt, that your best bet is an insanity defense, and you procure an eminent psychiatrist who tells you in private, "This is a very sick individual." What conclusions can you ask the doctor to testify to from the stand?[13]

---

[12] *See* United States v. Santos, 131 F.3d 16 (1st Cir.1997) ("Rule 704(b) has proved troublesome to administer and is not universally popular, because it complicates the provision of expert testimony and involves very difficult line drawing. . . . Whether much is changed by stopping the expert's testimony just short of the ultimate issue is open to doubt.").

[13] *See, e.g.,* United States v. Morris, 576 F.3d 661, 675 (7th Cir. 2009), *cert. denied,* 559 U.S. 916 (2010) ("It must be clear from the expert's testimony that he 'was merely identifying an inference that might be drawn from the circumstances surrounding the defendant's arrest, and

Rule 704(b) has been applied to drug cases in which police officers try to tie the evidence to common drug practices.

¶ **5.7:** Smart is on trial for possession of cocaine with intent to distribute, among other charges. Detective Tyrone Thomas testifies for the prosecution as an expert on illegal drugs. The prosecutor presents his with a "hypothetical" situation that mirrors all the facts of the case: A person walks directly to a spot near a building, picks up a large, white rock-like substance that turns out, when he is stopped, to be 25.5 grams of cocaine base. He is carrying a pager, $580 in small denomination bills, 56 empty Ziploc bags, and a 9 mm. handgun. The prosecutor asks with what activity, in the expert's opinion, these actions are consistent. The detective says that in his opinion the individual is engaged in a drug operation. "He met the elements," says the detective, and explains why each bit of information contributes to his conclusion. Should this testimony be allowed? If not, to what could the detective have properly been asked to testify?[14]

Though the traditional justifications for the ultimate issue rule seem unpersuasive, and the partial restoration of the rule in FRE 704(b) seems troublesome, there is at least arguably some merit to the rule in some circumstances. Often, an expert testifies without having any firsthand observations to offer about the particular case. Rather, she is offering her expertise in how to analyze, and what inferences to draw from, the

---

was not purporting to express an opinion as to the defendant's actual mental state.' " (citation omitted)); United States v. Finley, 301 F.3d 1000 (9th Cir. 2002) (reviewing cases and holding that "the defense was entitled to present evidence so that the jury could infer from the expert's testimony that the defendant lacked the necessary intent to defraud, but such a conclusion was not necessarily compelled by the diagnosis"); United States v. Diaz, 300 F.3d 66 (1st Cir. 2002) (experts did not violate Rule 704(b) in testifying that someone had set fire deliberately; experts did not testify that accused set fire or that he did so with malicious intent); United States v. Dennison, 937 F.2d 559, 565 (10th Cir.1991) (holding that testimony of an expert "that alcohol and drug consumption by a person with borderline personality disorder renders that person incapable of forming specific intent . . . is the type of opinion or inference testimony Rule 704(b) is intended to exclude"; even though the testimony was "premised on a hypothetical person" and "couched in terms of the characteristics of the illness itself, the necessary inference was that the instant defendant did not have the capacity"); United States v. West, 962 F.2d 123, 1246 (7th Cir.1992) (holding inadmissible testimony of psychiatrist that in his opinion defendant "knew what he was doing and knew it was wrong," but psychiatrist should have been allowed to testify that defendant was suffering from a severe schizoaffective disorder, together with description of manifestations).

[14] *See* United States v. Smart, 98 F.3d 1379 (D.C.Cir.1996), *cert. denied,* 520 U.S. 1128 (1997). *Smart* reviews the case law in this area, concluding that the expert may testify to common criminal practices, but that it is important that the jury be informed that the expert is not testifying to the ultimate issue of intent. The court held admission of this testimony to be improper, but harmless error—a very common result when prosecution evidence is challenged under Rule 704(b). *See also, e.g.,* United States v. Gonzales, 307 F.3d 906 (9th Cir. 2002) (holding that expert's testimony that a "person" possessing the evidence in question would, in fact, possess the drugs for the purpose of distributing did not violate Rule 704(b) because "[e]ven if the jury believed the expert's testimony, the jury could have concluded that [the accused] was not a typical or representative person, who possessed the drugs and drug paraphernalia involved).

evidence presented to the jury. Even if the expert did make some personal observations, it may be that her opinion is based in part on information that was provided to her in the course of the litigation and not in a way that she would usually receive information as part of her professional practice. It may therefore be inappropriate for her to say, "The blood found at the scene of the crime came from the defendant." It may be, rather, that she should say, "If the defendant left his blood at the scene of the crime and some of it were found, we would expect it to show up just about as it has in DNA tests. If someone else was the source of the blood, the chance that it would look like this would be very, very small."[15]

In other words, in the terms presented in Chapter 3, the expert should ideally testify in terms of a likelihood ratio or its components. Recall that a likelihood ratio is the probability of the evidence in question showing up given one hypothesis divided by the probability of that evidence showing up given the negation of that hypothesis. Assessing this ratio does not give what the jury ultimately must determine, the probability of the hypothesis given the evidence. To assess that probability also requires assessing the prior probability—the probability of the hypothesis as assessed without the evidence in question. And the expert has no particular expertise in assessing the prior probability; indeed, unless she attends the whole trial she may not have all the information the jury has. It may be, therefore, that if the expert gives an opinion on the ultimate issue, she is obscuring the fact that the opinion is based in part on her own perception of facts that the jury is perfectly able to assess, and might assess in a very different way.

¶ **5.8:** You are the prosecutor in a rape case. To prove that the complainant was in fact raped, you put on the stand Dr. Laura Klempay, a medical researcher and expert in rape trauma syndrome (RTS). She is prepared to testify that rape tends to cause certain psychological effects in its victims, and that the symptoms exhibited by the complainant, in the aggregate, form a classic case of RTS. You want to ask Dr. Klempay, "In your

---

[15] *See* Bernard Robertson, G.A. Vignaux & Charles E.H. Berger, *Interpreting Scientific Evidence* § 4.2 (2d ed. 2016); Richard D. Friedman, *Assessing Evidence*, 94 Mich. L. Rev. 1810, 1836 (1995). *But see* J.D. Jackson, *The Ultimate Issue Rule: One Rule Too Many*, [1984] Crim. L.R. 75 (contending that sound decisions based on the ultimate issue rule could be justified on other grounds, such as that the opinion is not helpful to the jury or that it is expressed in legally conclusory terms).

This analysis may perhaps cast a more charitable light than at first appears on cases like United States v. Schneider, 704 F.3d 1287 (10th Cir.), *cert. denied*, 133 S.Ct. 2868 (2013). In *Schneider*, involving charges of health care fraud, one expert testified that certain documents evidence "an intention to deceive and defraud the system," and another said that "this is a dishonest practice." The court said that "the rules do not prevent an expert from drawing conclusions about intent, so long as the expert does not profess to know a defendant's intent." For support, it pointed to an exchange in which one of the witnesses was asked, "Are you telling the jury what you know to be the Defendant's intent or are you stating what the evidence indicates to you?," and answered, "I'm stating what the evidence indicates to me. . . ."

[handwritten marginalia top: "Not a 704 objection b/c not about D, mental state of D, but 702 issue — does this help the trier of fact? does it go beyond witness' expertise? Can talk about common symptoms and symptoms here → do you believe she has PTS?"]

opinion, was Ms. Visser raped?" Should you be allowed to ask her that? Why or why not? If not, what question or questions should you ask instead?

¶ 5.9: (a) In a purse-snatching case, the prosecution puts on the stand the arresting officer, who came on the scene a few minutes after the incident. He testifies that when he arrived a crowd was holding down a suspect, whom he identifies as the defendant. May the officer testify that, in his opinion as a crime detection expert, the defendant committed the crime, and that he bases this opinion (as he usually does in forming opinions in his line of duty) on information provided to him by witnesses?

[handwritten: "Not any expert testimony being offered — relying on hearsay."]

(b) Is your answer any different if instead the case is a civil auto negligence action, and the officer is testifying, again on the basis of reports provided to him by witnesses, that the defendant jumped the light?

[handwritten left margin: "No. what's likelihood V was raped? How consistent what other possible causes of behavior you observed?"]

[handwritten left margin: "No! Beyond lay opinion."]

[handwritten left margin: "No. He jumping light is a component of negligence, not the ultimate issue."]

D. REPUTABILITY OF THE EXPERT EVIDENCE

When expert evidence is introduced, it almost inevitably raises a troubling paradox: By definition, the expert evidence is on a subject beyond the ken of laypeople, and yet when they are factfinders it is they, and not the experts, who must evaluate the expert's contentions. What is more, if one side offers expert evidence the other side likely will as well, and then we have a "battle of the experts." How is the layperson to resolve this? If you have ever had to make a significant decision and been given conflicting advice by different experts—lawyers, doctors, auto mechanics, whatever—you have some idea of the tension this situation creates.

In recent decades, the fear has often been expressed that juries tend too often to fall prey to "junk science."[16] But the concern that juries will not be able to deal satisfactorily with expert evidence is not a new one. Courts have long demanded that the expert's opinion must be in accordance with a theory that has achieved some threshold level of reputability. For many years, the dominant statement of this idea was the one in *Frye v. United States*, 54 App. D.C. 46, 47, 293 F. 1013, 1014 (1923), that the underlying "scientific principle or discovery . . . from which the deduction is made must be sufficiently established to have gained general acceptance in the particular field in which it belongs."

[handwritten: "as long as some community thinks it's legit!"]

---

[16] *See, e.g.*, Peter Huber, *Galileo's Revenge: Junk Science in the Courtroom* (1991). However widespread the phenomenon may be, it certainly exists. Consider, for example, the late anthropologist Louise Robbins, who testified widely that she could identify not only the shoe that made a given print but the wearer of the shoe. *See* Paul C. Giannelli, *The Abuse of Scientific Evidence in Criminal Cases: the Need for Independent Crime Laboratories*, 4 Va. J. Soc. Pol'y & L. 439 (1997).

some states still way onto this — MI uses Daubert

In 1993, however, the United States Supreme Court held that the Rules supersede the *Frye test. Daubert v. Merrell Dow Pharmaceuticals, Inc.*, 509 U.S. 579 (1993). The Court had no difficulty—indeed, it was unanimous—in reaching this sound conclusion; as Justice Blackmun's opinion said, the "austere standard" of *Frye* is incompatible not only with the language of Rule 702 but also with the liberal nature of the Rules in general. *Id.* at 589. State courts are not bound by *Daubert*, of course; though a significant number have decided to follow it, some states, including some that have adopted versions of the Federal Rules, still adhere to the *Frye* test.[17]

To hold that *Frye* does not survive the Federal Rules was relatively easy. Chief Justice Rehnquist, joined by Justice Stevens, dissented in part, believing the Court should stop there and "leave the further development of this important area of the law to future cases." *Id.* at 601. Justice Blackmun did go further, however, while limiting himself to the scientific context because that was the nature of the expertise offered in *Daubert*.

Confronting the argument that abandoning *Frye* might lead to "a 'free-for-all' in which befuddled juries are confounded by absurd and irrational pseudoscientific assertions," he expressed confidence in the capacity of the adversary system to deal with this problem without the "wholesale exclusion" of evidence under *Frye*; he also reminded courts of their power to grant judgment as a matter of law against a party when all the evidence considered together would not support judgment in that party's favor. *Id.* at 595–96. Facing the other direction, he made clear that "a gatekeeping role for the judge" remains, and defended this role in light of the realization that it "inevitably on occasion will prevent the jury from learning of authentic insights and innovations." Unlike scientific inquiry, he pointed out, law "must resolve disputes finally and quickly"; the Rules of Evidence are "designed not for the exhaustive search for cosmic understanding but for the particularized resolution of legal disputes." *Id.* at 597.

> ¶ **5.10:** Accepting that law must conclude cases before science resolves theoretical disputes, what bearing does that have on the question of whether the judge should exercise a substantial gatekeeping role? That is, does the existence of scientific debate weigh against the admissibility of scientific

---

[17] For a state-by-state breakdown, see Damian D. Capozzola, *Expert Evidence in Civil Trials: Effective Preparation and Preparation* (2015), § 2.46. States adhering to a version of *Frye* include California (which often refers to its version as *Kelly-Frye*, and which emphasizes the question whether the technique in question should be deemed "new," *see* People v. Cordova, 358 P.3d 518, 536 (Cal. 2015), *cert. denied*, 136 S.Ct. 1660 (2016)), Florida, Illinois, New York, and Pennsylvania.

Erin direction of not including confusion or bad science can use whatever you want

evidence? Could it just as well weigh in favor of admitting evidence on both sides of the debate?[18]

On its face, *Daubert* appeared to increase receptivity to expert evidence. After all, it reversed a judgment that had been entered, against the proponent of the challenged expert evidence, under a standard that the Supreme Court unanimously regarded as more "austere" than that prescribed by the Federal Rules. The additional discussion of the "gatekeeping" role, included over the objection of Chief Justice Rehnquist, was meant to provide assurance that the "wholesale exclusion" mandated by the rejected standard was not necessary to prevent a "free-for-all" of confusing evidence. Over time, however, it has become clear that since *Daubert* the federal courts at least have tended to become *less* receptive to expert evidence.[19] In large measure, this change may have been attributable to a change in political mood rather than to anything in *Daubert* itself; as just suggested, the most natural reading of *Daubert* is that it was more rather than less receptive to expert evidence than was the discarded *Frye* standard, but *Daubert*, like *Frye*, is malleable and subject to manipulation. Courts seeking a justification for implementing a tighter standard could, however, find some support in Justice Blackmun's attempt to articulate the "gatekeeping role," for he pronounced that, to be admissible, scientific evidence must be "not only relevant, but reliable," 509 U.S. at 589. This statement indicates that as a predicate for admissibility the court must satisfy itself as to the reliability of the evidence, and not merely, as suggested by *Frye*, depend on acceptance by experts in the field. The Court has since taken seriously Justice Blackmun's statement, repeating it prominently and giving it force in *General Electric Co. v. Joiner*, 522 U.S. 136 (1997), and *Kumho Tire Co., Ltd. v. Carmichael*, 526 U.S. 137 (1999).

Yes! Is it relevant? if it's not reliable.

¶ **5.11:** Does it make sense to say that evidence must be reliable to be admissible? As pointed out by the Chief Justice in *Daubert*, the Rules do not make reliability a general touchstone of admissibility, 509 U.S. at 599. Lots of nonreliable evidence is offered on many issues; in fact, trying to sort out the reliable from the unreliable is a large part of what trials are all about, and it is a function principally performed at the factfinding stage, not at the threshold of admissibility. Is there good reason to treat scientific evidence differently? If only reliable scientific

confusion, unfair prejudice

---

[18] *See* Richard D. Friedman, *The Death and Transfiguration of* Frye, 34 Jurimetrics J. 133 (1994).

[19] Lloyd Dixon & Brendan Gill, *Changes in the Standards for Admitting Expert Evidence in Federal Civil Cases Since the* Daubert *Decision* (Rand 2001).

evidence is admitted, does that mean that there can be scientific evidence only on one side of a given question?[20]

In thinking about these general questions, it may help to consider the example of microscopic hair comparison. It often happens that a hair apparently left by the perpetrator is found at the scene of a crime; if it is proven to come from the accused, that might be significant evidence that the accused is the perpetrator. Similarly, if a hair found on the clothes or person of the accused is proven to come from the victim, that might be significant evidence against the accused. The traditional method of analysis is by comparison under a microscope of the unknown sample with a known sample taken from the accused or the victim. Now it is usually, though not inevitably, possible to compare mitochondrial DNA of the two samples, and mtDNA comparison is generally considered to be very accurate. But, in large part because of cost and time considerations and in some cases because for some reason the mtDNA test cannot be performed or does not yield an unambiguous result, evidence of hair comparisons based on microscopic examination is still introduced quite regularly. The FBI continues to take the position that "microscopic hair comparison analysis is a valid scientific technique" and notes that it is "still conducted by the FBI Laboratory."[21] In an influential study, examiners were able to reach a conclusion—either "association" or "exclusion"—by both methods with respect to 95 pairs of hairs.[22] They broke down this way:

Table 5.a

		mtDNA results	
		Association	Exclusion
Microscopic examination	Association	69	9
	Exclusion	0	17

Assume for the sake of simplicity that the mtDNA results were all accurate, and that the results given above indicate the probability of each of the possible outcomes. Then an indication of exclusion by microscopic comparison appears to be quite reliable evidence, because in all 17 cases

---

[20] Note also a point made in Jennifer L. Mnookin, *Scripting Expertise: The History of handwriting Identification Evidence and the Judicial Construction of Reliability*, 8 Va. L. Rev. 1723 (2001), that judicial determinations with respect to given types of evidence may affect social perceptions of reliability. Mnookin demonstrates this phenomenon with respect to handwriting evidence.

[21] *FBI/DOJ Microscopic Hair Comparison Analysis Review*, https://www.fbi.gov/services/laboratory/scientific-analysis/fbidoj-microscopic-hair-comparison-analysis-review.

[22] Max M. Houck & Bruce Budowle, *Correlation of microscopic and mitochondrial DNA hair comparisons*, 47 J. Forensic Sci. 964 (2002).

in which the microscopic examination reported exclusion, the mtDNA test confirmed that the hairs were from different sources; looked at another way, in all 69 instances in which the hairs came from the same source, according to the mtDNA test, the microscopic comparison managed to pick this up. But the story is much different when the hairs are *not* from the same source: There is a substantial chance, 9/26, or 34.6%, that the microscopic comparison will inaccurately report that the hairs are in fact associated. Using these figures as a guide, we can thus say that an expert's report based on microscopic comparison that two hairs are associated has a likelihood ratio of about 2.89. The numerator of the ratio, the probability that if the hairs are from the same source the expert will report an association, is 100% (69/69), and the denominator, the probability that if the hairs are *not* from the same source the expert will nevertheless report an association, is 34.6%.[23]

¶ **5.12:** Given these figures, is it accurate to characterize as reliable a prosecution expert's report, based on microscopic examination, that there is an association between a hair found at a crime scene and one taken from the accused? *See* National Research Council, *Strengthening Forensic Science in the United States: A Path Forward* (2009) 161 (contending in part on the basis of this study that microscopic hair examination is not reliable). Is such a report *useful*?

However useful hair comparison analysis might be if properly presented, it now appears that, at least in the relatively recent past, prosecution experts have usually far overstated its significance. Indeed, an investigation of FBI experts, in which the FBI itself participated, revealed that in over 95% of the cases studied the expert did so; the tendency was to assert with certainty that the hairs came from the same source rather than pointing to microscopic similarities between hairs.[24]

¶ **5.13:** (a) A prosecution witness has performed a microscopic comparison of two samples and concluded that they are associated. Suppose you are the trial judge and you have decided to allow her to communicate her conclusion in some form. What will you allow her to say?

(b) Now consider whether, even given whatever you consider to be the optimal form in which the witness might give her testimony, you will in fact allow her to testify to the results of her microscopic examination. Consider the question under the

---

[23] *See* Richard D. Friedman, *Squeezing Daubert Out of the Picture,* 33 Seton Hall L. Rev. 1047, 1057–59 (2003).

[24] Dahlia Lithwick, *Pseudoscience in the Witness Box,* http://www.slate.com/articles/news_and_politics/jurisprudence/2015/04/fbi_s_flawed_forensics_expert_testimony_hair_analysis_bite_marks_fingerprints.html (2015).

alternative assumptions that: (1) the witness also did mtDNA *— just let in the best evidence* analysis, which also reported that the two hairs were associated; (2) the witness's lab tried to do mtDNA analysis but, for some *— ok* reason not attributable to wrongdoing by the lab, the test did not yield useful results; and (3) the lab never tried to do mtDNA *— fuck. off.* analysis.[25]

However sound Justice Blackmun's general insights in *Daubert* may be, attempting to make them operational is very difficult. He put great emphasis on Rule 702's use of the term "scientific knowledge" and operated from the premise that, to qualify as scientific knowledge, "an inference or assertion must be derived by the scientific method." 509 U.S. at 589–90. Accordingly, he set out to find indicia of what constitutes the scientific method. Without attempting "to set out a definitive checklist or test," and while emphasizing that "[t]he inquiry envisioned by Rule 702 is . . . a flexible one," he did offer some "general observations." *Id.* at 593, 594. Indeed, he laid out four criteria that should often enter into decision. We can refer to these as (1) testing, (2) peer review and publication, (3) error rates and standards and, in a partial resurrection of *Frye* (just a few pages after its apparent death), (4) general acceptance. We will consider each of these criteria in turn, though not in the order the Court presented them. We will start with general acceptance, the carryover from *Frye*.

General acceptance—Though the principal holding of his opinion was that the *Frye* test no longer governed, Justice Blackmun declared that " 'general acceptance' can yet have a bearing on the inquiry." *Id.* That is, the question of whether the expert testimony has a sufficiently accepted basis is no longer the determinative factor but it can be part of the mix of considerations used by a court in determining admissibility. "Widespread acceptance," the Court believed, can be important in showing reliability. *Id.* at 594.

The question of acceptance may be broken down into several parts. First, *what is it that must be "generally accepted"—the broad theory on which the expert bases her opinion, or the particular application?* If the former, we may wonder whether the rule has any teeth. If the latter, we may wonder whether it is realistic.[26] That is, scientists within a given

---

[25] Many courts have held hair comparison admissible. *See, e.g.,* Commonwealth v. Chmiel, 30 A.3d 1111, 1140–42 (Pa. 2011); State v. West, 877 A.2d 787, 807–08 (Conn.), *cert. denied,* 546 U.S. 1049 (2005) (reviewing cases and asserting that "the jurors were able to evaluate the evidence in light of its acknowledged limitations and to give that evidence whatever weight they deemed appropriate"); Johnson v. Commonwealth, 12 S.W.3d 258 (Ky. 2000) (holding that judicial notice could be taken of reliability of hair comparison evidence). But the evidence remains the subject of fierce contention, and even in states in which it is generally admissible it is possible to secure reversal of a conviction on the basis that the evidence was presented in a misleading manner. *See, e.g.,* Amelia Maxfield, *FBI Microscopic Hair Review,* 40 Champion 59 (Mar. 2016).

[26] *See* William C. Thompson & Simon Ford, *DNA Typing: Acceptance and Weight of the New Genetic Identification Tests,* 75 Va.L.Rev. 45, 57–58 (1989) ("a scientist may have no trouble

field—and, for that matter, pseudoscientists—are likely to agree on premises at a very general, abstract level. If that is all that must be "generally accepted," then the standard is not very demanding. The more detailed the question, the more likely experts are to disagree. But even among those who share basic premises and who have respect for each other's abilities, there may be sharp disagreement on particular issues of application. Moreover, if the question is particular enough, it is unlikely that widespread acceptance could be detected, because there might not have even been widespread *attention* to the precise question involved.

In *Daubert*, Justice Blackmun addressed this issue glancingly. "The focus, of course," he wrote, "must be solely on principles and methodology, not on the conclusions they generate." 509 U.S. at 595. The "of course" seems to suggest that this is an obvious, durable divide. But in *Joiner*, the Court's first opportunity to apply the distinction, the Court instead walked away from it.[27] Joiner and his wife claimed that he had contracted lung cancer in part as a result of exposure to PCBs[28] while working for GE.[29] He offered several animal and epidemiological (human statistical) studies to prove a link between PCBs and human cancer, but none of them individually provided strong support. Nevertheless, he had toxicologists who were willing to testify on the basis of the aggregation of the studies that exposure to PCBs probably promoted Joiner's cancer. Joiner argued that, in holding the expert evidence inadmissible, the trial court had rejected his experts' conclusions rather than their methodology, and so violated *Daubert*. "But conclusions and methodology are not entirely distinct from one another," wrote Chief Justice Rehnquist, now speaking for the Court. A court is not required "to admit opinion evidence which is connected to existing data only by the ipse dixit of the expert. A court may conclude that there is simply too great an analytical gap between the data and the opinion proffered."

[handwritten annotation: "he said it himself" i.e. based on the experts own statement]

---

accepting the general proposition that DNA typing can be done reliably, yet still have doubts about the reliability of the test being performed by a particular laboratory"); *compare* Coppolino v. State, 223 So.2d 68 (Fla.App.1968), *appeal dismissed*, 234 So.2d 120 (1969), *cert. denied*, 399 U.S. 927 (1970) (dispute whether decedent received a toxic dose of succinylcholine chloride, the presence of which in the body was previously believed impossible to detect; toxicologist testifies for the prosecution that, based on his procedures, some standard and others new, he concluded that she did receive such a dose; other experts testify both in support and in opposition; conviction affirmed), *with* People v. Young, 425 Mich. 470, 472, 485–86, 499, 391 N.W.2d 270, 270, 277, 283 (1986) (serological electrophoresis of dried evidentiary bloodstains has not achieved sufficient scientific acceptance, notwithstanding conceded reliability of electrophoresis of fresh blood).

[27] The issue actually presented to the Court in *Joiner* was what the standard of review is on *Daubert* questions. Unanimously, and rather unsurprisingly, the Court held that review is on an "abuse of discretion" standard, whether the trial court admits or excludes the evidence. Over the dissent of Justice Stevens, who thought the Court should have stopped there, the Court went on to hold that the trial court had not abused its discretion in excluding the evidence.

[28] Polychlorinated biphenyls, if you're interested.

[29] Joiner was a smoker and had a bad family history of lung cancer.

In dissenting from this portion of the opinion, Justice Stevens pointed out that one of Joiner's toxicologists, Dr. Daniel Teitelbaum, said this at his deposition:

> [A]s a toxicologist when I look at a study, I am going to require that that study meet the general criteria for methodology and statistical analysis, but that when all of that data is collected and you ask me as a patient, "Doctor, have I got a risk of getting cancer from this?" That those studies don't answer the question, that I have to put them all together in my mind and look at them in relation to everything I know about the substance and everything I know about the exposure and come to a conclusion. I think when I say, "To a reasonable medical probability as a medical toxicologist, this substance was a contributing cause," ... to his cancer, that that is a valid conclusion based on the totality of the evidence presented to me. And I think that that is an appropriate thing for a toxicologist to do and it has been the basis of diagnosis for several hundred years, anyway.[30]

¶ 5.14: Based on what you know about the case, was Teitelbaum operating on a sufficiently well accepted basis for his testimony to be admissible? What further information would you want to know to better answer this question?

A second aspect of the acceptance question is: *How broad is the relevant community in which acceptance is measured?* Can one define a field consisting of those who practice and believe in the efficacy of a given technique? As Justice Stevens suggested in his *Joiner* opinion, a phrenologist would not be allowed to testify to a defendant's future dangerousness based on the contours of the defendant's skull. And this would be so even if all the phrenologists in the world agree that the contour of the skull yielded such clues. Indeed, we would expect all the phrenologists in the world to agree to that, because that kind of belief is what makes them phrenologists.

The problem of defining the community is particularly significant because some techniques are principally practiced by forensic scientists, and they are usually testifying for the prosecution; indeed, their principal occupation may be assisting the police and prosecutors in criminal investigations.[31] For example, in *Williamson v. Reynolds*,[32] the district

---

[30] Dr. Teitelbaum was retained as an expert on toxicology, not on grammar. But this passage is a good indication of how garbled the syntax of even a very intelligent witness can sound when it is transcribed verbatim.

[31] Pettus v. United States, 37 A.3d 213, 218 (D.C. Ct. Apps. 2012) ("the relevant community for purposes of assessing *Frye* admissibility includes not just forensic scientists (including handwriting experts) but also others whose scientific background and training are sufficient to allow them to comprehend and understand the process and form a judgment about it") (citations and quotation marks omitted).

court, acting on a *habeas corpus* petition, decided that expert hair comparison testimony did not meet the *Daubert* standard; many courts have routinely admitted such evidence, but the judge may have been affected by the fact that this was a capital case.[33] "Not even the 'general acceptance' standard is met," the court said, "since any general acceptance seems to be among hair experts who are generally technicians testifying for the prosecution, not scientists who can objectively evaluate such evidence."[34]

Third, *how unanimous must consent be?* Taking *Frye* literally, it seems that exclusion of an opinion is warranted if there is a reputable body of persons in the field who disagree with that opinion, and some courts have treated the test that way.[35] Such a standard ensures that theoretical disputes will not be played out in front of a jury, but it seems unduly restrictive. Even while purporting to operate under *Frye*, some courts have found more flexibility in the term "general acceptance."[36] Note that *Daubert* used the term "[w]idespread acceptance" as well as "general acceptance." The former term seems preferable, suggesting that it suffices if there is a reputable body of persons in the field who would support the opinion to which the expert in question wishes to testify.

Fourth, *by what means, and how clearly, must acceptance be shown?* In some cases, particularly where he is attempting to litigate relatively cheaply, the proponent attempts to satisfy the acceptance standard merely by having the expert herself testify to the merits of her theory or

---

[32] 904 F.Supp. 1529 (E.D.Okl.1995), aff'd on other grounds, 110 F.3d 1508 (10th Cir.1997).

[33] The Court of Appeals reversed the ruling that the hair analysis was inadmissible, because the District Judge applied *Daubert* rather than the more lenient constitutional standard appropriate in *habeas* cases. 110 F.3d at 1522–23. In the course of its opinion, however, the appellate court did note that some authorities view hair analysis as "highly subjective and unreliable." *Id.* at 1520 n.13.

[34] 904 F. Supp. at 1558. Oklahoma, the state in which *Williamson* arose, is among those, *see* note 25 *supra*, that have adhered to the view that hair comparison evidence is admissible. Bryan v. State, 935 P.2d 338, 359 (Okla.Crim.App. 1997, *cert. denied*, 522 U.S. 957 (1997). *See also, e.g.,* State v. West, 877 A.2d 787, 807–08 (Conn. 2005) (reviewing cases and asserting that "the jurors were able to evaluate the evidence in light of its acknowledged limitations and to give that evidence whatever weight they deemed appropriate"). *Compare also, e.g.,* Robinson v. State, 47 Md.App. 558, 425 A.2d 211 (1981) (general acceptance within the field of forensic chemistry of electrophoretic techniques for identifying source of bodily fluids held sufficient, notwithstanding lack of wide use of techniques outside crime laboratories), *with* People v. Brown, 40 Cal.3d 512, 230 Cal.Rptr. 834, 726 P.2d 516 (1985) (casting doubt on *Robinson*), *reversed on other grounds,* 479 U.S. 538 (1987); *Young, supra,* 391 N.W.2d at 276 (rejecting for *Frye* purposes the "community of scientists having direct empirical experience with electrophoresis of evidentiary bloodstains").

[35] *See* People v. Shirley, 31 Cal.3d 18, 56, 181 Cal.Rptr. 243, 265, 723 P.2d 1354, 1376, *cert. denied,* 458 U.S. 1125 (1982) (issue whether hypnosis should be used to restore the memory of potential witness; court poses question as whether "scientists significant either in number or expertise publicly oppose [a technique] as unreliable").

[36] *See, e.g.,* Brodine v. State, 936 P.2d 545, 550 (Alaska Ct.App.1997) ("The *Frye* test does not require unanimous acceptance in the scientific community; it only requires general acceptance.").

technique and declare that it is generally accepted. Sometimes that will work, particularly if the type of evidence is one with which the court is familiar, but if the court is more dubious it may demand a demonstration of acceptance on the basis of academic literature.[37]

Testing—Ordinarily, Justice Blackmun wrote in *Daubert*, one "key question" is whether the theory or technique "can be (and has been) tested." Putting the "can be" part of this test another way, he suggested that a basic criterion is the "falsifiability" of the theory. 509 U.S. at 593. The Chief Justice said he was "at a loss" to understand what this means. *Id.* at 600. A serviceable answer is that a theory is falsifiable if a test can be performed to demonstrate that the theory is false, assuming hypothetically that in fact it is false. According to some philosophers of science, falsifiability is indeed one of the principal hallmarks of science, or even its sole distinguishing feature.[38]

But how much does this help? Let's think again about *Joiner*. One could imagine a test that would demonstrate definitively whether prolonged exposure to moderate levels of PCBs tends to promote lung cancer in humans. But it is not the type of test that is likely to satisfy the ethical standards of any Human Subjects Committee, and even if it did it is not likely to yield clear results for many years. So Joiner offered animal studies, based on massive injections of PCBs into the bellies of infant mice, and epidemiological studies, based on statistical analyses of the history of given groups of workers who had been exposed to PCBs or similar chemicals. The animal studies suggested a link between PCBs and cancer—but extrapolating from baby mice to grown-up humans is always troublesome—and the epidemiological studies, while suggestive, yielded very weak results. But that is not all Joiner presented. As we have seen, he also offered the testimony of toxicologists that, in their opinion based on all the evidence before them and all their experience, yes, they did believe that PCBs promote lung cancer and probably promoted Joiner's. It does not seem that there is any way of testing that inferential jump made by the toxicologists—but does that mean that the plaintiff is not entitled to have their opinions considered?[39]

Peer review and publication—Another relevant, but not dispositive, consideration set out by the *Daubert* Court "is whether the theory or technique has been subjected to peer review and publication." 509 U.S. at

---

[37] *Compare Coppolino, supra* (allowing testimony based on expert's own evaluation), *with Young, supra,* 391 N.W.2d at 283 ("General agreement . . . has not been achieved because independently conducted validation tests and control studies have not been undertaken").

[38] *See* Heidi Li Feldman, *Science and Uncertainty in Mass Exposure Litigation,* 74 Tex. L. Rev. 1, 9–10 (1995).

[39] *Cf., e.g.,* United States v. Scholl, 959 F.Supp. 1189, 1191 (D.Ariz.1997) ("Plainly Dr. Hunter could not provide any scientific evidence of falsifiability or the error rate of the distortion in thinking or denial"; testimony held inadmissible).

593. It is clear enough why this is often a valid consideration. We expect reputable scientific conclusions to be published, and most well regarded scientific journals (unlike most well regarded law journals!) depend on peer review to determine what gets published and what does not. But this standard, too, raises difficulties.

For one thing, it is by no means true that all good science gets published in peer reviewed publications, or that what gets published in peer reviewed publications is entitled to respect as good science. Peer reviewed publications tend to move slowly, sometimes too slowly for scientific developments. Particularly with the advent of the internet, some important results become widely disseminated, discussed, criticized, and used well before they are formally published. Whether disseminated by, before, or without formal publication, such after-the-fact commentary appears to be a far more important guarantor of the quality of scientific work than is the peer review process. And there are some journals that, though formally peer reviewed, are regarded by some scientists as essentially counterparts to vanity publishers.

Moreover, as with the "general acceptance" criterion, the criterion of peer review and publication faces a problem of ambiguity—just how broad a theory is it that must have been subjected to this process? Further, litigation often concerns questions of very narrow scope. The precise questions that arouse controversy in a given litigation—for example, what caused *this* patient's suffering, and how can that be determined?—may be of too parochial interest to warrant publication.

Even with respect to a recurrent problem, one that affects many people, there is no guarantee that analyses will be subjected to peer review and publication before they become of significance to litigation. Consider the constellation of litigation of which *Daubert* itself was a part.

Numerous children with serious birth defects claimed that these defects had been caused by their mothers' ingestion of Bendectin, an anti-nausea drug sold by Merrell Dow. Merrell Dow demonstrated beyond genuine dispute that there had been more than 30 published epidemiological studies, involving over 130,000 patients, examining the relation between Bendectin and human birth defects. In none of these studies did the authors find Bendectin to be capable of causing malformations in human fetuses. These studies had undergone full scrutiny from the scientific community.

In response, some Bendectin plaintiffs presented the testimony of several experts. These experts testified to studies, both *in vitro* (test tube) and *in vivo* (live), suggesting that Bendectin causes birth defects in animals; to pharmacological studies that purported to show similarities between the chemical structure of Bendectin and that of other substances known to cause birth defects; and to "meta-analyses" of the previously published epidemiological studies, suggesting that Bendectin can cause birth defects in humans. These meta-analyses were generated for the litigation itself by experts retained for the purpose, and had not been published in professional journals. Meta-analysis is a relatively new and increasingly important approach to statistical analysis that contends that the traditional "significance testing" approach is unduly cautious in drawing conclusions from multiple statistical studies. Meta-analysts attempt to accumulate knowledge across a series of studies. There are, as one review concluded, "many caveats in performing a valid meta-analysis, and in some cases a meta-analysis is not appropriate and the results can be misleading."[40] But meta-analysts insist that, when properly applied in an appropriate case, meta-analysis can provide much useful information.

Maybe? ¶ **5.15:** Should the meta-analysis in a *Bendectin* case be admitted? What further information would you want to know to inform your answer?[41] *what were the limitations of the epidemiological studies?*

Error rates and standards—An expert does not always discuss underlying theories. Sometimes a proponent wishes to present the results of some test, perhaps through a witness who does not understand very much about the theory but who has been trained in performing the technique. For example, in drunk driving cases the prosecution may offer the results of a Horizontal Gaze Nystagmus (HGN) test—which basically means that the arresting officer steadily moves a small object, such as a finger, pen, or pen-size flashlight, in front of the suspect's eyes, and then testifies as to how jerky the suspect's eye movements were.[42] To determine whether such a technique is reliable, the court might wish to understand the underlying theory, but its concerns must go to the level of application as well. *Daubert* indicated that in such a case the court should consider the "known or potential rate of error," and "the existence and maintenance of standards controlling the technique's operation." 509 U.S.

---

[40] Esteban Walker, et al., *Meta-analysis: Its strengths and limitations*, 75 Cleveland Clinic J. Med. 431 (2008). Among the difficulties are the "file drawer" problem, arising from the fact that studies showing negative results or insignificant ones are less likely to be published than studies showing affirmative results. Another is that meta-analyses tend not to reflect information on conflicts of interest in the underlying studies. Michelle Rosmean, et al., *Reporting of Conflicts of Interest in Meta-analyses of Trials of Pharmacological Treatments*, 305 JAMA 1008 (2011). There are also scholarly debates about the appropriate statistical techniques to be used in performing meta-analyses. For a helpful explanation of meta-analysis in the context of Bendectin litigation, see DeLuca v. Merrell Dow Pharmaceuticals, Inc., 911 F.2d 941, 946–49 (3d Cir.1990). On remand in *DeLuca*, the trial court granted summary judgment for the defense, 791 F.Supp. 1042, 1057 (D.N.J.1992), aff'd, 6 F.3d 778 (3d Cir.1993) (without opinion), *cert. denied*, 510 U.S. 1044 (1994). Wikipedia's article, *Meta-analysis*, https://en.wikipedia.org/wiki/Meta-analysis, is also very useful.

[41] Although the *DeLuca* plaintiffs submitted a meta-analysis purporting to show the effect of Bendectin in causing human birth defects, a published meta-analysis suggests that the effect is very slight, if it exists at all. *See* Joseph Sanders, *From Science to Evidence: the Testimony on Causation in the Bendectin Cases*, 46 Stan. L. Rev. 1, 24 (1993).

[42] *See* State v. O'Key, 321 Or. 285, 899 P.2d 663 (Or. 1995) (approving use; applying *Daubert* criteria).

at 594. The implication seems to be that if the technique is too error-prone (how much is too much?) or if proper (generally accepted?) operating standards are not followed, the evidence ordinarily should be inadmissible.

Once again, it is easy enough to see the appeal of these factors. If a technique, such as HGN or hair or handwriting identification, is no better than guesswork, the evidence it produces is valueless. If the technician who applied the method did not do so according to sound operating standards, the value of the evidence will be tainted; moreover, exclusion in such a case provides incentives for developing and adhering to sound procedures.

It is important, though, not to be too hasty in applying this criterion. Operating standards are very often a matter of intense debate among professionals. It does not always make sense for a court to exclude expert evidence as a mean of enforcing its choice of appropriate standards and adherence to them; it is sometimes better to admit the evidence and have these matters fought out in front of the jurors and taken into account by them in assessing the weight of the evidence.

As for error rates, it is important to recognize that a technique can produce a very high error rate and yet yield very valuable information. This, indeed, is what some medical "screening" tests do, in searching for a rare condition. Suppose such a test produces a large number of false positives, perhaps even many times the number of "hits" (accurate indications that the condition exists), and even a substantial number of false negatives. The screening test may yet be extremely valuable because the condition is hard to detect and this test is a cost-effective way of determining when further inquiry is warranted. Recall the hypothetical in ¶ 3.10 about an instrument that cheaply but not entirely accurately detects underground oil pools.

Bear in mind that *Daubert* explicitly disclaimed the intent to set out an exhaustive checklist of criteria for determining admissibility of scientific evidence. Some courts have nevertheless treated them almost as such, marching through them one by one on the path to a determination that the evidence either is or is not admissible. Others, though, while following the general analysis of *Daubert*, have added other considerations that seem material. For example, the Supreme Court of Texas, still emphasizing the non-exclusive nature of its list, added "the extent to which the technique relies upon the subjective interpretation of the expert" and "the non-judicial uses which have been made of the theory or technique." *E.I. du Pont de Nemours & Co. v. Robinson*, 923 S.W.2d 549, 557 (1995). In commenting on the 2000 Amendment to FRE 702, the Advisory Committee emphasized that it was not attempting to codify specific factors, that *Daubert* itself emphasized that the factors it listed were neither exclusive nor dispositive, that not all of the specific *Daubert* factors can apply to every case, and that additional factors may be appropriate in some cases.

Still, we must ask how helpful is the emphasis on whether the evidence constitutes "scientific knowledge." Rule 702, it is important to remember, does not make the question of whether knowledge is scientific dispositive; the Rule refers in very general terms to "scientific, technical, *or other* specialized knowledge" that "will help the trier of fact to understand the evidence or to determine a fact in issue." So why ask whether the evidence is scientific; why not simply ask whether it will, on balance, be helpful to the trier of fact?

Consider, for example, *United States v. Starzecpyzel*, 880 F.Supp. 1027 (S.D.N.Y.1995). It is not particularly important that you can pronounce or spell the name of the defendant, but the opinion is interesting. The question there was whether a forensic document examiner (FDE), given a large sampling of unquestionably genuine signatures of a person, could testify that two other documents were forgeries. The court worked through the *Daubert* criteria as they relate to the litigation-oriented expertise of FDEs. It concluded that this specialty has many of the "trappings of science"—including peer reviewed journals—but that it is not genuine science. Among other problems, there was no persuasive evidence that experts do better than laypeople in identifying forgers. Nevertheless, the court concluded that, considering the expertise as a nonscientific one, it was helpful to the jury, at least in a case like this, in which forgery detection, as opposed to forger identification, was at issue. Like harbor pilots, the court said, FDEs gather skill over the years, and can offer insights to the jury. They could, for example, be helpful to the jury in focusing on minute similarities and dissimilarities between two documents that laypeople might have missed. The court doubted that this was the type of evidence that would overwhelm the jury.[43]

The Supreme Court's latest foray into the field has confirmed that the critical question the trial court must ask is not whether the evidence should be deemed scientific. *Kumho Tire Co., Ltd. v. Carmichael*, 526 U.S. 137 (1999), the third case in the Court's expert-testimony trilogy of the 1990s, concerned an action brought against a tire manufacturer after a tire failure caused a fatal accident. The plaintiffs offered the testimony of an engineer, a tire analyst, who testified that on the basis of criteria he believed appropriate the most probable conclusion was that the tire failed because of manufacturing or design defect. The trial court worked through the *Daubert* criteria and concluded that the evidence was

---

[43]   To similar effect, see, e.g., United States v. Jones, 107 F.3d 1147 (6th Cir. 1997).

insufficiently reliable to be admitted. The plaintiffs contended that this analysis was erroneous, that *Daubert* applied only to scientific evidence, and they did not contend that the tire analyst's evidence was scientific. The court of appeals agreed. But the Supreme Court, resolving a question left open by *Daubert*[44] that split the lower courts,[45] held that the gatekeeping function prescribed by *Daubert* applies to all expert evidence, whether scientific or not. This is a point that the Advisory Committee emphasized when it explicitly wrote a reliability requirement into Rule 702:

> While the relevant factors for determining reliability will vary from expertise to expertise, the amendment rejects the premise that an expert's testimony should be treated more permissively simply because it is outside the realm of science. An opinion from an expert who is not a scientist should receive the same degree of scrutiny for reliability as an opinion from an expert who purports to be a scientist.

Note to 2000 amendment to FRE 702.

As the Advisory Committee did later, *Kumho* emphasized that the *Daubert* criteria are not binding on the trial court (though Justices Scalia, O'Connor, and Thomas wrote a brief separate concurrence to warn that in a given case failure to apply one or more of them might constitute an abuse of discretion). In the particular case, the Court—over the dissent of Justice Stevens, who would not have reached the issue—concluded that the trial judge acted within his discretion in holding the engineer's testimony inadmissible, a result that, as in *Daubert* and *Joiner*, resulted in summary judgment for the defense.

Consider whether you believe that ruling was correct. The witness, Denis Carlson, was an experienced tire engineer, who had worked for years for Michelin America, Inc., and then as a tire consultant. He testified that the inner tread of the tire had separated from the "carcass" and that this separation had caused the blowout; thus far, there does not seem to have been any dispute. He further testified that if a tire has not been subjected to "overdeflection" (underinflating it or causing it to bear too much weight) then usually the cause of separation is a defect in the tire, and that if the tire has been overdeflected he would expect to see certain physical symptoms. These would include (1) tread wear on the

---

[44] *See generally Daubert*, 509 U.S. at 599–600 (Rehnquist, C.J., dissenting) (asking whether the framework applies to "technical or other specialized knowledge," and if not, how they are distinguished from "scientific knowledge").

[45] *See, e.g.*, Bogosian v. Mercedes-Benz of North America, Inc., 104 F.3d 472, 479 (1st Cir.1997) (assuming *arguendo* that *Daubert* framework doesn't apply to technical expertise but still upholding exclusion of evidence as unreliable); Gier v. Educational Serv. Unit No. 16, 66 F.3d 940, 943–44 (8th Cir.1995) (applying *Daubert* to psychological evaluations in child custody cases).

tire's shoulder greater than in the center; (2) signs of a "bead groove," caused by the beads—wire loops that hold the cords together—being pressed too hard against the seat that holds them on the tire's rim; (3) sidewalls with physical signs of deterioration, such as discoloration; and (4) marks on the tire's rim flange. Absent at least two of these signs, and any less obvious cause of separation, Carlson said he concluded that a defect caused the separation. In fact, the tire in question bore each of the four symptoms to a limited degree, and it had two inadequately filled puncture marks in addition. But Carlson said that none of these were significant; wear was greater on one shoulder than in the center, for example, but he would have expected to see extra wear on both shoulders if overdeflection was the cause of separation. Carlson concluded that neither overdeflection nor the punctures caused the blowout, so that defect was the likely cause. However logical that might appear, there were numerous problems with Carlson's testimony. For example, he could not say with confidence whether the tire had traveled less than 10,000 miles or more than 50,000. Before he ever inspected the tire itself, as opposed to photographs of it, he issued a report concluding that the tire had not been overloaded or underinflated simply because the rim flange impressions were normal, a departure from the two-factor-out-of-four methodology that he later presented. The Supreme Court noted, 526 U.S. at 157,

> We have found no indication in the record that other experts in the industry use Carlson's two-factor test or that tire experts such as Carlson normally make the very fine distinctions about, say, the symmetry of comparatively greater shoulder tread wear that were necessary, on Carlson's own theory, to support his conclusions. Nor, despite the prevalence of tire testing, does anyone refer to any articles or papers that validate Carlson's approach. . . . Indeed, no one has argued that Carlson himself, were he still working for Michelin, would have concluded in a report to his employer that a similar tire was similarly defective on grounds identical to those upon which he rested his conclusion here.

¶ 5.16: Should Carlson's testimony have been excluded as insufficiently reliable? If so, what criteria should the trial court have used in making the determination? Do the *Daubert* criteria work well for the purpose?

¶ 5.17: Given the result in *Kumho*, should the hand-writing evidence in *Starzecpysel* be admitted?[46] Before admitting

---

46 *Compare* United States v. Saelee, 162 F.Supp.2d 1097 (D. Alaska 2001) (post-*Kumho* case, reviewing handwriting analysis cases and precluding testimony of expert even as to similarities and differences between known exemplars and documents in question, emphasizing

evidence that a latent fingerprint came from the same source as a known print, what would you want to know about fingerprint evidence?[47] How reliable? Testing? Acceptance? You know... the Daubert factors...

There is no doubt that courts must perform some gatekeeper role with respect to expert evidence—as with respect to all evidence. Some evidence, like that of the phrenologist, is just not worth the time and effort it would take to admit. But the plaintiffs' experts in cases like

insufficient empirical testing of proficiency of experts and lack of meaningful peer review); United States v. Brewer, 2002 WL 596365 (N.D. Ill. 2002) (relying on *Saelee* for similar conclusion), *with* United States v. Paul, 175 F.3d 906 (11th Cir. 1999) (holding, shortly after *Kumho*, that trial court did not abuse discretion in admitting testimony of handwriting expert that accused wrote extortion note or in excluding testimony of law professor critical of handwriting analysis); United States v. Gricco, 2002 WL 746037 (E.D. Pa. 2002) (allowing expert to testify as to match between writings on seized documents and known exemplar of accused's writing); In re Estate of Preutti, 783 A.22d 803 (Pa. Super. 2001) (holding admissible in will contest testimony of a handwriting expert who had testified over 200 times).

The academic literature on the proficiency of forensic document examiners is considerable and contentious. On the favorable side, see, e.g., Moshe Kam & Erwei Lin, *Writer Identification Using Hand-Printed and Non-Hand-Printed Questioned Documents*, 48 J. Forensic Sciences 1391 (2003). On the skeptical side, see, e.g., D. Michael Risinger et al., *Exorcism of Ignorance as a Proxy for Rational Knowledge: The Lessons of Handwriting Identification 'Expertise'*, 137 U.Pa. L. Rev. 731 (1999).

The field is likely to be transformed in coming years by computerized pattern recognition programs; developers claim they are capable of great accuracy in author recognition. *See, e.g.,* Proceedings of the 2nd International Workshop on Automated Forensic Handwriting Analysis (AFHA) 2013, http://ceur-ws.org/Vol-1022/ProceedingsAFHA2013.pdf; Sargur N. Srihari et al., *Individuality of Handwriting*, 47 J. Forensic Sci. 856 (2002), *Commentary* on that article, by Michael J. Saks, in 48 J. Forensic Sci. 916 (2003), and the *Authors' Response*, by Srihari, in 48 J. Forensic Sci. 919 (2003).

[47] In light of *Kumho* a highly respected district judge even placed in doubt the admissibility of expert opinion that a latent fingerprint came from the same source as a known print—though he later changed his mind. *United States v. Llera Plaza*, 2002 WL 27305 (E.D. Pa. Jan. 7, 2002), *vacated*, 188 F. Supp. 2d 549 (E.D.Pa. 2002). Although it is clear that fingerprints are unique to the individual and permanent, there is much less basis for concluding that a fingerprint expert can reliably determine whether a latent print matches with a known one. Arguably, a fingerprint expert should not be able to declare a match but only discuss the similarities shared by two prints. D.H. Kaye, *The Nonscience of Fingerprinting: United States v. Llera-Plaza*, 21 Quinnipiac L. Rev. 1073 (2003). But the track record of fingerprint evidence is extensive and on the whole good. I am tempted to conclude that if the treatment of fingerprint evidence does not square with *Daubert*—as some, including my collaborators in an academic exchange, have suggested, Richard Friedman et al., *Expert Testimony on Fingerprints: An Internet Exchange*, 43 Jurimetrics J. 91, 92 n.9 (2002)—the problem lies with *Daubert* and *Kumho* rather than with the way fingerprint evidence has been treated for decades. Having said that, I must acknowledge that in recent years fingerprint evidence has lost its appearance of inevitability; there have been cases in which convictions have been procured on the basis of incorrect declarations of fingerprint matches. See, for example, the case of Rickie Jackson on the National Registry of Exonerations, https://www. law.umich.edu/special/exoneration/Pages/casedetail.aspx? caseid=3318. But convictions on the basis of mistaken fingerprint identifications still appear to be very rare—though all we can really say for sure is that not many cases of false fingerprint identification have been exposed. *See Simon A. Cole, More than Zero: Accounting for Error in Latent Fingerprint Identification*, 95 J. Crim. L. & Criminology 985 (2005); *see also, e.g.,* D.H. Kaye, *Looking Backwards: How Safe Are Fingerprint Identifications?*, http://for-sci-law.blogspot.com/2014/07/looking-backwards-how-safe-are.html (2014). Fingerprints, of course, can demonstrate at most contact *at some point* in the past between a given person and a given object; especially when an object is easily moveable, the timing of that contact may be in doubt, and this factor may limit the usefulness of the fingerprint evidence. *See, e.g.,* United States v. Strayhorn, 743 F.3d 917 (4th Cir.), *cert. denied*, 134 S.Ct. 2689 (2014).

Daubert, Joiner, and *Kumho* should not be compared to phrenologists or other quacks.[48] They may have been overreaching, and their work may have had flaws, but these problems should not necessarily be dealt with at the admissibility stage. Suppose that in *Joiner* Dr. Teitelbaum gave his testimony by deposition and then died. Soon after, a new epidemiological study pointed more strongly—not compellingly, but persuasively enough that the issue should clearly reach the jury—to the conclusion that PCBs do indeed promote lung cancer in humans. The plaintiffs introduce evidence of that study, but they also offer Dr. Teitelbaum's evidence. In such a case it seems fairly clear that the Teitelbaum evidence should be admitted; it gives extra weight to the plaintiffs' case and so makes more probable the proposition for which it is offered to prove.

The implication of this analysis is that the weaknesses of scientific evidence in a case like *Daubert* or *Joiner* should be dealt with in determining *sufficiency* rather than *admissibility.* In these cases and many others, the scientific evidence at issue is crucial to the plaintiff's case; without it, the plaintiff cannot prevail. Often, the court holds the evidence inadmissible and then grants summary judgment for the defendant, there clearly being insufficient admissible evidence to support a verdict for the plaintiff.[49] Perhaps a more straightforward approach would be to be more receptive to admissibility, but still to consider whether the plaintiff has introduced enough evidence to withstand summary judgment. Such an approach might represent a fairly aggressive use of the summary judgment device—usually, if admissible testimony asserts a proposition, that is enough evidence to get to the jury on that proposition—but it is actually one approved by *Daubert.* Recall that in the portion of the opinion rejecting the *Frye* test, and so tending to minimize rather than maximize the gatekeeping role of the court, *Daubert* emphasized the power of courts to grant judgment as a matter of law against a party when all the evidence considered together would not support judgment in that party's favor. 509 U.S. at 595–96.[50]

Whether the courts operate against the evidence at the admissibility level or through summary judgment, the result may be much the same: judgment as a matter of law for the defendant. To some extent, in contexts such as mass or recurrent torts, that result might be motivated

---

[48] *See, e.g.,* Joseph Sanders, *From Science to Evidence: The Testimony on Causation in the Bendectin Case,* 43 Hastings L.J. 301, 346 (1992) (summarizing, though not advocating, "The Case Against Bendectin"); *see also* Joseph Sanders, *Scientific Validity, Admissibility and Mass Torts After* Daubert, 78 Minn. L. Rev. 1387, 1439–40 (1994) (arguing that presentation is a more serious problem than marginal science).

[49] The importance of summary judgment, and of pretrial proceedings in general, in the *Daubert* context is emphasized in Margaret A. Berger, *Procedural Paradigms for Applying the* Daubert *Test,* 78 Minn. L. Rev. 1345 (1994).

[50] This is an approach taken by some courts in Bendectin litigation. *See, e.g.,* Elkins v. Richardson-Merrell, Inc., 8 F.3d 1068 (6th Cir.1993), *cert. denied,* 510 U.S. 1193 (1994).

by a desire to generate a uniform rule of decision covering similar cases. And to some extent it might be motivated by belief that courts are better able than juries to evaluate difficult scientific issues. Whether there is really a significant differential in the sophistication of judges and juries in this area is unclear. The processes of judicial decisionmaking—with emphasis on reflection, written submission of materials and written articulation of the grounds of decision—are probably better suited than the awkward processes of jury decisionmaking for the evaluation of information that is beyond the ordinary ken of most laypeople, judges and jurors alike. On the other hand, judicial misunderstanding of the *Daubert* criteria appears to be rampant.[51] And we must always remember that the jury, within its realm, is the trier of fact designated by our adjudicative system—indeed, constitutionally designated in most American jurisdictions.

At base, the *Frye-Daubert* problem may be considered a matter of allocation of power among the jury, scientific establishment, trial judge, and appellate court. This is an enduring problem that doctrinal changes are unlikely to eliminate.[52]

E. PROCEDURAL CONSIDERATIONS

1. RECRUITING EXPERTS

In most litigation, only a few people—and sometimes no more than one—have personal observations that they can offer as testimony. Decisions and conduct of the parties do have some impact on who will actually become witnesses at trial; the parties may have to identify and locate the witnesses and secure their presence at trial, and often the parties will have some choices as to which witnesses to present. But usually the range of choices open to a party is relatively narrow; within bounds determined largely by cost and limits on the jury's attention, he wants anyone who can give admissible testimony that will help his case, and no one else. And the party usually can compel the testimony of these people, at trial if they are nearby and otherwise at deposition. The party may have to pay a witness fee, but it is nominal.

The situation is altogether different with respect to non-percipient experts—that is, those experts who can offer useful opinions but who have not personally observed the events at issue in the litigation. The fundamental principle that a litigant is entitled to "every person's

---

[51] S. Gatowski et al., *Asking the Gatekeepers: A National Survey of Judges on Judging Expert Evidence in a Post-*Daubert *World*, 25 Law & Hum. Behav. 433 (2001)).

[52] The literature on *Daubert* and related issues is, as you might expect, enormous. A good entry point is David H. Kaye, David E. Bernstein & Jennifer L. Mnookin, The New Wigmore: A Treatise on Evidence: Expert Evidence (2d ed. 2011 & 2016 Cum. Supp.).

evidence," *e.g., Jaffee v. Redmond,* 518 U.S. 1, 25 (1996), does not apply to these experts. They are professionals rendering a service, and for that they may negotiate a fee. In many settings, the party has a wide range of choice of which expert to try to recruit; anyone with the requisite specialized knowledge can potentially serve. But not all experts are created equal. They differ, among other ways, in how close their specialty lies to the subject matter of their prospective testimony; how close they live or work to the litigation forum; how capable and persuasive they are as witnesses; how favorable their testimony will be to the recruiting party; and how much they charge. Not surprisingly, matching up parties and experts has become a substantial business, much like any other head-hunting business.[53]

¶ **5.18:** You are representing a large corporation defending against a civil suit that charges it with an attempt to manipulate and monopolize the market for silver futures. Cost is no object to this litigation, at least on your side: You are instructed to do all that you can do to win, consistent with standards of professional responsibility. You investigate and find that, although there are several dozen economists who do substantial work on the commodity futures markets, three economists stand out as potential experts in this case, by virtue of their knowledge and experience with respect to the precious metals markets. How many of these experts should you attempt to retain?

2. EXPERTS BEFORE TRIAL

An expert may be retained simply to consult in preparation for the litigation, without the anticipation that she will testify. Such an expert is treated as part of the litigation team, and is usually immune from discovery. *See* Fed. R. Civ. P. 26(b)(4)(B).

If, however, an expert is retained for the purpose of testifying in a federal action, or she will do so as part of her regular duties for the party, the party may be required to file a report that states the opinions she will give, her grounds for them, and her qualifications. Fed. R. Crim. P. 16(a)(1)(E) gives a criminal defendant the option of asking for such a report; if he does so, the prosecution can then demand a reciprocal report. Fed. R. Crim. P. 16(b)(1)(C). Fed. R. Civ. P. 26(a)(2)(B) also requires such reports, though the court or the parties may work out other arrangements for a particular case. The report requirement, where it applies, is meant in large part to facilitate the opponent's task in attempting to impeach the expert; thus, the civil procedure rule requires a list of the expert's publications during the preceding ten years and a list of other cases in

---

[53] For a very helpful and thorough review of the entire process related to expert evidence, including the recruitment process, see Samuel R. Gross, *Expert Evidence,* 1991 Wis. L. Rev. 1113.

which she has testified as an expert within the last four years. The civil procedure rule also requires the inclusion of data considered by the expert in forming her opinions and the disclosure of any exhibits that she will use in testifying or that support her opinion.

In civil litigation, and in some criminal jurisdictions, the opponent may then take the expert's deposition; if he does so, he ordinarily would pay for the expert's time in preparing and attending the deposition. *See* Fed. R. Civ. P. 26(b)(4)(E). In some jurisdictions, it has become common practice for the *proponent* to take a video deposition of the expert, with the opportunity for the opponent to cross-examine at that time. The proponent then offers the deposition in lieu of the live testimony of the expert at trial.

¶ **5.19:** From the proponent's point of view, what is gained and what is lost by this procedure? Why do you suppose it is used especially for experts, and not generally for lay witnesses?

In a civil case, if a serious summary judgment motion is made, the expert may provide an affidavit, giving a full written forecast of the testimony she would provide if the case went to trial. The affidavit will typically include exhibits and may run many pages. Like the prospective trial testimony, and more than the original report, this affidavit is an attempt to persuade its audience.

These pretrial writings raise interesting questions concerning trial practice, which we will consider after we examine the current practice for taking testimony from experts at trial.

3.   QUALIFYING THE EXPERT

Because the question of the expert's qualifications is for the judge to decide, if the case goes to trial there must be a mini-hearing on that issue. Usually, the mini-hearing consists of nothing but the testimony of the witness herself. The proponent takes her through her professional history, showing that she has the training, skill, education, and experience to be considered an expert. In form, this demonstration is addressed to the judge, to persuade her that the expert really is qualified. Rarely does the judge conclude that the witness lacks sufficient credentials to testify within an area of her specialty. More often, the judge may rule that, although the witness may be qualified to testify on her specialty, the subject matter of her proposed testimony lies too far outside that specialty for her to testify. Most often, though, unless the expert fails to satisfy a statutory requirement, the judge does not prevent the expert from testifying on the ground that she is not qualified.

Thus, the proponent's real focus is on the jurors; she may be attempting to persuade them that they are privileged to be hearing from one of the World's Greatest Experts. The opponent then has a chance to question the witness on the preliminary question of whether she should be allowed to give her testimony. The opponent may ask no questions at all. If he does ask questions at this stage, he again will probably have in mind that the judge is not likely to hold the witness unqualified. His focus, too, is on the jurors. He may attempt to persuade them that the expert is not all that qualified, at least not on the precise subject at issue in this case. In the end, though, the opponent may not object to certifying the witness as an expert.

4. QUESTIONING THE EXPERT

Now let's assume that the court holds that the expert is qualified and that the opinion she wishes to deliver is an appropriate subject of expert testimony. Unlike the ordinary lay witness, an expert may have something to offer the jury even if she does not have information bearing closely on the historical facts in dispute.[54] She is on the stand because she has "specialized knowledge," and that knowledge may consist of an ability to process information provided to her and to yield an opinion that has some merit. She may be able to testify, in essence, "I examined the decedent and I can tell you he had cancer of the pancreas." But even if she does not have firsthand knowledge of this sort, she still has something to offer the jury if she can say, "I never saw the patient, but if all you say is true, then I would conclude, based on my long years of studying the area and practicing in it, that he had cancer of the pancreas." In other words, it may be not her observations in the current litigation (or not only those observations), but her analytical abilities, supported by the knowledge she has gained in her professional experience, that make her a useful witness.

What this means is that the usual firsthand knowledge rule does not apply, or at least applies differently, to experts; contrast the language in the first sentence of FRE 703—"data . . . that the expert has been made aware of or personally observed"—with the "rationally based on the witness's perception" language of Rule 701. This raises an immediate problem, however. What if the "data" on which the expert bases her opinion are themselves hotly in dispute? The expert may believe, for example, that if the decedent suffered a given series of symptoms, then he probably had pancreatic cancer. But perhaps the other side denies that he had any of these symptoms. If the expert never examined the patient, she is giving a contingent opinion, which has no value if the premises are not

---

[54] This may be something of an overstatement, in that some lay witnesses may be said no more than some experts to have information that bears closely on the historical facts—for example, the lay witness who knows nothing about the dispute but is able to identify a signature as the writing of one party. But this really emphasizes the point made at the end of Chapter 4 and explored further at the end of this chapter, that the line between lay and expert witnesses is far fuzzier than might be supposed.

true. It appears, therefore, that the expert must make clear just what those premises are, so that the jury can decide whether or not they are true and ignore the opinion if it finds that they are not.

This is where the hypothetical question comes in. A hypothetical question may be asked of an expert who has no first-hand knowledge of the particular case, or who has some first-hand knowledge that must be supplemented by other information to reach a useful opinion.

The hypothetical question is a logical necessity for an expert who is not able to testify totally on the basis of first-hand observation. But logic does not always control the law. The requirement of posing hypothetical questions present substantial practical difficulties; also, hypotheticals are often abused by lawyers as extra, sometimes very lengthy, arguments to the jury.

¶ **5.20:** Your expert witness examined the decedent and has told you, based on her observations and supplementary information that you have provided her, that she believes he died of pancreatic cancer. In all, she lists fifteen factors that led to her conclusion (skin color, fever, speed of death, blood tests, and so forth). In addition, you suppose that there are other factors— such as the absence of any other apparent cause of death—that must implicitly have been bases of her decision; that is, although she may not have been thinking about these factors, if they were different, her diagnosis likely would be different as well. In phrasing a hypothetical question, should you include all of these factors? If not, what are your criteria for selection? What is the danger of including too many factors in the question? Of including too few?

FRE 705 alters the common law approach. It allows hypotheticals but generally does not require them. Instead of asking a hypothetical, the attorney on direct may ask, "Do you have an opinion?", "What is that opinion?", and "What are the considerations that lead to that opinion?" But Rule 705 does not even require the expert, in answering the final question, to give the information that supports her opinion.[55] In most cases, she would want to; the opinion is unlikely to be particularly persuasive if the expert does not state the underlying data. But if the lawyer and the expert wish, the expert can testify in rather conclusory

---

[55] Originally, Fed.R.Evid. 705 said that the expert in testifying did not have to make "prior disclosure" of the information—but that appeared to conflict with the reporting requirement added in 1993 as Fed. R. Civ. P. 26(a)(2)(B), for that report would make the adversary aware before trial of the information on which the expert is basing her opinion. Hence, Rule 705 was amended to provide that unless ordered otherwise the expert could testify as to her opinions or inferences and reasons *without first testifying* to the underlying facts or data." We will consider later whether this provision may violate the Confrontation Clause when the evidence is offered against an accused.

form and leave it to the adversary to explore the underlying information. However the expert has testified, the adversary may want to probe that information base, trying to show that the expert's conclusions don't follow from the premises she used and also—if possible—that if the proponent's premises are not accepted then the expert would draw a different conclusion.

5. SOURCES OF THE EXPERT'S INFORMATION

We have seen that experts may draw conclusions in part on the basis of information provided to them. For example, our oncologist might depend in part on the report of a technician who has taken a blood test. Given that the physician did not take the test, there appear to be problems with her testifying to the results; testimony that "the white blood cell count was extraordinarily high" would lack personal knowledge, and testimony that "the technician told me . . . " would be hearsay. If the blood test is an essential predicate to the expert's opinion, therefore, it might appear that the technician would have to testify; furthermore, if several technicians reported information on which the expert based her opinion, they might all have to testify.[56] Obviously, this could create significant problems. And, as the Advisory Committee's note to FRE 703 suggests, strict adherence to theory would be foolish in some such situations; if experts can make life-and-death decisions depending on the reports of others, the courts might conclude that such reports are accurate enough to allow the experts to testify on the basis of the same information.[57]

Accordingly, Rule 703—reflecting a loosening of the law that had prevailed in some jurisdictions[58]—allows the expert to base her conclusion on data not admissible in evidence "[i]f experts in the particular field would reasonably rely on those kinds of facts or data in forming an opinion on the subject."[59] And because Rule 705 seems implicitly to provide that the expert may disclose the data underlying her opinion, and expressly provides that in some cases she must do so, it appears that the expert may testify to information that would otherwise be blocked by the personal knowledge requirement or by the hearsay rule.

---

[56] If, as is usually the case with a blood test, the information is provided to the expert in writing, and if that writing is still available, this problem could be eased by the "routinely kept records" exception to the hearsay rule. *See* FRE 803(6), *discussed in* Chapter 15.

[57] There are many other situations in which the drafters of the Federal Rules did not disturb the traditional law of evidence despite the fact that it is much more rigid than the informal process by which people draw conclusions in the outside world. Indeed, the entire law of hearsay may fit this description. But no one says that rulemakers have to be consistent.

[58] *See, e.g.,* Moore v. Grantham, 599 S.W.2d 287 (Tex.1980).

[59] Not all jurisdictions have gone along with this approach; *see* Michigan Rule of Evidence 703: "The facts or data in the particular case upon which an expert bases an opinion or inference shall be in evidence."

All this may be eminently sensible and practical; at the same time, bear in mind that such a result means that the jury can rely on the findings of a person, such as the technician, who has not testified in court and has not been subject to cross-examination. The most troubling concern, which did not become salient until relatively recently, is that in some circumstances operation of the Rule might in effect allow a prosecution witness to testify against an accused in violation of the Confrontation Clause, by filing a report rather than facing the accused and testifying under oath and cross-examination.

Even apart from the Confrontation Clause, it appears that Rule 703 can act in effect as a back-door exception to the rule against hearsay. Though the Rules can do what they want about the hearsay rule, that still left some courts uneasy. They varied in how they dealt with this situation, and in 2000 Rule 703 was amended to address it. The Rule now provides that if facts or data are otherwise inadmissible, "the proponent of the opinion may disclose them to the jury only if their probative value in helping the jury evaluate the opinion substantially outweighs their prejudicial effect." In other words, so long as the data satisfy the "reasonably rely" standard, the expert may *rely* on them, but the presumption is that she may not *testify* about them on direct. (The amendment does not interfere with the option of the opponent, recognized explicitly in Rule 705, to question the expert about the data on cross.) This presumption is the reverse of Rule 403; that Rule, you will recall, provides that evidence otherwise admissible may be excluded if its prejudicial effect substantially outweighs its probative value. Obviously, the amendment to Rule 703, which amounts to a thumb on one side of the scale, does not provide a complete solution to the problem, to which we shall return in Chapter 9, when we can better focus on the confrontation and hearsay considerations. *See* p. 244, ¶¶ 9.12–.15.

¶ 5.21: While in jail, Wells agreed to cooperate with the FBI by arranging a drug purchase from Slaughter. With Wells' consent, Wright, an FBI agent, monitored and taped phone conversations between Wells and Slaughter and monitored the sale, which occurred at a White Castle Restaurant. (It wasn't a very expensive sale.) At Slaughter's subsequent trial, Wells, a convicted felon and admitted perjurer, does not testify. Instead, Wright testifies about his extensive background and training as a narcotics agent, authenticates the tapes of the phone conversations, and explains that narcotics dealers often use code words to disguise the true nature of their conversations. He also offers the opinion that Wells and Slaughter had used code words for cocaine. Among those code words was "t-shirts." If pressed, Wright will acknowledge that he had never heard this specific code for cocaine. But he says that Wells told him it meant cocaine, and that he drew on this statement as well as on his experience with drug trafficking and the context of the conversation to reach his conclusion.

Should Wright be allowed to present his opinion that the references to "t-shirts" were really to cocaine? What questions should the prosecutor ask of Wright to satisfy the "reasonably rely" standard of FRE 703? Does it suffice to ask him, or should the prosecutor have to put another witness on the stand? What criteria should the judge use to decide whether the requirements have indeed been satisfied?

Assuming that Wright is allowed to offer that opinion, should he be allowed to testify that among the bases for the conclusion that "t-shirts" referred to cocaine is the fact that Wells told him so?[60]

6. COURT-APPOINTED EXPERTS

By now, you may have concluded that the entire mechanism for bringing expertise to bear at trials in our system makes little sense. What we want, you may think, is not experts who are essentially advocates for one side or the other. What we want instead is neutral, impartial expertise. If so, you may be drawn to the option of court-appointed experts, for which FRE 706 expressly provides. And if so, you will not be the first to find this possibility attractive. *See, e.g., Joiner, supra* (Breyer, J., concurring). In some settings, such as child custody disputes, court-appointed experts are used routinely, and the system seems to work reasonably well. But we must be careful before concluding that court appointment of experts is a panacea for the problem of expertise.

At the outset, it is worth asking: Given that courts have the unquestioned authority to appoint experts, why is it that they do so rather rarely apart from certain narrow settings? Part of the answer lies in practical factors. Recruiting the type of expert is not a snap-of-the-fingers job. It requires time, money, and the incentive to spend both. When the litigation has substantial stakes, the parties are far more likely than the judge to have all three.

Beyond this, even if the court has the ability and inclination to recruit an expert, it is not always clear that this is a good solution. Note that Rule 706(d) provides, "This rule does not limit a party in calling its own experts." This is very different from the procedure typical of Continental systems, in which the court will consider information only

---

[60] *See* United States v. Rollins, 862 F.2d 1282 (7th Cir. 1988). *Rollins* admitted Wright's testimony concerning what Wells told him, but consider how the 2000 amendment might affect the question.

from those experts it chooses to consult. Given our rights orientation towards litigation, it is unlikely that such a procedure would be tolerable in the United States. If the parties do call their own experts, then it is not clear that the court appointment of an expert has achieved any benefit; it has complicated rather than eliminated the "battle of the experts."

Whether or not the parties call their own experts, there are other factors that may diminish the appeal of court appointment. For one thing, in at least some contexts neutrality is an elusive concept at best. The expert comes to the case with her own views, perhaps with her own ax to grind. Even if she is not partial to one party or another, she may be a representative of one school of thought or another. The cloak of neutrality may shroud those leanings and give her unwarranted authority; arguably, it is better to keep matters out in the open, with her testimony sponsored by the party whom it favors.

Indeed, the institution of court-appointed experts fits uneasily in our adversarial system. If the court appoints an expert, it presumably expects to put heavy reliance on her opinion. And in a system that is largely based on party control, the parties may be very uncomfortable at the prospect that the decision will essentially be made by an expert who makes up her own mind behind closed doors.

Furthermore, when courts appoint experts, they have a tendency to go to the same well time after time. That practice has some benefits; the court is familiar with its source of information. On the other hand, it also tends to exalt the professional establishment, perhaps too much. Recall that *Daubert*, almost as much as *Frye*, puts great weight on establishment views, but the establishment does not have a monopoly on truth. Indeed, scientific advances often are by nature challenges to established views. Mirjan Damaska, a distinguished comparative scholar, has noted

> growing concern about the role of the Continental court-appointed expert. Even at this juncture judges are often unable to understand his arcane findings. The fear is spreading that courts are covertly delegating decision-making powers to an outsider without political legitimacy.[61]

This cautionary word is not meant to deny that court appointment of experts can, in some circumstances, be an extremely useful tool. But in this area, there are no easy answers.

¶ **5.22:** Prof. Samuel Gross has tentatively made a proposal that would operate along the following lines: As a precondition to presenting testimony of its own expert, a party must ask the

---

[61]   Mirjan R. Damaska, *Evidence Law Adrift* 151 (1997).

court to appoint a neutral expert. If asked, the court must do so. But neutral experts are chosen for appointment by the parties themselves or their nominees. If the parties agree and the chosen expert is willing, the court usually should honor the choice. Otherwise, the parties may each submit a list of suitable experts. If any expert appears on all lists, the judge may appoint her. If not, the judge forms a selection committee by choosing one person from each list. That committee then picks the expert for court appointment. At the conclusion of the case, the fees and expenses of the court-appointed expert may be charged as costs to the losing side—except that if the court-appointed expert is chosen by a selection committee, then those fees and expenses may only be charged to parties that submitted lists that did not include her name. *Expert Evidence*, 1991 Wis. L. Rev. 1113, 1227–29.

What advantages and disadvantages does this plan have? Should it be adopted?

F. THE LAY-EXPERT DIVIDE

Having explored the topics of lay and expert opinion, we will now focus on the divide between them. We will ask two inter-related questions: What is the standard for determining whether a given opinion should be characterized as expert or as lay? And what, if anything, depends on the distinction?

Perhaps the distinction seems clear-cut at first. If for some reason the eating habits of Jack Morris are relevant, we ordinarily wouldn't say that a witness who testifies to her knowledge of them from long acquaintance is doing so as an expert. On the other hand, if it is the habits of the Maori with which she's familiar, we would call her an expert. But notice that even if there are clear cases at one pole or another, there are fuzzy cases in the middle. Suppose the witness testifies from personal experience as to the eating habits of the McCoy clan. Is that expert testimony? Again, it may be that we should be thinking in terms not of a sharp binary lay-expert distinction but rather of a continuum.

The attractiveness of thinking about the matter that way may become more apparent if we consider the Advisory Committee's attempt to articulate the difference between lay and expert opinion. In its Note to the 2000 amendment to FRE 701, the Committee notes approvingly that "most courts have permitted the owner or officer of a business to testify to the value or projected profits of the business, without the necessity of qualifying the witness as an accountant, appraiser, or similar expert." "Such opinion testimony," the Committee adds, "is admitted not because of experience, training or specialized knowledge within the realm of an expert, but because of the particularized knowledge that the witness has by virtue of his or her position in the business." Does that help? The Committee appears to be drawing a rather mystifying distinction between "specialized knowledge" and "particularized knowledge": Recall that if an opinion depends on "specialized knowledge," then it may be appropriate for an expert to give under Rule 702—and the 2000 amendment to Rule 701 provides that it is not appropriate for a person other than an expert to give.

In an attempt to explain, the Committee says that a lay witness can testify that a substance appeared to be a narcotic, "so long as a foundation of familiarity with the substance is established," because this testimony "is based upon a layperson's personal knowledge" rather than upon "specialized knowledge within the scope of Rule 702." We might well wonder whether the type of knowledge on the basis of which a person can determine a substance to be a narcotic could be characterized as "specialized." By contrast, the Committee says, if the witness "were to describe how a narcotic was manufactured, or to describe the intricate workings of a narcotic distribution network, then the witness would have to qualify as an expert." Presumably this is so even if the witness's knowledge of these matters was based on personal experience and observation—but then what is the significance of that factor? Presumably a person can become an expert in a given (specialized? particularized?) field by making extensive observations of it over time.

The Advisory Committee seems to take another crack at the matter when it endorses the distinction drawn in *State v. Brown*, 836 S.W.2d 530, 549 (Tenn. 1992), that lay testimony "results from a process of reasoning familiar in everyday life," while expert testimony "results from a process of reasoning which can be mastered only by specialists in the field." That seems dubious. Is the expert testifying about narcotics manufacture really using a process of reasoning that can only be mastered by experts on the subject matter, or is it just that she has information that most people do not have?

An alternative approach endorsed by some commentators is to say that if the witness is testifying from the type of competence that most people have, she is giving a lay opinion, even if most people do not have the particular competence. Thus, a witness who says she recognizes her husband's voice on a recording is offering the type of opinion that most people can, though obviously most people would know other voices and not the husband's. Some courts and commentators would describe the wife in this case as a "skilled lay" witness.[62] But clearly there is a great deal of ambiguity in a standard that depends on the bounds of what is

---

[62]   *E.g.,* Cansler v. Mills, 765 N.E.2d 698 (Ind.App. 2002).

considered the same "type" of competence. And where does this analysis leave our business valuer? Certainly we cannot say that most people have competence at valuing a given type of business. Indeed, it seems dubious to say that most people have competence at valuing any business at all. Perhaps most people have some competence at valuing what they control; is that sufficiently narrow to be the same "type" of competence?

So the lay-expert distinction is not a simple one to draw. But what depends on the distinction? The courts articulate different standards for admissibility for lay and expert opinion. But it may have occurred to you that, though expressed in different language, the substantive standards are not all that dissimilar. We have seen that to be admissible a lay opinion must satisfy two principal requirements that cut in opposite directions: The opinion must be on a subject (1) with which the witness is familiar but (2) with which the jury is not (or at least not so familiar as the witness). We could say that a lay witness whose opinion satisfies these criteria has some expertise that is of value to the jury. And in fact, these two criteria express much of what a court should look for before allowing a witness to testify as an expert. The court may be more demanding the more expert-like the testimony appears, but that is a matter of degree and is compatible with the idea of a lay-expert continuum. And perhaps the determinative factor in deciding how much more demanding to be should not be whether the opinion is best characterized as lay or expert but how likely it is that the opinion will be difficult for the fact-finder to evaluate.[63]

¶ 5.23: *Brown* noted that a lay witness with experience could testify that a substance appeared to be blood, but that a witness would have to testify as an expert before testifying that bruising about the eyes is indicative of skull trauma. What would the proponent have to show before the witness could testify that

---

[63] The lay-expert distinction generates a difference not only in standards of admissibility but also in procedures. Perhaps such procedural incidents also should not depend on characterization of the testimony as expert but on standards geared to whether the incident is appropriate in the particular case. For example, only experts must file reports under Fed. R. Civ. P. 26(a)(2)(B). But it is not any expert who must file such a report, only one who is "retained or specially employed to provide expert testimony in the case or one whose duties as the party's employee regularly involve giving expert testimony." The court is much more likely to hold a hearing in the case of an expert opinion to determine whether the witness is competent to give the opinion. But here too the matter is one of degree; if the opponent objects to a witness's competence to offer a lay opinion, the court should hold whatever hearing it needs to rule on that matter as well before allowing the opinion. Perhaps the most significant procedural difference is that an expert witness cannot be compelled to testify and may be compensated at a negotiated rate for giving testimony. It is not clear that it is optimal to make these consequences depend on characterization of the testimony as expert; perhaps if the witness perceived events or conditions material to the case she should be subject to being compelled to testify to those matters and disallowed from negotiating compensation for that testimony, unless she perceived those events or conditions for the purpose of giving the testimony.

(a)   a substance was dog blood?

(b)   the area around a person's eyes bore a bruise indicative of a blow to that area?

In these cases should the expert be deemed to be testifying as a layperson or as an expert, or as something in between?

¶ 5.24: Would it be better for expert evidence to be submitted to the trial factfinder in writing, rather than presented orally the way most testimony is? (Continental courts usually secure the advice of experts in writing.) If you think it is important for the expert to appear in person at trial, would it be better if she answered questions only after the factfinder had read the written testimony?

¶ 5.25: You have temporarily been appointed Czar of the Universe. But you can't change human nature, economic reality, or the United States Constitution. What changes, if any, will you make in the American system for providing expert opinions in litigation?

CHAPTER 6

PRESENTING TESTIMONY

■ ■ ■

Now let us suppose that a witness is competent to give certain testimony and that the testimony would have substantial probative value with respect to a material proposition. The basic procedure for introducing testimony appears simple enough: The lawyer asks a question and the witness answers it.[1] The question must still clear several hurdles, however. Apart from the requirements studied later in this course—any necessary foundation must be supplied, and the question must not fall within any substantive exclusionary rule—the question must satisfy the two basic standards examined in this chapter: It must be in proper form, and it must be asked at the proper time in the trial.

A. NARRATIVE QUESTIONS

Additional Reading: McCormick, ch. 2, § 5; Mueller & Kirkpatrick, § 6.55

There is some appeal to the idea of calling a witness to the stand and saying to her, "Now, you know what this case is about. Please tell us whatever you know that bears on the dispute." Such a style of questioning would maximize our chances of getting fresh, unprompted testimony. It would tend to ensure that the fact that the matter is in litigation interferes as little as possible with the way in which the witness conveys the material information she has. And from the witness's point of view, this might be a particularly satisfying style of testimony, for she is able to tell her story in her own voice.

Nevertheless, this is not how witnesses usually testify in the common law tradition. The proponent will generally want some opportunity to prompt the witness's testimony to make sure the witness stays on track and doesn't forget anything important, and perhaps also to add a sense of pacing and drama to the testimony. But even if the proponent prefers the "Tell us what you know" approach, the court will probably resist it. It is not the function of the witness to decide what information the factfinder

---

[1] Actually, it is not quite so simple if the witness does not speak English. For a study of the problems that arise when testimony must be interpreted, see Susan Berk-Seligson, *The Bilingual Courtroom: Court Interpreters in the Judicial Process* (1990). On the problems created by a linguistic divide between lawyer and client, see Muneer I. Ahmad, *Interpreting Communities: Lawyering Across Language Difference*, 54 UCLA L. Rev. 999 (2007).

should hear; if evidentiary law is to be followed, the court must exercise control over the witness. And it is easier for the court to exercise such control—to make sure the testimony doesn't drift off into irrelevancies and doesn't sweep in inadmissible evidence—if the witness testifies in response to questions posed by counsel.

There is no hard-and-fast doctrine at work here, but rather common sense and judicial discretion. Some of counsel's questions may in fact be quite broad and call for the witness to relate a great deal of information. Even if the questioning calls for an extensive narrative response, courts generally allow it if it does not get out of hand; a witness who seems able to stay within bounds may get a good deal of leeway.

¶ 6.1: Your client Nina is a little-known choreographer who claims that the defendant Sun Dance Company, an equally little-known troupe, promised orally that if she created a full-length ballet that the company decided to use on a planned international tour it would pay her $5,000 plus 5% of the company's gross proceeds from any performance of the ballet, on the tour or afterward. Nina claims that she worked on the ballet for months, and that the company accepted it, with some revisions, but that the company denied ever agreeing to pay her more than the $5,000. As it happens, the ballet was a surprise success, and the company has continued performing it, to good reviews and before big crowds, since its return to the United States. Nina estimates that she is owed $50,000. Hence, she is suing. In an interview, Nina told you her story with some eloquence and considerable passion.

Pro: she can tell a good story

Con: might get led astray

(a) What advantages and disadvantages do you see in trying the "wind her up and let her go" method of interrogation?

(b) Suppose Nina is testifying at trial and you ask her, "Please tell us the story of your dealings with the Sun Dance Company." What should the court do? *Let her start. Interject if it gets out of hand.*

B. LEADING QUESTIONS

FRE 611(c), 614

Additional Reading: McCormick, ch. 2, §§ 6, 8; Mueller & Kirkpatrick, §§ 6.60–.61

The more usual objection to questions on direct examination is not that they give the witness too little direction but that they give too much—that is, that they are leading questions. We will focus on three basic questions: What are leading questions? When should a lawyer want to use them? When should they be disallowed?

1. WHAT ARE LEADING QUESTIONS?

The classic definition of a leading question is "one that suggests to the witness the answer desired by the examiner." McCormick, § 6. There is no bright line between the leading and the non-leading; indeed, "leadingness" is a matter of degree. We can see this by reformulating the definition slightly to say that a leading question is one that is in itself evidence to the witness of the answer desired by the questioner; the stronger evidence the question is, the more leading it is.[2] A question can be "evidence" of the desired answer if the witness says to herself, "I can see that she would likely ask me that question if she wanted answer X, but it is improbable that she would ask me the question if she wanted any other answer." Notice that this logic is really a form of the retrospective reasoning discussed in Chapter 3, in which a factfinder might say, "It's more likely that this evidence would turn up if the proposition at issue is correct than if it isn't, so the evidence makes the proposition more probable."

¶ 6.2: Consider whether, or to what extent, the following questions are leading:

(a) "How many times a year do rabbits have sex?" *open-ended*

(b) "Do rabbits have sex an average of 327 times per year?" *suggests an answer*

(c) [In the context of a Trivial Pursuits game] "How many times a year do penguins have sex?"

(d) "How many bottles, if any, were left in the six-pack?" *slight lead, suggests some left*

attorneys prob wouldn't object if it's only slightly suggestive

(e) "Were there several bottles left?"

(f) "Weren't there several bottles left?" *very leading*

(g) "Were there or weren't there several bottles left?" *open but confusing*

(h) "Was there more than one bottle left?"

(i) "Were there four bottles left?" *leading!*

LEAST leading: 1) Were there any bottles left? 2) How many?

2. WHEN WOULD A LAWYER WANT TO USE LEADING QUESTIONS?

As Nina's lawyer in ¶ 6.1, you wouldn't want to ask her leading questions, now would you? Why not? Nina is both cooperative and able, and her testimony will likely have maximum power if, for the most part, she is left to tell it with very little prompting. Leading a friendly witness like Nina may make it sound as if you were testifying rather than she,

---

[2] "Evidence" is being used here loosely, not in the technical sense of information presented to an adjudicative factfinder, but rather as information that tends to alter the probability of a proposition of interest.

and may therefore diminish not only the force of her testimony but also her credibility; it may appear that she is not testifying from her own memory but simply being cooperative with you and giving you the answers you want.

Sometimes, however, even with a friendly witness, you will want to ask some leading questions. You may want to get through preliminary materials quickly, or to direct the witness's attention to a new line of inquiry; or you may have a witness, such as a child, whose memory is faulty or who is so nervous that she needs some sort of prodding. In such cases you may be wise to use leading questions, and your opponent probably will not even object; if she does, the court will still probably allow you to lead the witness to some extent.

The chief use of leading questions, however, is to draw information out of hostile witnesses far more clearly and effectively than you are likely to be able to without such questions. With leading questions, you can state a factual proposition and ask the witness to confirm or reject it. Thus, affirmatively, you can get the witness to focus on the propositions that you want her to address; you minimize the wiggle room. And, negatively, you can prevent her from straying into areas that you would rather she not address, at least during your examination of her. Lawyers sometimes say that the ideal cross-examination is one in which the only possible answers are yes and no.

¶ 6.3: Farmer Smith sold a cow to Farmer Jones and is now suing for the unpaid balance of the purchase price. In his answer, Jones admitted that he did not make final payment. Jones contended, however, that the cow was barren, that Smith knew it to be barren, and that Smith fraudulently failed to disclose this fact, although he knew that Jones assumed the cow to be fertile. Smith has testified on direct that at the time of the sale he did not know the cow was barren. You represent Jones. Imagine a state of facts that seems to indicate that Smith did indeed know of the cow's condition, and prepare a series of questions designed to elicit this information from him on cross-examination.

3. WHEN SHOULD LEADING QUESTIONS BE DISALLOWED?

The discussion above suggests that sometimes a lawyer will find it advantageous to ask leading questions and sometimes not. The lawyer has a strong incentive to present the most persuasive possible evidence.

¶ 6.4: Given this, why should the court ever bar leading questions if that is the means that, under the particular circumstances, the lawyer deems best to present his case? Does it matter whether it is a jury or a bench trial? Need authentic voice, opp to judge credibility?

Traditionally, some courts operated on the premise that if you put the witness on the stand, she was your witness and (putting aside preliminary matters and the like) you should not be allowed to ask her leading questions. Sensibly, the Federal Rules of Evidence avoid such a dogmatic approach. Rule 611(c) states presumptive rules that leading questions are not allowed on direct examination, "except as may be necessary to develop the witness' testimony," and that they are allowed on cross. But these presumptions may be overcome.

It sometimes happens that a party finds it advantageous to put on the stand a witness whose interests are adverse to his own. In such a circumstance, leading questions on direct examination are very valuable, both to pry out of the witness information that she may be reluctant to surrender and to impeach her to the extent that she testifies unfavorably.[3] Rule 611(c) provides expressly that if a party calls to the stand "a hostile witness, an adverse party, or a witness identified with an adverse party," then direct examination may be conducted by leading questions, as if on cross-examination. Courts do not often meditate on what makes a witness hostile for purposes of this rule, but some factors entering into the determination are: the extent to which the testimony of the witness is unfavorable to the examining party; whether the witness has an interest in conflict with that of the examining party; whether the witness was likely to have cooperated with the examining party in preparing her testimony; whether the witness's testimony is less favorable to the examining party than might have been expected before she took the stand; and whether the witness's manner in answering questions indicates a lack of cooperativeness with the examining party. A witness may be deemed hostile to a party with respect to some matters but not with respect to others.

Correspondingly, if one party calls to the stand a witness identified with his adversary, the court might preclude that adversary's counsel from examining her by leading questions. Thus, the Advisory Committee said, in its Note to Fed. R. Evid. 611(c), "The purpose of the qualification 'ordinarily' is to furnish a basis for denying the use of leading questions when the cross-examination is cross-examination in form only and not in fact. . . ." But the matter is a discretionary one, and may depend in significant part on how favorable the testimony is to the adversary. A court that allows a party to ask leading questions of a friendly witness,

---

[3]   Rule 607, to be discussed below in Chapter 19, reverses the traditional law of many jurisdictions by allowing the party calling a witness to impeach the witness, without a preliminary showing of unusual factors, such as that the party has been surprised by the witness's testimony.

even though the examination is cross in name only, will not likely be reversed on that basis.[4] At least in this circumstance, pre-scripting of the testimony is made difficult by the fact that, immediately before the friendly lawyer examines the witness, the adversary will have had his turn.

¶ **6.5:** In ¶ 6.3, change the facts as follows: Jones paid in full, and he is the plaintiff, seeking to rescind the sale. In your case-in-chief, what witness will you want to call to the stand to prove Smith's state of mind at the time of the sale? Should you be allowed to ask leading questions? *Yes*

[margin: Smith's lawyer was also present... INL... Adverse party? Financial tie-/Self.]

¶ **6.6:** Green is on trial for distributing marijuana. Before trial, Porter, who was found in possession of marijuana, stated to a police officer that Green was his supplier. At trial, Porter is called to the stand by the prosecutor and testifies to his possession of marijuana. Asked by the prosecutor who his supplier was, Porter says, "I don't remember." May the prosecutor pursue the matter by asking leading questions? *Refresh collection instead?*

FRE 614(a) states a special rule for witnesses called by the court: All parties are entitled to cross-examine them, and the Advisory Committee Note makes clear that the right to cross-examine carries with it "all it implies," which at least ordinarily includes the right to ask leading questions. Even if the testimony of the court-called witness is favorable to a given party, that party does not control the witness, and there is no real concern that leading questions will help the lawyer hide from the court or the jury defects of the witness.

C. OTHER MATTERS OF FORM

Additional Reading: McCormick, § 7; Mueller & Kirkpatrick, §§ 6.56–.57

Other matters of form may make a question objectionable. Here are some of the more common ones.

1. ARGUMENTATIVE QUESTIONS

We expect our trials to be adversarial and confrontational. But it is not generally desirable for the lawyer to get into an argument with a hostile witness. Questions should ask simply for the facts, or for opinions that the witness is qualified to give. The witness should be protected from badgering by the lawyer. Also, to move things along expeditiously and to preserve decorum, most courts try to restrain lawyers from using the

---

[4] *See, e.g.,* Woods v. Lecureux, 110 F.3d 1215 (6th Cir. 1997); Morvant v. Construction Aggregates Corp., 570 F.2d 626 (6th Cir.), *cert. dismissed,* 439 U.S. 801 (1978).

examination of witnesses as an early opportunity to sum up their cases to the jury.

All these factors lead courts to hold some questions improper as being argumentative. Defining an argumentative question is not so simple. Basically, though, a question is argumentative if it is not asked in genuine hopes of getting an answer—perhaps because the witness is not competent to answer the question or because there is essentially no hope of getting an answer that will be favorable to the questioner—but rather because the question itself articulates propositions the questioner wants the factfinder to hear.

But once again, discretion is essential. A cross-examining party must be given considerable leeway to challenge the witness. And the cross-examiner is always entitled to hope that the witness, perhaps suddenly awakened to her obligation to testify truthfully or caught in the tightening coil of the cross-examiner's questions, will tell the truth (as the cross-examiner sees it), no matter how contrary to her own interests that might be. Your questioning will not often produce a transcript that culminates like this one:

Q: [W]ere you telling the truth then?

A: Then.

Q: So you're lying now.

A: All right. I'm lying.

But it happens occasionally,[5] and you are entitled to try. Indeed, one favorite type of question of some lawyers, when they feel they have caught the witness in a contradiction with a prior statement, is, "Are you lying now or were you lying then?" Courts often allow this kind of question.[6] And at least sometimes it must be proper, for if it is true that the witness must have been lying one time or the other the examiner is entitled to determine which one it is.[7] But if it is less clear that there is a contradiction, the statement might appear to be mere badgering.

---

[5] Annunziata v. Colasanti, 126 A.D.2d 75, 78, 512 N.Y.S.2d 381, 382 (N.Y. A.D. 1987).

[6] *E.g.,* Murdoch v. Castro, 489 F.3d 1063, 1071 (9th Cir. 2007) ("The concluding question on cross-examination of Dinardo seems obvious: 'Were you lying then or are you lying now?' "); U.S. v. Heaton 1996 WL 927703 (USN–MCCCA 1996) ("In light of these diametrically opposed and mutually inconsistent assertions, the next question likely to be raised by any competent litigator is, 'Were you lying then, or are you lying now?' "); Davidson v. Meier, 60 Ill.App.3d 386, 388, 17 Ill.Dec. 653, 655, 376 N.E.2d 799, 801–02 (Ill. App. 3 Dist. 1978) (harsh, but acceptable); *cf.* Smith v. Wainwright, 741 F.2d 1248, 1261–62 (11th Cir.1984) (trial court apparently disapproved of question in this form, but allowed inverted form, "Are you telling the truth now or when you testified to the police officers?"), *cert. denied,* 470 U.S. 1087, 1088 (1985).

[7] *Cf.* United States v. Bednar, 776 F.2d 236, 238 (8th Cir.1985) (per curiam) (*appellate court* declaring that witness must have been lying one time or the other).

¶ **6.7:** In the Smith-Jones case, ¶ 6.5, Farmer Smith testified at deposition that he "had no idea" when he sold the cow whether it was fertile. At trial, on direct, he has testified that he "believed the cow to be fertile" when he sold it. On cross, you confront him with his deposition testimony, and then ask, "Are you lying now or were you lying then?" Should this be allowed?

¶ **6.8:** Consider the following cases; in each, the court held the question improperly argumentative. Should it have done so?

(a) In a robbery case, the prosecutor asked the accused, "As a matter of fact, you drove the car that was parked outside the liquor store when he went in and stole some liquor; is that not a fact?" *See United States v. Cash,* 499 F.2d 26, 27 (9th Cir.1974).

(b) In a personal injury action, plaintiff's counsel asked an eyewitness who was a fellow employee of the plaintiff and who was testifying for the plaintiff, "Was there any other force of any kind, other than the suction created by the rapidly moving car, that would cause the rope to become entangled in the gearing of that car?" *See Johnson v. Wilmington City Ry. Co.,* 23 Del. 5, 76 A. 961 (1905).

(c) In a prosecution for mayhem, defense counsel asked a witness (apparently one for the prosecution), "Isn't it a fact that [defendant's] mouth is so small that he could not reach up and get it wide enough open to get [the complainant's] ear in there?" *See White v. State,* 22 Okla.Crim. 131, 210 P. 313 (1922).

2. QUESTIONS THAT ASSUME FACTS NOT IN EVIDENCE

A lawyer will sometimes ask a question that assumes, implicitly or explicitly, that a given factual proposition is true, even though a factfinder does not yet have any basis for inferring that predicate proposition. In some cases, such a question is problematic because it conveys to the jurors information that should be presented by evidence. Suppose, for example, a witness has testified, "I left for New York on Thursday." If counsel then asks, "When you flew to New York, how were you dressed?" the question would be objectionable as assuming a fact not yet in evidence. If the assumed fact is not important to the question, the opposing lawyer may not even object. But suppose that, perhaps out of caution, she does. Then the examining lawyer should probably at least rephrase the question without reference to that fact: "When you left for New York, how were you dressed?" And if the assumed fact is important, then counsel should first establish it: "When you left for New York, how did you go?" In some cases, the objection runs deeper than a matter of pure form, because the question would not even be relevant unless the predicate proposition is true.

Assumes:
1) married
2) cheated
3) stopped

¶ **6.9:** You want to ask a witness, "When did you stop cheating on your spouse?" What three facts does this question assume? Before you ask this question, what preliminary questions should you ask? What would be wrong with asking the "When did you stop . . . " question first?

3.   COMPOUND AND VAGUE QUESTIONS

Ideally, everyone involved—not only the questioning lawyer and the witness but also the opposing lawyer, the judge, the jury, and an appellate court—understands the questions asked by the lawyer. As you prepare your questions, it is crucial that you bear in mind how they, and the witness's answer, will be understood in court and how they will look on paper.

Sometimes, the potential danger of a vague question is mitigated by its open-endedness. In such a case, the witness's answer will stand on its own, even if it is not particularly responsive. Thus, if the lawyer asks, "Please tell us about your relationships with your colleagues," everybody in the courtroom might wonder just what it is that the lawyer wants to know, but whatever the witness answers will presumably be comprehensible on its own terms. The court might therefore rule, "If the witness understands the question, she may answer it." If the answer reveals that the witness did not understand the question, and did not give the lawyer the information she wanted, the lawyer can try again— assuming she has been listening carefully enough to be aware of the problem. This is not an ideal way of proceeding, of course, but the problem is relatively benign.

The more serious problem arises when the wording of the question creates a risk that the meaning of the answer will be unclear; this might arise because the question is vague or ambiguous, or because it is compound, rolling two or more questions into one. Here, the judge is more likely to intervene so that the jury and the courts, both trial and appellate, will understand what the witness has testified to. Sometimes, as the examining lawyer, you might not be all that unhappy with a certain amount of vagueness. You may feel that if your questions were sharper the limited nature of the answer might be clearer; if an affirmative answer to "Was it bigger than a breadbox?" is the best you can do—and if your adversary and the court let you get away with that—then you are better not trying to be more precise. But vagueness is more likely to hurt you than help you when you are trying to establish a proposition. Don't let sloppiness in your own questions result in testimony that will fail to give the jury the information you need to provide and that, when read by a reviewing court, will fail to support a verdict in your favor.

¶ **6.10:** What objections might be raised to these questions? Should they be sustained?

(a) "Was he driving safely or was he going over the speed limit?"

(b) "Please describe the intersection where the accident occurred."

4. "ASKED AND ANSWERED"

There is no hard-and-fast rule against asking a question a second time. Especially on cross-examination, you are allowed to press the witness. For example, if one of her answers sounds inconsistent with an earlier one, you can ask if she still adheres to her earlier testimony. Or you may ask a slightly different question to try to get as much precision as possible. But at some point the judge will say, "You've been through this enough, counselor. Move on."

¶ **6.11:** Be prepared to do the direct examination of Nina, from ¶ 6.1. Bear in mind that your presentation of her testimony will be much more effective if it is not cluttered by objections to improperly phrased questions.

D. A NOTE ON QUESTIONS AT DEPOSITION

Deposition questions need not be proper questions for trial; remember that the deposition has several purposes, only one of which is to produce a transcript that might be introduced at trial.[8] Indeed, if at the time of trial the witness is readily available to testify, the deposition transcript will likely be excluded as hearsay. *But see* Arizona R. Civ. P. 32(a) (generally allowing use of deposition transcripts at trial without a showing of unavailability). On the other hand, one of the purposes of a particular deposition, or of a particular portion of a deposition, may be to create or preserve evidence for trial; hence, even at deposition, you must be aware of the form of your questions and of your adversary's.

Bear in mind that there is ordinarily no judge or magistrate at deposition, and even if there were it would be premature for her to rule on the admissibility of evidence.[9] If a party states an objection to a question, the objection is made for the record, for later use at trial. But the witness

---

[8] *See* Chapter 12, discussing use of depositions at trial.

[9] The parties may recess the deposition to get a ruling from the judge or magistrate on the *discoverability* of some information—that is, on whether the questioning party is entitled to get an answer to his questions—but that, of course, is a much different matter from *admissibility* at trial.

answers the question, unless advised not to do so on limited grounds (such as that the question is privileged) by her lawyer.

Under Fed.R.Civ.P. 32(d)(3), and common practice in state courts, a rather sharp distinction is drawn between the treatment of objections to the form of a question and other objections. In rough terms, objections to the form are those that focus on how the question is phrased, such as its leading character; substantive objections focus on the content of the information given by the witness.

Under Fed.R.Civ.P. 32(d)(3)(B), objections to the form of a question must be made at deposition or they are waived; that is, if the deposition question and answer are otherwise admissible at trial, an objection to the form made for the first time then will not keep it out of evidence. Why not? Problems with the form of a question can be spotted at the time the objection is made, most often simply by listening to the question itself. And, because they are only problems with the form of the question, they can be fixed right then. It would be wasteful of information to allow an adverse party to sit back, knowing that the deposition question was in improper form, and then state the objection for the first time at trial, when it is too late to do anything about it.[10]

Thus, if your adversary is asking questions at deposition, it is important—if you think there is a chance she will want to use the transcript at trial—that you be alert to any problems of form and state any objections you wish to preserve. By the same token, if you are doing the questioning and your adversary states an objection to form, take care. If you are confident that the question is in good form, or you are sure you will not want to use this portion of the deposition at trial, proceed. But if you are less sure, and particularly if one of your purposes is to preserve the testimony of a favorable witness,[11] ascertain what the problem is and if necessary fix it on the spot. If you ignore the objection and later offer the transcript at trial, you will be sorely disappointed if the judge agrees with your adversary.

---

[10] For baseball fans, this may bring to mind the incident in which Billy Martin, manager of the New York Yankees, noticed that George Brett of the Kansas City Royals had too much pine tar on his bat, but did not raise an objection until after Brett had hit a home run. Overruling the umpires, the president of the American League ruled that the homer was valid; Martin's remedy, which he could have exercised before Brett swung, was to have the bat removed from the game. For extensive discussions of the jurisprudential implications of this episode, see the symposium, *The Jurisprudence of Pine Tar*, 5 Cardozo L. Rev. 409 et seq. (1984); Raymond Belliotti, *Billy Martin and Jurisprudence: Revisiting the Pine Tar Case*, 5 Alb. Gov't L. Rev. 210 (2012); Joseph Lukinsky, *Law in Education: A Reminiscence with Some Footnotes to Robert Cover's* Nomos and Narrative, 96 Yale L.J. 1836 (1987); Michael J. Yelnosky, *If You Write it (S)he Will Come: Judicial Opinions, Metaphors, Baseball, and "the Sex Stuff"*, 28 Conn. L. Rev. 813 (1996).

[11] You may be taking a deposition of a favorable witness because you believe she may be unavailable at trial. Or it may be that your adversary took her deposition and you are asking some "clean up" questions at the end.

More substantive objections, including those to the "competence" (which should be understood to mean admissibility) of testimony are generally preserved for trial "unless the ground for [the objection] might have been corrected" if raised at deposition. Fed.R.Civ.P. 32(d)(3)(A). Why? Substantive objections cannot always be spotted so easily. For example, it may not be clear at the time the question is asked whether the information it seeks will be relevant to a material issue at trial. Furthermore, if the answer would not be admissible there is usually is nothing the questioner can do about it at deposition. Thus, it is too much to ask the other party to pose substantive objections at deposition, and such objections will not do any good then anyway. Indeed, the Federal Rules actively discourage parties from littering depositions with premature objections.

¶ **6.12:** An objection that a question assumes a fact not in evidence would probably not be deemed waived if not made at deposition. Why? On the other hand, an objection that a question implicitly assumes the witness's belief in a fact as to which she has not yet testified might be considered a formal objection that would be deemed waived if not made at deposition. Why?

¶ **6.13:** On what grounds may a lawyer legitimately advise a witness not to answer a deposition question?

E. REFRESHING RECOLLECTION

FRE 612

Additional Reading: McCormick, ch. 2, § 9; Mueller & Kirkpatrick, §§ 6.66–.69

If your witness's memory fails, you may be allowed to ask leading questions—but then again, you may not be, and in any event you may be reluctant to. Even without leading questions, you may be able to jog the witness's memory by presenting her with some stimulus. There is no particular limit on what you can use for this function, which is akin to waving smelling salts in front of the witness. Anything (within reason) that does the trick of reawakening the witness's memory—including waving smelling salts in front of her—can in principle be used. Most often, though, the stimulus is not so exotic, but rather a document, such as notes previously taken by the witness or somebody else.

But if the notes have the information that you want the jury to learn, why not simply introduce them? Sometimes that is possible, but not always. As you will later understand in depth, depending on who wrote the notes, when, and why, they may pose a problem under the Confrontation Clause if they are offered against a criminal defendant, because introducing them may effectively allow a witness to testify in

.writing against an accused. Also, if the notes are offered to prove the truth of assertions made in them, they are hearsay; the notes cannot be cross-examined, because they are not a live witness testifying from the witness stand. In some cases, an exemption from the hearsay rule, such as the one for past recollection recorded; *see* FRE 803(5), may apply and allow the notes themselves to be made evidence.

But if a confrontation or hearsay problem remains, you cannot introduce them into evidence to prove what they assert; it is only the witness's ordinary live testimony, revived by the notes, that is admissible evidence. If the witness testifies that the document revives her memory, and so allows her to testify fully, then ordinarily she will be allowed to do so—whatever the origin of the document was, even if you wrote the notes yourself. But because the notes themselves have not been admitted into evidence, you will not be able to show them to the jury.

¶ **6.14:** You are representing McCoy, who has been accused of manslaughter. Ruskin is the chief prosecution witness against him. Her testimony contradicts statements she made in a conversation of which McCoy has procured a tape recording. The recording was made surreptitiously by a third person with an electronic eavesdropping device, in violation of the Federal Wiretap Act, 18 U.S.C.A. § 2510–2521 (1994), and the judge has ruled that the tape is inadmissible. You believe, however, that you may be allowed to use the tape to "refresh" Ruskin's memory. You want to get the maximum impact you can out of the tape, but you also want to act ethically. What should you do and say?

Sometimes, it is not the proponent but the other side that will want to show the document to the jurors, to convince them that, far from testifying from a freshly revived memory, the witness was simply reading a crib sheet. Thus, the adversary must be given an opportunity to cross-examine with the document, and, if he deems it helpful, to introduce the document into evidence. Note that Fed. R. Evid. 612 generally gives him the right to do this if the witness uses a writing to refresh her memory while testifying. If you refresh your witness's memory, you will want if at all possible to avoid giving your adversary the opportunity to create a transcript that looks approximately like this:

Q: Now, Ms. Witness, when you told my friend that you first learned of the impending marriage at 4:30 p.m. on January 24th, isn't it true that you were simply reading the note she scrawled after you had been unable to answer her prior questions on that point?

A: That is correct.

Q: And now I present to you Defendant's Exhibit 1 marked for identification. This is that note, correct?

A: Yes, it is.

Q: Thank you. Your honor, I ask that Defendant's Exhibit 1 be introduced into evidence and shown to the jury.

Whereupon Defendant's Exhibit 1 [a note bearing the inscription "4:30 on Jan. 24th, stupid!"] was admitted into the evidence and shown to the jury.

¶ 6.15: True story: One afternoon, a lawyer noticed that a witness put on the stand by the other side was paying a great deal of attention to his wrist during his testimony. On cross-examination, he asked why, and was gratified to get the answer that the witness had taken notes during a lunchtime conference with the witness's lawyers in preparation for his testimony. What could the cross-examining lawyer have done at this point? Would it have been more effective than what the lawyer did, which was simply to ask, "Have you written anything on any other parts of your body?"

The Advisory Committee would have provided that even if the witness has refreshed her recollection *before* she actually takes the witness stand by reviewing a writing, the other party has a right to have the document produced. The House Judiciary Committee softened this aspect of the Rule, so that if the witness refreshes her recollection using a document before testifying the court has discretion as to require production. The Committee expressed concern that required production of documents used before testifying "could result in fishing expeditions among a multitude of papers which a witness may have used in preparing for trial." The Committee further noted its intention that "nothing in the Rule be construed as barring the assertion of a privilege with respect to writings used by a witness to refresh his memory." The courts have *not* treated this comment as establishing a flat rule preserving the attorney-client privilege and the work-product protection to documents that the witness consults in preparing for her testimony. In fact, some courts have treated such consultation as creating an automatic waiver. Most courts, however, have treated the matter as one for balancing, weighing the opposing party's valid interest in seeing a document that the witness used to refresh her recollection before testifying against the proponent's interest in preserving the privilege and work-product protection. *E.g., Coryn Group II, LLC v. O.C. Seacrets, Inc.,* 265 F.R.D. 235 (D. Md. 2010); *Thomas v. Euro RSCG Life,* 264 F.R.D. 120 (S.D.N.Y. 2010). A court might be more likely to require production if the witness relied on the document heavily, if she examined it shortly before testifying, if she is testifying as an expert, if parts of the document have already been disclosed, if there is some basis for believing that evidence has been concealed, or if the document was prepared for the specific purpose of preparing her for testimony. The court might be more likely to protect the document if the witness appears to have had a great need to refresh her memory or if the document reveals thought processes of the lawyer. These factors are by no means exclusive.[12] In light of the conflicting and legitimate interests at stake, the balance to be drawn by the court is often difficult and delicate.

¶ **6.16:** After being fired from her job, Packard hired a lawyer to pursue discrimination and other charges. Shortly afterwards, she wrote a long letter to the lawyer, laying out the factual basis for her complaint. The letter was based in part on numerous documents, some of which Packard later misplaced and eventually lost. The lawyer did not act immediately, and two months later, when she began to draft an affidavit for Packard to sign in conjunction with a proceeding before the Equal Employment Opportunity Commission (EEOC), she and Packard sat down together to review the case. They used the letter as the basis for this conversation. A year later the EEOC proceeding was concluded. Dissatisfied with the outcome, Packard fired her lawyer and hired another, who brought a Title VII action in her behalf. Packard reviewed the letter with the new lawyer before he drafted the complaint, again two days before she gave a deposition, and again one week before she testified at trial. Examining the letter *in camera*, the court concludes that it is much more detailed, and in some cases less favorable to Packard's case, than is her testimony. Should the court grant the employer's motion that Packard be ordered to produce the letter to it? *Cf.* Woodward v. Avondale Industries, Inc., 82 Fair Empl. Prac. Cas. (BNA) 1345, 2000 WL 385513 (E.D.Pa.) (opinion of Magistrate J.) (ruling that plaintiff there "waived any attorney-client privilege by relying extensively on the statement to prepare her EEOC affidavit").

[handwritten margin note: ½ - No! used to prep, not during trial. Attorney client-privilege weighs heavily in keeping this out]

By its terms, FRE 612 applies only to writings. Just what the scope of a writing is for purposes of the Rule is uncertain.[13] But it should not matter, because the principle—that the adverse party must have a chance to inspect the stimulus, cross-examine it, and if he wishes introduce it to show the witness's reliance on it—should apply whether the stimulus is documentary or not.

---

[12] *See generally, e.g.,* Woodward v. Avondale Industries, Inc., 82 Fair Empl. Prac. Cas. (BNA) 1345, 2000 WL 385513 (E.D.Pa.2000) (opinion of Magistrate J.); Nutramax Laboratories, Inc. v. Twin Laboratories, Inc., 183 F.R.D. 458 (D.Md. 1998) (opinion of Magistrate J.).

[13] Compare the comprehensive joint definition of writings and recordings in Rule 1001(1) for purposes of the so-called "best evidence" rule, discussed in Section D of Ch. 7.

F. CROSS-EXAMINATION

FRE 611(a)–(b)

Additional Reading: McCormick, ch. 4, §§ 19–27, 29–31; Mueller & Kirkpatrick, §§ 6.62–.65

1. THE IMPORTANCE OF CROSS; CONSEQUENCES OF ITS DENIAL

Cross-examination is a fundamental part of our trial system. Wigmore called cross-examination "beyond any doubt the greatest legal engine ever invented for the discovery of truth." 5 John Henry Wigmore, *Evidence* § 1367, at 32 (Chadbourn rev. 1974). That may be in some doubt. Certainly sometimes cross-examination leads toward the truth, exposing flaws in a witness's testimony that may not have been apparent before. On the other hand, in some circumstances cross might obstruct the truth-determination process, flustering a truthful witness and making her appear suspicious. Indeed, many trial lawyers will tell you that they regard it as their obligation to try to raise doubt about the testimony of a witness even if they are confident that the witness is telling the truth. Moreover, the threat of cross may intimidate a truthful witness from taking the stand in the first place, if she has any choice in the matter.

In the end, the most important justification for cross-examination may not be that it helps lead the adjudicative system toward the truth. It may be, rather, that unless a party, especially a criminal defendant, has had an opportunity to cross-examine the witnesses against him we cannot say with confidence that he has had an adequate opportunity to test—to try—the evidence. As we shall see later, the opportunity to cross-examine is now considered an essential aspect, perhaps the most essential aspect, of the criminal defendant's right to be confronted with the witnesses against him. And the rule against hearsay is based in large part on the perceived inadequacy of out-of-court statements; it may be that, if the problem were characterized not as the presumptive *unreliability* of statements that had not been cross-examined, but on the impropriety of using *testimonial* statements as to which the adversary did not have an adequate opportunity for cross-examination, the law of hearsay would be in much better shape than it is.

In any event, the right to cross-examine an opposing witness is so fundamental that if for some reason a party does not have this opportunity after the witness has testified on direct, it may be necessary to strike the direct testimony, or even to declare a mistrial. *See Commonwealth v. Kirouac*, 405 Mass. 557, 562 & n. 5, 542 N.E.2d 270, 273 & n. 5 (1989) (collecting authorities).

What to do in this situation is a complicated issue, depending on various factors:

Has the denial of the opportunity to cross-examine been total, or only partial? For example, it may be that a witness answers some questions and then refuses to answers others, or that she becomes ill or dies part way through the cross-examination. In such a case, it may be that no remedy is necessary; indeed, in some circumstances the witness's refusal to answer a question will give the cross-examining party about all he could have hoped for.

Is the problem temporary or permanent? If it is only temporary, then perhaps a continuance of the trial will solve the problem.

Did either party cause the witness's unavailability for cross? If the proponent of the witness's testimony did, then the testimony will almost certainly be struck; correspondingly, if the opponent did, then the direct testimony will almost certainly be allowed to stand.

What is the nature of the witness's unavailability for cross? If it is the witness's own refusal to answer questions, or her voluntary disappearance, the court will be more inclined to strike the testimony— even if the witness is a criminal defendant—or, if necessary, declare a mistrial. If it is apparent illness, the court might be suspicious. If it is death, the court might be more inclined to let the direct testimony stand—but that depends a great deal on the following factors.

Who is the party that has been denied the ability to cross? If the party is a criminal defendant, then the court will be far more inclined to hold that, at a minimum, the testimony must be struck. Even McCormick, who is inclined not to view the loss of opportunity for cross as fatal to the testimony, acknowledges that in this situation striking may be required by the defendant's rights under the Confrontation Clause of the Sixth Amendment to the Constitution, or by the comparable provisions of state constitutions. McCormick, § 19.

How significant, and how disputable, is the testimony? If the testimony seemed subject to reasonable dispute, so that cross might likely have been effective, the court will be more likely to strike it at least. If it was important to the case, the court will be more likely either to strike it or to declare a mistrial.

¶ **6.17:** Douglas Kirouac is on trial for indecent assault and battery of his daughter Valerie. She was 4 years old when she first described the acts allegedly perpetrated by Kirouac, and is 6 at the time of trial. Valerie's mother and other witnesses have testified to conversations they had in which Valerie described various acts of sexual assault; during a lengthy videotaped interview with a female state trooper, Valerie described, in childish language and with the help of an anatomically correct doll, conduct amounting to rape. At trial, Valerie is called to the stand by the prosecution. She testifies reluctantly, but she does say that "Dougie" had touched her on her "tookie." She then announces that she is tired, and soon after court is adjourned for the day. The next day, she testifies again. The prosecutor fails to obtain any further inculpatory testimony. Here is a sadly representative portion of the cross-examination:

Q: Valerie, do you remember yesterday you talked about some things that happened to you? Do you remember that?

A: No.

Q: You don't remember that?

A: (Witness shaking head)

Q: Do you remember talking about Dougie at all?

A: (Witness shaking head)

Q: Is that 'No'?

A: I forgot.

Q: Is that 'No' or 'Yes'?

A: No.

Q: You didn't talk about Dougie?

A: I'm tired. I wish I could go to my nanny's. * * *

Q: You don't remember talking about that at all, Valerie?

A: I'm trying to get this.

Q: You're trying to take your panda's jacket off?

A: Yeah, because he's hot.

Q: He's hot, yeah.

[VICTIM-WITNESS ASSISTANT]: I don't think it comes off.

A: Yes, it does. It came off in my bed yesterday.

[VICTIM-WITNESS ASSISTANT]: You have to answer [defense counsel's] questions, then we can take care of panda. * * *

A: I want my nanna. I got two quarters.

Q: Do you want some more water, Valerie?

A: It spilled on the floor.

Q: That's okay. Do you remember yesterday when you talked about Dougie, Valerie?

A: No.

Q: You don't remember that?

A: No.

Q: Do you remember talking about something that happened to you, Valerie?

A: I want to go to nanny's.

Q: Valerie, you're tired?

A: (Witness nodding).

* * *

(a) Is the defense entitled to any remedy? *Try again. Want to ask about "rookie"? Δ will argue this isn't sufficient*

(b) Assume that the defense has made all appropriate motions, that the court has denied them all, and that Kirouac has been convicted. What should the appellate court do? *See* *Kirouac, supra.* *Wh... did have a chance... mistrial — can't unhear what kid said! and it's a criminal case*

2. THE SCOPE AND CONDUCT OF CROSS

There is a long-standing controversy over the proper scope of cross-examination. Many jurisdictions follow some form of a restrictive rule in which cross-examination is limited to the subject matter of the direct examination. Other jurisdictions follow a "wide open" rule that allows the cross-examiner to ask any question that is proper in the case, whether or not it relates to the subject matter of the direct. Sometimes the difference between these approaches determines whether the cross-examining party can, or will, examine the witness at all with respect to certain matters; sometimes it determines whether leading questions are allowed; and sometimes it determines only the timing of questions.

For three reasons, the difference between these approaches may be less crucial than might appear. First, courts following a restrictive approach usually tend to view the scope of the direct rather broadly. The cross-examiner is entitled to explore all inferences that might be drawn from the direct testimony.

Second, even under the restrictive view, matters affecting the credibility of the witness are deemed a proper subject of cross, whether they otherwise bear on the subject matter of the direct testimony or not. Indeed, some questions are proper because they test the witness's credibility even if they have no other relation to the subject matter of the lawsuit. As you will come to appreciate in studying Chapter 19, a good deal of evidentiary law is concerned with the issue of what kind of credibility-attacking evidence, presented on cross-examination or otherwise, is permissible.

Third, even under the restrictive view, a court may in some circumstances allow the cross-examining party to ask questions that go beyond the scope of direct by "making the witness his own." Assume for the moment that, if cross is restricted, the cross-examining party could later recall the witness to the stand as his own witness. As a matter of convenience, the court might allow the cross-examiner to avoid this step, with the proviso that when his questioning goes beyond the bounds of the direct examination he must conduct the examination *as if* he had put the witness on the stand and were now conducting her direct examination.

Note that this variation of the restrictive approach is the position adopted—after considerable debate in the drafting process—by Fed. R. Evid. 611(b). (Many states that have adopted codifications modeled on the Federal Rules, however, have taken other positions, more or less rigid, on this matter.) The proviso in Rule 611(b) that the additional inquiry must be conducted "as if on direct examination" means that ordinarily the examiner must avoid leading questions. But recall that the court has discretion to allow leading questions on direct if the witness is a hostile one.[14] If the court favors the cross-examiner with a double dose of discretion—"All right, I'll let you go now beyond the scope of the direct, and what's more I'll let you treat this witness as a hostile one, so you can continue to ask leading questions"—then the court has, for this examination, effectively re-created the wide-open approach.

But now let's consider what happens if the court does say, "No you can't ask that now. It goes beyond the scope of the direct."

¶ 6.18: McLaughlin is on trial for bank fraud and for conspiracy to commit bank fraud with Bruce and Wood. The Government offers evidence that the three conspired to defraud the Bank of New England. McLaughlin sought a loan from the bank, supposedly for the purchase of a Caterpillar from Bruce, and as collateral he offered that Caterpillar and another that he supposedly owned; for proof of ownership, he presented serial numbers that had been supplied to him by Wood. Part of the Government's case is presented through the testimony of a customs agent and an FBI agent who participated in the investigation of the case. McLaughlin's principal defense theory is that he was the innocent dupe of Bruce and Wood, who had used a similar scam to defraud the Bank of Marlborough.

---

[14] *See, e.g.,* MDU Resources Group v. W.R. Grace & Co., 14 F.3d 1274, 1282 (8th Cir.1994) (tort defendant should not be allowed to attempt to establish statute-of-limitations defense by leading questions of plaintiff's witness, unless the witness' testimony bears significantly on the limitations issue or defendant can sufficiently demonstrate that the witness is hostile).

McLaughlin seeks to cross-examine the agents about the Bank of Marlborough incident, which they did not mention in their direct. Should he be allowed to do this? *See United States v. McLaughlin*, 957 F.2d 12 (1st Cir.1992) (holding that questioning would exceed scope of direct). *Seems relevant. Should use discretion to allow. Most federal judges will allow it.*

If the court does bar the cross as going beyond the scope of direct, what are the consequences? First, assume that the cross-examiner *could* later put the witness on the stand as part of his own case. Then the restrictive approach will at least have the consequence of delaying the additional questioning; it may also prevent the additional questioning from being conducted by leading questions. As a practical matter, moreover, the party might say, *More efficient than calling the witness back again for the A*

> I would have been glad to ask her these questions as part of my cross-examination, particularly because I was delaying my adversary's presentation of his case. If I hadn't gotten anything useful out of the witness on this point, I would have made a brave face and just sat down; the jury might never have noticed the fuzzy line where I went beyond the scope of direct. But if I have to do it as part of my own case, it's not worth the trouble. If I don't get anything useful out of the witness, I'm going to have egg all over my face, because the jury is going to wonder why I bothered to call her back to the stand.

As this discussion may suggest, the choice in this context between the wide-open and restrictive systems is a close one. The wide-open system has the virtues of simplicity and of allowing free-wheeling cross-examination. On the other hand, we must recognize that cross-examination is an obstruction to the proponent's ability to present his side of the case. It is an obstruction that we encourage so long as the adversary is staying on the subject matter that the proponent presented. But arguably we should tell the adversary that, if he wants to raise subject matters that the proponent did not, he should do it on his own time. As in so many areas of evidence law, this is an area best treated by discretionary judgment rather than by rigid rules.

Now consider the possibility that, if the adversary is not allowed to ask a set of questions on cross-examination, he will *not* be able to bring her to the witness stand later. Occasionally the problem might be one of practicality—the witness might be about to leave the jurisdiction, for example—and if so the adversary might be able to take her testimony immediately by deposition. But the far more frequent problem arises when the adversary is not entitled to take the witness's testimony, and this problem arises most often when the witness is a criminal defendant: If the prosecutor is not allowed to ask a set of questions as part of a cross-examination, she will be foreclosed altogether from doing so. In this setting, dicta by the Supreme Court suggest, in effect, that the Self-Incrimination Clause of the Fifth Amendment to the Constitution may impose the restrictive rule on the scope of cross-examination. The defendant has a right not to be compelled to testify. If he does testify, he must answer questions on cross-examination, but arguably he waives his privilege only "with respect to the testimony he gives," *Harrison v. United States*, 392 U.S. 219, 222 (1968);[15] by the scope of his testimony on direct he "determines the area of disclosure and therefore of inquiry" and he opens himself to cross-examination "on the matters relevantly raised by that testimony," *Brown v. United States*, 356 U.S. 148, 155 (1958). The matter has not been definitively resolved, however.

¶ **6.19:** Jackson is on trial for armed robbery. He made a videotaped statement at the local sheriff's office admitting to participation in the crime. At a pretrial hearing, in support of a motion to suppress the taped statement, Jackson testified that it was not voluntary. The court denied his motion, and the statement was admitted as part of the prosecution's case at trial. State law provides that a defendant "may testify in support of a motion to suppress without being subject to examination on other matters," but that "[i]f the defendant testifies before the jury at the trial on the merits, he can be cross-examined on the whole case." Jackson seeks to testify at the trial only on the voluntariness of the statement, and to bar cross-examination about other aspects of the case. What result?[16] *Crossed on whole case!*

Prosecution can't call the ∆, so have to be able to cross on it.

G. REDIRECT AND SUBSEQUENT EXAMINATIONS

Additional Reading: McCormick, ch. 4, § 32

Redirect and subsequent examinations do not offer second and third bites at the apple; rather, they offer an opportunity to inquire into matters that were opened up on the prior examination. Thus, for redirect the general requirement is that the questioner must be addressing new matters raised on cross. Roughly speaking, then, you must not ask for a repetition of the testimony given on direct, but you cannot be raising a new matter, and your adversary must have asked about it on cross. The range of allowable questions continues to narrow in like fashion through re-cross and any later examinations; usually these examinations are very brief, if they are allowed and occur at all.

---

[15] *Cf.* Kansas v. Cheever, 134 S.Ct. 596, 601 (2013) ("when a defendant chooses to testify in a criminal case, the Fifth Amendment does not allow him to refuse to answer related questions on cross-examination").

[16] *See* State v. Jackson, 523 So.2d 251 (La.Ct.App.), *cert. denied*, 530 So.2d 565 (La.1988) (adhering to view that the state law is constitutional).

If a court is overly restrictive in its conception of the proper scope of redirect, it will exclude valuable evidence that might have helped to explain, clarify, qualify, or avoid testimony given on cross. It may also make lawyers feel that they have to cover everything in great detail on direct, lest they miss something and not be able to cover it later. The lawyer examining on direct may not know just where the attack on cross-examination will come, and it is reasonable enough for her to have enough flexibility that, even if she covers a matter quickly or vaguely on direct, she will have a chance to address it in more depth if it is a focus of cross. Moreover, prejudice to the adversary from the direct examiner's return to a matter can usually be avoided by use of re-cross. On the other hand, if the court is excessively lenient, the trial could become ragtag. Parties might use redirect to cover soft spots they left by sloppiness or failure to prepare. The adversary may be blindsided, not knowing how to present cross because she thinks the proponent has presented on direct all she has to offer from the witness. Perhaps moderate lenience, recognizing the difficulties facing the trial lawyer, is the soundest approach. Most lawyers already have strong incentive to present a good but reasonably compact direct, and additional pressure from the court might be counterproductive.

¶ 6.20: Keesser died of injuries suffered in a fight at a birthday party, and Holder, 16 years old at the time of the incident, is on trial for killing him. The Medical Examiner testifies as part of the prosecution case, and during this testimony Holder reacts with visible emotional distress. Holder testifies in his defense, denying guilt, and is then cross-examined. The defense then seeks on redirect to have Holder testify as to why he was grieved by Keesser's death; this testimony, his counsel says, is necessary to dispel any conclusion that his manifest distress reflected a consciousness of guilt. If the prosecution objects, how should the court rule? Assuming the court sustains the objection and Holder is convicted and appeals from the court's ruling, what should the result be on appeal?[17]

Redirect is potentially extremely useful, in helping to undo some of the damage caused by cross. But it also is potentially very dangerous. On direct, assuming you are well prepared, you should not be surprised by your witness's testimony. When you cross-examine an opposing witness, you may get some unpleasant surprises, but, after all, she is an opposing witness; the jury will not expect her testimony to please you, and a good poker face may help cover the extent of your displeasure. On redirect,

---

[17] *See* Holder v. State, 692 A.2d 882, 887 (Del.1997)(upholding exclusion of evidence, which was beyond scope of cross and could have been presented on direct).

though, it is your witness and you may be shooting blind—unless you are very well prepared.

¶ 6.21: Recall ¶ 5.8, in which you presented the testimony of Dr. Klempay, an expert on rape trauma syndrome, as part of a rape prosecution. Assume that she has been allowed to explain the syndrome and to testify that, in her opinion, the symptoms exhibited by the complainant form a classic case of RTS. On cross, defense counsel asks, "Are there any possible causes of RTS other than rape?" Dr. Klempay responds, "Well, yes, there are." On redirect you rise and smugly ask, "Dr. Klempay, is it plausible that one of those other causes could account for the symptoms in this case?" According to Murphy's law, what response will she necessarily give? Into what hole shall you then crawl? What could you have done to avoid this result?

Don't ask unless you know (have practiced).

Just waive re-direct.

Or, you mentioned other ... what is your opinion about most likely cause of RTS?

CHAPTER 7

PRESENTING OTHER FORMS OF EVIDENCE

■ ■ ■

A. REAL, DEMONSTRATIVE AND EXPERIMENTAL EVIDENCE

Additional Reading: McCormick, ch. 21; Mueller & Kirkpatrick, §§ 9.32–.37

Not all evidence is testimony. Frequently you may want to present tangible evidence—documents, photographs, pistols, and so forth. In addition, you may want to present evidence that is neither testimony nor in tangible form; you may, for example, want the jurors to view a demonstration of how a machine works, or see what difficulty a personal injury plaintiff has in raising her arm. Often you will find that non-testimonial evidence is more attention-grabbing, memorable, and generally effective than the droning of a witness. If nothing else, it provides a little bit of variety, which can be important. (Even law students perk up at audio-visual aids; we law teachers console ourselves with the thought that if we used such aids all the time you would get tired of them and beg to hear us talk more.)

There is no limit to the types of evidence you may present. You must, of course, satisfy the judge that the evidence has sufficient probative value to warrant admissibility in light of the time it will take to present and any dangers of prejudice or confusion that it creates. And you must also satisfy the procedural requirements discussed in this chapter.

The term *demonstrative* evidence is sometimes used to include pretty much all evidence other than a witness testifying live in court. But the term is often used in a narrower sense, to distinguish it from *real* evidence. This discussion will use that narrower sense of "demonstrative," employing it in contradistinction to "real." And indeed, we will also distinguish out a third sort of evidence that is not in-court testimony, *experimental* evidence.

Let's start by focusing on the distinction between real and demonstrative evidence. An item of real evidence, in this usage, is one that assertedly played a role in the story of the event being litigated. The obvious, frequently used, example is a murder weapon. Thus, if a witness says that *this* particular gun, People's Exhibit 3, is the very gun that Blivet used to shoot Blodgett, then the gun is real evidence. If the witness merely says that the exhibit resembles the gun used in the shooting, or is of the same type, then it is demonstrative evidence; this particular item has no special connection to the case but is useful to help the witness demonstrate her testimony.

To be considered real evidence, an item need not have been one of the causes of the litigated event; it may, indeed, have been created by that event. Suppose that the prosecution contends that Blivet's bullet, after passing through Blodgett's body, also passed through the back of the chair in which Blodgett was sitting. The chair would be real evidence as well. Plainly, it did not cause Blodgett's misfortune, but it is part of the story. The hole in the chair is, in the prosecution's view, a trace left by the episode, and perhaps an aid in reconstructing it. In the same way, skid marks on a road would be real evidence that might help reconstruct an auto accident.

The distinction between real and demonstrative evidence is helpful in some circumstances in determining what the proponent must show about the evidence as a foundation for its admission. Suppose the prosecution wants to show the jury a photograph of Blodgett sprawled across his chair. One way is to present the testimony of the photographer, or someone else who can say how the photograph came to be. Such a witness does not even need to remember what the scene looked like. The photograph itself is a *silent witness* of the events. That is, it is real evidence, the result of light reflecting off Blodgett—the very Blodgett who is the victim in this case—his clothing, his blood, and so forth, into a small darkened chamber and then onto either (a) a sheet or roll of a flexible cellulose material that is covered with a substance sensitive to light and is then subjected to a series of chemical processes that yields an image, or (b) a collection of thousands of tiny light-sensitive diodes that convert photons into electrons, each of which creates an electrical charge that records the intensity of one color of light at a given site, this data then being reassembled by computer software to create an image.[1]

Now suppose that the witness is Wooten, who had nothing to do with the creation of the photograph, but who remembers the incident vividly. Wooten could testify, "Instead of trying to tell you what it looked like in a thousand words or so, let me draw you a picture. Here, I'll start with my red crayon." This evidence is clearly demonstrative, a *pictorial aid to testimony*. But if Wooten lacks the artistry to draw an accurate picture, she could take one drawn by the prosecutor, saying, "Yes, that's just what it looked like." (Note that presenting the picture to the witness and asking whether it looks like the scene is in a sense a very leading

---

[1] *See generally* Andrea Roth, *Machine Testimony* (forthcoming) (distinguishing among evidentiary uses of machines as tools, as silent witnesses, and as "declarants"; in the latter capacity, they make "explicit assertions about events perceived by them, in the form of symbolic output readable to human observers").

question, but given the extent to which this technique can aid testimony courts do not usually worry about this problem.) And if the prosecutor has a photograph of the scene, Wooten can say the same thing about that. Note that the witness does not have to testify to how the prosecutor's drawing or photograph came to be; all she has to be able to say is that the evidence is a "fair and accurate representation" of what she saw. Indeed, if the photo isn't really one of Blodgett, but of a mannequin dressed to look like him, that would be all right, too—so long as Wooten testifies that the scene looked like the photo in material respects. Of course, if the jury sees a photo described as a fair representation of the scene, it will assume that it is seeing a photo of the scene, even though that is not what the testimony is; perhaps this is the reason that some old-fashioned courts have purported to allow only a limited role to evidence admitted under this "pictorial testimony" theory.[2]

¶ 7.1: You are prosecuting Donohue for theft of cash from an automatic teller machine. There were no witnesses to the theft—human witnesses, that is. You want to introduce a series of photographs taken by an automatic camera that shows someone looking like Donohue breaking into the machine. What preliminary evidence must you offer to introduce the photos?

¶ 7.2: You are trying a case involving an auto accident that occurred at a complicated intersection. Wisely, you use a map to help your presentation. You ask a witness, "Is this a fair and accurate representation of Washington Circle?" and your leadable witness answers, "Yes, it is." Your smirking adversary objects to admission of the map, saying,

> There's been no foundation laid that the witness had anything to do with the creation of this map. Moreover, this obviously isn't an accurate representation of Washington Circle. The Circle is three-dimensional, and tangible; it's not just lines drawn on a sheet of paper. And that's significant here, because a question here is whether the buildings blocked the sun at the time of the accident.

How do you respond?

Now let's focus on experimental evidence. As we are using the term, experimental evidence subjects a person or thing—which may be the person or thing actually involved in the litigated dispute or may be a reasonably close surrogate—to a given stimulus, in expectation of yielding a given type of response. If you give the accused a glove and ask him to

---

[2] For an interesting discussion of the history of the treatment of photographic evidence, see Jennifer Mnookin, *The Image of Truth: Photographic Evidence and the Power of Analogy*, 10 Yale J. L. & Hums. 1 (1998).

try it on, in the hope of showing that it fits, that is a form of experimental evidence. (Beware: It might not fit, in which case the jury may well acquit.) If Atticus suddenly throws a ball at Tom, who catches it with his right hand, and asks Bob to sign his name, which Bob does with his left hand, then Atticus has effectively used experimental evidence to increase the relative probability that Bob rather than Tom hit Mayella on the right side of her face. Now notice the nature of this experiment. Atticus has not asked Tom or Bob to hit Mayella, or anybody else. But the experiment nevertheless has value *if* asking each to perform a designated task sufficiently recreates the two hypothesized versions of reality—Tom or Bob motivated to hit Mayella—that it yields probative evidence that Tom would have used his right hand and Bob would have used his left.

¶ **7.3:** Taylor was driving Otte in Taylor's auto when they got into an accident. Otte is now suing Taylor, and alleges that Taylor was under the influence of two Nembutal tablets that he had taken shortly before the accident. Taylor puts on the stand a physician who testifies that the pills would not likely make a driver drowsy within an hour and who takes two Nembutals himself, testifying an hour later that he is not drowsy.

(a) Should this experiment be allowed?[3] No'. unfair-prejudice? Not specific to Taylor actually

(b) Assuming the experiment is allowed, and that during maybe you the physician's testimony a bottle of Nembutals was admitted can. with into evidence, should the bottle be sent to the jury room during its deliberations? If so, with what instructions? No... don't ingest!

Let's distinguish now between *animations* and *simulations*. Animations are motion pictures designed to recreate how an event occurred. They are a form of demonstrative evidence: A witness can testify, "It happened this way," and use the animation, rather than just words or still pictures or a combination of the two, to illustrate how. Simulations, by contrast, are a form of experimental evidence; they try to prove that, given certain assumptions about a situation, a given set of consequences would follow. Here is a general description of how a computerized simulation of a vehicle accident may be created:

First, variable sets representing the coordinates of objects present at the scene are inputted. Next, the information is processed and synthesized to calculate the motion of each object involved in the incident. Finally, the information inputted yields

---

[3] *See* Otte v. Taylor, 180 Neb. 795, 146 N.W.2d 78 (1966) (no abuse of discretion to allow evidence).

output in the form of a visual presentation that conforms to the laws of science and physics.[4]

And here is a more particular description of how a simulation of an aircraft accident might be created:

> The computer is programmed with aircraft velocity, heading and rates of climb or descent or, conversely, the entering of known physical locations and times from which the computer will determine the aircraft velocity, heading, and rate of climb or descent. The computer program already has built into it all of the physics associated with banks and turns so that if a bank angle is specified the computer determines the rate of turn and the turn radius, or, conversely, the entering of aircraft headings at known times from which the computer computes the bank angle, rate of turn and turn radius.... [W]hile the laws of science provide the rules by which the evidence of the specific incident must abide, the computer provides the best fit within these rules for the complex data handed to it.[5]

¶ **7.4:** If you are the trial judge and a simulation of an aircraft accident prepared along the lines suggested above is offered, what information would you want before deciding whether it should be admitted? If you are the opposing attorney, what lines of cross-examination might you consider?

[handwritten margin notes: "who made it?", "How reliable?", "Daubert like", "Daubert factors", "other options", "Reliability"]

B. THE PROCEDURE FOR OFFERING EXHIBITS; THE AUTHENTICATION REQUIREMENT

FRE 901—903

Additional Reading: McCormick, ch. 22; Mueller & Kirkpatrick, §§ 9.1–.31

As you might have gathered from the discussion in Section A, ordinarily you cannot simply present tangible evidence to the factfinder—"Here's the murder weapon. Take my word for it." In most cases, you will need a witness to explain what the evidence is. Some trial lawyers use a mnemonic for remembering the procedure to introduce tangible evidence: **MIAO,** standing for **M**ark; **I**dentify; **A**uthenticate; **O**ffer.

(1) Mark the Exhibit—There may be more than one black Smith & Wesson .38 with two notches on the side. But there's only one "People's Exhibit 3; People v. Blivet, Podunk District Court, No. 17–CRIM–1432."

---

[4] Betsy S. Fiedler, Note, *Are Your Eyes Deceiving You?: The Evidentiary Crisis Regarding the Admissibility of Computer Generated Evidence*, 48 N.Y.L. Sch. L. Rev. 295, 297 (2004) (footnotes omitted).

[5] Adam T. Berkoff, Note, *Computer Simulations in Litigation: Are Television Generation Jurors Being Misled?*, 77 Marq. L. Rev. 829, 831 n.9, 831 (1994).

Hence, the exhibit must be marked, with a tag or a stamp (which may be electronic if the evidence itself is being offered in electronic form), to ensure that there is no ambiguity when later reference is made to it, at trial or on appeal.

Marking for identification is just that; it does not suggest that the exhibit is admissible. Hence, the judge usually does not get involved, and it is sometimes said that the court clerk will mark the defendant's leg if a party asks. To save time in trial, marking is often done before the trial.

(2) Identify and (3) Authenticate the Exhibit—These two steps may sometimes occur together; indeed, FRE 901(a) draws no distinction between them. A witness should be asked to identify the exhibit—that is, to say what it is. And then she should be asked to explain, if it is not already obvious, how she knows the exhibit is what she says it is. Thus, to authenticate a document does not mean to prove that what the document says is the truth; rather, authentication means merely proving that a piece of evidence is "what the proponent claims it is." FRE 901(a). In some cases, it may be necessary to present evidence showing that the evidentiary item has not been altered since the time of interest; with respect to digitalized evidence the proof required on that point may be quite elaborate.[6]

(4) Offer the Exhibit—Show the exhibit to your adversary, if she has not just had an opportunity to examine it; this gives her an opportunity to object, if she wishes to, or to cross-examine the witness about the exhibit after you are done with direct. Then say something clever like, "Your Honor, I offer People's Exhibit 3 into evidence." If your adversary does object, the judge will presumably hear argument and then rule whether the exhibit is admissible.

Now let's focus on the most crucial and troublesome aspect of this procedure, the authentication requirement. Although the need for authentication is most obvious with respect to tangible evidence, it is not limited to such evidence. Notice that FRE 901(a) is worded generally, and note the illustration of telephone conversations in FRE 901(b)(6).

Authentication may be accomplished in various ways. Suppose the exhibit has been marked and the witness has given the following testimony:

Q: I show you People's Exhibit 3 for identification. Do you recognize it?

A: Yes.

Q: What is it?

---

[6] *See, e.g.,* George L. Paul, *Foundations of Digital Evidence* 132–34 (2008).

A: That's the gun I saw Blivet use to shoot Blodgett. [Note: The Exhibit has now been identified.]

Q: How do you know that this is the same gun?

At this point, there are various answers the witness may give. Among them are the following:

- *Recognition of distinguishing features*—"I recognize it because as I saw Blivet shoot it I noticed those two unusual notches it has on the side."

- *Marking or tagging*—"After I picked it up, I scratched these two notches in the side so that I would recognize it later."

- *Chain of custody*—"I picked the gun up immediately, and put it in my locker, to which only I have a key. It remained there until this morning, when I brought it to court and put it on the counsel table. I have kept an eye on it continuously ever since. I have not even blinked with both eyes simultaneously." This is an exaggeration, of course. The exact standard, whatever it is, is significantly more lenient. An analogy: Suppose you pack your bags for a trip and leave them in the front closet of your home. You then have a visitor, who so far as you are aware has no reason to know you are about to travel and whom you leave in the living room near the front door for a couple of minutes while you go into the kitchen. When an airline agent asks whether your bags have been in your custody at all times since you packed them, you are probably in the clear if you answer in the affirmative.

There are other ways of authenticating an exhibit; the idea is simply to prove that the exhibit is what you claim it to be, and how you do that depends on the particular exhibit involved and the circumstances of the case. FRE 901(b) contains a catalogue, not meant to be exhaustive, of authentication methods.

¶ 7.5: Larry Loper is on trial for possession of cocaine. Detective Ruth Ramirez has testified as follows: She arrested Loper after finding on Loper's possession an envelope, inside of which were two plastic packets containing a white powdery substance. At Police Headquarters she put the envelope and the two packets into a large clear plastic bag that she closed with a twist tie (of the sort used on garbage bags). She marked her name and date on the bag and delivered it personally to Chloe Charlton, a chemist on the police staff.

Charlton is prepared to testify as follows: After she received the bag from Ramirez she took it back to her desk, which is against the east wall in the lab at Headquarters. Her work area has partitions on the north and south sides separating it from her neighbors' areas, and there is a windowless wall on the east side, but the west side is open to a corridor. A guard on the floor ensures that only police personnel and other authorized persons with visitors' passes enter the lab. Charlton took the plastic packets containing the powder out of the large bag and weighed them. They each weighed almost exactly one-half kilogram. Charlton's work day was ending, so she put the packets back in the bag, closed it again with the twist tie, and left it on her desk. When she returned at 8:30 the next morning, the bag was in the position in which she had left it, still tied closed. Once again she removed the packets. This time she tested the substance and determined that it was cocaine.

Loper made a timely motion to suppress Charlton's testimony on the grounds that the prosecution had not "sufficiently established that the packets that Charlton tested were the same packets, in unaltered condition, that Ramirez had found on Loper's possession." How should the court rule?

The requirement of authentication may appear overly restrictive at times. This is particularly evident with respect to the authentication of writings. Most often in our ordinary affairs we assume that a writing is what it purports to be. Suppose you receive in the mail a document bearing at the top the letterhead "Schmertz Realty," near the bottom the handwritten words "Jacqueline Schmertz," and underneath that the typewritten words "Jacqueline Schmertz, President." In the absence of more information on the point, you will probably conclude that Jacqueline Schmertz, who is the president of Schmertz Realty, has sent you a letter. And it certainly seems clear that on the question of whether Jacqueline Schmertz, President of Schmertz Realty, made statements that appear on the face of this document, the document is far more probative than prejudicial, even without any additional proof: There is the letter, and if it is genuine then Schmertz, purporting to act as President of Schmertz Realty, *did* make the statements, because they're in the letter. But traditional evidence law and Rule 901(b) tend to be stickier. The court will usually demand affirmative proof, apart from the contents of the letter itself, that the letter is what the proponent contends it is.

The requirement is not always burdensome. For example, it should be enough if you are able to present testimony:

(a) of a witness who knows Ms. Schmertz and recognizes her signature (though note that if your witness is not an expert she will probably have to testify on the basis of familiarity acquired before litigation, *see* FRE 901(b)(2)), or

(b) demonstrating that the letter has information knowable only by Ms. Schmertz, or

(c) demonstrating that the letter was in response to one written to Ms. Schmertz. *See* FRE 901(b)(4) and Advisory Committee Note.

But sometimes it will be difficult to assemble such authenticating evidence—and it will very likely be difficult to do so if you do not prepare until the time you are trying to introduce the document. As this discussion suggests, authentication usually requires the testimony of a witness; what is more, for reasons that we will discuss in Chapter 8, her authenticating testimony itself must be in admissible form. If the witness who is testifying at the time you want to introduce the document happens to be able to provide the necessary testimony, you are in luck—but this will not always be the case.

¶ **7.6:** Peter Plaintiff is suing Doran Developers, Inc., claiming that Doran's made fraudulent representations on which he relied in deciding to buy a house in a Doran development. Peter will testify that he had looked at the house but was worried about a nearby factory; he later called Doran's asking about it, and while on the phone the employee with whom he was speaking, whose voice he recognized from his prior visit, told him that the factory would soon be torn down. Satisfied by this representation, he bought the house without further ado; as it turned out, there was no prospect that the factory would soon be torn down. Doran's denies that any person representing it made the alleged misrepresentation, and denies information sufficient to form a belief as to whether the alleged misrepresentation was made at all. Plaintiff would like to introduce evidence that Doran's made a similar misrepresentation to Winny Witness. In each of the following cases, is the misrepresentation sufficiently authenticated as having been made on behalf of Doran's?

(a) Winny will testify that she had been thinking of buying a house in the development when she received an unsolicited call from a man who identified himself as a salesman for Doran's. The man, whose name she did not catch, urged Winny to buy a house in the development, and when she expressed concern about the factory told her that it would soon be torn down.

[handwritten margin note: N aye – not a call back, no name, doesn't know voice]

(b) Winny's testimony would be that she received an unsolicited letter from Doran's. Plaintiff offers into evidence a piece of stationery bearing what purports to be Doran's letterhead and containing the same representation that the factory would soon be torn down.

[handwritten margin note: Nope. How do we know it's really Doran's? Easy to fabricate!]

(c) Now Winny would testify that she took the initiative herself: She looked Doran's number up on-line and called the number; a man answered "Doran's" and, in response to her questions, made the misrepresentation. Yes!. Known # _ no name matter?

(d) The final cell in the 2 x 2 matrix. This time Winny's testimony would be that she wrote a letter to Doran's, at the address she found on its website, and that she received a letter from Doran's containing the fateful misrepresentation. Plaintiff offers into evidence a piece of stationery that bears what purports to be Doran's letterhead and that she claims is the offending letter. Yes!

Why does the law insist on affirmative authenticating evidence, apart from the document or thing itself? One answer sometimes given is that the common law has a traditional fear of forgery and other forms of fakery. If the idea is that, absent any other information about the document purporting to be a letter from Schmertz, we cannot say it is probably a letter from Jacqueline Schmertz, then it certainly seems misguided. Forgery exists, to be sure, but at least in the absence of contrary evidence a jury would be justified in regarding it as highly likely that the document is what it purports to be. Perhaps the more serious concern is a dynamic one—that if documents such as this one are admissible without other proof of authenticity then interested persons will have too great an incentive for the fabrication of evidence. Still, we may wonder whether this is a sufficiently great problem to warrant the authentication requirement. Even given the opportunity, most people will not forge evidence, and if they do there is usually an adverse party with the incentives and the tools to expose the deed.

A second answer is that, even if the contents of the letter are adequate in themselves to demonstrate to the requisite level of confidence that the document is what it purports to be, the proponent could probably produce better evidence of that proposition, and excluding the document unless he does so will give him an inducement to do so. But if the document itself is sufficient proof of its own authenticity, and if the proponent is satisfied to rely on that without having to present extra authenticating evidence, then perhaps that should be enough; arguably it should be left to the opponent to present evidence *challenging* the authenticity of the document if he chooses to.

A third answer is that for several centuries the common law has relied heavily on testimony. "Nuth'n walks itself into evidence," the sagacious (but fictitious) Mr. Dooley once said. We generally expect tangible evidence to have a sponsoring witness.

The issue is made more intriguing by the fact that, with respect to a limited set of documents, the law has in fact done away with the authentication requirement, by calling them self-authenticating. That is, if on the face of the document it appears to satisfy certain criteria, testimony establishing authenticity is not required. Traditionally, this treatment was essentially limited to documents purporting to have been vouched for by some official. Notice, however, that FRE 902 creates new categories of self-authenticating documents, including "[p]rinted material purporting to be a newspaper or periodical." The question then arises why the category of self-authenticating documents should be so limited. Perhaps any document or tangible item should be treated, at least presumptively, as self-authenticating.

¶ **7.7:** Consider whether FRE 901(a) should be replaced by either of the following alternatives:

Alternative A: If proffered evidence has sufficient probative value to warrant admissibility, there shall be no separate requirement of authentication or identification as a condition precedent to admissibility unless there is substantial doubt that the proffered evidence is what its proponent claims, and the proponent of the evidence is reasonably able and substantially better able than the opponent to produce evidence bearing on that question. *[handwritten: IDK... at least show your work in case newer/appeal]*

Alternative B: If the proponent of a tangible item of evidence contends that it is what it appears or purports to be, no separate authenticating evidence is necessary, and any adverse party may introduce evidence tending to show that the item is not what it purports to be.[7] *[handwritten: Ok]*

¶ **7.8:** Consider the eased requirements for authentication of ancient documents, as expressed in FRE 901(b)(8).

(a) McCormick argues, § 225, that "[a]ge itself may be viewed as giving rise to some inference of genuineness in that inaccuracies might have already been discovered, and an instrument is unlikely to be forged in order for a goal to be realized at a time in the distant future." Are you persuaded? *[handwritten: No! Fakes and forgeries ancient!]*

(b) Should the first two requirements of FRE 901(b)(8)— that the document "(A) is in such condition as to create no suspicion concerning its authenticity, [and] (B) was in a place where it, if authentic, would likely be"—be sufficient for authentication without proof of the third requirement, that the

---

[7]   *See* Richard D. Friedman, *Conditional Probative Value: Neoclassicism Without Myth*, 93 Mich. L. Rev. 439, 476–77 (1994); Dale A. Nance, *Conditional Probative Value and the Reconstruction of the Federal Rules of Evidence*, 94 Mich. L. Rev. 419, 445–53 (1995); Richard D. Friedman, *Refining Conditional Probative Value*, 94 Mich. L. Rev. 457, 464–65 (1995)

document "(C) has been in existence 20 years or more at the time it is offered"? *Yeah 20 feels arbitrary*

At the time of this writing, the Advisory Committee for the Federal Rules of Evidence has proposed two new rules, which would be FRE 902(13) and (14), providing for the authentication, respectively, of certain records generated by an electronic process or system and for certain data copied from an electronic device, storage media, or file. The proposals are characterized as instances of self-authentication, but that is arguably a misnomer, because in each case a separate certification is required (as is already true with respect to FRE 902(11) and (12)). Whether these rules, which arguably pose Confrontation Clause problems in some circumstances, will be adopted is not yet clear.

In Chapter 8 we will again refer to authentication, in the context of a general analysis of decisions of preliminary facts. We will discuss there who decides whether the authenticating fact is true and how persuasive the evidence must be.

C. THE RULE OF COMPLETENESS

FRE 106

Additional Reading: McCormick, ch. 6, § 56; Mueller & Kirkpatrick, §§ 1.17–.18

When you offer a document or part of one into evidence, be aware that the rule of completeness may apply. *Beech Aircraft Corp. v. Rainey*, 488 U.S. 153 (1988), the one relatively recent Supreme Court case that has considered the rule, provides a set of facts helpful to understand it.

Lt. Comm. Barbara Ann Rainey, a Navy flight instructor, and her student, Ens. Donald Knowlton, were killed when their training aircraft, manufactured by Beech, crashed during exercises. The Navy investigated, concluding that pilot error was the most probable cause of the accident. Lt. Comm. Rainey's husband John, himself a Navy flight instructor, conducted his own investigation and outlined his conclusions in a letter to the chief Navy investigator. Rainey sued Beech, and as part of Beech's case-in-chief it called him as an adverse witness. In response to questions by Beech's counsel, he admitted that in his letter he had written that (1) his wife had attempted to cancel the flight, in part because Knowlton was tired and emotionally drained, and (2) either she or Knowlton had initiated a hard right turn when another aircraft unexpectedly came into view. As you will learn more fully in Chapter 14, John Rainey's prior statements come within the doctrine of party admissions, because he was a party, and these were his own statements offered against him; accordingly, objections to these statements that otherwise may have been valid, on the grounds of the hearsay or opinion rules, did not apply.

Though Rainey's letter did include these statements, it also said: "The most probable primary cause factor of this aircraft mishap is a loss of useful power (or rollback) caused by some form of pneumatic sensing/fuel flow malfunction, probably in the fuel control unit." His counsel's attempt to ask him about this conclusion was met by the objection that the conclusion was an opinion. The trial judge sustained the objection. (Note that admissions doctrine did not help Rainey because the rules of evidence apply asymmetrically in this context: It was Rainey himself, not his adversary, who was offering the statement on rollback, and so admissions doctrine did not apply.)

Perhaps not surprisingly, the Supreme Court held that this ruling was an abuse of the trial judge's discretion. Beech's questioning had given a distorted view of the letter, and Rainey was entitled to overcome that by offering evidence concerning another part of the letter that might not have been admissible but for Beech's evidence. Thus, in this case, the need for completeness "trumps" the exclusionary rule, as Professor Nance has put it in a pair of extremely thoughtful and comprehensive articles on completeness.[8]

Note that the trial judge in a case like this has three basic options, none of which is perfect: (1) Exclude all the evidence (or strike the proponent's evidence if it has already been admitted), thus potentially denying the factfinder important information. (2) Admit the proponent's evidence but exclude the opponent's, thus adhering to the evidentiary rules applicable to each but potentially creating unfairness and distortion. (3) Admit the opponent's evidence as well as the proponent's, thus providing the factfinder with full information but potentially overriding the considerations supporting the rule that appears to exclude the opponent's evidence. An argument in support of Option 3—that the proponent has "opened the door" by presenting its own evidence[9]—is not entirely satisfactory because it begs the question; it is by no means clear, for example, that by presenting evidence of one conversation the proponent should be held to have waived a privilege with respect to another conversation. But in a case like *Rainey*, it appears clear that Option 3 is the best, at least once the proponent's evidence has been

---

[8]   Dale A. Nance, *Verbal Completeness and Exclusionary Rules Under the Federal Rules of Evidence*, 75 Tex. L. Rev. 51 (1996); *A Theory of Verbal Completeness*, 80 Iowa L. Rev. 825 (1995).

[9]   The "open the door" phrase is also used often in connection with the doctrine of curative admissibility. This is the idea that, if a piece of evidence is for some reason improperly admitted, the opponent should be allowed to introduce evidence that might not have been admissible on its own, to correct any prejudice created by the first piece of evidence. The proponent of the first piece has "opened the door" and cannot object to the second piece. This doctrine is not the same as the rule of completeness, which does not depend on the premise that the first piece of evidence was improperly admitted, but clearly the two are related. In a sense, the doctrine of curative admissibility is the rule of completeness together with a rule of estoppel: The original proponent cannot object that the predicate for admitting the second piece of evidence was the improper admission of the first piece, because it was the proponent who offered that first piece.

admitted; Beech, having offered evidence of Rainey's opinion as expressed in the letter, does not have any persuasive basis for objecting to another expression of opinion by Rainey in the same letter that may correct a distortion created by Beech's own evidence.

Apart from the trumping function, as Nance points out, the rule of completeness performs a timing function: If the adversary can present completing evidence (whether it was admissible independently or by virtue of the trumping function), the rule allows the opponent to introduce that evidence *now*, without waiting for presentation of its case—or even, arguably, for cross-examination. Thus, FRE 106 provides that when one party introduces all or part of a document, her adversary can "require the introduction *at that time* of any other part" of the document, or any other document, that "ought in fairness to be considered contemporaneously with it." Thus, when one part of a writing is introduced and another part is necessary for completeness, the opponent should at least arguably be able to compel the proponent to introduce the two portions together. Some jurisdictions accord the rule of completeness *only* this timing function; this conception of the rule allows the adversary to advance the time for presenting the completing evidence but does not render evidence admissible that otherwise would be inadmissible.

You might also have noticed one other potentially troublesome feature of Rule 106: By its terms it applies only to the introduction of documentary evidence, broadly construed. In *Beech Aircraft*, the evidence at stake *concerned* a writing, but the only evidence actually introduced was Rainey's testimony. Thus, there was doubt about whether Rule 106 itself applied, and the Court avoided the issue, holding that the completing evidence should have been admitted under general principles. And indeed, there does not seem to be any very good reason to limit the principle of completeness to documentary evidence.[10]

> ¶ **7.9:** Ko is accused of murdering his old girlfriend, Hong, to placate and impress his new girlfriend, Seong. In its opening, the defense refers to a statement made by Seong that a bloody shirt found at the murder scene was hers. The prosecution seeks to introduce other statements by Seong made in the same conversation, to the effect that Ko often wore the shirt and that bloody pants found at the scene were his. If it were not for the opening statement, the prosecution could not introduce this evidence because it would violate the Confrontation Clause. Has Ko opened the door? *See Ko v. Burge*, 2008 WL 552629 (S.D.N.Y. 2008). Can't open door to confrontation clause issue!
>
> And... 106 is limited to writings. Doesn't apply to convos.

---

[10] *See, e.g.,* U.S. v. Haddad, 10 F.3d 1252, 1258 (7th Cir. 1993) (holding that although "by its terms [Rule 106] refers to written or recorded statements[,] Rule 611(a) gives the district courts the same authority with respect to oral statements and testimonial proof").

¶ **7.10:** Parton is suing Dabney for wrongful discharge. As part of her case, Parton wishes to prove that Dabney thought well of her work until she confronted him with allegations that some of his senior officers were sexually harassing women workers. Parton presents a properly authenticated e-mail message written at 2:07 pm on January 15, several weeks before the confrontation, by Thurman, then one of Dabney's employees but now deceased. The message includes the following: "Dabney said at today's staff meeting that Parton seemed to be doing a terrific job at Personnel." The defense objects to the memo as hearsay, but the court holds that it is admissible as an agency admission. *See* FRE 801(d)(2)(D), removing the hearsay bar for certain statements of an agent (in this case, Thurman) offered against the agent's principal (Dabney). Defense counsel says, "Your Honor, if that's admitted, then I'd like to have Thurman's e-mail message of January 22 at 3:05 pm admitted as well at this time." That message includes this passage: "Dabney seemed slightly tipsy, and very giddy, last week. Perhaps that's why he was so uncharacteristically generous to the whole staff. He's never had a nice word to say about Parton before; three months ago, he couldn't even remember her name." If Parton had not offered the first message, Dabney would be precluded by the rule against hearsay from offering this second one; the exemption for agency admissions applies only to statements offered against the agent's principal. Parton objects to admission of the second message, saying, "This is inadmissible hearsay. Besides, the defense should wait until we rest before they introduce their evidence." What result?

D. THE DEMAND FOR ORIGINALS— THE "BEST EVIDENCE" RULE

1. AN OVERVIEW

Additional Reading: McCormick, ch. 23, §§ 2230–232; Mueller & Kirkpatrick, § 10.1

It is sometimes tempting to think that certain evidence should be excluded because another type would be better proof of the disputed fact. Suppose, for example, that in an armed robbery case the complaining witness testifies that the assailant wore blue jeans with a heart shaped patch on the seat, and that another witness testifies that the defendant has a pair of jeans meeting that description. You might think in such a case that the prosecution should be required to secure the jeans themselves, if it can, rather than rely on the second witness' account.

Whether soundly or not, such an argument is usually met by this basic principle: A party is not required to prove its case in any particular manner. It may usually—subject, of course, to the various exclusionary rules—present whatever evidence it wishes that rationally advances the propositions it hopes to prove. And, by the same token, the party, rather than the court, may decide in most settings which evidence it will *not* produce. It may, for example, decide that, although certain evidence would be very probative on a given issue, the issue is too unimportant, or is already sufficiently well proven, to warrant the expense of producing that evidence. Although a party may find it necessary to explain to the jury why it failed to present a particular type of evidence, the evidence that the party does offer is not objectionable because other evidence would have been better. In short, notwithstanding some old comments and some stray modern ones, there is no general "best evidence" rule.

Having said this, we should also acknowledge that, as we have already seen in several settings, there are various outcroppings in evidentiary law of a "best evidence" principle (though perhaps it should be called a "better evidence" principle). Under this principle, some evidence, though more probative than prejudicial, is nevertheless excluded in hopes that doing so will induce the proponent to produce evidence that is better yet. To some extent, the rule requiring personal knowledge manifests this principle. A testimonial statement drawing an inference beyond the personal observation of the witness may be acceptable if nothing better can be secured (if, for example, the statement was made before trial but in a way that it does not run afoul of the rule against hearsay), but courts will exclude testimony with gratuitous inferences in hopes that this will result in more purely factual testimony. Restraints on leading questions also reflect this principle. And at least arguably, as we have just seen, so too does the requirement of authentication. We will see also that the rule against hearsay may in part be a reflection of this principle: A statement made out of court and asserting a proposition may be useful evidence of the proposition, but it would be better to have the declarant appear live as a witness in court.

Apart from these, there is a rule of relatively narrow scope that is commonly referred to as the "best evidence" rule. McCormick provides a useful short statement of the rule: "In proving the content of a writing, recording or photograph, where the terms of the content are material to the case, the original document must be produced unless it is shown to be unavailable for some reason other than the serious fault of the proponent, or unless secondary evidence is otherwise permitted by rule or statute." § 231 (footnotes omitted).

Note that this rule applies only to certain recorded evidence—in the terms used by McCormick and by FRE 1002, to a "writing, recording, or photograph." We will use "document" as a shorthand description of the type of thing to which the rule applies—that is, a writing, recording, or photograph. Thus, the first question in understanding the rule, addressed in Subsection 2, is: What is a "document" within the meaning of the rule?

Once we have determined that a thing is a document within the meaning of the rule, we must then decide whether its contents are in issue—that is, whether the proponent is "proving the content" of the document, so that the rule applies. Subsection 3 addresses this issue. Subsection 4 then analyzes when production of documents other than the original, such as photocopies and summaries, might satisfy the demands of the rule. Subsection 5 considers what reasons for nonproduction of the document are excusable. Subsection 6 closes the discussion by posing broader questions about the proper role of best evidence principles in evidentiary law.

2.   IS THE THING A DOCUMENT?

FRE 1001, 1002

Additional Reading: McCormick, ch. 23, § 233; Mueller & Kirkpatrick, § 10.2

That a memorandum, whether on paper or recorded electronically, is a document within the best evidence rule, and that a pair of blue jeans is not, are easy enough propositions. But then there is a large body of intermediate cases. When should an inscribed chattel—such as a license plate or a policeman's badge—be considered a document?

To answer this question, we must consider what the policies underlying the best evidence rule are. Traditionally, the rule was justified as an attempt to prevent fraud. More broadly, it may limit mistaken transmission of information from the document. But these concerns are applicable to tangibles in general, not just to documents; a witness could mistakenly or fraudulently describe the blue jeans she saw, as well as the document she read. In general, if we want to know the contents of a thing—whether a document or not—the best way is to look at the thing itself. Even if secondary evidence of the contents of the thing is not bad, excluding such evidence gives the proponent an incentive to produce the better evidence. And yet in some cases it will be more sensible than in others to require a party to produce the thing in court.

With respect to some things, there is a particular need for precision; knowing precisely what the contractual language is, for example, may be critical in a particular case.

In some instances, secondary evidence may not satisfactorily transmit the necessary information about a thing. A witness who easily remembers "blue jeans with heart-shaped patch" may have difficulty remembering precise and extensive contractual language; thus, there may be a large differential between the value of primary and secondary evidence. On the other hand, a witness who has a reasonably clear memory of the terms of a document will usually be able to convey them to the jury, because the information is already in verbal form, the form by which witnesses usually communicate testimony; it is more difficult to convey verbally information about such factors as size, shape, and color.

In some cases, producing the thing will not do much good because it may have changed in a material respect since the event in question. We would allow a plaintiff to testify that the banana peel he slipped on was very slippery, without requiring him to bring in the formerly slippery peel's year-old remains. No matter how yellow the passage of time makes a document, however, it is unlikely to change the document in the respect that is usually most material—the contents of the text.

In some cases, producing the thing may be very difficult. To determine that a car is red, we would not ordinarily want to force a party to bring the car into the courtroom. Producing a piece of paper, on the other hand, is usually quite easy, and so is retaining it in court records.

There are three basic approaches we could take to handling these various considerations. First, we could have a very flexible rule, giving the trial court discretion to decide on a case-by-case basis whether production should be required. Second, at the opposite extreme, we could carve out a simple classification of materials—"documents"—as to which the policies supporting required production tend to prevail, and then require production for all materials within that classification; the question in a given case would be whether the particular thing is within the definition of document, not whether required production appears appropriate. Third, in the middle, we could define the materials as to which production is required, but allow courts to define the precise bounds of the definition by reference to the underlying policy considerations.

So far, at least, the law has not adopted the first, wide-open approach—though as we have seen the best evidence principle does appear in various contexts of evidence law, and one leading scholar has argued powerfully that it actually underlies more of the rules of evidence than has been recognized.[11] The black-letter law seems to be close to the second approach—note the categorical definitions in FRE 1001 and the simple requirement of production in FRE 1002. But, inevitably, courts feel pressure to introduce some flexibility into the rule.

¶ 7.11: If the question is what a car looked like, the best evidence rule does not apply. Under the FRE, however, if the

---

[11] *See* Dale A. Nance, *The Best Evidence Principle*, 73 Iowa L.Rev. 227 (1988).

question is what a photo of the car looked like, the rule does apply. Does this make sense? *In an adversarial system where we're not actually seeking truth, sure.*

¶ 7.12: Yamin is on trial for various counts relating to trafficking in counterfeit watches. Two of the counts allege sales to particular customers, who testify that they bought watches from Yamin bearing counterfeit trademarks. These watches are not introduced (though the Government does introduce 324 counterfeit watches seized from Yamin's store). Does the best evidence rule apply?[12] *Not a writing, recording, or photo... so... no? Is a trademark... Is a writing? Is it authenticating an item? NO! Introducing to show others more exact ... but makes more likely... IDK why can't the others be introduced? Bad faith?*

¶ 7.13: Seiler sues the producers and creators of the movie *The Empire Strikes Back*, alleging they copied drawings of his "Garthian Striders" and used them as models for the "Imperial Walkers" that appear in the film. Plaintiff does not produce what he contends are the original drawings and instead offers reconstructions. Does the best evidence rule apply?[13] *most suspicious testimony... but doesn't fall w/in the rule! Arg for no: not writing, recording, or photo. #1, 3rd + the actual drawings in Q*

¶ 7.14: Duffy is on trial for transporting an auto from Florida to California, knowing it to have been stolen. Duffy was not found in possession of the car. Among the prosecution evidence is the testimony of a police officer and an FBI agent that a suitcase found in the car's trunk contained a shirt imprinted with a laundry mark reading "D-U-F." Does the best evidence rule apply?[14] *But not necessary Is a writing ... to enter.*

3. ARE THE CONTENTS OF THE DOCUMENT IN ISSUE?

Additional Reading: McCormick, ch. 23, § 234; Mueller & Kirkpatrick, §§ 10.6–.7

Suppose a storekeeper was temporarily put out of business by a fire that she claims her landlord negligently caused. At trial against the landlord, her lawyer asks her, "How much business did you do the month before the fire?" Of course, her sales records might well be better evidence on the point than her testimony from memory. Perhaps, therefore, as a matter of her own litigative self-interest, she should introduce the records instead of, or in addition to, her testimony. But she is *not* required to by the best evidence rule. Here, she is trying to prove the actual sales information—the underlying data—rather than the contents of the

---

[12] *See* United States v. Yamin, 868 F.2d 130, 134 (5th Cir.1989), *cert. denied*, 492 U.S. 924 (1989).

[13] *See* Seiler v. Lucasfilm, Ltd., 808 F.2d 1316 (9th Cir.1986), *cert. denied*, 484 U.S. 826 (1987).

[14] *See* United States v. Duffy, 454 F.2d 809 (5th Cir.1972).

records, and so even if the hearsay rule is satisfied, the best evidence rule never comes into play.[15]

One reason for this result is that it is not always clear whether a document is better evidence of a proposition that it recites than is in-court testimony of the same proposition. The document is, however, (almost) unambiguously better evidence of its own contents than is any other statement about the document.[16] Thus, suppose the plaintiff's lawyer asks her, "What did the lease say about whose responsibility it was to maintain the premises?" Now a best evidence objection would be proper. The contents of the document itself, rather than some proposition that the document is offered to prove, are in issue.

¶ 7.15: In a drug prosecution, Government informants testify as to the substance of conversations they had with the defendants, but the Government does not introduce recordings it made of these conversations. Does the best evidence rule apply?[17]

¶ 7.16: Parsons brings a slip-and-fall case against Downtown Cinemas, Inc. Parsons testifies that he bought a ticket, gave it to the ticket-taker, and fell on some slippery tiles several steps inside the theater. Downtown objects to the testimony concerning the ticket. What ruling?

Bear in mind that saying the contents of the document are in issue is *not* the same thing as saying that the truth of the document is in issue. For example, the lease provision on maintenance of the premises really has no truth value—it does not report facts but rather provides terms for the future. And suppose a plaintiff in a securities fraud action wants to prove that the defendant made a fraudulent statement in writing. The contents of the writing are very definitely in issue—they are the linchpin of the case—even though the plaintiff is clearly *not* trying to prove the truth of the statement. Thus, the best evidence rule would apply. But the writing would not be hearsay, because it is not offered to prove the truth of what it asserts. On the other hand, suppose the plaintiff wrote a memo describing a meeting he had just attended with the defendant. If the plaintiff wants to prove what occurred at the meeting, the best evidence rule would not require production of the memo; the contents of the meeting, rather than of the memo, are in issue. If, though, the plaintiff *wants* to introduce the memo to prove the factual assertions it recites, the ban on hearsay will prevent him unless he finds an applicable exception.

---

[15] *See* Herzig v. Swift & Co., 146 F.2d 444 (2d Cir.1945), *cert. denied*, 328 U.S. 849 (1946).

[16] The "almost" is necessary because it is possible that the document has been altered since the material time. *The Verdict*, a movie starring Paul Newman, involved a best-evidence ruling that failed to take alteration properly into account.

[17] *See* United States v. Gonzales-Benitez, 537 F.2d 1051, 1053–54 (9th Cir.1976).

And even if an exception does apply, the plaintiff would presumably not be allowed simply to testify, "I wrote a memo saying. . . ." That would be putting the contents of the memo at issue, and so the best evidence rule *and* the rule against hearsay would apply, requiring production of the original.[18]

4. WHAT MUST THE PROPONENT PRODUCE TO SATISFY THE RULE?

FRE 1001(3), (4), 1003, 1005, 1006

Additional Reading: McCormick, ch. 23, §§ 235, 236, 241; Mueller & Kirkpatrick, §§ 10.2–.5, .8–.9

Although the best evidence rule, when applicable, generally requires production of the "original," unless excused, this rule has to be applied sensibly. *First*, several originals may be created at once. Thus when a contract is executed, the parties will customarily sign more than one copy, with each counterpart intended to have the same effect. If the contract is later involved in litigation, any of the copies will do; the first one signed is not considered the only original. Note the first sentence of FRE 1001(d).

Second, it may be that a document is not in tangible form. Note the provision of FRE 1001(d) with respect to output of data stored by computer: A printout is considered an original, but so too is "any other output readable by sight," so long as "it accurately reflects the information." Many transactions are now completed electronically, without any paper.[19] Indeed, in the Electronic Signatures in Global and National Commerce Act, sometimes referred to as the E-Sign Act, 15 U.S.C. 7001 et seq., Congress has given a big boost to this development, providing in broad terms, though subject to some limitations, that

> [n]otwithstanding any statute, regulation, or other rule of law . . . with respect to any transaction in or affecting interstate or foreign commerce—
>
> > (1) a signature, contract, or other record relating to such transaction may not be denied legal effect, validity, or enforceability solely because it is in electronic form; and

---

[18] There is an ironic result, though, if the basis for avoidance of the rule against hearsay is that the memo qualifies under the Federal Rules' version of the exception for recorded recollection, FRE 803(5). Then the memo would be read into evidence but—under an amendment made by the original Advisory Committee to the Reporter's first draft of what became Rule 803(5)—would not itself be admitted as an exhibit, unless it was offered by an adverse party. Thus, the best evidence rule would require production of the original, but the jury would never see it. These rules do not necessarily make sense alongside one another.

[19] *See, e.g.,* John Robinson Thomas, Note, *Legal Responses to Commercial Transactions Employing Novel Communications Media,* 90 Mich. L. Rev. 1145, 1167–68 (1992).

(2) a contract relating to such transaction may not be denied legal effect, validity, or enforceability solely because an electronic signature or electronic record was used in its formation.

¶ 7.17: Buyer routinely ordered paint drums from Seller by e-mail. Seller delivered 9000 drums on June 9, and Buyer refused to accept delivery. Buyer contends, "I told Seller in my purchase order that if I didn't get delivery by June 8 it would be too late." If Buyer wishes to prove this contention, does the best evidence rule apply? If so, what, if anything, must Buyer produce to satisfy it? See FRE 1001(3).

Third, the original for purposes of the best evidence rule is not necessarily the first document in which the contents were written; what constitutes an original depends on the context of the case.

¶ 7.18: On June 1, Buyer writes out "Rush Order" for paint drums and sends it to Seller by fax. Seller telephones Buyer and says, "We'll fill your order promptly." On the same day, Buyer photocopies the piece of paper on which he wrote out the order and mails the photocopy to Seller, keeping the original in his files. On June 2, Seller ships 4000 drums of paint to Buyer, and on June 9 Buyer receives the shipment. Buyer complains to Seller, saying that he had ordered 9000 drums. On June 10, Seller receives the mailing from Buyer, which does indeed ask for 9000 drums. Seller says that Buyer's handwriting was unclear, and that on the fax the 9 looked like a 4. Buyer sues Seller for damages caused by the delay in shipment.

(a) Which is the original for purposes of the best evidence rule?

(b) Seller testifies that she photocopied the fax she received from Buyer, so that she would have an extra copy of the order. May she introduce the photocopy of the fax?

Fourth, the law gives the status of originals, or something close to it, to properly created duplicates. If for some reason it is significant what the Eleventh Edition of the Encyclopedia Britannica said on a given point, we would not demand that the proponent bring in the original plates; any copy of the Eleventh Edition should do. The FRE extend this principle sensibly in Rule 1001(e) to cover photocopying and other accurate means of reproduction. Copies produced by such methods are considered "duplicates" and, subject to the qualifications in FRE 1003, are admitted to the same extent an original would be: Basically, the duplicate may be admitted unless there is some good reason to demand the original.

¶ 7.19: A Japanese importer is plaintiff in a civil fraud case. In an attempt to prove damages, it introduces photocopies of its business records. The originals are in Japan, and the copies were made during the course of the litigation. Should a best evidence *yes* objection succeed?[20] *know they were going to be used... why not make originals?*

Fifth, when a great volume of original documents would be necessary to prove a narrow point, FRE 1006 allows the offering party to introduce a summary instead. Notice, however, that this rule provides only partial relief from the best evidence rule: It relieves the party from having to offer the originals in evidence, but it still requires that the originals be made available to the other party. This rule can obviate the need for a stultifying presentation of documentary evidence. It also preserves the ability of the other party to examine the originals and, if necessary, introduce them into evidence.[21]

> ¶ 7.20: Suspecting that Dave Christensen was not fully performing his promise to make monthly payments to several employee trust funds, Paddack and the other trustees of the funds commissioned an auditor to monitor Christensen's compliance. In preparing its report, the auditor relied on (1) the reports Christensen filed with the funds, (2) Christensen's payroll and personnel records, and (3) information from the employees' union indicating that an employee had worked for Christensen but was not on his records. The report showed a large deficiency, and the trustees sued. What must the trustees establish to overcome a best evidence objection to introduction of the auditor's report?[22] *Voluminous docs reviewed to write report*

5. WHEN IS FAILURE TO PRODUCE EXCUSABLE?

FRE 1004

Additional Reading: McCormick, ch. 23, §§ 237–240; Mueller & Kirkpatrick, §§ 10.10–.14

Recall that the idea behind the best evidence rule is not that secondary evidence of a document's contents is inadequate; it is that the document itself is better. Accordingly, if the proponent fails for some

---

[20] *Cf.* Toho Bussan Kaisha, Ltd. v. American President Lines, Ltd., 265 F.2d 418, 422–24 (2d Cir.1959).

[21] Often a court admits charts or other summaries—in addition to originals—to assist the jury in understanding the originals. *See, e.g.,* United States v. Scales, 594 F.2d 558, 562 (6th Cir.1979), *cert. denied,* 441 U.S. 946 (1979). In doing so, the court may instruct the jury that the summary is not in itself evidence but is only an aid in evaluating evidence. *Id.* at 564. (A non-expert witness' statement that the summary is a "fair and accurate" representation of the originals should probably not be allowed weight if the jury can feasibly evaluate the originals.) Similarly, although a transcript made from a tape recording would be subject to a best evidence objection if offered in lieu of the recording, it may, when properly authenticated and offered with the recording itself, be admissible to assist the jury in understanding the recording. *E.g.,* United States v. Slade, 627 F.2d 293, 302–03 (D.C.Cir.1980), *cert. denied,* 449 U.S. 1034 (1980).

[22] *See* Paddack v. Dave Christensen, Inc., 745 F.2d 1254, 1257–61 (9th Cir.1984); *cf.* White Industries, Inc. v. Cessna Aircraft Co., 611 F.Supp. 1049, 1070 (W.D.Mo.1985).

excusable reason to produce the document, secondary evidence is admissible. The key question, of course, is what is an excusable reason for nonproduction.

If the document no longer exists, plainly the proponent cannot produce it. Accordingly, this is a satisfactory excuse, even if she lost or destroyed it herself (say, as part of routine file-cleaning)—so long as she did not lose or destroy it in bad faith, in an attempt to prevent it from being admitted. *See* FRE 1004(a). If she says she lost it, the question arises of whether she has made sufficient efforts to find it.

If the document is in the possession of her adversary, or of a third party, and the proponent has made reasonable efforts to procure it (such as by giving timely notice to the adversary) but has failed, she will not be charged with its nonproduction. FRE 1004(b), (c). What is reasonable is, of course, open to dispute.

Finally, even if the proponent has no good reason for failure to produce the document, she will not be required to do so if the court deems that it is involved only collaterally—or, in the terms of FRE 1004(d), if it is "not closely related to a controlling issue." This, too, is an open-ended issue.

¶ **7.21:** Kaiser claims that Knapp owed it money and that in Year 1 Ottumwa promised to pay this debt if Knapp failed to. At the end of Year 1, Knapp was unable to pay Kaiser, and Ottumwa refused. Kaiser sues Ottumwa in April of Year 2. At trial, it offers an exhibit, prepared in December of Year 1, summarizing activity on Knapp's account through December 14 of that year. Kaiser does not offer all the original documents on which the exhibit was based. It explains that in February of Year 2 it sold the subsidiary that had maintained the Knapps' account, and that the documents in question were lost in a later transfer of records to other Kaiser offices. Should the exhibit be admitted? Who bears the burden on the question of whether the records were lost in good faith?[23]

Shouldn't Kaiser have anticipated litigation and kept better records? If they want to introduce should they show not lost in bad faith?

Nope! Other party has burden to show b/c they're making the accusation—presumption of good faith

¶ **7.22:** Prudence Bank is suing Duckworth, claiming that Duckworth fraudulently represented his financial position in a letter seeking a loan. Prudence does not offer the letter; that appears to be in the possession of a former officer, Nyquist, who has moved back to his native Sweden with many of his files. Nyquist is on bad terms with Prudence, and if Prudence wants to secure the letter it will have to ask the court for a letter rogatory, requesting the Swedish authorities to depose Nyquist

---

[23] *See* Kaiser Agricultural Chemicals v. Ottumwa Prod. Credit Assn., 428 N.W.2d 681, 683 (Iowa App. 1988).

and require production of the letter. The cooperation of the State Department will probably be essential to secure cooperation of the Swedish authorities. Prudence has an internal memorandum, made shortly after the time of Duckworth's letter and quoting the key language of it.

[margin: pretty onerous and time-consuming to produce]

(a) Prudence offers the memo. Should a best evidence objection prevail?

[handwritten: Prob not. Not concerned about authenticity, whether info presented was accurate. That should be reflected in memo. X]

(b) Instead of the memo, Prudence offers the testimony of Kilson, an officer of the bank. Kilson says she read Duckworth's letter the day Prudence received it and she is prepared to testify as to its key language. Is her testimony admissible? Is your answer altered if Kilson was the author of the memo?

[margin left: Nope. This is about the content of the writing. None of the available always apply so best evidence rule actually would Key in out memo... (a)]

[margin right: can testify from her own memory. then isn't the memo even better? yes, but she's still testifying to the comms NOT to the memo so it should be old - no, content is at issue]

¶ 7.23: Jones is on trial for unlawful ownership of fighting pit bulldogs. Officer Carter wants to testify for the prosecution that, while he was posing as a prospective purchaser, Jones showed him an album of photographs of fighting dogs, including some engaged in fights; when he returned with a search warrant, he was unable to find the album. The prosecution has not given Jones notice of its intention to offer evidence concerning the album at trial.

(a) Should a best evidence objection be allowed? *[handwritten: Well... isn't there an available judicial process to request the album from Jones?]*

(b) Now suppose that Jones denies that the album exists. How does that affect the best evidence ruling?[24] *[handwritten: Need to be put on notice of use at trial]*

[margin right: (b) No available judicial process - 1006]

¶ 7.24: In *Duffy, supra* ¶ 7.14, the prosecution offers the following evidence in addition to the testimony concerning the shirt: Duffy worked in the body shop in Florida from which the auto was stolen. He and the auto disappeared over the same weekend, and both were found in California, though not together. The person found in possession of the car testified that he had bought it from Duffy. Duffy's fingerprints were found on the rear-view mirror of the car. Duffy and two other witnesses testify in his defense, attempting to establish that he had worked on the car in the Florida body shop, but did not steal it or transport it, and that he hitchhiked to California.

The prosecution argues that, even if the shirt is within the scope of the best evidence rule, it should be admissible as collateral. What ruling?

[handwritten: Yes? seems insignificant relative to all the other evidence.]

[handwritten: Is it collateral w/in meaning of 1004 (d)?]

[handwritten: No! It does relate to a controlling issue. But... would be a harmless error given all the other available evidence.]

---

[24] *See* Jones v. State, 473 So.2d 1197, 1202–03 (Ala.Crim.App.1985).

6.   REFLECTIONS: WHAT ROLE FOR BEST EVIDENCE PRINCIPLES?

Additional Reading: McCormick, § 230; Mueller & Kirkpatrick, § 10.1 (review)

If you are careful and well prepared, you will not often be tripped up by the best evidence rule, because you will either produce the original (or a satisfactory duplicate) or be prepared to account for your inability to do so. At the same time, the rule can be a trap for the sloppy lawyer who has not thought out ahead of time precisely what documents she must bring to court. Thus, it is important at a technical level for a trial lawyer to be aware of the best evidence rule.

The rule also has a broader interest for us. Even putting matters of rules aside, the proponent has a strong incentive to introduce the best possible evidence in support of its case, and the opponent has an equally strong incentive to demonstrate any defects in the proponent's evidence. Thus, if the contents of a document are what the proponent contends they are, the proponent is motivated to produce the original if doing so is feasible; producing the original eliminates virtually all doubt about the contents. At the same time, if the proponent fails to produce the original and there is substantial doubt about the contents of the document, the opponent is motivated to present evidence (which might be the original itself) suggesting that the contents of the document are not what the proponent contends. Within its scope, however, the best evidence rule suggests that sometimes the court cannot rely completely on these incentives; sometimes the court excludes certain types of evidence so that the offering party will have an incentive to bring in other evidence deemed better.

It is certainly debatable how persuasive this approach is. Arguably, it should not be applied as rigorously as traditional law does to induce the production of documentary originals. But arguably also it should be applied more broadly to other contexts as well. And to some extent, as this chapter has suggested, perhaps it already is. As we study the exclusionary rules, especially hearsay, you should consider to what extent they are based on unarticulated best evidence principles.

¶ 7.25: Consider whether you think a state should adopt either of these rules:

(a)   "The best evidence rule is abolished."

(b)   "Whenever the court deems that evidence offered to prove a proposition is less satisfactory, in securing just and efficient resolution of the disputed matter, than other evidence of the same proposition that the offering party could procure without undue expense or inconvenience, the court shall exclude the offered evidence unless (i) the party introduces the other evidence, and (ii) given the admission of the other evidence, the initially offered evidence has sufficient probative value to warrant admission."

CHAPTER 8

DECIDING PRELIMINARY FACTS

■ ■ ■

FRE 104, 1008

Additional Reading: McCormick, ch. 6, §§ 53, 58; Mueller & Kirkpatrick, §§ 1.10–.13

We have seen that, to render evidence admissible, certain preliminary factual propositions must often be supported. For example, a witness will not be allowed to testify to a scientific opinion unless it appears that she has sufficient expertise; her expertise is therefore a preliminary matter. Similarly, the plaintiff in an auto negligence case ordinarily cannot introduce a photo of a car crash without offering some proof that the photo represents the crash in issue; that the photo represents the crash is therefore a preliminary factual issue.

This chapter considers four basic questions concerning such preliminary facts: (1) In a jury trial, who decides whether these facts are proven? (2) To what extent must that decisionmaker be persuaded? (3) Must the proof of that preliminary fact itself conform to the rules of evidence? (4) When do the parties present evidence supporting and opposing the preliminary fact? The first question is the most fundamental; answering it will help us answer the others.

You may find the material covered by this chapter rather abstract. But it is crucial to understanding the roles of judge and jury at trial and the procedures by which evidence is admitted or excluded.

A. WHO DECIDES?

On the one hand, it is the judge's role to rule on the admissibility of evidence; thus, if the evidentiary ruling requires determination of a factual issue, it would seem to be the judge's responsibility to make that determination. On the other hand, the jury is the factfinder in the trial. In some cases, if the judge makes a factual determination she may be stepping on the prerogative of the jury. So we cannot answer "judge" or "jury" to the question of who decides preliminary facts; we have to sort out "judge questions" from "jury questions."

1. EXCLUSIONARY RULES OF EVIDENCE

Many of the rules of evidence are specifically designed to keep evidence from the factfinder. Sometimes, as in the case of much of hearsay law, this is supposedly for fear that the jury will overlook the flaws of the evidence and so give it too much weight (though when we study hearsay law we shall question this perspective). Sometimes, as in the case of evidence of prior misconduct of a criminal defendant, exclusion is based most soundly on fear that the evidence would bias the factfinder, perhaps causing it to reach a determination of guilt in the face of substantial doubt. Sometimes, as in the case of privileged evidence or of some evidence collected by unconstitutional means, it is important to keep the evidence from the factfinder because the policy behind the exclusionary rule would be undercut if the factfinder gave the evidence any weight at all. Sometimes exclusion is necessary to enforce procedural demands of the system, such as that witnesses testify live at trial rather than, say, by writing out their testimony. And sometimes, perhaps more often than has been commonly recognized, it is because exclusion of the evidence will induce the proponent to present evidence that the adjudicative system regards as better in some respect.

Bear in mind that much of this evidence, though inadmissible, has great probative value; indeed, as just suggested, in some cases the fear, whether well founded or not, is that the jury will quite rationally give it weight. It therefore probably would not work well to tell the jury, "Now, jurors, before you can consider the evidence of the accused's confession on the merits you must first decide whether it meets the criteria of admissibility, on which I will now instruct you. If you decide that it does not, you must shut your ears to the confession and decide the case as if you had never heard it."

In fact, this is in effect what a trial judge is supposed to tell herself when she sits as the factfinder in a bench trial; she must rule on admissibility and then is supposed to put out of mind the evidence that she determines to be inadmissible, however probative it might be. We might well question the extent to which trial judges actually perform this mental gymnastic; in part because it is so difficult to perform, many judges tend to apply exclusionary rules very loosely when they are sitting as factfinders. For jurors, less trained than a judge, and perhaps less inclined to put aside significant evidence for long-term reasons having little to do with the case before them, the exercise would be more difficult yet.[1] In any event, the division between judge and jury avoids the

---

[1] The witty law professor Thomas Reed Powell is said to have commented, "If you can think of a subject which is interrelated and inextricably combined with another subject, without knowing anything about or giving any consideration to the second subject, then you have a legal mind." Thurman Arnold, Fair Fights and Foul: A Dissenting Lawyer's Life 20–21 (1965).

difficulty: The judge determines questions related to admissibility, and if she decides that the evidence is inadmissible the jury simply does not hear the evidence.

Not only is there good reason for the jury *not* to decide factual questions bearing on the applicability of exclusionary rules, but usually there is no particular reason why the jury *should* decide them. Suppose, for example, the admissibility question is whether a particular letter written by a client to his lawyer is privileged. That might depend on whether the author intended the letter for other recipients besides his lawyer. But *that* issue probably has very little to do with the facts that the jury must resolve in determining the dispute being litigated. So by both criteria, this preliminary question is for the judge—it's important to keep the question from the jury, and there's no need for the jury to decide it.

Sometimes, the preliminary issue that must be resolved for determining the applicability of an exclusionary rule *is* similar to, or even identical with, an issue that the jury must resolve. For example, suppose the question is whether a criminal defendant who made a confession did so voluntarily. The court must resolve that issue for the purposes of determining whether the confession is admissible. If the court decides that the confession was not made voluntarily, it is inadmissible. But if the judge decides that the confession was voluntary and admits it, the question of voluntariness does not drop out of the case; the defendant still has an opportunity to argue to the jurors that the confession was involuntary and therefore they should give it little or no weight. (Recall ¶ 6.19, in which the accused sought to testify at trial only about the voluntariness of his confession.) There does not seem to be any anomaly in the judge and jury both considering this issue; they are doing so for different purposes.

Now turn the hypothetical around and suppose that the judge excludes the confession as involuntary. Suppose further that a juror learns about this later and complains, "The judge usurped our function. If we'd had a chance, we might have concluded that the confession was voluntary and given it substantial weight." But the complaint is not valid, because it is still true that the judge considered the issue of voluntariness with respect to an issue that is separate from the jury's function. The judge is given the responsibility of determining whether involuntariness renders the confession inadmissible, and given that the judge has decided that question in the affirmative, the jury simply should not hear the confession. We might say that the factor that renders the confession inadmissible trumps the jury's consideration of the confession.

2.   CONDITIONAL RELEVANCE

We have just discussed factual questions that bear on the applicability of exclusionary rules of evidence. Now consider the fundamental rule, discussed in Chapter 4, that evidence that is not relevant is not admissible. See FRE 402. This might also be considered an exclusionary rule, even the most important one, but it is better to think of it in separate terms; recall James Bradley Thayer's statement, quoted in Chapter 3, that this principle is "not so much a rule of evidence as a presupposition involved in the very conception of a rational system of evidence."

Now we will examine an elaboration on the theme of relevance, what is commonly called conditional relevance. This idea, as classically conceived, means that the relevance of one fact depends on whether another fact is true. For example, consider this variation of the supermarket slip-and-fall case discussed in Chapter 4. The plaintiff claims that the supermarket was negligent in not cleaning ketchup off the floor sooner. The supermarket contends that it had no notice of the spill. The plaintiff offers testimony of a witness that another shopper called out, "There's ketchup on the floor!" Call this Evidence **A**. It is relevant to the notice issue, but only if Fact **B**—that an employee of the supermarket heard the yell or a report of it—may be true. So the classical idea is that Evidence **A** is relevant *conditionally* on proof of Fact **B**; **B** is a preliminary (or predicate or foundational or threshold) fact for Evidence **A**, not because of any technical exclusionary rule of evidence but because of the logic of the situation.

This classical conception is somewhat overly rigid. Even absent affirmative proof of Fact **B**, Evidence **A** is *relevant* under the minimal conception of relevance expressed in FRE 401; so long as it is *possible* that **B** is true, then **A** is relevant because it increases the probability of notice to some extent. That is, even in the absence of further evidence bearing on **B**, learning **A** should cause us to increase our evaluation of the probability of notice. But it may be that, absent significant proof of **B**, Evidence **A** has insufficient *probative value* to warrant admissibility. Thus, a more refined analysis would speak of *conditional probative value* rather than of conditional relevance. The latter term, though, is the prevailing one.

Now, if evidence of the shopper's call is presented to the jury but it is then proven that none of the store's employees heard it, is there a substantial danger that the jury will give much weight to the evidence? Probably not; here the reason to discount the evidence is not some legal policy that may be unappealing to the jury, but rather the fact that the evidence has no value.

Furthermore, if there is substantial evidence that an employee heard the shopper's call, it is affirmatively important that the jury be allowed to consider the preliminary fact, because that is part of the historical story that it is their job to determine. If the judge rules, "I'm not going to allow the jury to decide the question of whether any employee heard the call, because I don't believe that any did," she is essentially saying, "I don't believe that the defendant got notice in the way that the plaintiff claims, so I'm taking this issue away from the jury." If the jury could reasonably have found that the defendant did receive notice in this way, that ruling is a usurpation of the jury's role.

But recall the argument that we have just seen in connection with the voluntariness of a confession—that the judge can decide the factual question for purposes of admissibility and the jury can decide the same question on the merits of the lawsuit. That argument doesn't work in this context. Why not? The *only* reason admissibility of the evidence of the shopper's call is dependent on proof that a store employee heard it is that without such evidence the call lacks sufficient probative value to warrant admissibility. But if the jury *could* plausibly find that a store employee heard the call, then the evidence of the call has sufficient value in proving the plaintiff's version of events, even if the judge personally would not conclude that an employee did hear the call.

In this case, the question of whether an employee of the defendant heard the shopper's call is plainly one of the facts in dispute in the case, and therefore one that is for the jury to resolve. The same type of logic, we shall now see, applies even when the preliminary fact concerns the origins of evidence, including the authenticity of tangible evidence.

Once the evidence has been presented to the jury, there is ordinarily no real dispute about *what* evidence has been presented to it, but usually there is a real dispute about *how* the evidence got there. Indeed, in a broad sense, the jury's job may be conceived as resolving that evidentiary dispute, by asking, for example, "How did this evidence most likely come to be placed before us as it was, by a course of events consistent with the defendant's liability to the plaintiff or by a course of events inconsistent with such liability?" This means that the jury must make judgments about events not only at the time at issue, but also before and after.

Thus, if in a contracts suit the plaintiff introduces a piece of paper bearing defendant's name on the bottom and admitting her liability, the jury must ask itself, "How did this paper get here? Was it indeed written by the defendant and sent to the plaintiff? Or is it perhaps a forgery created after the fact by the plaintiff?" Or suppose the plaintiff in a paternity case offers the results of a DNA test. Critical questions for the jury may be: "How did the report presented here come to be? Is it in fact the result of DNA tests properly performed on samples taken from the child and the defendant respectively? Or is it possible that the lab mistakenly swapped the sample from the child with a second sample from the defendant, as he contends?" What happened in the lab is far removed from the fact that the jury must ultimately determine—whether the defendant fathered the child. But it is an essential issue that the jury must face in its task of historical reconstruction.

To sum up: When Evidence **A** is significantly probative conditional on the truth of Fact **B** (which may be a proposition concerning how Evidence **A** came to be created and presented in court), it is for the jury to determine whether Fact **B** is true or not. If there is no other reason to exclude Evidence **A**, therefore, the judge should allow the jury to consider the evidence even though she is not persuaded that Fact **B** is true. We must, however, qualify this statement in one important respect, to be more fully explored soon, when we discuss burdens of proof on preliminary questions: Evidence **A** should be admitted only if a jury would be *reasonable* in finding Fact **B** to be true (or at least plausible). Thus, *even on what we are here calling jury questions the judge has a substantial role.*

Often two facts are each probative conditionally on proof of the other. For example, suppose that Fact **A** is that semen traces found on a rape victim contain Type A blood, and Fact **B** is that the defendant has Type B blood. Individually, neither of these pieces of evidence has much, if any, probative value; taken together, they obviously have great, perhaps even conclusive, significance.

3.   PUTTING IT TOGETHER

We have seen that there are two different types of preliminary factual questions—(a) predicates for exclusionary rules of evidence, and (b) predicates for conditionally relevant evidence—and that they are dealt with in fundamentally different ways. Now study FRE 104(a) and 104(b). Notice how these Rules draw the distinction, and how they treat the two types of predicate facts differently. Rule 104(b) expresses the classical concept of conditional relevance. The discussion above has suggested that this conception is somewhat too rigid in speaking of relevance rather than of probative value, and we will see other respects in which the Rule is overly restrictive. But the separation between these two Rules is basically a sound one. Also study FRE 1008, which provides some further elaboration of the distinction in the context of writings, records, and photographs.

It is important, therefore, when a factual issue arises in deciding the admissibility of a piece of evidence, to determine which type of evidentiary rule is at stake.

¶ **8.1:** You are prosecuting David Dimson for the murder of his friend Farley. Dimson claims that he did not see Farley on the day of his death. Weathers comes into your office shortly before trial and tells you that on the day in question, about two hours before the apparent time of death, she had a phone conversation with Dimson in which Dimson said, "I'm going over to visit Farley in a little while." What foundational facts must be supported for Weathers' testimony of this conversation to be admitted? Are these factual questions for the judge or for the jury? Be prepared to conduct a direct examination that would allow you to elicit this testimony.

[handwritten margin note: confirm voice of speaker]

¶ **8.2:** You are representing the plaintiff, Patricia Paxton, in an auto negligence action. You want to present the testimony of Warren Wilson that a short time after the accident he came up to the scene and heard Paxton say, "I had the light and was waiting to make a turn when this bozo comes out of nowhere and rams me in the side!" This testimony is hearsay, but might be admissible under the bizarre "excited utterance" exception, which applies to a statement "relating to a startling event or condition, made while the declarant [here, Paxton] was under the stress of excitement that it caused." FRE 803(2) (discussed in Chapters 9 and 15). What foundational questions should you ask Wilson? Does the judge or the jury decide whether the foundational facts are established?

[handwritten margin note: demeanor How short? Judge? (yes) 104 (a)]

¶ **8.3:** Recall ¶ 5.4, an obstetric malpractice case, in which Leslie Rosberg, a physician, is prepared to testify that ordinarily a Cesarean is not necessary for a breach birth and that sound medical practice requires that other alternatives be exhausted before performing a Cesarean. Before eliciting this testimony, what other questions will you have to ask Dr. Rosberg? Who should decide, judge or jury, whether Dr. Rosberg is sufficiently qualified to give this opinion?

[handwritten margin note: Lay foundation to qualify as witness judge 702/Daubert — no junk science]

¶ **8.4:** The prosecution in a rape case wants to prove that the DNA profile in blood found in semen traces on the victim matches the profile of the defendant. The defense has evidence suggesting that the police lab may have accidentally switched samples so that the sample taken from the defendant was tested twice and the other sample not at all. Who should decide whether the two profiles are what the prosecution claims them to be?

[handwritten margin note: Jury need to tell jury... that it could be but I.T. says it is, but jury determines if it actually is or not — judge could issue a limiting instruction when it comes in]

Consider now *Huddleston v. United States*, 485 U.S. 681 (1988). Guy Huddleston was tried and convicted for possessing and selling stolen Memorex videocassettes. One of the elements of the crime, and the only genuinely disputed issue at trial, was the proposition that Huddleston knew the cassettes were stolen. The Government offered evidence of other sales made by Huddleston of appliances that he had received from the same source, Leroy Wesby. Under FRE 404(b), prior acts of a person may not (with exceptions discussed in Chapter 18 but not here relevant) be offered on the ground that, because he acted in a given way on one occasion in the past, he more likely acted in the same way on the occasion that is the subject of the litigation. Prior acts may, however, be admitted for other purposes, such as to show the person's knowledge or intent or lack of mistake. Huddleston did not challenge in the Supreme Court the Government's evidence concerning one attempted sale of appliances— refrigerators, ranges, and icemakers—that he had received from Wesby and that were determined to have been stolen. But the Government also offered evidence that previously Huddleston had sold, for $28 apiece, 38 TVs that he had obtained from Wesby, that he had said he could obtain several thousands of them, and that he had not presented a bill of sale. Huddleston's objection to this evidence reached the Supreme Court. The Court noted: "The Government's theory of relevance was that the televisions were stolen, and proof that petitioner had engaged in a series of sales of stolen merchandise from the same suspicious source would be strong evidence that each of these items, including the Memorex tapes, was stolen." 485 U.S. at 686. The Court also said that the evidence that Huddleston offered the TVs for sale "was relevant under the Government's theory only if the jury could reasonably find that the televisions were stolen." *Id.* at 689. [Note that perhaps the Court should have added "Huddleston knew that" before "the televisions" in this passage.] Huddleston argued that the trial judge should have declined to admit the TV evidence unless it made a preliminary finding that the TVs were stolen. The Court, unanimously per Chief Justice Rehnquist, rejected this argument. *Id.* at 682, 686–87.

¶ 8.5: Should it have?

Recall that sometimes a predicate issue that is important in determining the applicability of an exclusionary rule may also have a bearing on the factual decisions the jury must make. Furthermore, in some cases the same predicate fact may have a bearing on both the applicability of an exclusionary rule and a question of conditional relevance. Thus, in some cases the judge and jury must consider the same predicate issue, but for different purposes.

¶ 8.6: Dahlberg Co., defending against an antitrust action, presents the testimony of its employee Enders, who was a participant in a key meeting. Enders' memory of the events is dim, and Dahlberg seeks to have read into evidence the text of a memo that Enders wrote sometime after the meeting describing it. The plaintiff objects that the memo is hearsay. Dahlberg acknowledges that it is hearsay but contends that it falls within the hearsay exception for recorded recollections, FRE 803(5). That exception applies only if the events the writing describes were fresh in the writer's memory at the time she made the writing. Dahlberg contends they were, and the plaintiff contends that they were not. Who decides this issue—judge, jury, or both? If both, what is the role of each?

judge to let in, jury as part of assessment of credibility/weight

Rule 104

¶ 8.7: Harlan is accused of being an accomplice in a bank robbery. The prosecutor wishes to offer the testimony of Gordon, the arresting officer, that he gave Harlan the *Miranda* warnings and that Harlan then said, "I drove Jack to the bank. That's all I'll say." The defense seeks to suppress this statement, claiming that it was not voluntary, but was made under threats of harsh treatment if he did not cooperate. Again, who decides the question of voluntariness—judge, jury, or both? If both, for what purpose should each decide it? *See Jackson v. Denno,* 378 U.S. 368 (1964).

judge - exclude it it gets in, jury decide how much weight

just b/c something comes in, doesn't mean we can't continue to question

validity

Once we have decided whether the predicate issue bears on an exclusionary rule or on a problem of conditional relevance (or both), so that we know whether the issue is one for the judge or for the jury (or both), the other questions posed at the outset of this chapter can more readily be answered.

- end -

B. BURDENS OF PROOF ON PRELIMINARY QUESTIONS

1. JUDGE QUESTIONS

If an exclusionary rule is at issue, so that predicate factual questions are for the judge, ordinarily she must decide them according to the "preponderance of evidence" standard, which we will study more closely in Chapter 21. This standard is basically understood to mean that the judge must decide whether she believes that the asserted fact is more likely true than not. This is usually the standard in a civil case, and in a sense it is the "default" standard, applicable if no other standard clearly applies (just as a constitutional provision saying that "the legislature shall decide" would ordinarily be taken, absent language to the contrary, to mean by majority vote). The preponderance standard might, however, have different meanings in different contexts.

¶ 8.8: Recall variation (d) of ¶ 5.4, the obstetrics malpractice case in which Dr. Rosberg, the purported expert, is a general practitioner. Suppose now you are the judge deciding whether Dr. Rosberg will be allowed to testify. Suppose further that, if you were the factfinder, you would not rely on her opinion

[handwritten left margin: You wouldn't, — but would jury? If so, let in.]

because of her limited obstetric experience. Is that dispositive of whether you should allow her to testify? What if you believe it is more likely than not that the jury will not find her testimony helpful? *[handwritten: Then don't let it in.]*

¶ 8.9: (a) Griesback is on trial for tax fraud. The prosecution's case is built around records that it claims his agents kept for business purposes. The records are inadmissible hearsay but for the potential applicability of two doctrines: They are admissible as what are traditionally known as party admissions if indeed they were kept by agents of Griesback, *see* FRE 801(d)(2)(D), and as business records if they were kept in the ordinary course of business, *see* FRE 803(6). Griesback denies the applicability of either of these doctrines. Under FRE 104(a), the resolution of these preliminary questions is for the judge. Griesback argues, "This is a criminal case. The preponderance standard cannot apply." Do you agree? *See Bourjaily v. United States*, 483 U.S. 171, 175–76 (1987) (applying preponderance standard).

[handwritten right margin: no evidence doesn't have to come in BARD... JTH would be if it 1st ard... in the trial? still preponderance? why would it change?]

(b) Now suppose that it is Griesback who seeks introduction of the records. They are inadmissible unless the business records doctrine applies. What burden of proof applies?

¶ 8.10: Review ¶ 8.7. Assume that Harlan is challenging admissibility of his statement on the grounds that the *Miranda* warnings were never given, as well as on his contention that the statement was not voluntary. In deciding these predicate factual issues, what burden of proof should the Constitution be construed to demand? The Supreme Court has held that the Constitution only demands application of the preponderance burden. *See Lego v. Twomey*, 404 U.S. 477 (1972). Do you agree? Should a court apply a greater burden, even though not compelled to do so constitutionally? *Cf. State v. Phinney*, 117 N.H. 145, 370 A.2d 1153 (1977).

[handwritten right margin: Yeah. It's a lower prong... if something higher. If all the bricks are weakly nailed, won't hold.]

On preliminary facts, as on the ultimate questions in the case, proof is often scanty. In such cases, the judge's role in deciding preliminary facts is not so much a matter of weighing conflicting evidence; rather, it is a matter of attempting to draw inferences from the circumstances and allocating the risk of failing to produce evidence.

¶ 8.11: Derrick is about to go on trial for stealing the gold chain of Patrick, an acquaintance of his, in a brawl. He has moved to suppress a note he wrote to Patrick shortly after his arrest, in which he said, "I don't have your chain any more, but I can get it back if you will agree not to press charges." Assume that the decisive question in determining whether the note should be suppressed is whether it was intended as a private communication.

At the suppression hearing, the arresting officer testified that when Derrick was brought to the station house, he asked if he could speak with Patrick. On being told he could not, Derrick asked if he could send Patrick a note. He was told that he could, and he wrote the note in question, which he then gave to the police officer to deliver. The officer read it, and eventually referred it to the prosecutor. On being asked at the hearing whether the note was either rolled up or folded over, the officer said, "I don't remember." It is apparent from a crease mark that, at some point, the note has been folded. Derrick did not testify at the suppression hearing. Should the note be suppressed? *No. Nothing tipping in favour of it being folded before officer had it... although... no ev that it was folded after or reason offered why .. suppress b/c that's the most logical reason for crease and party seeking to introduce has burden*

2. JURY QUESTIONS

If an evidentiary problem is one of conditional relevance, so that a preliminary factual issue is a jury question, it might seem that the judge does not have to be persuaded at all on the preliminary fact. But, as you know, we do not allow a jury to reach a conclusion (except for a conclusion of no guilt in a criminal case) unless the conclusion would be justified on some reasonable view of the evidence. This is the law of judgments as a matter of law, which you have probably studied in Civil Procedure: A case doesn't go to the jury unless there is sufficient evidence for the jury to find reasonably that the plaintiff has proven his claim. And in Chapter 21 of this book we will see essentially the same point, under the rubric of burdens of production: If a party does not present enough evidence to meet her burden of production on a proposition, she does not get to the jury on that proposition. Courts usually apply the same principles when the proposition that a party seeks to present to the jury is of a preliminary fact rather than of an ultimate issue in the case.

Thus, the classical rule appears to be that if Evidence **A** has insufficient probative value to warrant admissibility unless Fact **B** is true, proof of Evidence **A** should not be admitted unless the jury can reasonably conclude that Fact **B** is true. FRE 104(b) reflects the ordinary statement of this rule: Admission of Evidence **A** requires that "proof . . . be introduced sufficient to support a finding that [Fact **B**] does exist." The judge need not find that the predicate fact is true—she needn't be convinced that it is more likely than not true, but only that a jury could reasonably find the fact true. Note that FRE 901(a), speaking of authentication, uses very similar language ("the proponent must produce evidence sufficient to support a finding that the item is what the proponent claims it is"), and FRE 1008 explicitly refers to Rule 104(b) in prescribing that certain issues in implementing the best-evidence rule are for the jury.

¶ **8.12:** MDU, a utility company, has discovered that its office building is releasing harmful asbestos fibers. It sues Grace, which manufactured the fireproofing that was installed in the building in September of 1968. To show that as of this time Grace was aware of the dangers of asbestos, MDU offers its exhibit P–83A. This is a summary of a 1966 article published by the American Insurance Association, entitled *Asbestosis*, that discusses the cancer risks of asbestos. P–83A is the last of five pages that, during the discovery process, were found stapled together in a file folder in a Grace office. The other four bear dates of 1967, and it is apparent that at least one of them was furnished to Grace by its insurance carrier. These five were found near the front of a folder that contained 197 pages of paper in all. The few pages found in front of P–83A bear dates before September 1968. Just over half—100—of all the pages in the folder bear dates of September or before. Four pages bear dates after September 1968. The others are undated.

Should P–83A be admitted? *See MDU Resources Group v. W.R. Grace & Co.,* 14 F.3d 1274, 1281–82 (8th Cir.), *cert. denied,* 513 U.S. 824 (1994). Yes. Sufficient evidence jury could find before Sept. 1968 — pages stapled to it more relevant than others in folder

The FRE 104(b) formulation often works, but in several respects it is overly rigid. We have already discussed one of these respects, the Rule's reference to relevance rather than to probative value. Another is that in various contexts the predicate fact, **B**, appears obvious, or at least highly probable, even in the absence of any substantial affirmative proof. In such circumstances, the law is sometimes, as shown by the discussion of authentication in Chapter 7, somewhat more rigorous on this score than common sense would require. But it is not altogether irrational; in many circumstances, a predicate fact appears sufficiently probable even in the absence of affirmative proof that a court will not require such proof. Consider the following problem.

¶ **8.13:** Jack sues Jill. He is prepared to testify that she hit him in the head with a sledgehammer and that he has suffered loss of memory and certain motor functions, headaches, double vision, and depression. Jill objects to this evidence, saying that it is irrelevant without proof that these injuries are the type that could be suffered by reason of a sledgehammer blow. What result? We can use common sense on this, druh.

This problem should make you consider the possibility that the probative value of every fact depends on the truth of one or more other facts; as some scholars have put it, all relevance is conditional relevance. Unless jurors are to be treated as blank slates, to whom the parties must teach even the most elementary facts of nature, the jurors must be allowed to draw some factual conclusions even without evidence. How to sort those facts out from others that need proof is a substantial problem that we will examine in discussing inference and "factfinder notice" in Chapter 21; we shall not address it further here. For now, it is enough to say that FRE 104(b), if taken literally, is overly restrictive in that it sometimes seems to require evidence where none is really needed.

¶ **8.14:** In *Huddleston,* see ¶ 8.5, the Government's argument that Huddleston knew the TVs involved in the prior incident were stolen was based in part on the low price of the TVs and the large quantity offered for sale. The Government also pointed to the apparent absence of a bill of sale: If Huddleston could produce a bill of sale issued to him or to his supplier, or even if he had seen such a bill, that would make it less probable that the TVs were stolen, and that he knew it; on the other hand, if Huddleston never had a bill of sale issued to him, and never even asked to see one issued to his supplier, that would make theft, and his knowledge of it, more probable. Assume that no evidence at all was introduced regarding a bill of sale for the TVs, neither evidence that Huddleston had seen one nor evidence that he had not. In the determination of the admissibility of the TV evidence, should the absence of any evidence that Huddleston had seen a bill of sale count in the Government's favor? Assuming the TV evidence was admitted, should the Government have been allowed to argue to the jury on the basis of that absence of evidence?

[handwritten margin notes: No- need to raise that issue if you're the one seeking to introduce the evidence]
[handwritten note: yes - can shift burden if arguing absence?]

A further way in which FRE 104(b) may be overly restrictive is that it requires sufficient evidence to support "a finding" of the predicate. Unless the jury were asked to give a special verdict, it presumably never would make a formal finding of the predicate. But the Rule seems to require the judge to act *as if s*he were deciding whether or not to submit the case to the jury for a finding on the predicate, which she should do only if the jury could conclude reasonably that the predicate is more likely true than not. Sometimes, however, the jury may reasonably accord significant probative value to Fact **A** if there is substantial evidence of Fact **B**, even though the jury is ultimately not persuaded that **B** is true. Consider the following problems.

¶ **8.15:** (a) Oswalt is accused of committing a robbery at approximately 10:10 p.m. on Tuesday, December 22. He does not take the stand but presents an alibi defense. His first witness is Rice, owner of a restaurant named The Rice Bowl located three miles from the scene of the robbery. She testifies that Oswalt had been a regular at the restaurant until about September, and then had not come in for a few months, but that he came in one evening in December—she cannot remember the exact date—

about 8:30, and stayed until closing, at 11 p.m. Silver, one of Rice's servers, then testifies that she remembers seeing Oswalt in the restaurant on December 22. She says she is certain about the date because she remembers that it was in the week before Christmas—they chatted about their plans for the holiday weekend—and Tuesday was usually the only evening she worked at the restaurant. Silver says, though, that her shift ended at 9:00, and she left the restaurant then, with Oswalt still there. Both witnesses are subjected to a rigorous cross. Juror Jergins concludes that Rice is more likely than not lying about when Oswalt left the restaurant, and that Silver may be mistaken about the date, but she is not confident on either score.

What use should Jergins make of the testimony? Should the judge instruct the jury as to what standard it should apply? Is an instruction necessary to ensure that the jury acts in a sensible way? Are the jurors likely to obey such an instruction if it conflicts with their instincts?

(b) Now consider whether your answers change at all if the case is altered as follows: The robbery occurred at 11:30 p.m. Oswalt testifies that he took a train out of town at 10:15. The prosecution offers Silver's and Rice's testimony to defeat the alibi. The prosecution also has some powerful evidence linking Oswalt to the crime—his fingerprints were found at the scene, and what appears to be part of the stolen property was found in his home.

¶ 8.16: In ¶ 8.7, the judge finds that Harlan's statement was made voluntarily, and so admits it into evidence. Should the judge be required, as a matter of constitutional law, to instruct the jury that, if they do not find the statement to have been made voluntarily, they should ignore it? *See Lego v. Twomey*, 404 U.S. 477 (1972) (holding in the negative). Apart from any constitutional requirement, should the judge give such an instruction?

¶ 8.17: In *Huddleston*, see ¶ 8.5, the court of appeals originally held that the TV evidence should not have been admitted unless the Government proved by clear and convincing evidence that the TVs were stolen. On rehearing, the court applied a "preponderance of the evidence" standard, and affirmed the conviction. The Supreme Court held that in applying FRE 104(b) the trial court "simply examines all the evidence in the case and decides whether the jury could reasonably find the conditional fact—here, that the televisions were stolen—by a preponderance of the evidence." 485 U.S. at

690. What standard—one of these or some other—do you think should apply? *preponderance seems fine - just trying to keep junk away from jury*

By now, you may well have concluded that understanding the exact meaning of conditional relevance, or conditional probative value, is more difficult than it might at first appear; indeed it has been suggested that the whole idea should be discarded.[2] The view presented here is that the classical concept is too rigid but that the basic idea has clear merit and is indeed fundamental: Sometimes proof of one proposition will not have sufficient probative value to be admitted unless substantial and plausible proof of another proposition is also offered. Even if it is true that all relevance, or probative value, is conditional, that does not sap the notion of conditional relevance, or conditional probative value, of usefulness, for the essential question remains: conditional on what?

C. DOES PROOF OF THE PRELIMINARY FACT HAVE TO CONFORM TO THE RULES OF EVIDENCE?

1. JUDGE QUESTIONS

The Advisory Committee Note to FRE 104(a) suggest some of the practical problems that would arise if the rules of evidence generally applied to the proof submitted in support of a predicate factual issue that the judge must decide. One of those difficulties is particularly glaring: Some of that proof would raise its own evidentiary questions, and presumably predicate factual issues, which could raise their own evidentiary questions. The court would be bogged down in a mire—theoretically endless—of preliminary issues, most having little or nothing to do with the merits of the dispute. Moreover, to the extent that the exclusionary rules arise from distrust of the jury—a factor that this book suggests is less important than is often thought—it may be anomalous to apply them to judge-made decisions.

¶ 8.18: FRE 104(a) provides that in deciding preliminary questions, "the court is not bound by evidence rules, except those on privilege." Why the exception? Should other rules—such as the provision of FRE 408 that offering to compromise a disputed

---

[2] *Compare* Vaughn C. Ball, *The Myth of Conditional Relevancy*, 14 Ga. L. Rev. 435 (1980); Ronald J. Allen, *The Myth of Conditional Relevancy*, 25 Loy. L.A. L. Rev. 871 (1992), *with* Dale A. Nance, *Conditional Relevance Reinterpreted*, 70 B.U. L. Rev. 447 (1990). And note also the following exchange: Richard D. Friedman, *Conditional Probative Value: Neoclassicism Without Myth*, 93 Mich. L. Rev. 439 (1994); Peter Tillers, *Exaggerated and Misleading Reports of the Death of Conditional Relevance*, 93 Mich. L. Rev. 478 (1994); Dale A. Nance, *Conditional Probative Value and the Reconstruction of the Federal Rules of Evidence*, 94 Mich. L. Rev. 419 (1995); and Richard D. Friedman, *Refining Conditional Probative Value*, 94 Mich. L. Rev. 457 (1995).

claim "is not admissible . . . to prove liability for, invalidity of, or amount of a claim that was disputed as to validity or amount"— also be excepted?

¶ **8.19:** Greathouse, an informant working for the FBI, arranged to sell a kilogram of cocaine to Lonardo, on the understanding that Lonardo would find other individuals to distribute the drug. When the arrangements were nearly complete, Lonardo told Greathouse by phone that he had a "gentleman friend" who had some questions. In a later conversation, Lonardo agreed that he and his "friend" would meet Greathouse for the exchange at a designated parking lot. Lonardo came to the designated spot with Bourjaily. After the cocaine was put in Bourjaily's car, Lonardo and Bourjaily were arrested. The agents found over $20,000 in cash in Bourjaily's car.

Bourjaily was charged with conspiracy to distribute cocaine and possession with intent to distribute. At his trial, the court considered that Lonardo's statements referring to the "friend" would be inadmissible hearsay but for the conspirator exemption to the hearsay rule, FRE 801(d)(2)(E). That rule would allow the statements to be admitted against Bourjaily if they were made (1) by a person who was in a conspiracy (2) of which Bourjaily was also a member, (3) during the course of and (4) in furtherance of the conspiracy.

In deciding whether these predicates were substantiated, could the court properly rely, in part or in whole, on Lonardo's statements themselves? *See Bourjaily v. United States*, 483 U.S. 171 (1987), and the last part of FRE 801(d)(2), as added in 1997.[3]

2. JURY QUESTIONS

Once again, the situation is different when the predicate fact is significant for a conditional relevance problem. Remember that the predicate fact, like the evidence that depends on it for its relevance, is part of the story the jury must determine. Indeed, as we have already seen, sometimes the two are mutually dependent for their relevance;

---

[3] Reversing pre-Rules law, the *Bourjaily* Court held that the trial court can rely in part on the statements themselves, but reserved the question of whether the trial court can rely *solely* on the statements. The 1997 amendment to FRE 801(d)(2) answers that latter question in the negative. This is the conclusion that most post-*Bourjaily* courts had reached—though, as further discussed in Chapter 14, it is dubious whether a case in which the prosecution seeks to rely *solely* on the prior statements in establishing the predicates ever exists. *See* James Joseph Duane, *Some Thoughts on How the Hearsay Exception for Statements by Conspirators Should—and Should Not—Be Amended*, 165 F.R.D. 299, 353 (1996).

recall from Section A.2 the hypothetical of exculpatory blood-typing evidence in a rape case.

Thus, to prove a predicate fact on which the relevance of other evidence is conditional, the proponent must comply with the rules of evidence just as with any other factual issue that bears on the merits of the case. Now recall that authentication is a problem of conditional relevance; this means that the proof authenticating an exhibit must in itself be admissible evidence. Note again the similarity between FRE 104(b) and FRE 901(a), the basic authentication rule. Both use the "sufficient to support a finding" language.

D. PRESENTING EVIDENCE FOR AND AGAINST THE PREDICATE FACT

It seems rather clear that evidence supporting the predicate fact must ordinarily be presented before the judge decides whether to admit it or not. There is one major qualification to this rule, however. Note that FRE 104(b), where applicable, provides that the judge may admit the foundational proof after the proffered evidence. Thus, the attorney promises to "link it up" by providing the necessary proof.

¶ **8.20:** (a) Why might an attorney want to present proof of the predicate fact after the evidence whose relevance depends on the predicate fact? What happens if the attorney doesn't keep her promise? Are there situations in which, as a logical matter, the attorney must present a piece of evidence before presenting evidence supporting a predicate fact on which the relevance of the first piece depends? (Hint: A woman gave her son two shirts, one red, one blue. The next morning, he came downstairs wearing the red one. The mother asked, "The blue one you don't like?")

(b) Does the "linking up" procedure apply in the authentication context? Note that FRE 901 has nothing comparable to the second sentence of FRE 104(b).

(c) Are there circumstances in which a predicate issue is a judge question, but the judge may admit the evidence subject to later proof of the predicate fact?

Now, how about evidence opposing the predicate fact? If the ultimate evidentiary question is one that the judge must decide, because an exclusionary rule may prescribe that the jury should not hear the evidence, then it seems clear that, at least ordinarily, the opponent must get her chance to disprove the predicate fact before the evidence is presented to the jury. Thus, the judge must hold a "mini-hearing" on the admissibility of the evidence. This is sometimes called a "*voir dire*" (the same term, inconveniently enough, used to describe examination of potential jurors), and sometimes called "traversing" the evidence. Furthermore, if the hearing itself would allow the jury to know what the evidence is, or otherwise pose potential problems of prejudice, then the hearing should be conducted outside the presence of the jury; on this point, note FRE 104(c). Sometimes this is done by sending the jury out in the middle of the trial. Often, if the issue can be anticipated, it is more efficient, and poses less danger of tipping off the jury, if the suppression hearing is held during a recess in the trial or—the more common practice when prosecution evidence is challenged on constitutional grounds—before the trial.

Once again, the rules are different with respect to predicate issues in the conditional relevance context. Recall that the judge does not have the responsibility of deciding whether the predicate fact is true or not; she only has to decide whether there is sufficient evidence for the jury to find it true. That decision she can make after the proponent has presented his evidence. It is not necessary for her to hear the opposing evidence, for if the proponent has presented sufficient evidence the matter will go to the jury even if the judge believes the opposing evidence. The opponent will still have an opportunity to present his evidence concerning the predicate fact—on cross-examination or as part of his case.

¶ 8.21: Suppose Huddleston is prepared to testify that in fact he had seen a bill of sale issued to his supplier, but that he did not keep a copy. Should the prosecution's evidence relating to his sale of the TVs be admitted before he has given this testimony?

* * *

The issues raised by this chapter are difficult and abstract, but pervasive and important. The most fundamental question is determining why the admissibility of a piece of evidence depends on a given factual proposition. If the reason is that the evidence lacks sufficient probative value to warrant admission unless that proposition is true, the proposition is for the jury to determine. If the reason is that unless that factual proposition is true an exclusionary rule applies, then the proposition is for the judge to determine. Once the preliminary factual issue is determined to be a jury question, on the one hand, or a judge question, on the other, several consequences follow—the burden of proof on that preliminary issue, the applicability of evidentiary rules in deciding it, and the procedures for that decision. And all along we must take into account the possibility that the same factual proposition (or a pair of very similar propositions) is significant for two different purposes, and is to be decided by the judge for one and by the jury for the other.

PART II

CONFRONTATION AND HEARSAY

■ ■ ■

CHAPTER 9

BASIC PRINCIPLES OF CONFRONTATION AND HEARSAY

■ ■ ■

Additional Reading: McCormick, ch. 24; Mueller & Kirkpatrick, §§ 8.1–.23, .83–.89

A. INTRODUCTION

This unit explores two crucial and related matters. First is the *confrontation principle*. The Confrontation Clause of the Sixth Amendment to the Constitution provides: "In all criminal prosecutions, the accused shall enjoy the right . . . to be confronted with the witnesses against him." This right long predates the Clause; for centuries in the common law system (and for millennia before, in some ancient systems) a criminal defendant has been able to demand that witnesses against him testify in his presence. In modern times, the right has come also to mean that the defendant (through counsel) must have an opportunity to examine the witness. Furthermore, if reasonably possible, the opportunity for confrontation must be offered at trial; only if the witness is unavailable to testify at trial will the record of prior testimony, taken subject to confrontation, be an acceptable substitute. Although the Confrontation Clause runs only in favor of criminal defendants, the same principle generally applies in favor of other parties to litigation, though probably without the same degree of force: Witnesses testify in the presence of the adverse party, and subject to cross-examination. This principle is best conceived as a fundamental rule of procedure, governing how witnesses give their testimony. It is enforced, very imperfectly, by an exclusionary rule of evidence that—usually but not always, and with a great deal of collateral damage—prevents testimony not given under the requisite conditions from being admitted.

And that exclusionary rule is the second focus of this unit, the *law of hearsay*, which renders presumptively inadmissible evidence that is characterized as hearsay. The basic definition of hearsay includes any out-of-court declaration offered to prove the truth of a matter asserted in the declaration. This is a vast category of evidence. Any out-of-court statement can be hearsay if it is offered to prove a factual proposition that the statement asserts. That is so whether or not the statement was made as part of or in anticipation of litigation, and however it was made, whether orally, in writing, or by some other means. A complete exclusion of hearsay would be intolerable. Over the years, therefore, courts and rulemakers have developed numerous exemptions to the rule against hearsay—and beyond all the categorical exemptions, courts have discretion to exempt a particular statement from the exclusionary rule on the basis of factors specific to that case. The commonly accepted doctrine, articulated vigorously by Wigmore, is that the general factors determining whether a statement ought to be exempted from the rule against hearsay are (1) the reliability (or trustworthiness) of the statement and (2) the necessity for it in litigation. Hearsay law is complex, multi-faceted, and often confusing. Sometimes it is also bizarre.

One reason that the confrontation principle and the law against hearsay are related is that they overlap in the values they protect. Both reflect the idea that it is better to have a person testify to a proposition in court, in the presence of the adverse party and the trier of fact, and subject to the oath and cross-examination, than to present secondary evidence of what that person said at an earlier time. But the confrontation principle is relatively narrow: It does not apply to all prior statements the person may have made, but only to statements she made acting as a witness. On the other hand, the confrontation principle is much more rigorous than the rule against hearsay; for example, a court should not excuse the failure to afford an accused an opportunity to confront an adverse witness on the basis that the witness's testimony was highly reliable.

Until recently, however, courts and rulemakers have failed to express adequately what the confrontation right is about. They knew that there had to be some right; after all, it is stated expressly in the Sixth Amendment. But they tended to perceive it as merely a constitutionalization of the law of hearsay. If hearsay law—including all the exemptions to the rule against hearsay, and including individualized consideration of case-specific factors if no categorical exemption applied—allowed admissibility of a statement, then usually the Confrontation Clause posed no obstacle. One result, naturally, was that the Clause was far weaker than it should have been. And another result, I believe, was that hearsay law became far more restrictive than it would be ideally. Because the nature of the confrontation right was not articulated separately from that of hearsay law, but decision-makers had a residual sense that certain uses of secondary evidence would be fundamentally alien to our system, they tended to rely on hearsay law for protection against intolerable results. But, because hearsay law did not articulate the confrontation right, it was a clumsy tool for the purpose.

This unsatisfactory state of the law has had an important pedagogical manifestation. Typically, Evidence coursebooks spend a great deal of space on hearsay law, with all its rich complexities, and then, almost as an afterthought near the end of the unit, bring in the Confrontation Clause. Until recently, this approach was pardonable, because it was difficult to see just what effect the Clause had. But now, as a result of *Crawford v. Washington*, 541 U.S. 36 (2004), matters have changed drastically.

Crawford separated out the confrontation right from hearsay law. It recognized that the Confrontation Clause is not a general rule of hearsay; rather, it deals with persons who act as "witnesses" against an accused. And a witness is a person who makes a "testimonial" statement. The Court did not define "testimonial," but it made clear that some testimonial statements are made out of court; the one in *Crawford* was made to the police in the station-house the night of the alleged criminal event. With respect to testimonial statements, the Court held, a judicial determination of reliability would not satisfy the Confrontation Clause. Such a statement could be admitted against an accused only if the accused had an opportunity to confront and examine the witness—that is, the maker of the testimonial statement. And that opportunity would have to be offered at trial, rather than beforehand, unless the witness was not available to testify at trial.

Crawford quite properly puts the Confrontation Clause on an independent footing. It articulates what the right is all about—it is a protection of the conditions under which witnesses give testimony—and it does so without depending on hearsay law. Operationally, this means that in many cases, even though the hearsay law of a jurisdiction would tolerate admissibility of a given statement, the Confrontation Clause does not.

This also means that we can take a fresh look at hearsay law. In many cases, I believe, the sometimes strange-looking lines drawn by hearsay law now appear to be gropings in the dark, in an attempt to protect a dimly understood confrontation right. Now that the right is better understood, and protected without reliance on hearsay law, we can re-evaluate whether the constraints of hearsay law are necessary, and if so how they should be shaped. My own view is that now—so long as the confrontation right is independently articulated and protected—hearsay law should become far more lenient, and considerably less doctrinaire and with a much different orientation, than in the past. *See generally* Richard D. Friedman, *The Mold That Shapes Hearsay Law*, 66 Fla. L. Rev. 433 (2014).

All of this suggests not only that the Confrontation Clause demands far more emphasis than in traditional textbooks, but also that the unit should be organized much more around the Clause than around hearsay law. And that is the approach taken here. We will study basic concepts of the confrontation principle, and along the way we will see how hearsay law has handled them. The bulk of the discussion of hearsay law in most Evidence coursebooks is organized around *seriatim* treatment of the hearsay exceptions; most of our discussion of those exceptions will come as we examine how well they fit with the confrontation principle.

As we go along, bear in mind that, to the extent we are discussing current doctrine, two separate bodies of law are at play—the Confrontation Clause and the rule against hearsay. If a prosecutor offers evidence of a statement made out of court, *each* of these presents a potential hurdle to admissibility. In other contexts, the Confrontation Clause does not apply, but hearsay law may still block admission.

B. HISTORICAL BACKGROUND

A rational system of proof must depend in large part on the testimony of witnesses. And that pretty much means that the system must establish conditions for how witnesses give their testimony. One condition that most systems in the Western world have required is that a witness must give her testimony under oath. Another condition in many systems is that witnesses—especially accusing witnesses in a criminal case—must give their testimony in the presence of the adverse party and, if reasonably possible, of the trier of fact.

Thus, for example, the Book of Deuteronomy includes this prescription:

> If a malicious witness rises against any man to accuse him of wrongdoing, then both parties to the dispute shall appear before the Lord, before the priests and the judges who are in office in those days; the judges shall inquire diligently, and if the witness is a false witness and has accused his brother falsely, then you shall do to him as he had meant to do to his brother; so you shall purge the evil from the midst of you.

Deut. 19:16–19. The immediately preceding verse prescribed that two or three witnesses were required to convict a person. Now, suppose someone committed the same crime repeatedly, but each time there was only one witness to it. Would that be enough to support a conviction? Yes, said the Essenes, the people of the Dead Sea Scrolls. But suppose that by the time the defendant committed the later crimes the witnesses to the earlier crimes were no longer available. The Essenes developed a solution: If there were just one witness to the commission of a crime, he should be brought into the presence of the defendant, and his testimony should be recorded; it could then be used to support a conviction if the crime was repeated. This appears to be the first known example of what we would now call a deposition to preserve testimony—and notice that the witness had to testify in the presence of the accused.

The Romans, too, required that witnesses testify against the person accused. In the Book of Acts, 25:15–16, the Roman governor Festus reports to King Agrippa on how he handled charges against the apostle Paul:

> When I was in Jerusalem the chief priests and the elders of the Jews brought charges against him and demanded his condemnation. I answered them that it was not Roman practice to hand over an accused person before he has faced his accusers and had the opportunity to defend himself against their charge.

In the middle ages, however, proof was generally not by witnesses in the modern sense; instead, courts sought to ascertain the judgment of God by various ordeals. A hot iron might be pressed against a defendant's hand, for example; if it appeared to be healing within a few days that was taken as a sign of innocence, and if not of guilt. Or the defendant might be weighted down and placed in water; if he sank, that was seen as an indication of innocence (requiring a quick rescue), and if he floated of guilt. In 1215, the Catholic Church, in the Great Lateran Council, decided that its clergy would no longer participate in these ordeals, and so Western systems had to come up with another method of proof.

The English courts, like their counterparts on the European Continent, returned to reliance on witnesses. It therefore became important to determine the conditions under which testimony should be given, and both in England and on the Continent courts insisted that testimony be given under oath. But the systems diverged sharply from there. In the Continental systems, purportedly for fear of intimidation by the parties, a witness gave her testimony to court officials out of the presence of the parties, though the parties could prepare in advance questions that the court would pose to the witness; a record of this deposition was later presented at the trial. English witnesses, by contrast, gave testimony in open court, in the presence of the adverse party. A description by Sir Thomas Smith of an English criminal trial in the mid-sixteenth century describes it as an "altercation" between accuser and accused. Over the course of centuries, numerous English commentators proclaimed the open English style of giving evidence as one of the great glories of the English system of justice, especially in criminal cases.

¶ **9.1:** What purposes does the English style serve? What disadvantages does it have? In addition to the systems for giving testimony already mentioned, what other possibilities are there?

¶ **9.2:** From the historical account given so far, what indication is there that the right to confront witnesses does not depend on the use of a public prosecutor or of a jury as trier of fact?

To be sure, the norm of confrontation was not always respected. In particular, in treason trials—which were highly charged politically and, unlike most criminal trials, were prosecuted by agents of the Crown—the norm was often disregarded. But beginning at least in the early 16th century, treason defendants often demanded that their accusers be brought to court, and sometimes this was done. The case of Walter Raleigh in 1603 is perhaps the most notorious, but not the only one, in which it was *not* done. Raleigh, arguing passionately that his chief accuser, Lord Cobham, should be brought before him, contended that this was standard procedure in mundane cases: "If there be but a trial of five marks at Common Law," he pointed out, the witnesses would have to testify before the accused. "Good my lords, let my Accuser come face to face. . . ." Within decades, Parliament came to the defendants' side, repeatedly passing statutes that called for treason witnesses to be brought "face to face." By the middle years of the 17th century, the right was established, and judges even solicitously asked of treason defendants if they had any questions to pose to the witnesses.

Furthermore, some courts in England followed the Continental system. Most notorious of these was the Court of the Star Chamber, which did not survive the political upheavals of the 17th century. But the courts of equity did survive, and there was a curious development. Though the common law courts generally sneered at the equity practice of taking testimony by pre-trial deposition, if a witness was unavailable at the time of trial the common law courts found that those depositions taken in an equity court could be very useful, and in that circumstance, at least in civil cases, they treated the depositions as an acceptable substitute for live testimony at trial. Indeed, by the middle of the 17th century the courts developed a sophisticated body of law on when depositions could be admitted at a later trial; as we will see, this law has stayed remarkably stable through the centuries, though the rubric under which it is expressed has changed substantially.

One other setting in which the common law courts departed from the usual norm for giving testimony involved 16th century statutes, passed during the reign of Queen Mary (and so often referred to as the Marian statutes), that required a justice of the peace to take a statement from an accusing witness in a felony case. It appears that ordinarily the accused was present at the JP's inquiry. Robert Kry, *Confrontation Under the Marian Statutes: A Response to Professor Davies*, 72 Brook. L. Rev. 493 (2007). These statements were not intended for testimonial purposes, but early on a practice manual advised JPs to take the statements under oath so that they could be used as a substitute for trial testimony if the accuser was unavailable to testify at trial. This practice appears to have largely died out by the late 18th century, and in England it was eliminated by statute in 1842.

Not surprisingly, the confrontation right traveled to America—and not surprisingly it was often trampled on by a Crown eager to maintain control of its colonies. Most of the earliest state constitutions, adopted immediately after the Declaration of Independence, established the right of criminal defendants to confront the witnesses against them. Some used the time-honored "face to face" formula; others used the confrontation language that a decade and a half later, when the nation adopted a Bill of Rights, was included in the Sixth Amendment to the Constitution.

Let's emphasize several points that may emerge so far from this brief historical survey. First, the confrontation right was meant to ensure not merely that criminal defendants would have a right to examine those witnesses who testified against them at trial. Indeed, the essence of the right was to ensure that witnesses *would* testify at trial, or if this was not reasonably possible then at some earlier proceeding at which some form of confrontation was possible.

Second, the confrontation principle is not merely an evidentiary rule. Rather, it is a fundamental aspect of our adjudicative procedure. Procedural rights are often categorical and unequivocal, and the confrontation right appears to be one of those. The Sixth Amendment does not provide, for example, that the accused has a right to counsel and to a jury *unless* it appears that these rights would not advance the determination of truth in the particular case—and neither does it say that the accused has a right to be confronted with the witnesses against him unless their testimony appears to be highly reliable.

Third, this account has not referred to the rule against hearsay. The definition of hearsay, as we have already seen, is very broad, but the focus of the confrontation principle is relatively narrow: The basic definition of hearsay includes any out-of-court statement that a party offers at trial to prove the truth of what it asserts—casual comments to a friend, routine reports in a newspaper or almanac, and so forth—but the confrontation right expresses a rule as to how *testimony* shall be given. The Confrontation Clause was not intended as a constitutionalization of the law of hearsay, and it could not have been, for at the time the Clause was adopted the rule against hearsay was still in nascent form, not well articulated or developed.

In the decades just before and after adoption of the Confrontation Clause, the rule against hearsay developed rapidly and took the basic form that has remained in place to this day. The driving force appears to have been the increasing role of criminal defense lawyers, who until then, at least in England, had not been a major presence. If a person makes an out-of-court statement that is later used at trial against a party, that party's lawyer will want to cross-examine the maker of the statement (who is called the declarant), whether or not the declarant was acting as a witness in making the statement. And so by the early 19th century courts and commentators articulated a rule that any out-of-court statement offered to prove the truth of what it asserted is hearsay and presumptively inadmissible.

To understand the rule against hearsay, it is important to keep in mind this focus on cross-examination. Despite what may be the lay conception, the chief problem with hearsay is not that the in-court witness may be reporting inaccurately what the declarant said; concerns over the accuracy of the in-court witness's testimony may be addressed in the usual ways, principally by cross-examination. Rather, the principal concern is that, however well it may be proven that the declarant made the hearsay statement, the declarant cannot be cross-examined with respect to the statement. Thus, the category of hearsay includes not only a witness's testimony of what the declarant said; it also includes a written statement made by the declarant, or in modern times an electronically recorded one.

In earlier days, criminal defendants complained if witnesses did not testify in their presence. Now their lawyers tended to complain more about their inability to cross-examine declarants, including declarants whose statements were made without any contemplation of litigation.

The apotheosis of this development occurred in the famous case of *Wright v. Tatham*, 5 Cl. & F. 670, 7 E.R. 559, 47 Rev. Rep. 136 (H.L. 1838). John Marsden, a person of great wealth but limited mental capacity, had issued a will naming George Wright, his steward, as principal beneficiary. Admiral Sandford Tatham, a cousin of Marsden, challenged the will on the ground that Marsden was incompetent. In support of his contention that Marsden was competent, Wright offered several letters addressed to Marsden that appeared on their face to treat him as a person of ordinary abilities. One was from another cousin, Tatham's brother Charles, who had migrated to America, reporting at length on his experience there; another was from a neighbor, suggesting that Marsden get engaged in a local dispute; and the third was a fulsome letter of thanks from a local cleric about to leave his position, which had been under Marsden's sponsorship. These letters were written long before Marsden died, and long before there had been any threat of litigation. The case eventually reached the House of Lords, which in 1838 decided that the letters were inadmissible hearsay.

An exclusionary rule as broad as the one suggested by the result in *Wright v. Tatham* would not be tolerable if it were applied rigorously. From the beginning, the rule against hearsay was subject to a series of exceptions, and courts, rulemakers, and legislatures have developed more exceptions over time. The Federal Rules of Evidence continued the trend, articulating the well-known exemptions, usually in rather liberal terms, and including a residual exception that could be used for a case-by-case determination of hearsay statements not fitting within any other exemption.[1]

Glance over Rules 801 to 807 to understand their basic structure.

• Rules 801(a)–(c) contain what we will refer to as the *basic definition* of hearsay—as an out-of-court assertion offered to prove the truth of what it asserts.[2] Note that this definition is limited to assertions, meaning that the rule of *Wright* is rejected.

• Rule 802 states the presumptive rule that hearsay is excluded except as otherwise provided.

• Rule 801(d)(1) provides an exemption to the exclusionary rule by taking out of the definition of hearsay certain prior statements made by a person who is a witness at the current trial; note that if the prior statement of a witness does not fall within one of these categories it is still hearsay, for reasons that we will discuss later, notwithstanding that the declarant is now a witness.

• Similarly, Rule 801(d)(2) withdraws from the definition of hearsay statements made by the party against whom they are offered, and other statements that for one reason or another the law treats as effectively attributable to that party.

• Rule 803 contains a long list of exceptions to the rule against hearsay that apply without respect to the status of the declarant—that is, they apply if the declarant (a) testifies at the current trial; (b) could be made a witness at the current trial but

---

[1] I sometimes use the word exemption because the Federal Rules withdraw from the definition of hearsay certain prescribed categories of statements even if they are offered to prove the truth of what they assert. *See* Fed. R. Evid. 801(d) (certain prior statements of a witness; party admissions). Because these categories are definitionally not hearsay, the exclusionary rule does not apply to them. The term exemption is meant to include these categories as well as statements that do fall within the definition of hearsay but are excepted from the exclusionary rule.

[2] Rule 801(c) defines hearsay as

a statement that

    (1) the declarant does not make while testifying at the current trial or hearing; and

    (2) a party offers in evidence to prove the truth of the matter asserted in the statement.

The "does not make" language, introduced by the 2011 restyling amendments, may be confusing. A statement will not be hearsay unless the declarant makes it—but it will also not be hearsay if she makes it while testifying at the current trial or hearing. The pre-restyling wording was that hearsay "is a statement, other than one made by the declarant while testifying at the trial or hearing, offered in evidence to prove the truth of the matter asserted."

has not been made one; or (c) is unavailable to testify at the current trial.[3]

•   Rule 804(b) provides a shorter list of exceptions that apply only if the declarant is unavailable to be a witness at the current trial. Rule 804(a) contains a definition of unavailability.

•   Rule 807 (which was created from pieces taken from Rules 803 and 804) states a "residual" exception, which the court can invoke if it believes the particular statement should be admitted but it does not fit within any of the other exemptions.

•   Rule 805 addresses hearsay within hearsay—for example, A testifies that B reported what C said, and the evidence is offered to prove that what C allegedly said is the truth. The basic rule is that the evidence is not admissible for this purpose unless each link fits within an exemption.

•   Finally, Rule 806 provides rules for the impeachment and support of a declarant of a statement that fits within the basic definition of hearsay but also within an exemption.

So running alongside each other are two principles that limit the use of out-of-court statements—the relatively narrow but categorical procedural principle that witnesses must testify subject to confrontation, and the broad, amorphous, and hole-ridden rule against hearsay. For the most part, a court inclined to exclude evidence of an out-of-court statement has not had to rely on the language of confrontation; the rule against hearsay would be broad enough to reach the situation. And so courts have spoken mainly in the language of hearsay rather than of confrontation. The result has been that the hard-edged confrontation principle got virtually lost within the broader but softer hearsay doctrine.

Matters might have continued indefinitely in this way, except that in *Pointer v. Texas*, 380 U.S. 400 (1965), the Supreme Court held that the Confrontation Clause is applicable against the states, by virtue of the Fourteenth Amendment. This holding makes it matter what the scope of the Confrontation Clause is: If a state court admits an out-of-court statement in violation of the Confrontation Clause, a federal court might grant relief to the accused, on direct review in the Supreme Court or on *habeas*. But a federal court, including the Supreme Court, cannot grant relief on the ground that the state court has violated the state's law of hearsay, or that the decision would have violated the federal law of hearsay had the case been tried in federal court.

---

[3]   One of the exceptions in this Rule, however, the one for prior recollection recorded, FRE 803(5), requires that a person who made or adopted the proffered statement be a live witness. Accordingly, this exception would probably be better placed in Rule 801(d)(1).

The impact of the Confrontation Clause was limited, however, by the fact that the Supreme Court did not have a good conception of what the Clause meant. The Clause seemed to require the exclusion of some hearsay, but it could not practicably be treated as excluding all hearsay. The Court floundered, eventually articulating in *Ohio v. Roberts*, 448 U.S. 56 (1980), a rationale that the Clause was meant to exclude only unreliable hearsay, and leaning heavily on the established and expanding body of hearsay exemptions to determine what was reliable. Consequently, the Clause still had only a very limited effect. The lower courts usually could find a basis for admitting a statement, either by fitting it within an exemption or making a case-specific determination of reliability. And, though the Supreme Court occasionally swooped down and held the admission of a given statement to be a violation of the Clause,[4] the law was highly unpredictable because it was not rooted in any solid underlying theory.

A few justices expressed dissatisfaction with this state of the matter, and then, in *Crawford v. Washington*, 541 U.S. 36 (2004), a criminal defendant asked the Court to reconsider the framework of *Roberts*.

C. THE *CRAWFORD* TRANSFORMATION

Michael Crawford was tried in a Washington state court on charges arising from his stabbing another man. His wife Sylvia was present at the incident, and that night in the police station she made a statement that tended to discredit his claim of self-defense. Sylvia did not testify at Michael's trial, because Michael refused to waive his spousal privilege, and so, over his objection, the prosecution presented the audiotape and transcript of Sylvia's statement. Michael was convicted.

The Washington Supreme Court held that Sylvia's statement was sufficiently reliable to satisfy the Confrontation Clause. The United States Supreme Court granted Crawford's petition for *certiorari*.

The principal issue raised by Crawford was whether the Court should discard the *Roberts* doctrine and instead adopt a "testimonial" approach to the confrontation right, under which a statement deemed to be testimonial in nature could not be introduced against an accused unless he had an adequate opportunity to be confronted with and examine the witness who made the statement. The Court granted *certiorari* without limitation, and in briefing the case Crawford focused on this broad theoretical issue, which also occupied most of the Court's attention at oral argument. Ultimately, the Court decided unanimously that introduction of Sylvia's statement against Michael violated the Confrontation Clause. Seven members of the Court, in an opinion by Justice Scalia, voted to

---

[4]   *E.g.*, Lilly v. Virginia, 527 U.S. 116 (1999); Idaho v. Wright, 497 U.S. 805 (1990).

adopt the testimonial approach. The remaining two members, Chief Justice Rehnquist and Justice O'Connor, concurred only in the result, which they did not think required such a wholesale doctrinal change.

The majority opinion rejected the *Roberts* approach, which it held was applied erratically and ignored core values of the Confrontation Clause. A review of the history persuaded the Court of two main propositions. The first was that "the principal evil at which the Confrontation Clause was directed was the civil-law [i.e., continental] mode of criminal procedure, and particularly its use of *ex parte* examinations as evidence against the accused." Second, "the Framers would not have allowed admission of testimonial statements of a witness who did not appear at trial unless he was unavailable to testify, and the defendant had had a prior opportunity for cross-examination." The Court drew the inference that the Clause is mainly addressed to testimonial statements. As to such statements, the rule is clear: **A testimonial statement may be admitted against an accused to prove the truth of what it asserts *only* if the witness is unavailable to testify at trial *and* the accused has had an adequate opportunity for cross-examination.** No exceptions are made because the statement is deemed reliable by the court; the confrontation right is a procedural one, and the required procedure cannot be replaced by a judicial determination of reliability. The Court did explicitly endorse the principle that the accused might forfeit the right by wrongful conduct that renders the witness unavailable, and it also held out the possibility that the "dying declaration" exception to the hearsay rule might, for historical reasons, create an exception to the confrontation right.

¶ **9.3:** (a) Was the result in *Crawford* correct?

(b) Was the Court justified in adopting a testimonial approach to the Confrontation Clause?

(c) The Court emphasized prosecutorial abuse as a basis for the Confrontation Clause. Do you think this was correct?

(d) Why is it significant under *Crawford* whether or not the witness is unavailable?

Crawford suggested that testimonial statements are the primary focus of the Confrontation Clause, but it did not definitively resolve whether the Clause applies at all to out-of-court statements that are not testimonial. Subsequently, the Court has answered this question clearly, in the negative. *Davis v. Washington*, 541 U.S. 813, 823–26 (2006); *Whorton v. Bockting*, 549 U.S. 406, 420 (2007). Thus, whether a statement is characterized a testimonial is critical: If the statement is testimonial and certain other criteria are met, then it falls within a hard-edged Confrontation Clause, but if it does not, the Clause is simply not applicable.

¶ 9.4: Under *Roberts*, the Confrontation Clause could apply to any hearsay statement. Under *Crawford*, as subsequently elaborated, it *only* applies to testimonial statements. Does this make sense? The Clause refers to witnesses. What do witnesses do? They testify.

Crawford and successive decisions, we can see, make crucial for application of the Confrontation Clause the following questions, which we will use to frame most of the discussion in this unit.

1.   *Is the evidence in question evidence of a statement made out of court and offered to prove the truth of what it asserts?* (We will address this question in the following subchapter.) If the answer is negative, then the evidence creates no problem under the Confrontation Clause, and it is not hearsay. If the answer is affirmative, then the statement is hearsay and rendered presumptively inadmissible by the rule against hearsay (though it may fit within an exemption that lifts the hearsay bar), and the statement may raise a confrontation problem, depending on the answers to the following questions.

2.   *Is the statement testimonial in nature?* (We will address this question in subchapter E of this chapter.) If the answer is negative, then the Confrontation Clause does not apply; if it is affirmative then, depending on the answers to the other questions, there may be a violation of the Clause. This is the most complex question under the Clause. Hearsay law does not explicitly make the answer to this question determinative, but as we will see hearsay doctrine is far more receptive to non-testimonial statements than to testimonial ones.

3.   *Is the maker of the statement a witness at trial?* (Chapter 10) If so, then under *Crawford* there is no violation of the Confrontation Clause. But, as we shall see, the presence of the witness does not necessarily give the party against whom the witness's prior statement is presented an adequate opportunity to cross-examine her if she does not stand behind the substance of the prior statement. And traditionally, the hearsay bar against an out-of-court statement was not relieved by the presence at trial of the maker of the statement. The Federal Rules of Evidence take a hedged view, exempting from the hearsay rule some but not all prior statements of a witness.

4.   *Is the maker of the statement unavailable to be a witness at trial?* (Chapter 11)

5.   *Did the accused have an adequate opportunity for cross-examination?* (Chapter 12) Even if an out-of-court testimonial statement is offered to prove the truth of what it asserts and the witness who made the statement does not testify at trial, there is no Confrontation Clause violation *if* the witness is deemed unavailable to be a witness *and* at some point the accused had an adequate opportunity to cross-examine her. In

this respect, the law of confrontation is essentially the same as a generally applicable principle of hearsay law that has been stable for hundreds of years.

6. *Did the accused forfeit the confrontation right—or does the statement qualify as a dying declaration?* (Chapter 13) If the accused's own wrongdoing accounts for his inability to be confronted with a witness against him, he may be held to have forfeited the confrontation right. The Supreme Court has also held out the possibility that there is an exception to the confrontation right for certain dying declarations. And ordinary hearsay law includes a doctrine of forfeiture and a dying-declaration exception.

D. STATEMENTS PRESENTED FOR THEIR TRUTH

Neither the Confrontation Clause nor the rule against hearsay is implicated unless the evidence in question is of a statement that is presented to the trier of fact to prove that an assertion made by the statement is true. The proponent of the evidence will therefore often contend that the basis on which it is offering the statement should not be deemed to be proving the truth of a matter asserted in the statement. Often, indeed, the proponent will be perfectly happy if the jury were to use the statement as proof of a matter asserted in it but will recognize the need to cite some other purpose for which the statement might be properly used—that is, the proponent will contend that the fact that the statement was made has significant probative value to the case without relying on it as a truthful report.

The question of whether a statement is presented for its truth—or, to put it another way, whether there is a basis for admitting the statement that does not depend on its being a truthful report—is critical for both the law of confrontation and hearsay doctrine. It is important at the outset to understand why. Suppose you are chatting with your friend Allison and she tells you, "Barbara tells me that David beat Charlie up." If you then evaluate this information, you might call it hearsay. And you might say, in part, "Allison is only telling me what she heard Barbara say. And Allison might have misunderstood what Barbara said or reported it incorrectly."

This lay understanding does not square with the concept of hearsay as applied in the law of evidence; nor does it reflect the confrontation principle. Suppose now that Allison testifies in court that Barbara told her that David beat Charlie up. Allison's testimony would be regarded as hearsay so far as it is offered to prove that David had indeed beaten Charlie up: Barbara's statement was made out of court and it is being offered to prove that the proposition that it asserted—that David beat Charlie up—is true. And, depending on the circumstances, the use of the testimony for that purpose might also be a violation of David's confrontation right. But the principal perceived problem under both hearsay and confrontation doctrine is not that Allison, the witness in court, misunderstood what she heard or reported it incorrectly. Allison is in the position of most witnesses in court: She is reporting something that she observed but the jury did not, so that the jurors must rely on her observations, rather than on their own sense impressions, to determine what happened. This does not pose a serious difficulty, however; we expect the jury to rely on the reports of witnesses and, if the witness is testifying incorrectly, the party opponent has significant tools that, we hope, will help reveal the inaccuracy. Thus, Allison, like any other witness in court, must give her testimony face-to-face with the adverse party; she is subject to cross-examination and under oath, and the jury can observe her demeanor in giving her testimony.

The principal problem, according to the prevailing doctrine, is that *Barbara*, the declarant whose out-of-court statement is being offered to prove the truth of what it asserted, is not present as a witness in court. Thus, if Barbara was acting as a witness when she made her statement— that is, if the statement was testimonial in nature—then admission of Allison's testimony would effectively mean that Barbara was allowed to testify against David without having to confront him. And even if Barbara's statement was not testimonial, so that the confrontation right does not come into play, we still may be concerned that the ordinary truth-determining tools cannot be used with respect to Barbara. And that usually means that the truth-determining process can operate less well than if Barbara were a live witness, testifying from her own memory.[5] The basic rule against hearsay, expressed in FRE 801(c), implements this concern by treating an out-of-court statement offered to prove the truth of the matter it asserts as hearsay, and so presumptively inadmissible.

Notice further two aspects of this logic. First, the confrontation right, and the definition of hearsay, extend even to statements that were written or otherwise recorded before trial. Vary the hypothetical, so that we are presented with a written statement bearing what we recognize to be the signature of Barbara and reciting that David beat Charlie up. Or suppose that we have what is without doubt a videotape of Barbara making the same statement. In common parlance, we probably would not think of the writing or of the videotape as hearsay; after all, we see the statement of Barbara before us, and do not have to rely on the testimony

---

[5]   Now, assuming that Barbara was not acting as a witness when she made her statement (suppose her statement was made without contemplation of use in litigation), one might ask, "So what? Why should the admissibility of evidence of her statement be restricted because it does not satisfy the standards for testimony?" There is force to this resistance, and we will explore the matter further later. But we should also note that the search for truth probably would be advanced if Barbara *were* a live witness; the hearsay is a second-best kind of evidence.

of Albert to prove what Barbara has asserted. But in evidentiary law, the writing does not address the difficulty. Even if we had hundreds of clergy members, of all denominations, swearing that Barbara had written the statement or made the video recording, that does not relieve the main problem, which is that Barbara is not a witness testifying face-to-face with David in court. So, as much as an oral statement, a written statement can violate the confrontation right and can be deemed hearsay—even though it was never literally heard. And the same holds true for a recording in which the jurors can see or hear for themselves that the declarant made the statement at issue.

Second, the confrontation right does not come into play, and the principal problem perceived with hearsay does not apply, if the fact that the declarant made the statement has significant probative value irrespective of whether it is true. If an event has probative value in a litigation—a car rushing into an intersection, or a fight between a homicide victim and the defendant—we expect it to be proved by the reports of persons who observed it. Some such events are acts of communication—for example, the making of a contract offer—and they may be proved like any other event: If a witness observed it, she may testify to it, and if the act of communication was embodied in a document, that document—like any other tangible evidence, subject to the authentication and best evidence rules—may be introduced.

¶ 9.5: Street is on trial for murder. The prosecution has relied on a confession that Street made to the sheriff. Street has testified that his confession was coercively derived from that of an accomplice, Peele; he contends that the sheriff read from Peele's confession and directed him to say the same thing. On rebuttal, the prosecution wants to call the sheriff to the stand, have him read Peele's confession, and then elicit testimony emphasizing the differences between that confession and Street's. Should it be allowed to do so? *See Tennessee v. Street*, 471 U.S. 409 (1985) (holding in the affirmative).

To elaborate on the point, let's try a variation on the ketchup-on-the-supermarket-floor scenario we discussed in Chapter 4. Sam Shopper sues a grocery store for injuries allegedly suffered in a fall caused by the store's negligently leaving spilled ketchup spread over the floor. As in Figure 4.a, which we saw in discussing the capacities of witnesses, let **SPILL** represent the proposition that there was indeed ketchup on the floor; suppose further that the defendant store denies that this is true. Sam then offers the testimony of another shopper, Wilma Witness, that a third shopper, Deborah Declarant, told a fourth, Bob Bystander, "There's ketchup all over the floor!"

Here the testimony is being offered to prove that **SPILL**—the proposition asserted by the declaration—is true. But the jury does not see the ketchup in place; it cannot confirm **SPILL** with its own eyes. Nor does the jury even know from its own senses that **DECLARATION(SPILL)**—the proposition that Declarant has declared **SPILL**—is true. What the jury does hear, and so knows to be true, is **TESTIMONY(DECLARATION(SPILL))**—the proposition that Witness has testified that Declarant declared **SPILL**. In order to conclude **SPILL** from this evidence, the jury must decide not only that the witness before it is telling the truth about what she claims to have heard—that is, that the proposition **DECLARATION(SPILL)** is true—but also that Declarant told the truth about what she claimed to have seen.

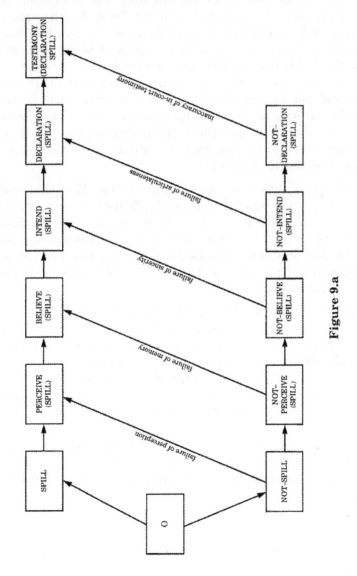

Figure 9.a

Figure 9.a illustrates the problem. This diagram is very similar to Figure 4.a, but with an extra set of nodes. In Figure 4.a what we called the "truth path" led to **TESTIMONY(SPILL)**. But here we don't have testimony of **SPILL**. Instead, the truth path leads to **DECLARATION(SPILL)**—meaning that Declarant accurately perceived a spill, remembered it, intended to communicate it, and did accurately communicate a spill. From there the truth path leads to **TESTIMONY (DECLARATION(SPILL))**—meaning that in addition Witness accurately reported the declaration.

As in Figure 4.a, there are other paths by which events may have led to the known point. In particular, Declarant might have erred. One possibility is that ketchup was not all over the floor, but Declarant *inaccurately perceived* ketchup to be on the floor. Another possibility is that Declarant did not perceive ketchup to be on the floor but *inaccurately remembered*, and so at the time of her statement believed, that ketchup was on the floor. A third possible error is that Declarant was *insincere* in that she attempted to communicate that ketchup was on the floor even though she did not believe that to be true. It might also be that, even though Declarant was not attempting to communicate that ketchup was on the floor, she did so because she was *inarticulate*. Finally, it is possible that Declarant did not in fact declare **SPILL** to be true, but Witness nevertheless testified that she did.

Figure 9.a is a model, and so a simplification. We could make it far more detailed in many ways. For example, failure of memory could occur at stages, over time, not all at once. Or the diagram could show all the possibilities of what Witness, as well as Declarant, perceived, remembered, and intended to communicate. For our present purposes, however, that won't be necessary, because possible error by Witness is not now our principal concern.

The jury must determine whether **SPILL** or **NOT-SPILL** is true. Hence, it must determine whether events more likely proceeded via the truth path, through **SPILL**, or via one of the alternative paths that go through **NOT-SPILL**. The jury must therefore assess the relative likelihood of each of these paths. One of the alternate paths is the one involving the possibility that Witness was inaccurate in testifying that she heard Declarant assert **SPILL**. That possibility, as we have seen, is one the judicial system is confident it can handle. A large part of the jury's ordinary job is to decide whether it believes the witness in front of it is telling the truth about what he claims to have perceived firsthand. This task is not necessarily any more difficult because what the witness claims to have perceived was a communicative act rather than some other fast-moving event.[6]

But the other possibilities—that Witness's testimony is not a product of inaccuracy on her part but of a failure of perception, memory, sincerity, or articulateness on the part of Declarant—are, under the received theory, more troublesome. How is the jury to evaluate these if Declarant is not testifying before it,[7] under oath, and subject to cross-examination? Each of these possibilities thus reflects a *hearsay danger*. Sam is essentially asking the jury to discount these dangers, and so to take Declarant's word, even though Declarant isn't a witness. Witness's testimony of Declarant's statement is therefore considered hearsay, and under the rule against hearsay, articulated in FRE 802, it is rendered presumptively inadmissible. It is only *presumptively* inadmissible because an exemption to the hearsay rule may apply, but for now we are focusing on the basic rule.

Even assuming that the hearsay dangers render the evidence problematic—and you may well wonder how great the hearsay dangers are in a case of this sort—why should the result be a rule presumptively excluding it? Suppose the jury understands the dangers and discounts the evidence appropriately, saying in effect, "It's hard to tell whether Declarant really told the truth, because she isn't here and isn't subject to cross-examination, so even assuming Declarant made the statement Witness says she did we'll count the evidence for less than if Declarant testified to the statement at trial and stuck to her guns under cross-examination." In that case, it appears that the truth-determining goal of the trial would probably be aided by admitting the statement for whatever probative value it has rather than by excluding it. But, in the first half of the 19th century, as the modern hearsay rule began to gel, courts and commentators began asserting that hearsay must presumptively be excluded because jurors would likely overvalue it.[8] The

---

[6]   The best evidence rule, requiring the production of an original in many circumstances, may be based in part on the idea that certain types of information, including verbalizations, are more difficult to convey accurately than are others. Recall that, as in most formulations, the Federal Rules' version does not apply to tangible evidence in general; rather, it only applies to an item deemed to be a "writing, recording, or photograph." See Chapter 7 above.

[7]   Note, however, Olin Guy Wellborn III, *Demeanor*, 76 Cornell L. Rev. 1075 (1991), reviewing experimental evidence and casting doubt on the value of demeanor evidence in assessing credibility, and Jeremy A. Blumenthal, *A Wipe of the Hands, A Lick of the Lips: The Validity of Demeanor Evidence in Assessing Witness Credibility*, 72 Neb. L. Rev. 1157 (1993), agreeing in part with Wellborn.

[8]   A famous expression of this view was that of Chief Justice Mansfield in *Re Berkeley*: "[I]n England, where the jury are the sole judges of the fact, hearsay is properly excluded, because no man can tell what effect it might have upon their minds." 4 Camp. 401, 415, 171 E.R. 128, 135 (1811). Mansfield distinguished the situation in Scotland, where judges were the finders of fact, and could "trust themselves entirely" to give hearsay such weight as they thought it deserved. *See* Richard D. Friedman, *No Link: the Jury and the Origins of Confrontation Right and the Hearsay Rule*, in John W. Cairns & Grant McLeod (eds.), THE DEAREST BIRTH RIGHT OF THE

theory is suspect on its face: Even if jurors do give hearsay evidence more value than it is worth, they would have to give it *much* more value than it is worth if excluding the evidence altogether will tend to lead the jurors closer to the truth than will admitting the evidence. What is more, there is no good support for the conclusion that jurors tend systematically to over-value hearsay, and in some settings they seem to *under*-value it.[9]

Now let's change the case somewhat. Suppose that the intended recipient of Declarant's warning was not Bystander but Sam the plaintiff himself, and that it is the defendant that offers the evidence. Plainly, whatever the store's stance with respect to the truth of **SPILL**—it may stipulate that the proposition is true, it may deny the truth of that proposition, or it may take no position at all—the store has no desire to prove **SPILL** to be true. But here **DECLARATION(SPILL)**—the proposition that the declaration was made—is itself relevant without regard to any support it provides for the truth of **SPILL**. It tends to prove that, whether or not **SPILL** was actually true, the plaintiff was on notice that it might be true. To conclude **DECLARATION(SPILL)** does not require the jury to follow the route diagram all the way back to **SPILL** or **NOT-SPILL**. So far as this use of the testimony is concerned, there is no need for the jury to distinguish among the routes leading to **DECLARATION(SPILL)**. Even if that point was reached through, say, a failure of Declarant's perception or memory, the fact remains that—assuming Witness is telling the truth—she made the declaration. Because the fact that Declarant made the declaration is in itself relevant—for some reason other than that, if she made the declaration, what she declared is more likely true—Witness's testimony that she made the declaration is not considered hearsay.

In short, in determining whether evidence of an out-of-court declaration is hearsay, you should ask yourself: "Assuming the evidence presented in court is accurate, so that the statement was in fact made, does that fact have relevance to some material proposition, without regard to whether the out-of-court declarant was reporting accurately?" If the answer to that question is affirmative, the evidence will not be hearsay so far as it is offered to prove that material proposition.

The standard American encapsulation of this idea, found in FRE 801(c), is that hearsay is a statement, not made by the declarant while testifying at the current proceeding, that "a party offers in evidence to prove the truth of the matter asserted in the statement." By implication,

---

PEOPLE OF ENGLAND: THE JURY IN THE HISTORY OF THE COMMON LAW, 93 (2002); American Law Institute, MODEL CODE OF EVIDENCE 36 (Foreword by Edmund Morgan), 221 (1942).

[9]   *E.g.,* Roger C. Park, *Visions of Applying the Scientific Method to the Hearsay Rule,* Mich. St. DCL L. Rev. 1149 (2003).

a statement offered for some other purpose is not hearsay. You should get used to this formulation, but it poses several difficulties.

First, "*the* matter asserted" is potentially misleading. A statement may assert more than one proposition; a simple example would be, "I went to the butcher's, then to the baker's, then to the candlestick maker's." If the statement is offered to prove any of these propositions then, to that extent, it is hearsay. Replacement of "the" by "any" would be an improvement.[10]

doesn't have to assert all matters stated — any is sufficient to be hearsay

Second, many students find the "truth of the matter asserted" language syntactically confusing. What it means is that if the probative value of the out-of-court statement depends on its being true, then to that extent the statement is hearsay. One way of thinking about this is that if a proposition that the statement asserts is the same as a proposition that the statement is offered to prove, then to that extent the statement is hearsay; thus, if the statement is "Defendant ran the light," and it is offered to prove that Defendant ran the light, it is hearsay. But be careful. Suppose the statement is, "Defendant was running out of the bank." You will not escape a hearsay objection by arguing, "The proposition asserted in the out-of-court statement is that Defendant was running out of the bank. But I am offering it to prove that he robbed the bank."[11] Only if the statement is true does it tend to prove that Defendant robbed the bank; the proposition asserted by the statement (that Defendant was running out of the bank) is an inferential stepping stone to the ultimate proposition, that Defendant robbed the bank. Thus, the statement is hearsay for the purpose for which it is offered.

Third, the formulation may disguise the fact that the statement may be offered at the same time both to prove "the matter asserted"—for which it would be hearsay, though perhaps within an exemption to the exclusionary rule—and for some other purpose. For example, suppose Declarant's statement that there was ketchup on the floor was made to an employee of the store sometime before Sam's accident. Sam might offer it to prove *both* that there was ketchup on the floor, for which it is hearsay, and that the defendant had prior notice of the condition, for which it is not. Presumably, in that circumstance, the statement would be admitted to prove notice but—unless it fit within an exemption—not to prove that there really was ketchup on the floor. In that case a limiting instruction

---

[10] This is the formulation in the leading modern English treatise on the law of evidence, describing the common law rule (now supplanted by statute): "[A] statement other than one made by a person while giving oral evidence in the proceedings was inadmissible as evidence of any fact stated." Colin Tapper, *Cross & Tapper on Evidence* 551-552 (12th ed. 2010; repr. 2013).

[11] The example is taken from Roger C. Park, McCormick on Hearsay *and the Concept of Hearsay: A Critical Analysis Followed by Suggestions to Law Teachers*, 65 Minn. L. Rev. 423, 430 (1981).

would be appropriate, and the evidence could not be used to support a finding that ketchup was indeed on the floor.

Fourth, as to some significant types of statement, the formulation simply does not fit. Suppose that Landlord is suing Tenant on a lease, and that Tenant contends that he terminated the lease pursuant to its terms by giving notice. Tenant offers a letter that he wrote to Landlord saying, "I am hereby notifying you of my intent to terminate the lease as of sixty days from today." The statement is literally offered to prove the truth of what it asserts. But it is not hearsay. The making of the statement is itself an event of significance to the litigation, without respect to the Tenant's reportorial ability, and it is capable of being proved like any other material event.[12]

Fifth, the standard formulation is not particularly informative. There is a good deal of truth in the following fictitious exchange among lawyers:

> "Oh, [Judge Feckler] can recite the magic words as well as any other judge," said Tucker, "but that doesn't mean he really understands them. If the other side objects to your evidence as hearsay, all you have to say is, 'It's not for its truth, your honor,' and Judge Feckler will overrule the objection. It works every time." * * *

> That's when Frank Logan said, "Wait a second. Suppose you're on the receiving end of this. How do you get the judge out of the trap so he will rule in your favor?"

> "You've got to make the judge understand that just because the other side says the evidence is not offered for its truth doesn't make it so," said Angus.[13]

---

[12] Professor Park distinguishes usefully between assertion-oriented and declarant-oriented definitions of hearsay:

> An assertion-oriented definition focuses on whether an out-of-court assertion will be used to prove the truth of what it asserts, while a declarant-oriented definition focuses on whether the use of the utterance will require reliance on the credibility of the out-of-court declarant.

Id. at 424 (footnotes omitted); *see also* Roger C. Park, *The Definition of Hearsay: To Each Its Own*, 16 Miss. Coll. L. Rev. 125 (1995) (pointing out that there is a continuum of definitions between these two poles).

The hypothetical presented here suggests a problem with an assertion-oriented definition that is not faced by a declarant-oriented definition. On the other hand, declarant-oriented definitions face other problems in that other types of statements may raise significant hearsay dangers even though they are not considered to be hearsay. Park's favorite example is a demonstrably false statement offered to prove that the declarant had something to hide. The statement raises hearsay dangers because it loses probative value if it was a product of failure of memory, perception, or communicative ability rather than of sincerity. *Concept of Hearsay*, 65 Minn. L. Rev. at 426.

[13] To similar effect, it should not be a sufficient response to a hearsay objection to say that the evidence has probative value on the ground "that the statement was made," *cf., e.g.*, Taylor v. Molesky, 63 Fed.Appx. 126, 2003 WL 21089147 (4th Cir. 2003); United States v. Moss, 9 F.3d

"Absolutely," said Barbara Swanson. "I like to say, 'Judge, if this evidence is no good for its truth, then what is it good for? The plaintiff has got to tell us why he is offering it.'"

James W. McElhaney, *It's Not for Its Truth*, 77 A.B.A. J. 80, 80–81 (Oct. 1991).[14]

Here, then, are some overlapping categories of statements or other utterances that might be admissible on non-hearsay grounds—that is, other than for their truth.

1. *Utterances without truth value.* As one court has said, "An order or instruction is, by its nature, neither true nor false and thus cannot be offered for its truth." *United States v. Shepherd*, 739 F.2d 510, 514 (10th Cir.1984). So Winken's command, "Blinken, sell Nod two packs," would not be hearsay as offered to prove that Winken and Blinken were in a conspiracy to sell drugs to Nod.[15] Similarly, a question—if it is really only a question—does not have truth value. The matter is not always unambiguous, however; sometimes, as we shall see, an utterance that in form is an imperative or a question is in fact, at least in part, a declaration that may have truth value.

2. *Statements of operative significance.* Some statements, like Tenant's notification to the Landlord, are themselves part of the story to be proved in court. Similarly, contract offers and acceptances, and often negotiations themselves, are part of the case to be proved. Sometimes, also, an alleged tort or crime, such as fraud or undue influence, may have been consummated or furthered by a statement; plainly, the plaintiff or proponent must be able to prove that the statement was made. And, as in the case of Winken, Blinken, and Nod, statements made to further a conspiracy are part of the story the prosecution wants to tell of how the conspiracy operated.[16] Finally, some statements help determine the

[handwritten margin note: words that do something e.g. seal a contract]

543, 550 (6th Cir.1993). If the reason why the fact "that the statement was made" is relevant is that this tends to prove that the declarant believed in the truth of a proposition asserted by the statement, and this conclusion is a stepping stone to proving that the proposition is true, the statement is hearsay. For the statement not to be deemed hearsay, the proponent should demonstrate that the making of the statement has sufficient probative value to warrant admissibility without relying on its truth.

[14] Of course, some judges do get the point. *See, e.g.,* United States v. Evans, 216 F.3d 80, 85 (D.C. Cir.2000) ("But if [an FBI agent's] testimony about the FBI's 'information' [that the defendant was involved in drug trafficking] did not go to the truth of that assertion, to what did it go?").

[15] Sometimes the point is made by distinguishing between "performative" and "illocutionary" utterances, the former being those that "do not make any truth claims" and the latter being those that "narrate, describe, or otherwise convey information, and so are judged by their truth value." United States v. Montana, 199 F.3d 947, 950 (7th Cir. 1999) (Posner, C.J.). The term "performative utterances" is also sometimes used more broadly to include utterances, described below and sometimes labeled "verbal acts," that may have truth value but are offered for their operative significance.

[16] Depending on the circumstances, such a statement may be exempted in any event from the rule against hearsay as a personal admission, *see* Fed. R. Evid. 801(d)(2)(A), or as the

nature of the conduct they accompany; for example, the statement, "I'm giving you this pen as a present" helps make the transfer a gift. In each of these cases, the probative value of the statement does not depend on the declarant's reporting accuracy. Statements in these circumstances are sometimes called verbal acts or, in the last type of case, verbal parts of acts. If you find these labels helpful, all well and good. But bear in mind on the one hand that all communication requires conduct—speaking is an act—and on the other hand that not all communicative acts that might have operative significance to a case are verbal. On the floor of a commodity exchange, for example, a wave of the hand might communicate, "I accept your offer to sell me 5000 pounds of pork bellies."

3. *Statements that provide context for other acts or parts of a conversation.* Suppose, for example, that Accuser says to Accused, in the presence of Witness, "You're a thief. You've been robbing me blind for years," and Accused says, "So you finally found me out." As we shall see later, if Accused is prosecuted for the theft, his statement would be exempt as a personal admission from the rule against hearsay. But Accused's statement by itself makes little sense standing by itself. So Accuser's statement would be considered non-hearsay so long as it is offered only to place Accused's statement in context, without the jury putting weight on Accuser's credibility.

4. *Statements significant* (*because of their impact on a recipient,* or, effect on the listener) Tenant's statement gave notice to Landlord. Similarly, in a negligence case, a statement made before the accident at issue to the defendant about past accidents of a similar nature might show that the defendant had notice of a dangerous condition and was in a position to do something about it. The making of other statements might demonstrate that the recipient had cause to fear a person, or a motive to commit a crime.

5. *Statements significant because of what they show about the state of mind of declarant.* Suppose now that in the negligence case it is a statement by the defendant before the accident at issue that refers to prior accidents of an earlier nature. This statement tends strongly to prove that the declarant had notice of those accidents. Similarly, if the motive, intention, fear, or taste of the declarant is a material issue, a statement by the declarant may help to prove them. Thus, if Donald kills Victor and claims that he acted in self-defense, his statement "Victor is a violent person" is not hearsay as offered to prove that Donald feared Victor.

Unlike statements in most of the other categories, statements offered to prove the state of mind of the declarant do raise some hearsay dangers:

---

statement of a conspirator, *see* Fed. R. Evid. 801(d)(2)(E), but these questions need not be reached if the statement is not hearsay.

The statement may not prove what it is offered to show if the declarant was speaking insincerely (perhaps joking) or unclearly. But the problems of misperception and of failed memory are not present. Even if these possibilities explain how the declarant came to make the statement, that does not diminish the probative value of the statement, because the issue for which the statement is offered is what was in the mind of the declarant, not whether the declarant was accurately reporting some outside reality.

Another complexity is that sometimes a statement will not only reveal a state of mind but assert it. Suppose, for example, that Donald says, "I believe Victor is a violent person." This statement is offered to prove its literal truth. But it doesn't make much sense to say that the inclusion of the "I believe" tag at the beginning of the statement should change the determination of whether or not the statement is admissible. And in fact, though the statement would probably be considered hearsay, it would also fit within an exception, for statements asserting the declarant's state of mind. *See* FRE 803(3). There is no substantive difference between admitting a statement as non-hearsay proof of the declarant's state of mind apparent from but not asserted in the statement and admitting it as hearsay within the exception for statements of the declarant's state of mind.

6.   *Statements offered on the ground that they are false.* In some cases, a party wishes to prove that a statement was made and then prove by other evidence that the statement was false. *E.g., Anderson v. United States*, 417 U.S. 211, 220 (1974). Making the false statement may be the way that some wrong, such as fraud, was consummated. Or it may be that the making of the statement suggests that the declarant was detached from reality; a classic illustration is that of a woman who declared, "I am the pope." Or the statement may show that the declarant had bad judgment or something to hide.

7.   *Statements that show the ability or manner of expression of the declarant.* If there is doubt as to whether the declarant was alive after an accident, her statement after the accident, "I'm alive" would not be hearsay on that point. Neither would the statements, "I'm dead" or "That hurt"—all on the same ground that dead people don't talk. In the movie *Mr. Deeds Goes to Town*, two old ladies testify, in a hearing on Deeds's competence, that he is "pixillated," but the force of this testimony is diminished when they assert that *everyone* is pixillated—except them. Alternatively, if Deeds's counsel had not been able to secure that acknowledgment from the ladies at trial, he might have put on the stand a witness to testify that the ladies had called all their neighbors pixillated. This testimony would be non-hearsay to show the ladies' use of the term.

8. *Statements inconsistent with the testimony of a witness.* If a witness testifies to **Not-X** and previously made a statement asserting **X**, the previous statement will be considered non-hearsay when offered to impeach the witness's testimony. The distinction between admitting the prior statement for impeachment and for its truth is subtle and elusive, and will be discussed below in Chapter 10. For now, it is enough to point out that, if a party has the burden of proving **X**, he cannot help satisfy that burden by introducing the witness's prior statement of **X** merely to impeach her current testimony of **Not-X**. Only if the prior statement is admissible, notwithstanding the rule against hearsay, to prove the truth of what it asserted, **X**, will it help satisfy that burden.

9. *Statements offered in support of an opinion.* Recall that Fed. R. Evid. 703 provides that an expert witness may base an opinion on information "that the expert has been made aware of or personally observed." Moreover, in a departure from the prior common law, the Rule provides: "If experts in the particular field would reasonably rely on those kinds of facts or data in forming an opinion on the subject, they need not be admissible for the opinion to be admitted." Thus, for example, if physicians reasonably rely in large part on statements by a patient in forming a diagnosis, then this Rule allows them to testify to a diagnostic opinion based in part on a patient's statement, even though that statement would not be admissible on its own. Moreover, the Rule now provides that "if the facts or data would otherwise be inadmissible," the proponent may nevertheless introduce them "if their probative value in helping the jury to evaluate the opinion substantially outweighs their prejudicial effect." This Rule therefore can operate in effect as an end-run around the rule against hearsay: The proponent might say, "I'm not offering this statement for the truth of what it asserts; I'm offering it to show the support for the expert's opinion." In some cases, that distinction might be clear. For example, if an expert offers an opinion that a particular product is not marketable, she might base that opinion in part on statements by potential consumers assessing the product's features. In most cases, though, the statement does not provide any real support for the opinion unless the statement is true; the report of a blood test might support a diagnostic opinion, but presumably only if it is accurate. So far as Rule 703 is concerned, this does not matter; the Rule allows the expert to testify to an opinion based on the report and, subject to its balancing test, allows the report itself to be admitted. But if the statement made to the expert is testimonial and offered against an accused, does the rationale of Rule 703 relieve a Confrontation Clause problem? The last problems presented below address this issue.

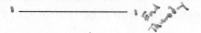

¶ **9.6:** Let's start with some simple problems to test your understanding of the discussion above. Which of the following comes within the basic definition of hearsay? Do not worry at this point about whether the statement would actually be admissible.

(a) To prove that the Defendant in an auto accident case ran a red light, Plaintiff offers testimony of Witness that soon after the accident Declarant said to Witness, "Defendant ran the light." *Yes. Used for truth.*

(b) Same as (a), but Plaintiff offers a properly authenticated writing signed by Declarant in which Declarant says, "Defendant ran the light." *Still used for truth.*

(c) Same as (a), but Plaintiff offers a properly authenticated videotape recording that shows Declarant saying, "Defendant ran the light." *Still a statement!*

(d) To impeach Prime-Witness, who has testified that Plaintiff ran the light, Plaintiff offers the testimony of Secondary-Witness that Prime-Witness previously said, "Defendant ran the light." *NOT for truth. For impeachment!* *which is ok b/c we can grill the witness if they remember correctly/other testimonial incapacities*

(e) The testimony is as in (d), but offered to prove that Defendant ran the light. *Nope, that's hearsay, bruh.*

(f) To prove that there was a dangerous condition that injured Tenant, Tenant offers the testimony of Employee that, shortly before the accident, Neighbor said to Landlord, "That porch is in bad shape." *Using for truth*

(g) To prove that Landlord had notice of the dangerous condition, Tenant offers the evidence in (f). *Does show notice... but isn't also being offered to show porch is in bad shape too?. really just goes to notice*

(h) To prove that Landlord had notice of the dangerous condition, Tenant offers the testimony of Employee that, shortly before the accident, Landlord said, "The porch on the house Tenant is renting from me is in bad shape." *This def goes to notice. only difference with (g) is who made the statement* *Maybe Neighbor said it, but its not in bad shape.*

(i) In support of the contention that Henry and Sergeant conspired to kill Thomas, Eliot's testimony that Henry said to Sergeant, "Won't somebody whack Thomas for me?" *Sure its a question, but still used for truth? NOPE. there's no assertion!*

¶ **9.7:** Tom Testator has died, and his nieces, Brenda and Barbara Beneficiary, are fighting over his will. Barbara offers testimony that, shortly before Tom's death, he said to Brenda, "You're a witch." Admissible? What if the testimony is that Tom said, "I think you're a witch"? What if the statement was in writing? *Not for truth.* *and maybe it's a statement of operative significance, too* *same diff* *state of mind exception 803*

so technically this is being offered to show TOMA, that Tom thinks X, but, it comes in anyway b/c

¶ **9.8:** (a) Smith sold Jones his cow, Bessie. Jones now sues Smith, claiming that Smith fraudulently represented Bessie's condition. Jones has offered evidence that Bessie is barren. He now wants to offer his own testimony that just before he agreed to buy Bessie, Smith said to him, "This is one fertile cow." Is this testimony hearsay? *Used for misrepresentation, not truth. statement offered (yup! ☺) on the ground that it is false*

(b) Now assume instead that Jones is claiming that Smith breached a contract to sell Bessie, and that Smith is contending that there was no contract. Jones wants to testify that Smith said, "I'll sell you Bessie for $500," and that he responded, "I accept." Is this testimony hearsay? *too! No. Statements of operative significance. No truth value.*

However tricky you may have found these problems to be, they are actually quite cut-and-dried so far as standard doctrine is concerned. The following ones pose more difficulty.

¶ **9.9:** Hanson and Schrik agreed to split 50–50 the corn that Schrik harvested from land that he leased from Hanson. Schrik sold a crib of corn that Hanson claimed belonged to him, and Hanson's executor has sued the purchaser for conversion. *could be* Can Schrik testify that when Hanson came to the farm Schrik *an operative* pointed to the other crib and said, "This is your corn"? What if *any statement,* Schrik's testimony is that he said, "I've divided the corn as we *a statement* agreed. That's yours"? *Compare Hanson v. Johnson*, 161 Minn. *of division* 229, 201 N.W. 322 (1924). *What does the question assert? of the corn*

¶ **9.10:** Recall Knapp from our discussion of probabilistic *w/ the "?"* evidence. He is on trial for murdering a marshal and pleads that *not an issue* he killed in self-defense. He contends that he was in fear for his life, in part because he had heard that the marshal had killed an old man in another town. For each of the following variations, be prepared to discuss whether the offered evidence is admissible, and if so, for what proposition or propositions.

(a) Wembley's testimony for Knapp that Knapp told him, a day before killing the marshal, "The marshal clubbed an old man to death." *Used to show Knapp's fear*

(b) Same as (a), but Wembley's testimony is that Knapp said, "I believe the marshal clubbed an old man to death." *none used to show man clubbed to death* *Now it is being used for truth. State of mind exception!*

(c) Knapp's testimony that, shortly before he killed the marshal, the marshal told him, "I clubbed an old man to death." *Same used for effect on the listener*

(d) Winters' testimony that he overheard the conversation in (c).[17] *same*

---

[17] *See* Richard D. Friedman, *Route Analysis of Credibility and Hearsay*, 96 Yale L.J. 667, 702–07 (1987).

(e) Winters' testimony that Wembley told her that Wembley had told Knapp about the clubbing. *still fear... actually... no... being used to show Wembley said X. Wembley isn't on the stand, can't cross-examine them / test their testimonral incapacities*

¶ **9.11:** Recall the *Bridges* case, in which Sharon, a young girl, allegedly described the room in which Bridges molested her. Independent evidence shows that Bridges' apartment meets Sharon's description, and that Sharon probably wasn't in Bridges' apartment on any other occasion. Assume now that Sharon is unwilling or unable to testify at all. Can Sharon's mother testify for the prosecution that

(a) Sharon told her that she was molested in a bedroom that had a television near the door, a large bed, and a reclining chair? *No. used to show molestation.*

(b) Sharon told her that she was molested in a bedroom that had a stuffed hammerhead shark on the wall, a mangy ficus tree in one corner, a large mirror on the ceiling, and a poster of Donald Trump in a basketball uniform on another wall? *No. used to show molestation.*

(c) Sharon brought home from school a story that she had written, which the mother is able to authenticate, and which tells about a birthday party and includes a description of a room as in (a)? *No... ble not relevant?*

(d) Same as (c) but the room description in the story is the one given in (b)?[18] *Yes. shows she knows room. Linked to molestation, but that's not the assertion.*

¶ **9:12:** Goldstein, who suffers from schizophrenia, killed Kendra Webdale, a woman he did not know, by pushing her into the path of an oncoming subway train. He pleads insanity to a murder charge. The principal witness against him is Hegarty, a forensic psychiatrist, who testifies that Goldstein's schizophrenia is relatively mild and that he uses it as an excuse for violent and predatory acts against women. In reaching this conclusion, Hegarty relied on her own examination of Goldstein, on voluminous clinical records, and on her interviews of several people. One, John P., was a security guard at a supermarket who describes an attack by Goldstein on a woman about two years before the killing; according to P., Goldstein said right after the assault that he was sick and should go to the hospital, as he did after the killing. Second, Kimberly D., an acquaintance of Goldstein's, told of a woman named Stephanie H., who strikingly resembled Webdale, worked in a strip club, and teased Goldstein

---

[18] *See* Bridges v. State, 247 Wis. 350, 19 N.W.2d 529 (1945) (holding admissible mother's testimony that daughter described some features of apartment matching defendant's). For contrasting analyses of *Bridges,* see Friedman, *Route Analysis,* 96 Yale L.J. at 681–83 & n.40; Park, *Concept of Hearsay,* 65 Minn. L. Rev. at 437–41, 439 n.50.

sexually. Third, Serita G., a former landlady of Goldstein's, told Hegarty that he exposed himself to one of her maids. Fourth, Isaac V., a former roommate of Goldstein's, described him as "a little weird" but "never violent."

(a) Should Hegarty be allowed to testify to her expert opinion as to the extent Goldstein's schizophrenia played a role in the killing, given that the opinion is based in significant part on these and other interviews? *Yes, thats dble thats how experts get opinions*

(b) Assuming the answer to (a) is affirmative, should Hegarty be allowed to support her opinion by testifying to what P., D., G., and V. told her? *See People v. Goldstein*, 6 N.Y. 3d 119, 843 N.E.2d 727 (2005). *No, then using for truth, not as basis of opinion*

¶ 9.13: Szymanski is accused of having committed arson in an apartment. The prosecution offers the testimony of a fire inspector to a statement made to him the night of the fire by the tenant of the apartment. In the statement, the tenant, who died before trial of unrelated causes, described the condition of the apartment before she left it that evening. The statement was made after the fire had been extinguished and as part of an investigation into a possible crime. The prosecution contends that the statement is not testimonial, and that in any event it does not pose a confrontation problem because it is not offered to prove the truth of what it asserted "but only to show what the inspector did and what information he relied upon in forming the opinion that the fire was intentionally set by human hand." How should the court rule? *See Szymanski v. State*, 166 P.3d 879 (Wyo. 2007). *Admissible? No! Expert can use as basis of opinion, but can't relate the hearsay. Hearsay and confrontation clause issue.*

Now consider *Williams v. Illinois*, 132 S.Ct. 2221 (2012). After a rape in Chicago, the Illinois State Police (ISP) sent a vaginal swab taken from the victim, referred to as L.J., to a private forensic lab, Cellmark, in Germantown, Maryland. The ISP did this to help it relieve a backlog of DNA samples that it wanted tested. Cellmark sent the ISP a report, signed by two lab supervisors, containing the profile of male DNA of material that it said was found on the swab. An ISP analyst was able to match this profile with that of Williams, whose profile was in the database as the result of an arrest on unrelated charges made several months after the rape. This was a cold hit. That is, before this hit, there had been no specific suspect for the crime. L.J. identified Williams, albeit somewhat uncertainly, and he was charged with the rape. At trial, with the judge sitting as fact-finder, the state proved Williams' DNA profile through the testimony of Karen Abbinanti, a lab analyst who had performed a test on blood taken from Williams. But the state did not present anyone from the Cellmark lab; nor did it even introduce the report. Instead, it offered the testimony of Sandra Lambatos, another lab analyst, that both she and a computer program had determined that Williams's profile matched the one reported by Cellmark. Williams objected on Confrontation Clause grounds. The case ultimately turned on the votes of five justices that the Cellmark report was not testimonial. But it also presented the issue of whether the lab report was offered for the truth of what it asserted. Speaking for a group of four, Justice Alito concluded that it was not; the other five justices vigorously disagreed. Justice Alito's basic argument was this: The prosecution asked its expert, Lambatos, whether in her opinion there was a match between the profile reported by Cellmark and Williams' known profile. Lambatos's testimony therefore did not relay the contents of the Cellmark report; rather, it took that content as a premise. (And because this was a bench trial, Justice Alito assumed that the judge would draw the distinction; in a jury trial, it might be a different story.) But, Justice Alito recognized, that testimony would be irrelevant if there were no other proof of the contents of that report—or as he put it, of "the source of the sample that Cellmark tested" and "the reliability of the Cellmark profile." What was there, given that no one from Cellmark testified at trial? Justice Alito noted that the prosecution presented conventional chain-of-custody evidence, including that the vaginal swabs were sent to Cellmark and then returned to the ISP lab. Moreover, he emphasized, the match between the profile reported by Cellmark and Williams' was itself strong confirmation both that Cellmark deduced its profile from the semen on the vaginal swabs and that it did so accurately: There was no plausible explanation as to how "shoddy or dishonest work in the Cellmark lab" could have produced a DNA profile that just happened to match that of Williams, whom the victim identified at a lineup. Note that the logic here is much like that suggested above in ¶ 9.11, presenting variations on the *Bridges* case; that is, the fact-finder is not being asked to rely on the reporting accuracy of the out-of-court witness but on the remarkable coincidence that her statement matches a conjunction of features associated with the accused.

¶ 9.14: Suppose the *Williams* case is replayed, and you are representing the defense. The trial judge has ruled that she will allow the prosecution to present Lambatos's opinion on the basis suggested in the paragraph above. What kinds of statements by the prosecutor as to Cellmark and the report will you allow the prosecutor to make in argument without objection? And what kinds of statements will you try to prevent the prosecutor from making?

¶ 9.15: Katso is on trial for rape. The prosecution offers the testimony of Davenport, a DNA expert, that in his opinion Katso's DNA profile matches that of DNA found on a vaginal swab taken from the alleged victim. Davenport had no role in the testing; the samples taken from Katso and from the alleged victim were sent to a forensic lab, and one analyst, Fisher, worked on both and prepared a report of the tests he performed. The prosecution does not offer Fisher's report into evidence. Is Davenport's testimony proper? *See United States v. Katso*, 74 M.J. 273 (CAAF 2015), *cert. denied*, 136 S.Ct. 1512 (2016).

Now that we have examined closely the question whether a statement is being offered to prove the truth of a matter that it asserted, we can see that the determination is often straightforward, but not always. And sometimes when we determine that the statement *is* being offered to prove the truth of a proposition it asserts we might wonder what the significance of that is, because the hearsay dangers do not appear all that great and there is no good reason to believe that the jury will be so unable to consider those dangers that excluding the evidence is better than admitting it. But now consider the matter through the lens of the confrontation principle—that if a testimonial statement is to be used against a party, it should be made in a way that an adverse party (especially a criminal defendant) has a right to confront and cross-examine the witness who made the statement. That principle is not threatened, or at least is not likely to be threatened seriously, unless the testimonial statement is offered to prove that what the witness said is true. In this context, then, drawing a line between offering a statement for the truth and for other purposes makes a great deal of sense. This may be an area—we will see many others—in which hearsay law seems implicitly to reflect the confrontation principle.

Finally, consider whether the problem of defining hearsay would be much diminished if, instead of classifying a species of out-of-court statements as hearsay and rendering them presumptively inadmissible, the law recognized the existence of hearsay dangers when they exist and prescribed an appropriate treatment depending in part on the extent of the dangers. Such an approach might lack some of the predictability of a categorical, definitional approach—but as we study hearsay consider whether current doctrine truly achieves with sufficient regularity results that are both predictable and sound. An open-textured hearsay rule would not protect the confrontation right—but the essential contribution of *Crawford* is to recognize that the confrontation right must stand on its own, and not be protected by hearsay doctrine. One may wonder whether a categorical hearsay rule has persisted so long because until recently courts failed to articulate a confrontation right independent of it.

Some force might be added to this last observation by focusing on one important aspect of hearsay doctrine that we have noted but not squarely addressed: Modern American hearsay doctrine rejects the rule of *Wright v. Tatham* and instead limits hearsay to *statements*. Recall that Wright, attempting to prove that the testator Marsden was competent, offered three letters written long before the litigation arose—one from a cousin, reporting on his experiences in America, one from a neighbor, asking that Marsden get involved in a local dispute, and one from a departing cleric thanking Marsden for his sponsorship. None of the letters *asserted* that Marsden was mentally competent, but each arguably reflected the writer's belief in this fact. The House of Lords held that the letters were hearsay when offered to prove Marsden's competence. Their Lordships were correct in understanding that as evidence the letters had some of the same defects that hearsay does. And yet the Federal Rules would no longer classify the letters as hearsay when offered to prove Marsden's competence, because they do not assert the proposition that Marsden is competent. So how should a modern court take into account the evidentiary defects of the letters in deciding whether they should be admitted? In the same way that it does with respect to most evidence—by engaging in a case-specific, non-doctrinaire balance of probative value, prejudice, and other costs. And so that might make us wonder whether, *so long as the confrontation right is separately protected*, we ought to trust the same type of open-ended judgment in determining the admissibility of evidence that, because it is of a statement, does constitute hearsay under the modern definition.

¶ 9.16: (a) Elucidate the reasoning that underlay Wright's contention that the letters were probative. How did they tend to prove that Marsden was a competent person? How might the authors have come to write them even if Marsden were *not* competent at the time they wrote? Put another way, what hearsay problems does the evidence create? Which is better evidence that Marsden was competent—one of these letters, or an affidavit by its author stating explicitly that Marsden was competent? Did it make sense to treat the letters as hearsay and presumptively inadmissible? Were the letters testimonial in nature?

(b) Consider a hypothetical discussed in *Wright*: A ship captain thoroughly inspects the ship and then boards it with his wife and children for a long sea voyage. Should evidence of this conduct be admissible to prove that the ship was seaworthy? Is this evidence hearsay? If not, on what basis might a court conclude that the evidence should not be admitted?

(c) Suspecting that Humphrey was running an illegal bookmaking operation out of his house, government agents secured a warrant to search his house. While they were there, they answered the phone several times. The unknown callers gave directions for placing bets on various sports events. At trial, the Government seeks to introduce evidence of these calls. Should it be admissible?[19] *See. Not saying Humphrey is doing X...but makes it more likely X was happening.*

(d) Two women are on the sidelines of a youth soccer game. As one player grabs the ball and charges downfield with it, one of the women says to the other, "Look at my daughter run." Would evidence of this utterance be hearsay if offered to prove that the girl with the ball was indeed the declarant's daughter? In deciding, what more information might you want to know?

Yes?.

E. WHAT STATEMENTS ARE TESTIMONIAL?

We have just addressed a significant respect in which the confrontation principle and hearsay doctrine are substantially the same: Neither comes into play unless the statement in question is offered to prove the truth of a matter that it asserts. Now we will address the most significant respect in which they differ: The confrontation principle applies only to statements that are testimonial in nature—that is, to statements that were made by a person who was effectively acting as a witness in doing so. Hearsay doctrine is not so limited—the basic definition of hearsay applies to all out-of-court statements offered for their truth, whether testimonial or not—but during the course of this unit we will see that the exemptions to the rule against hearsay tend to relieve the hearsay bar from non-testimonial statements and to leave it in place with respect to testimonial statements.

Crawford, while making clear that the term "testimonial" is central to Confrontation Clause doctrine, declined to give a comprehensive definition of it. The Court did refer to three definitions of the term that it said "share a common nucleus":

• "ex parte in-court testimony or its functional equivalent—that is, material such as affidavits, custodial examinations, prior testimony that the defendant was unable to cross-examine, or similar pretrial statements that declarants would reasonably expect to be used prosecutorially";

• "extrajudicial statements . . . contained in formalized testimonial materials, such as affidavits, depositions, prior testimony, or confessions";

• "statements that were made under circumstances which would lead an objective witness reasonably to believe that the statement would be available for use at a later trial."

---

[19] *See* United States v. Zenni, 492 F.Supp. 464 (E,D, Ky. 1980) (extensive discussion, concluding that evidence is not hearsay under Federal Rules); *cf.* R. v. Kearley, 2 App. Cas. 228, 2 All E.R. 345, 2 W.L.R. 656, 95 Crim. App. 88 (H.L. 1992) (reaffirming *Wright*). Various issues related to *Kearley* are discussed by fifteen scholars, mainly Americans, in *Symposium on Hearsay and Implied Assertions: How Would (or Should) the Supreme Court Decide the* Kearley *Case?*, 16 Miss. Coll. L. Rev. 1 (1995). *Kearley* has been effectively nullified by the Criminal Justice Act 2003.

More than by presenting definitions, *Crawford* gave guidance by listing categories of statements that are clearly testimonial:

> Whatever else the term covers, it applies at a minimum to prior testimony at a preliminary hearing, before a grand jury, or at a former trial; and to police interrogations.

The Court emphasized that it "use[d] the term 'interrogation' in its colloquial, rather than any technical legal, sense," and that "Sylvia's recorded statement, knowingly given in response to structured police questioning, qualifies under any conceivable definition." It is important to bear in mind that, in listing clear cases of testimonial statements, *Crawford* did not purport to define the outer bounds of the category of testimonial statements.

The testimonial approach represents a fresh way of thinking about confrontation matters, but in most contexts it does not change the results reached under the *Roberts* regime, which largely incorporated the rules of hearsay. Consider the case of statements by conspirators. Suppose, for example, that Conspirator speaks to Undercover Informant, not knowing U.I.'s role, and tells U.I. that Defendant is going to provide some of the cash with which Conspirator hopes to buy cocaine from U.I. *Crawford* indicated that such a statement is not testimonial. This appears correct. Conspirator is not acting as a witness in making this statement; he is simply going about his conspiratorial business, and even after *Crawford* the Confrontation Clause does not pose any obstacle to admission of the statement. Traditional hearsay law reaches the same result—and so too did Confrontation Clause jurisprudence under *Roberts*—but by a remarkably attenuated chain of logic. Statements by a party are admissible against that party—that is what has traditionally been known as the doctrine of party admissions, resting on the ground that a party has no need to cross-examine himself. Fed. R. Evid. 801(d)(2)(A). This theory was traditionally extended to statements made by an authorized agent of the party. Fed. R. Evid. 801(d)(2)(C). And members of a conspiracy are deemed to be agents of each other when acting in furtherance of the conspiracy, so statements of one conspirator in furtherance of the conspiracy are admissible against another conspirator. Fed. R. Evid. 801(d)(2)(E). Wow!

Now look at the other side: Statements made by a conspirator about the subject matter of the conspiracy but *not* in furtherance of the conspiracy often *will* be testimonial. In particular, suppose a conspiracy member knowingly makes a statement to the police exposing the conspiracy. That statement is almost certainly testimonial, and so under *Crawford* the Confrontation Clause would presumably require its exclusion. The statement would also presumably be excluded by the hearsay rule: Exposing the conspiracy certainly did not further it, so the exemption for conspirators' statements does not apply.

¶ 9.17: Here is an excerpt from the oral argument in *Hammon v. Indiana.*

JUSTICE BREYER: When, for example, there's an undercover agent, a law enforcement officer—let's think of the mafia or the Ku Klux Klan reveals himself. One of the co-conspirators during the ongoing conspiracy switches sides. But no. He doesn't switch. He's still in the conspiracy. Makes a whole lot of statements. Those are all inadmissible, though they'd come in now because they would be in the furtherance of the conspiracy.

MR. FRIEDMAN: Statements in furtherance of a conspiracy, if I understand—

JUSTICE BREYER: Yes. There—but there's—in other words, I've got your definition and all I've tried to do is create a circumstance where, while it fits your definition, it's made by a person that is in the conspiracy. So I make him undercover, the law enforcement officer.

MR. FRIEDMAN: If it's an undercover law enforcement—

JUSTICE BREYER: But known.

MR. FRIEDMAN: By—by known, I mean to the declarant.

JUSTICE BREYER: Yes.

MR. FRIEDMAN: By known, I mean to the declarant. So if it's—

JUSTICE BREYER: Yes.

MR. FRIEDMAN: —if it's an undercover agent and so it's a statement to an undercover—

JUSTICE BREYER: So you're saying my hypothetical could never come up. What I'm trying to do is—it seems to me that your hypothetical is going to take statements that would come in that are pretty far removed from the prosecution that are in odd circumstances, are not just testimonial at all in anybody's thought, but it keeps them out.

MR. FRIEDMAN: I—I'm afraid I—I don't fully understand the hypothetical. If the—if the officer is not known to the declarant as a law enforcement officer, then there's no problem. Then—then the statement could—

JUSTICE BREYER: He's known.

> MR. FRIEDMAN: If he's—he's known to the law enforcement officer and the member of the conspiracy is making a—
>
> JUSTICE BREYER: It's continuing.

If you were arguing the case, what would you say now? *How does this further the conspiracy?*

As noted above, though *Crawford* fundamentally altered the way courts *conceptualize* the confrontation right, it leaves most *results* unchanged from those prescribed by prior doctrine. But it certainly does change *some* results. Since *Crawford*, there has been little doubt that statements made in formal judicial proceedings are testimonial. For example, if Defendant One pleads guilty to a crime and makes a statement at a plea hearing, that would be considered testimonial and so could not be admitted, absent live testimony by Defendant One, at a trial of Defendant Two. In this respect, *Crawford* has clearly altered the practice of the *Roberts* era, when many courts were willing to characterize such statements as reliable and therefore admissible notwithstanding the confrontation right. But in doing so, *Crawford* restored a rule that had been clearly established since the 17th century, in the *Case of Thomas Tong*, Kelyng J. 17, 18, 84 Eng. Rep. 1061, 1062 (1662)—that an out-of-court confession may be used against the confessor, but not against his conspirators.

Treating these statements as testimonial has not been controversial since *Crawford*. But in two other contexts, very different from each other—fresh accusations and forensic lab reports—the meaning of "testimonial" has been very controversial and the Supreme Court has repeatedly attempted to give the lower courts guidance.

Davis v. Washington, 547 U.S. 813 (2006), addressed the first of these contexts. *Davis* decided a pair of cases, each of which grew out of a trial that was held before the Supreme Court issued its decision in *Crawford*. Each of the two involved an accusation of domestic violence, made to a state agent shortly after the alleged incident, by a woman who did not appear at trial. In each one the trial court admitted the accusation under the "excited utterance" or "spontaneous declaration" exception to the rule against hearsay; as expressed in Fed. R. Evid. 803(2), this exception applies to "[a] statement relating to a startling event or condition made while the declarant was under the stress of excitement caused by the event or condition."

Some historical background might be useful here. As the rule against hearsay crystallized in the early 19th century, a statement was not exempted on the basis that it reported on a fresh event; courts may have been aware, at least implicitly, that if they created such an exemption then witnesses would effectively be allowed to testify by making accusations or other important testimonial statements right after the event. But a doctrine gradually emerged that a statement might be admitted as part of what was called the *res gestae*—that is, if it was not merely a report on events but part of the event itself, then that provided a basis for admission. So, for example, if before a fatal blow was cast the victim made an accusation against the defendant, then the making of the accusation might be admitted as helping set the scene for the blow. For a time, courts adhered rigorously to this limitation. In the latter half of the 19th century, for example, *R. v. Bedingfield,* 14 Cox Crim. Cas. 341 (Crown Ct. 1879), held that a statement by a young woman, made while running out of a house seconds after having her throat slit and accusing the ultimate defendant of having committed the crime, was not within the doctrine. But this case was controversial from the start, and by the time Wigmore published his treatise at the beginning of the 20th century he claimed that for at least a generation there had been a hearsay exception for certain statements made soon after an event. Wigmore placed emphasis on the stress of excitement rather than on strict simultaneity as being the principal criterion for the exception. Most courts followed Wigmore's lead, but by the time the Federal Rules were drafted there was enough support for a simultaneity-based exception that the Rules incorporated both.

¶ 9.18: Read the hearsay exceptions for present sense impressions and excited utterances, FRE 803(1) and (2). How are they different? In what respect is each more generous than the other? Suggest a case that satisfies the first but not the second, and one that satisfies the second but not the first.

¶ 9.19: As stated by Wigmore, the "excited utterance" exception applied to statements that were made while the declarant was so affected by the startling event that she could not have had time to concoct a falsehood. As expressed in the Federal Rules, the exception seems to be considerably broader, but it is still based on the idea that a declarant is unlikely to blurt out a falsehood when speaking under the stress of a startling condition.

(a) Is this rationale persuasive?

(b) Can you make any generalization about whether a declarant is likely to be acting as a witness if she makes a statement immediately after a stressful event?

Under the pre-*Crawford* decision of *White v. Illinois,* 502 U.S. 346 (1992), a "spontaneous declaration" exception was deemed "firmly rooted," and therefore statements falling within it satisfied the reliability requirement of *Roberts*—and, the Court held, the Confrontation Clause posed no problem irrespective of whether the declarant was unavailable to testify. As a result, in many cases, especially ones involving domestic violence, the prosecution proved the crime merely by introducing evidence of an out-of-court accusation made shortly after the alleged event. *See* Richard D. Friedman & Bridget McCormack, *Dial-In Testimony*, 150 U.PA. L. REV. 1171 (2002). Indeed, prosecutors often spoke of "evidence-based prosecutions," a curious term referring to prosecutions marked particularly by one piece of evidence that was *missing*—the live testimony of the complainant. If the trial court determined that the complainant made a statement shortly after the events and that she was very upset when she did so, that was usually enough to guarantee admission of the statement, without demonstrating why the witness was not testifying in court.

In one of the two cases decided under the *Davis* caption, *Davis* itself, the accusation was made in a 911 call, begun while the caller was in distress and unprotected and the accused was not only at large but still in the house. At the beginning, the caller, Michelle McCottry, spoke in the present tense: "He's here jumpin' on me again." The operator asked for the assailant's name, and McCottry gave his last, first, and middle names. After she reported that Davis had left, the operator told her, "Stop talking and answer my questions." McCottry gave further information about Davis, including his birthday, and described the background to the incident.

In deciding this case, the Court once again declined to offer a comprehensive definition of the term "testimonial." It did, however, announce this principle:

> Statements are nontestimonial when made in the course of police interrogation under circumstances objectively indicating that the primary purpose of the interrogation is to enable police assistance to meet an ongoing emergency. They are testimonial when the circumstances objectively indicate that there is no such ongoing emergency, and that the primary purpose of the interrogation is to establish or prove past events potentially relevant to later criminal prosecution.

Although this language sounds as if the purpose of the interrogator is the key factor, other passages make it appear that the perspective of the declarant ultimately governs, and that the purpose of the interrogator is significant only so far as it casts light on the understanding of the declarant. *See, e.g.,* 547 U.S. at 822 n.1 ("even when interrogation exists, it is in the final analysis the declarant's statements, not the interrogator's questions, that the Confrontation Clause requires us to evaluate"); *see also* Richard D. Friedman, Crawford, Davis, *and* Way *Beyond*, 15 J.L. & Pol. 553, 568–72 (2007) (arguing that a perspective based on the declarant's understanding rather than an interrogator's purpose is preferable and consistent with *Davis*). As we will see, the Court addressed this issue five years later.

In deciding *Davis*, the Court pointed to these facts: (1) The complainant was speaking as events "were actually happening"; (2) her call "was plainly a call for help against bona fide threat"; (3) the statements elicited were necessary to help resolve the emergency rather than merely learn what had happened in the past; and (4) the setting was frantic, rather than "tranquil, or even (as far as any reasonable 911 operator could make out) safe." Accordingly, the Court concluded that the beginning of the call was primarily an attempt "to enable police assistance to meet an ongoing emergency." This characterization included the complainant's identification of the assailant, which the Court believed might help the dispatched officers to know whether they were encountering a violent felon. But, the Court said,

> after the operator gained the information needed to address the exigency of the moment, the emergency appears to have ended (when Davis drove away from the premises). The operator then told [the complainant] to be quiet, and proceeded to pose a battery of questions. It could readily be maintained that, from that point on, [the complainant's] statements were testimonial.

The Court regarded the other case, *Hammon v. Indiana* (in which I represented the petitioner), as "much easier." In *Hammon*, the woman made the accusation in her living room to a police officer, while her husband was restrained by another officer, an indeterminate amount of time after the incident; immediately after she made her oral statement, the officer asked her to complete an affidavit to similar effect, and she did so. (The state supreme court acknowledged that the affidavit was testimonial but ruled that its admission was harmless error.) The Supreme Court held 8–1 (Thomas, J., dissenting), that this statement was clearly testimonial. "It is entirely clear from the circumstances," the Court noted, "that the interrogation was part of an investigation into possibly criminal past conduct.... There was no emergency in progress...." The Court regarded it as significant that the complainant was describing past events and that when she made her statement police officers were separating her husband from her. And it indicated that some initial inquiries at a crime scene, intended to enable the police to assess the situation, might produce non-testimonial statements.

¶ **9.20:** Prepare to discuss the following questions, based on the descriptions given above.

(a) Was the result in *Davis* correct? In *Hammon*?

(b) What constitutes an "ongoing emergency"? Was the Court justified in concluding that the first part of the statement in *Davis* was made in response to such an emergency? If so, precisely when, if at all, do you believe McCottry's statements began to be testimonial? In answering these questions, take into account this additional fact: Near the end of the conversation, the 911 operator said, "They're gonna check the area for him first, and then they're gonna come talk to you."

[handwritten margin note: Dude's still at large, but not in house... one told to stop talking / start answering Qs.]

(c) In some portions of the opinion, the *Davis* Court appears to emphasize the purpose of the questioner in determining whether a statement is testimonial. Is this appropriate? How should the question of whether a statement is testimonial be determined when it is not made in response to questioning?

[handwritten margin note: Does purpose matter if not known to declarant?]

(d) Must a statement be formal to be considered testimonial? (Justice Thomas took the position that it must be, and this was the basis of his dissent in *Hammon*.) If so, what does formal mean?

[handwritten margin note: No? Ppl talk to police informally]

The Supreme Court returned to the area of fresh accusations, but with different results, in *Michigan v. Bryant*, 562 U.S. 344 (2011). Responding to a radio dispatch concerning a shooting in Detroit, police found Anthony Covington near a gas station, lying on the ground, bleeding from the chest and stomach areas, and in considerable pain. As each officer arrived, he asked Covington what had happened, who had shot him, and where the shooting had occurred. In response, Covington told the officers that Bryant—who had supplied Covington with drugs for years—had shot him about 30 minutes before and about six blocks away, at Bryant's house and through the front door, and that he had driven himself to the gas station. Covington expressed concern about when medical help would arrive, but gave no suggestion that anyone was in danger of further violence; the officers did not draw their weapons or search the scene for a gunman. Covington died several hours later; at the time he made the statements, he was apparently unaware that he was so close to death. Bryant was eventually found and tried for Covington's murder. Evidence of Covington's accusatory statements was introduced over Bryant's objection, and Bryant was convicted. The Michigan Supreme Court held that Bryant's confrontation right had been violated, but the United States Supreme Court took the case and reversed, 6–2, with Justice Sotomayor writing the majority opinion and Justices Scalia (caustically) and Ginsburg in dissent. (Justice Kagan was recused.) The majority held that Covington's statements were not testimonial.

Before considering the merits of the case, note that the fact that Covington died before trial, and by gunshot wounds, creates a great temptation to admit his statements. We have already referred briefly to two doctrines that might be thought to bear on a case of this sort—dying declarations and forfeiture—but for reasons that we will explore later neither was available here. The fact that Covington was unavailable to testify at trial made inadmissibility of his statements a singularly unappealing result, but on the face of it (though perhaps not in reality), the Supreme Court did not take this factor into account in determining whether those statements were testimonial. The Court's decision that the statements were not testimonial therefore would have rendered the Confrontation Clause inapplicable even if Covington had fully recovered from his wounds, was living around the corner from the courthouse, and simply decided that he did not wish to appear at trial.

Justice Sotomayor's opinion contained some language suggesting that some of the justices may be having buyer's remorse over *Crawford*. "[T]here may be other circumstances, aside from ongoing emergencies," she wrote, "when a statement is not procured with a primary purpose of creating an out-of-court substitute for trial testimony." Moreover: "In making the primary purpose determination, standard rules of hearsay, designed to identify some statements as reliable, will be relevant." And further: "Implicit in *Davis* is the idea that because the prospect of fabrication in statements given for the primary purpose of resolving that emergency is presumably significantly diminished, the Confrontation Clause does not require such statements to be subject to the crucible of cross-examination." And, she indicated, the logic here is "not unlike that justifying the excited utterance exception in hearsay law," which is based on the idea that statements falling within the exception because made under the stress caused by the event described in the statement, "are considered reliable because the declarant, in the excitement, presumably cannot form a falsehood."

¶ 9.21: You can assume that Justice Sotomayor accurately stated the traditional justification for the excited-utterance exception. Are you persuaded by it? Do you believe that her discussion of *Davis* is accurate?

Subsequent developments, though, indicated that Justice Sotomayor, at least, did not mean to resuscitate a reliability test for the Confrontation Clause.

Bryant addressed the issue of how the "primary purpose" test of *Davis* should be implemented. Justice Sotomayor indicated repeatedly that the inquiry is an objective one: "[T]he relevant inquiry is not the subjective or actual purpose of the individuals involved in a particular encounter, but rather the purpose that reasonable participants would have had, as ascertained from the individuals' statements and actions and the circumstances in which the encounter occurred." The reference to "participants" was not accidental, for she also wrote that "*Davis* requires a combined inquiry that accounts for both the declarant and the interrogator." Often, she said, "the primary purpose of the interrogation will be most accurately ascertained by looking to the contents of both the questions and the answers." For example, she noted, if the police say, "Tell us who did this to you so that we can arrest and prosecute them," and the victim answers, "Rick did it," the question gives the context to indicate that the statement is testimonial. Justice Sotomayor further contended that "[t]he combined approach also ameliorates problems that could arise from looking solely to one participant," most notably the problem of mixed motives on the parts of both interrogators and declarants.

¶ 9.22: (a) In a case like *Bryant*, what motives might the interrogator have? The declarant? *— Frame someone . . . or just make an accusation*
Find assailant

(b) It certainly seems correct that determination of whether a statement is testimonial should take account of all the circumstances, and that the nature of a question might be a key factor in determining whether the response is testimonial. But what does it mean to speak of the "purpose of the interrogation" as opposed to the purpose of one or the other of the parties? Does such an approach genuinely ameliorate the problem of mixed motives? (Justice Scalia regarded the idea as bizarre.) What if the motives of the parties are different? In *Bryant*, what do you suppose the purpose of the police was in asking Covington what happened? What was Covington's purpose in answering? If an officer begins questioning with little idea of what happened, but the declarant knows that a crime has been committed, that there is no immediate danger of further crime, and that by speaking he is making an accusation that may lead to the arrest, and be used in the prosecution, of the person accused, should that statement be considered testimonial? *Yes! It's testimonial!*

(c) Suppose a person sends directly to the court a written statement describing criminal activity. Should that statement be considered testimonial? In considering this question, bear in mind that at the time of the Sixth Amendment there was nothing resembling a modern police force, and at least in England most crime was still privately prosecuted, as had been the norm for centuries. *Yes! Purpose = give info to court*

In discussing the particular circumstances of the case, Justice Sotomayor emphasized that the conversations were informal—though she noted that "informality does not necessarily indicate the presence of an emergency or the lack of testimonial intent." Given Covington's grievous condition and his concern for medical care, she could not conclude "that a person in Covington's situation would have had a 'primary purpose' 'to establish or prove past events potentially relevant to later criminal prosecution.' "

¶ **9.23:** Are you persuaded? What did making the statements do to relieve Covington's condition or secure medical help? Not persuaded. Seems like he's making an accusation.

As for the police, Justice Sotomayor wrote that at the outset of the encounter they had a report of a shooting, but they "did not know why, where, or when the shooting had occurred. Nor did they know the location of the shooter or anything else about the circumstances in which the crime occurred." The questions they asked were precisely of the sort that police might ask in a fluid, unresolved situation to assess the danger to themselves, to the victim, and to the public. Covington's statements were therefore deemed not to be testimonial and therefore were outside the reach of the Confrontation Clause.

¶ **9.24:** What perverse incentive might this resolution provide for the police? Not gather info before questioning

¶ **9.25:** Suppose *Hammon* were to arise now. Would the result be the same? Yes? Primary purpose still seems testimonial... what am I missing?

And so the law governing the Confrontation Clause and fresh accusations may be in some flux, with a recent backslide in the direction of *Roberts*. Meanwhile, the Court has repeatedly addressed the other key area in which disputed Confrontation Clause issues often arise, that of forensic lab reports. This has been an area of persistent friction, and now also of considerable confusion.

The foundation case was *Melendez-Diaz v. Massachusetts*, 557 U.S. 305 (2009). This was a mundane drug prosecution. Pursuant to a state statute but over the accused's objection, the prosecution proved that the substance in question was cocaine by introducing attested certificates of laboratory reports to that effect. Note that even apart from the Confrontation Clause, absent such a statute there is a potential hearsay problem with introducing such certificates, for they are clearly being used to prove the truth of what they assert. Before *Crawford*, some courts held that the hearsay problem is avoided by the hearsay exception for records of regularly conducted activities, *see* Fed. R. Evid. 803(6), often referred to as the "business records" exception, or the exception for public records, *see* Fed. R. Evid. 803(8). The first of these is generally justified on the basis that if a type of record is routinely kept by an organization and relied on by it, then it is presumably trustworthy. However true that may be, it does not address the question of whether the record is testimonial for purposes of the Confrontation Clause—but note that *most* regularly kept records are made without litigation being in the offing. Indeed, one may well wonder whether the same trustworthiness argument applies if the particular type of record—a forensic lab report—is routinely kept *for the purposes of litigation* and the organization that keeps it relies on it only in the sense that the organization uses it in litigation. The public-records exception is also usually based on trustworthiness, and the same caveats apply. Indeed, note that the Rule itself takes them into account. Subpart (A)(ii) does not extend to "a matter observed while under a legal duty to report" if the observer is "law-enforcement personnel" (raising for some courts the question of whether a forensic lab independent of the police and prosecution but routinely used by them to prepare prosecutions counts as "law-enforcement personnel"), and subpart (A)(iii), applying to "factual findings from a legally authorized investigation," cannot be invoked by a prosecutor. Note also FRE 803(7) (absence of business record), (9) (public records of vital statistics), 10 (absence of public record).

But of course the question before the Supreme Court concerned the Confrontation Clause rather than ordinary hearsay law. By a 5–4 vote, per Justice Scalia, the Court held that the certificates were testimonial and that admitting them, without offering the accused an opportunity for cross-examination, violated his confrontation right. The certificates were in essence affidavits, and affidavits were within the core class of testimonial statements described by *Crawford*. In addition, applying the third of the three definitions of "testimonial" presented by *Crawford*, the Court held that the certificates were clearly "made under circumstances which would lead an objective witness reasonably to believe that the statement would be available for use at a later trial." Indeed, noted the Court, under Massachusetts law "the *sole* purpose" of the certificates was to provide proof of the composition, weight, and quality of the analyzed substance. Thus, the majority regarded the case as a "rather straightforward application of *Crawford*." But the majority went on to respond to a "potpourri" of counter-arguments offered by the Commonwealth and the dissent.

[handwritten margin note: prepared for trial – may have lab tech to have testify – but Δ usually just stipulates to it better to have it on paper instead of a PhD in a white coat talk about it]

¶ 9.26: Among these counter-arguments were the following:

(a) The certificates should not be deemed testimonial because they were not accusatory. *[handwritten: but... important part of case against]*

(b) The certificates should not be deemed testimonial because they were routine business or official records, and *Crawford* had noted that business records "by their nature" are not testimonial. (Given the result of *Melendez-Diaz*, is this another circumstance in which, at least until relatively recently, the rules of hearsay law (at least if properly construed) conformed to the confrontation principle, crafting exceptions that generally tolerate the admissibility of non-testimonial hearsay while generally excluding testimonial hearsay?) *[handwritten: This kinds sounds lgit to me...]*

(c) The lab technicians were not conventional witnesses: (1) Their statements were nearly contemporaneous with their observations; (2) they did not observe the crime or any human action related to it; and (3) their reports were not made in response to interrogation. *But knew intended purpose*

(d) The certificates reported on a scientific test. *So?*

(e) The expense of requiring lab technicians to testify in court would be very burdensome. *So? That's not an exemption for a constitutional right...*

Do you think the Court was right to reject each of these arguments?

In any event, *Melendez-Diaz* was only the beginning of the story. The four dissenters—Chief Justice Roberts and Justices Kennedy, Breyer, and Alito—have sought repeatedly to undercut it.[20] In *Bullcoming v. New Mexico*, 564 U.S. 647 (2011), the state, in presenting a lab report indicating a very high blood alcohol content, did call a live witness from the lab—but not the analyst who prepared the report, for he had been placed on unpaid administrative leave. By 5–4—over the votes of the same four dissenters—the Court held that this did not suffice.

¶ **9.27:** Was this the correct result? *Sure. They're available, call them.*

In *Williams v. Illinois*, 132 S.Ct. 2221 (2012), the *Melendez-Diaz* dissenters achieved some success—the lab report involved there was held not to be testimonial, but no group of five justices agreed as to why. The facts of *Williams* are summarized before ¶ 9.14. Recall that this was a cold-hit DNA case in which the Illinois State Police sent a commercial lab in Maryland, Cellmark, a vaginal swab taken from a rape victim, and Cellmark sent back a report, signed by two lab supervisors with the profile of male DNA that it said it had found on the swab. At trial, no one from Cellmark testified, and the lab report was not introduced, but Lambatos, a lab analyst testified that both she and a computer program had determined that Williams's profile matched the one reported by Cellmark.

¶ **9.28:** Does the fact that the state did not offer the Cellmark report into evidence preclude an objection based on the Confrontation Clause? What witness testified against Williams *Yes?*

---

[20] Four days after deciding *Melendez-Diaz*, the Court granted certiorari in *Briscoe v. Virginia*, in which the state contended that it could present a certificate of lab results at trial because a statutory procedure gave the accused the right to call the lab analyst as his own witness if he chose. The grant was surprising—including to me, who represented the petitioners—because the Court seemed to have resolved the issue, in favor of the accused, in *Melendez-Diaz*. There was widespread speculation that the dissenters were hoping to take another shot: By longstanding custom, it only takes four justices to grant certiorari, Justice Souter had announced his retirement, and Judge Sonya Sotomayor, already nominated to replace him, was a former prosecutor. But at argument, it became plain that the new justice was not about to vote to undercut a seven-month precedent, and two weeks later the Court did what most observers had assumed it would do right after *Melendez-Diaz*—vacate the decision below in *Briscoe* and remand for further proceedings in light of *Melendez-Diaz*. Briscoe v. Virginia, 130 S.Ct. 1316 (2010).

without his having a chance for confrontation? If the prosecution in *Crawford* had introduced a police officer's summary of what Sylvia Crawford had said, rather than a tape recording of her statement, would that have avoided the confrontation problem? What standards should govern the question of when a statement is sufficiently presented to the trier of fact for the Confrontation Clause to be invoked?

Justice Alito, writing for himself and the three other *Melendez-Diaz* dissenters, concluded that the Cellmark report was not a testimonial statement. He wrote that the abuses that prompted adoption of the Confrontation Clause "involved out-of-court statements having the primary purpose of accusing a targeted individual of engaging in criminal conduct." But the primary purpose of the Cellmark report, he determined, "was to catch a dangerous rapist who was still at large." It was not to accuse Williams, who was then neither in custody nor under suspicion, nor to create evidence for use at trial. Indeed, he pointed out, no one at Cellmark could have known that the profile it produced would inculpate Williams. There was no reason to fabricate "and no incentive to produce anything other than a scientifically sound and reliable report." Moreover, the foursome found significant the division of responsibilities at Cellmark—numerous technicians working on a given sample, so that each was motivated simply to do his or her job as prescribed—the knowledge that defects in a DNA profile are often detectable from the face of the profile itself, and the "beyond fanciful" possibility that mistake or fraud would lead to a DNA profile of a person who would be picked out of a lineup by the victim. These factors led them to the conclusion that "the use at trial of a DNA report prepared by a modern, accredited laboratory" does not resemble the historical practices that the Confrontation Clause was meant to eliminate.

Five justices—Justice Thomas writing for himself and Justice Kagan for the other four—vigorously rejected this reasoning.

¶ 9.29: Suppose you were assigned the responsibility of drafting an opinion rejecting the reasoning of this portion of Justice Alito's opinion. What would your draft say? Begin by considering whether Justice Alito's analysis is consistent with *Crawford*.

Nevertheless, Justice Thomas agreed with the Alito foursome that the Cellmark report was not testimonial. He did so entirely on the basis that the report was not sufficiently formal to be considered testimonial. Why not, given that it was a report of a DNA test sent to a state police lab, signed by two reviewers, bearing case numbers and referring to "evidence"? "Nowhere," he wrote, "does the report attest that its statements accurately reflect the DNA testing processes used or the results obtained"; the reviewers "neither purport to have performed the DNA testing nor certify the accuracy of those who did." The report therefore lacked the "indicia of solemnity" that mark a testimonial statement. Justice Thomas was not worried that such a standard would "result in a prosecutorial conspiracy to elude confrontation by using only informal extrajudicial statements against an accused." Using less formal statements comes at a price, because they tend to be less persuasive to the fact-finder. Moreover, he believed the Confrontation Clause should be construed to reach "bad-faith attempts to evade the formalized process."

¶ **9.30:** Are you persuaded by this reasoning? Suppose you are confident that Justice Thomas's view represents the law, and representatives of a state's legislature, prosecutors, and police ask you for advice as to how they might take advantage of it. What would you tell them? How should a court go about determining whether a state has engaged in "bad-faith attempts to evade the formalized process"? Suppose after Sylvia Crawford came to the police station, an officer said to her,

Please sit in this nice, comfy chair. Would you like some milk and cookies? Now please tell us what happened. Don't worry, we're very informal here. I'm not taking notes or recording what you say, and I won't ask you to sign a statement. If it turns out that this matter goes to trial and you don't feel like testifying then, I'll just tell them what you tell me.

Should her statement then be deemed testimonial? What would Justice Thomas say? *Cf. Ohio v. Clark,* 135 S.Ct. 2173, 2185 (2015) (Thomas, J., concurring in the judgment) (emphasizing solemnity rather than formality).

The Alito opinion did not go so far as to hold that the Cellmark report was not formal, but it did contain some discussion of formality. It said that every post-*Crawford* case but *Hammon* in which the Court had found a violation of the confrontation right, "involved formalized statements such as affidavits, depositions, prior testimony, or confessions"; in *Hammon*, it said, "an informal statement was held to violate the Confrontation Clause"—though in *Hammon*, joined by every member of the foursome, the Court said that the circumstances in which Amy Hammon spoke made the statement "formal enough" to invoke the Confrontation Clause. This is a further indication that these four justices might be feeling buyer's remorse about *Hammon*, and perhaps even about *Crawford*.

So where do matters now stand? Dissenting for herself and three others in *Williams*, Justice Kagan wrote:

The five Justices who control the outcome of today's case agree on very little. Among them, though, they can boast of two accomplishments. First, they have approved the introduction of testimony at Williams's trial that the Confrontation Clause, rightly understood, clearly prohibits. Second, they have left significant confusion in their wake. What comes out of four Justices' desire to limit *Melendez-Diaz* and *Bullcoming* ... in whatever way possible, combined with one Justice's one-justice view of those holdings, is—to be frank—who knows what. Those decisions apparently no longer mean all that they say. Yet no one can tell in what way or to what extent they are altered because no proposed limitation commands the support of a majority.

The Supreme Court's latest brush with the meaning of "testimonial" came in the *Clark* case, cited above in ¶ 9.30. *Clark* involved a statement by a three-year-old child, and we will postpone consideration of it to Chapter 20, which will address the perplexing problem of how statements by children should be treated. We'll close this chapter with one more issue that it appears, sooner or later, the Supreme Court will have to [bad-pun alert] confront.

¶ **9:31:** Craig is accused of murder. The prosecution offers against him the report of an autopsy conducted by Ruiz, a pathologist who is now retired from the medical examiner's office. Koehler, the current medical examiner, consults with Ruiz and then testifies at trial. She relays to the jury what the report says, and drawing in large part on the report estimates the time of death, a crucial factor in implicating Craig. The text of the report is admitted. Ruiz is not called to testify. Has Craig's confrontation right been violated? *See, e.g., State v. Craig*, 853 N.E.2d 621 (Oh. 2006), *cert. denied*, 549 U.S. 1255 (2007). Does your answer depend on the purposes for which autopsy reports are usually prepared? Does it depend on how long after the murder Craig was identified as a suspect, or charged with the murder? Yes, all that matters. changes whether testimonial or not.

[handwritten margin note: It's accusatory to say cause of death is murder. SCOTUS hasn't ruled on this issue yet.]

[handwritten note: End Tuesday]

CHAPTER 10

PRIOR STATEMENTS OF AN
IN-COURT WITNESS

■ ■ ■

Additional Reading: McCormick, ch. 24, § 251; Mueller & Kirkpatrick, §§ 8.24–.26

A. INTRODUCTION

Suppose Green is on trial for distributing illegal drugs. The prosecution puts on the stand Porter, and asks him, "Who was your supplier?" He says, "I don't remember." If the prosecution does not have substantial other evidence that Green was Porter's supplier, then Green may successfully move for a judgment of acquittal as a matter of law; the case will never get to the jury.

But now suppose that previously Porter had told a police officer, Wade, that Green was his supplier. After receiving Porter's profession of failed memory, the prosecutor wants to prove, perhaps through Porter or perhaps through Wade, that Porter had said Green was his supplier. If the prosecution is allowed to prove this statement, and it is admitted to prove the truth of the assertion that Green was Porter's supplier, then the prosecution has enough evidence to get to the jury. Should this be allowed?

The traditional answer is no. And the reason traditionally given is that Porter's statement is hearsay. That is confusing to many students— how can the statement be hearsay if Porter is in court, actually testifying from the witness stand? But note that the basic definition does not treat as hearsay a declaration offered for the truth of what it asserts if it was made *by someone who is not now a witness*. Rather, the definition more broadly sweeps in the statement if it was made *other than from the witness stand*.

But to call the statement hearsay merely begs the question: *Why* shouldn't the statement be admissible, given that Porter is on the stand and subject to cross-examination?

There is a persuasive answer, I believe, at least in a situation precisely like this one: Porter's prior statement is testimonial in nature and it is being offered against a criminal defendant. For reasons discussed below, although Porter is on the stand, Green's ability to cross-examine him with respect to the earlier statement is severely hampered if, when the cross-examination begins, Porter is not still adhering to the substance of that statement. Thus, Green does not have a full opportunity for confrontation. But the force of this logic has not always impressed itself on modern courts and commentators, and so there has been a general drift away from the traditional rule.

Indeed, *California v. Green*, 399 U.S. 149 (1970), the case from which this hypothetical was adopted, involved a provision then new, California Evidence Code § 1235, which creates an exception to the rule against hearsay for prior inconsistent statements of a witness. And in that case the Supreme Court held that this provision did not violate Green's confrontation right. *Crawford* specifically preserves this aspect of *Green*, and asserts broadly that "when the declarant appears for cross-examination at trial, the Confrontation Clause places no constraints at all on the use of his prior testimonial statements." 541 U.S. at 59 n.9. So, for better or worse, that's that, at least for now, so far as the Confrontation Clause goes. But that's not the end of the story.

The Federal Rules of Evidence, which were in formation when *Green* was decided, do not go to this constitutional limit. They modify the traditional rule—but they still begin with the premise that an out-of-court statement offered to prove the truth of what it asserts is hearsay notwithstanding the fact that the declarant is now a witness in court. Recall that under the basic definition, as expressed in FRE 801(c), hearsay is a statement *that the declarant does not make while testifying at the current trial or hearing* and that is offered in evidence to prove the truth of the matter asserted in the statement. The italicized words express the traditional law, which are surprising to many students. This language means that a statement made *before* the current proceeding and offered for the truth of what it asserts is presumptively hearsay even though the declarant is now a witness at that proceeding. Thus, if Wendy testifies, "Dina told the police that Tom punched Jerry," that statement is hearsay to prove that Tom punched Jerry, even if Dina now testifies. Indeed, even if the declarant is the witness who testifies as to the making of the statement, the statement is presumptively hearsay. Thus, if Dina testifies, "I told the police that Tom punched Jerry," that is also hearsay to prove the punch.

FRE 801(d)(1) modifies the traditional rule, and limits the reach of FRE 801(c), by treating *certain* prior statements of a witness as not hearsay. But do not be misled by the boldface heading. It is not all prior statements of witnesses that are withdrawn from the definition of hearsay. Rather, the Rule provides three relatively narrow categories of statements that, if made by a declarant who is now a witness subject to cross-examination at the current proceeding, are deemed not to be hearsay. In essence though not in form, these carve-outs from the definition of hearsay amount to exceptions from the rule against hearsay; we will sometimes use the more neutral term *exemption* to describe rules that make the rule against hearsay inoperative with respect to some statements that fall within the basic definition of hearsay expressed in Rule 801(c).

Section B of this chapter considers the merits of the traditional view that the presence of a witness at trial does not relieve a problem under the Confrontation Clause or the rule against hearsay. Section C addresses the modifications made by the Federal Rules and some other evidentiary regimes. Section D will tentatively suggest how the law in this area might be revamped. My view is that *Green* and *Crawford* have failed to understand that the confrontation right is impaired when the prosecution introduces a testimonial statement and the declarant testifies at trial, but not to the full substance of the earlier statement. This remains an area in which hearsay law is doing work that should be performed by the Confrontation Clause.

B. THE TRADITIONAL VIEW AND CHALLENGES TO IT

The Confrontation Clause ordinarily requires that a witness testify live, subject to oath and cross-examination. Even when the Clause does not apply, the rule against hearsay expresses a general preference that the same conditions be imposed whenever the trier of fact is asked to rely on the truth of a person's assertion. So, if a person makes a statement and then testifies at trial, is there good reason to exclude the prior statement? The traditional view, in the affirmative, was stated forcefully by the Minnesota Supreme Court in an oft-quoted passage in *State v. Saporen*, 205 Minn. 358, 362, 285 N.W. 898, 901 (1939):

> The chief merit of cross-examination is not that at some future time it gives the party opponent the right to dissect adverse testimony. Its principal virtue is the immediate application of the testing process. Its strokes fall while the iron is hot. False testimony is apt to harden and become unyielding to the blows of truth in proportion as the witness has opportunity for reconsideration and influence by the suggestions of others. . . .

¶ **10.1:** Do you accept the logic of this passage? Which type of false statement is a declarant more likely to back down on during cross-examination: one he has just made under oath or one that he made some time before, probably not under oath? Is any generalization possible?

Clearly, as *Saporen* suggests, once direct testimony given at trial is admitted, the opponent has a strong interest in cross-examining immediately rather than later, and cross will ordinarily not be postponed significantly. But that seems not to be the question when a party offers the prior statement of a witness; if there is cross-examination, it will be now. The question seems to be whether the opponent is substantially prejudiced by the fact that the substantive statement being cross-examined, rather than being testimony just given, is a statement made at a prior time out of court.

Since the beginning of the 20th century, the ascendant view has been that this question should be answered negatively. Because the role of the Confrontation Clause was poorly understood throughout most of the century, the discussion was conducted mostly in terms of the hearsay rule. Wigmore, the most influential evidentiary scholar of all, initially adhered to the traditional view but later opposed it vigorously; he said that if the declarant is present and subject to cross-examination "[t]he whole purpose of the Hearsay rule has been already satisfied" because "[t]here is ample opportunity to test him as to the basis for his former statement."[1] Learned Hand similarly contended that evaluation of the prior statement was not significantly hindered by loss of demeanor evidence:

> If, from all that the jury see of the witness, they conclude that what he says now is not the truth, but what he said before, they are none the less deciding from what they see and hear of that person and in court.

Di Carlo v. United States, 6 F.2d 364, 368 (2d Cir.1925).

The Wigmore view was expressed in § 503(b) of the Model Code of Evidence, adopted in 1942:

> Evidence of a hearsay declaration is admissible if the judge finds that the declarant * * * is present and subject to cross-examination.

The Model Code was not adopted in any state, but Rule 63(1) of the original Uniform Rules of Evidence, adopted in 1953, provided a similarly broad hearsay exception for "[a] statement previously made by a person who is present at the hearing and available for cross-examination with respect to the statement and its subject matter, provided the statement would be admissible if made by declarant while testifying as a witness." Kansas adopted this rule, Kan. Stat. Ann. § 60–460(a) (1982), and at least one other state provided by decision in general terms that the hearsay rule does not prescribe exclusion of a prior statement by a witness who is subject to cross-examination at trial. *Jett v. Commonwealth*, 436 S.W.2d 788 (Ky.1969); *compare* Ky. L. Evid. 801 (1992).

---

[1]   2 John Henry Wigmore, *Evidence* § 1018 (2d ed. 1923), at 460 (noting that the first edition had approved the traditional view); *accord, id.* at 996 (Chadbourn rev. 1970).

Two evidentiary codes adopted in the 1960s—New Jersey's, which was based closely on the Uniform Rules, and California's, which borrowed heavily from it—took a somewhat more cautious stance. Each adopted the traditional definition of hearsay but provided that the rule against hearsay would not exclude certain designated categories of prior statements made by a person who testified as a witness at the current proceeding.[2] In *California v. Green*, 399 U.S. 149 (1970), discussed below, the Supreme Court upheld a key part of the California codification against constitutional attack.

When the Court decided *Green*, the Federal Rules of Evidence were in preparation. The Advisory Committee for the Rules expressed skepticism about the traditional view; see the Note to Rule 801(d)(1). Nevertheless, like the New Jersey and California drafters, the Committee maintained the traditional classification of prior statements as hearsay but with significant exceptions.

Adoption of the full-blast Model Code view would mean that in lieu of direct examination at trial a witness could prepare a written statement and have it read into the record. That appears to be a rather dramatic alteration of trial procedure, moving closer to the model followed in Continental Europe, in which witnesses testify primarily by making written statements and then may answer some questions in court. Interestingly, English civil litigation, which is almost always tried without a jury, has moved towards this procedure in recent decades: Witnesses typically prepare written testimony, and then appear at trial mainly to face cross-examination. And in the 1998 Microsoft antitrust trial, the judge adopted the same procedure.

¶ 10.2: What advantages and disadvantages do you see in adopting this procedure for American litigation?

Probably the more significant issue, though, is whether cross-examination regarding a prior statement of the witness provides (in Wigmore's view) "ample opportunity" to test the witness's testimonial capacities. That is the crucial question when the confrontation right is at stake—that is, when a prosecutor offers a prior testimonial statement by a witness who now takes the witness stand at trial. In other circumstances, it is not the only consideration that should determine the admissibility of the prior statement. After all, some statements by declarants who are unavailable altogether at trial are admitted, when the confrontation right is not an issue, even though the adverse party may have had no opportunity for cross-examination, or a less than ideal one. And arguably evidentiary rules should be even more lenient than they are with respect to such statements. But if the question of the adequacy of the

_____

2   Cal. Ev. Code §§ 1235–1238; Former N.J. Evidence Rule 63(1).

opportunity to examine the declarant is not the only question, it certainly is an important one, even with respect to non-testimonial statements.

Thus, we can consider both testimonial and non-testimonial statements in asking: What shall our standard be for determining the adequacy of the opportunity offered to examine a witness-declarant when she is in court and her prior statement is offered? An obvious, though not inevitable, benchmark is the opportunity that the party opposing admissibility of the statement would have had if the witness had made the statement immediately before, from the witness stand, rather than at an earlier time. And a balanced answer, not surprisingly, is that sometimes the opportunity for adverse examination is markedly hindered by the fact that the witness made the statement at a prior time, and sometimes it isn't.

Consider first the witness who claims to remember the events perfectly well, and whose memory is in perfect accord with her prior statement. Suppose, for example, that White is prepared to testify, "I saw the blue car run the red light," and also that at an earlier time she asserted the same information to Taylor. Here, given White's assertion of a clear memory, there does not seem to be any serious impediment to cross-examination if the prior statement is admitted. That does not necessarily mean the statement should be admitted, though. Given that White is prepared to testify to the substance of the prior statement, the value of the prior statement may be dubious. The factfinder needs to know what White observed, not what she said about it at an earlier time, and it probably is better to require the proponent first to ask directly what she saw.

In light of that testimony, does proof that she previously made a statement to the same effect have sufficient probative value to warrant admissibility? If she made the statement immediately before the trial to the proponent's counsel, it probably does not; it may be little but distracting and time-consuming bolstering of the witness. But if the statement was made significantly earlier, and particularly if it was made shortly after the events it describes, then it is more likely to have substantial value. In that situation, it may well dispel the inference that some failure in testimonial capacity—perhaps loss of memory attributable to the passage of time, or perhaps bias created by some influence that arose or strengthened after the events at issue—accounts for the witness's testimony.[3]

---

[3]   The Advisory Committee confused matters somewhat by saying, "If the witness admits on the stand that he made the statement and that it was true, he adopts the statement and there is no hearsay problem." Notes to Rule 801(d)(1). The text of Rule 801(d)(1) itself does not seem to suggest this result, which conflicts with some pre-Rules case law. *See, e.g.,* Goings v. United States, 377 F.2d 753, 761 (8th Cir.1967), *cert. denied,* 393 U.S. 883 (1968). Suppose a witness does adopt the prior statement—"I said it before, and it was true then and it's true now." The

Now suppose that the witness does not testify to the full substance of the prior statement. It may be that the statement and the testimony are inconsistent in a material way, or it may be that, even apart from any inconsistency, the prior statement asserts relevant information that the current testimony does not. Such extra information means that, if the witness's current testimony to the substance of the prior statement would have significant probative value, then almost surely the prior statement itself will as well. But in this setting, it is not clear that the party opponent had sufficient opportunity to examine the declarant.

¶ 10.3: Green is on trial for furnishing marijuana to Porter, a minor, in violation of state law. Porter was arrested for selling marijuana to an undercover agent, and four days later told Officer Wade that Green was his supplier. A week later, Porter testified to similar effect at Green's preliminary hearing, which was held to determine whether there was sufficient evidence to hold Green for trial. Two months later, at Green's trial, Porter testified again, but this time he was markedly evasive and uncooperative. After he claimed an inability to remember the events, the prosecution introduced evidence of his prior statements. Porter testified that he recalled making the statements, and that he had been telling the truth when he made them, but he also insisted that he was unable to remember the actual events. The prosecution presented no other evidence clearly identifying Green as Porter's supplier. *See California v. Green*, 399 U.S. 149 (1970). Should the evidence of the prior statements have been admitted? If you believe the answer is negative, do you think admission of the prior statements should be deemed to be a violation of the confrontation right?

In *Green*, the Supreme Court upheld against Confrontation Clause attack the California statute, Evidence Code § 1235, that excepts prior inconsistent statements from the rule against hearsay. *Green* held that the Clause does not require exclusion of a declarant's out-of-court statements "as long as the declarant is testifying as a witness and subject to full and effective cross-examination." *Id.* at 158. If the defendant is able to make such cross-examination, the Court declared,

---

adoption amounts to testimony of the substance of the prior statement. But the prior statement itself still appears to be hearsay. In most cases, this would not matter very much. As explained in the text, the prior statement may have probative value, even given the current testimony, because it helps dispel the conclusion that some later reportorial failure accounts for the testimony. If so, the statement probably ought to be admitted to support the witness's credibility, and if not admissibility of the prior statement probably will not do much harm. But it is generally better for a witness to be asked first what she recalls rather than merely to endorse a prior statement—in part because, as we shall see, significant problems may arise if the witness in fact fails to endorse the entirety of the prior statement.

the inability to cross-examine the witness at the time he made his prior statement cannot easily be shown to be of crucial significance. . . . The most successful cross-examination at the time the prior statement was made could hardly hope to accomplish more than has already been accomplished by the fact that the witness is now telling a different, inconsistent story, and—in this case—one that is favorable to the defendant.

Id. at 159.

¶ 10.4: Is this logic persuasive?

Ironically, the situation addressed by the Court's argument in *Green*—the witness who testifies *inconsistently* with the prior statement—did not fully reflect the facts of the case, because Porter professed *inability to remember* who his supplier was. Toward the end of its opinion, the Court recognized that this might be a significant difference, and so it remanded the case. Eighteen years later, the Court resolved the issue it had left open.

¶ 10.5: On April 12, Foster, a correctional counselor at a federal prison, was attacked and brutally beaten with a metal pipe. As a result of his injuries, his memory was severely impaired. A week later he was unable to remember his attacker's name. On May 5, however, he was able to describe the attack. He named Owens as the attacker and identified Owens from an array of photographs.

At Owens's trial, Foster recounted his activities just before the attack and described feeling the blows to his head and seeing blood on the floor. He said he clearly remembered that in the May 5 interview he identified Owens as the assailant. But on cross-examination he acknowledged that he could not remember seeing his assailant, and he could not remember whether any of his visitors in the hospital had suggested that Owens was the assailant. Defense counsel unsuccessfully sought to refresh his recollection with hospital records, including one indicating that Foster had attributed the attack to someone other than Owens.

Owens moves to strike Foster's testimony on the grounds that it violates his confrontation rights and is hearsay not within FRE 801(d)(1). Should the motion be granted? *See United States v. Owens*, 484 U.S. 554 (1988).

California v. Green indicated that, so far as the Confrontation Clause is concerned, jurisdictions are free to adopt the Model Code-Wigmore view. The Confrontation Clause does require that a witness who testifies for the prosecution about his own prior statement, like any other prosecution witness, be subject to cross-examination. Similarly, while

FRE 801(d)(1) provides significant qualifications to the traditional view that a prior statement is not taken out of the definition of hearsay by the fact that the declarant is now a witness, a predicate for invoking each of these qualifications is that the declarant be ".subject to cross-examination concerning the statement." *Owens* holds that this requirement, under both the Confrontation Clause and the Federal Rules, may be satisfied even if the statement is as to a belief the witness no longer has and the basis for which he cannot recall. With respect to the Confrontation Clause, the Court said: "It is sufficient that the defendant has the opportunity to bring out such matters as the witness' bias, his lack of care and attentiveness, his poor eyesight, and even (what is often a prime objective of cross-examination), the very fact that he has a bad memory." *Id.* at 559 (citation omitted). Similarly, the Court held that the Rules' requirement is ordinarily satisfied if the declarant "is placed on the stand, under oath, and responds willingly to questions." *Id.* at 561. Although "limitations on the scope of examination by the trial court or assertions of privilege by the witness may undermine the process to such a degree that meaningful cross-examination within the intent of the rule no longer exists," that is not true if the witness asserts memory loss—which "is often the very result sought to be produced by cross-examination, and can be effective in destroying the force of the prior statement." *Id.* at 561–62.

Let's examine the perspective of *Green* and *Owens* carefully. There is no doubt that, in general, if a witness previously asserted a proposition harmful to the party opponent, the opponent would rather the witness testified inconsistently with that proposition than that the witness reaffirmed the substance of the prior statement from the witness stand. But this is just to say that the opponent is better off facing wobbly evidence rather than sturdy evidence; this does not seem to be an illuminating comparison. The important issue is whether the opponent has had an adequate opportunity to expose fully the weakness of whatever evidence is actually presented. Even though the witness's current testimony is favorable to the party opponent, she might do him harm that he will have difficulty counteracting.

Suppose that the witness is testifying for the prosecution in a criminal case and that the jury is inclined to believe that her prior, pro-prosecution version is accurate and that she changed her tune for some improper reason, such as intimidation. The defendant is then in a jam. It will be counterproductive for him to suggest that the witness is not currently inclined to tell the truth. And even though the witness is purportedly willing to assist in impeaching her own *past* inclination to tell the truth, she may in fact impede these efforts; the jury will be getting the witness's version of why the prior statement was untrue, and that may not be as persuasive as the version that the jury would infer if it saw the defendant confronting a hostile witness. The witness may in effect be winking at the jurors, suggesting that they accept the prior statement even though, for some reason, the witness is not willing to testify to it now. It is almost as if there were two witnesses: One is in court, subject to examination, casting doubt on the prior statement, and so outwardly helping the accused, but in a suspicious manner wholly unpersuasive to the factfinder. The other, the one who has done the damage, is not in court and is impervious to adverse examination.[4]

To see how the adverse examiner's tools are blunted when the witness's prior statement makes an assertion that the witness does not reaffirm at trial, consider the two variations in the following problem.

¶ **10.6:** The prosecution wishes to prove that the defendant, Dreier, was part of a brief meeting held in the parking lot at The Gathering, a local restaurant. A participant in the meeting, Washington, has told the police that she was there for the entire meeting and that Dreier joined in after the beginning.

(a) Variation 1: At trial, Washington testifies in accordance with his prior statement. On cross-examination, Dreier's counsel asks Washington, "Does Dreier have a red convertible?" Washington answers truthfully, "Yes." Counsel then asks, "Did Dreier arrive at The Gathering in the convertible?"

(1) Washington has three basic answers—"Yes", "No", and "I don't remember." For each of these answers, imagine information that Dreier's counsel might have that could help her trap Washington if Washington is not telling the truth.

(2) What is the most that counsel can hope for from cross-examination? If she gets it, what is the effect of Washington's testimony?

(b) Variation 2: At trial, Washington disappoints the prosecution by denying that Dreier was at The Gathering. The prosecution then offers evidence of her prior statement. Whether in accordance with or despite the law of the jurisdiction, the court admits the statement, both to impeach Washington and for the truth of what it asserts. What use of the convertible evidence can Dreier make now?[5]

---

[4]   *See, e.g.,* People v. Chavies, 234 Mich. App. 274, 593 N.W.2d 655 (1999) (upholding homicide conviction based on grand jury testimony of witnesses who claimed inability to remember at time of trial; reviewing cases and adhering to majority rule that uncorroborated prior inconsistent statement can provide the sole support for conviction).

[5]   See generally Ruhala v. Roby, 379 Mich. 102, 124–28, 150 N.W.2d 146, 156–58 (1967); Richard D. Friedman, *Prior Statements of a Witness: A Nettlesome Corner of the Hearsay Thicket,* 1995 S. Ct. Rev. 277, 293–301.

The hindrance to cross-examination may be even greater if to any difficult question the witness answers, "I don't recall." The *Owens* Court seems misguided in concluding that demonstrating the witness's professed inability to remember will be of great assistance to the party opponent.

¶ 10.7: (a) In *Green*, when Porter professed inability to remember who his supplier was, was the jury likely to believe him and count this acknowledgment against the credibility of his prior statement? What other explanations might the jury believe would account for Porter's testimony? In *Owens*, what factor would the jury likely believe explained Foster's inability to remember at the time of trial? To what extent would this factor likely undercut the persuasive force of Foster's prior statement?

(b) Compare *Delaware v. Fensterer*, 474 U.S. 15 (1985) (*per curiam*). Fensterer was charged with the murder of his girlfriend, Swift. A key question was whether hairs believed to be Swift's and found on a cat leash that may have been the murder weapon had been forcibly removed. Robillard, an FBI agent, testified to his opinion that they had been forcibly removed—but he acknowledged that, on review of his notes, he was unable to determine the basis on which he drew that conclusion. Should a motion to strike Robillard's testimony have been granted?

¶ 10.8: Blunt is on trial for killing Ford. Two days after the incident, Williams testified to the incident before the grand jury, inculpating Blunt. At trial, Williams is noticeably distressed from the beginning of her testimony, and she acknowledges that she is under stress and afraid to testify again. Asked about the incident, Williams says repeatedly that she doesn't remember; she contends that reading her grand jury testimony does not refresh her recollection, though she says that it was accurate when given. The trial judge finds that her claimed memory loss is feigned.

(a) May the grand jury transcript be admitted? *See United States v. Blunt*, 959 A.2d 721 (D.C. 2008).

(b) What if in response to any question about the incident, Williams had said, "I respectfully decline to answer because I am afraid"?

(c) What if instead Williams had said, "I respectfully decline to answer because of my privilege against self-incrimination"? *Douglas v. Alabama*, 380 U.S. 415 (1965).

When the witness professes inability to remember, her presence in the courtroom means very little, and there is a strong argument that we should treat her as if she were not only absent from the court but unavailable to testify. In fact, the Federal Rules appear to do this, because FRE 804(a)(3) classifies as a species of unavailability the situation in which the declarant actually takes the stand but "testifies to not remembering the subject matter." In that circumstance, the proponent may invoke any of the exceptions listed in Rule 804(b), which apply only if the declarant is unavailable.

¶ 10.9: Foster clearly was unavailable as a witness within the meaning of Rule 804(a)(3) (and his statement did not fall within any of the exceptions stated in FRE 804(b)). Thus, Owens argued that Foster should not have been considered "subject to cross examination" within the meaning of FRE 801(d)(1). The Court responded by suggesting that Rule 804—which was then headed "Hearsay Exceptions; Declarant Unavailable"—could alternatively be described as applying to cases of "unavailability, memory loss, and other special circumstances." 484 U.S. at 563. Do you find this response persuasive? What quality is common to the "special circumstances" listed in Rule 804(a)?

The limited reach of *Green* and *Owens* should be emphasized. Both cases concern the Confrontation Clause, which only sets an outer bound for what is admissible; even if the Clause does not require exclusion of a given piece of evidence, a jurisdiction is free to exclude it. *Owens* also involves the Federal Rules, but they only govern the federal courts. Other courts, even those that have adopted codifications based on the Federal Rules, are free to conclude that a witness asserting profound memory loss should not be considered "subject to cross examination."

The discussion in this Subsection has suggested that—*Green* and *Owens* notwithstanding—the party opponent will be hindered in his ability to examine a witness with respect to a given proposition if the witness asserted the proposition at a prior time and did not reassert it as part of her testimony at the present proceeding. At least when a criminal defendant's confrontation right is at stake—that is, when a prior testimonial statement is offered against him—this factor should probably result in exclusion of the evidence. But this result does not seem appropriate in all other circumstances. If the party opponent is not a criminal defendant, then the Confrontation Clause does not apply. The more general confrontation principle still does apply if the prior statement is testimonial, but it lacks the constitutional force of the Clause. And if the prior statement is not testimonial, whether the party opponent is a criminal defendant or not, then the power of the demand for an adequate opportunity for cross-examination is muted considerably. The prior statement is likely to have significant probative value. It may be, given that the declarant is a witness in the current proceeding, that the proponent of her prior statement has done all that could be reasonably expected of him to preserve the ability of the party opponent to examine the declarant. Moreover, though the opponent's opportunity to examine the witness with respect to a proposition is hindered by the fact that the witness has not reasserted the proposition, the opportunity is not necessarily useless; the opponent may be able to explore the basis on which the witness made the prior statement.

Suppose that a witness in a car accident case made a casual prior statement that Blue Car rammed Green Car, but that her testimony now is in essence:

> I really don't remember which car rammed which, but I remember very well seeing the accident. I had a great view of it, because I was just crossing First Avenue on the south side of Main Street, there were no obstructions in my way, and my eyesight is very good. I got home within twenty minutes, and I told my husband what I had seen. No, I had no motive to lie, because I had no interest in the dispute and no reason to mislead my husband. I don't remember just what I said, but if I said the blue car rammed the green one I must have meant just that, because I speak the English language as it is customarily spoken hereabout; what then, Swedish?

It seems here that the prior statement has significant probative value, and that, although Blue Car's ability to cross-examine might be hampered by the declarant's inability to remember, there is still significant scope for cross-examination. The case would be much the same if instead of the last sentence the witness testified in essence:

> I remember very well saying Blue Car rammed Green Car, and that must have been just what I meant. But to be absolutely honest, I still don't have any recollection, independent of the fact that I made the statement, of which car rammed which.

¶ 10.10: In *Owens*, (a) what might Owens reasonably hope to achieve from cross-examination of Foster?

(b) How might the hindrance of Owens's ability to examine Foster be attributable to Owens himself?

(c) What might the prosecution have done to better protect Owens's ability to examine Foster?

This is a surprisingly complex area. Try to suspend judgment for now as to whether, or when, prior statements of a witness ought to be admitted. You may have different views after you study the Federal Rules' solution and consider it against the backdrop of what you already know of the confrontation right.

C. QUALIFICATIONS TO THE TRADITIONAL VIEW

Under the decisions of the Supreme Court, the Confrontation Clause allows courts to depart completely from the traditional rule: Even if an out-of-court testimonial statement is offered against a criminal defendant, there is no violation so long as the witness testifies at trial. Most jurisdictions have taken advantage of this leeway—but only in part. Most of the states now follow the structure of the Federal Rules of Evidence: They adhere to the traditional doctrine that a prior statement of a witness is generally considered hearsay when offered to prove the truth of what it asserts but limit that doctrine by important qualifications. The states, of course, do not all adhere to the precise bounds drawn by the Federal Rules. In fact, while all but a few of the states have adopted codifications based on the FRE, this is one area in which they vary widely; the states cover the entire spectrum, a few still adhering full force to the traditional rule and a few admitting all prior statements of a witness. For simplicity we will focus on the Federal Rules, discussing in turn each of the three lettered clauses of Rule 801(d)(1).

Clause (A)—prior statements of the witness inconsistent with her testimony in court. It is important to understand that this clause does not state limitations on when prior inconsistent statements can be used for impeachment. Indeed, the clause does not apply at all to that use; if the statement is used merely to undermine the witness's credibility by showing that she has been inconsistent, rather than to prove the truth of the statement, it does not come within the basic definition of hearsay in FRE 801(c). As we will see in Chapter 19, pretty much any prior statement inconsistent with the testimony of the witness may be used for impeachment.[6] Thus, the significance of clause (A) is to set forth the circumstances in which the prior inconsistent statement may, *in addition to* its use for impeachment, be used to prove its truth.

> ¶ 10.11: Sometimes, the substantive tail may seem to be wagging the impeachment dog. In *California v. Green*, ¶¶ 10.3, .4, did the prosecution have any need to impeach Porter's testimony? In *Owens*, ¶ 10.5, would it have been a valid argument that the prosecution needed to impeach Foster's testimony?

It is not self-evident just what counts as an inconsistency. This matter will be explored when we discuss impeachment, but a brief examination may be helpful here. Logical incompatibility between the prior statement and the current testimony will suffice, at least ordinarily:

---

[6] As we shall see, if the inconsistency is on a matter deemed "collateral," the impeaching party may be precluded from introducing extrinsic evidence of the inconsistency—that is, evidence other than the witness's own testimony. But that limitation need not concern us here.

If Washington now testifies that Dreier was at The Gathering and previously said that Dreier was not, that is a clear inconsistency. But logical incompatibility does not exhaust the possibilities of inconsistency. Roughly speaking, if a witness has testified to a proposition and the fact that she made a prior statement suggests that at that earlier time she did not believe the proposition to be true, the prior statement may be considered to have impeachment value as inconsistent.

¶ 10.12: Before the grand jury, Washington testified in the course of a long narrative, "Archer called me up, and told me to meet in the parking lot at The Gathering. I did that, and Archer told me just how to do the deal. Baker was there, too, and warned me not to mess up." At trial, Washington testifies that Dreier was also present in the parking lot. May the defense use the grand jury statement? For what purpose?

¶ 10.13: Dreier lives in Dallas. The prosecution needs to prove that on October 3 Dreier was in Houston. To its disappointment, his former girlfriend, Waxman, testifies that on October 3 Dreier stayed around her house in Dallas all day. Previously, Waxman said to the police, "In the evening of October 2, I saw Dreier off for a flight to Houston." May the prosecution use this statement? If so, for what purpose?

¶ 10.14: If the prior inconsistent statement may be used only for impeachment, then presumably the proponent of the witness's testimony is entitled to a limiting instruction to that effect. What does this instruction mean? That is, how can the jury give the prior statement importance in judging the credibility of the witness and yet not weigh it in favor of the proposition that it asserts? Is it likely that the jury will do so?

Apart from a jury instruction, what else might be at stake over the question of whether the prior inconsistent statement may be used substantively? What would have happened in *California v. Green* if the prior statements could not have been used substantively?

Some jurisdictions, notably California, pose no hearsay obstacle to any prior inconsistent statement of a witness; recall that California Evidence Code § 1235, involved in *Green*, is of this type. The Federal Rules provide that prior inconsistent statements satisfying certain conditions are removed from the hearsay bar.

¶ 10.15: Under either the California or the Federal rule, at least some prior statements that would not otherwise be admitted to prove the truth of what they assert may be so admitted if they are inconsistent with the current testimony of the witness. Does this make sense? That is, given that the declarant is a witness subject to cross-examination, should the fact that the prior statement is inconsistent with the witness' present testimony give the prior statement a *better* chance of admissibility? If so, is it because

- the inconsistency means that the opponent of the prior statement has some compensation for the inability to cross-examine at the time that statement was made, in that the current testimony contradicts it?

- as suggested by the California Law Revision Commission in a passage quoted by the Advisory Committee's Note to FRE 801(d)(1)(A), this rule protects a party "against the 'turncoat' witness who changes his story on the stand and deprives the party calling him of evidence essential to his case"?

- given the inconsistency, the jury will hear the prior statement in any event for impeachment?

The legislative history shows that the limitations in clause (A)—the requirement that the prior statement have been "given under oath subject to the penalty of perjury at a trial, hearing, or other proceeding, or in a deposition"—were hotly disputed in the drafting of the Rules. The Reporter's first draft adopted the full-blast Model Code view—so long as the declarant was present at trial and subject to cross-examination concerning the statement, the rule against hearsay would not apply. The Advisory Committee cut back very substantially on this treatment and introduced the approach, which has endured, of designating only certain categories of prior statements of a witness as falling outside the definition of hearsay. But as the Rule was presented to Congress, it provided a flat exemption for prior inconsistent statements of a witness; in essence, if the statement could be used for impeachment, then it could be used substantively as well. The Senate supported this version, but the House did not; the House version, adopted after considerable tinkering, would have allowed substantive use only if the prior statement was made subject to cross-examination. The Rule as ultimately enacted was a compromise drafted by the Conference Committee. Richard D. Friedman & Joshua A. Deahl, *Federal Rules of Evidence: Text and History* 319–332 (2015).

¶ 10.16: What is the significance of the difference between the House version and the clause as eventually adopted? That is, in what circumstances would a prior inconsistent statement be admissible for substantive purposes under the clause as adopted but not under the House version? Put another way, in what circumstance does a statement satisfy the condition that it have been "given under penalty of perjury at a trial, hearing, or other proceeding or in a deposition," even though it was *not* subjected to cross-examination at the time it was made?

Interestingly, the long-standing exception for prior testimony of an unavailable declarant, codified in Rule 804(b)(1), reflects the principal concern that motivated the House in considering Rule 801(d)(1)(A); even if the prior testimony was under oath, Rule 804(b)(1) will not allow its admission if the party against whom it is now offered did not have an opportunity to examine the declarant. This, of course, is what the Confrontation Clause demands when a testimonial statement is offered against an accused. We will be studying Rule 804(b)(1) later, in Chapter 12. Do not confound it with Rule 801(d)(1)(A); the two rules apply in different circumstances, and to different categories of statements.

¶ 10.17: Rule 804(b)(1) applies only if the declarant is unavailable. Rule 801(d)(1)(A) applies to a somewhat broader category of statements, but only if the declarant is not only available but actually testifying. Is there any rational basis for having two such rules? What is the reason for leniency if the declarant is unavailable? If the declarant is available and testifying? What circumstance do these rules leave uncovered? What is the reason for relative harshness in that circumstance?

Note the wide range of choices open to rulemakers (given constitutional leeway) in dealing with prior inconsistent statements. They might adopt (among other possibilities):

(1) the Model Code-Wigmore view, so that all prior statements of a witness subject to cross-examination at trial, whether inconsistent with the current testimony or not, would escape the hearsay rule;

(2) the Senate version of FRE 801(d)(1)(A), similar in effect to Cal. Evid. Code § 1235, so that all such statements that are inconsistent with the trial testimony would be exempted from the rule;

(3) the oath requirement of FRE 801(d)(1)(A) but not the requirement that the prior statement have been given "at a . . . proceeding or in a deposition," thus allowing affidavits but not unsworn statements to be admitted on the merits;

(4) FRE 801(d)(1)(A) as is, thus allowing grand jury testimony but not affidavits to be admitted on the merits;

(5) FRE 801(d)(1)(A) in the form favored by the House, thus allowing prior inconsistent cross-examined testimony but not grand jury testimony to be admitted on the merits; or

(6) the traditional rule, in which prior inconsistent statements are not admissible on the merits.

¶ 10.18: What are the arguments for and against each of these options? Which one—or what other solution—do you prefer?

¶ 10.19: Peratis, a police chemist, makes a statement at a deposition in a murder case that, as it turns out, is harmful to the prosecution: He states that in performing some blood tests he used 7 ml. of blood, an amount that would leave some blood unaccounted for and possibly available for framing the defendant. The deposition is introduced at trial, because Peratis is very ill. The prosecution takes a videotaped statement from Peratis, at his bedside, in which he says that the 7 ml. measurement was only an approximation. May the statement be admitted under the Federal Rules? Under California law? If so, for what purpose?[7]

¶ 10.20: The day after a serious industrial accident, an investigator hired by a lawyer retained in the hospital by several prospective plaintiffs interviews various witnesses and then drafts statements for them to sign. If the witnesses give testimony at trial that varies significantly from the statements, should the plaintiffs be able to use the signed statements? For what purposes?

Clause (B)—prior statements of the witness consistent with her testimony in court. When the witness's prior statement is consistent with, rather than inconsistent with, her trial testimony, the problem takes on a different cast. Recall that, if the prior statement would be merely duplicative of the current testimony, then the prior statement doesn't really raise any serious confrontation or hearsay concerns; but, then again, it may not have significant incremental probative value, and so there may be no good reason to admit it. Thus, note this asymmetry: Although prior inconsistent statements of a witness may generally be used to impeach the witness's testimony, prior consistent statements may *not* generally be used to bolster her testimony.

¶ 10:21: Why not? That is, why can't a witness say, "This is what happened, and I've said the same thing consistently since the events occurred"?

There are some situations in which a prior consistent statement *may* be used to support the witness's testimony. For example, suppose that the adverse party contends that the witness fabricated her story after she had

---

[7]   *See* State v. Simpson, Official Transcript of Closing Arguments for Defense at xi–2, 8, State v. Simpson (No. BAO9721), *available at* 1995 WL 697930.

a motive to lie; if Wendy is testifying against her sister's former husband, his attorney may argue that Wendy is just trying to support her sister's desire for vengeance. In this case, it would be proper to offer evidence that, back when things seemed to be lovey-dovey between sis and hubby, Wendy said the same thing she is now testifying to. Similarly, if the ex-brother-in-law contends that Wendy's testimony is the product of stale memory, then a prior statement consistent with the testimony would—to the extent that it was made close to the time of the events it described—tend to dispel the contention.

In Chapter 19, we will examine more closely such uses of prior consistent statements to rehabilitate a witness. For now, we are concerned principally with the issue of the "substantive" or "independent" admissibility of these statements—that is, the question of whether the rule against hearsay bars admissibility of such a statement to prove the truth of what it asserts (or whether the Confrontation Clause should). Traditionally, most courts held that such statements might be admissible for rehabilitation but not substantively.

What does that distinction mean? Suppose a witness testifies to **A**, is then impeached on cross-examination, and on redirect testifies that she previously asserted **A**. An instruction telling the jurors to consider the prior statement only for rehabilitation of the witness and not for the truth of the matter that it asserts will probably be greeted with bafflement. Given that the witness asserted **A** in her current testimony, if a juror is using the prior statement to support the witness's credibility, is she not also using it to prove **A**? A conceptual distinction might be drawn—perhaps the juror is supposed to rely on the prior statement only to dispel the argument that a testimonial failure, such as improper motive, accounts for the witness's current testimony, and not give extra credence to the statement because it reflects a fresher memory than the current testimony. But this distinction is so wafer-thin, and so dubious in merit—why *shouldn't* the juror take into account the fact that the prior statement reflects fresher memory?—that jurors could not be expected to follow it.

Nevertheless, there is a valid concern underlying the traditional distinction. Often, the rehabilitating statement contains more information than the current testimony. Put schematically, the witness testifies to **A** and the prior statement is **A & B**. Consider this variation on ¶ 10.13. Waxman testifies, "On the evening of October 2, I drove Dreier to the airport." The defense impeaches her, on the ground of recent hostility to Dreier, and the prosecution then introduces a statement she made on October 3: "Last night I took Dreier to the airport for his flight to Houston." That statement tends to dispel the contention that newfound hostility to Dreier accounts for Waxman's professed memory that she drove Dreier to the airport on October 2. But note that the prior statement has an "overhang," some extra information that the current testimony does not include—that she drove Dreier *for his flight to Houston,* a crucial matter for the prosecution. And given that Waxman has not testified from her current memory to this proposition, Dreier's ability to cross-examine her on *that* proposition may be severely hampered, for reasons we have already seen. In some cases of this sort, it appears that substantive admissibility of the overhang, and not the supposed need for rehabilitation, is the main benefit that the prosecution seeks by introducing the prior statement. And if the prior statement is testimonial in nature, offered against an accused, and critical to there being sufficient evidence on a given proposition to support a conviction, then it seems there should be a very serious Confrontation Clause concern.

The Supreme Court's statement in *Crawford* that there is no Confrontation Clause violation if the witness testifies at trial brushes away this concern. And also in apparent disregard of it, FRE 801(d)(1)(B) departs significantly from the traditional law. That Rule exempts a statement from the rule against hearsay if the declarant is a witness at trial subject to cross-examination concerning the statement, the statement is "consistent with the declarant's testimony," and it is offered to rehabilitate the declarant's credibility after it has been attacked. Thus, this Rule eliminates the distinction between admissibility for rehabilitation and for substantive purposes.

¶ **10.22:** A young girl testifies that her father sexually abused her. She is nervous on the witness stand and manages only to describe one incident of improper touching, and even that in quite vague terms. The father suggests in cross-examination that the girl had been biased against him by her mother, from whom he is divorced. The prosecution then offers to prove that, before the relationship between the parents turned bitter, the girl made a statement describing in detail several acts of sexual molestation, involving contact by his fingers and mouth with her vaginal area. The defense objects. What should the court do? *See generally* Mueller & Kirkpatrick § 8.25 (stating that the Rule "should not let a party prove important details lying beyond [the] testimony merely because statement and testimony are consistent in general tenor").

As it stood before 2014, the Rule was more limited; it did not contain what is now subdivision (B)(2), and so applied only if the prior statement was offered "to rebut an express or implied charge that the declarant recently fabricated [the testimony] or acted from a recent improper influence or motive in so testifying." The amendment was made to ensure that the Rule would apply to all situations in which a prior consistent statement might be admissible for rehabilitation—for example, if the impeacher's contention was simply that the current testimony was a product of faulty memory. (Many states, of course, still have the older formulation.)

The amendment retained the confusing word "consistent". A prior statement may have the prescribed rebuttal effect even if there is a small logical incompatibility between the statement and the testimony; if, for example, there is an insubstantial difference in the time at which the witness puts an event in the two versions, the statement may still help dispel the conclusion that some late-arising testimonial failure led to the essence of the witness's current testimony. The intent of the Rule appears to be that if the statement has sufficient rehabilitative effect to warrant admissibility on that ground, then it should be deemed to be consistent with the current testimony and should be substantively admissible as well, notwithstanding the rule against hearsay; it is not clear how much work the term "consistent" does in this chain of reasoning.

¶ 10.23: Can a prior statement be considered neither inconsistent with the current testimony for purposes of clause (A) nor consistent with the current testimony for purposes of clause (B)? Can it be considered both? *See - it covers different topic*

Although Rule 801(d)(1)(B), as amended in 2014, makes clear that it reaches beyond cases in which the basis of impeachment is a charge of fabrication or improper influence or motive, those still constitute a significant set of cases within the ambit of the Rule. Usually, a prior statement will not help rebut a charge that the witness's testimony was a product of an improper influence or motive unless the statement was made before the improper motive or influence arose. Consider *Tome v. United States*, 513 U.S. 150 (1995). Tome was charged with sexually abusing his four-year-old daughter, decorously referred to by the Court as A.T. At trial, A.T., several months shy of her seventh birthday, testified very haltingly. The prosecution then offered several prior statements that she had made, describing incidents of sexual molestation in some detail. Tome contended that A.T. made these statements as part of an attempt to live primarily with her mother, from whom Tome was divorced, rather than with Tome, who was the primary custodian. The Court held, 5–4, that Rule 801(d)(1)(B) incorporates an absolute pre-motive requirement: A statement cannot be introduced under the Rule if it was made after the improper motive or influence allegedly arose. The Court further held the Rule did not support admissibility of A.T.'s prior statements; although the Court's discussion was not entirely clear, its rationale seems to have been that there was no showing that A.T.'s desire to live with her mother had changed between the time of the statements and the time of trial. 513 U.S. at 165.

The *Tome* Court was clearly correct that a statement made after the improper motive or influence allegedly arose will not usually have substantial rehabilitative value. But it is another matter whether there is any need for an absolute rule enforcing this generalization of probative value—and now there is a question of how this pre-motive rule should be enforced. *Tome*, of course, is only a decision on the Federal Rules, and the states are free to disagree. Some have done so. *See, e.g., Cook v. State*, 7 P.3d 53 (Wyo. 2000). The Federal Advisory Committee, however, made clear in recommending the 2014 amendment that it had no intent to undo the result in *Tome*: The amendment was intended to expand the scope of the Rule but not to alter its operation within its prior scope.

¶ **10.24:** In each of the following cases, consider whether the statement ought to be admissible, and whether it could be admissible consistent with *Tome*.

(a) In *Tome*, the prosecution argues that, even if A.T. wished to live with her mother at the time she made the prior statements, the spontaneity of the statements suggests they could not have been the result of a calculated scheme by a four-year-old girl to effect a change in custody arrangements. *See* the Tenth Circuit's original decision, 3 F.3d 342, 351.

(b) Prosecution Witness has a grudge against Defendant. At the time of a prior consistent statement, the basis for the grudge had appeared, but the grudge was not yet as strong as it is now. *See Holmes v. State*, 116 Md. App. 546, 556, 698 A.2d 1139, 1144 (1997).

(c) Prosecution Witness has a grudge against Defendant, and did at the time of the prior consistent statement, which she made confidentially to her most intimate friend.[8]

¶ **10.25:** What does "recent" in Rule 801(d)(1)(B) mean?

To the extent that Rule 801(d)(1)(B) appears to set limits on when a prior statement can be used for rehabilitation, it is an oddity, because it is placed in the portion of the Federal Rules dealing with hearsay. We will consider the Rule again when we focus on rehabilitation of witnesses in Chapter 19.

Clause (C)—prior statements of the witness identifying a person. This clause was also a controversial one during the passage of the Federal Rules. It was part of the Rules as they were proposed to Congress, but it was deleted from the Rules as passed at the beginning of 1975. The principal objector was Sen. Sam Ervin of North Carolina, who feared that a person could be convicted solely on the basis of a statement of

---

[8]   See generally Friedman, *Prior Statements*, 1995 Sup. Ct. Rev. at 310–12.

identification that the identifying witness did not affirm at trial. Later in the year, with Sen. Ervin retired, Congress restored this provision to the Rules.

The Rule seems to be a strange one. Unlike Clauses (A) and (B), it does not depend on the relationship of the prior statement to the in-court testimony. It does not require that the prior statement be inconsistent with the in-court testimony, nor that it was made under any particular circumstances. Nor does it require that the prior statement be consistent with the current testimony or have rehabilitative value. The prior statement may be inconsistent with the in-court testimony, or it may be consistent with the testimony in the strong sense that they both assert the same propositions, or—as in *Owens*—it may provide information as to which the witness simply does not testify. The Rule is shaped by the subject matter of the statement. A prior statement of identification might be one picking out a photograph, or picking out a live person at a lineup, or naming or verbally describing someone who participated in an incident.

¶ **10.26:** Why should a prior statement of a witness be considered not hearsay just because it identifies a person? Are such statements particularly trustworthy? Is there a greater need for such statements than for others?

The Advisory Committee cited "the generally unsatisfactory and inconclusive nature of courtroom identifications as compared with those made at an earlier time under less suggestive conditions." Does this persuade you? If a witness has made one statement of identification, is *any* request for her to make a subsequent identification statement inherently suggestive? Could courtroom identifications be made more satisfactory and less suggestive than they usually are? If the basis for allowing testimony of the prior identification is that it was made "at an earlier time," when the events were fresher in the witness's mind, wouldn't this logic apply equally well to any prior statement by the witness? Alternatively, could an earlier identification be made in such a way as to provide the defendant with much the same rights that he has when the witness makes an in-court identification? Are you satisfied that prior statements of identification, such as statements at police lineups and one-subject showups, are *not* highly suggestive? *See, e.g., Stovall v. Denno*, 388 U.S. 293 (1967).

There is some ambiguity as to what constitutes a statement of identification. Suppose a witness testifies in court, "Someone killed Roger Rabbit," and previously she made a similar statement and was asked, "Who did it?" In that case, her answer, "Donald Duck did it," would clearly be a statement of identification: That statement provides no information about *what* was done beyond what is present in the witness's trial testimony; it just tells (perhaps confirming the trial testimony, perhaps not) *who* committed those acts. But now suppose that the witness's trial testimony contains less information, merely "Roger Rabbit is dead." The prior statement "Donald Duck killed Roger Rabbit" identifies who committed an act, but it does much more, carrying with it the substance of what that person did—substance to which the witness has not testified. Courts seem not to have worried about this issue very much, but we should: The exemption for prior statements of identification is sometimes used effectively as a hook to bring in all sorts of information describing what a person did rather than merely who did it.

¶ **10.27:** Dugan was tried for robbing a liquor store. He was convicted but the first trial was thrown out for ineffective assistance of counsel. At the second trial, three years later, Loudon, the store owner, testifies for the prosecution and identifies Dugan as the robber. The prosecution seeks to offer a sketch that bears some resemblance to Dugan, along with the following testimony of Loudon: The day after the robbery, Loudon met with a police artist, and described the robber to her. The artist used a kit of transparent overlays, each bearing a different facial feature, to put together a rough portrait; she then filled in some of the smaller details by hand.

May this testimony, along with the portrait itself, authenticated by Loudon, be admitted? Would your answer be different if at trial Loudon was unable to identify Dugan?

D. REFLECTIONS

One can hardly avoid the conclusion that the rulemakers and courts have not yet solved the problem of prior statements by a witness who actually appears and testifies in court. This is an extremely tricky area, and this Section, building on the previous ones, will offer some tentative musings as to how it may be approached.

Consider first the witness who claims a clear memory and who testifies to the complete substance of the prior statement. In this case, we have seen, the party opponent's ability to cross-examine is not hampered. But the question is whether the prior statement has sufficient probative value to warrant admissibility. That will depend in large part on the timing and circumstances of the statement. If they tend to dispel the conclusion that some reportorial failure accounts for the testimony—perhaps loss of memory or fabrication in response to an improper motive—then the statement very likely should be admissible. In any event, it seems preferable to hear the live testimony of the witness first before deciding whether the prior statement should be admitted.

Now consider the witness who does *not* testify to the complete substance of the prior statement; perhaps she actually says something inconsistent with the prior statement, or perhaps her testimony is less complete than that statement. In this setting, to the extent that the witness does *not* reaffirm the substance of the prior statement, the party opponent is likely to be hindered in examining the witness: He is attempting to challenge her with respect to a proposition that she is not asserting, and he will lack the foothold necessary for a maximally effective examination.

But so what? First, let us assume that the prior statement in question is not testimonial in nature—and for simplicity let us assume that this means that the statement was not made in anticipation of its use in litigation. (For the moment at least, the term testimonial is being used to include statements made in anticipation of use by any litigant, a civil party or criminal defendant as well as a prosecutor.) Given that the prior statement was not testimonial, it need not satisfy the conditions ordinarily required for testimony. And this means that, although the opponent's opportunity to cross-examine the declarant will be impaired by the fact that the opportunity occurs at a time when the witness is no longer asserting the substance of the prior statement, the statement ought usually to be admitted. One way of thinking about this is to say that a non-testimonial statement ought to be admitted unless either (1) it does more harm than good to the truth-determining process or (2) exclusion is necessary to induce the proponent to produce substantially better evidence.

As to the first point, assume that if the witness had testified live to the extra propositions—those asserted by the out-of-court statement but not by the actual testimony—that would be more probative than prejudicial; if this is not true, then the out-of-court statement presumably should be excluded without reaching the hearsay issue. If the assumption is true, then in most cases the out-of-court statement also will be more probative than prejudicial. The prior statement, after all, reflects a fresher memory than does the in-court testimony. Moreover, the declarant is at least subject to some cross-examination, which is better than nothing. And, even if (as is not clear) the jurors would likely give too much weight to the statement, failing to discount its value because of the hindrance to cross-examination, it seems highly unlikely that they would so overvalue the statement that truth determination would be better served by shutting their ears to it; that is overvaluation to a very high degree.

As to the second point, the fact that the declarant is a live witness in court suggests that the proponent has done all that could be expected of him to protect the opponent's ability to cross-examine. This is not inevitably so. It could be that the proponent might have had some indication that the declarant would not adhere to the full substance of the prior statement at trial, because of either forgetfulness or changing motive. If so, perhaps the proponent could have ensured that the opponent had a chance to examine the declarant at a deposition while the declarant was still adhering to that substance. But, given ample discovery, it may also be—depending on the precise circumstances—that the opponent was able to protect himself by arranging for a deposition, if he truly believed that worthwhile.

This analysis suggests a receptive attitude to non-testimonial prior statements of a witness, after the witness is asked for her current recollection.

Now consider the case in which the prior statement was testimonial in nature and is offered by a criminal prosecutor. In this setting, more than the truth-determining process is at stake, and there is what courts *should* regard as a serious Confrontation Clause problem (though the Supreme Court does not so regard it): For reasons presented in this chapter, the right to confront an adverse witness is seriously compromised if the accused does not have a chance to exercise it until a time at which the witness no longer stands by the statement. The accused has a powerful argument that he has a right not to be convicted on the basis of a testimonial statement made by someone who no longer stands by it at the time the accused examines her. *See* Stanley A. Goldman, *Guilt by Intuition: The Insufficiency of Prior Inconsistent Statements to Convict,* 65 N.C.L.Rev. 1 (1986).

Under this view, in other words, the prosecution would bear the risk that a declarant who had made a favorable statement of a testimonial nature would not adhere to the substance of it at trial, even if she did become a witness there. But a cautious prosecutor could often protect herself against this eventuality in much the same way that she might protect against the possibility that a potential witness will be unable to testify at trial altogether—by taking the witness's deposition, subject to cross-examination, before trial.[9] If at trial the witness was forgetful or

---

[9] In most jurisdictions, depositions are not now routinely taken in criminal litigation. Some states do have extensive criminal discovery, however. Even in jurisdictions that do not, depositions are allowed under Fed. R. Crim. P. 15, and the comparable provisions that apply in most states, at least when extraordinary circumstances require the preservation of testimony. Also, those states that hold a preliminary hearing to test the sufficiency of evidence provide a routine mechanism for pretrial examination that bears some similarities to the deposition. Moreover, some states now provide for the videotaping of depositions of children's allegations of sexual abuse, with a view to the possible use of the deposition at trial in lieu of live testimony. In Chapter 20, we shall consider the validity of statutes that allow children in some circumstances

spoke inconsistently, the deposition could be used substantively; the defendant's confrontation rights would presumably be preserved because he had a chance to cross-examine the witness when she believed the prior statement.

Whatever the merits and demerits of such a system, it appears improbable that the Supreme Court will impose it; *Crawford* confirms that, at least for now, the Confrontation Clause of the Federal Constitution will not be read to require that the witness believed the statement at the time the defendant examined her. But the states, of course, are free to adopt such a system if they wish.

Now consider statements that are testimonial in nature and offered in a civil case. Suppose, for example, that after an accident the plaintiff's lawyer interviews a witness and drafts a statement for her to sign. At trial the witness testifies more favorably to the defendant, and plaintiff's counsel offers the earlier statement, relying on it to defeat the defendant's motion for judgment as a matter of law. Arguably, a testimonial statement should not be admissible to prove the truth of a proposition even against a civil litigant if he has not had an adequate opportunity to examine the witness at a time that she is asserting that proposition. But if the defense was given notice of the earlier signed statement and either took the witness's deposition at a time when she was still asserting the proposition, or declined an opportunity to do so, then arguably (given that this is civil litigation) the opportunity should be deemed significant.

Perhaps by now you are persuaded at least that this whole area of prior statements of an in-court witness is a difficult one. It may well change considerably in the coming decades. A key to a sound resolution is to recognize that sometimes the ability of an opponent to cross-examine is impaired by the fact that the witness did not make the statement in question shortly before cross begins.

---

to testify either by videotaped deposition or by closed circuit television out of the presence of the defendant.

One might argue that it would even be sufficient for the prosecutor to give the defense notice of the prior statement, and of her intent to use that statement if the declarant did not testify to similar effect at trial, and to ensure that the declarant is available for a deposition if the defense wishes to take it. But the better result seems to be that the prosecution rather than the defense should have the burden of assessing the risk that a given prosecution witness will not testify in accordance with the prior statement—that is, it ought to be the prosecutor rather than the defense that has the burden of taking a deposition to insure against the situation that a prosecution witness will fail to testify at trial to the full substance of her prior statement.

The question of which of these pre-trial opportunities to examine the witness should be deemed sufficient if the witness does not testify at trial is discussed below, ¶ 12.9.

CHAPTER 11

UNAVAILABILITY

■ ■ ■

Additional Reading: McCormick, ch. 24, § 253; ch. 31, § 302; Mueller & Kirkpatrick, §§ 8.63–.67

Chapter 10 has just considered the situation that arises when the maker of an out-of-court statement is brought to trial as a witness. Now suppose instead that the person is unavailable to be a witness at trial. We should emphasize at the outset that unavailability does not mean simply that the person *is not* a witness at trial; rather, it means that the person *could not be* made a witness at trial, or at least could not be made a satisfactory witness without imposing an undue burden on her or one or more parties or the judicial system.

The opponent may contend that unavailability of the declarant weighs against admissibility of the statement because it means that the opponent will be foreclosed altogether from examining the declarant. "If she had only been available," the opponent might say, "and her hearsay statement were admitted, I could and would have called her as a witness to examine her" (though we may well doubt, for reasons explored later, whether the opponent really would have done so). "But given that she is unavailable, I can't do so, and I have no opportunity to examine her if the hearsay is admitted."

More often, though, unavailability has appeared to be a factor weighing in favor of admissibility. The proponent will contend that it does so because excluding the statement presumably will not induce him to present the live testimony of the declarant. (I say presumably because it may be that if an exclusionary rule was in place and the proponent knew about it, the proponent could have taken steps to prevent the unavailability.) Accordingly, Fed. R. Evid. 804 provides several hearsay exceptions that apply only if the declarant is unavailable.

Unavailability also played a role in the now discarded Confrontation Clause regime of *Ohio v. Roberts*; there, the Court said that ordinarily a hearsay statement could not be introduced against a criminal defendant unless the declarant was unavailable. But that requirement—which was set in the context of a view that the scope of the Confrontation Clause was as broad as that of the rule against hearsay—was impractical from the start, and the Court soon drew back from it. Indeed, in some cases it seemed to suggest that the unavailability requirement only applied to statements fitting within the exception for former testimony. This seemed perplexing; to fit within that exception, under Rule 804(b)(1) and the law of most jurisdictions, a statement must have been subjected to cross-examination, a crucial requirement not applicable to any of the other exceptions in Rules 803 or 804. So why were statements fitting within that exception alone subject to the unavailability requirement?

Under the *Crawford* regime, which of course limits the scope of the Confrontation Clause to statements that are testimonial in nature, the role of unavailability is clear: If the witness is unavailable to testify at trial, but the accused had an adequate opportunity to cross-examine her in an earlier proceeding, then the prior testimonial statement may be admitted as a good second-best substitute for live testimony. But if the witness is available to testify at trial, the prior testimonial statement may not be admitted, even if the accused did have that opportunity; if the prosecution wants to use the statement, it has to bring the witness in to trial. This doctrine actually conforms quite closely to the traditional rule on prior testimony of a witness who is now unavailable—a rule that is several hundred years old and is now expressed in Rule 804(b)(1).

It is easy enough to see why, under the second-best theory, Rule 804(b)(1) applies only if the witness is unavailable. But consider Arizona Rule of Civil Procedure 32(a), which provides:

> At the trial or at any hearing any part or all of a deposition, so far as admissible under the rules of evidence applied as though the witness were then present and testifying, may be used against any party who was present or represented at the taking of the deposition or who had reasonable notice thereof, and had an opportunity and similar motive to develop the testimony by direct, cross, or redirect examination. The party who seeks admission of the testimony by deposition may do so without proof of the deponent's unavailability to testify at trial. Nothing contained in this Rule shall be construed to limit, in any way, the right of any party to call the deposed witness to testify in person at trial.

¶ 11.1: Should other jurisdictions adopt this Rule?

It is also easy enough to see why unavailability is required for Rules 804(b)(2), the exception for dying declarations, and 804(b)(6), the forfeiture exception, which makes the rule against hearsay inapplicable when wrongdoing by the opponent rendered the declarant unable to testify live at trial. Why unavailability is necessary for Rules 804(b)(3), the exception for declarations against interest, or 804(b)(4), the exception for statements of personal and family history, is more mysterious and historically contingent.

In any event, we have to address the matter of unavailability for analysis under both the Confrontation Clause and hearsay law. The basic question is when a person should be deemed unavailable. Unavailability is a conclusory term; whether a declarant should be deemed unavailable or not is, at least in large part, a matter of definition. FRE 804(a) offers a multi-part definition; the declarant must fit at least one of its categories for the hearsay exceptions in FRE 804(b) to apply. This definition is also useful in considering unavailability for confrontation purposes, though it will not necessarily bind the Court in defining unavailability in that context. Read Rule 804(a) carefully, and bear in mind these points:

(1) Unavailability is not always symmetrical: It may be that one party could produce the declarant far more readily than could the other party. Indeed, in some cases one party could produce the declarant quite readily but the other party is altogether foreclosed from doing so. This is particularly so in criminal cases. If a declarant is asserting her privilege against self-incrimination, the accused has no way of requiring her to testify. The prosecution has tools at its disposal, however—if it chooses to use them. It can give the declarant immunity; it can plea bargain with her, giving lenient treatment in return for her testimony; and sometimes it can try her first, so that by the time it needs her testimony her case has been resolved, one way or the other, and she can no longer claim the privilege.[1] On the other hand, if the accused is the declarant, the accused can choose to testify but the prosecution cannot compel him to. Similarly, if the accused and the declarant have a close relationship, it may be that the declarant is asserting the privilege primarily to accommodate the accused's desire that she not testify, and the accused could, if he wished, persuade her not to invoke the privilege.

(2) Unavailability is often a matter of degree. Though a dead declarant is absolutely unavailable at the time of the trial, other declarants may be more or less available—depending on how much effort and cost, financial or otherwise, the proponent or the court is willing to undergo to procure the declarant's testimony. A declarant who might be considered unavailable if she made a seemingly trustworthy statement of peripheral importance to the case might be considered available if her statement was dubious and of crucial significance. But note that this is not the way the Federal Rules work, at least on their face: Except for the reference in Rule 804(a)(5) to "other reasonable means," the definition of

---

[1] *See* John G. Douglass, *Admissibility as Cause and Effect: Considering Affirmative Rights Under the Confrontation Clause,* 21 Quinnipiac L. Rev. 1047, 1068 (2003) (arguing that, where declarant is unavailable only because of assertion of privilege against self-incrimination, court should put prosecutor to the choice of granting use immunity or forgoing the use of hearsay).

unavailability in Rule 804(a) is categorical, insensitive to the context of the case.[2]

(3) Unavailability is often a matter of timing. Even a declarant who is dead, or otherwise unavailable at the time of trial, might have been more readily available at an earlier time, and if so her testimony might have been taken and recorded under oath and subject to cross-examination.

(4) Unavailability is also sometimes a matter of parts. In order to produce a person as a witness, a party must identify her, locate her, procure her attendance, and persuade her to testify. In some cases a party can perform some of these tasks but not others; the other party may be able to perform the tasks that the first one cannot, or to give the first party the necessary information to do so.

(5) Unavailability is sometimes a matter of fault. We will discuss this matter in detail in conjunction with the doctrine of forfeiture, which is now expressed for the Federal Rules in FRE 804(b)(6): If the opponent has wrongfully procured the unavailability of the declarant, he ought not be able to exclude evidence of a statement made by the declarant on the grounds that he has not had a chance to cross-examine her. The last sentence of Rule 804(a) refers to the reverse situation, in which the proponent of the evidence wrongfully procures the unavailability of the declarant. It seems clear that in this circumstance the proponent ought not be able to invoke a hearsay exception based on that unavailability; for that matter, the proponent probably ought to be held to have forfeited introduction of the hearsay altogether.

(6) Sometimes, as in many other evidentiary contexts, decisions on the issue of unavailability must be made in the face of a glaring lack of information.

With these comments in mind, let us consider problems raising unavailability issues. Some useful ones are presented by Supreme Court cases involving a defendant's contention that his confrontation right was violated by use of former testimony without an adequate showing that the witness was unavailable. For example, in *Barber v. Page*, 390 U.S. 719 (1968), Barber and Woods were jointly charged in Oklahoma with armed robbery. Woods testified at a preliminary hearing, incriminating Barber. Barber's counsel did not cross-examine Woods. When Barber was tried

---

[2] The "or other reasonable means" language has not always been given much force. Note Murray v. Toyota Motor Distributors, Inc., 664 F.2d 1377, 1380 (9th Cir.), *cert. denied*, 457 U.S. 1106 (1982), saying, "Garrett resided in California, beyond the reach of a subpoena from the district court in Montana, and was therefore 'unavailable' within the meaning of Fed.R.Evid. 804(a)." The court seems not to have inquired whether Garrett's attendance could have been procured by "reasonable means"—such as friendly persuasion or perhaps reimbursement of travel expenses—other than a subpoena. By contrast, note *Barber v. Page*, summarized below.

seven months later, Woods was residing in Texas. That in itself would not preclude the State from securing Woods' presence. Indeed, there is a Uniform Act for just that purpose—the aptly and lengthily named Uniform Act to Secure the Attendance of Witnesses from Without a State in Criminal Proceedings, *reprinted in* 11 U.L.A. That Act, which has been adopted in one form or another by every state, provides a mechanism under which a court in a state where a witness is found compels the witness—in custody, if necessary—to give testimony in another state. The situation with respect to Woods was made more complex by the fact that his residence was a prison. Again, that should not have been a showstopper.[3] But there was one further complication: Woods was a *federal* prisoner, and the Uniform Act does not apply to the federal government. Thus, the State offered the transcript of Woods' preliminary hearing testimony; it made no effort to obtain Woods' presence at trial, because it had no way of compelling federal authorities to produce him. That did not resolve the case, however. Quoting Judge Bailey Aldrich's dissent in the Court of Appeals, 381 F.2d at 481, the Supreme Court rightly emphasized that "the possibility of a refusal is not the equivalent of asking and receiving a rebuff," 390 U.S. at 724, and so held that the hearing transcript should not have been admitted.

Four years later, in *Mancusi v. Stubbs*, 408 U.S. 204 (1972), with substantially different membership and on facts stronger for the prosecution, the Court was less demanding. Stubbs was tried in state court in Tennessee for kidnaping Alex Holm and his wife and murdering Mrs. Holm. Alex Holm testified for the prosecution, telling the story of the kidnaping and murder. Stubbs was convicted, but the judgment was thrown out on federal habeas corpus on the ground that he had been denied the effective assistance of counsel, his lawyer having been appointed only four days before the trial. At the retrial, Holm's son testified that his father, an American citizen, had returned to Sweden, his native land, and was a permanent resident there. At the time, 28 U.S.C. § 1783(a) allowed a federal court to compel the appearance "before it of a national or resident of the United States who is in a foreign country. . . ." Thus, as the statute then stood, the federal court could not compel Holm's appearance before a state court. (Several months later, Congress corrected the problem by amending the statute to read "before it, or before a person or body designated by it, . . .") The trial court admitted the transcript of Holm's testimony from the first trial, and the United States Supreme Court, in affirming a later conviction of Stubbs as a second

---

[3] Because some states were not willing to apply the Act to Secure the Attendance of Witnesses to prisoners, another Uniform Act, the Uniform Rendition of Prisoners as Witnesses in Criminal Proceedings Act, was promulgated in 1957 to address the problem. That Act is still on the books in some states, but the Uniform Law Commissioners, believing that interpretations of the earlier Act make the subsequent one unnecessary where it has not already been adopted, have withdrawn it.

offender, held that this did not violate the Confrontation Clause. The Court declared that "the State of Tennessee, so far as this record shows, was powerless to compel his attendance at the second trial, either through its own process or through established procedures depending on the voluntary assistance of another government." 408 U.S. at 212; note how this last clause pushes against *Barber*. In dissent, Justice Marshall, joined by Justice Douglas, wrote, *id.* at 223:

> At a minimum, the State could have notified Mr. Holm that the trial was scheduled, and invited him to come at his own expense. Beyond that, it could have offered to pay his expenses. Finally, it could have sought federal assistance in invoking the cooperation of Swedish authorities, as a matter of international comity.

¶ 11.2: (a) Should Holm have been deemed unavailable to testify at the second trial?

(b) Would your answer to (a) be different if the witness in Sweden was not Holm but a former neighbor who said he noticed Stubbs looking at the Holms' house the week before the kidnapping?

(c) Should Holm have been deemed unavailable to testify at the second trial if he told the prosecutors that he would come to the second trial, but only if the State paid his transportation costs? If he said he would come only if the State paid his transportation costs and reimbursed him for all his expenses, including lodging in a first-class hotel and three-star meals? If, in addition to the above, Holm demanded compensation of $1,000 per day for his time?

¶ 11.3: Roberts was tried in March 1976 for forgery and possession of stolen credit cards belonging to Bernard and Amy Isaacs. He testified in his defense that the Isaacs' daughter Anita had given him her parents' checkbook and credit cards with the understanding that he could use them. In rebuttal, the State offered the transcript of testimony given by Anita at the preliminary hearing in January 1975. There, Anita testified that she had permitted Roberts to use her apartment for several days while she was away, but that she had refused to give him access to the checks and credit cards. Soon after the preliminary hearing, Anita left her home in Ohio for Tucson, Arizona. In about April or May 1975, her parents received a form relating to a welfare application she had filed in San Francisco. They telephoned the social worker assigned to Anita's case and through that social worker they spoke to Anita the same day. Since then, they had only one contact with her by the time of Roberts' trial, when she called them, sometime during the summer of 1975, from an unidentified place outside Ohio. Amy Isaacs testified at *voir dire* that she knew the name of a person whom Anita had known in Tucson, but that she did not know how to get in touch with that person, and that she did not know how to get in touch with Anita. The prosecution issued five subpoenas to Anita at her parents' home, but they were all returned without service; three of the subpoenas were apparently served after Amy told the police that she was not living there. No one on behalf of the prosecution made an attempt to reach the person in Tucson or the social worker in San Francisco. Should the transcript have been admitted? See *Ohio v. Roberts*, 448 U.S. 56 (1980) (holding Anita unavailable for purposes of Confrontation Clause analysis).

¶ 11.4: Consider *Lee v. Illinois*, 476 U.S. 530 (1986). The prosecution wishes to use against Lee a statement that Thomas made to the police inculpating both Lee and himself in a gruesome double murder. Assume that admissibility of the statement depends on whether Thomas is unavailable. The prosecution contends that Thomas is indeed unavailable because he is invoking his privilege against self-incrimination. The defense responds that the prosecution could, if it wished, nullify the privilege. Should Thomas be deemed unavailable?[4]

Would your answer change if Thomas's involvement was, at most, as an accessory after the fact (he gave Lee a place to stay when she was on the run), and the prosecution is unsure of whether it wished to charge him?

¶ 11.5: Yida is charged with conspiracy to import ecstasy into the United States. A key witness against him at trial is Renziniano, who is subject to a deportation order; he has been detained on a material witness warrant, and his deportation delayed, so that he could testify against Yida. The jury reaches an impasse, on April 13 the judge declares a mistrial, and 13 days later the judge sets a new trial to begin in July. Renziniano and his lawyer work out a deal with the Government providing for his immediate deportation to Israel. Renziniano promises as part of the deal that if asked he will return to testify at the second trial, at the Government's expense. But when the time for the second trial comes, guess what—Renziniano says he can't travel, and the Government has no means to compel him to do

---

[4] Note that under *Crawford* the statement would be inadmissible in any event because Lee never had an opportunity to cross-examine Thomas. The *Lee* Court, pre-*Crawford*, held it inadmissible on other grounds; four dissenting justices, reaching an issue that the majority did not, would have held that Thomas was unavailable for Confrontation Clause purposes.

so. Should Renziniano be deemed unavailable to testify at trial? *See Yida v. United States*, 498 F.3d 945 (9th Cir. 2007).

¶ **11.6:** Consider *R. v. Forbes*, 171 Eng. Rep. 354 (1814), in which a lingering murder victim identified Forbes as the killer. If the authorities do not arrange for Forbes to be present and to have an opportunity for cross-examination when the victim makes the statement, should the victim be deemed unavailable for purposes of confrontation or hearsay doctrine? Does the victim's condition at the time he makes the statement, or his knowledge of his condition, affect your answer?

¶ **11.7:** In each of the following cases, the witness is the alleged victim of the crime charged. She testified, subject to cross-examination, at a preliminary hearing, and at trial she takes the stand, but now she is reluctant to testify substantively. What means of persuasion or compulsion, if any, should the court use in an attempt to persuade her to testify before declaring her unavailable?

(a) Domestic violence. The witness is the defendant's wife and insists that she wants to preserve their marriage.[5]

(b) Child sex abuse. The witness is the defendant's seven-year-old daughter, and she "clams up" when she takes the stand.

(c) Rape. The witness and the defendant are strangers (as in a substantial minority of rape cases), and the witness says that she still finds the episode highly traumatic and does not want to relive it.

(d) Extortion. The defendant is allegedly a mobster and the witness was paying him large sums as part of a protection scheme until she decided to go to the police. She had intended to testify but she has received an intimidating phone call warning her not to.

¶ **11.8:** After an earthquake, a 25-year-old school building collapsed, killing several children. The parents are suing the school district, claiming that the building collapsed because the mortar was insufficient to withstand even minor shocks. The plaintiffs offer the testimony of Gribald, who used to be a foreman for Mix Masters, Inc., the contractor that supplied the mortar for the school. Gribald is prepared to testify that, a year after the school was built, Morton Matthews, the sole owner and proprietor of Mix Masters, told him, "I shaved a little bit on the

---

[5] *See* Cheryl Hanna, *No Right to Choose: Mandated Victim Participation in Domestic Violence Prosecutions*, 109 Harv. L. Rev. 1850 (1996).

mortar for that school. Let's hope for the best. Now that I'm back on my feet, I can do the next one right." Gribald stopped work for Matthews, who was then 60 years old, soon after. He did not stay in touch with Matthews at all after leaving his employ. Mix Masters dissolved twenty years ago, and there is no local telephone listing for a Morton Matthews. Assume that Matthews' statement would be excepted from the rule against hearsay as a declaration against interest, *see* Fed. R. Evid. 804(b)(3)—if he is deemed unavailable. Should he be? If you were the judge, what more, if anything, would you need to know before deciding?

¶ **11.9:** Consider Arizona Rule of Civil Procedure 32(a), which provides:

> At the trial or at any hearing any part or all of a deposition, so far as admissible under the rules of evidence applied as though the witness were then present and testifying, may be used against any party who was present or represented at the taking of the deposition or who had reasonable notice thereof, and had an opportunity and similar motive to develop the testimony by direct, cross, or redirect examination. The party who seeks admission of the testimony by deposition may do so without proof of the deponent's unavailability to testify at trial. Nothing contained in this Rule shall be construed to limit, in any way, the right of any party to call the deposed witness to testify in person at trial.

Should other jurisdictions adopt this Rule?

CHAPTER 12

OPPORTUNITY FOR ADVERSE EXAMINATION

■ ■ ■

FRE 804(b)(1)

Additional Reading: McCormick, ch. 31; Mueller & Kirkpatrick, §§ 8.68–.70

A. BACKGROUND AND RATIONALE

As you know, unavailability of the witness is significant under *Crawford* because *if* she is unavailable *and* the accused had an adequate prior opportunity to examine her, then the prior statement, though testimonial, may be introduced against him without violating the Confrontation Clause, as a second-best substitute for live testimony.

In this respect, confrontation doctrine is closely in accordance with the hearsay exception for former, or prior, testimony, which the Federal Rules express in FRE 804(b)(1). That exception has a very long history. Indeed, in a sense, it was established before the rule against hearsay itself. If that seems odd, the key is to recognize that this doctrine, like the Confrontation Clause after *Crawford*, is limited to testimonial statements, and it provides an alternative means for the presentation of testimony.

For at least four hundred years, the common law system has depended primarily on the live testimony of witnesses, presented in open court. But alongside the common law courts in England was another system, eventually known as equity, with its procedures based on those of continental and canonical (church) courts. Testimony for equity proceedings was not taken in open court or before the parties. On the contrary, these courts feared intimidation of witnesses by the parties, and so an officer of the court took the deposition of the witness in a closed proceeding, out of the presence of the parties. The parties did have a right to pose questions for the witness in writing. The deposition transcript was the evidence used by the equity court in determining the facts.

Common law courts came to realize that depositions had a great advantage: If the witness was unavailable to testify at trial, the deposition transcript could be used as a substitute. By the middle of the seventeenth century, a sophisticated body of doctrine grew up in civil cases governing the circumstances in which depositions taken in equity might be presented at a common law trial. The essentials of the doctrine were that the witness must be unavailable at trial—for if she were available her live testimony would be preferred—and that the party against whom the evidence was offered, or a predecessor in interest, must have had an adequate opportunity to pose questions for the witness.

This seventeenth-century doctrine was remarkably similar to the modern hearsay exception for prior testimony. It was not then conceptualized as an exception to the rule against hearsay, however. There was then no well-developed rule against hearsay, and the term hearsay was generally understood to mean a witness's testimony about a statement she had heard; a deposition transcript presented in court would not be considered hearsay. The rules on use of deposition transcripts were rather a part of procedural law, a limitation on the manner in which testimony might be taken and presented.

The exception for prior testimony is therefore different in nature from most of the other hearsay exceptions. Most of the other exceptions are purportedly based on a perception that some circumstance renders the declaration particularly trustworthy, and so makes the absence of cross-examination tolerable. The view taken here is that most of the exceptions are actually warranted, to the extent they are, by the fact that the statements included in them are not testimonial in nature. (That's not true of the exception for dying declarations, but other considerations, which we'll discuss in the next chapter, apply with respect to it.) This exception, by contrast, is based on the fact that the statement at issue is in fact a form of testimony that was taken at an earlier time, perhaps in the same proceeding or perhaps in another, subject to oath and cross-examination (or some other form of questioning that, for present purposes, has filled the same need). Whether or not the prior testimony seems trustworthy, the logic goes, it has already been subjected to most of the same protections as live testimony at trial, and so it is a good substitute if the witness is unable to appear at trial.

On the other hand, introducing a transcript of the prior statement— traditionally the best possible way to present the statement at the current trial—does not give the factfinder the opportunity to observe the demeanor of the declarant. How important is that? Social psychology research indicates that nonverbal conduct accounts for a great deal of the information communicated by a speaker to another person concerning the speaker's emotions and attitudes, particularly in emotional situations.[1]

---

[1] One researcher even attempted to numerify the matter, concluding that 55% of a speaker's expression of feelings, and vocal clues for another 38% is conveyed by factual clues. Albert Mehrabian, *Nonverbal Communication*, 182 (1972). But even if numerification of this

Moreover, some experts conclude that when a listener perceives that a speaker's statement and the accompanying metacommunication clues are in conflict, the listener tends to disbelieve the statement. It appears, though, that people tend to vastly overrate their ability to discern a person's truthtelling ability from her demeanor; the sweat and shifty eyes that we tend to regard as indications of lying may in fact reflect nothing more than nervousness, and the collected and self-confident manner and apparent strength of conviction that we tend to regard as indications of truthfulness may in fact be the stock in trade of a skilled liar.[2]

Consider also that in most cases the absence of demeanor evidence is more likely to hurt the proponent—the one attempting to convey the message—than the opponent of prior testimony. The proponent is usually happier with the vividness of live testimony than with a relatively dry transcript of prior testimony. This factor might seem to favor admissibility of the prior testimony when the witness is unavailable. At the same time, it seems to cut against admissibility when the witness is available; if the proponent *could* present the live testimony of the witness but chooses to present a paper transcript instead, we may well wonder whether the proponent has some reason to believe that in fact the witness's demeanor would suggest that her testimony was false.

In modern times, a new consideration has entered the picture: Sometimes, testimony is videotaped—whether at deposition, in a trial, or in another proceeding—in which case a subsequent factfinder, rather than being limited to a transcript, can observe an electronic transmission of it.

¶ 12.1: To what extent should videotaped testimony taken at an earlier time be considered a full substitute for testimony given live at trial, even if the witness is available? What advantages does it have over live testimony? What disadvantages and costs does it pose? Should the possibility of videotaping testimony mean that a transcript is not an adequate substitute?

We shall later consider in more depth videotaped testimony in the context of child witnesses. For now, though, it is important to note that the possibility of videotaped testimony highlights a concern apart from demeanor that is raised by prior testimony. Even assuming that taped

---

matter has meaning, such overall numbers do not seem helpful; the importance of nonverbal clues is very context-dependent.

   [2] *See generally* Charles F. Bond, et al., *New Findings in Non-Verbal Lie Detection*, in Pär Anders Granhag, et al., eds. *Detecting Deception: Current Challenges and Cognitive Approaches* (2015), at 37–58; Max Minzer, *Detecting Lies Using Demeanor, Bias, and Context*, 29 Cardozo L,. Rev. 2557 (2008); Jeremy A. Blumenthal, *A Wipe of The Hands, A Lick of the Lips: The Validity of Demeanor Evidence in Assessing Witness Credibility*, 72 Neb. L. Rev. 1157 (1993); Olin Guy Wellborn III, *Demeanor*, 76 Cornell L. Rev. 1075 (1991) (reviewing experimental evidence).

testimony gives the factfinder every bit as good an opportunity to observe the demeanor of the witness as does live testimony, or even better, previously taped testimony may be significantly less satisfactory than live testimony in one important respect. The fact that the testimony was taken at an earlier time means that counsel may not have had all the information she does at trial to prepare cross-examination.

And so, in part perhaps because of the demeanor concern and in part because of this timing concern, the view still prevailing is that prior testimony is a substitute for current testimony at trial, but generally a second-best substitute to be used only if taken under satisfactory conditions and if current testimony is unavailable. This viewpoint is apparent in FRE 804(a)(5), part of the definition of unavailability. Note that this provision allows the proponent to invoke the prior testimony exception if he has been unable to procure the declarant's attendance at trial by reasonable means, but it allows the proponent to invoke the other Rule 804 exceptions only if he is not reasonably able to procure the declarant's "attendance *or testimony*," (emphasis added). In rough terms, the Rules appear to set up a hierarchy applicable to these other exceptions: If you can get the declarant's prior testimony, taken under the conditions required for proper testimony, you should use that rather than a declaration not given under those conditions. And if you can get the declarant to show up in court, you should do that instead of using the prior testimony. In short, prior testimony appears to be more satisfactory than an unexamined out-of-court declaration, but not as satisfactory as in-court testimony, and so only if in-court testimony is unavailable should the prior testimony be admitted.

B. OPPORTUNITY AND MOTIVE FOR PRIOR EXAMINATION

The central issue, both for this aspect of confrontation doctrine and for the hearsay exception for prior testimony, is whether the party opponent has had an adequate opportunity to examine the witness. Sometimes the term "opportunity and motive" is used; it is not sufficient that the party have had the legal right to examine the witness if at the time he had no incentive to do so. *See* FRE 804(b)(1)(B) ("opportunity and similar motive to develop" the testimony).

Sometimes it is easy to determine that a prior opportunity for cross was adequate. Suppose, for example, a witness testifies against an accused at trial and is then subjected to a full cross-examination by able counsel. The case goes to the jury, which deadlocks and is dismissed. The prosecution decides to retry the accused, but in the interim the witness has died, of natural causes. The prosecution offers into evidence at the second trial a transcript of the witness's testimony from the first trial.

Ordinarily, the evidence should be admitted; on the face of it, the accused had an adequate opportunity to be confronted with the witness, who is now unavailable.

¶ 12.2: Suppose you are representing the accused in a case like *Mancusi v. Stubbs*, ¶ 11.2 and accompanying text, or *Yida*, ¶ 11.5, in which the witness testified subject to a full cross-examination at the first trial but was arguably unavailable at a retrial. Can you imagine facts under which you might have a plausible argument that the opportunity for cross-examination at the first trial should not be deemed adequate?

Situations other than prior trials are more likely to create difficult questions as to whether the opportunity and motive for examination were adequate.

¶ 12.3: In *California v. Green*, 399 U.S. 149 (1970), Porter identified Green as his supplier not only in a conversation with Officer Wade but also at a preliminary hearing, the purpose of which was to determine whether there was sufficient evidence to hold Green for trial. The Supreme Court said that Porter's preliminary hearing testimony was

> given under circumstances closely approximating those that surround the typical trial. Porter was under oath; respondent was represented by counsel—the same counsel in fact who later represented him at the trial; respondent had every opportunity to cross-examine Porter as to his statement; and the proceedings were conducted before a judicial tribunal, equipped to provide a judicial record of the hearings.

Suppose then that Porter absconded before trial and that despite good-faith efforts the prosecution was unable to locate him.

(a) Should admission of his preliminary hearing testimony be deemed to violate the Confrontation Clause?

(b) For better or worse, the Supreme Court stated in *Green* that there would be no violation in this setting. How might this ruling affect your conduct if you are representing the accused at a preliminary hearing?

(c) Suppose that as defense counsel you have no desire to engage in a full cross-examination at the preliminary hearing (and you suspect the court has no interest in your doing so, either), but you don't want to prejudice the interests of your client by failing to do so. What might you do? Hint: Perhaps in the end, the statement in *Green* as to the adequacy of the opportunity for cross at the preliminary hearing is nothing more than a trap for the unwary.

Alternatively, suppose that as a criminal trial is approaching, the prosecution realizes that a key witness is dying and may not survive until trial, or be strong enough to testify then. So the prosecution may arrange for a deposition for the preservation of evidence. Traditionally, this, rather than discovery, was the main purpose for which depositions were used by the common law, in civil as well as criminal litigation. Such depositions, sometimes called *de bene esse*, are still allowed, where circumstances warrant, even in jurisdictions that do not allow depositions for criminal discovery. In most jurisdictions, they are not routine, but perhaps as a result of *Crawford* they will become more so.

¶ 12.4: (a) Amy Hammon makes a statement in her living room to a police officer accusing her husband Hershel of having assaulted her. The prosecutor recognizes in light of her experience in domestic violence cases that by the time trial comes around, which may not be for several months, she may be unable for a variety of reasons to produce Amy as a live witness. Should the prosecutor take Amy's deposition a month after the incident, giving Hershel notice and an opportunity to cross-examine? If so, and Amy does not testify at trial, should the deposition transcript be admitted?

(b) Suppose that the prosecutor does depose Amy—and, believing that she has only a narrow time window in which Amy will be willing to testify in front of Hershel, the deposition is held 24 hours after the incident. Sure enough, Amy does not testify at trial, and the prosecutor offers the deposition. Has Hershel had an adequate opportunity to cross-examine Amy—or can one tell on the facts given?

¶ 12.5: (a) Lopez, a convicted felon, is charged with possession of a firearm. He denies the charge. The state lists Moroni as a trial witness, indicating that he will testify that Lopez possessed a firearm. The state allows criminal defendants to take depositions of listed prosecution witnesses for discovery purposes, and Lopez avails himself of the opportunity. After the deposition and before trial, Moroni absconds. The state offers a statement Moroni made to a police officer to the effect that Lopez possessed a firearm. Lopez objects on Confrontation Clause grounds. May the statement be admitted against him? *Compare State v. Lopez*, 974 So.2d 340 (Fl. 2008), *with Howard v. State*, 853 N.E.2d 461 (Ind. 2006).

(b) Suppose instead that the prosecutor wrote Lopez's counsel saying, "We have taken a statement from Moroni. Here it is. We intend to use it if he does not appear at trial, which may be likely because he is in bad health." Lopez does not take Moroni's deposition, and Moroni dies before trial. May the statement be used?

(c) Suppose instead that the prosecutor makes a general practice of writing defense counsel, "Here is a list of our witnesses, and the substance of the testimony we expect them to present at trial. If for any reason any of these witnesses is not available to testify at trial, we expect to introduce proof of the statements she has made to us. You may wish to avail yourself of the opportunity to take the depositions of all these witnesses." If Lopez does not take Moroni's deposition and Moroni dies before trial, may the prosecution offer Moroni's statement?

¶ 12.6: (a) The body of a young girl is found. A medical examiner who is near retirement performs an autopsy and prepares a report, which indicates (1) when the girl died, (2) that she was strangled to death, and (3) that she was raped before she was murdered. Suspicion centers on five men; Craig is the prime suspect. But there is inadequate evidence to charge anyone at this time. The prosecutor hopes that further evidence might eventually turn up, allowing a case to be brought against the murderer; there is no statute of limitations on murder. She also recognizes that the medical examiner may not be around to testify live at such time as a case is brought. What should she do? Should this be effective if in fact sufficient evidence turns up to prosecute Craig, and by that time the medical examiner is dead? Do you have enough information to answer that question? *Cf.* Fed. R. Civ. P. 27 (providing procedure perpetuating testimony by taking deposition before civil action can be brought; requiring notice to persons whom the petitioner expects to be adverse parties).

(b) Same facts, but suppose the prosecutor is unable at the time of the murder to limit attention to a narrow set of suspects. Does this alter your answers? *See People v. Wilkey*, 2004 WL 576659 (Mich.App. 2004).

Usually the opportunity for examination that is assertedly adequate was on cross-examination, but this is not necessarily so.

¶ 12.7: Painter sued Dallek in an auto negligence case. Dallek put Wesmer on the stand, and to his disappointment she said he was going "quite fast." Dallek's counsel asked some further questions to try to limit the damage. Now Pointer is suing Dallek for damages arising from the same incident.

Wesmer is dead. May Pointer introduce the transcript of Wesmer's testimony from the Painter trial?

¶ **12.8:** Temple was a truck driver employed by Drovers, Inc. He ran a Drovers truck, which he had not personally loaded, into a wall. Drovers sued Temple. In that action, Whitson testified for Drovers that Temple was driving very fast and that the truck was overloaded. Whitson then died. Now Jackson is suing Drovers for damages arising from the accident. May Jackson introduce against Drovers, under the hearsay exception for former testimony, the transcript of Whitson's testimony?[3] Could it invoke any other doctrine to avoid the rule against hearsay?

And the argument is sometimes made that there may be an adequate opportunity for adverse examination if the adverse party can bring the witness to trial.

¶ **12.9:** Briscoe is being tried for possession of cocaine. Critical evidence against him is a certificate of a lab analysis indicating that a substance found on his possession is cocaine. Pursuant to a state statute, the prosecutor offers the certificate without presenting its author as a live witness. The statute gives Briscoe the right to call the author as his own witness, but to ask her leading questions, if he wishes to do so. Briscoe declines to do so.

(a) Is the statute constitutional? *See Melendez-Diaz v. Massachusetts*, 557 U.S. 305, 324–25 (2009); *Briscoe v. Virginia*, 130 S.Ct. 1316 (2010). In thinking about this question, consider whether, if the author had testified at trial, Briscoe likely would have asked her any questions on cross. If the answer is yes, then why do you suppose Briscoe failed to call the author as a witness to ask such questions?

(b) Assume the statute is unconstitutional and consider whether a statute along the following lines would be constitutional: *If the prosecution gives notice at least thirty days before the trial date that it intends to introduce a lab certificate, then it may do so, without presenting the author as a live witness, unless at least ten days before trial the accused demands that the prosecution presents the author.*

(c) One argument made in favor of statutes like the one in *Briscoe* is that requiring the lab analyst who wrote the report to testify at trial would be unduly expensive—especially given that by the time of trial she is unlikely to have any clear recollection

---

[3] In Chapter 14, we will consider whether the evidence might be admissible in a situation like this under the doctrine of adoptive admissions.

of the particular case, and therefore cross-examination is unlikely to be valuable. Is this argument persuasive? Would the problems to which it points—expense and limited value of cross—be mitigated if the state offered the accused a deposition of the lab analyst three weeks after the test was completed? Now suppose the deposition were one day after she has completed the report. Has he had an adequate opportunity to cross-examine her—or can one tell on the facts given?

C. "PREDECESSORS IN INTEREST"

The confrontation right is personal: A court should not hold that you have no right to cross-examine a witness because another defendant has done so. But on the civil side the matter is not quite so restrictive.

Suppose the party against whom prior testimony is offered was not a party at the first proceeding. If the present opponent is a party to the case because he has succeeded in interest to a party in the prior case—such as by inheritance, or by purchasing a company—then it is easy to see that the hearsay exception should still apply. Suppose, for instance, that Target Co. sues Proponent, and that at trial Proponent offers the testimony of Witness, whom Target cross-examines. The judgment of the trial court is eventually reversed and the case sent back for retrial. Before the second trial, however, two things happen. First, Raider Co. buys Target and dissolves it, turning Target into one of its own divisions; the litigation continues under the new caption *Raider Co. v. Proponent*. Second, Witness dies. At the retrial, Proponent offers the transcript of Witness's testimony from the first trial. Raider's argument that the transcript should not be admitted because it did not have an opportunity to cross-examine Witness would be rejected rather scornfully. In effect, when it bought Target, Raider also bought into Target's cross-examination of Witness.

The traditional law went only so far as this narrow concept of "predecessor in interest"; put another way, testimony could be offered against Party 2 because Party 1 in a prior action had an opportunity to examine the witness only if the two were *in privity* with each other. If the two did not have this relationship, Party 2 could argue, in effect, "Don't introduce against me the earlier testimony of a witness whom I have not had a chance to examine just because somebody else cross-examined her back then. Why should I be stuck with cross-examination by somebody I don't control?"

The drafters of the Federal Rules attempted to build on a trend more hospitable to admissibility. They would have made the exception applicable so long as a party "with motive and interest similar to those of the party against whom [the statement is] now offered" had an adequate opportunity to examine the witness at the prior proceeding. 56 F.R.D. at 321; Richard D. Friedman & Joshua A. Deahl, *Federal Rules of Evidence: Text and History* 414–16 (2015).[4] The House Committee on the Judiciary, however, appeared to revert to the more traditional rule: "The Committee considered that it is generally unfair to impose upon the party against whom hearsay evidence is being offered responsibility for the manner in which the witness was previously handled by another party." The only exception, in the Committee's view, occurs when, *in a civil proceeding*, the party's predecessor in interest "had an opportunity and similar motive" to examine the witness. The Committee amended the Rule to reflect this principle. The Senate adhered to the House's language, but a passage in the report of its Committee on the Judiciary left the matter in some confusion:

> Although the committee recognizes considerable merit to the rule submitted by the Supreme Court, a position which has been advocated by many scholars and judges, we have concluded that the difference between the two versions is not great and we accept the House amendment.

¶ **12.10:** Ruggles Company recently designed and now manufactures an intrauterine device. Lawton, Inc. also manufactures the device under license from Ruggles. Women in several states have brought actions against one company or the other, claiming that the device caused pelvic inflammatory disease.

(a) In one trial against Ruggles, a Dr. Ervin testified for Ruggles that the device was incapable of causing the disease. Dr. Ervin died shortly afterwards. Can the transcript of her testimony be introduced by Ruggles against another plaintiff in a subsequent action?

(b) Now suppose instead that in the first trial Dr. Ervin had testified for the plaintiff and against Ruggles, to the effect that the device was capable of causing the disease. May a subsequent plaintiff introduce against Ruggles the transcript of her testimony?

(c) Now suppose that Dr. Ervin's testimony was as in (b), but the first trial was against Lawton. May the plaintiff in a

---

[4] The drafters also rejected an old-fashioned rule of mutuality that A could not offer prior testimony against B unless B could have offered the testimony against A. This rule bears some resemblance to the old mutuality rule in the context of issue preclusion, or collateral estoppel, which you most likely have studied in Civil Procedure. It probably has less justification in the context of prior testimony than in the context of issue preclusion (where it has been significantly weakened, though not altogether eliminated), and in the former context it was significantly undercut even before the Federal Rules were passed.

subsequent action against Ruggles introduce the transcript of her testimony?[5]

¶ 12.11: Why does the "predecessor in interest" provision of Rule 804(b)(1), however broadly it might be interpreted, only come into play "in a civil action or proceeding"? Presumably the House Committee, which drafted this limitation, had in mind the common situation in which a prosecutor might wish to introduce testimony given at an earlier trial of another defendant. *Cf.* Friedman & Deahl, *supra,* at 415 (Reporter's Comment, raising question "whether the accused must himself have been a party to the original proceeding or whether a similarly situated person will serve the purpose"). But consider also this situation: Barrett is being tried on federal charges of bank robbery. The circumstances in which he committed an earlier homicide have become (circuitously and dubiously) relevant, and to prove that he then acted in self-defense he wishes to introduce transcripts of testimony that was given by witnesses that he called at his state court trial on the homicide charge. The witnesses are no longer available. Should the prior testimony be admitted?[6]

* * *

Let's look back over the ground we've covered so far, just so far as it bears on the structure of the confrontation right. If a statement is testimonial in nature, it is presented against an accused for the truth of what it asserts, and the witness who made the statement does not testify at trial, then—unless the witness is unavailable to testify at trial *and* the accused had a prior opportunity for cross-examination—there is a presumptive violation of the confrontation right. But we cannot yet say that the right has been violated; in particular, as we shall see, it may be that the accused forfeited the right, and (what is arguably the same thing) certain statements made by a dying person may probably be admitted against an accused notwithstanding the right. We will turn to these issues now.

---

[5] *Compare, e.g.,* Clay v. Johns-Manville Sales Corp., 722 F.2d 1289, 1293–95 (6th Cir.1983), *cert. denied,* 467 U.S. 1253 (1984) (broad view of "predecessors in interest" akin to that favored by Advisory Committee); New England Mutual Life Insurance Co. v. Anderson, 888 F.2d 646, 651–52 (10th Cir.1989) (applying broad view, but finding it not satisfied, in insurance fraud case arising out of murder of husband of minister's lover); *with* In re IBM Peripheral EDP Devices Antitrust Litigation, 444 F.Supp. 110 (N.D.Cal.1978) (narrow view, like that of the House Committee); Acme Printing Ink Co. v. Menard, Inc., 812 F.Supp. 1498, 1525–26 (E.D. Wis. 1992) (summarizing debate and adopting narrow view).

[6] *See* United States v. Barrett, 766 F.2d 609, 618–19 (1st Cir.), *cert. denied,* 474 U.S. 923 (1985) (upholding exclusion; United States was not a party in prior trial).

CHAPTER 13

FORFEITURE AND DYING DECLARATIONS

■ ■ ■

Additional Reading: McCormick, ch. 24, § 253, ch. 32; Mueller & Kirkpatrick, §§ 8.71, .78, .90

There is a quality known in Yiddish by the term *chutzpa*, which is best understood by the story of the man who killed both parents and then asked the court to have mercy on a poor orphan. *That* is *chutzpa*. Another example of *chutzpa* is the person who engages in wrongful conduct that prevents a potential witness from testifying against him, and then argues that a statement that she previously made should not be admitted against him because he hasn't had a chance to cross-examine her. At least in some circumstances, an appropriate response is: *"You* are responsible for her unavailability, and therefore if she cannot come to court you have forfeited the right to cross-examine her." Courts have in effect given this answer in a variety of situations—most commonly when the accused has caused the unavailability of the declarant by killing or intimidating her, but also when he has concealed her or wrongfully persuaded her not to testify.[1] The principle is applicable generally, not just when the evidence is offered against a criminal defendant, but that is far and away its most common application and the one on which we shall focus. *Crawford* explicitly preserves forfeiture doctrine, saying that in contrast to

---

[1] *See, e.g.,* Reynolds v. United States, 98 U.S. 145, 158 (1878); Steele v. Taylor, 684 F.2d 1193, 1201 & n. 10 (6th Cir.1982), *cert. denied,* 460 U.S. 1053 (1983) (summarizing case law from United States and England); United States v. Mastrangelo, 693 F.2d 269 (2d Cir.1982), *cert. denied,* 467 U.S. 1204 (1984); United States v. Thevis, 665 F.2d 616, 627–31 (5th Cir.1982), *cert. denied,* 459 U.S. 825 (1982); People v. LaTorres, 186 A.D.2d 479, 480, 590 N.Y.S.2d 187, 188 (1st Dept.1992).

Among my writings on forfeiture are several postings on the Confrontation Blog, www.confrontationright.blogspot.com, *Giles v. California: A Personal Reflection,* 13 Lewis & Clark L Rev. 733 (2009); *Forfeiture of the Confrontation Right After Crawford and Davis,* 19 Regent U. L. Rev. 489 (2006–07); and *Confrontation and the Definition of Chutzpa,* 31 Israel L. Rev. 506 (1997) (available on the Confrontation Blog). Writings by other authors on forfeiture include the other articles in the symposium in the Fall 2009 issue of Lewis & Clark Law Review; James A. Flanagan, *Foreshadowing the Future of Forfeiture/Estoppel by Wrongdoing: Davis v. Washington and the Necessity of the Defendant's Intent to Intimidate the Witness,* 15 J. L. & Pol. 863 (2007); Andrew King-Ries, *Forfeiture by Wrongdoing: a Panacea for Victimless Domestic Violence Prosecutions,* 39 Creighton L. Rev. 441 (2006); Paul T. Markland, Comment, *The Admission of Hearsay Evidence Where Defendant Misconduct Causes the Unavailability of a Prosecution Witness,* 43 Am. U. L. Rev. 995 (1994); Kenneth W. Graham, Jr., *The Right of Confrontation and the Hearsay Rule: Sir Walter Raleigh Loses Another One,* 8 Crim. L. Bull. 99, 139 (1972) ("A defendant who murders a witness ought not be permitted to invoke the right of confrontation to prohibit the use of his accusation.").

exceptions to the hearsay rule that purport to identify reliable types of hearsay it "extinguishes confrontation claims on essentially equitable grounds." 541 U.S. at 62. The doctrine was not originally expressed in the Federal Rules of Evidence, but now it is, in Rule 804(b)(6).

Running alongside forfeiture doctrine for more than two centuries has been a hearsay exception for dying declarations. Suppose a murder victim lingers before dying, and during that interval, while aware that she is on the verge of death, she makes a statement about the circumstances leading to her incipient death; the statement may identify the killer. Then, according to doctrine going back at least to the late 18th century, the statement is excepted from the hearsay rule; no one, it is sometimes said, would want to meet his Maker with a lie upon his lips.[2] The dying-declaration exception is expressed in FRE 804(b)(2).

Crawford explicitly preserved the possibility that, notwithstanding the fundamental transformation that it wrought in the doctrine of the Confrontation Clause, there is a similar exception to the confrontation right for dying declarations. The Court noted that in general, at the time the Sixth Amendment was adopted, the extant hearsay exceptions did not extend to testimonial statements that had not been subject to confrontation. The "one exception" of which it was aware, the Court noted, was the one for dying declarations. The Court declined to decide "whether the Sixth Amendment incorporates an exception for testimonial dying declarations." And, it added, "If this exception must be accepted on historical grounds, it is *sui generis*."

In my view, there should be no dying-declaration exception as such to the confrontation right—and there is no need for one, because a properly constructed forfeiture doctrine should yield similar results in most cases, without undermining the structure of the doctrine of the Confrontation Clause. I shall outline the argument in the following pages—but for now it is principally of academic interest, because of the Court's decision in *Giles v. California*, 554 U.S. 353 (2008).

A. THE BASIC FORFEITURE PRINCIPLE AND THE DYING-DECLARATION EXCEPTION

The basic forfeiture principle seems well-founded. An accused's conduct at trial may be so intolerable that he forfeits his right to be in the courtroom when witnesses testify, *Illinois v. Allen*, 397 U.S. 337 (1970). A corresponding principle is that he should forfeit the right to confront a

---

[2]   Queen v. Osman, 15 Cox Crim.Cas. 1, 3 (Eng.N.Wales Cir.1881) (Lush, L.J.) ("[N]o person, who is immediately going into the presence of his Maker, will do so with a lie upon his lips").

declarant if his misconduct prevents the confrontation by keeping *the witness* away from the courtroom.

So let's suppose that a criminal defendant knows that a witness is about to testify against him at trial. "Not going to happen," says the defendant, and shoots the witness to death as she is headed to the courthouse. But as it happens, the witness made a testimonial statement to the police shortly beforehand. Lacking a live witness, the prosecution now offers a police officer's rendition of what the witness then said. "Objection! Confrontation!" says the defendant. There is no real doubt that *if* it made a finding that in fact the defendant murdered the witness, the court would overrule the objection on forfeiture grounds. It is sometimes said that forfeiture is necessary because no one should profit from his own wrong. But that doesn't seem to get the matter quite right. A more precise statement is that the defendant should not be able to complain about the foreseeable consequences of his own wrongdoing. (Should it be the intended, rather than merely foreseeable consequences, of the wrongdoing? Let's postpone that issue.)

¶ **13.1:** What's wrong with the "No one should profit" language? In what circumstances could it be that forfeiture of the confrontation right is unnecessary to prevent the defendant from profiting from his own wrong? In what circumstances would forfeiture be insufficient to prevent that result?

The result presumably wouldn't change if the witness is the victim of the original crime. But now suppose that the crime with which the defendant is charged is also the wrongdoing that assertedly rendered the witness unavailable. To take the most obvious example, the victim is struck with what ultimately proves to be a fatal blow. Some time before dying, she makes a statement describing the assault and identifying the eventual defendant as the attacker. At the defendant's murder trial, the prosecution offers this statement.

The Framing-era cases exhibit a notable pattern in these circumstances. If death did not appear imminent at the time of the statement, the accused was ordinarily brought into the presence of the victim when she made the statement—and the statement was held inadmissible if this was not done. In one case, for example, the accused was brought into the victim's presence part-way through the giving of the deposition, so only the portion before that was held admissible.[3] If, however, the victim appeared to understand that she was on the verge of death when she made the statement, then the statement was admitted as a dying declaration. The gates of Heaven appeared to be opening when

---

[3]   R. v. Forbes, Holt 599, 171 E.R. 354 (1812); *cf.* R. v. Smith, Holt 614, 171 E.R. 357 (1817) (after defendant appeared, the justices of the peace reswore the declarant and read the statement over to him, and he assented to its truth; entire statement admitted).

the victim spoke, and that sufficed. Even in the modern day, courts have recited this rationale. *See Idaho v. Wright*, 497 U.S. 805, 820 (1990) (asserting that exception is "based on the belief that persons making such statements are highly unlikely to lie," and that therefore "the test of cross-examination would be of marginal utility").

¶ 13.2: (a) Is that rationale persuasive? Is it as plausible to suppose that a person knowing that death is imminent would conclude that there are no negative consequences of telling a self-interested lie, perhaps evening out old scores?

(b) Suppose you are the defense lawyer in a murder case. The prosecution contends that your client shot the victim to death. Before dying, the victim made a statement to the police implicating your client. By special arrangement, the court offers you the possibility of a one-day visa, to travel wherever the victim may be, in this world or another, and take her deposition. Would your response be, "Not worth the bother. She knew she was about to die, so cross would hardly be worthwhile"? If you did decide to take her deposition, what possibilities that might have led to an inaccurate statement would you like to explore? *See People v. Taylor*, 741 N.W.2d 24 (Mich. 2007).

(c) Note also the elements of the dying-declaration exception as stated in Fed. R. Evid. 804(b)(2): Not only must the statement be made by the declarant "while believing the declarant's death to be imminent," but it must be "made about its cause or circumstances." If the gates-of-Heaven rationale were truly persuasive, should the exception be applicable to *any* statement made by the declarant while believing death is imminent?

Another view of these old cases is possible. The cases requiring that the accused be present when the witness is deposed suggest that, even if the accused's wrongdoing is responsible for the witness being unavailable to testify at trial, the state has an obligation to *mitigate* the problem to the extent reasonably possible, taking available measures to preserve as much of the confrontation right as best as it reasonably can; the fact that a witness is dying does not give the state an excuse to avoid confrontation altogether. But at some point, it becomes impractical or inhumane or both to arrange for confrontation; the point where the victim realizes that death is imminent is not a bad test—or at least it is not a bad proxy—for determining that point.

In this view, there should not be a dying-declaration exception as such to the confrontation right. Rather, dying-declaration cases may be seen as instances of forfeiture: If the court finds that the defendant's wrongdoing is the cause of the witness's unavailability, and the state did not forgo any reasonable measures that might have mitigated the problem, then the witness's testimonial statement should be admissible against the defendant even though he never had an opportunity to be confronted with the witness. This approach would avoid the need for *any* exception to the confrontation right, because forfeiture is not really an exception but rather a rule, like waiver, as to how the right may be lost.

But as we will see, this view has not prevailed, at least not for now.

B. THE *GILES* CASE

¶ **13.3:** Giles is accused of murdering his former girlfriend, Avie. He admits killing her but contends that he did so in self-defense. The prosecution wishes to offer a statement made by Avie to a police officer several weeks before the killing. In that statement, Avie said that Giles had attempted to strangle her. The circumstances in which she made that statement strongly resembled those in *Hammon*. State hearsay law poses no obstacle to admitting this statement, but Giles objects to it on Confrontation Clause grounds. The prosecution contends that Giles forfeited the confrontation right by killing Avie and thereby rendering her unavailable to testify at his trial. Assume that the trial court would, if the issue is significant, conclude that Giles clearly killed Avie without justification. How should the court rule?

In *Giles v. California*, 554 U.S. 353 (2008), the Supreme Court held 6–3 that it was insufficient for a determination of forfeiture that Giles murdered Avie. In addition, the Court held, the state would have to show that his conduct was designed, or intended (the words are not necessarily synonymous), to render her unavailable as a witness.

The lead opinion—part but not all for a majority—was written by Justice Scalia. The principal reason purportedly leading him to the outcome was his reading of history. If the mere fact that the accused killed the victim without justification was enough to lead to a conclusion of forfeiture, then why did the courts of the Framing era go to so much trouble to determine whether the dying declaration exception, which includes an imminence requirement, applies?

¶ **13.4:** If you were arguing on behalf of California, how might you respond?

A second factor influencing the justices in the majority was what Justice Souter, concurring along with Justice Ginsburg, called the "near circularity" of the state's argument—"evidence that the defendant killed would come in because the defendant probably killed." *See also* majority opinion (per Justice Scalia) ("a principle repugnant to our constitutional system of trial by jury: that those murder defendants whom the judge considers guilty (after less than a full trial, mind you, and of course before the jury has pronounced guilt) should be deprived of fair-trial rights, lest they benefit from their judge-determined wrong."). "The only thing saving admissibility and liability determinations from question begging," wrote Justice Souter, "would be (in a jury case) the distinct functions of judge and jury: judges would find by a preponderance of evidence that the defendant killed (and so would admit the testimonial statement), while the jury could so find only on proof beyond a reasonable doubt."

¶ **13.5:** (a) Are you persuaded by this logic? Complete the following sentence: "The only thing saving noon from darkness is the ___." Topologically, what is a near circle?

(b) The "design" or "intent" standard adopted by the majority does not completely avoid the "repugnant" result identified by Justice Scalia, though it reduces the circumstances in which it would occur. Can you explain?

(c) In what other context have we seen what Justice Souter regards as a nearly circular result—that is, evidence is admitted to prove proposition **X** if the court finds that **X** is probably true?

Third, Justices Souter and Ginsburg believed that, without proof of "intent to prevent the witness from testifying" it would not be equitable to apply forfeiture doctrine.

¶ **13.6:** Suppose *Giles* arose in a state allowing the defendant to testify at a hearing on evidentiary matters without his testimony being admissible against him on the merits. At a hearing on forfeiture, Giles testifies, "Yes, I killed Avie. I did so because she was interfering with my relationship with my new girlfriend. The thought that killing her would prevent her from testifying in a prosecution of me never occurred to me." Would it be inequitable to apply forfeiture doctrine?

Having established a requirement of design, or intent, the Court softened its impact considerably in the context of domestic violence. Justice Scalia wrote for the Court:

Acts of domestic violence often are intended to dissuade a victim from resorting to outside help, and include conduct designed to prevent testimony to police officers or cooperation in criminal prosecutions. Where such an abusive relationship culminates in murder, the evidence may support a finding that the crime expressed the intent to isolate the victim and to stop her from reporting abuse to the authorities or cooperating with a criminal prosecution—rendering her prior statements admissible under the forfeiture doctrine. Earlier abuse, or threats of abuse, intended to dissuade the victim from resorting to outside help would be highly relevant to this inquiry, as would evidence of ongoing criminal proceedings at which the victim would have been expected to testify.

Justices Souter and Ginsburg, whose votes were necessary for the majority, came closer to suggesting a *per se* rule in the context of domestic violence:

> [T]he element of intention would normally be satisfied by the intent inferred on the part of the domestic abuser in the classic abusive relationship, which is meant to isolate the victim from outside help, including the aid of law enforcement and the judicial process. If the evidence for admissibility shows a continuing relationship of this sort, it would make no sense to suggest that the oppressing defendant miraculously abandoned the dynamics of abuse the instant before he killed his victim, say in a fit of anger.

> ¶ 13.7: What does it mean to say that the crime "expressed the intent" to isolate the victim? If the crime was designed to prevent testimony regarding a prior incident, why does that—as opposed to any other illegitimate motive for homicide—satisfy the majority that forfeiture is appropriate? Assuming that domestic abuse was (primarily? substantially?) intended (designed?) to isolate the victim, does that mean that the murder was as well—or does it appear that for some reason the abuser changed course?

As you might have guessed, I believe that *Giles* is a bad decision. There are several problems. One is the simple matter of principle: I believe that a defendant who engages in serious misconduct that has the predictable impact of rendering a witness unavailable to testify *ought* on equitable grounds be held to have forfeited the confrontation right.

Beyond that, I believe that *Giles* has the inevitable effect of distorting confrontation doctrine. If a court believes that the defendant's misconduct accounts for the unavailability of a witness, but it is not allowed to hold that he forfeited the confrontation right, the court will be strongly tempted to find another way to secure admissibility of the witness's statements. It was predictable when *Giles* was decided that the chief way in which this would happen would be to give an unduly narrow construction to the term "testimonial"—a construction that will then apply beyond the situation in which the accused should arguably be held to have forfeited the confrontation right. The beginning of this effect appears in *Giles* itself. The majority, making the point that its rule has less impact than might be supposed, points out (correctly) that the rule matters only with respect to testimonial statements—and then it casually tosses off a dictum that statements to treating physicians are not testimonial. Whoa!! That's a significant issue, one very much in dispute. I don't think the fact that the audience of a statement is a physician who is treating the declarant should be enough in itself to cause the statement to be characterized as non-testimonial. It may be, for example, that the declarant and the physician know full well that the physician is under a legal and professional obligation to pass on to the authorities any accusation of serious crime that the declarant makes. If such statements are deemed non-testimonial, then we have created a system by which a witness can self-consciously create narrative evidence for trial by speaking to a physician who has some therapeutic purpose in meeting with her. The Court's dictum on this point should not settle the matter, but it does suggest how an unduly narrow view of forfeiture might contribute to an unduly narrow view of "testimonial"—which may be a consequence of far greater importance.

The chief demonstration of this effect, though, is *Michigan v. Bryant*, which we have discussed in Chapter 9. Recall that there the victim, Covington, knowingly made statements to police officers accusing Bryant of shooting him. Given the lack of urgency with which Covington made the accusations, and with which the officers received them, one might have thought that the statements were clearly testimonial. But Covington died hours afterwards of his wounds; the temptation to admit his statements became very strong. Given *Giles*, the only way the Court could get around the Confrontation Clause was to hold the accusations non-testimonial—a conclusion that may affect many fresh-accusation cases even when the declarant is available to testify at trial. Now imagine what would have happened if *Giles* had come out the other way. In all probability, the trial court could have concluded that Bryant's serious intentional wrongdoing was foreseeably responsible for Covington's unavailability, that the state had no opportunity to mitigate the problem because Covington died so soon afterwards (and also because Bryant had absconded), and that therefore Bryant had forfeited the confrontation right. The outcome of the case would have been the same—admissibility of Avie's statement—even if the court held that the accusation was testimonial, but in fact no court would ever even have had to reach that question.

Another means of evading *Giles* is to stretch the dying-declaration exception beyond its appropriate bounds. An example of this is *State v. Jensen*, 727 N.W.2d 518 (2007). This case reached some notoriety—Julie Jensen, afraid that her husband Mark might poison her, left a note indicating that if she should die unexpectedly suspicion should be cast on Mark. The trial judge, explicitly anticipating the outcome in *Giles*, held the note to be a dying declaration. I believe this is a rather outlandish application of the dying declaration doctrine—Julie did not believe herself on the verge of death when she wrote the note—but it may become typical under *Giles*.

Indeed, *Giles* makes it essentially inevitable that there will be a dying-declaration exception to the confrontation right, in addition to forfeiture doctrine; courts would not likely tolerate a doctrine that required exclusion of the dying words of a murder victim, identifying the killer, on the ground that the murder was not committed for the purpose of rendering the victim unavailable as a witness.[4] But what is the theoretical justification for incorporating a dying-declaration exception into confrontation doctrine? *Crawford* states none other than that the exception existed at the time of the Framing. The rationale traditionally given for the exception is principally a reliability one—that the prospect of imminent death guarantees trustworthiness of the statement. But one of the essential propositions of *Crawford* was that reliability of a testimonial statement, or a category of statements, is not a ground for admitting it absent an opportunity for cross-examination. The Court has therefore complicated and undermined the general theory of the Clause, and that will likely make it less robust—because more complicated, less easily understood, and less rational—in the long run. If *Giles* had come out the other way, by contrast, it would be possible to enunciate a theory of the Confrontation Clause under which there are no exceptions to it; forfeiture, like waiver, is not really an exception to the right, but a factor causing estoppel against exercise of the right.

There are other reasons as well to regard the result in *Giles* as unfortunate.[5] And in the end, it may turn out that the *Giles* test is rather easily satisfied. Time will tell, but I believe that most courts are (as they should be) strongly inclined to admit statements made by a witness who was precluded from testifying in court by the defendant's own wrongful conduct. (Indeed, most courts are inclined to admit testimonial statements by unavailable witnesses even when that condition, which

---

[4] At the argument in *Bryant*, however, Justice Scalia questioned whether there was a dying-declaration exception to the Confrontation Clause—even though it was his opinion in *Giles* that seemed to rest in part on the assumption that there was such an exception.

[5] See the discussion at the very end of this chapter of how *Giles* inhibits development of a potential doctrine of responsibility to mitigate a forfeiture problem.

Giles also takes away a potential basis for challenging the rule of *United States v. Owens*, 484 U.S. 554 (1988), which we discussed in Chapter 10. Recall that *Owens* holds that the Clause is satisfied so long as the witness who made the statement testifies at trial, even if the witness does not remember the underlying facts. And recall that in this situation the ability of the accused to cross-examine the witness is seriously undermined, a factor that the *Owens* Court did not recognize. *Owens* itself could be explained on the basis of forfeiture, if there were no purpose requirement attached to forfeiture doctrine; the trial court might have concluded that the reason Foster could not remember the underlying facts was that Owens had bashed his head in. But I do not believe the *Giles* standard could be satisfied in the *Owens* situation. There is no indication that Owens bashed Foster's head in for the purpose of rendering Foster unavailable to testify at trial; it was the bashing itself for which Owens was tried, which means that before the assault there was presumably no prospect of Foster testifying adversely to Owens in any proceeding.

should justify admissibility, is not present.) The key passages quoted above from the majority opinion and from Justice Souter's concurrence may give courts a way to find that the *Giles* standard is met in the domestic violence context, by emphasizing the abuser's control over the victim. Non-lethal domestic violence that intimidates the witness is probably the most common context in which the accused might commit serious intentional misconduct that has the predictable consequence of rendering the witness unavailable even though the misconduct was not clearly and primarily directed towards that end. In other words, in the most common context in which the *Giles* issue will arise, it may be that the *Giles* test will usually not benefit defendants, but only make for a more extensive process.

C. WHAT KINDS OF CONDUCT LEAD TO FORFEITURE?

Beyond the *Giles* issue, there are numerous complexities in applying the forfeiture principle. One is the question of what kinds of conduct it covers. Certainly it covers murder and intimidation—but how far does it extend?

¶ **13.8:** Sister was arrested on drug conspiracy charges and made a statement to the police describing Brother's role in the conspiracy. The prosecutor proposes that she testify against Brother in return for lenient treatment on the charges pending against her. Sister is inclined take the deal, but before she agrees to it Brother speaks to her, appeals in gentle terms to her sense of family loyalty, and reminds her of her right not to testify.[6] Sister tells the prosecutor, "No deal." In the case against Brother, may the prosecutor use the statement Sister made to the police?[7]

¶ **13.9:** Szerlong's girlfriend made statements to the police, to a close friend, and to her sister, that he had grabbed her by the throat while she was asleep and held a knife to her throat. Eight days after the alleged attack, Szerlong was charged with assault by means of a dangerous weapon, among other crimes. Fifteen days after that, the couple were married; they had not been engaged before the alleged attack. After that, Szerlong's new wife refused to testify against him on grounds of spousal privilege. Assuming the privilege is available to her,

---

[6] Assume the prosecutors are either not authorized by state law or are unwilling to give Sister use and derivative use immunity.

[7] In *Crawford*, the Washington Supreme Court held that the accused did not lose the confrontation right by invoking his privilege to prevent his wife from testifying. The United States Supreme Court did not question that conclusion.

notwithstanding that the crime alleged was one committed against her, may the prosecution offer evidence of her out-of-court statements at trial? *Commonwealth v. Szerlong*, 933 N.E.2d 633 (Mass. 2010) (invoking forfeiture doctrine); *see also United States v. Marchini*, 797 F.2d 759, 762–65 (9th Cir.1986) (defendant in tax evasion case marries secretary to claim spousal privilege; hearsay evidence of her statements held admissible under residual exception).

D. THE ACCUSED'S INVOLVEMENT

For forfeiture doctrine to apply, what must the involvement of the accused be in the conduct that renders the declarant unavailable? Note that FRE 804(b)(6) speaks of the party having "wrongfully caused—*or acquiesced* in wrongfully causing—the declarant's unavailability as a witness." The idea behind that clause seems fair enough. Suppose Mob Underlings tell Big Boss that they will take measures to ensure that Witness does not testify against him. Big Boss does *not* say words to the effect of, "Don't do that. It wouldn't be right, and I'll be very upset if it happens." Sure enough, Underlings render Witness unavailable to testify. In this case, it seems appropriate to hold Big Boss accountable, because he was in a position to prevent the wrongful behavior and did not.

¶ **13.10:** (a) West is on trial on drug charges. Before the grand jury, Brown, a drug dealer who had cooperated with the Government to avoid a pending charge against him, testified in detail about drug transactions he made with West. There is ample corroboration of Brown's testimony, because drug enforcement agents had wired him for his meetings and had conducted surveillance of them, by photographs and other means. Before trial, Brown was murdered in a manner clearly suggesting a contract killing. May Brown's grand jury testimony be admitted against West, absent additional evidence suggesting West's involvement in the killing? *See United States v. West*, 574 F.2d 1131 (4th Cir.1978).

(b) Now suppose that there is evidence persuasive to the court that East and West were in an ongoing conspiracy to distribute drugs, and that East was involved in the killing of Brown. The prosecution argues, "East killed Brown within the scope of and in furtherance of the drug conspiracy. The murder was a foreseeable part of this ongoing conspiracy. Therefore, you should hold that West is liable for this action of his conspirator, and therefore he has forfeited the confrontation right. *See United States v. Cherry*, 217 F.3d 811 (10th Cir. 2000)." How should the court rule?

E. THE STANDARD OF PERSUASION

Closely related to the question of what the accused's involvement must be is another question: What standard of persuasion must the prosecutor satisfy as to the accused's involvement? As noted by *Davis*, most courts use the "preponderance of the evidence," or "more likely than not," standard. But a plausible argument can be made that a more rigorous standard, like "clear and convincing evidence," should apply.[8]

The difficulties of proving the accused's involvement—even his acquiescence—are very substantial, because conduct of this sort is not committed in the open. Deciding the preliminary factual question of whether the defendant committed misconduct amounting to a forfeiture could require a side-trial as extensive as the main trial. And sometimes it is immensely frustrating: Often the accused's clear motive to have the declarant out of the way strongly suggests that the accused was involved in the misconduct, but there is no other substantial evidence linking him to that conduct; even if it was his associates who committed the misconduct, it may be that they were doing a favor for him behind his back, without his knowledge. Accordingly, there is some temptation to do away altogether with a requirement that the accused be linked to the misconduct. Indeed, English law, subject to some qualification, now allows a statement made to an investigating authority and embodied in a document to be admitted if "the person who made it does not give oral evidence through fear or because he is kept out of the way." Criminal Justice Act 1988 (c. 33), § 23(3).[9]

F. MAY THE STATEMENT ITSELF BE USED IN DETERMINING FORFEITURE?

Suppose that, among the proof that a prosecutor wants to use to demonstrate that the accused forfeited the confrontation right and the

---

[8]   *See, e.g.,* United States v. Thevis, 665 F.2d 616, 627–31 (5th Cir.1982), *cert. denied,* 459 U.S. 825 (1982); People v. Geraci, 85 N.Y.2d 359, 625 N.Y.S.2d 469, 649 N.E.2d 817 (1995).

[9]   This provision was meant to expand on § 13(3) of the Criminal Justice Act 1925, which referred to witnesses "kept out of the way by means of the procurement of the accused or on his behalf." *Cf.* R. v. O'Loughlin & McLaughlin, [1988] 3 All E.R. 431, 85 Cr. App. Rep. 157, 161–62 (1986) (failing to find sufficient proof that threats were made by or on behalf of the defendant, and refusing to hold that threats "with the defendant's interests at heart" would suffice). But the 1988 statute did not merely remove the need for proof of the defendant's involvement. The disjunctive wording can be satisfied by proof of spontaneous fear, not attributable to any affirmative conduct by the defendant or anybody else; one court has held that the fear need not be reasonable but that the court should be "sure that the witness is in fear as a consequence of the commission of the material offense or of something said or done subsequently in relation to that offense and the possibility of the witness testifying to it." R. v. Acton Justices ex p. McMullen, 92 Cr. App. Rep. 98, 105–06 (1990). *See generally* Colin Tapper, *Cross and Tapper on Evidence* 609 (12th ed. 2010; repr. 2013) (statute does not explicitly require that the fear "need be related to the accused, or even to the offence being tried").

hearsay objection is the statement itself, the one that the prosecutor is trying to introduce into evidence.

¶ **13.11:** In *Giles*, suppose the prosecution tries to use Avie's statement to demonstrate forfeiture, and therefore secure admission of the statement. The prosecution argues, "The fact that Avie made the statement gave Giles a motive to kill her. And the fact reported by the statement shows that Giles was willing and inclined to use deadly force on Avie. Accordingly, the statement makes it substantially more likely that Giles committed wrongdoing that was intended to and did procure the unavailability of Avie." Should use of the statement for these purposes be allowed? *Cf.* FRE 801(d)(2)(E) (conspiracy exemption).

G. A MITIGATION REQUIREMENT?

Finally, consider whether the prosecution has any burden, if it wants to invoke forfeiture doctrine, to mitigate the problem by doing what it can to preserve as much of the confrontation right as possible. The doctrinal basis for a mitigation requirement might be like that for the "last clear chance" doctrine in torts: Even if the defendant engaged in wrongdoing that prevented the witness from coming to court, is it fair to say that the defendant caused the witness's unavailability when the state had available to it, but did not take advantage of, reasonable opportunities to preserve the confrontation right in substantial part?

Thus, courts could develop a set of rules governing steps that the state must take in given circumstances to preserve the confrontation right of the accused to the extent reasonably possible notwithstanding the accused's wrongful conduct. For example, if the wrongful conduct is murdering the witness, who while dying made a testimonial statement, then mitigation doctrine would require the state, as a precondition to invoking forfeiture doctrine, to offer the accused an opportunity to take the witness's deposition, so long as there was a practical, humane opportunity to do so. If the wrongful conduct is intimidation, a mitigation requirement might require the state to make certain efforts to ascertain the extent to which confrontation might be preserved; for example, the state might be required to bring the witness to chambers to explore whether she might be willing to testify there, subject to cross-examination by counsel. Procedural rules of this sort would likely be less easily avoided than substantive standards that a judge could manipulate around.

¶ **13.12:** Silvia Woodcock was allegedly murdered by her husband William. Suppose Silvia lingers for several weeks before dying. She never appears to be out of danger, but at times she is perfectly lucid and able to carry on a conversation. During one of these intervals, a stenographer comes to her bedside and records a statement about the assault. The stenographer transcribes the statement, and Silvia signs it, under oath. In William's trial for murder, should the statement be admitted? Note *R. v. Forbes*, Holt 599, 171 E.R. 354 (1814), presented in ¶ 11.6, asserting the accused's right to be present at the deposition of a dying victim and to cross-examine.

¶ **13.13:** Suppose that William is charged with assaulting but not killing Silvia. Shortly after the incident, Silvia made a detailed statement about it to a police officer. The state subpoenas her for trial, but on the day of trial she does not appear. The prosecutor tells the judge that she spoke to Silvia earlier that morning, and that Silvia is too scared to appear and testify at trial. Should Silvia's statement be admitted? If you think the answer is negative, what more should happen or should have happened? Among the possibilities:

(a) Require the prosecution to present admissible evidence supporting the proposition that William intimidated Silvia.

(b) Bring Silvia into court, and ask her whether she is scared to testify, and if so, why.

(c) Bring Silvia into chambers, and ask her whether she is scared to testify, and if so, why.

(d) Require that Silvia's statement be given under oath.

(e) Require that Silvia's statement be given subject to cross-examination by defense counsel.

(f) Require that Silvia's statement be given with William able to watch and listen by one-way video connection.

(g) Require that Silvia's statement be given with William and Silvia both able to see each other, and William able to hear, by a two-way video connection.

(h) Require that the state have offered a deposition of Silvia promptly after she made her initial statement.

(i) Threaten Silvia with contempt if she does not testify subject to conditions prescribed by the court.

(j) Jail Silvia if she does not testify subject to conditions prescribed by the court.

(k) Promise Silvia strong measures of protection if she testifies subject to confrontation.

Under the historical theory of forfeiture that I have presented, dying-declaration cases should be seen as a manifestation of forfeiture doctrine confined by a requirement that the state mitigate the problem of a dying witness by taking a deposition, until it becomes impractical or inhumane or both, which might occur when death appears imminent. Had *Giles* adopted a view of forfeiture unconfined by a requirement that the forfeiting conduct have been designed to render the witness unavailable, it probably would have made at least the start of adopting a mitigation requirement; otherwise it would be hard to explain, given the availability of a broad forfeiture requirement, why courts have always insisted that a dying declaration is admissible only if death appeared imminent. *Giles* does not preclude adoption of a strong mitigation doctrine, but given a relatively narrow doctrine of forfeiture and a dying-declaration exception that contains its own imminence requirement, it will be a much harder sell.

CHAPTER 14

ADMISSIONS

■ ■ ■

A. THE BASIC IDEA AND RATIONALES

FRE 801(d)(2), 1007

Additional Reading: McCormick, ch. 25, §§ 254–258; Ch. 23, § 242; Mueller & Kirkpatrick, § 8.27

We have organized the discussion of this unit so far around confrontation principles. Was the statement testimonial? Was it offered for the truth of matter it asserted? Was the witness present at trial? If not, was the witness unavailable at trial and did the adverse party have another opportunity for confrontation? Did the adverse party forfeit the right to confront the witness by wrongful conduct that rendered her unavailable to testify?

Along the way, we have addressed many of the principles of hearsay law, some of them thoroughly enough that we do not need to return to them. You should understand that (1) the basic definition of hearsay extends to any statement—not just testimonial ones—that was made out of court and is offered to prove the truth of a matter that it asserts, (2) hearsay is presumptively inadmissible, but it may fit within one of a long list of exemptions, and (3) a statement is not *per se* exempted from the hearsay rule by the fact that the declarant is a witness at trial, but under the Federal Rules certain categories of prior statements of witnesses are defined as not hearsay and so exempted from the rule. Now we will focus on other exemptions from the hearsay rule; we use the term exemptions to cover both statements defined as not hearsay and statements that are hearsay but fall within an exception to the rule.[1] We begin in this chapter with the most fundamental of the exemptions, what traditionally have

---

[1] There is little operational significance to the distinction between an exclusion from the definition of hearsay and an exception to the hearsay rule. McCormick), § 254 n. 8, does claim a distinction: The residual exception, FRE 807, in attempting to articulate a standard of admissibility, refers back to the guarantees of trustworthiness in the exceptions enumerated in Rules 803 and 804, and the McCormick text contends that "[t]he inclusion of admissions, which possess no objective guarantee of trustworthiness, as an exception would not have been consistent with this pattern." This argument is open to question from both ends: Arguably, admissions *do* possess some guarantee of trustworthiness, and even if the enumerated exceptions do possess some such guarantees the exceptions clearly vary so much that it is virtually impossible to draw from them a useful standard for applying the residual exception.

been known as admissions or party admissions—statements made by or attributable to a party and offered against that party. These, too, are defined by the Federal Rules as not being hearsay, though they could just as easily be considered an exception to the hearsay rule. In the next chapter, we will look at the long list of hearsay exceptions.

In some cases, the exemptions and the rationales usually given for them may seem odd to you. As you study them you should ask yourself: Assuming there are good reasons for a rule presumptively excluding hearsay, is there good reason to exempt this category of statements from the rule? Often you may say not. But what you may find is that many of the exemptions describe rather well categories of statements that are not testimonial. Thus, admitting them into evidence does not threaten to create a situation in which a witness can testify without the adverse party having an opportunity to cross-examine.

The basic definition of party admissions is very simple; do not overcomplicate it. If an out-of-court declaration that would otherwise be inadmissible hearsay is a statement by, or otherwise attributable to, a party, and is offered against that party, it is an admission. One reason we are studying admissions before all the exceptions is that you should look for them first, once you have decided that the evidence is analytically within the basic definition of hearsay—and sometimes even before. And one reason you should look for them early is that they are usually easy to spot. First determine whether the declaration is a statement made by, or attributable to, a party to the litigation. Usually there can be no real debate as to whether or not the statement was made *by* a party. Often, however, difficulties arise in determining whether a statement not actually made by a party should nevertheless, for purposes of admissions doctrine, be attributed to the party. The second step is to determine whether the statement is being offered against the party to whom it is attributable. If the answer is yes—and ordinarily this question, too, is not debatable—then the statement is an admission, and so is not barred by the hearsay rule. Period.

Again: to qualify as an admission, the statement must be one by (or otherwise attributable to) a party, and offered against (not by!) that party. Unfortunately, the label "admissions" is rather confusing, because it seems to connote that the statement acknowledges some fact that is unpleasant for the declarant. But there is no requirement that the statement have been against the party's interest when it was made. (In part for this reason, the restyling of the Federal Rules did away with the term; Rule 801(d)(1) now refers to "[a]n opposing party's statement". We will stick with the traditional term, not only because it is concise and well entrenched in the case law and the rules of most states but also because the phrasing of the Federal Rules is also misleading; bear in mind that some statements are admitted under this doctrine even though they are not made by a party.) There *is* an exception to the hearsay rule for declarations against interest, which is codified in FRE 804(b)(3) and which we will study in Chapter 15, but you should not confuse it with admissions doctrine. Courts often speak of "admissions against interest", but this is a confusing term because it confounds the two doctrines. Avoid it.

¶ **14.1:** Drake, a farmer, also works part-time as a potter. He sells his wares, generally for cash, out of his home. On an application for a bank loan, he stated that he had earned $75,000 from his pottery sideline in the previous year. On his tax return, however, he indicated $5000 net earnings from the pottery business. Drake is now on trial for tax evasion. The prosecution seeks to introduce the bank application. One of the requirements for the declaration-against-interest exception is that the declaration have been against the declarant's interest when made. Is the bank application admissible on this theory? As a party admission?

[handwritten margin note: Yes. Was made in their interest, now being offered against their interest.]

¶ **14.2:** Same facts as in ¶ 14.1, except that Drake claimed $5000 net pottery earnings on the bank application as well as on his tax return, and the IRS is now claiming that he actually earned $75,000. Who will want to introduce the bank application? Is it admissible as a party admission?

[handwritten margin note: Drake would want to introduce, but it's not being offered against his interest so NO, not a party admission. Might be admissible as prior consistent statement if TT will say fabrication of $5000.]

¶ **14.3:** Patrick, the owner of a bar, is suing Duke, seeking to recover damages allegedly caused by Duke and Ward when they got into a fight in the bar. Duke contends that the fight caused no substantial damage. Patrick offers into evidence a letter written by Ward shortly after the fight, saying, "Sorry we made so much of a mess. I'll pay whatever is necessary—though of course I think Duke should split the bill." Ward died shortly after writing the letter. Is the letter admissible as a party admission? As a declaration against interest?

[handwritten margin note: It's a declaration against his own interest. Also implicates Duke, but they're not co-conspirators, so NO. Maybe could come in under 804(b) - statement against interest and Ward unavailable.]

Also, do not confuse admissions doctrine with the rules on prior inconsistent statements. One of those rules, which we will study in depth in Chapter 19, allows a witness to be impeached with her prior statements that are inconsistent with her current testimony; in some cases, as we have already seen in Chapter 10's discussion of FRE 801(d)(1)(A), another rule also allows introduction of such a prior statement to prove the truth of what that prior statement asserts. Unlike the prior inconsistent statement rule, <u>admissions doctrine</u> requires that the declaration be by, or otherwise attributable to, a party, and <u>does *not* require that the declarant be a witness</u>. Moreover, if the declarant *is* a witness, the admissions rule does not require that the prior statement be inconsistent with the declarant's testimony. The rationale for generally allowing proof of prior inconsistent statements for impeachment—that in judging a witness's credibility the factfinder should know that the witness previously made statements inconsistent with her current testimony—is inapplicable to admissions. It is sometimes said that for a declaration to qualify as an admission it must be inconsistent with the position asserted by the party—in testimony or by other means, such as counsel's argument—at trial. Under the Federal Rules, at least, there is no such requirement, but if there were it would not have much impact; if a statement is offered against, and objected to by, a party, it will almost always be inconsistent with the position asserted at trial by the party. (Note that a declaration can be both an admission and a prior inconsistent statement, but if it is an admission there is ordinarily no need to determine whether it is a prior inconsistent statement, because the hearsay rule will not prevent its being admitted to prove the truth of what it asserts.)

¶ **14.4:** Packer is suing Decker for failure to deliver wheat pursuant to an oral contract. Packer claims that the contract was for 200 tons, but Decker's bookkeeper, Becker, has testified for Decker that he was on the phone when the deal was made and that it was for only 100 tons. Packer wants to introduce evidence that two days after the deal was made Becker wrote Packer a note saying, "This confirms that we have agreed to sell you 200 tons of wheat." Under what theory or theories can the evidence be admitted? For what purpose or purposes?

Spotting admissions is usually easy, but determining the rationale for their admissibility is somewhat harder than it might appear. A frequently stated rationale, given by Wigmore, is that the concern behind the hearsay rule never comes into play if the declarant is the adverse party, because he "does not need to cross-examine himself." 4 John Henry Wigmore, *Evidence* § 1048, at 4 (Chadbourn rev. 1972) (emphasis deleted). There is certainly force to this argument. This book takes the view that the driving force behind much of hearsay law is the right of a party (a constitutional right in the case of criminal defendants and at least a strong norm in the case of civil parties) to confront a witness who makes a testimonial statement against him—but if that witness was the party himself, he has no basis for complaint. He cannot complain that the witness made the statement out of his presence, and presumably he has as much opportunity as he wants to put himself on the stand to discuss the statement (though a criminal defendant may not be eager to avail himself of the opportunity). If he misperceived or his memory failed, or if he was joking, lying, or using words in an unorthodox manner, perhaps he can persuade the factfinder of this.

Moreover, this rationale is at least consistent with one of the limitations on admissions doctrine: Although anything a party previously said may be used against him, it is not conclusive against him. Once again, the "admissions" label may be misleading. Evidentiary admissions should not be confused with stipulations (sometimes called "judicial admissions," *see* 9 Wigmore §§ 2588–2589), admissions in response to requests under Fed. R. Civ. P. 36 and similar rules, pleas of guilty, pleadings or admissions to pleadings, all of which will bind a party absent judicial relief. By contrast, an evidentiary admission, like live testimony, is merely evidence—powerful evidence perhaps, but still merely evidence that potentially can be undercut. Do not be confused by the language you will sometimes find in judicial opinions to the effect that a party is "bound" by his admission. He has to live with it, in the sense that it is likely to be admissible against him and he has to explain how his version of events is consistent with the fact that he made the statement. But the fact that he made the statement does not, as a legal matter, limit the positions he may advocate in court.[2]

¶ 14.5: Pauline is suing Daniel for injuries arising from an auto accident. In her initial complaint, Pauline claimed $500,000 in damages, attributable to an alleged neck injury. Shortly after filing that complaint, Pauline switched lawyers, and soon after that she filed an amended complaint. The amended complaint claimed $1 million for the neck injury and also $1 million for an alleged lower-back injury. Can Daniel present the initial complaint to the jury? On what theory? For what purpose? With what effect? *See generally* Sherman J. Clark, *To Thine Own Self Be True: Enforcing Candor in Pleading Through the Party Admissions Doctrine*, 49 Hastings L.J. 565 (1998).

¶ 14.6: (a) Denton, charged with criminal fraud in the sale of shares in a real estate syndication, pleaded guilty. While he was awaiting sentencing, he reconsidered and asked to change his plea. The court granted his request, and Denton is now on trial. Can the prosecution introduce the former plea and the transcript of the initial hearing, at which Denton acknowledged his understanding of the charge and admitted his guilt? *See* FRE 410.

(b) Now assume instead that Denton pleaded nolo contendere (no contest) to the criminal charges, and was sentenced to a fine and probation. He is now defending a civil

---

[2]   Indeed, the better view is that a party may attempt to rebut testimony that he himself has just given at the trial. Obviously, one would rather not be in a position in which his lawyer feels the need to tell the jury, "My client testified inaccurately on that point." But it is easy enough to see how as a result of forgetfulness, or confusion in recalling fast-moving events, or of the peripheral importance of a particular matter, the client might testify contrary to a proposition his lawyer is advocating. The range of solutions to this problem is well presented in McCormack § 258.

suit brought by Post, one of the purchasers whom he allegedly defrauded. May Post introduce the nolo plea? *No · No contest is not an admission of guilt. (not discussed)*

¶ **14.7:** Temple is a driver for Drovers, a trucking company. In January, while driving a Drovers flatbed truck, Temple slammed into Green's garden wall. In April, Green sued Drovers for $20,000. In his complaint, Green asserted that at the time of the accident Temple was driving in the course of his employment, and in its answer to the complaint Drovers admitted this allegation. In May, Jackson sued Drovers for $5 million, claiming that she was driving in the other direction when Temple's truck went out of control, and that she had to turn so sharply to avoid hitting Temple that she seriously injured her spine. (Jackson did avoid contact and continued driving; until she filed her complaint, neither she nor her lawyer communicated with Drovers.) In its answer to Jackson's complaint, Drovers denied that Temple was driving on its business at the time of the accident. May Jackson use Drovers' answer to Green's complaint? With what effect? *It is an admission against them run / it just admitted to / b/c low $, not worth fighting / (can explain it but still bound in)*

¶ **14.8:** In Pauline's auto accident case against Daniel, *supra* ¶ 14.5, Pauline is claiming that Daniel was speeding. Daniel denies this. Can Pauline introduce proof that Daniel, who lives 700 miles from the place of the accident, pleaded guilty to a speeding charge brought in connection with the accident and paid a $100 fine? *Cf. Ando v. Woodberry,* 8 N.Y.2d 165, 203 N.Y.S.2d 74, 168 N.E.2d 520 (1960) (allowing proof of guilty plea to traffic offense to be admitted in subsequent civil action). *Yes · Guilty plea / litigation strategy / withdrawn admitted / (not discussed)*

Although useful, the no-need-to-cross-examine-himself rationale for admissions does not seem complete, in at least two respects.

First, admissions doctrine is not limited to statements by the party himself. As we will explore in considerable depth, it has been extended quite generously to certain statements made by a person who, on one theory or another, was considered an agent of the party. (Thus, the restyled Federal Rules' use of the term "[a]n opposing party's statement" seems quite misleading.) The party may definitely have an interest in examining such a declarant. But by the time of trial the declarant may be dead, otherwise unavailable, or—worse yet (from the point of view of the party)—hostile. See Section D below.

The second respect in which the "explain it away" rationale is incomplete is that it fails to explain all the consequences of admissions doctrine. In general, showing that a piece of evidence is not barred by the hearsay rule does not remove other barriers to admissibility; it does not, to take the most obvious example, relieve the proponent of the burden of showing the relevance of the evidence. But in the treatment given by

Wigmore and some other treatises writers, admissions doctrine is a topic independent of hearsay law, because some of the consequences of admissions doctrine extend beyond the bounds of the hearsay rule. In particular, admissions are generally exempted from competency requirements, most notably the rule against lay opinions and its close relative, the rule requiring a witness (or hearsay declarant) to have personal knowledge of the subject matter of which she speaks. Furthermore, under the Federal Rules, written admissions are exempted from the "best evidence rule" generally requiring the production of documentary originals.

¶ **14.9:** Hannah badly injured her hand while operating a power saw in Jerome's mill. Jerome was not present when the accident occurred, but he rushed to the hospital as soon as he heard about it and told Hannah, "It appears this was our fault." Subsequent attempts to settle Hannah's claim failed, and Hannah has sued Jerome, claiming that the saw was negligently maintained. Jerome now contends that the accident was caused by Hannah's negligence in operating the saw. Can Hannah introduce Jerome's bedside statement?

¶ **14.10:** Karen is a real estate developer. One of her holdings is an amusement park. While she was in the park one day, she witnessed a roller coaster accident, in which a four-year-old child, Larry, was injured. Karen immediately went up to Larry's parents and said, "I'm sorry. The operator was running the roller coaster too fast." Larry has sued Karen, and Karen has denied liability. Can her statement be introduced against her?

¶ **14.11:** In the two cases just above, in-court testimony by the party would probably be held objectionable. Is there any justification for so holding and yet admitting the prior statements? In this connection, consider also the following case: Young Douglas was hit in an auto accident, and his father brings an action as Douglas's guardian against the driver who hit Douglas and others. The court rules that Douglas is too young to testify at trial. The defendants ask the father whether Douglas made any statement after the accident about what caused it. Plaintiff's counsel objects. How should the court rule?[3]

¶ **14.12:** Seller is suing Buyer, claiming that Buyer ordered via fax 1000 drums of paint but only paid for 500. The color was an unusual one, which Seller prepared specially for the order, and Seller has been unable to sell the remaining 500 drums to

---

[3]   *See* Berggren v. Reilly, 95 Misc.2d 486, 488, 407 N.Y.S.2d 960, 962 (Sup. Ct. 1978); *see also* Freda F. Bein, *Parties' Admissions, Agents' Admissions: Hearsay Wolves in Sheep's Clothing,* 12 Hofstra L. Rev. 393, 402–03 nn. 61–64 (1984).

another buyer. Buyer contends that he only ordered 500 drums, and that the paint was defective. Seller has neither produced the faxed order nor satisfied the court that he could not. Consider whether Seller should be able to introduce any of the following: *but party admission does not trump best evidence*

(a) Her own testimony that Buyer said over the phone a week after receiving the order, "I wrote an order for 1000 drums, but I'm only going to be able to pay for 500." *It's an admission, but isn't this unless a best evidence issue? Yes (1004) falls - Jim 1007*

(b) A letter written by Buyer, making the statement in (a). *Yes, let it in.*

(c) An <u>interrogatory answer</u> by Buyer, saying he ordered 1000 drums. *Yes, let it in.*

all reliable, know Buyer actually made statement, is against interest *see Rule 1007*

(d) Buyer's testimony at deposition, "Yes, I ordered 1000 drums, but it was terrible paint."[4] *Let it in.*

Thus, relief from the hearsay rule is just one—albeit perhaps the most important—consequence of a statement being a party admission. And that in turn suggests that at least part of the rationale for the receptive attitude towards admissions is not related to the hearsay rule. A broader rationale is emphasized by the Advisory Committee in its Note to FRE 801(d)(2), which may be ironic because it is probably the placement of admissions doctrine in that Rule, as a part of the definition of hearsay, that has encouraged us to think of admissions as a subordinate part of hearsay doctrine. This argument, based on the role of the evidence in an adversary system, could be addressed to the adverse party in terms such as these:

> Your adversary is contending for a proposition that you deny. (If you don't deny it, you should be willing to stipulate to it anyway, and there really isn't a problem.) Well, at an earlier time, either you or someone who was in a position to act for you asserted that proposition. If that statement was made before the lines were clear in this litigation, it probably has significant probative value in undercutting your present denial of the proposition; and if the statement was made *after* the lines were clear, so that it cut against your interest when it was made, it has all the more probative value. Perhaps you have a good explanation for the statement, or some reason for believing that it does not have the significance that your adversary ascribes to it. If so, present it to the jury, by evidence or argument or both, and hope for the best. Perhaps you are hampered in your ability to present the explanation—because, for example, the person who actually made the statement is not available as a witness. If so, that's tough luck, but not tough enough to keep the statement away

---

[4] *See* Freitas v. Emhart Corp., 715 F.Supp. 1149, 1151–52 (D.Mass.1989); McCormick § 242; Mueller & Kirkpatrick § 10.16; FRE 1007.

from the jury. This is a statement that comes from your side of the fence in this litigation but that helps the other side, and for that reason it's worthy of attention, and almost certainly you are not substantially *less* able than the other side to present the declarant as a witness.

But another part of the rationale must satisfy the confrontation principle. So far as personal admissions are concerned, that's easy: As Wigmore said, a party does not need to cross-examine himself. And so far as admissions doctrine extends to representative admissions, as we will see, it generally stops short of testimonial statements.

As we proceed through this chapter, you should consider whether there is good justification for a *per se* rule exempting admissions from the hearsay rule, as well as from the opinion rule, the first-hand knowledge requirement, and (in part, at least) the best evidence rule. *See generally* Roger C. Park, *The Rationale of Personal Admissions*, 21 Ind. L. Rev. 509 (1988).

B. ADMISSIONS ACTUALLY MADE OR ADOPTED BY THE PARTY

FRE 801(d)(2)(A), (B)

Additional Reading: McCormick, ch. 25, § 261; Mueller & Kirkpatrick, §§ 8.27, .29

If the party is an individual, and the statement offered against her is one that she made herself, then it is clearly an admission. *See* FRE 801(d)(2)(A). That's easy.[5]

Sometimes, though, the statement was not actually uttered or written by the party, and yet the party took some action to make the statement her own. This is what is known as an adoptive admission. If the adoption was clear, this raises few problems. For example, if a defendant signs a statement, it should be considered her own even though it was a police officer or an insurance investigator who drafted it. So far as admissions doctrine is concerned, the drafting of the statement is merely a predicate for the adoption, the adoption amounting to the making of the statement by the party.

---

[5]　Well, there is one potential complication. Suppose a declarant, speaking for no one but herself, makes a statement and then is sued in her capacity as representative of an estate. Or conversely, suppose she makes a statement in her representative capacity and is then sued individually. Traditional law applied admissions doctrine only if the declarant had made the statement in the same capacity in which she was a party to the litigation. *See* 4 Wigmore § 1076; Unif. R. Evid. 63(7) (1953) (superseded). But FRE 801(d)(2)(A) does away with this distinction, providing that the statement is an admission of the party if it is offered against her and was her statement made "in an individual or representative capacity."

¶ **14.13:** In ¶ 14.5, Pauline previously submitted an affidavit that claimed only the neck injury, not the back injury. Daniel has introduced the affidavit. Can Pauline introduce her testimony that she had signed the affidavit at the urging of her prior attorney, who told her that it was accurate, and that she had not bothered to read it? *Sure, shows she didn't really adopt the statement. She can explain it, but still comes in as a party admission since she signed it.*

Sometimes, it is not so clear that the party has adopted the statement.

¶ **14.14:** Trampton constructed a building on property adjoining Braxton's. As Trampton was nearing completion of the project, he received a call from Braxton, who said, "Your construction has caused a cave-in on my property!" Trampton responded, "Uh huh." Braxton then added, "The west wall of my gazebo has collapsed! It's going to cost me $10,000 to replace!" And Trampton then responded, "Uh huh. I'll get back to you." But Trampton did not get back to Braxton, and Braxton has sued. Can Braxton introduce his testimony of this conversation? *No- it's vague. Not necessarily an admission. Problem here is who is offering. Braxton can't get in his own statements!*

Compare Matthew 27:11, in which Pilate, the Roman governor, asks Jesus if he is the King of the Jews. The King James Bible translates Jesus's response as "Thou sayest." In the English Standard Version, it is, "You have said so." And the New American Standard Bible gives the response as "It is as you say." *This adopts*

¶ **14.15:** Reconsider ¶ 14.9. Suppose now that Jerome's statement was, "I understand that this was our fault." Should it be admissible? What if his statement was, "Everybody tells me this was our fault"? What if it was, "I hear it was our fault"? *None of these are admissions / adoptions - just acknowledging that others say* *vague - I heard that? I know that? Also, hearsay within hearsay* *NOPE! Actually, these can possibly the adopting the statements.*

¶ **14.16:** Recall ¶ 14.7, in which Temple, a driver for Drovers, slammed into a wall while driving a Drovers flatbed truck. Before Drovers realized that Jackson would be making a claim, Temple sued Drovers, claiming that he was injured because the truck had been overloaded by another Drovers employee, and so was unstable. In that suit, Drovers presented the testimony of Whitson, who is not one of its employees, that Temple was driving "very fast" when he slammed into the wall. On cross-examination, Whitson testified, "The truck looked unstable. It was way overloaded." The case was settled soon after Whitson completed his testimony. *NOT stuck w/ what the witness says on cross*

(a) In Jackson's suit, can she introduce the transcript of Whitson's testimony about Temple's speed? About the load on the truck? *No. Not an employee. Drovers introduced evidence, doesn't mean it's adopted.* *Nope! If you put on the testimony you're adopting it?*

(b) Would your answer regarding the testimony about the truck load be affected if that part of the testimony had also been given on direct? *Maybe? Still doesn't feel like a statement from Drovers.*

(c) Now suppose that when Temple's case came to trial Whitson was temporarily out of the jurisdiction, and that what Drovers introduced at the Temple trial was excerpts of the transcript of Whitson's deposition. Does this change your answers? *whitson still isn't a party ... and how its not being used against D. shouldn't come in!*

¶ **14.17:** In considering cases like the four problems immediately above, is it for the judge or for the jury or both to decide whether the party adopted the statement? *Judge should play gate-keeping — end- rule- it's a question of admissability not weight.*

C. TACIT ADMISSIONS

FRE 801(d)(2)(B)

Additional Reading: McCormick, ch. 25, §§ 262–265; Mueller & Kirkpatrick, §§ 8.29–.30

If a party expressly adopts another's statement as his own, then it is easy enough to see why that statement can be considered to be an admission that can be offered against him. But now suppose that in response to the statement the party neither affirms nor denies it. In some circumstances—just when is the tricky question—his responsive conduct, while not being an *adoption* of the statement, nevertheless can be considered a *tacit* admission of it. The following problems may help focus on this rather subtle distinction.

¶ **14.18:** Gruber has a six-year-old daughter, Lindsay. At a neighborhood barbecue, Gruber accosted Dubler and said, "You dirty pig, you molested my daughter!" Dubler simply looked down at the ground, saying nothing, while several other neighbors pulled Gruber away. Lindsay is now suing Dubler for assault. Dubler denies the claim. Can Lindsay's counsel introduce evidence of the barbecue incident? *Not saying anything seems to be saying something*

on its own, this is hearsay - but -ith Dubler's reaction, it can come in as an admission

silence is nonverbal conduct - not intending to assert anything, but manifests belief in statement 801(d)(2)(B)

¶ **14.19:** Dark, a well-known lawyer, is on trial for fraud in connection with a bank of which he was the chairman. He has not taken the stand, and may not. His defense is essentially that he was a dupe. According to his lawyer's opening statement, the bank's backers sought him out as chairman because his international trade work had made him a very visible and well-regarded figure; he had slight involvement with bank matters and no more than a superficial understanding of banking regulations; and he understood virtually not at all the transaction at issue. The prosecution wishes to introduce an audiotape of a radio interview that Dark gave two years after he had become chairman of the bank and a year before the challenged transaction. The show's hostess described Dark as "a well-known expert on international trade and banking law."

Dark did not respond to this description, but answered numerous questions posed by the hostess, some of which concerned the bank's basic goals and operations and others of which bore on international trade matters. Should the tape be admissible?

¶ 14.20: Sleazy is suing Beazley for failure to pay for a shipment of disposable widgets. Beazley rejected the shipment, saying that he did not make the order.

(a) Can Sleazy introduce evidence that, three weeks after the alleged order, he sent Beazley a properly addressed e-mail message that said, "This is to let you know that the hundred tons of disposable widgets that you ordered are on their way," and that Beazley never responded?[6]

(b) Now suppose that Sleazy's note said, "This is to let you know that the hundred flidgets and the hundred widgets that you ordered are on their way. The bill is $30,000 for the flidgets and $250 for the widgets, including delivery." To this, Beazley responded, "You're crazy. I never ordered any flidgets." Can Sleazy introduce this exchange in support of his claim for the widgets?

(c) Same problem as (b), but now the figures are reversed— the $30,000 bill was for the widgets and the $250 bill for the flidgets.

¶ 14:21: Doyle was arrested for selling marijuana, and was given the *Miranda* warnings. He remained silent. At trial, he testifies that he was framed. May the prosecutor offer proof revealing that the defendant remained silent after the arrest?[7]

---

[6] In some circumstances, silence or inaction in response to an offer may be deemed as a matter of contract law to constitute acceptance. Roughly speaking, this is so if (a) the offeree takes the benefit of an offer though he could have rejected it and he should have known that the offeror expected compensation; (b) the offeror had given the offeree reason to understand that silence or inaction may manifest acceptance, and the offeree intends by the silence or inaction to accept; or (c) "because of previous dealings or otherwise, it is reasonable that the offeree should notify the offeror if he does not intend to accept." *See* Restatement (2d) Contracts § 69(1). Thus, the silence or inaction may have operative significance. If it does, then plainly Beazley's responsive conduct or inaction in the problem would be admissible. But we can assume here that his conduct or inaction would not have such significance, not only on the ground that none of the conditions of Restatement § 69(1) appear to be satisfied but also because Sleazy is not purporting to make an offer but rather to report on the progress of previously made offer. So the issue is whether Beazley's conduct or inaction may be admitted for its *evidentiary* significance in indicating a prior acceptance.

[7] *See* Doyle v. Ohio, 426 U.S. 610 (1976) (holding that post-*Miranda* silence is "insolubly ambiguous").

Would your answer change at all if Doyle had not been given the *Miranda* warnings?[8]

No - right exists with or without warning

¶ **14.22:** (a) Janson stabbed and killed Ruffing. Within the hour, the police put out an All Points Bulletin for Janson's arrest, and several local radio stations reported this. Janson turned himself in to the police two weeks later. At trial, Janson testifies that he killed Ruffing in self-defense. May the prosecutor cross-examine Janson about his failure to turn himself in earlier, and argue to the jury that this suggests that Janson was guilty?[9]

Yes - Janson can offer an alternative explanation

No - there's no hearsay problem here. Not assertion. Not - conduct. Not adopting any statement. Is the conduct relevant? Yes!

(b) Same problem as (a) except that, instead of simply failing to turn himself in, Janson fled the jurisdiction.[10]

Yes - same

If in the above cases you are inclined to regard the evidence as admissions, it may not be because you believe the party has implicitly adopted the statement. In at least some of these cases, it does not appear that the party intended to communicate agreement with the statement. Rather, it may be more accurate to say that the party's reaction merely reflected his belief that the statement was true. Recall the discussion in Chapter 9 of conduct offered to prove the truth of a belief apparently reflected by the conduct. Now note a theoretical problem in FRE 801(D)(2)(B), which speaks of a statement that "the party manifested that it adopted *or* believed to be true" (emphasis added). This phrasing suggests that another person's statement should be admissible against a party if the party's reaction manifested his belief in the statement, even if it did not amount to an adoption of the statement. But if the party opponent did *not* adopt the statement, then what we have is a statement made by someone other than the party—and so not itself an admission—and conduct by the party that, because it is not assertive, does not even fall within the basic definition of hearsay. So which is the admission, the statement by a non-party, or the conduct by the party that is not even hearsay? Or does it matter?

¶ **14.23:** Given that the *statement* is deemed not to be within the definition of hearsay, does that mean that the factfinder may legitimately be asked to rely on the credibility of the non-party who made the declaration?

---

[8] *Cf.* Fletcher v. Weir, 455 U.S. 603 (1982) (no constitutional violation to allow impeachment of the defendant by silence after arrest and before affirmative assurances such as those in the *Miranda* warnings are given).

[9] *Cf.* Jenkins v. Anderson, 447 U.S. 231 (1980).

[10] *See* United States v. Amuso, 21 F.3d 1251, 1257?61 (2d Cir.), *cert. denied,* 513 U.S. 932 (1994) (analyzing evidence of defendant's flight after indictment on one set of charges and continued absence after learning he might be subjected to murder-related charges).

¶ **14.24:** Whose decision is it—the judge's or the jury's or both—whether the party has made a tacit admission? What criteria should be used in making the decision?

A NOTE ON ADMISSIONS BY CONDUCT

As often conceived, a tacit admission involves a statement made by another and a silent reaction from the party. But other forms of non-communicative conduct, as well as silence, may indicate a party's belief in a proposition. Indeed, the distinction between silence and conduct is not really useful, because even silence is always accompanied by some type of conduct; if something as simple as looking down, as in ¶ 14.18, cannot be found, then at least we can say that the party continued to breathe while he remained silent, and that he invested the mental energy necessary to understand the statement and somehow dealt with a world altered by the fact that the statement was made.

Moreover, the context for conduct by a party that tends to reveal the party's belief in a proposition need not be a statement made by another person asserting that proposition. Thus, tacit admissions may be considered a subset of a broader category that is sometimes called admissions by conduct. Unfortunately, for reasons suggested above, the label "admissions by conduct"—indeed, the whole concept—may be misleading, at least within the modern hearsay framework embodied in the Federal Rules (and rejecting the rule of *Wright v. Doe d. Tatham*). If the party's conduct is not communicative, it—as opposed to any statement that it admitted—should not be considered hearsay at all under the FRE approach. That is not to say that there are no serious problems that might render doubtful the admissibility of such evidence. But the most interesting of these problems tend to be the ordinary ones of probative value, in which we ask the basic questions, "How likely is it that this evidence would arise if the hypothesis is true?" and "How likely is it that the evidence would arise if the hypothesis is not true?" Indeed, the type of behavior that is often referred to as an admission by conduct sometimes has significant probative value even if the person who engaged in it was someone other than the party against whom it is offered. Under the FRE approach, such evidence should not raise a hearsay problem at all.

¶ **14.25:** (a) Reconsider ¶ 14.22. Assume now that the APB was not put out on Janson, but that there were witnesses to the stabbing. Do your answers change at all?

(b) Now assume that immediately after the episode Janson sought out the police. May Janson introduce proof of this? Is he entitled to an instruction regarding this?

(c) Now assume that Larson as well as Janson got into the fatal fight with Ruffing. Janson claims that Larson, not he, committed the murder. To prove this, may he introduce evidence that shortly after the episode Larson fled the jurisdiction?[11] *should be able to! How is classified as hearsay???*

¶ 14.26: (a) Donald, a municipal official, is on trial on charges that he took a bribe from Citak, a city contractor. May the prosecution offer evidence that, shortly after the indictment was filed, Donald

(i) attempted to persuade a potential witness to give perjured testimony?[12] *Yes!*

(ii) attempted suicide? *No! i mean... ith... is conduct, speech if you're only introducing it to*

(b) Now assume that Donald's suicide attempt was successful and that Citak is on trial for bribery. May the prosecution offer *show their response!* proof of the suicide? *Yes*

Some types of evidence that are sometimes classified as "admissions by conduct"—such as offering to compromise a claim or taking remedial measures after an accident—raise policy issues apart from the question of how much probative value they have. These are important, but they are not really hearsay issues (note that the Federal Rules address them in the 400 series);[13] we will consider them in Chapter 17.

D. REPRESENTATIVE ADMISSIONS

FRE 801(d)(2)(C)–(E)

Additional Reading: McCormick, ch. 25, § 259; Mueller & Kirkpatrick, §§ 8.28, 8.31–.34

1. AGENCY ADMISSIONS

People often act through other people as their agents. And entities that are not individuals almost inevitably conduct most of their activities through individuals; although the Board of Directors of a corporation might make many of its decisions, it is unlikely to conduct most of the business of the corporation. Often, then, the proponent of an out-of-court statement will contend that it should be admissible as an admission of the party opponent because it was made by an agent of that party.

---

[11] *Cf.* State v. Piernot, 167 Iowa 353, 149 N.W. 446, 448 (1914) ("Flight, if proved, is nothing more than a confession by another, and the defendant was not entitled to the use of this testimony in his own defense.").

[12] *See* McQueeney v. Wilmington Trust Co., 779 F.2d 916 (3d Cir. 1985) (suborning perjury is indicative of weakness of case, because "a party knows better than anyone else the truth about his own case").

[13] A significant, and perhaps the primary, basis for the rules on subsequent remedial measures and compromise is the desire not to inhibit socially useful action. These rules *exclude* evidence, and their logic applies most forcefully if the person who took the action in question is the party against whom the evidence is offered—precisely the situation in which admissions doctrine applies to *allow* admissibility.

We have already referred to representative admissions in passing, for they pose in very stark form the question of what justification underlies admissions doctrine; recall that it is the relationship of the agent to the party opponent at the time of the statement, rather than at the time of trial, that determines whether the statement is an admission. But even putting aside this issue of change of relationship, there is a basic question: To what extent should the statements of the agent be treated for purposes of hearsay law as if they were the statements of the principal, and so admissible against it?

We are familiar with the substantive principle of agency law of *respondeat superior*, that a principal is liable for the authorized acts of its agent. Courts around 1800, while refusing to recognize a doctrine of agency admissions, did recognize that the principal might be substantively liable for communicative acts, as well as noncommunicative ones, authorized by the principal and committed by the agent. Thus, a corporation is bound substantively by a sales offer made by its clerk who is authorized to make offers of that type. Soon courts made a natural extension, holding that if the principal authorized the agent, explicitly or implicitly, to make a statement, the statement might be admitted against the principal on an admissions theory. That is, if the authorized statement was merely narrative, so that it appeared to be hearsay, it could be admitted against the principal to prove the truth of what it asserted. FRE 801(d)(2)(C) expresses this traditional view based on *respondeat superior*. Note, though, that, at least when the principal is an individual, this doctrine is already a departure from the confrontation principle: Although the agent may have been under the control of the principal at the time of the statement, they are nevertheless separate persons, and there is no guarantee that the principal controls the agent at the time of trial. Therefore, the principal may well have a significant interest in cross-examining the agent.

Drawing on then-recent developments, the drafters of the Federal Rules went beyond the traditional authorization-based theory of agency admissions. Rule 801(d)(2)(D) treats as an admission "a statement by the party's agent or servant concerning a matter within the scope of the agency or employment, made during the existence of the relationship." It appears this Rule virtually or entirely swallows up subdivision C; it is difficult or impossible to come up with a statement that would fit within subdivision C but not within subdivision D. Most American jurisdictions—some that have not yet adopted codifications based on the Federal Rules as well as virtually all that have—now extend their doctrine of agency admissions as far as subdivision D. There are exceptions, however, including California.[14]

Subdivision D lacks the intellectual simplicity of subdivision C: If the agent's statement was authorized by the principal, then it is easy enough to say that the statement was, in effect, a statement *of* the principal; statements by a public relations agent or by a lawyer speaking on behalf of her client are often good examples. But this characterization seems inappropriate if the statement was *not* authorized by the principal. Subdivision D has some practical advantages, though. It eliminates the often-difficult question of whether an employee who was paid principally to do rather than to talk should be deemed to have had authority to talk about what she did. And usually—though hardly always—when an agent makes a statement about a matter within the scope of the agency she is familiar with the subject matter of the statement, and her interests are in accord with those of the principal; at least the statement was presumably in her own interests, which might accord with those of the principal. Usually, then, if the statement supports the position taken at trial by the principal's opponent, it has substantial probative value. Moreover, usually the principal is no less able than its opponent to produce the agent as a witness at trial. McCormick argues, "Typically the agent is well informed about acts in the course of business, the statements are offered against the employer's interest, and while the employment continues, the employee is not likely to make the statements unless they are true." § 259. The last of these assertions may be doubted in some cases; the agent may not be on the hook, either to the boss or to the adverse party, for any wrongdoing in the case, and the agent may be willing to be very sympathetic at the expense of the boss's money. But most often the agent will be accountable at least to the boss if liability-creating trouble arose in relation to the agent's function. As a general rule, statements fitting within subdivision D are of substantial assistance to the truth-determining process even though they were not authorized by the principal.

¶ 14.27: (a) Priscilla is suing Dodgson, a trucking firm, for damages arising from an accident in which she collided with a Dodgson truck driven by Tompkins. Dodgson denies liability. Priscilla offers her testimony that, twenty minutes after the accident and while they were waiting for a police officer to

---

[14] Cal. Evid. Code § 1222 (requiring authorization); *see, e.g.,* Cabaluna v. Hoag Memorial Hospital Presbyterian, 2014 WL 2447330 (Cal.App.4th Dist. 2014) (noting that § 1222 has been interpreted "as only applying to high-ranking organizational agents who have actual authority to speak on behalf of the organization"); Wash. R. Ev. 801(d)(2)(iv) (statement by an agent or servant "acting within the scope of the authority to make the statement for the party"). The trend in Illinois is to adopt the federal view, *see, e.g., Garcia v. 6653–55 North Seeley Bldg. Condominium Ass'n,* 2013 WL 1296242 (Ill.App. 1st Dist.), *appeal denied,* 996 N.E.2d 15 (2013), but the state supreme court has not resolved the matter.

arrive, Tompkins said calmly, "Gee, I'm sorry. I was reaching down to get a beer and a joint, and I must have taken my eye off the road. These things happen, you know." Admissible?

(b) Now assume that Priscilla is suing Tompkins as well. When she offers her testimony of Tompkins' statement against him, his counsel objects, saying, "If Tompkins did indeed say this, he said it as an employee of Dodgson and in the course of that employment. It should not be admissible against him individually." How should the court rule?

Broad though the bounds of subdivision D are, sometimes questions do arise as to whether the subject matter of the statement should be considered to be within the scope of the agency.

¶ 14.28: Wilkinson was hurt on a cruise ship when an electric sliding door in the pool area malfunctioned. The ship owner defends against her tort action on the ground that it had no prior notice of any problem with the door. Wilkinson offers the testimony, via deposition, of her cabin-mate that shortly after the accident a steward "felt real bad and said that they had been having problems with the door and that he was hoping they would get it fixed before it happened to a child." The defense presents unchallenged evidence that the steward's job was primarily to clean the cabins, that he had nothing to do with the sliding door, and that he was prohibited from being in the pool area of the ship. Should the testimony be admitted? How, if at all, would your answer be affected if the steward's job had nothing to do with the sliding door, but he was responsible for cleaning the area around the pool?[15]

Another difficulty that sometimes arises, either under the Federal Rules approach or the more traditional one, is determining whether the relationship of declarant to party should be treated as that of agent to principal.[16] The following problems highlight a sample of the issues.

¶ 14.29: At JFK Airport in New York for a flight from Brazil, Da Silva responds to routine questions by a customs agent in English. He is arrested for drug smuggling and, because

---

[15] See Wilkinson v. Carnival Cruise Lines, Inc., 920 F.2d 1560 (11th Cir.1991); cf. Preston v. Lamb, 20 Utah 2d 260, 436 P.2d 1021 (1968) (slip-and-fall case; statement by waitress that floor had been waxed the night before).

[16] Sometimes a procedural problem arises: Should the court be able to use the proffered statement itself in determining that the agency relationship existed? The problem is considered below in the context of conspirator statements, in which it most often arises; the analysis in the context of non-conspiratorial agencies should be essentially the same. Cf. FRE 801(d)(2) (providing that "[t]he statement must be considered but does not by itself establish the declarant's authority under (C); the existence or scope of the relationship under (D); or the existence of the conspiracy or participation in it under (E)") & Advisory Committee's Note.

Da Silva is more comfortable speaking in Spanish than in English, the DEA provides an interpreter, Customs Inspectional Aide Mario Stewart. Da Silva says, "Thank God" when he learns that Stewart speaks Spanish. After being given the *Miranda* warnings in Spanish, Da Silva indicates that he understands his rights and is willing to respond to inquiries. Stewart then translates the conversation. At trial, the interviewing officer testifies for the prosecution but Stewart does not. Da Silva objects to the officer's testimony of Stewart's translation on the ground that it is hearsay: The translation was an assertion, and it is offered to prove the truth of that assertion—that is, that Da Silva did in fact say what the interpreter reported. The prosecution responds that the translation should be considered an agency admission. How should the court rule?[17]

¶ **14.30:** In 1974, the Department of Justice, through its Antitrust Division and in the name of the United States, brought a civil action to break up AT & T. (AT & T eventually agreed to a partial break-up.) AT & T offered statements made in proceedings before the Federal Communications Commission by senior officials of agencies of the Government other than the Department of Justice; one was by the Administrator of General Services and others were from the Defense Department. In response to a hearsay objection, AT & T contended that these statements were agency admissions by the plaintiff United States. How should the court have ruled?[18]

¶ **14.31:** Santos, charged with assaulting a federal officer, attempts to introduce an affidavit made by an agent of the Federal Bureau of Narcotics who was present at the incident. He too contends that the statement is an agency admission by the United States. How should the court rule?[19]

Recall that in determining whether the party opponent and the declarant were in a principal-agent relationship, the key time is when the statement was made, not the time of trial. If the declarant was an agent of the party when she made the statement, the statement can be an admission even if she is no longer one by the time of trial (and if she was

---

[17] *See* United States v. Da Silva, 725 F.2d 828, 832 (2d Cir.1983); *compare* Kalos v. United States, 9 F.2d 268, 271 (8th Cir.1925).

[18] *See* United States v. American Tel. & Tel. Co., 498 F.Supp. 353, 356–58 (D.D.C.1980).

[19] *See* United States v. Santos, 372 F.2d 177 (2d Cir.1967); *compare* United States v. Morgan, 581 F.2d 933, 937–38 (D.C.Cir.1978); Randolph N. Jonakait, *The Supreme Court, Plain Meaning, and the Changed Rules of Evidence*, 68 Tex. L. Rev. 745, 774–778 (1990).

not an agent when she made the statement, becoming an agent subsequently will not turn the statement into an admission).[20]

Agents are often employees of substantial organizations, and often they make statements within the organization. If we were to anthropomorphize the organization—analogize it to a person—these intraorganizational statements would be the counterparts of private thoughts, rather than of statements to the outside world. The trend in recent decades, accelerated by the Federal Rules, has been to treat such statements as admissions.

¶ 14.32: Burton, a manufacturer of compact disc players, sues Krypton, a manufacturer of discs as well as of players. Burton claims that Krypton violated the antitrust laws when it introduced its new "110 Compact System," the centerpiece of which was a new type of disc that provides better sound quality and is cheaper than previous ones. Burton contends that Krypton gained an improper advantage in the market for compact disc players, because Krypton included features ensuring that at first only Krypton could make players compatible with the new 110 discs. Burton seeks to introduce a memo written by Marshak, a lab scientist at Krypton, to his boss, the chief scientist in the product development division, while the company was about to bring the new system to market. Marshak wrote: "We're crazy if we introduce these discs. Their durability stinks. The sound quality is not as good as we had hoped. We risk damaging our reputation over the long run if we try to push these on the market."

(a) Is this memo admissible notwithstanding the fact that (until Burton received it in discovery) it was not sent to anyone outside Krypton? Notwithstanding the fact that it was not approved by any of Marshak's superiors? Does admissibility follow from the rationales underlying admissions doctrine?

(b) Now assume that the memo is admitted and that you are representing Krypton. How are you going to try to explain the memo away?

The Federal Rules approach frequently poses the question of whether agency admissions, like personal admissions, should be exempted from the rules on lay opinions and personal knowledge. Note that the Advisory Committee, in referring to the exemption of admissions from these requirements, did not distinguish among the various types of admissions.

---

[20] *See, e.g.,* United States v. Chappell, 698 F.2d 308 (7th Cir.) (statement of agent, deceased by time of trial, admissible under FRE 801(d)(2)(D)), *cert. denied,* 461 U.S. 983 (1983).

¶ **14.33:** Patterson was discharged from her job and is now suing her former employer, claiming age discrimination. Which of the following should she be allowed to offer, and on what foundation?

(a) A statement to Patterson by Manton, her manager, made when he informed her of his decision to let her go: "This is a job for a younger person."

(b) A statement to Patterson by Manton, "I was told by those in charge, 'This is a job for a younger person.'"[21]

(c) A statement to Patterson by Collins, a friend of hers who worked in the personnel department: "You got shafted. They're trying to get rid of everybody over 45 not up at the very top."

(d) A statement to Patterson by O'Neill, the chief operating officer of the corporation, when she went to him to complain about the discharge: "It appears that the managers in your division felt somebody younger would be more appropriate."

2. CONSPIRATOR STATEMENTS

a. Rationales for Admission

In a criminal case, the prosecutor often wishes to introduce a statement by a person who allegedly was a member of a conspiracy along with the accused. At least theoretically, the substantive law of conspiracy makes each member of the conspiracy liable for the acts of every other member taken to further the conspiratorial design. The idea is that conspirators, like partners, are each agents of the other, implicitly or explicitly authorized to take action in furtherance of the conspiracy. Courts have thus traditionally applied the doctrine of agency admissions to statements made by those who have conspired with a party.

How far should the application extend? Consider whether the exemption for party admissions from the personal knowledge requirement should apply to conspirator statements.

¶ **14.34:** Tinker, Evers, and Chance are on trial for conspiracy to purchase a large quantity of crack cocaine. On June 1, Tinker had a telephone conversation with Stallings, who unbeknownst to Tinker was a government informer recording the call. Tinker said he would like to buy some crack, and Stallings said that he had a shipment for sale, but would need

---

[21] *See* Cedeck v. Hamilton Sav. & Loan Assn., 551 F.2d 1136 (8th Cir. 1977) (holding comparable statement inadmissible because identity of initial declarant was not given).

$500,000. Tinker said he could put up $100,000 and would try to raise the rest.

No conspiracy yet so question.

On June 2, Tinker called Stallings back; again the call was recorded. Tinker told Stallings that Evers was interested in the deal, and would put up $250,000, but that Evers wanted "to come over today to look at the stuff." (Stallings is prepared to testify that later that day Evers came over to his place and tested a sample of the crack.)

Now Evers is in; statement furthering conspiracy

Around noon on June 3, Tinker called Stallings again, and again the call was recorded. Now Tinker said that Chance would put up the remaining $150,000. Stallings said that they should come over to his apartment at 5 p.m. that day with the cash.

Stallings will testify that, at about 5 p.m. that day, Tinker, Evers, and Chance arrived at his apartment. Stallings invited the three to come back to his bedroom. Only Tinker did; the others waited in the living room. In the bedroom, Stallings and Tinker made the exchange. As they emerged, Stallings said, "A pleasure doing business," and three policemen emerged from a closet and arrested Tinker, Evers, and Chance.

The prosecution wants to introduce the testimony of Maranville, a convicted drug dealer now on parole, that he had a conversation with Evers on the morning of June 3 during which Evers said, "Tinker is trying to raise money for a big deal. He's going to try to get some from Chance, but I don't know that Chance is good for it." The defendants all object to this testimony. Chance's lawyer argues, "There's no foundation showing that Evers was speaking from personal knowledge." What ruling?[22]

The drafters of the Federal Rules treated statements of conspirators separately from other agency admissions, however. Rule 801(d)(2)(E) exempts a statement that "was made by the party's coconspirator during and in furtherance of the conspiracy."[23] The "in furtherance" requirement, which reflects the earlier case law, makes clear that this subdivision E does not go as far as subdivision D. The Advisory Committee noted that the expanded theory of subdivision D "might suggest wider admissibility

---

[22] *Cf.* United States v. Ammar, 714 F.2d 238, 252–54 (3d Cir.), *cert. denied,* 464 U.S. 936 (1983).

[23] The Federal Rule uses the term "coconspirator." But James Joseph Duane, *Some Thoughts on How the Hearsay Exception for Statements by Conspirators Should—and Should Not—Be Amended,* 165 F.R.D. 299, 304–12 (1996) [hereinafter *Some Thoughts*], argues at some length that we should speak instead of a party's conspirators. Largely on the basis that if someone puts so much energy, learning, and rhetoric into such a point he may well be right, this text will adhere to Duane's locution.

of statements of co-conspirators," but concluded that "the agency theory of conspiracy is at best a fiction and ought not to serve as a basis for admissibility beyond that already established." This statement is ironic, because by limiting the reach of the exemption for statements by conspirators to those that further the conspiracy, the drafters continued one of the limitations imposed by agency theory—a limitation that is not applicable to agency statements that fit within subdivision D.

You might well ask why the fictitious nature of the agency theory bothered the drafters in the context of conspirator statements and not in the more general context of agency admissions. A quick answer, which probably contains a good deal of truth, is that conspirator statements are nearly always introduced against criminal defendants.

As we study conspirator statements, you will probably come to the conclusion that they are not more reliable than the run of the hearsay mill. Indeed, as one perceptive commentator noted many years ago, "It is no victory for common sense to make a belief that criminals are noted for their veracity the basis for law." Joseph H. Levie, *Hearsay and Conspiracy*, 52 Mich. L. Rev. 1159, 1166 (1954). Justice Marshall quoted this statement in his dissent in *United States v. Inadi*, 475 U.S. 387, 404–05 (1986), in which he also spoke of conspirator statements as including "the boasts, faulty recollections, and coded or ambiguous utterances of outlaws." *Id.* at 411.

Moreover, criminal defendants are generally not more able than the prosecutor, the proponent, to produce the declarant of a conspirator statement as a live witness in court. On the contrary, very often the defendant is significantly *less* able than the prosecutor to produce her former conspirator as a witness. In the typical case, the declarant-conspirator is asserting her privilege against self-incrimination and is completely unavailable to the defense. The prosecutor, however, has at least the theoretical possibility of compelling her to testify, by granting her immunity, entering into a plea bargain with her, or simply trying her first.

Why, then, apart from the fiction of agency, is the law hospitable to conspirator statements? Here is the sketch of a possibility that depends on a rejection of the usual doctrinal assumption that most hearsay is insufficiently reliable to warrant admission. Let's assume instead for the moment that most hearsay, whether reliable or not, has sufficient probative to justify admission if live testimony by the witness would be admissible. Conspirator statements, even if far from trustworthy, do tend to have significant probative value. Criminals don't lie *all* the time, and what they say while they are going about their criminal business is often quite helpful to the truth-determination process. Now let's say the conspiracy is broken up, and one of the conspirators talks to the police about it. That statement might still be very probative, but it is no longer the statement of a conspirator going about her business; now it is a testimonial statement, because the declarant likely knows she is talking to the police and, if the law allows it, ultimately to a trier of fact. In this view, the doctrine of conspirator statements does not select out an unusually reliable form of hearsay from the run of hearsay statements. Rather, it helps police the line between mundane (albeit crime-serving) hearsay, which is made without any anticipation of use at trial, and testimonial statements that are made without an opportunity for confrontation by the defendant.

b. The Existence, Membership and Duration Requirements

For a statement to come within the exemption for conspirator statements, the following requirements must be satisfied: (1) There must have been a conspiracy. (2) Both the declarant and the party opponent must have been members of the conspiracy. (3) The declarant must have made the statement during the course of the conspiracy. (4) The statement must have been made in furtherance of the conspiracy. This subsection will discuss each of these requirements but the last.

Though the meaning of conspiracy for purposes of the exemption is not necessarily the same as its meaning for purposes of substantive criminal law, many courts have tended to give it a substantially similar definition, such as "a joint venture for an illegal purpose, or for a legal purpose using illegal means." *United States v. Gil*, 604 F.2d 546, 549 (7th Cir.1979). Other courts have gone further and stated that Rule 801(d)(2)(E) covers lawful joint ventures as well as illegal combinations. *E.g., United States v. El-Mezain*, 664 F.3d 467 (5th Cir. 2011).[24]

Courts and commentators have often said that the gist of the crime of conspiracy is a wrongful agreement. The requirement is a rather loose one, however. No writing, or even express verbalization, is necessary; a mere tacit understanding is sufficient. In the evidentiary context, however, it might be better to focus not so much on the act of agreement as on a common enterprise; alternatively, one might define agreement in terms—such as "the continuous and conscious union of wills upon a

---

[24] This doctrine is criticized in Ben Trachtenberg, *Confronting Coventurers: Conspirator Hearsay, Sir Walter Raleigh, and the Sixth Amendment Confrontation Clause*, 64 FLA. L. REV. 1669 (2012). For a response, see Richard D. Friedman, *The Mold That Shapes Hearsay Law*, 66 FLA. L. REV. 433 (2014). Why would courts try to jam a lawful joint venture in to the exemption for conspirators' statements even though a broad exemption for agency admissions is already available? Precedent indicates that the agency exemption would not allow a statement by a General Motors employee in Kuala Lumpur to be introduced against a General Motors employee in Detroit with whom she had no prior relationship and who was unaware of her existence. By speaking of the exemption for conspirator statements, however, a court might manipulate its way around that limitation, because that exemption has been extended to situations in which declarant and party opponent had no genuine relationship with each other except that they were members of the same far-flung enterprise.

common undertaking"[25]—that emphasize the continuity of enterprise (even if over a short period) rather than the act of agreement. A focus on a common enterprise squares better with the way courts tend to use the word conspiracy in this context, "to refer not to a crime, which by definition must be an act, but rather to a group—the body of [people] who are guilty of the crime of conspiring with one another."[26] It also squares with the reality of the modern enterprise conspiracy,[27] and particularly of those large conspiracies in which any given member, say the accused, may have had no contact with, and even been unaware of the existence of, any other given member, say the declarant. Furthermore, this approach emphasizes a factor that tends to enhance the probative value of a statement by a co-venturer, whether a criminal conspirator or not—that the statement was made by a person who presumably shared an interest, with respect to the subject matter of the statement, with the party against whom it is offered. The act of agreeing to unlawful conduct may be the gist of what makes conspiracy a crime, but it does not seem to have much bearing on whether a statement ought to be admitted.

A focus on the enterprise, rather than on an agreement, may help explain the tendency of courts to say that a statement of a conspirator may be admitted against the defendant even though the defendant was not yet part of the conspiracy. The standard theory is that a conspirator who joins the conspiracy after it has started adopts all prior acts and declarations that have been committed in furtherance of the conspiracy, *e.g., United States v. Liefer*, 778 F.2d 1236, 1250 (7th Cir.1985), but this fiction does not seem a particularly persuasive basis for admissibility.

Even assuming that the *party opponent* need not have been a member of the conspiracy at the time of the statement, standard doctrine clearly requires that the conspiracy have been *in existence* by then and that the *declarant* have been a member.

¶ **14.35:** In the Tinker-Evers-Chance case, ¶ 14.34, the prosecution seeks to introduce over the defendants' objections each of the three phone calls between Tinker and Stallings of June 1, 2, and 3. To what extent, if any, should these objections prevail? Should the result depend on whether the jurisdiction, like several states but not the federal courts, has adopted the "unilateral" theory of conspiracy, advanced by § 5.03(1) of the Model Penal Code, under which a person may be guilty of conspiracy even if there is only one other party to the agreement

---

[25] *Developments in the Law—Criminal Conspiracy*, 72 Harv. L. Rev. 920, 926 (1959).

[26] *Id.* at 928.

[27] This is a term that has emerged in RICO litigation. *E.g.*, United States v. Sutherland, 656 F.2d 1181, 1192 (5th Cir.Tex.1981), *cert. denied*, 455 U.S. 949 (1982).

and that person, unbeknownst to the first, is a government agent or informant?[28] *Yes?*

¶ 14.36: Bob Burke and Seth Sailor are on trial for distributing cocaine. The prosecution evidence indicates that Sailor solicited Germond, an undercover agent; phoned Burke's house to say he had a customer; and arranged to bring Germond to Burke's house in two hours. The prosecution wants to introduce Germond's testimony that when they arrived at Burke's house, Burke's housemate, Robin Rawlings, said, "Bob phoned a while ago to say he's been held up getting what you need, but he expected to be back by now. Why don't you make yourselves comfortable? I'm sure he'll be back in a few minutes." Should this testimony be admitted? Would it make a difference if Rawlings was Burke's wife?[29] *what evidence that this is part of the conspiracy?*

Very frequently, the court must face the question of whether the conspiracy should still be deemed to have been in existence at the time of the statement. The Advisory Committee's Note to FRE 801(d)(2)(E) said that the Rule is "consistent with the position of the Supreme Court in denying admissibility to statements made after the objectives of the conspiracy have either failed or been achieved." Obviously, this standard carries a great deal of ambiguity and depends in large part on factual questions involving the intentions of the conspirators. If they failed, did they intend to try again? If they succeeded, did they intend to repeat their conduct? The typical drug conspiracy, for example, might be termed an iterative conspiracy; after it completes one drug transaction it does not disband but moves on to the next.

In the federal courts and those of some states, the matter is complicated by a doctrine tracing to *Krulewitch v. United States*, 336 U.S. 440 (1949), that a conspiracy that has either attained or abandoned its "chief objective" is not deemed to continue merely because its members are engaging in acts intended to conceal their prior conduct. Courts have found a variety of ways to evade this doctrine—such as concluding that

---

[28] *Cf.* United States v. Liefer, 778 F.2d 1236 (7th Cir.1985); United States v. Coe, 718 F.2d 830, 839–40 (7th Cir.1983).

[29] *Cf.* United States v. Bulman, 667 F.2d 1374 (11th Cir.), *cert. denied*, 456 U.S. 1010 (1982) (expressing doubt about, but declining to characterize as clearly erroneous, trial court's ruling that showing another member the way to the airport was not sufficient to constitute defendant a member of conspiracy); United States v. Hassell, 547 F.2d 1048, 1053 (8th Cir.), *cert. denied*, 430 U.S. 919 (1977) (though mere association with conspirators, or knowledge of or even acquiescence in the conspiracy is not enough to constitute one a conspirator, here there was enough to characterize the wife of a prime conspirator as a member; it was then for the jury to determine whether she was "a mindless hostess or a knowing participant"); Miller v. United States, 382 F.2d 583, 587 (9th Cir.1967), *cert. denied*, 390 U.S. 984 (1968) (declining, for substantive purposes, to characterize traveling companion of conspirator as a member of conspiracy; it may have been that, "totally unaware of her companion's activities, [she] merely went along for the ride").

the conspiracy is a continuing one; construing the "chief objective" of the conspiracy broadly; generously concluding that that objective has not been either attained or abandoned; perceiving secrecy as essential to achieving the goals of the conspiracy and not merely to protection against investigation and prosecution; finding an agreement to conceal as part of the original conspiracy agreement; simply disregarding *Krulewitch* or shrugging it aside;[30] and, an old standby at the appellate level, concluding that a violation of *Krulewitch* was harmless error.

When courts work so hard to avoid a doctrine, there is good reason to believe that it is ill-founded. *Krulewitch* might provide a good basis for determining when the statute of limitations should begin to run on a conspiracy crime,[31] but that is not the evidentiary issue in determining the applicability of the hearsay exemption for conspirator statements. Concealing the crime, or at least the identity of the perpetrators, so that investigation and prosecution may be avoided is usually one of the chief common interests of the members of a conspiracy. Statements made in furtherance of that objective ought to be considered within the exemption.

More broadly, though, it appears that, so long as the conspirators are working for the benefit of the conspiracy—whether by trying to achieve their original objective or by covering up their crime—their statements are almost certainly not testimonial, and the confrontation principle does not apply. But if they are talking about the conspiracy but no longer working for its benefit, it may well be that their statements are made in the anticipation of prosecutorial use, in which case they are probably testimonial.

¶ 14.37: Contracting Wife hires Hitman to kill Unwanted Husband. At some point after Hitman fulfills his part of the contract, he and Wife have a conversation. Hitman complains that he has not been paid. Wife reminds him of their agreement that he will be paid when she receives the proceeds of an insurance policy on Husband's life. She also complains that he botched the job by leaving incriminating evidence behind. Should this conversation be admissible against either Wife or Hitman or both? When should the conspiracy be deemed to have ended for purposes of the hearsay exemption for conspirator statements—

---

[30] *See, e.g.*, Commonwealth v. Winquist, 2016 WL 3245061 (Mass. 2016).

[31] There are other non-evidentiary issues as well that depend on when the conspiracy is deemed to be in existence. For example, in United States v. Jimenez Recio, 537 U.S. 270 (2003), the Court held that a conspiracy does not end when the Government, unbeknownst to some of its members, frustrates the objective of the conspiracy, in this case by seizing the drugs that the conspiracy sought to distribute; thus, given proof that the defendants participated in the conspiracy, the Government did not have to prove that they joined it before the seizure.

when Husband is killed? When Wife receives the insurance proceeds? When Hitman is paid? Never?[32] *Don't they have incentive to always keep it secret/continue?*

¶ **14.38:** Rivera, a would-be bank robber working in conjunction with Rucker, flees in panic before attempting the robbery. Rucker persuades him to try again two days later. On that day, Rivera does go back to the bank, but flees again before even presenting a demand note to the teller. He then asks a friend to help him get rid of his clothes. Assuming this statement would be inadmissible hearsay unless it fits within the exemption for conspirator statements, does it fit within the exemption?[33] *Does friend know why?*

Note that under prevailing doctrine the status of the conspiracy as of the time of trial, and the relationship at that time of the declarant and the accused, do not matter. Nor does it matter if the declarant is then dead or otherwise unavailable to the accused. Indeed, it is very common that a statement is introduced under this exemption even though the declarant is unavailable to the accused because she is asserting her own privilege against self-incrimination—and even though the prosecution could remove the privilege, if it were so inclined, by plea bargaining with the declarant, or immunizing her, or trying her first.

¶ **14.39:** Consider whether this is appropriate in the context of Bourjaily's case, which we examined in ¶ 8.19. Bourjaily is being tried for conspiracy to distribute cocaine. According to the prosecution's case, Bourjaily conspired with Lonardo, the front man in dealing with a supplier, Greathouse. In one conversation Lonardo told Greathouse by phone that he had a "gentleman friend" who was interested in the transaction, and in another he told Greathouse that he and his friend would meet Greathouse for the exchange. Bourjaily showed up with Lonardo at the designated parking lot, and took possession of the cocaine—but they were arrested, because it turns out that Greathouse is a Government informant. However cooperative Bourjaily and Lonardo were with each other earlier, by the time of Bourjaily's trial, they are each protecting their own interests. Lonardo exercises his right not to testify. The prosecution wishes to introduce statements made by Lonardo, allegedly made during the conspiracy. Should introduction of this evidence be held consistent with hearsay law and with Bourjaily's confrontation

---

[32] *Cf.* People v. Hardy, 2 Cal.4th 86, 145, 5 Cal.Rptr.2d 796, 828, 825 P.2d 781, 813, *cert. denied,* 506 U.S. 987 (1992), 506 U.S. 1056 (1993); People v. Leach, 15 Cal.3d 419, 124 Cal.Rptr. 752, 541 P.2d 296 (1975), *cert. denied,* 424 U.S. 926 (1976); People v. Saling, 7 Cal.3d 844, 103 Cal.Rptr. 698, 500 P.2d 610 (1972).

[33] *See* United States v. Rucker, 586 F.2d 899, 906 (2d Cir.1978) (holding in the affirmative).

right? *See Bourjaily v. United States,* 483 U.S. 171 (1987) (holding in the affirmative). ⸮

c. The Nexus Between the Predicate and the Substantive Issues Being Tried: The "In Furtherance" Requirement

In understanding some of the complexities of conspirator statements, it is helpful to focus on a double nexus. At the crux of both nexuses is the predicate for the conspirator exemption, a showing that the statement was made during the course of and in furtherance of a conspiracy of which both the declarant and the defendant were members. One nexus is between the predicate and the substantive issues being tried. The other is between the predicate and the matter asserted by the statement.

First, consider the nexus between the predicate for the exemption and the substantive issues being tried. Conspirator statements can be offered in any kind of case, civil or criminal, and the conspiracy that assertedly justifies introduction of the statement need not be part of the case on the merits at all. But in the overwhelming majority of cases, it is a prosecutor who offers the statement, and usually the conspiracy that is a predicate for the admissibility of the conspirator statement is at least a large part of what the case is all about.

This nexus raises an interesting logical point. Many statements that are offered under the conspirator exemption to the rule against hearsay could be admitted under a nonhearsay theory. To fit within the hearsay exemption, the statement must have been made "during and in furtherance of" the conspiracy. But if the statement satisfies that standard, then there is probably at least a plausible argument—assuming that the same conspiracy is of substantive importance to the case—that the statement is admissible to show the existence of the conspiracy and how it operated. Most courts fail to note this point. Indeed, often courts struggle with the question of whether a given statement fits within the conspirator exemption without pausing to consider whether the statement is being offered on a hearsay theory. For example, suppose Customer-Informant is prepared to testify that Drug Salesman said, "Come meet my source, Mr. Big." Embedded within that utterance is an assertion that Mr. Big is the speaker's source. But the utterance may also have substantial probative value in showing the sales and recruitment operations of the conspiracy. Informing Customer-Informant who the supplier was may have been part of those operations. And, apart from the assertion, the fact that Drug Salesman invited Customer-Declarant to meet Mr. Big might, depending on what other evidence the prosecution presents, have considerable probative value in demonstrating the conspiracy's outreach attempts. To the extent the utterance is an invitation—an imperative rather than declaratory sentence—it has no truth value and so cannot be hearsay.

¶ **14.40:** Tinker, Evers, and Chance, from ¶ 14.34, now argue that Maranville's testimony should not be admitted because the statement it reports was not made in furtherance of any conspiracy. What result? *Doesn't come in?*

¶ **14.41:** Jack and Jill are on trial for bank robbery.

(a) For each of the following consider whether the offered testimony is admissible against Jack and whether it is admissible against Jill.

(1) Weber's testimony that, the day before the robbery, Jill said to him, "Jack and I need a car to use in a bank job tomorrow. Think you could help us find one? It'll be worth your while." [Do not consider yet the possibility that this statement fits within the exception for declarations against interest.] *Against both*

(2) Warburg's testimony that, later that day, Jill told him, "Weber helped Jack and me rip off an old Chevy. We're gonna use it in a bank job tomorrow." *Against both Jill only — talking about conspiracy ≠ furthering conspiracy*

(3) Teller Weller's testimony that Jill came up to her window at the bank and handed her a note, written in a [masculine hand,] saying, "Hand over $50,000 in small bills. Don't even think about pressing the alarm button." Apparently Jill retrieved the note with the money. *what even is that?* *Against both, b/c still in conspiracy?*

(4) Officer Warden's testimony that, one day after she arrested both Jack and Jill, Jill asked to see her and said, "OK, OK, we did it. I got the cash and Jack drove the getaway car." *Against Jill only — conspiracy over once thwarted* *conspiracy doesn't work with police investigation* *It's an opposing statement* *NOT hearsay*

(b) If, in any of the cases in (a), you think that the evidence is admissible against one defendant but not against another, what remedy is appropriate?

The nexus between the predicate for the hearsay exemption and the substantive issues being tried means that, to decide whether the statement should be admitted, the trial court must first decide issues that the jury has to decide in determining guilt. That may seem troublesome, but it is not a particularly difficult problem. The judge has her job and the jury has its own, and they perform them in a substantially different manner. In *Bourjaily v. United States*, 483 U.S. 171 (1987), the facts of which we have just considered in ¶ 14.39, the Supreme Court, interpreting the Federal Rules of Evidence, held that the standard governing the judge's determination of the predicate was preponderance of the evidence—more likely than not—rather than any more elevated standard. It also held that, in making this determination, the judge has the freedom accorded by FRE 104(a) and is not limited to admissible evidence.

¶ 14.42: Are these conclusions sound?

If the judge decides that the evidence supports a conclusion that the statement fits within the conspirator exemption, she should admit the statement, but she need not comment to the jury on why she has done so. She should not announce, "Ladies and gentlemen, I have decided that this statement was made in furtherance of a conspiracy between Accused and Declarant, and therefore I have admitted it. Later, it will be up to you to decide whether you believe these two people conspired. But don't be swayed by my determination."

d. The Nexus Between the Predicate and the Substance Asserted by the Statement: The Bootstrapping Problem

Now consider the nexus between the predicate for the hearsay exemption and the substance asserted by the proffered statement itself. In many cases, the statement tends to prove all or part of the predicate— that the statement was made during the course of and in furtherance of a conspiracy of which the declarant and the defendant were both members. It may, for example, flatly assert that the defendant and the declarant are planning some criminal operation together. The traditional law, before the Federal Rules, was that in determining the applicability of the exemption the trial court must rely completely on evidence other than the statement itself; otherwise the statement would "bootstrap" itself into admissibility. *See Glasser v. United States*, 315 U.S. 60, 74–75 (1942).[34] In *Bourjaily*, however, the Court, interpreting the Federal Rules, rejected this doctrine. We have seen this aspect of *Bourjaily* in ¶ 8.19. Basically, *Bourjaily* took the view that, in determining a preliminary evidentiary issue, FRE 104(a) allows the judge to consider all non-privileged evidence; it does not explicitly exclude the item of evidence being offered, and there is no reason to treat that item alone, among all non-privileged evidence, as being beyond the court's purview.

This aspect of *Bourjaily* has proved controversial, and has not been adopted by all of the states. An amendment to FRE 801(d) promulgated in 1997 was intended to confirm *Bourjaily*'s rejection for the federal courts of the broad ban on bootstrapping, by providing that "[t]he contents of the statement shall be considered. . . ." Much of the public commentary made before the amendment was formally proposed by the Advisory Committee

---

[34] It is not quite true that under the broad rule against bootstrapping a court could not *consider* the substance of the statement in determining its own admissibility; in most cases the court would have to take into account the substance of the statement to determine whether it was made in furtherance of the conspiracy. What the rule prohibited was a court relying on the truth of an assertion in the statement—that is, making a hearsay use of the statement—in determining whether the statement avoids the rule against hearsay.

was hostile to this part of the amendment; a summary of this commentary is published along with the Advisory Committee's Note on the amendment.

At the same time that it confirmed the rejection of a strong rule against bootstrapping, however, the amendment purported to retain— again, for the federal courts only!—a partial ban on bootstrapping. This resolved an issue left open by *Bourjaily*. Though *Bourjaily* held that the proffered statement could be part of the basis on which the judge decides that the predicate for the hearsay exemption is made out, it declined to say whether the court could rely "solely" on the proffered statement in determining that the statement satisfies the predicate for the hearsay exemption. All the federal courts that had considered this issue since *Bourjaily* had concluded in the negative, and that is the position taken by the 1997 amendment, which, as restyled in 2011, provides that the proffered statement "does not by itself establish the declarant's authority under (C); the existence or scope of the relationship under (D); or the existence of the conspiracy or participation in it under (E)." (Note from this language that, though the issue most often arises with respect to conspirators' statements, it can arise with respect to other representative admissions as well.)

But this issue of whether the statement can lift itself *entirely* by its own bootstraps seems to be a fanciful one, and indeed it appears never to have been critical to the resolution of an actual case. It is not even clear that it is theoretically possible for the statement itself to be the *only* evidence of the predicate—or even of any aspect of the predicate—for applicability of the hearsay exemption; there will always be some piece of information that makes it more likely than it would be without that information that the declarant and the defendant were both members of a conspiracy. Theory aside, it seems that as a practical matter this is at least virtually always so. After a thorough canvass of the cases, Professor James Duane concluded that "the prosecutor always has something other than the mere contents of the proffered statement, even if it is only some barely probative detail about the context in which the statement was made that renders it ever so slightly more trustworthy than an anonymous note slipped through the United States Attorney's transom in the middle of the night." Duane, *Some Thoughts*, 165 F.R.D. at 353.

¶ **14.43:** Reconsider *Bourjaily*, summarized in ¶ 14.39, and suppose it arises in a jurisdiction not bound by federal law. In deciding whether Lonardo's statements satisfied the exemption for conspirator statements, do you think the court should rely, in whole or in part, on Lonardo's statements themselves?

Doesn't Lonardo showing up for the deal also show evidence of conspiracy?

¶ **14.44:** (a) Is there any way of giving the "does not by itself establish" language of the 1997 amendment, as since restyled, any force without restoring the strong rule against bootstrapping that prevailed in the federal courts before *Bourjaily*?

(b) Suppose a prosecutor argued, "True, I don't have any evidence, other than the statement itself, that the defendant was a member of the conspiracy, but I have lots of other evidence that there was a conspiracy and that the declarant was a member." Should that argument be accepted? *See* Duane, *Some Thoughts*, 165 F.R.D. at 330–31. *Yes?*

¶ 14.45: Louie is on trial for ordering a gangland murder. An eyewitness testifies that the murderer attached a note by knife to the victim's body. The note reads, "Regards from Louie." Admissible? With what foundation? *Literally any connection from Louie to murder* *implied assertion of involvement in murder*

¶ 14.46: Jeffrey Archer, the novelist and then a deputy chairman of Britain's Conservative Party, got himself into an unfortunate position in October 1986. Reports began circulating that Archer was having an affair with a prostitute named Monica Coghlan. Archer offered to pay her off if she would leave the country quietly. They arranged for her to meet his representative at Victoria Station. Unknown to Archer, Ms. Coghlan arrived for the meeting wired—in the electronic sense— and also accompanied by a reporter from the *News of the World*, then a well-known tabloid. Somewhat imprudently, as it appeared in retrospect, Archer had chosen as his envoy a public relations man, named Michael Stacpoole. Stacpoole recognized the reporter, but did not put two and two together. A public relations man to the core, he said to the reporter:

> "I'm here to do a favor for a very important political friend. He's having a spot of bother, and he wants my help to smooth it out."

Lelyveld, *Jeffrey Archer Quits His Tory Post Amid Vice Scandal*, N.Y. Times, Oct. 27, 1986, at A1.

(a) Now suppose that the payment, if authorized by Archer, was illegal, that Archer is on trial, and that he denies having authorized the payment. Suppose the reporter offers to testify to his encounter with Stacpoole and to Stacpoole's statement. Would that be admissible? If so, what predicate would be necessary? *Yes — Stacpool is envoy ... knows what's up*

(b) Now suppose the reporter's account is that Stacpoole said, "Keep this confidential, but I'm doing a favor for Jeffrey Archer, who's had himself a spot of bother." Admissible? *Yes*

(c) Suppose that the facts are as in (a), and that Stacpoole, testifying for the prosecution, asserts that he was acting on

Archer's behalf. Would that be a sufficient foundation to admit the statement Stacpoole made at Victoria Station? Yes

(d) Who decides, for purposes of determining whether the jury can use the evidence, whether agency has been proven? What burden of proof applies?[35] Judge - preponderance -end-

E. PRIVITY-BASED ADMISSIONS

Additional Reading: McCormick, ch. 25, § 260

Suppose that a statement was made by the predecessor in interest of a party, such as the assignor of a claim or the decedent in a tort suit brought by his estate. Should that statement, which would be an admission if offered against the predecessor, be admissible against the successor, now the actual party? This is the problem of "privity-based" admissions.

The party opponent is not the same person as the declarant and cannot necessarily put the declarant on the stand; of course, that is true with respect to agency admissions as well. And at least the successor in interest will ordinarily be no less able than the proponent to produce the declarant. To the extent that admissions doctrine is based on the idea that evidence that originated on one side of the dispute but that aids the other tends to have significant probative value, the rationale does apply to privity-based admissions.[36] And of course a doctrine of privity-based admissions can only apply in a civil case; a criminal defendant does not succeed to criminal liability from anyone else.

Note that the Federal Rules do not make a provision for privity-based admissions—even though they were rather well established at common law. This is a rare instance of a case in which the FRE tightened up on the law. Or did they? *Huff v. White Motor Corp.*, 609 F.2d 286, 290–91 (7th Cir.1979), refused to read FRE 801(d)(2) as allowing privity-based admissions. Under a rather expansive reading of the residual exceptions, however, the court held that the statement in that case should have been admitted. *Id.* at 295.

¶ 14.47: *Huff* was a wrongful death action in which Mrs. Huff claimed that her husband was fatally injured because the faulty design of the fuel system of a White truck-tractor caused a fire. Mr. Huff's statement, made several days after the accident,

---

[35] Archer, by the way, was made a member of the House of Lords in 1992; in 2001 he was convicted of perjury on charges arising out of the Coughlan scandal.

[36] If a doctrine of privity-based admissions is not applied, it opens a loophole to evade admissions doctrine—but not one that we would expect to be used frequently. Conceivably, where a claim is very large but the claimant made a highly significant admission that would be admissible against him if he pursued the claim yet not admissible against a successor in interest, the claimant might find it worthwhile to assign the claim to someone else.

was that just before the collision his pants leg had caught fire. Before holding that Rule 801(d)(2) does not make a provision for privity-based admissions, the court rejected an argument that there was no privity between the Huffs. Some states have survivorship statutes, in which the estate of the decedent sues for the damages that the decedent would have been entitled to had he lived. In Indiana, by contrast, the action is not derivative; Mrs. Huff's claim was for the injury *she* suffered by reason of her husband's death. Thus, she argued that there was no privity between her and her husband. The court rejected this argument, saying that it represents "a hypertechnical concept of privity." *Id.* at 290. Do you agree?

CHAPTER 15

THE HEARSAY EXCEPTIONS

■ ■ ■

We are now going to take a quick canvass of some of the most important hearsay exceptions. We have already touched on some of these.

Wigmore stated that the criteria for exceptions to the hearsay rule are necessity and trustworthiness. As we work through the exceptions, consider how they measure up against these criteria. Do the exceptions carve out categories of particularly trustworthy statements? Is there more of a need for them than for most hearsay statements? And consider whether the criteria make sense. Should we demand that hearsay be trustworthy before admitting it? Isn't there always a need for good evidence?

A. SPONTANEOUS STATEMENTS

Additional Reading: McCormick, ch. 26, §§ 268–272.1; Mueller & Kirkpatrick, §§ 8.35–.36

We have already examined the hearsay exceptions for present sense impressions and excited utterances, which are stated in Fed. R. Evid. 803(1) and (2), respectively. *See supra* ¶¶ 9.18, .19.

> ¶ 15.1: In thinking about hearsay exceptions that appear similar to one another, it is useful to think of a type of statement to which on exception would apply but not the second, and of a type to which the second would apply but not the first. Can you do this with these two exceptions?

As these exceptions first emerged, the required spontaneity made them unlikely to reach testimonial statements, at least in ordinary course. But courts gradually gave them more expansive constructions. Before *Crawford*, it became common practice to use these exceptions to admit statements made to authorities by the victim of a crime, even if the victim did not testify in court. Such cases took on the ironic name of "evidence-based prosecutions"—ironic because they were characterized by the major piece of evidence, the live testimony of the prosecution, that was *not* presented. Given the holdings in *Davis v. Washington* and *Michigan v. Bryant*, it is still possible to use these exceptions to secure admissibility against an accused of a spontaneous statement, if the court is willing to deem the statement to have been made primarily to resolve an ongoing emergency.

B. STATEMENTS OF CURRENT PERSONAL CONDITION

Additional Reading: McCormick, ch. 26, §§ 273–276; Mueller & Kirkpatrick, §§ 8.37–.41

Now read FRE 803(3), the exception for statements of then-existing mental or physical condition of the declarant. Note that this is in a sense a subset of FRE 803(1)—it covers present sense impressions about the declarant herself. Recall that this exception is virtually a necessary consequence of the doctrine that statements offered to prove the speaker's state of mind are not hearsay: It would make little sense if Tom's statement "Brenda is a witch" is not hearsay to prove that Tom did not like Brenda, but by tacking on "I think" at the beginning of the statement, so that it is literally offered to prove the truth of what it asserts, Tom transforms the statement into inadmissible hearsay.

¶ **15.2:** (a) Is this exception justified on any other basis?

(b) Why do you suppose the exception generally does not include "a statement of memory or belief to prove the fact remembered or believed"? Hint: There is an exception to this exception-to-the-exception, for statements relating to the declarant's will, and it pretty much does away with the hearsay rule in such cases.

(c) Trowell, a trucker, banged into Pernick. Pernick is suing Trowell's employer, Drovers. Drovers contends that it is not liable because Trowell was on a "frolic and detour" when the accident occurred. The day after the accident, Trowell made a statement to his brother saying that he was just trying to make his delivery and he had chosen Route 9, where the accident occurred, even though he knew it would be 15 miles longer than Route 20, because he thought it would be quicker at that time of day. Trowell died shortly afterwards. The jurisdiction follows most of the Federal Rules, but not Rule 801(d)(2)(D). Is the statement admissible under Rule 803(3)? *See Garford Trucking Corporation v. Mann,* 163 F.2d 71 (1st Cir. 1947).

The Rule specifically indicates that among the states of mind that it includes is intent or plan. Consider *Mutual Life Ins. Co. v. Hillmon,* 145 U.S. 285 (1892). Sallie Hillmon sued on life insurance policies on her husband. The insurance companies contended that the body offered by Sallie was not Hillmon but one Walters, and that Hillmon had murdered Walters so that he could produce a body to achieve insurance fraud. The companies presented a letter by Walters to his fiancée in which he expressed the intention of leaving Kansas "with a certain Mr. Hillmon, a sheep trader, for Colorado, or parts unknown to me." The Court, in an opinion by Justice Gray (who had consulted with the notable Evidence scholar James Ripley Thayer), said that the letter would be admissible, notwithstanding the hearsay rule, "as evidence that, shortly before the time when other evidence tended to show that he went away, [Walters] had the intention of going, and of going with Hillmon, which made it more probable both that he did go and that he went with Hillmon than if there had been no proof of such intention."

In drafting the Federal Rules, the Advisory Committee said it intended to leave the result of *Hillmon* undisturbed; the House Judiciary Committee said it disapproved of the result so far as it applied to the conduct of a person other than the speaker. In coming to grips with this issue, consider the following problems.

¶ **15.3:** (a) If Walters said he intended to go by himself, should it be admissible to show that he acted in accordance with his intention? What hearsay dangers does it raise? What other possibilities are there as to how Walters could have come to make the statement and yet not acted in accordance with his intention? Is a statement like that of Walters testimonial?

(b) Can a person's statement of her intent to do something be probative as to the later conduct of another person? In what circumstances? Consider what, if anything, these statements should be admissible to prove:

(1) Don Quixote says, "I'm going to La Mancha, with my saddle bags, my horse, and Sancho Panza."

(2) Sancho Panza says, "I'm going to La Mancha, with my saddle bags, my horse, and Don Quixote."

(3) Benjamin Braddock says to his parents, "I'm going to marry Elaine Robinson."

(c) Dalton is accused of soliciting bribes while serving as commissioner of public works of a large city. The prosecution offers the testimony of Barbara Barton that her father, Jack, a building contractor, told her over lunch one day, "Dalton says I've got to make a large 'campaign donation' if I want a chance to get the contract for the city hall renovation. So I guess I will pay to play." Is the statement admissible, and if so, for what purpose or purposes? *Cf. United States v. Annunziato*, 293 F.2d 373, 378 (2d Cir. 1961) ("True, inclusion of a past event motivating the plan adds the hazards of defective perception and memory to that of prevarication; but this does not demand exclusion or even excision, at least when, as here, the event is recent, is within the personal knowledge of the declarant and is so integrally included in the declaration of design as to make it unlikely in the last degree that the latter would be true and the former false.").

C. STATEMENTS FOR PURPOSES OF MEDICAL DIAGNOSIS OR TREATMENT

Additional Reading: McCormick, ch. 27; Mueller & Kirkpatrick, § 8.42

Read FRE 803(4). In a sense this was an offshoot of the exception for statements of bodily condition. As the exception developed over the course of the 20th century, and as it was expressed in the Federal Rules, it applies to statements of past condition, and statements of causation, as well as to statements of present symptoms. Note also that it applies to statements "made for purposes of medical diagnosis or treatment." Thus, by its terms, it covers a statement made to a doctor hired for the purpose of giving a diagnosis for use in litigation. Some courts, though, have adopted an intermediate position—that it applies to a statement made for purposes of diagnosis as long as the diagnosis is sought for eventual medical use.

¶ 15.4: Suppose a 4-year-old girl makes a statement to a pediatrician to the effect that her step-father had attempted to rape her, and had ejaculated near her vagina. Does this statement satisfy this exception? Should the pediatrician's testimony that the girl had made the statement be admitted?

D. PRIOR RECORDED RECOLLECTION

Additional Reading: McCormick, ch. 28; Mueller & Kirkpatrick, § 8.43.

Read FRE 803(5). Note that this exception might perhaps better be placed within FRE 801(d)(1)—because it requires the maker (or adopter) of the statement to be a witness at trial, and thus subject to at least some cross-examination. Why does the Rule allow the memorandum to be read into evidence but does not allow it to be offered as an exhibit by the proponent? The ambivalent attitude is reminiscent of this exchange:

"Why are you sitting there in your underpants?"

"No one's going to come visit me."

"Then why are you wearing a good shirt?"

"Someone might come."

The halfway approach might also suggest that the rulemakers recognized—in a way that the Court did not in *United States v. Owens,*

484 U.S. 554 (1988), ¶ 10.4—that cross-examination is impaired when the witness does not recall the events described in his prior statement.

Recall the difference, already referred to in Chapter 6, between this hearsay exception and the rule allowing a party to refresh a witness's recollection. A refresher (or its text) does not itself become evidence at the instance of the proponent; the evidence is the refreshed recollection. By contrast, when this hearsay exception is invoked, the text of the memorandum is the evidence. Some courts require counsel to attempt to refresh recollection before using this exception.

E. REGULARLY KEPT RECORDS AND PUBLIC REPORTS

Additional Reading: McCormick, chs. 29–30; Mueller & Kirkpatrick, §§ 8.44–.54

Read FRE 803(6)–(9). A record kept as part of a routine and not in anticipation of litigation is the quintessence of a non-testimonial statement that is very valuable to the truth-determination process. And in most settings, if a record is routinely prepared, then it is *not* made in anticipation of litigation. But among the routinely prepared records that are *offered in litigation*, a significant portion of those that are introduced in litigation are prepared *in contemplation of that (or other) litigation*. *Melendez-Diaz* deals with certificates of laboratory analysis and holds that they are testimonial for purposes of the Confrontation Clause. Arguably, *Melendez-Diaz* stands for a broad proposition that reports that are made routinely *as part of the prosecutorial process* may not be admitted against a criminal defendant, absent the live testimony of the author. So, just as *Davis v. Washington* cuts back on a prosecutor's ability to use the exception for spontaneous declarations, *Melendez-Diaz* does the same with respect to the exception for regularly kept records; to what extent that remains so after *Williams v. Illinois* remains to be seen.

The hearsay exception for routinely kept records applies no matter how many people within the organization take a hand in the creation of the record. If the organization sets up its affairs so that *A* reports to *B*, *B* to *C*, *C* to *D*, and then *D* finally makes a record, so be it. The logic still is that the record is one produced by the organization as a routine matter, based on firsthand observations by persons reporting in the performance of their duties; the facts that there is a chain of such observations, and that what some of the observers in that chain are reporting is what they have been told by others, do not defeat the exception.

But now consider the widely recognized doctrine identified with the case of *Johnson v. Lutz*, 253 N.Y. 124, 170 N.E. 517 (1930). That was a civil action arising out of an auto accident. The court ruled inadmissible a policeman's accident report because it relied on information provided by a bystander. The bystander was not a member of the police organization, and so was under no duty to report. Accordingly, the court held the exception inadmissible. If the bystander's statement had fit within a hearsay exception of its own, then the report would have been admissible by linking the exceptions together.

The Advisory Committee's draft of FRE 803(6) rather clearly endorsed *Johnson v. Lutz*; it spoke of a document made "by, or from information transmitted by, a person with knowledge, *all* in the course of a regularly conducted activity." And the Advisory Committee itself, in its Note on the Rule, explicitly endorsed *Johnson*: "The rule follows this lead in requiring an informant with knowledge acting in the course of the regularly conducted activity." During the legislative consideration of the Rules, this Rule was altered, without comment by either House, in a way that seems on its face not to incorporate *Johnson*; as it stood until 2011, the Rule provided that the document must have been made "by, or from information transmitted by, a person with knowledge, *if kept* in the course of a regularly conducted business activity." But the courts have not worried about this change, and have continued to apply *Johnson* as if the text of the Rule clearly called for that result.[1] Presumably the 2011 stylistic revision will have no impact on application of the Rule.

Sometimes, though, the courts have wriggled around *Johnson*. That may be especially true when it is clear that the record was made without anticipation of litigation in which the organization would be a party. (In *Johnson* itself, the record was clearly made in anticipation of litigation, but the police officer was acting essentially as a neutral scribe.) *United States v. McIntyre*, 997 F.2d 687, 699–701 (10th Cir.1993), *cert denied*, 510 U.S. 1063 (1994), is typical. The prosecution was trying to prove a conspirator's presence at a motel, and so offered the motel's log, which was filled in by a motel employee based on information provided by the guest. The court said that even though this document depended on information provided by one not under a business compulsion to provide it, the business records exception could still be applicable if the business entity had "adequate verification or other assurance of accuracy of the information provided by the outside person";[2] a policy of the organization to verify the information, as by checking identification, would suffice,[3] as would a strong self-interest in the accuracy of the log on the part of the business entity. In this case, the court was not satisfied that the log did

---

[1] *E.g.*, United States v. Emenogha, 1 F.3d 473, 483–84 (7th Cir., 1993), *cert denied*, 510 U.S. 1080 (1994); *cf.* 5 John Henry Wigmore, *Evidence*, § 1561a, at 490, § 1561b, at 507 (Chadbourn rev. 1974) (criticizing the *Johnson* doctrine).

[2] Apparently the prosecution failed to make the argument that the statement of identification by the conspirator should come within the exemption for conspirators' statements.

[3] Thus, the court held admissible records from another motel that, according to the testimony of its office manager, enforced a policy of verifying the identity of guests by examining driver's licenses.

have adequate guarantees of trustworthiness—but the defendant had not objected below, and the court refused to rule that admission of the log was plain error. Conviction affirmed.

¶ **15.5:** Blue Car v. Yellow Car. The defendant (driver of the yellow car) offers a report of the accident filed in the station house by Officer Jones the day of the accident. Officer Jones was not present at the time of the accident, but arrived ten minutes afterward and recorded what she was told there. Determine whether each of the following extracts from the report is admissible.

(a) "A woman said that she had seen everything and that the blue car ran the light."

(b) "The driver of the yellow car told me that the driver of the blue car ran the light."

(c) "The driver of the blue car said that the sun was in his eyes." [Other evidence will show that in fact the sun had set shortly before the accident.]

(d) "The driver of the blue car said that he had been hurrying to get across town."

(e) "The driver of the yellow car told me that she had a bad headache since the accident."

(f) "Officer Smith told me that she had seen everything and that the blue car ran the light."

(g) "Officer Smith told me that she heard the crash and arrived within thirty seconds afterward, and that the driver of the yellow car said that the other car had run the light."

(h) "Officer Smith told me that she heard the crash and arrived within thirty seconds afterward, and that a woman there said that she had seen everything and that the blue car had run the light."

Before 2000, Rule 803(6) required a witness to lay the foundation for a statement to fit within this exception. To save time, money, and trouble, the rulemakers added a provision that the foundation for the exception—and also the requirement of authenticating the document—can be satisfied by a certificate of a custodian or other qualified person.

¶ **15.6:** Should a prosecutor be allowed to take advantage of this provision?

¶ **15.7:** Jakobetz, a truck driver for Wildcat Construction Co., is on trial for kidnapping. The prosecution offers an expense report submitted by Jakobetz to his employer, including a receipt, bearing a time-stamp of 3:28 a.m., June 14, for the Throgs Neck Bridge. The kidnap victim was released at about 3 a.m. on June 14, about a thirty minute drive from the bridge. The Government offers as an authenticating witness the custodian of Wildcat's records, but no one with firsthand knowledge of the bridge's record system. Is the receipt hearsay? Is it admissible, and if so on what theory?[4]

¶ **15.8:** The Advisory Committee has proposed a new subsection (13) to Rule 902. The proposal would prescribe for self-authentication of records meeting the following description:

> **Certified Records Generated by an Electronic Process or System.** A record generated by an electronic processor system that produces an accurate result, as shown by a certification a qualified person that complies with the certification requirements of Rule 902(11) or Rule 902(12). The proponent must meet the notice requirements of Rule 902(11).

Should this proposal be adopted?

Now consider the rather broad exception for public records and reports offered by FRE 803(8). Statements falling within one of the three categories set out in subdivision (A) come within the exception unless, pursuant to subdivision (B), the opponent shows a lack of trustworthiness. Subparagraphs (A)(i) and (ii) apply to records describing what the agency has done and observed, respectively; (i) refers to "the office's activities," and (ii), with qualification, to "a matter observed while under a legal duty to report." Subparagraph (iii), again with qualifications, applies to "factual findings from a legally authorized investigation."

¶ **15.9:** In what sense is subparagraph (i) broader than subparagraph (ii)? In what sense narrower?

Note that subparagraph (ii) is limited in the criminal context; the Rule expressly does not cover "in a criminal case, a matter observed by law-enforcement personnel." The basic reason for this exclusion is easy enough to understand; absent some such exclusion, the prosecution could prove its case by introducing a police report or equivalent document. From the perspective of the *Crawford* era, we can say that such reports are testimonial in nature because they are made in contemplation of prosecution, and admitting them would presumably violate the Confrontation Clause. It is somewhat mysterious why no such exclusion is present in subparagraph (i)—perhaps one should be read into that

---

4   *See* United States v. Jakobetz, 955 F.2d 786, 800–01 (2d Cir.), *cert. denied*, 506 U.S. 834 (1992) (holding the evidence admissible, because it was integrated into the employer's business).

Rule—and why the exclusion in subparagraph (ii) is different from the one in subparagraph (iii), which does not bar a criminal defendant's use of a report. (Of course, in writing subparagraph (ii), the drafters were no doubt focused on the most common case, in which it is the prosecution that seeks to offer a police report, but occasionally such a report will favor a defendant.)

One recurrent question under subparagraph (ii) is who, besides police officers, should be regarded as "law-enforcement personnel"; for example, does a pathologist on the staff of the medical examiner's office qualify? When it is the prosecution offering the statement, though, the Confrontation Clause should often make moot the question of how the hearsay provision should be construed.

Another recurrent issue is whether, or the extent to which, a prosecutor may offer records that are prepared by a law enforcement officer and that purport to record matters objectively observed by the officer as part of some routine *before* a crime has been committed. For example, officers might record the license plates of all cars passing a given checkpoint, without contemplation that this recording will be significant in prosecuting the driver of any given car. Rule 803(8)(A)(ii) seems to offer the prosecutor no assistance. But if the matter is truly routine—and some courts are generous to the prosecution in concluding that—the court may be willing, in essence, to take part of the rationale behind Rule 803(6)—the extra reliability suggested by the routine nature of the records—and used it to soften the exclusion in Rule 803(8)(A)(ii).

The third part of Rule 803(8)(A), subparagraph (iii), has the broadest potential reach in civil actions. Plainly, this Rule was meant to apply to at least some matters that (ii) does not; thus, it applies to factual findings made by the agency even though no member of the agency or its staff actually observed the facts. This is a powerful rule. Once again, it is obvious enough why this provision does not apply in favor of the prosecution in a criminal case. Perhaps the more serious question is why a governmental investigative report should be admitted even in a civil case.

Consider *Beech Aircraft Corp. v. Rainey*, 488 U.S. 153 (1988), another aspect of which we considered in Chapter 7, Section C. Lt. Comm. Barbara Ann Rainey and her flight student were killed when their naval training aircraft crashed during exercises. The surviving spouses brought an action against the companies that made and serviced the plane. At trial, the only seriously disputed issue was whether pilot error or equipment malfunction caused the crash. The defense presented an investigative report prepared by Lt. Comm. William Morgan on order of the training squadron's commanding officer and pursuant to authority granted in the Manual of the Judge Advocate General. This "JAG Report" was divided into sections labeled "finding of fact," "opinions," and "recommendations." The "opinions" section included the statement that, because of the deaths of the two pilots and the nearly total destruction of the aircraft, "it is almost impossible to determine exactly what happened to Navy 3E955 from the time it left the runway on its last touch and go until it impacted the ground." Nevertheless, the report offered a "possible scenario," concluding that pilot error was "[t]he most probable cause of the accident."

Were these conclusions "factual findings" within the meaning of the Rule? The Supreme Court, unanimous on this point, held in the affirmative, asserting that the phrase "includes conclusions or opinions that flow from a factual investigation." *Id.* at 164. The Court emphasized the "provision for escape" now found in subdivision (8)(B), taking the report out of the exception if it appears to be untrustworthy.

¶ **15.10:** Bear in mind that *Beech Aircraft* is a nonconstitutional decision that has no binding authority outside the federal courts. How should a state court operating under a rule similar to FRE 803(8)(A)(iii) rule in a similar case? How about a court operating in the absence of a codification?

¶ **15.11:** Suppose you are sitting as a federal trial judge in a case just like *Beech Aircraft*. What information will you want to know to determine whether the report should be excluded under the "lack of trustworthiness" clause of FRE 803(8)(B)?[5]

F. DECLARATIONS AGAINST INTEREST

Additional Reading: McCormick, ch. 33; Mueller & Kirkpatrick, §§ 8.72–.76

The exceptions discussed so far in this canvass apply even if the declarant could testify in court—and for that matter even if the declarant is testifying. Indeed, FRE 803(5) *requires* the declarant to testify. But remember that there are several exceptions, listed in FRE 804, that apply only if the declarant is unavailable. We have already fully discussed the exceptions for former testimony, dying declarations, and forfeiture, expressed in FRE 804(b)(1), (2), and (6), respectively. The exception for statements of personal or family history, expressed in FRE 804(b)(4), is not particularly controversial or illuminating. (Note, though, that ordinarily statements fitting within that exception are not testimonial.)

---

5 *See, e.g.,* In re Air Disaster at Lockerbie, Scot. on Dec. 21, 1988, 37 F.3d 804 (2d Cir.1994), *cert. denied,* 513 U.S. 1126 (1995); In re Paducah Towing Co., Inc., 692 F.2d 412 (6th Cir.1982); Fraley v. Rockwell Int'l Corp., 470 F.Supp. 1264 (S.D.Ohio 1979); Note, *The Trustworthiness of Government Evaluative Reports Under Federal Rule of Evidence 803(8)(C),* 96 Harv. L. Rev. 492 (1982).

That leaves the exception for declarations against interest, expressed in FRE 804(b)(3).

Read that Rule. If one accepts the premise that hearsay exceptions are meant to select out statements likely to be reliable, this exception certainly makes a good deal of sense. The idea is that in some settings one can say that the declarant's interests would be so adversely affected by making a statement (perhaps especially if the statement were untrue) that it is difficult to understand why the declarant would make the statement unless it were true. Traditionally, the exception was limited to statements against pecuniary or proprietary interest. Why? Probably specifically to exclude statements against penal interest—which are very likely testimonial in nature. But as part of the general loosening of hearsay rules in the 20th century, this Rule was drafted to include statements that expose the declarant to civil or criminal liability. Indeed, as drafted by the Advisory Committee, the Rule would apply to statements adverse to any type of interest at all, including "statements tending to expose declarant to hatred, ridicule, or disgrace." Adv. Comm. Note. But Congress limited the reach of the Rule to designated types of interest.

Now consider what may be called the audience problem. Suppose a declarant makes two statements acknowledging participation in a criminal activity and including in her narration another person, the defendant in the case ultimately charged. One of the statements is made to a close confidante, and the other to the police. Which one can more clearly be characterized as against the declarant's interest, in the sense that one would not expect her to make the confession unless it were true? You might think that the one to the police would be, because it is likely to lead to punishment. And yet the Advisory Committee cautioned that a statement made in this setting might be too untrustworthy, because it might be an attempt to "curry favor" with the authorities, while a statement to an acquaintance might "have no difficulty in qualifying." Is this backwards? The "curry favor" concern may be forceful in some cases, though when the declarant confesses to playing an important role in a serious crime it seems usually not to have great force. The real problem with confessions made to the authorities, as should be obvious after *Crawford*, is that they are clearly testimonial. It has been established since *Tong's Case* in 1662 that a confession by Defendant 1 cannot be admitted against Defendant 2 if Defendant 1 does not testify in the presence of Defendant 2. But the laxness of hearsay law, and the virtual submergence of confrontation law before *Crawford*, occluded this fact.

An indication of the difficulties created by failure to recognize the confrontation issue that these statements raise is *Williamson v. United States*, 512 U.S. 594 (1994). Harris made a statement to the police acknowledging possession of cocaine and attributing ownership to

Williamson. He refused to testify at trial. After *Crawford*, it would be obvious that the Confrontation Clause prevents the statement from being introduced against Williamson (at least unless Williamson forfeited the right), but acting before *Crawford* the Supreme Court resolved the case without even mentioning the Clause. The acknowledgment of possession was clearly against Harris's interest, but the attribution to Williamson— the key aspect so far as the prosecution of Williamson was concerned— was not. Thus arose the question of severability—to what extent should the exception be applied to assertions that are not in themselves against interest, because they are associated with assertions that are? The Court, contrary to the great weight of precedent interpreting the exception, adopted a narrow interpretation, under which the exception applies to a "single declaration or remark." This decision has the unfortunate result of narrowing the exception in cases where no confrontation issues are involved; in many cases, even though the assertion at issue is not against the declarant's interest, the fact that it is associated with assertions that clearly are against interest makes it unlikely that the declarant would tell the truth about the against-interest matters and yet lie about the subject matter of the assertion at issue. The Court's rule also is difficult to apply: Taking the Court seriously, "We owned the cocaine [understood to refer to Williamson as well as the speaker]" would be within the exception, and presumably "Williamson and I owned the cocaine" would be as well; "I was an owner of the cocaine; so was Williamson" would not be. *Williamson* may be an unfortunate leftover from the pre-*Crawford* era, an example of hearsay law being tightened to do the work that confrontation doctrine ought to.

¶ **15.12:** Assume that the following is true, as in the *Williamson* case: Harris was stopped while driving on the highway, purportedly because he was weaving. He consented to a search of his trunk, which revealed 19 kilograms of cocaine. Harris was then arrested. He made a series of statements, the upshot of which was that he was transporting the cocaine to Atlanta for Williamson. Harris said that Williamson had been traveling ahead of Harris in another rental car and turned around after Harris was stopped and observed the search of the trunk. Harris, who said he was afraid of Williamson, refused to sign a written version of his statement, and at Williamson's trial he refused to testify, even though he was given use immunity and held in contempt. Now assume that, unlike the actual *Williamson* case, the trial is in state court. How much, if any, of Harris's statements should be admissible against Williamson? *See Williamson, supra*; Emily F. Duck, Note, *The Williamson Standard for the Exception to the Rule Against Hearsay for Statements Against Penal Interest*, 85 J. Crim. L. & Criminology 1084 (1995).

Rule 804(b)(3)(B) presents another oddity. Until 2010, the last sentence of Rule 804(b)(3) provided: "A statement tending to expose the declarant to criminal liability and offered to exculpate the accused is not admissible unless corroborating circumstances clearly indicate the trustworthiness of the statement." This provision may seem anomalous in that it imposes a requirement on pro-defense evidence that is not imposed on pro-prosecution evidence. The provision is based on the fear that it is too easy for Accused to come up with a Witness who will testify, "Absent Declarant said he did it, not Accused." But even if that is so, and even if the jury cannot be trusted to see through the ploy, it is somewhat mystifying why the Rule demands corroboration of the trustworthiness of the *statement* by Declarant, rather than of the testimony by Witness. A 2010 amendment expanded this provision, now subdivision (B) of Rule 804(b)(3), by making it applicable to statements that tend to inculpate the accused as well as to those that tend to exculpate him. That is, the amendment requires corroboration of a statement that is offered under this exception by either party in a criminal case and that tends to expose the declarant to criminal liability. This change eliminates the perceived inequity of the provision, but it leaves in place, and indeed expands, the curious feature of requiring corroboration of the out-of-court statement because of doubts about the veracity of the in-court witness.

G. THE RESIDUAL EXCEPTION

Additional Reading: McCormick, ch. 34; Mueller & Kirkpatrick, §§ 8.81.

Glance over FRE 803(11) through (23). There are a whole lot of hearsay exceptions we haven't even discussed. Some of them can be significant at times. Any time you see such a long list of narrow rules, especially a list of exceptions, you should suspect that the doctrine is not doing a very good job of explaining its underlying rationale. You also should expect that perhaps the list should not be closed; perhaps it is just illustrative, and other cases will provide occasions for similar treatment.

Indeed, the initial drafts of the Federal Rules did not provide a closed list of exceptions to the rule against hearsay but rather general standards under which the hearsay rule should not result in the inadmissibility of evidence. In the Reporter's first draft, Rule 8–03(a) provided:

> Evidence is not admissible under the hearsay rule if, regardless of whether the declarant is unavailable as a witness, the nature of the statement and the special circumstances under which it was made offer assurances of accuracy not likely to be enhanced by calling the declarant as a witness.

And the Reporter's first draft of Rule 8–04(a) provided:

> Hearsay is not inadmissible under the hearsay rule if the declarant is unavailable as a witness and the special circumstances under which it was made offer assurances of reasonable accuracy.

Each of these draft rules was accompanied by a section (b), which gave a list of illustrations introduced by the following language:

> By way of illustration and not by way of limitation, the following exemplify the application of this rule:

Richard D. Friedman & Joshua A. Deahl, *Federal Rules of Evidence: Text and History* 345–46, 411 (2015).

¶ 15.13: Was this a sound approach? Were the different standards articulated in Draft Rule 8–03 (applying regardless of the declarant's unavailability) and Draft Rule 8–04 (applying only in case of the declarant's unavailability) sensible ones? Why or why not?

After receiving public commentary in response to its Preliminary Draft, however, the Advisory Committee retreated somewhat. It adopted the current structure of Rules 803 and 804—Rule 803 provides a closed list of exceptions applying whether or not the declarant is available,[6] and Rule 804 provides a shorter list applicable only if the declarant is unavailable. But the Committee recognized that these lists could not set forth a complete set of circumstances in which the hearsay rule should not bar the admissibility of hearsay. And so they added a catch-all, or residual, exception to Rule 803 and an identical one to Rule 804; they thought they needed two exceptions because, though the wording of each was identical, each of them referred to the list of exceptions in its respective Rule as a point of reference. Ultimately, in 1997, the rulemakers decided to move the residual exceptions out of Rules 803 and 804 and to combine them in a new Rule 807. Their stated rationale—"to facilitate additions to Rules 803 and 804"—is a little scary.

The Rule is articulated in a rather curious fashion; one may well wonder whether the Reporter's first draft came closer to setting out useful standards. First, subdivision (a)(1) requires "equivalent circumstantial guarantees of trustworthiness" to the exceptions in Rules 803 and 804. What does that mean? It would be hard to say that those exceptions provide a uniform level of guarantee of trustworthiness. So should the court attempt to determine an overall grand mean level of guarantees of trustworthiness? Or determine whether the offered statement has at least

---

[6] Recall, though, that Rule 803(5), the exception for recorded recollections, requires that a person who made or adopted the statement actually be a witness.

as strong guarantees of trustworthiness as the least trustworthy statement that fits within one of those exceptions? Probably most courts apply a pretty simple standard: Is the statement sufficiently trustworthy to warrant admission?

The Rule then states three additional criteria. Those in subdivisions (2) and (4) add little or nothing—if the statement weren't of a material fact, or if admitting it were contrary to the general purposes of the Rules or the interests of justice, the court presumably would not be considering admitting it.

Subdivision (3) requires that the statement be "more probative on the point for which it is offered than any other evidence that the proponent can obtain through reasonable efforts." This clause reflects the idea that necessity is, along with trustworthiness, one of the hallmarks of hearsay that should be admissible.

This clause is a plain invocation of the best-evidence principle. The principal issue to which it refers is the availability of the declarant. If the declarant is readily available but the proponent has not produced her, the court might say that evidence more probative than the hearsay—the live testimony of the declarant—can be produced through reasonable efforts. In this situation, if the court were applying the exception rigorously, there would not usually be much room for its operation. Even if the proponent responds, "But judge, this happened a long time ago, and her statement reflects clearer memory than her live testimony would," a plausible response would be, "Well, bring her in, and then we can have her live testimony *and* if need be the prior statement." Indeed, if the proponent produces the declarant as a live witness but the prior statement still has significant probative value, perhaps because her memory is no longer clear, that is a factor that courts have found to weigh significantly in favor of admitting the prior statement.[7] On the other hand, producing a witness is not cost-free, and unavailability is a matter of degree; thus, a court might find in a given case that if the statement appears to be accurate, or if the declarant's memory of the facts is likely to be stale, or both, that any incremental benefit form requiring production of the declarant is not worthwhile.

If the declarant is unavailable, that too weighs in favor of admissibility; as in the case of the declarant whom the proponent produces but who does not have a good memory, it appears—at least on the surface—that the proponent has done the most that could be expected of him.

---

[7] *E.g.,* United States v. Iaconetti, 406 F.Supp. 554, 559 (E.D.N.Y.1976) (Weinstein, J.), *aff'd,* 540 F.2d 574 (2d Cir.), *cert. denied,* 429 U.S. 1041 (1977); State v. Edward Charles L., 183 W.Va. 641, 398 S.E.2d 123, 138 (1990).

¶ **15.14:** (a) Ellsworth testified before a grand jury as to McHan's role in a mob hit of Vernor. Ellsworth was gravely ill at the time and died soon after. At McHan's trial on murder charges, he objects to admission of the grand jury testimony. He points out that the Government knew Ellsworth was unlikely to survive until trial, and that, knowing it was contemplating a prosecution of McHan, could have taken Ellsworth's deposition. What result? *Cf. United States v. McHan*, 101 F.3d 1027, 1037 (4th Cir.1996), *cert. denied*, 520 U.S. 1281 (1997); *compare R. v. Forbes*, Holt 599, 171 E.R. 354 (1814), presented in ¶ 11.6.

(b) Now suppose that McHan is acquitted but Vernor's widow brings a wrongful death action against him. She seeks offers Ellsworth's grand jury testimony. Should it be admitted?

If the proponent has either produced the declarant or the declarant is unavailable, this "more probative . . . than any other evidence" clause will not usually have much effect. It certainly would not make any sense to exclude the hearsay because the proponent already has (or is going to) produce evidence from a source other than this declarant that is more probative on the proposition at issue. Unless that other evidence puts the proposition beyond genuine dispute, there is still a need for other probative evidence. And if the proponent is *not* offering a given piece of other evidence, usually the court will not second-guess the decision and say, "Use that other evidence instead of the hearsay."

Note that the concept of unavailability implicit in Rule 807, depending entirely on an assessment of "reasonable efforts," is more flexible than that in Rule 804(a). Thus, if the court is persuaded that a child declarant could easily be put on the witness stand but that she could not be induced to testify usefully, at least without causing undue trauma, it might well decide that her prior statement is "more probative on the point for which it is offered than any other evidence which the proponent can procure through reasonable efforts." Whether introduction of the prior statement should be deemed to satisfy the defendant's confrontation right is of course another matter.

Finally, Rule 807(b) requires pretrial notice of intent to use the statement. The rationale appears to be that, while the party opponent may expect to have to face an offer of hearsay coming within one of the specific exemptions, the opponent is more likely to be surprised by hearsay admitted under the residual exception, which is more flexible and (supposedly) less frequently used, and so (supposedly) less predictable. This rationale may be rather dubious; many statements offered under the residual exception are crucial to the case, and the opponent is not surprised by the offer. The real reason for the notice requirement may be that an articulated, codified residual exception is a device of the modern age, and in the modern age, with liberal discovery in civil cases and in some criminal ones as well, we have come to appreciate the advantages of pretrial notice of adverse evidence. Notice provisions have been included in other provisions of the Federal Rules, including Rule 412(c) (introduction of evidence excepted from the rape shield rule), Rules 413–15 (allowing evidence of sexual misconduct in some circumstances), Rule 609(b) (impeachment of conviction by old crimes), and the 2000 amendment to Rule 902 (authentication by certification of regularly kept records).

In any event, courts have sometimes been lenient with respect to the notice requirement. Sometimes they have held that the proponent was not negligent in giving late notice; for instance, the issue that made the hearsay material may have arisen during the trial itself. Also, if the opponent is not prejudiced by the delay in notice—if, for example, he has enough time to discover whatever material information he would likely have learned about the declarant even given more time—the lateness may be excused. Similarly, it may be excused if a continuance of the trial appears practical and likely to avoid whatever prejudice the late notice has created. And if the opponent fails to object contemporaneously, not only to the offer of the evidence but to the lateness of notice, he may find that he is foreclosed from raising the notice issue on appeal.

Taking all this into account, you should also be aware that occasionally courts *do* refuse to admit evidence under the residual exception because the proponent did not give adequate notice.[8] The conscientious lawyer will make sure that, if there is a plausible possibility that she will be relying on the residual exception for the admissibility of a statement, she gives her adversary adequate notice of her intent to offer the statement.

H. REFLECTIONS ON REFORMATION OF HEARSAY LAW

Crawford separated confrontation law out from hearsay law. Now that the rule against hearsay need not be relied upon to do the work that the Confrontation Clause should do, the big questions over the long run are what role remains for the law of hearsay and what shape that law might take.

Let's begin with non-testimonial statements. Admitting them does not threaten the procedures by which witnesses testify. But will it hurt the truth-determining process? For all the talk of the defects of hearsay evidence, it appears for the most part that, if live testimony by a declarant to a proposition would be more probative than prejudicial, then

---

[8]   *See, e.g.,* State v. Carrigan, 589 S.E.2d 134 (N.C. Ct. Apps. 2003).

hearsay evidence of the declarant's assertion of that proposition probably is as well; there is no persuasive evidence that juries systematically over-value hearsay; in fact, they may tend to *under*-value it.[9] If that is true, then perhaps non-testimonial hearsay ought to be presumptively admissible. And arguably this presumption should not be overcome unless the proponent is substantially better than the opponent to perform one or more of the functions necessary to produce the declarant as a live witness—identifying the declarant, locating her, ensuring her presence in court, and inducing her to testify.[10] If the proponent is substantially better able than the opponent to perform one of these functions, the disparity might, depending on the circumstances, be mitigated or eliminated by advance notice and by the proponent providing appropriate information to the opponent. And balance in favor of admissibility might be enhanced significantly if the court adopts the following procedure: If the proponent gives advance notice of intent to introduce the hearsay, the court determines whether it appears to be more probative than prejudicial. Assuming the answer is affirmative, the court rules that the hearsay will be admitted unless the *opponent* timely produces the declarant, ready and able to testify. But if the opponent does so, the *proponent* must put the declarant on the witness stand as part of his case, or forgo use of the hearsay. An approach based on such principles would not only be far more receptive to non-testimonial hearsay than is current law—and therefore considerably cheaper, in that it would not require the production of live witnesses as frequently—but it would also be considerably more flexible and less doctrinaire.

¶ 15.15: (a) What advantage is there to putting the burden on the *opponent* of producing the declarant, assuming he is substantially as able as the proponent to do so?

(b) What advantage is there to providing that if the opponent does produce the declarant, the *proponent* must put her on the stand as part of his case or forgo use of the hearsay?

Now consider testimonial statements made out of court. If the statement is offered against an accused, we know the basic answer: Unless the witness who made the statement testifies at trial, or she is unavailable to do so but the accused has had a prior opportunity for confrontation, then, with very narrow qualifications, the confrontation right precludes use of the statement for its truth.

---

[9]   *See, e.g.*, Peter Miene, Roger C. Park & Eugene Borgida, *Juror Decision Making and the Evaluation of Hearsay Evidence*, 76 Minn. L. Rev. 683 (1992).

[10]   For elaboration of this approach, see Richard D. Friedman, *Toward a Partial Economic, Game-Theoretic Analysis of Hearsay*, 76 Minn. L. Rev. 723 (1992); Richard D. Friedman, *Improving the Procedure for Resolving Hearsay Issues*, 13 Card. L. Rev. 883 (1991).

The right applies only in favor of a criminal defendant, but what if a proponent other than a prosecutor offers a statement that is testimonial in nature and that has not been subjected to an opportunity for examination by the party opponent? For example, suppose a civil plaintiff offers an affidavit prepared by an observer of the key events who would rather not appear at trial. The confrontation principle, though not the right, still has force in such a situation; it is a general premise of our system that witnesses testify in the open, under oath, face to face with the adverse party, and subject to cross-examination. But the principle should not be as unyielding when the party opponent is not an accused. Given that civil litigation is a far more symmetrical matter than is a criminal prosecution, and given the ample opportunities for discovery in civil litigation, a court might take the attitude that a non-accused opponent, rather than the proponent, ought to bear the risk that the witness is unable to appear for reasons not attributable to the fault of either party. And in the case of an available witness, a jurisdiction might adopt a notice-based doctrine: An out-of-court testimonial statement cannot be admitted for its truth unless the proponent gives the opponent enough notice, and other necessary information, to allow the opponent to produce the witness in a timely manner—but if the opponent does so, then, as suggested above with respect to non-testimonial statements, the proponent must put the witness on the stand or forgo use of the statement.[11]

¶ **15.16:** If such a system were adopted with respect to testimonial statements offered by a party other than an accused, what changes would it likely cause in the way evidence is presented at trial? Would those be for the better?

No jurisdiction is close to adopting an approach resembling the one suggested here. But most of the common law world outside the United States has drastically curtailed the application of hearsay law outside the criminal context. And over the next few decades, judges, lawyers, rulemakers, and scholars may get used to a world in which the confrontation right—the force of which is considerably bolstered in the United States by its expression in the Bill of Rights—stands on its own footing without any need for a doctrinally complex hearsay rule. After a while, perhaps many of them will ask, "Now, just what do we need this rule for?"

---

[11] *See* Richard D. Friedman, *Jack Weinstein and the Missing Pieces of the Hearsay Puzzle*, 64 DePaul L. Rev. 449, 469–72 (2015).

PART III

OTHER EXCLUSIONARY RULES

■ ■ ■

CHAPTER 16

PRIVILEGES

■ ■ ■

Proposed (Deleted) FRE 501–506, 510–513; Unif. R. Evid. 501–505, 509–512

Additional Reading: McCormick, chs. 8–12; Mueller & Kirkpatrick, ch. 5

The term "privilege" has a range of meanings. Sometimes it is used loosely to cover exclusionary rules like the one generally barring admissibility of compromise negotiations. A narrower use of the term, covering rules preserving a right to keep certain relevant information from one's adversaries, would include the work-product doctrine and the right against self-incrimination under the Fifth Amendment to the Constitution. We will concentrate here primarily on rules fitting an even narrower concept of privilege—rules excluding evidence of, and preserving the confidentiality of, information received in the course of certain relationships, such as attorney to client, doctor to patient, cleric to penitent, and spouse to spouse.

Many of the exclusionary rules studied in this course are based, at least in part, on the perception that the evidence in question is in some sense defective, and so tends to lead to inaccurate factfinding; perhaps the evidence would bias the factfinder, or (so the standard rhetoric holds) be overvalued by the factfinder, or perhaps excluding the evidence would give the proponent an incentive to produce better evidence. Privileges are different. They often block the admissibility, and even the disclosure, of information that has great probative value and little prejudicial potential. At least in their immediate effect, they represent a sacrifice of part of the judicial system's truth-determining ability, in an attempt to serve other types of goals.

Section A of this chapter explores what those goals are, and at the same time the broadest question in the law of privileges: To what relationships ought a privilege apply? Sections B through F examine other substantive questions concerning whether a privilege is applicable. Section B considers the subject matter of the privilege—communications, with respect to most of the privileges—and Section C and D address respectively the requirement that the communication or other privileged activity must be in the course of the privileged relationship and that it be confidential. Section E explores the possibility of waiving or forfeiting a privilege and Section F discusses exceptions to privileges. Section G then considers procedural issues in the determination of privilege questions. These sections focus principally, but not exclusively, on the attorney-client privilege, the one with which you will probably have most contact. Section H closes by comparing the attorney-client privilege to the work-product doctrine.

Before we get into the meat of this chapter, it is helpful to note briefly the history of the Federal Rules of Evidence on privilege. As initially approved by the Supreme Court, the Rules included an extended Article V providing rules of privilege. But this proved to be one of the most controversial portions of the Rules and Congress deleted it. Because of the sensitive nature of privilege rules, Congress also provided that any evidentiary rule "creating, abolishing, or modifying an evidentiary privilege shall have no force or effect unless approved by Act of Congress." 28 U.S.C. § 2074(b). In place of the Advisory Committee's Article V, Congress left a very brief Rule 501. Thus, for many years the only guidance that the FRE gave in the area of privilege was that Rule's prescription that state privilege law shall be followed with respect to state law claims, and that privilege questions for federal claims shall be decided, in the absence of other governing law, "by the principles of the common law as they may be interpreted by the courts of the United States in the light of reason and experience." In 2008, on the advice of the rulemakers, Congress enacted an intricate Rule 502, which deals in detail with unintentional and inadvertent waiver of the attorney-client privilege and work-product protection, but the Federal Rules still lack a comprehensive set of provisions codifying the law of privileges. The original Advisory Committee's draft of Article V, representing an intelligent effort to articulate a body of law in this area, offers a useful text to study, as do the somewhat different corresponding portions of the Uniform Rules of Evidence, which were modeled on that draft. As this history suggests, the law of privileges can be politically controversial, and so it remains today.

A. NATURE AND PURPOSES OF A PRIVILEGE; COVERED RELATIONSHIPS

We begin with the premise, endorsed by many courts over the centuries, that a litigant is entitled to every person's evidence. (In older days, though women were competent to testify, the familiar expression was "every man's evidence"; for citations going back to parliamentary debates in 18th century England, see *Jaffee v. Redmond*, 518 U.S. 1, 9 n.8 (1996)). That a witness finds it difficult or inconvenient or embarrassing to testify does not enable her to beg off. Privileges operate in derogation of this principle. Why?

One of the purposes for creating a privilege, and the one emphasized by Wigmore, is what we will call the *instrumental* rationale, to encourage communications in certain relationships. If Alan knows that Barbara will eventually testify to anything he tells her, Alan will be very hesitant to say anything that might be harmful to him. In certain settings, we want to encourage Alan to talk freely to Barbara without fear that he will be hurting himself in litigation.

In most settings, though, it would never occur to Alan that what he said might later be the subject of litigation; even if it did, Alan might not be sufficiently aware of the law of evidence to know both that absent the privilege Barbara might testify to their conversation and that the privilege would prevent such testimony; and even if he were so aware, that knowledge might not alter his behavior. In short, most communications that are made outside the litigation context and under the protection of a privilege would be made without that protection. This point is supported by empirical studies of the patient-psychotherapist and client-attorney relationships: In most settings, the willingness of patients and clients to communicate freely depends more on their confidence in the ethics and confidentiality standards of the professional with whom they are dealing than on the existence of an evidentiary privilege. In particular settings, the instrumental rationale may have more force; absent a privilege, for example, it appears that sophisticated clients might be less willing to communicate with their lawyers in writing, and presumably they would be more likely to withhold some information altogether if litigation were in the offing or actually pending. But in general there is no good basis for thinking that absent a privilege desirable communications within the prescribed relationships would be significantly impaired.[1] Even assuming the law wants to encourage free communications in the relationship, unburdened by the specter of litigation, a privilege carries a high cost, because it keeps away from the factfinder potentially valuable information that it would otherwise have.

And yet there are other important rationales for privileges, emphasized by McCormick among others. Some relationships seem sufficiently intimate that the legal system hesitates to enforce its usual rule that a litigant is entitled to the testimony of every person who might have useful evidence to give. This *intimacy* rationale is not based on an

---

[1] For a very helpful survey and analysis of studies on the psychotherapist-patient and attorney-client privileges, see 1 Edward J. Imwinkelried, The New Wigmore: A Treatise on Evidence: Evidentiary Privileges § 5.2.2 (2d ed. 2010). Among the studies described by Prof. Imwinkelried is a notable one on the attorney-client privilege, Vincent C. Alexander, *The Corporate Client-Attorney Privilege: A Study of the Participants*, 63 St. John's L. Rev. 191 (1989). *See also* Edward J. Imwinkelried, *Questioning the Behavioral Assumption Underlying Wigmorean Absolutism in the Law of Evidence*, 65 U.Pitt. L. Rev. 145 (2004) (finding that the robustness of professions is not undermined by making privileges conditional or qualified rather than absolute).

assumption that the privilege will affect people's behavior; rather, it takes their behavior as a given, and counsels against intruding without very good cause, because of fear that the relationship would be hurt by disclosure of confidences. Closely related to this intimacy rationale, applicable in an overlapping set of contexts but with different consequences, is an *oppression* rationale, that it would be intolerable for governmental authorities to compel (or perhaps even to permit) one party to the relationship to testify against the other or otherwise impair the other's interests.[2]

¶ **16.1:** In each of the following settings, should Alan have a privilege to prevent Barbara from testifying as to his communications to her? If so, on what rationale or rationales?

(a) Barbara is a criminal lawyer and Alan is her client. Alan is on trial for murder, and he told Barbara his version of the incident. Note in connection with this question Jeremy Bentham's argument that the attorney-client privilege (i) is not necessary for the client who is in the right, because he has nothing to lose by disclosure of his communications, and (ii) obstructs justice when it is exercised by the client who is in the wrong.[3] Are you persuaded?

(b) Barbara is a real estate lawyer, and Alan is her client. In the course of making a friendly deal with Caroline that has now gone sour, Alan made some statements to Barbara about his understanding of how the deal would work out.

(c) Same as (b), except that Barbara is Alan's accountant.[4]

(d) Barbara is Alan's physician. Over the years, Alan has made many statements to Barbara about his health. Alan had a heart attack while piloting a small plane and crash landed, injuring his passenger. The passenger is now suing him, claiming that he should not have been flying because his health

---

[2]   Another rationale, stressed by Prof. Imwinkelried, is that privileges may foster autonomy with respect to fundamental life preferences. One difficulty with this rationale is that it does not clearly distinguish between relationships that frequently or usually are privileged and those that are not.

[3]   Bentham's argument is quoted at length in 8 John Henry Wigmore, *Evidence* § 2291 (McNaughton rev. 1961), which also offers a lengthy response.

[4]   Compare Couch v. United States, 409 U.S. 322, 335 (1973) (no federal privilege), *with, e.g.,* Fla. Stats. Ann. § 90.5055; Col. Rev. Stats. Ann. § 13–90–107(f)(I), Ariz. Rev. Stats. Ann. § 32–749 (creating privilege). Note 26 U.S.C. § 7525, added by Pub.L. No. 105–206 (1998), which extends a privilege for tax advice to communications between a taxpayer and a federally authorized tax practitioner to the same extent as privilege would apply under common law if the adviser were an attorney.

was too poor.[5] (If the instrumental rationale is deemed necessary to encourage patients to communicate freely with their physicians, does that run counter to the argument that the hearsay exception for statements made for medical diagnosis or treatment, FRE 803(4), is justified because people's self-interest ordinarily impels them to tell the truth to their doctors?)

(e) Barbara is a licensed clinical psychologist and is Alan's psychotherapist. Over the last six years, Alan has made numerous statements to Barbara about his relationship with his wife and children. Alan and his wife are now divorcing, and they are litigating custody of the children.[6]

(f) Same as (e), except that Barbara, while legally practicing as a psychotherapist, is not a clinical psychologist but a licensed social worker.[7]

(g) Same as (f), except that Barbara, while legally practicing as a psychotherapist, has no professional license or degree of any sort; state law does not require it.

(h) Same as (e), except that Barbara is the Dean of Students at the law school that Alan attended beginning seven years ago, and she is the school official to whom students are generally directed when they have a problem that might interfere with their studies.

(i) Barbara is a minister and Alan is a member of her congregation. As part of their ritual of penitence, Alan, who is now on trial for murder, made some statements to Barbara regarding the incident.[8]

(j) Alan contends that he was raped, and Barbara is a sexual assault counselor with whom he consulted.[9]

---

[5] See Unif. R. Evid. 503 (physician and psychotherapist-patient privilege). Note that the proposed Federal Rules on privilege did not include a physician-patient privilege; see the Advisory Committee Note to Deleted FRE 504.

[6] See, e.g., Deleted FRE 504; Unif. R. Evid. 503.

[7] Cf. Jaffee v. Redmond, supra (recognizing a psychotherapist privilege, and extending its scope to licensed social workers, as well as to psychiatrists and psychologists, in the course of psychotherapy); id., 518 U.S. at 18–36 (Scalia, J., dissenting) (objecting to creation of privilege and to extension to social workers).

[8] See Deleted FRE 506 (privilege for communications to clergymen acting in professional character as spiritual adviser); Unif. R. Evid. 505 (similar). Cf. Hughes v. Wehr, 1993 WL 176979 (Ky. App.1993) (holding over dissent that letters to diocese complaining about sexual molestation by a priest are privileged confidential communications), action dismissed as moot sub nom. Commonwealth v. Hughes, 873 S.W.2d 828 (Ky.1994).

[9] Compare, e.g., Commonwealth v. Wilson, 602 A.2d 1290, 1297 (Pa. 1992), cert. denied, 504 U.S. 977 (1992) (upholding against constitutional attack absolute privilege for sexual assault counselors' records), with People v. Stanaway, 521 N.W.2d 557, 577 (Mich. 1994) (complainant's testimony may be precluded if records of counselor contain information necessary to defense and

(k) Alan is an alcoholic who attends Alcoholics Anonymous ("AA") meetings. AA is a very effective "self-help" program for acknowledged alcoholics that depends in large part on attendance and participation at confidential meetings and on members' adherence to a twelve-step series of principles, the second of which is belief that "a Power greater than ourselves" could overcome the problem; others among the principles refer to dependence on "God, as we underst[an]d him." At an AA meeting, Alan confessed to committing a murder. Barbara is another AA member who attended the meeting.[10]

(l) Alan and Barbara are husband and wife. While they were in bed one night, Alan, who is now on trial for murder, made some statements to Barbara regarding the incident.[11]

(m) Alan and Barbara are husband and wife. One night six years ago, Alan expressed distaste for his boss. Alan is now charged with murdering his boss last year.

(n) Same as (m), except that Barbara is Alan's closest friend, and promised to treat their conversation confidentially.

(o) Same as (m), except that Barbara is Alan's daughter.

(p) Same as (m), except that Barbara is Alan's mother, and Alan was 14 when he made the statement.

(q) Alan is 24 and Barbara is his mother. A plaintiff who has sued Alan's boss for sexual harassment has sought Alan's testimony, in the belief that Alan also was engaged in a sexual relationship with the boss. Alan told details of the relationship to his mother.[12]

(r) Barbara is a journalist who has written a series of articles on municipal corruption. Alan, a city employee, was her

---

complainant does not waive statutory privilege); *see* Maureen B. Hogan, Note, *The Constitutionality of an Absolute Privilege for Rape Crisis Counseling: A Criminal Defendant's Sixth Amendment Rights Versus a Rape Victim's Right to Confidential Therapeutic Counseling,* 30 B.C. L. Rev. 411 (1989).

[10] *See* Cox v. Miller, 296 F.3d 89 (2d Cir. 2002) (overruling habeas corpus decision that communication was privileged).

[11] *See, e.g.,* Deleted FRE 505 (spousal privileges); Unif. R. Evid. 504 (similar).

[12] *See* Mueller & Kirkpatrick § 5.33 (noting that [as Monica Lewinsky's mother learned] few common-law decisions recognize a parent-child privilege, which is common in Continental European systems). A few states have privileges of varying types that apply to the relationship between a parent and minor child. *See* Idaho Code § 9–203(7) (providing in general that parent may not be required to disclose communication made by minor child in a proceeding to which child is a party); Mass. Gen. L. Ann. ch. 233 § 20 (prohibiting unemancipated minor child living with parent from testifying in criminal proceeding against parent, except where victim is member of parent's family or lives in parent's household); Minn. State. 595.02(j) (providing in general that absent waiver neither minor child nor parent may be examined as to any communication made in confidence by the child to the parent).

chief source, but because Barbara promised him confidentiality, he is known to readers of Barbara's paper, including the local prosecutors, only as "a source in city government." City officials named in the article are now being prosecuted for corruption.[13]

(s) Barbara is a prosecutor. Alan is a member of a drug ring who has provided Barbara with information on the membership of the ring and who has participated in conversations with his confederates while wearing a wire kindly provided by Barbara. Two of the other members of the ring have been arrested and they have asked Barbara to provide them with the name of the informant who provided her with information.[14]

(t) Alan is a faculty member who was asked by Barbara, the chair of his department, to review the published works of two junior colleagues, Cathy and David, for the purpose of determining whether or not to grant them tenure. David was granted tenure, Cathy was not, and Cathy has sued, claiming sex discrimination.[15]

(u) Alan is chairman and chief executive officer of Downjohn, Inc., a pharmaceutical company. Barbara is secretary and general counsel of the company. They spoke about his concerns that some employees were making improper payoffs to foreign governmental officials.

(v) Alan is chairman of his state's Environmental Protection Agency. The agency is being sued by members of the legislature for failure to enforce an environmental statute. The plaintiffs seek discovery of conversations about the statute that Alan had with Barbara, general counsel of the agency.[16]

(w) Alan is President of the United States. He is being investigated for possible obstruction of justice in connection with a failed land deal in which he participated and in connection with a civil suit against him for sexual harassment, in which it is claimed that he encouraged a potential adverse witness to

---

[13] *Cf.* Branzburg v. Hayes, 408 U.S. 665 (1972) (declining to construe First Amendment as creating privilege); In re Farber, 78 N.J. 259, 394 A.2d 330, *cert. denied*, 439 U.S. 997 (N.J. 1978) (holding that statutory privilege violates criminal defendant's Sixth Amendment rights if, as in this case, defendant can show materiality of the reporter's information, need, and the absence of a less intrusive means of access).

[14] *See, e.g.*, Deleted FRE 510 (privilege for identity of informant); Unif. R. Evid. 509 (similar).

[15] *Cf.* University of Pennsylvania v. EEOC, 493 U.S. 182 (1990) (refusing to recognize either a privilege under the common law, through FRE 501, or a First Amendment right to withhold peer review materials prepared as part of tenure process).

[16] *See* Melanie B. Leslie, *Government Officials as Attorneys and Clients: Why Privilege the Privileged?*, 77 Indiana L.J. 469 (2002).

perjure herself. The independent counsel investigating the first charge asks Barbara, who is Deputy White House Counsel and a friend of Alan, for the substance of conversations she had with Alan about the sexual harassment matter.[17]

(x) Same as (w), except that Barbara is Alan's scheduling secretary, and the independent counsel and the plaintiff in the civil suit have asked Barbara for information concerning all communications by Alan or his private secretary as to persons with whom he was meeting during a six-month period.[18]

(y) Same as (x) except that Barbara is a Secret Service agent who was assigned to protect Alan, and the independent counsel seeks Barbara's testimony of intimate conversations of Alan's that Barbara overheard.[19]

(z) Barbara is a state supreme court justice and Alan is her clerk. The court recently decided a case involving discipline of a lawyer, and a local newspaper published a column that accused the court of playing "a little political shimmy shammy" with the case. The chief justice has sued the newspaper company and the columnist, claiming libel. In discovery, the defendants seek all written communications between Barbara and Alan that relate to the underlying case.[20]

As you might suppose, the question of which relationships should be the subject of a privilege has proved a controversial one, especially because a profession appears to gain a certain cachet, an official status symbol, if it is accorded the special treatment of a privilege. That special treatment might cause lay people to hold the profession and its members in higher regard; we may wonder whether, from the public point of view, that is good or bad.

---

[17] *See* In re: Bruce R. Lindsey (Grand Jury Testimony), 158 F.3d 1263 (D.C. Cir.), *cert. denied sub nom.* Office of the President v. Office of the Independent Counsel, 525 U.S. 996 (1998).

[18] *Cf.* United States v. Nixon, 418 U.S. 683 (1974).

[19] *In re* Sealed Case 148 F.3d 1073 (D.C. Cir.), *cert. denied sub nom.* Rubin v. United States, 525 U.S. 990 (1998) (over dissents by Ginsburg and Breyer, JJ.).

[20] *See* Thomas v. Page, 837 N.E.2d 483 (Ill. App. 2005) (adopting "a judicial deliberation privilege protecting confidential communications between judges and between judges and the court's staff made in the course of the performance of their judicial duties and relating to official court business"; extending privilege to conversations between judges, between judges and clerks (whether or not the clerk works for the particular judge), and between clerks; holding privilege absolute); U.S. Navy-Marine Corps. Court of Military Review v. Calucci, 26 M.J. 328 (U.S. Ct. Mil. Apps. 1988) (asserting that privilege is qualified and "sometimes must yield to other considerations" but upholding application in the instant case); Kevin C. Milne, Note, *The Doctrine of Judicial Privilege: The Historical and Constitutional Basis Supporting a Privilege for the Federal Judiciary*, 44 Wash. & Lee L. Rev. 213 (1987); Archibald Cox, *Executive Privilege*, 122 U. Pa. L. Rev. 1383, 1406 (1974).

Now, there are two different basic types of privileges. The most common type, and the one on which we will be focusing primarily, is what might be called a *privilege against disclosure*. If (a) the relationship in question is one covered by a privilege; (b) the evidence in question is within the basic scope of the privilege as outlined in Sections B through D—loosely speaking, a confidential communication (or, more broadly in some circumstances, a confidential information transmittal) in the course of the relationship; (c) the privilege has not been waived or forfeited, as described in Section E; and (d) no exception, as described in Section F, is applicable, then the evidence is privileged. The basic consequence, according to standard doctrine, is that the holder of the privilege has a comprehensive right of nondisclosure. That is, the privilege-holder, whether or not a party to the action, has a right to refuse to disclose the substance of the communication, even in response to an otherwise valid discovery request or question at trial, and to prevent disclosure by any other person (typically the other party to the privileged conversation) of the communication or of information learned in the communication.[21] And this right of nondisclosure applies no matter how valuable may be the information that it cloaks.[22]

Note that this rigid protection is better suited to the extent that a privilege is based on the instrumental rationale. To achieve its purpose, such a privilege must be simply stated and easily predictable, because otherwise people will not be able to rely on it in guiding their behavior. The intimacy rationale, on the other hand, does not purport to be based on hopes of affecting people's behavior. Thus, it can abide a more after-the-fact type of rule, in which a court decides on the basis of all the circumstances whether the intrusion on the relationship is worth the sacrifice of probative evidence in the particular case. Nevertheless, even for the patient-physician privilege, which, at least in many settings, seems much more clearly based on the intimacy rationale than on the instrumental rationale, courts that apply the privilege do not usually indulge explicitly in such case-by-case balancing.[23] But they achieve much the same results by using broad exceptions and concepts of waiver.

---

[21] Even when the trial judge is deciding a preliminary question on which admissibility of other evidence depends, the privilege applies: FRE 104(a) says that in making its determination the court "is not bound by evidence rules, except those on privilege." If the court is deciding whether a given piece of evidence is itself privileged, then there may be an endless loop problem—should it deem the evidence privileged for purposes of determining whether it is privileged? As we will see in Section G, courts sometimes cut through the problem by conducting *in camera* review.

[22] *But see, e.g.*, Priest v. Hennessy, 51 N.Y.2d 62, 68, 431 N.Y.S.2d 51, 514, 409 N.E.2d 983, 986 (1980) ("even where the technical requirements of the privilege are satisfied, it may, nonetheless, yield in a proper case, where strong policy requires disclosure").

[23] Some do, however. *See, e.g.,* In re Grand Jury Subpoena, 839 A.2d 837 (N.H. 2004) (suggesting circumstances in which medical privilege can be overridden).

In the limited situations in which it applies, the oppression rationale justifies another type of privilege, a *privilege against testimony*. This kind of privilege gives one party to the relationship a right not to testify against the other, or it may give one party a right to preclude testimony by the other against him.

B. THE SUBJECT MATTER OF THE PRIVILEGE

That Alan's relationship to Barbara is the type covered by a privilege does not mean that all testimony by Barbara against Alan, or about their relationship, is privileged. To the extent that the privilege is guided by the instrumental rationale—attempting to encourage communication between Alan and Barbara—it is only such communication that should be protected. And even to the extent that the privilege is determined by considerations of intimacy, not all testimony that Barbara might give would be considered an undue intrusion. If Barbara is Alan's lawyer, for example, it would not intrude unduly on the relationship to reveal that Alan was wearing a red jacket when they went to a ballgame together. Nor has the legal system concluded that the client-attorney relationship is such that it would be unduly oppressive to require Barbara to testify about such a matter.

Thus, the attorney-client privilege is generally applicable only to communications—most traditionally those from client to attorney, but also those running the other way. (This extension may be justified as necessary to prevent revelation of the client's statements, but also because the lawyer would often be inhibited in giving advice if she could then be forced to testify about it.) It does not prevent Barbara from testifying about the red jacket. Nor would Barbara ordinarily be prevented from testifying about the fact that Alan retained her, or about the general purpose of the retainer.

It is crucial to emphasize that only the communication is privileged. This means that neither client nor lawyer can be required to testify about the substance of the communication—in any proceeding or at any stage. Nor can either be required to testify about what he or she learned as a result of the communication. But the underlying information communicated is not privileged. Suppose that Alan gives Barbara a document while saying, "This is a copy of a letter I wrote to Cynthia," and that the document later becomes material to a suit by Cynthia against Alan. Alan cannot be required to testify to the conversation. Nor, absent a waiver of the privilege by Alan, can Barbara testify about the conversation, or about what she learned in the conversation. But Cynthia's counsel can secure copies of the document in discovery from either Alan or Barbara, can introduce the document (or a proper copy) into evidence, and can ask Alan, "Is this a letter you wrote Cynthia?" In other words, a client cannot "cleanse" information by passing it on to the lawyer.[24] The privilege does not prevent disclosure of information that would be discoverable if the communication were never made.

¶ 16.2: Instead of giving Barbara the memo, Alan told her about it. In response to a proper discovery request,

(a) should Alan answer questions about the memo?

(b) should Barbara?

(c) should Alan produce the memo?

Usually it is only the substance of the communication between client and attorney that is protected by the privilege; the fact that there was a communication is generally not protected. But in some cases that fact itself must be protected to serve the purposes of the privilege. Furthermore, from the very act of communicating with the client the attorney may learn significant information about the client even though the client does not attempt to communicate that information to the attorney. Sometimes that is the type of information that anybody who communicated with the client might learn, but in other cases it is information that a person in the position of acting as attorney is much more likely to have learned.

¶ 16.3: Baird is an experienced tax attorney, well known within the tax bar. He was approached by accountants and an attorney for a group of taxpayers who had an unpaid tax bill. These taxpayers wanted to pay the taxes, with interest, but not reveal their identities to the IRS, for fear of prosecution. Baird was told nothing about the identities of these taxpayers, except that they were a group of able and responsible businessmen engaged in a legitimate business. After consultation, the other attorney delivered to Baird a cashier's check for a sum of nearly $13,000, representing the amount that the accountants had determined to be the unpaid tax bill plus interest to a date shortly in the future. Baird passed this letter on to the IRS, explaining in a letter that he did not know who the taxpayers were. Should the IRS be able to compel Baird to reveal the names of the accountants and the other attorney?[25]

¶ 16.4: Dikes is on trial for kidnapping. The prosecutor offers a ransom note left by the kidnapper and asks Atkins, who was Dikes' attorney in connection with a previous felony charge

---

[24] *See, e.g.,* In re Six Grand Jury Witnesses, 979 F.2d 939, 945 (2d Cr.1992) (although communication is protected by the privilege, the "underlying information" is not, even though it was "developed in anticipation of litigation" and at the direction of counsel), *cert. denied,* 509 U.S. 905 (1993).

[25] *See Baird v. Koerner,* 279 F.2d 623 (9th Cir.1960) (holding in the negative), *discussed in* McCormick § 90 and Mueller & Kirkpatrick § 5.19.

that was eventually dropped before trial, to identify the handwriting. Can Atkins be required to do so if she is familiar with Dikes' handwriting from having read confidential notes written to her by Dikes in connection with that representation? What if the previous charge was forgery, and Atkins became familiar with Dikes' handwriting because Dikes provided her with specimens?

¶ **16.5:** Henderson brings a habeas corpus proceeding, in which a key issue is whether he knowingly waived objections to seized evidence. His trial lawyer submits an affidavit stating that Henderson was "alert and attentive.... [H]e understood and comprehended [my] explanations in regard to the seized evidence." Is submission of this affidavit to the court a violation of privilege?[26]

The attorney-client privilege is a protection only against disclosure. Now consider the spousal privilege. There are actually two separate doctrines at play here. One is a privilege against *spousal testimony*. This doctrine is very unlike most of the others we are studying in this chapter—though it may resemble a parent-child privilege to the extent that jurisdictions adopt one. At common law, and persisting into the modern era, the rule was that if one spouse was a party to litigation, the non-party spouse—as well as the party spouse—was incompetent to testify, for or against the party spouse. For obvious reasons, an exception was drawn for cases in which the party spouse was charged with a crime against the non-party spouse. This doctrine of incompetence eventually wore away, but many jurisdictions retained a narrower rule in which a criminal defendant could bar the other spouse from testifying *against* him, again excepting narrow categories of cases depending largely on the identity of the victim of the crime. *See, e.g.,* Deleted FRE 505. Many jurisdictions and courts, including the United States Supreme Court, have narrowed the doctrine further yet, so that the defendant spouse cannot keep the other spouse off the stand, but the other spouse can decline to testify. *See Trammel v. United States*, 445 U.S. 40 (1980).[27] This doctrine is based on the oppression rationale, the idea that it intrudes unduly into a marriage if the government requires one spouse to testify, involuntarily, against another in a criminal case. Thus, the right lasts only as long as the marriage. Even though the narrower form of the doctrine only gives the non-party spouse a right not to testify, and does not prevent her from testifying, many jurisdictions still draw exceptions

---

[26] *Compare Henderson v. Heinze*, 349 F.2d 67, 70 (9th Cir.1965) (holding in the negative), *with Gunther v. United States*, 230 F.2d 222, 223–24 (D.C.Cir.1956) (holding in the affirmative).

[27] The Washington statute, by contrast, provides that one spouse cannot be examined for or against the other without the consent of the party spouse. RCW 5.60.060.

depending on the identity of the victim of the crime. We will discuss these in Section F.

The second doctrine is the privilege against disclosure of *marital communications. See, e.g.*, Unif. R. Evid. 504(a). This privilege fits the mold of most of the others that we are discussing in this chapter: It protects against disclosure of confidential communications made during the course of a particular relationship, in this case a marriage. The privilege lasts, with respect to communications already made, even if the marriage does not. The privilege applies to any litigation, civil or criminal, and whether or not either spouse is a party. It is usually limited by exceptions akin to those for the spousal testimony privilege, and discussed in Section F.

We have seen that the reach of the attorney-client privilege extends to some information that the attorney learns in the course of communication with the client, even if it is not information that the client affirmatively attempted to communicate. A similar phenomenon is observable in the case of the marital communications privilege. Indeed, some courts have slid in the direction of according privilege to all information that the testifying spouse would not have learned absent the marital relationship. Perhaps this is taking the privilege too far; the McCormick text, § 79, advocates limiting the privilege rather strictly to communications. An intermediate position is possible. If a wife learns information about her husband that she would not have learned but for the fact that she was married to him, and thus often in his company, yet others were in a position to learn the same information, there is no powerful reason to uphold the privilege. On the other hand, if she has learned information only by virtue of the confidential nature of the relationship, there is a much stronger argument for the privilege, even if the information was not actually communicated by the husband.[28] Bear in mind that the most persuasive argument in favor of the marital communications privilege is not that it encourages marital communications but that it prevents undue intrusions.

> ¶ 16.6: Can Menefee, standing trial for robbery, claim privilege to prevent his wife from testifying that (1) he left home before the time of the robbery, came home some time after, and placed a pistol on the mantelpiece, and (2) she drove with him a few times after the robbery to the vicinity where the stolen property (a safe) was hidden?[29]

---

[28] *Cf.* Commonwealth v. Byrd, 689 S.W.2d 618, 620 (Ky.App.1985) (distinguishing between acts done in private, as to which the spousal privilege may attach, and those that "may have been known or seen by any person," which are not privileged).

[29] *See Menefee v. Commonwealth*, 189 Va. 900, 55 S.E.2d 9 (1949) (upholding claim of privilege).

¶ **16.7:** Mrs. Pierce learned about her husband's birthdate by looking at the family Bible. Is this an appropriate subject of privilege?[30]

The physician-patient privilege also is often articulated in terms of communications and yet extended to other information learned by the physician in the course of the relationship. A physician often observes information about the patient that the patient does not actually communicate; we would be hard pressed to call a patient's pulse rate a communication. But to the extent—if any—that the instrumental rationale makes sense for this privilege, it may be as necessary to encourage people to expose themselves (often literally) to the doctor's observation as to encourage them to communicate to the doctor. More significantly—because the intimacy rationale provides stronger support for this privilege—a patient may have as great an intimacy interest in the physician's observations as in what the patient said to the physician.

¶ **16.8:** Blair has brought a suit against her Blue Cross carrier, claiming that it was wrongful in refusing to pay her medical expenses for treatment of psoriasis. She serves on Blue Cross an interrogatory asking for the names, addresses, and telephone numbers of all other subscribers who had recently filed claims for psoriasis treatment. Blue Cross contends that the claim forms are necessary for medical treatment and therefore privileged. What result?[31]

→ C. THE COURSE OF THE RELATIONSHIP

Suppose you are golfing with your tax attorney and you say, "Let me tell you about the armed robbery I attempted last week. No, don't start running your meter. I didn't get anything of value, so there's no tax implications. Just a good story I thought you'd find amusing. Hey, nice putt." This would not be privileged. Although it is a conversation between client and attorney, it is not a part of that relationship; the attorney is not acting as attorney.

¶ **16.9:** A potential client comes to you to discuss a personal injury case he thinks he might have. You offer a free consultation. After a few minutes, you decide that it is not worth your while to represent him, especially because you do not think

---

[30] *See Prudential Insurance Co. v. Pierce's Administratrix*, 270 Ky. 26, 109 S.W.2d 616, 617 (1937) (holding in the affirmative; privilege extends to "all knowledge obtained by reason of the marriage relation and which would not have been known but for the confidences growing out of the relation").

[31] *See* Blue Cross of Northern California v. Superior Court, 61 Cl.App.3d 798, 132 Cal.Rptr. 635 (1976) (upholding claim of privilege).

he has much chance of success. Accordingly, he never retains you. Was your conversation privileged? *—consultation ... seems like expectation of privilege—*

If a statement fell within the attorney-client privilege when made, then the privilege will persist even after the end of the relationship—and even if the relationship ends only with death. *instrumental rationale*

¶ **16.10:** Foster was a lawyer whose boss was being investigated for possible improprieties related to activities with which Foster was connected. When federal prosecutors began investigating the matter, Foster consulted with a lawyer, Hamilton. Hamilton took notes. Nine days later, Foster committed suicide. The prosecutors sought Hamilton's notes. Hamilton claimed privilege. Should the claim be (a) rejected without further inquiry because of Foster's death, (b) upheld without further inquiry, or (c) determined on the basis of a balance of the need for the information against Foster's presumed interest in maintaining posthumous confidentiality? *See Swidler & Berlin v. United States,* 524 U.S. 399 (1998). *privilege extends beyond death*

Now consider the important case of *Upjohn Co. v. United States,* 449 U.S. 383 (1981), which you may have studied in Civil Procedure. There, Upjohn management discovered that a subsidiary may have made improper payments to foreign governmental officials. The Chairman sent a letter to "all foreign and general area managers," enclosing a detailed questionnaire that the employees were to send to Gerard Thomas, whom the Chairman identified as "the company's General Counsel" (and who was also Vice President and Secretary of the company). The Chairman cautioned the employees to treat the investigation as "highly confidential" and not to discuss it with anyone other than Upjohn employees who might be helpful in providing the requested information. As part of an investigation of the tax consequences of the payments, the IRS sought production of the questionnaire answers. In determining whether those answers should be regarded as privileged, the Supreme Court seems to have assumed that Thomas was acting as a lawyer.

¶ **16.11:** Is this assumption valid? Try to construct an argument that Thomas was not acting as a lawyer.[32] If he is *—not giving legal advice— wrong? He company and doing an internal investigation*

---

[32] *Cf.* In re Witness before The Grand Jury, 631 F.Supp. 32 (E.D.Wis.1985), which cautioned:

> [W]here the attorney acts as a business advisor or collection agent, gives investment advice, or handles financial transactions for his client, the communications between him and his client are not protected by the privilege. . . . Although preparation of tax returns by itself may require some knowledge of the law, it is primarily an accounting service. Communications relating to that service should therefore not be privileged, even though performed by a lawyer.

Id. at 33 (citations and internal quotation marks deleted). *See also* SR Internat'l Business Insurance Co. Ltd. v. World Trade Center Properties LLC, 2002 WL 1455346 (S.D.N.Y. 2002) ("No privilege attaches to an attorney's communications when the attorney is hired to give

deemed to have been acting as a lawyer, does that open the door to abusive claims of privilege? *[handwritten note]*

Now, let's assume that Thomas was acting as a lawyer, and let's assume also—because it is no longer commonly contested—that a corporation or other entity (including a governmental entity[33]) can have a privileged relationship with a lawyer. But that does not settle the case. Were the employees who responded to the questionnaire acting as clients? The court of appeals in the *Upjohn* case adopted a form of the widely used "control group" test. The idea behind that test is that only those who would play a role in deciding what action to take in response to legal advice should be part of the privileged circle; in some forms of this test, it includes not only top management but those who advise management and on whose opinions management relies. *See, e.g., Consolidation Coal Co. v. Bucyrus-Erie Co.,* 89 Ill.2d 103, 59 Ill.Dec. 666, 432 N.E.2d 250 (1982). While disclaiming any intent to select a standard of its own, the Supreme Court in *Upjohn* rejected the "control group" test as inadequate. It noted that even lower level employees may have information that is important to the corporation in securing legal advice; if a trucker driving for General Motors gets into an accident it is he, and not the CEO, who has the information the corporation needs to defend itself. The Court took the view that the privilege was necessary to protect the flow of information from such employees to the attorney. Though *Upjohn* has proved controversial, its approach appears to have gained the upper hand; if the "control group" test is not yet totally dead, it appears to be dying.[34]

¶ 16.12: One criticism sometimes made of *Upjohn* is that "a lower level corporate employee sufficiently sophisticated to factor an evidentiary privilege into his decision to communicate with a corporate attorney is unlikely to be assured by a privilege which is waivable in the exclusive discretion of the corporation. At a minimum, the privilege should apply only to corporate employees who either have, or are expressly conferred, the power to assert

---

business or personal advice, or to do the work of a nonlawyer"; holding that information gathering, though supervised by in-house counsel, was in course of business rather than in anticipation of litigation); In re Grand Jury Subpoenas Dated March 9, 2001, 179 F.Supp.2d 270 (S.D.N.Y. 2001)(holding, in a grand jury investigation into President Clinton's last-minute pardon of a fugitive financier, that employment of a lawyer in preparing a petition for a Presidential pardon submitted outside executive clemency guidelines amounts to lobbying rather than legal representation; the court speaks of the proceeding as being *ex parte* rather than adversarial, but this seems to confuse the analysis).

[33] *See, e.g.,* Mueller & Kirkpatrick § 5.18; *but see* Melanie B. Leslie, *Government Officials as Attorneys and Clients: Why Privilege the Privileged?,* 77 Ind. L.J. 469 (2002) (arguing that "[a]t most, government entities should be able to claim a limited litigation privilege that enables them to shield communications made in furtherance of trial preparation").

[34] The test is still good law in Illinois. *See* Does v. Township High School Dist. 211, 34 N.E.3d 652, 672–73, 393 Ill. Dec. 451, 471–72 (App. Ct. 1st Dist. 2015); Sterling Finance Management, Inc. v. UBS Paine Webber, Inc., 336 Ill. App. 442, 782 N.E.2d 895, 270 Ill. Dec. 336 (App. Ct. 1st Dist. 2002). A 1998 amendment to Tex. R. Ev. 502 discarded the test.

the privilege." McCormick § 87.1 (footnotes omitted). Do you agree?

(skip)   ¶ **16.13:** One issue left unresolved by *Upjohn* was whether the privilege should be applicable to statements made to counsel by former employees concerning activities during their period of employment. *See Upjohn*, 449 U.S. at 395 n.3. What do you think?

Upjohn involved a demand for information by an entity with no ties to the corporation. But another complication arises when it is shareholders who demand the information.

(skip)   ¶ **16.14:** A group of plaintiffs purporting to act on behalf of a class of people who bought stock in Burnco Corp. during Year 2 bring suit against Burnco, its wholly owned subsidiary Kane Corp., and Glenn Burley, CEO of both Burnco and Kane. Plaintiffs contend that during Years 1 and 2 the defendants caused Burnco to publish fraudulent information putting a falsely favorable light on Kane's financial condition, and therefore artificially inflating the price of Burnco stock. In particular, the plaintiffs focus on Burnco's annual reports in Years 1 and 2, in which Burnco presents a generally optimistic outlook for products liability litigation in which Kane is a defendant. Plaintiffs seek discovery of communications between Burley and Burnco's corporate counsel relating to the outlook for this litigation. Defendants resist on grounds of privilege. Should the claim of privilege be upheld for communications in Year 1? In Year 2? Now suppose instead this was a shareholders' derivative action against Burley, seeking to recover from him for payments made by Burnco in satisfaction of liability to a bank for fraudulent statement of Kane's financial health. Would your analysis change?[35]

Issues as to whether a communication (or, more broadly, information transmittal) is part of a privileged relationship also arise in other contexts besides attorney-client.

---

[35] *See, e.g.,* Garner v. Wolfinbarger, 430 F.2d 1093, 1103–04 (5th Cr.1970) (holding that in litigation between corporation and stockholders on charges of acting inimically to stockholder interests, stockholders should have opportunity to show good cause why privilege should not be invoked, and listing criteria that may enter into the decision) *cert. denied,* 401 U.S. 974 (1971); In re Bairnco Corp. Securities Litigation, 148 F.R.D. 91 (S.D.N.Y.1993) (reviewing decisions applying *Garner* doctrine, including split as to whether it should be limited to the context of stockholder derivative actions, and concluding that doctrine may be applied even if discovering plaintiffs were not shareholders during the time of the communications at issue); National Football League Properties, Inc. v. Superior Court, 65 Cal. App.4th 100, 75 Cal. Rptr.2d 893 (6th Dist. 1998) (rejecting *Garner*, finding no shareholder exception to privilege under California Evidence Code).

¶ **16.15:** Herman and his wife Wendy were partners in a dry goods business. One evening as they were getting undressed for bed, Wendy said to Herman, "I'm not at all happy about that last shipment we sent Pete. We were really rushed, and I think our quality control might have slipped a little." Sure enough, Pete came to the same conclusion, and has sued Herman and Wendy.

(a) Is the conversation privileged? *Yes - testimonial privilege*

(b) Would your answer to (a) be affected if, by the time of Pete's lawsuit, Herman and Wendy were divorced?[36] *Privileged e time./*
(They've given up testimonial privilege) Cano wasn't ded

¶ **16.16:** As part of a custody battle, Wilma claims that Henry is psychologically unfit. Per court order, Henry submits to an examination by a psychologist chosen by Wilma. Henry also submits to an exam by another psychologist, selected by his lawyer, who may testify in his behalf at trial. Are Henry's statements to either psychologist protected by the psychotherapist-patient privilege? If not, what argument can Henry make that his statements to the second psychologist are covered by the attorney-client privilege?[37] *+ Psych agent of attorney?*

why would it be privileged if it is done for the purpose of litigation?

relationship came in?

no showing that matter what kind of info sought for spouse

¶ **16.17:** (a) Morales and Montalvo have been convicted of murder. In support of a *habeas* petition, they offer the testimony of Towle, a Catholic priest, to the following effect:

> Jesus Fornes asked Towle to visit him at his house. There, they had a "heart to heart" talk, during which Fornes confessed that he was involved in the murder and that Morales and Montalvo had nothing to do with it. Fornes asked for advice as to what to do, and Towle suggested that Fornes confess to the authorities. Before leaving, Towle granted Fornes absolution for his sins.

Fornes never did confess to the authorities, and he has since died. May Towle testify to what Fornes told him? *See Morales v. Portuondo*, 154 F. Supp.2d 706 (S.D.N.Y. 2001) (holding in the affirmative); Jordan B. Woods, *Morales v. Portuondo: Has the Seal of the Confessional Sprung a Leak?*, 42 Cath. Lawyer 105 (2002) ("The meeting as described lacked several crucial

Yes!.

---

[36] *See* McCormick § 85; Mueller & Kirkpatrick § 5.32; Unif. R. Evid. 54(a).

[37] *See* McCormick § 99; Mueller & Kirkpatrick § 5.34; *cf.* Linde Tomson v. Resolution Trust Co., 5 F.3d 1508, 1512–15 (D.C.Cir.1993) (assuming that Missouri law would protect some of client's communications with insurer under attorney-client privilege, and acknowledging that "where the insured communicates with the insurer for the express purpose of seeking legal advice with respect to a concrete claim, or for the purpose of aiding an insurer-provided attorney in preparing a specific legal case" the privilege would apply, but holding that federal law applies to the case and the privilege does not; "if what is sought is not legal advice, but insurance, no privilege can or should exist").

elements of a sacramental confession, including contrition for the murder, satisfaction in the form of a penance, and the proper location as set out in Canon 964 [which provides that "[t]he proper place for hearing sacramental confessions is a church or oratory" and that "[e]xcept for a just reason, confessions are not to be heard elsewhere than in a confessional"].); Uniform R.Evid. 505(b).

(b) Now suppose instead that Fornes is living, that he is being tried for the murder, and the prosecution wants to introduce Towle's testimony. What result? *No - clear that he intended it in a clergy/privileged way*

D. CONFIDENTIALITY

Even if a communication is made in the course of a relationship that is the subject of a privilege, the particular communication is not privileged if it was not confidential. Neither the instrumental nor the privacy rationale is invoked if the speaker did not intend the communication to be confidential. Recall that privileges are created in derogation of the usual rule that a litigant is entitled to every person's evidence. Accordingly, privilege law creates a sort of "second most favored nation" status for the litigation system. That is, the privilege holder is entitled to keep undisclosed a communication that is confined to the privileged relationship. But the privilege holder cannot selectively extend the range of the communication. If he includes anybody else in the communication—if, for example, a client speaks to his lawyer in an elevator, clearly in the earshot of a third person—then a litigant is entitled to discover and introduce evidence of the conversation. It is important to realize that an absence of confidentiality bursts the bubble of privilege completely: Not only the stranger in the elevator but both the client and the lawyer can be compelled to testify about the conversation.[38]

Older decisions essentially created a "no fault" rule with respect to eavesdroppers: If an eavesdropper heard the conversation, it was not privileged, and tough luck on the would-be privilege holder who failed to take sufficient precautions—running water, secure lines, surreptitious meeting places, whatever—to prevent the eavesdropping from happening. Modern decisions generally impose on the parties to the privileged communication only a duty of taking reasonable precautions to ensure confidentiality. *See* McCormick § 74; Mueller & Kirkpatrick § 5.13. Note also FRE 502(b), discussed further below.

¶ **16.18:** The conversation occurred not in an elevator but in a taxicab. The glass partition between the front and back seats

---

[38] McCormick § 101 mentions and criticizes some cases that ignore this principle in the context of the physician-patient privilege.

[handwritten: Not good enough. Tatitart.]
[handwritten: probably destroy privilege]

was closed, and the passengers did not think that the cabdriver could hear—but he could. Is the privilege breached? Does it matter whether the reason the driver could hear was that he had particularly good hearing, or that, because he found it amusing to eavesdrop on his passengers, he had installed a small microphone in the back seat? *[handwritten: ok this is closer call, but still gloss!. This is not a private setting!]*

[handwritten margin: No]

¶ **16.19:** Now suppose instead that the communication was conducted by e-mail, without encryption. Because skilled hackers are able to intercept e-mail messages they have no business reading, sending such a message has been compared to sending a postcard through the mails. Is the message privileged if

[handwritten: probably bk if they do what is normally ...]

(a) it has not in fact been intercepted? *[handwritten: Yes]*

(b) it has in fact been intercepted?[39] *[handwritten: Hmmm... by what means?]*

¶ **16.20:** Now suppose that the communication was by phone, when the client was in prison. As a condition of using the telephone, the client had to sign a statement acknowledging that, for security purposes, all of his conversations on the phone would be recorded. Is the conversation privileged?[40] *[handwritten: Nope!. Get a legal call, bud!.]*

The classic model of privilege involves one person on either side of a communication. But, as the *Upjohn* problem has already suggested, the world is not that simple. Sometimes the client is a multi-person entity. Often clients, and professionals as well, need the assistance of others to conduct the communication effectively. Courts will generally allow a claim of privilege so long as the communication was confined to those reasonably necessary to effectuate the rendering of services.[41]

¶ **16.21:** A reprise of ¶ 1.1: You have a general commercial law practice. Your spouse practiced law for three years but now works for a foundation. Ted, a successful playwright and a good friend of your spouse, calls up one Saturday morning and asks to come visit you. As he sits down in your living room, he tells you and your spouse how, ten years ago, when he was hard up for cash, he agreed with his publisher, Splashy Publishing Co., to waive all his future royalties in return for an immediate cash payment. Ted now believes the deal was one-sided in favor of Splashy and seeks to renegotiate it.

---

[39] Mikah K. Story, *Twenty-First Century Pillow-Talk: The Applicability of the Marital Communications Privilege to Electronic Mail*, 58 S.C.L. Rev. 275 (2006) (reviewing cases, concluding that attorney-client privilege is not defeated by use of unencrypted e-mail, but arguing that marital communications privilege stands on a different ground).

[40] *See* United States v. Hatcher, 323 F.3d 666 (8th Cir.2003) (attorney-client privilege does not attach); United States v. Madoch, 149 F.3d 596 (7th Cir.1998) (same with respect to marital communications privilege).

[41] *See, e.g.,* McCormick § 91; Mueller & Kirkpatrick § 5.13.

(a) Do you ask your spouse to leave the room? *[handwritten: Yes - not retained as lawyer]*

(b) Would your decision be any different if your spouse were your secretary rather than an attorney? *[handwritten: Yes - he can stay]*

(c) Suppose Ted brought his secretary to the meeting. Should you ask the secretary to leave the room? *[handwritten: Uhh... this should be ok but I still feel like maybe no? — agency relationship]*

¶ 16.22: (a) Wolfle dictates to his secretary a message to his wife, in which he says, referring to some associates, "I am going to rob every last one of them blind." Wolfle is charged with doing just that, and the prosecution seeks to introduce the secretary's testimony as to this assertion by Wolfle. Wolfle objects on grounds of the spousal privilege. What result? *See Wolfle v. United States*, 291 U.S. 7 (1934) (no privilege). *[handwritten: No privy! ✓ gave up by dictating]*

(b) Would the answer be any different if instead Wolfle made the assertion orally to his wife at the family dinner table, with the only other person present being their son Oliver, if

(i) Oliver was 3 years old. *[handwritten: Yes - probably not going to understand — privilege reasonable / not taking / oops to ensure privacy]*

(ii) Oliver was 14 years old and was playing games on his phone at the time. *[handwritten: No - those assholes still hear — no privy]*

(iii) Oliver was 18 years old. *See* Martin J. McMahon, *Presence of Child at Communication Between Husband and Wife as Destroying Confidentiality of Otherwise Privileged Communication Between Them*, 39 A.L.R. 4th 480 (1985). *[handwritten: No]*

¶ 16.23: Neal is accused of robbery and homicide. After the events at issue, Neal and his wife engaged in some phone conversations, which Neal took some care to assure that nobody could overhear. In fact, his wife, fearful for her own criminal exposure, had agreed to cooperate with the police, and the conversations were being recorded. In the conversations, Neal made damaging admissions. May the recordings be <u>introduced</u> <u>against</u> him at trial? Assume they can be authenticated without testimony by the wife. *Compare <u>United States v. Neal</u>*, 532 F.Supp. 942 (D. Colo. 1982), *with <u>People v. Schultz</u>*, 1998 WL 1988666 (Mich. Ct. Apps. 1998). *[handwritten: No! He still thinks it's confidential/ privileged. NOPE! Can be waived by either party - not by participating w/ police — came out the other way / Morris case]*

¶ 16.24: (a) You and your friend Rachel are each representing individuals who have been made targets of an investigation for embezzlement. No charges have yet been brought. You and Rachel agree to meet with your clients to review the case and plan strategy. Is this conversation privileged?[42] *Yes*

(b) Now assume that both clients have been indicted. You have made a successful motion to have the trials severed. You have your strategy meeting shortly before the first trial. Is the conversation privileged? *No longer common interest, so, no?*

Even if a communication was made privately, if it was made with the intention that the substance of it would be disclosed outside the privileged circle, courts will generally hold that it was not privileged.[43]

¶ 16.25: In ¶ 16.15, in which Pete is suing Herman and Wendy for a defective dry goods shipment, suppose that Wendy's statement was, "You'd better bear down on Jack to improve the quality control. I let that shipment to Pete go out because we were in a rush, but I wasn't happy about it." Is this privileged?

Assumption that they'll talk about it so... not privileged

Confidentiality has significance beyond the question of privilege. The bar and most of the other professions covered by the privilege impose an ethical obligation to maintain confidentiality. There is no necessary congruence between the privilege and the obligation of confidentiality. For example, in its Comment 5 on Model Rule of Professional Conduct 1.6, the ABA says, "The confidentiality rule applies not merely to matters communicated in confidence by the client but also to all information relating to the representation, whatever its source." What happens if a lawyer believes she has an obligation to maintain confidentiality with respect to a matter that the court holds the privilege does not cover? In the ABA's older Model Code of Professional Responsibility, DR 4–101(C)(2) provided that the lawyer may reveal confidences when "required by law or court order." Comment 19 to the Model Rules is somewhat more hedged: "The lawyer must comply with the final orders of a court or other tribunal of competent jurisdiction requiring the lawyer to give information about the client."

¶ 16.26: Under the Model Rules, if a trial court orders the lawyer to reveal a matter as to which the lawyer believes she has an obligation to maintain confidentiality, what should she do?

Be willing to... contempt? need? comply on appeal?

---

[42] *Compare* Unif. R. Evid. 502(b)(iii) (speaking of communication by "the client or a representative of the client or the client's lawyer to a lawyer or a representative of a lawyer representing another party in a pending action and concerning a matter of common interest therein") *with* Deleted FRE 503(b)(3) (speaking of communication "by [the client] or his lawyer to a lawyer representing another in a matter of common interest").

[43] *See* McCormick § 80 (discussing context of marital communications: "The fact that the communication relates to business transactions may show that it was not intended as confidential. . . . Usually such statements relate to facts which are intended later to become publicly known."); Mueller & Kirkpatrick § 5.13 (discussing context of attorney-client privilege).

Note that in some settings a professional has a legal obligation of *non*-confidentiality—that is, of disclosure. This arises if the professional receives information indicating that the client may be a serious danger of violence to himself or to others. The classic case, which you may have studied in torts, is *Tarasoff v. Regents of the University of California*, 17 Cal.3d 425, 551 P.2d 334, 131 Cal. Rptr. 14 (1976). And sometimes the matter is addressed by legislation. *See, e.g.,* Mass. G.L.A. 119 § 51A (requiring a report by anybody who, in a long list of professional capacities, including some that are part of privileged relationships, has reason to believe that a child is suffering substantial injury from abuse). The duty to warn has been kept separate from the privilege. That is, a psychiatrist must make whatever disclosures are necessary to fulfill the duty to warn, but having done so she is not authorized to testify against her patient in subsequent legal proceedings. *See United States v. Hayes*, 227 F.3d 578 (6th Cir. 2000).

E. WAIVER AND FORFEITURE

Even if a communication is confidential and made as part of a privileged relationship, so that it is privileged when made, the privilege may be waived later. The privilege holder may waive the privilege, and in some circumstances the other party to the privilege may be authorized, either implicitly or explicitly, to waive it. Suppose, for example, a civil plaintiff meets with his attorney and gives the attorney some information about the case. The information itself is not privileged, but the attorney's receipt of it is, and she cannot be forced to tell what she has learned. But now suppose the attorney sits down with the defendant's lawyer to try to settle the case. In that conversation she might reveal some information that her client has provided her, emphasizing the strength of the case. Thus, the privilege has been waived to that extent. Perhaps her client expressly authorized her to pass that information on, but even if he did not an implicit authorization would likely be found, because the attorney performing her job in settlement negotiations must convey the strength of the case to the other side.

You must be extraordinarily careful with respect to waiver of privilege. Waiver is voluntary relinquishment of a known right. But in some circumstances, although the act that arguably constituted a waiver was clearly voluntary, the actor did not fully realize the potential consequences of the act. Indeed, in some cases the conduct causing loss of the privilege may perhaps better be characterized as forfeiture, because even if the privilege holder did not voluntarily relinquish the privilege, the law may deem his conduct to be incompatible with retention of the privilege. We will not focus further on the waiver-forfeiture distinction here.

The physician-patient privilege, in those states recognizing it, is particularly subject to waiver. Many states provide that by putting one's medical condition in issue as part of a claim or defense a person waives this privilege.[44] That is reasonable enough, given that the privilege is based principally on the desire to protect privacy concerning medical condition; a party cannot say, in effect, "I am willing to make intimate details of my medical condition the subject of litigation, in hopes of getting money—but you can't inquire into what I told my doctor about the condition or what she saw about it."

¶ **16.27:** Deanna, a young child, suffered severe problems from birth. Through her parents, she brings a malpractice action against the treating obstetrician and the hospital where she was born. The defense contends that Deanna's problems are the result of a genetic disorder. It seeks discovery of the medical records of Deanna's younger sister Kimberly, who appears to be suffering from similar problems. The girls' parents claim privilege on behalf of Kimberly. How should the court rule?[45]

¶ **16.28:** Recall the custody battle between Henry and Wilma from ¶ 16.16. In defending against Wilma's charge that he is unfit to maintain custody, Henry puts on the stand Schick, who was his psychotherapist from 2000 to 2003. Schick testifies as to privileged conversations. Should Wilma now be able to ask Gillette, who was Henry's psychotherapist from 1997 to 2000, similar questions about her conversations with Henry?

¶ **16.29:** In Neal's case, see ¶ 16.23 supra, assume that instead of a telephone conversation it was a letter from Neal to his wife that contained the damaging admissions, and that Neal's wife gave the letter to the police. Should the privilege be deemed waived or forfeited? What if Neal's wife showed the letter to her best friend and confidante? See 1 Imwinkelried, Evidentiary Privileges, § 6.6.5.

¶ **16.30:** Assume that in Upjohn the company believes that, if the matter were litigated fully, the IRS might succeed in its attempt to compel production of the questionnaire answers. It would rather not battle the matter out with the IRS, especially because it does not believe its exposure in the tax litigation is very great. Accordingly, it negotiates an agreement with the IRS under which it will furnish the documents to the IRS, but they

---

[44] Alternatively, they may speak of a patient-litigant exception to the privilege. See generally McCormick § 103–04; Mueller & Kirkpatrick § 5.34.

[45] See Dierickx v. Cottage Hospital Corp., 152 Mich.App. 162, 393 NW.2d 564 (1986) (holding privilege not waived by institution of the older sister's suit, because the right to assert the privilege is personal to the patient).

will be treated as "confidential, privileged, and proprietary materials." Shareholders now bring a derivative action against the company's management and certain of the foreign managers, and they seek the questionnaire answers in discovery. The defense responds that the documents are privileged. The plaintiffs answer that Upjohn waived the privilege by turning the documents over to the IRS. The defense argues that this was not a general disclosure, but only to one government agency, and that it was not truly voluntary, but only made under pressure. The plaintiffs respond that the defense cannot disclose selectively and that the disclosure should be deemed voluntary, if that factor even is material, because Upjohn did not have to disclose when it did and presumably it received some consideration for disclosing. What result?[46]

Waiver of privilege is particularly a concern for young litigators in commercial practice. If you do this kind of work, chances are you will spend considerable time engaged in discovery, and supervising production of documents for it. There are few worse feelings than realizing you have handed over to your adversary a document that hurts your side and that should have been withheld as privileged. Cases of inadvertent waiver of privilege arise with some regularity; there is a considerable range of degrees of inadvertence. In 2008, Congress added FRE 502, which, without defining inadvertent waiver, treats it generously: Where applicable, Rule 502(b) provides that inadvertent disclosure does not operate as a waiver of a privilege, or of work-product protection, if "the holder of the privilege or protection took reasonable steps to prevent disclosure" and "the holder promptly took reasonable steps to rectify the error...." This provision may be regarded as Congress's gift to overworked junior litigators. But it is important to recognize that this is just a federal rule, and it will not be applicable to disclosures made without any connection to a federal office, agency, or proceeding. And even when it is applicable, though the Rule gives you the ability to fight against the conclusion that the disclosure was inadvertent, it does not guarantee that you will win.

---

[46] The majority view does not allow selective waiver; as United States v. Mass. Inst. of Technology, 129 F.3d 681, 684 (1stCir.1997), put it, "where the client chooses to share communications outside [the] magic circle, the courts have usually refused to extend the privilege." Some courts, and some scholars, take a contrary view. *See* 2 Imwinkelried, Evidentiary Privileges § 6.12.4 (summarizing cases). Westinghouse Elect. Corp. v. Republic of the Philippines, 951 F.2d 1414 (3d Cir.1991), endorsed a useful distinction between two types of limited waiver. *Selective* waiver, such as is sought in this problem and in *Westinghouse*, would allow the party to disclose a communication to some entity outside the privileged circle but then claim the privilege when another entity seeks evidence of it. *Partial* waiver allows the party to disclose part of a set of communications and claim privilege with respect to another part. *See* ¶¶ 16.32–.33 *infra*.

¶ **16.31:** Your client Shirley, a hardware supplier, terminated Ralph as a retailer, and Ralph brought an antitrust suit, claiming that the termination was part of a price-fixing conspiracy. Shortly after you answered the complaint, Ralph's counsel served a document request on you. You reviewed the request with Shirley and got from her copies of all documents that she thought might be responsive to it. You then asked Leonard, a paralegal in your office, to sort through the documents, sorting out those that clearly had to be produced, those that clearly did not, and those as to which he was doubtful; you personally decided whether to produce the documents from the third pile. Leonard retains a copy of each document produced. At Shirley's deposition, you are horrified when Ralph's counsel asks her about three documents. Each was clearly privileged. Consider with respect to each one whether the privilege has been waived, and how the problem might have been averted.

(a) The first is a letter from Atkins, your predecessor as Shirley's counsel, and it says, "Terminating Ralph creates a serious antitrust risk." You have never seen this document. Red-faced, you ask Leonard how it could have been produced. Redder-faced, Leonard searches through the retained copies of the produced documents, and realizes that Atkins' letter was stapled to the back of a harmless letter, production of which was clearly required, written by Shirley to Ralph. Leonard had not noticed Atkins' letter—but evidently your super-efficient clerk, who did the photocopying and assembled the documents, did not miss it.

(b) The second document consists of photocopied notes, in Shirley's hand, of a meeting with Ralph two years before the litigation. This document was in Leonard's doubtful pile, and you personally reviewed it and decided that, although you were not happy about its contents, it had to be produced. What you did not realize, because there was nothing on the document to indicate it, was that Shirley wrote these notes to Atkins to keep him informed, and sent a photocopy to her files. Had you known this, you certainly would have claimed privilege.

(c) The third document is a copy of a letter that Shirley wrote to you. You remember seeing this document, and remember making certain to keep it out of the document production, because it was clearly privileged. Gloating, Ralph says that he found the document by searching through the garbage outside Shirley's office.[47] *Not point doing in ... .*

Often, when the privilege is waived with respect to one communication, questions arise as to whether it has been waived with respect to other communications that are closely related to the first. Subsection (a) of Rule 502 addresses this issue, and like subsection (b) it tends (when applicable) to weigh against waiver: The waiver extends to matter not disclosed only if the waiver is intentional; the disclosed and undisclosed communications "concern the same subject matter," and "they ought in fairness to be considered together."

¶ 16.32: Ralph's claim is based principally on conversations he had with Shirley in October and December. At trial, Ralph's counsel has suggested that Shirley's version of the October conversation was a recent fabrication. In response, you have introduced a letter she wrote to Atkins shortly after that conversation, giving a version consistent with her current testimony. If Ralph's counsel now demands production of another letter that Shirley wrote to Atkins giving her rendition of the December conversation, how should the court rule? [Note: How would Ralph even be aware of the other letter?] *than if he knows about it? petition.*

¶ 16.33: After Claus was acquitted of the attempted murder of his wife Martha, his lawyer, Alan, wrote a book about the case, with Claus' encouragement; Claus even helped Alan promote the book. The book revealed portions of four conversations between Claus and Alan relating to such matters as the development of new leads and Claus' ability to refute the testimony offered by Martha's children from a prior marriage. Meanwhile, Martha, through her children, sued Claus civilly for assault. The civil plaintiffs would like to make some use of Alan's book.

(a) Has Claus waived his privilege with respect to:

(i) the portions of the conversations revealed in the book? *yes ✓*

(ii) the balance of those conversations? *10k what this means*

(iii) all other conversations between Claus and Alan to the extent that they dealt with the same subject matter as the four revealed conversations? *| No*

---

[47] *Cf.* Suburban Sew 'N Sweep, Inc. v. Swiss-Bernina, Inc., 91 F.R.D. 24 (N.D.Ill.1981) (rejecting claim of privilege for papers found in trash; client could have taken surer measures, such as shredding the papers). A leading opinion presaging the more moderate test of FRE 502 is Hydraflow, Inc. v. Enidine Inc., 145 F.R.D. 626 (W.D.N.Y. 1993).

(iv) all other conversations between Claus and Alan relating to the case? *See In re von Bulow*, 828 F.2d 94 (2d Cir.1987).

(b) Would your answers to (a) change if, instead of publishing the book, Alan had testified in the civil trial, narrating portions of his conversations with Claus?

(c) Would your answers to (a) change if Claus had urged Alan not to write the book?[48]

Finally, recall from ¶ 6.16 and the discussion before it in Chapter 6, Section E, that in some circumstances courts will find that a witness waived a privilege by consulting and relying on privileged documents in preparing testimony.

F. EXCEPTIONS

Even if a communication was confidential and within a privileged relationship, it may not be privileged if it fits within an exception. It is impossible to summarize the law of exceptions briefly, because it varies greatly from one jurisdiction to another and from one privilege to another. Most of the important exceptions, though, might be put under one of two headings.

First, some exceptions make the privilege inapplicable in certain types of action. Some jurisdictions, for example, make the patient-physician privilege inapplicable altogether in criminal cases where the patient is a victim, witness, or defendant. Or, to take a far different example, if a lawyer and his client wind up in litigation against each other—including a lawsuit brought by the lawyer to collect her fee—the privilege does not exclude evidence of communications between the two. *See* Uniform R.Evid. 502(d)(3). Similarly, if two clients retain a lawyer jointly, conversations that either had with the lawyer would not be privileged in a suit by one against the other. *See* Uniform R.Evid. 502(d)(5). And on similar grounds, it makes little sense to apply a spousal privilege if the two spouses are litigating against each other. Nor does it make sense to apply the privilege if one spouse is being tried criminally for battering the other—even though the allegedly battered spouse is not technically a party to the prosecution. But it is not always so simple to determine in which cases the privilege ought to apply and in which it ought not.

---

[48] During the investigation of President Clinton, Bob Woodward published a book, *Shadow*, that purported to reveal conversations between the President and his private attorney, Robert Bennett. Had the matter ever reached litigation, it would have raised interesting questions of whether the disclosure to Woodward was an authorized waiver and, if so, what was the scope of the waiver.

¶ 16.34: Unif. R. Evid. 504(d)(3) makes the marital communications and spousal testimony privileges inapplicable in any proceeding in which

> one spouse is charged with a crime or tort against the person or property of the other, a minor child of either, an individual residing in the household of either, or a third person if the crime or tort was committed in the course of committing a crime or tort against the other spouse, a minor child of either spouse, or an individual residing in the household of either spouse.

Obviously, this provision reflects many choices; the exception can be drawn more narrowly or broadly in various respects. Does the exception go far enough? Does it go too far? In particular, was it a good choice to make the exception

(a) applicable both in criminal and civil cases? ✓

(b) applicable whether the crime or tort is against a person or against property? ✓

(c) applicable to cases of crimes or torts committed against some persons other than the other spouse? ✓

(d) applicable in a case in which the crime or tort was committed against a minor who is a child of the defendant spouse but who is not a child of the other spouse? ✓

(e) inapplicable in general if the crime or tort was committed against an adult child of either spouse? *Yeah, they're not in their care*

(f) applicable if the crime or tort was committed against a person (other than a minor child of either spouse) who was residing in the same household of the other spouse? ✓

(g) applicable if the crime or tort was committed against a person (other than a minor child of either spouse) who was residing in the same household of the defendant spouse? ✓

(h) applicable if the crime or tort against a third person in the course of committing a crime or tort against a person falling in one of the other enumerated categories? ✓

(i) inapplicable if the crime or tort was committed against someone not in any of the enumerated categories? *idk nm I don't think it makes sense in general)*

¶ 16.35: In the midst of a domestic dispute that turned violent, Wanda calls 911. The police arrive within minutes and find that Wanda has a bruise on her cheek and finger marks near her throat. Pursuant to a local ordinance, Wanda's husband

Harry is locked up for 20 hours. The police take photographs of Wanda's injuries.

Now suppose you are the county prosecutor. Wanda, an intelligent and well educated woman, has told you that she does not want charges pressed against Harry. She tells you that the couple has two children, that they are determined to restore their family life, and that if Harry, who is well known locally, were to be prosecuted it would put a terrible strain on them. You tell Wanda that you believe it is important to bring the charges, because Harry is in danger of repeating his assault, possibly with far worse consequences, and because it is necessary to send a public message that domestic violence is intolerable and is not simply a private matter. Wanda remains adamant and says she will not cooperate.

(a) Should you bring the prosecution?

(b) If you do bring the prosecution, should you attempt to compel Wanda to testify?

(c) If you ask, may the court require Wanda to testify, subject to contempt if she refuses? If so, should it? (We have considered similar problems in ¶¶ 11.7(a) and 13.13(i).)[49]

¶ 16.36: Booth is charged with having murdered Lincoln. The prosecution claims that, while making his getaway, Booth fell from some height and broke his ankle. The night of the shooting, Booth was treated by Dr. Mudd, who set Booth's ankle and also noticed some powder burns on Booth's hands. Should Booth have a privilege to bar Mudd's testimony?[50]

Second, some exceptions are addressed to the communication itself, removing the privilege no matter what the litigation context.[51] Most prominent of these is the exception to the attorney-client privilege that arises "if the services of the lawyer were sought or obtained to enable or aid anyone to commit what the client knew or reasonably should have known was a crime or fraud." Uniform R.Evid. 502(d)(1).[52] Note that this

---

[49] *See* Cheryl Hanna, *No Right to Choose: Mandated Victim Participation in Domestic Violence Prosecutions*, 109 Harv. L. Rev. 1849 (1996) (advocating use of compulsory means, where necessary, to secure victim testimony).

[50] See McCormick § 104; Mueller & Kirkpatrick § 5.34 (noting that some jurisdictions make the physician-patient privilege inapplicable in criminal cases and other designated types of cases).

[51] *See, e.g.*, Cal. Evid. Code § 1006 (making privilege inapplicable to "information that the physician or the patient is required to report to a public employee").

[52] Note that this is one area in which the law of privilege and the professional obligation of confidentiality are not congruent. Disciplinary Rule 4–101(c)(3) of the old ABA Model Code of Professional Responsibility allowed a lawyer to reveal "[t]he intention of his client to commit a crime and the information necessary to prevent the crime." Rule 1.6(b) of the ABA's more recent

exception depends on the client's intent; even if the lawyer was pure of heart and mind, the exception applies if the client's purpose in procuring services was to aid in the commission of a crime or fraud. *See, e.g., In re Sealed Case,* 162 F.3d 670 (D.C. Cir. 1998) (consultation by Monica Lewinsky with lawyer for purpose of committing perjury and obstructing justice; no suggestion of impropriety by her lawyer).

¶ **16.37:** (a) Your client Doan comes into your office and says, "Here is the gun with which I shot Jordan to death. Please dispose of it properly." Whereupon he puts a pistol on your desk and leaves your office. What should you do?[53]

(b) Assume you have successfully and ethically resolved your problem with respect to Doan's gun. But now Innes is on trial for the murder that Doan has told you he committed.

    (i)   What should you do?

    (ii)   Suppose that Innes, suspecting you might have something to offer, has called you to the stand in his trial. Does the privilege apply?

¶ **16.38:** You are defending a chemical company in a toxic tort case. During the course of your representation, you become persuaded that your client probably is committing a nuisance, contaminating ground water and increasing the risk of cancer for people who live in the vicinity. May you reveal this information? Must you in response to a proper discovery request—or on your own initiative?

Model Rules of Professional Conduct has been a frequent source of contention in the ABA, and it has been amended twice to address this issue. As it originally stood, that Rule allowed disclosure only if the lawyer believed a criminal act by the client would likely cause "imminent" death. Subsections (1) to (3) of the Rule now allow disclosure if the lawyer reasonably believes it necessary

    (1) to prevent reasonably certain death or substantial bodily harm;

    (2) to prevent the client from committing a crime or fraud that is reasonably certain to result in substantial injury to the financial interests or property of another and in furtherance of which the client has used or is using the lawyer's services;

    (3) to prevent, mitigate, or rectify substantial injury to the financial interests or property of another that is reasonably certain to result or that has resulted from the client's commission of a crime or fraud in furtherance of which the client has used the lawyer's services.

Rule 16(b)(1)–(3) is not as broad as the "crime-fraud" exception to the privilege. Accordingly, a lawyer could have a presumptive obligation under these rules to keep confidential information that a court deems non-privileged. But recall from Section D that a valid and final court order trumps the obligation of confidentiality, at least after all appeals have been exhausted.

[53] *Cf.* Clark v. State, 159 Tex.Crim. 187, 261 S.W.2d 339, 347 (holding advice to get rid of murder weapon "admissible as not within the realm of legitimate professional counsel and employment") *cert. denied,* 346 U.S. 855 (1953).

G. PROCEDURAL ISSUES

Often a court cannot easily decide whether a given communication was privileged without knowing the substance of the communication. But revealing the communication, even in camera to the court, abrogates the privilege in part, by intruding on the confidential relationship.

The Supreme Court confronted this difficulty in *United States v. Zolin*, 491 U.S. 554 (1989). The IRS, as part of an investigation of the tax returns of L. Ron Hubbard, sought the production of tapes containing confidential attorney-client conversations. The Church of Scientology, which Hubbard had founded, and his widow, Mary Hubbard, resisted production and asserted attorney-client privilege. (A former member of the Church, Gerald Armstrong, had gotten possession of the tapes, illegally according to the Church; the Church sued Armstrong in state court, and the tapes were in the possession of the state court's clerk when the IRS issued its subpoena.) The IRS contended that the communications were in furtherance of future illegal conduct.

So now how should the trial court proceed? An obvious possibility is that the court should examine the tapes *in camera*, outside the presence of the requesting party.[54] Recall that FRE 104(a) provides that preliminary determinations concerning "the existence of a privilege" are made by the court, and that in doing so the court "is not bound by the rules of evidence except those with respect to privileges." Thus, if the court wants to consider the document in question to determine whether or not it is privileged, the opponent argues, "Under Rule 104(a), you can't consider it. It's privileged."

¶ **16.39:** So does this Rule create an endless loop, precluding *in camera* inspection? Put another way, should a document as to which a claim of privilege has been made be deemed privileged for purposes of this Rule? What if, as in *Zolin*, it appears clear that the materials sought contain confidential attorney-client communications, made in the course of the relationship, and there has been no waiver, the only substantial question being whether the privilege fits within an exception? *SeeZolin, id.* at 565–70 (holding that *in camera* inspection is not absolutely precluded by the Rule).[55]

---

[54] An additional precaution in some cases is to have the litigation of privilege issues be conducted, for the adversary of the party claiming privilege, by an attorney who is "walled off"from the rest of the office representing the party. *See, e.g.,* United States v. Stewart, 2002 WL 1300059 (SD.N.Y. 2002).

[55] The *Zolin* Court distinguished FRE 104(a) from California Evidence Code 915(a), which provides presumptively that a court "may not require disclosure of information claimed to be privileged . . . in order to rule on the claim of privilege." This presumptive rule, which California courts previously found very confining, has been substantially weakened by an amendment that applies to hearings in responses to search warrants seeking documents held by lawyers, among

Now let's assume that *in camera* review is permissible in some circumstances. The discovering party seeks production of a communication, the opposing party resists on the grounds of privilege, and the discovering party answers that it does not believe the document is privileged—perhaps because the communication never fell within the basic scope of the privilege, perhaps on the ground that the privilege was waived or, as in *Zolin*, the communication fell within an exception. The discovering party says production should be ordered, without need for *in camera* review. The opponent, by contrast, argues that in the circumstances the claim of privilege should be upheld without even a need for *in camera* review. So what threshold showing, if any, must be made, and by whom, before the court decides to conduct *in camera* review? The *Zolin* Court said that before conducting *in camera* review to determine the applicability of the crime-fraud exception, the trial judge should first require a factual basis adequate to support a good-faith belief by a reasonable person that such review may reveal evidence to establish the applicability of the exception. If that showing is made, the court should exercise its discretion as to whether to conduct *in camera* review, assessing such matters as the importance of the allegedly privileged information to the case, the volume of material for which review is sought, and the likelihood that the exception will be established without need to look at the allegedly privileged material. *See Zolin* at 570–72.

¶ **16.40:** (a) Do you think this is an appropriate standard? In deciding whether to conduct *in camera* review, the court obviously must consider the presentation made by the party challenging the privilege; should it also consider a presentation made by the party claiming the privilege?[56]

(b) Apparently by legal means, the IRS had obtained partial transcripts of the tapes from an undisclosed confidential source. Would it be proper for the trial court to consider these transcripts in determining whether the tapes are privileged?[57]

(c) When the court reviews the assertedly privileged evidence *in camera*, what standard should it apply in deciding whether the evidence falls within the crime-fraud exception? "More likely than not"? A more stringent standard? A less stringent one? *See Zolin* at 563 n. 7 (declining to resolve issue).[58]

---

other professionals. *See, e.g.*, Deukmejian v. Superior Court, 103 Cal.App.3d 253, 259–60, 162 Cal.Rptr. 857, 861–62 (Cal.App.2d Dist.1980); *cf.* Lipton v. Superior Court, 48 Cal.App.4th 1599, 1619–20 56 Cal.Rptr.2d 341, 352–53 (2d Dist.1996).

[56] *See* Haines v. Liggett Group Inc., 975 F.2d 81, 96 (3d Cir.1992) (holding in the negative).

[57] *See Zolin* at 573–74 (holding that if the transcripts were not privileged the trial court could consider them).

[58] An epilogue to *Zolin*: Eventually, a federal court ordered the state court clerk to turn the tapes over to the IRS and the clerk complied. The Church appealed from that order; the federal

Standing issues frequently arise in connection with privileges. With respect to a professional privilege, the privilege-holder is usually the client, the person who received the services. Thus, if a lawyer is being investigated for fraud and her clients waive the privilege, she cannot refuse to disclose confidential communications with them.

¶ 16.41: Dyer, on trial for murder, contends that he was nowhere near the scene. He believes that statements he made in confession to his priest shortly after the murder will lend weight to his alibi. The priest declines to testify, citing the sanctity of the confessional. May he be compelled to testify?[59]

If a party to an action seeks evidence as to which her adversary has a privilege, the adversary, as privilege-holder, may of course object. Not all cases fit this simple pattern, however. Sometimes, for instance, a party to an action in which the privilege-holder is not a party seeks to compel testimony from the other participant in the privileged communication. That other participant, such as a lawyer, is generally permitted to claim the privilege on behalf of the privilege-holder, assuming there has been no waiver. Indeed, as discussed in Section D, most professions covered by a privilege have an ethical obligation to maintain confidentiality and so to assert the privilege absent waiver.[60]

If, however, the privilege-holder is not a party and the other participant in the conversation does not assert the privilege, the question of whether anyone else may assert the privilege may become important. Of course, even if the opponent of the evidence has no standing to assert the privilege, there is nothing to prevent him from calling the privilege to the attention of the court, and the court may decide on its own motion that the privilege should be protected. The more serious question is what happens if the trial court refuses to invoke the privilege. The question then becomes whether the opponent of the evidence may appeal on the basis that the court should have applied a privilege belonging to someone else. *See* McCormick § 73.1(a) (arguing in the negative).

---

appeals court held the appeal moot because the tapes had already been produced, but the Supreme Court reversed, holding that (assuming the tapes were in fact privileged) the Church still had an interest in ending the continued possession of them by the Government. Church of Scientology of California v. United States, 506 U.S. 9 (1992). Ultimately, the entire litigation settled, on unusual terms that included a payment of $12.5 million by the Church but a grant to it of tax-exempt status. Douglas Frantz, *$12.5 Million Deal With I.R.S. Lifted Cloud Over Scientologists*, N.Y. Times, Dec. 31, 1997.

[59] *See* Deleted FRE 506(c) and Uniform R.Evid. 505(c), both of which provide that the privilege belongs to the communicating person and set out a presumption that the clergy member is authorized to claim the privilege on his behalf. The Uniform Rule is more explicit that the clergy member may claim the privilege "only on behalf of the communicant."

[60] *Cf.* Scott v. Henry Ford Hospital, 199 Mich.App. 241, 501 N.W.2d 29 (1993) (the physician-patient privilege is "all the more sacred" after death; personal representative of deceased's estate may waive privilege, but plaintiff's widow, who had not yet been appointed representative, cannot).

¶ **16.42:** Macumber is on trial for murder. Two attorneys are willing to testify for him that a client of theirs, now deceased, confessed the crime to them.

(a) May the court invoke the privilege on its own motion?[61]

(b) May the testimony be excluded by the prosecution's invocation of the privilege?

¶ **16.43:** Shirley Maillian is on trial for the murder of her estranged husband Ronnie. In an attempt to show Shirley's motive, the prosecution presents the testimony of Ronnie's domestic relations lawyers concerning conversations they had with him. Ronnie isn't around to object and his lawyers decide not to. Shirley does.

(a) Should her objection be sustained?

(b) Assume the objection is overruled and that Shirley is convicted and appeals. Should Shirley have standing to seek reversal on the basis that evidence of Ronnie's conversations should not have been admitted?[62]

¶ **16.44:** Frank Winterfield was cashier of a bank and embezzled from it. When the bank discovered his chicanery, he promised to make good on his debt, and gave the bank a deed, signed by his wife Louisa and him, to their residence. Soon after, Frank committed suicide. Louisa then brought an action against the bank to quiet her title. She claims that she knew nothing of Frank's wrongdoing, and that he had told her that the papers she was signing were simply necessary to insure the home. The bank objects to her testimony about this conversation on the ground of privilege. How should the court rule?[63]

¶ **16.45:** In Blair's case against Blue Cross, see ¶ 16.8, she argues that Blue Cross should not be able to claim privilege on behalf of its subscribers, because they are its potential adversaries: The subscribers might wish either to join as named plaintiffs, or to participate as unnamed class members, in her action on behalf of all subscribers denied coverage for psoriasis. What result?

---

[61] *See* State v. Macumber, 112 Ariz. 569, 544 P.2d 1084 (1976) (holding in the affirmative, but reversing on another ground).'

[62] See State v. Maillian, 464 So.2d 1071, 1077 (La.App.), *cert. denied,* 469 So.2d 982 (1985) (no standing; privilege could be invoked only by client or his lawyer).

[63] *Cf.* Sommerfeld v. Griffith, 173 Minn. 51, 216 N.W. 311 (1927) (stating conclusorily—where the husband was still alive and testifying—that conversation was not covered by the marital communications privilege).

Now suppose a party is thwarted from offering a potentially important item of evidence by her adversary's claim of a privilege. The offering party sometimes seeks the consolation of being able to ask the jury to draw an adverse inference from the claim of privilege. Whether, or when, such an argument should be allowed has been a matter of dispute for many years.[64] Deleted FRE 513(a) and Unif. R. Evid. 512(a) take a hard line against allowing adverse inference.

¶ 16.46: Consider this argument by the privilege-holder:

If my adversary could argue on the basis of our claim of privilege, it would severely undercut the value of the privilege, and so the policies underlying it, because it would make exercise of the privilege very costly. Besides, just about every time a party had a conversation with his lawyer, we'd have to go through this charade—put the party on the stand, ask about the privileged conversations, and then after the privilege is claimed ask the jury to draw an inference from that.

And now by the offering party:

I'm just asking that the jury be allowed to draw the ordinary inference from the failure of a party to put on evidence within his control. Sure, the privilege gives him a right not to testify—he can't be compelled to do so. But he doesn't have a right to be immunized from the unpleasant consequences of the choice that he's made, one of which is a mere matter of common sense inference. This point is important enough to warrant a small amount of trial time.

(a) Which way do you come out? Does your answer depend on what the privilege is, on whether the case is criminal or civil, or on any other circumstance?

(b) Assuming that no adverse inference is allowed, would you nevertheless allow the offering party to call the privilege-holder to the stand, so that the privilege must be invoked in front of the jury?

H. THE ATTORNEY-CLIENT PRIVILEGE AND THE WORK-PRODUCT DOCTRINE COMPARED

Closely associated with the attorney-client privilege, and sometimes loosely considered part of it, is the doctrine covering work product, or materials prepared in anticipation of trial. This doctrine, enunciated in

---

[64] *See* McCormick § 74.1; Mueller & Kirkpatrick § 5.4.

Hickman v. Taylor, 329 U.S. 495 (1947), and now partially codified in Fed.R.Civ.P. 26(b)(3), is thoroughly covered in most Civil Procedure courses, so here we will look at it only briefly, to emphasize its relationship to, and distinction from, the attorney-client privilege.

The work-product doctrine extends far beyond the privilege in one important respect—it is not limited to the communication of confidential matter between client and attorney. The doctrine is necessary to curb what would otherwise be the unacceptable consequences of liberal discovery and broad relevance rules in our adversary system: It would be impossible for a party, his attorney, and other representatives to prepare for trial if they had reason to fear that everything about the case that they put down on paper, or assembled, or said, or even thought, was subject to discovery by the other side. So the work-product doctrine is simply a rule of discovery. Rule 26(b)(3) provides that materials prepared for litigation—not only by the lawyer but also by other representatives or by the party himself—are ordinarily not discoverable. And although on its face Rule 26(b)(3) only extends protection to "documents and tangible things," the holding of *Hickman* clearly extends immunity from discovery to oral or mental preparations for litigation whether or not they are incorporated in a document or other tangible thing; moreover, as discussed below, Rule 26(b)(3)(B) provides particularly stringent protection for mental impressions in those circumstances in which tangible work product is disclosed. Because the rule is one of discovery, its protection is not necessarily waived by disclosure of the documents to a third party.

Thus, in some respects the work-product protection is more extensive—that is, it has broader coverage—than that of the privilege. But in another sense, the work-product doctrine is less extensive: Though doubts have been raised on this score, the doctrine, unlike the privilege, ordinarily applies only to evidence prepared during, or in anticipation of, litigation. Geoffrey C. Hazard, Jr., et al., *Civil Procedure* 345 (6th ed. 2011). Furthermore, the protection provided by the work-product doctrine is considerably less intensive than that of the privilege. If a communication is privileged, most courts treat it as absolutely protected, no matter how probative it may be. (Of course, when the issue is a close one a court might be tempted to characterize highly probative evidence as not privileged—not within the scope of the privilege—or waived, or within an exception.) By contrast, in certain circumstances material may be considered work product yet nonetheless subject to discovery: Where the other side has a real need for the information contained in the materials and has no other way of getting it, the court may order discovery.[65] But in

---

[65] Courts are sometimes generous in finding "substantial need." *See, eg.*, Duck v. Warren, 160 F.R.D. 80 (E.D.Va.1995) (per Magistrate Judge) (§ 1983 action alleging unjustified shooting

doing so, the Rule provides that the court "must protect against the mental impressions, conclusions, opinions, or legal theories of a party's attorney or other representative concerning the litigation." Suppose, for example, that the plaintiff in an auto accident case was unable to find eyewitnesses because he was unconscious at the time.[66] A court might order the defendant to produce transcripts of interviews with such eyewitnesses, but only in extremely rare cases, if at all, should the court order the defendant to produce notes on such interviews prepared by the defendant's investigator. *See Upjohn, supra,* 449 U.S. at 401–02.

Rule 26(b)(3)(C) allows a person—whether a party or not—to obtain from a party, without making the usually required showing, a statement that she made to a party about the subject matter of the litigation. And Rule 26(b)(4) has special provisions with respect to experts. If an expert is retained with the anticipation that she will testify at trial, then discovery of that expert is appropriate, as it would be for a non-expert witness. If, however, the expert is retained for the litigation but without the expectation that she will testify, then she is in much the same position as a lawyer or investigator, a member of the party's litigation team, and so discovery would be appropriate only in exceptional circumstances. Obviously, there are delicate factual and ethical issues concerning when an expert is "expected to be a witness at trial."

¶ **16.47:** (a) Given the work-product doctrine, is the traditional attorney-client privilege necessary?

(b) Alternatively, consider a unified doctrine along these lines:

> Protect only materials within the work-product doctrine as it stands, but for those materials provide the protection that they get under current privilege or work-product law. That is, if the materials do not also fit within the current attorney-client privilege, they receive only the protection now offered by the work-product doctrine. If, however, the materials fit the attorney-client privilege as well as the current work-product doctrine—essentially, if they are communications between client and lawyer made in

---

by a police officer; court allows discovery of documents that were part of internal affairs investigation, on grounds that these would likely yield useful impeachment evidence); Doubleday v. Ruh, 149 F.R.D. 601, 608 (E.D.Cal.1993) (per Magistrate Judge) (§ 1983 action alleging improper arrest; court allows discovery of district attorney's file used to prosecute plaintiff; finding "substantial need" because "the passage of time and the present, potential bias of the defendants may color recollections such that what was said at the time cannot be accurately deciphered").

[66] This scenario approximates the facts of Newell v. Capital Transit C., 7 F.R.D. 732 (D.D.C.1948).

anticipation of litigation—they receive the greater protection that the privilege now gives them.

Should such a doctrine be adopted?[67] Who would complain?

---

[67] *Cf.* Leslie, *supra*, 77 Ind. L.J. at 550 ("At most, government entities should be able to claim a limited litigation privileges that enables them to shield communications made in furtherance of trial preparation.").

CHAPTER 17

THREE CATEGORICAL RULES
OF EXCLUSION

■ ■ ■

The rules of evidence give the trial judge an enormous amount of leeway in deciding whether the probative value of a piece of evidence outweighs the various costs of admitting it. The rulemakers do not attempt to prescribe the outcome for every conceivable case, in part because it would be impossible to do so. The balance—in trying to weigh such matters as the perceived likelihood of prejudice, the financial cost of presenting evidence, and the delay it entails—depends on the particulars of the given case, which are not predictable. Some evidentiary problems, however, recur sufficiently often that the rulemakers have felt justified in prescribing a general rule. Furthermore, some recurring situations raise policy related to the effect that admissibility is likely to have on the parties or other persons. Such concerns tend to lead to *per se* rules that leave relatively narrow discretion to the trial judge.

Probably the most important rule of this sort, to be discussed in the next chapter, is the general prohibition against evidence offered to show the propensity of a person. This chapter discusses several other rules of this type. Section A discusses evidence of compromises of disputes, and of offers and statements made in attempts to reach settlement. Section A also discusses closely related types of evidence, apologies and the payment or offer to pay one's expenses arising from an injury. Section B discusses evidence of measures, taken after an accident or other similar event, that might have prevented the event had they been taken before. Finally, Section C discusses evidence that a person was or was not insured against liability.

Although substantively unrelated, the rules covered in this chapter are similar in nature; probably for that reason the Federal Rules' versions of them are grouped together, in FRE 407–411.[1] Each of them prescribes a *per se* rule of exclusion, but only when the evidence is offered to prove a particular type of proposition: If the proponent can show that the evidence is relevant to another material proposition, these absolute rules do not apply. Nevertheless, the prejudicial impact of the statement with

---

[1] The basic propensity rules are grouped alongside in FRE 404–406, with later-added rules that qualify them in FRE 412–415.

respect to the particular proposition would presumably still be applicable in making the general balance of prejudice versus probative value. Each of the rules reflects a concern that the prejudicial impact of the evidence may outweigh its probative value. That alone would probably not be enough to warrant a *per se* rule. But each of the rules (the insurance rule less so) also reflects an external policy—that is, one most directly related not to the truthfinding process of the trial but to the desirable conduct of people in the outside world.

A. COMPROMISES: SETTLEMENTS, OFFERS, STATEMENTS MADE IN NEGOTIATIONS, AND PAYMENT OF EXPENSES

FRE 408–410

Additional Reading: McCormick, Ch. 25, § 266m, § 267 (*"Payment of medical expenses"*); Mueller & Kirkpatrick, §§ 4.25–.29, .35

1. SETTLEMENTS, OFFERS AND ACCOMPANYING STATEMENTS: THE CIVIL SIDE

First, we consider offers to settle, and actual settlements of, disputed claims. FRE 408(a) expresses the well-accepted rule, that such offers and settlements are not admissible "either to prove or disprove the validity or amount of a disputed claim."

Such evidence might be offered if the settlement negotiations break down. Then one side wants to let the jury know, "See, they were willing to settle this case on terms much less advantageous than they're demanding now." And whether the settlement goes through or not, it might be offered in litigation involving another party: "See, they paid my next door neighbor a whopping amount to settle this case. So how can they deny liability for the sludge in our back yards?" Note that there is something to these arguments, for this type of evidence can have significant probative value. Offering to settle a dispute on terms less advantageous than those demanded in litigation might reflect the party's awareness of the weakness of his litigation position, and that might reflect his awareness that the facts do not support his side.[2]

Nevertheless, Rule 408(a)(1) prevents this type of evidence from being introduced to prove that the facts were against the party who made

---

[2] Thus, such offers and settlements have traditionally been called *admissions by conduct.* And so the McCormick book, § 266, continues to label them, and to consider them within the hearsay unit, despite the facts that (1) they are not in themselves assertive and so not hearsay according to the prevailing modern definition, (2) the most significant rule of evidence in this area is one of inadmissibility, not (as with admissions) one of admissibility, and (3) evidence of this sort need not (though it usually does) concern the conduct of the party opponent.

the settlement offer.[3] Why? One reason is that a party's decision to try to settle does not necessarily reflect a belief that his case is weak. Let's focus on the defendant's side; the plaintiff's side is roughly symmetrical. Put in simplified terms, a defendant will accept a settlement offer if the cost of the settlement is less than the cost of continuing litigation plus the probability of losing judgment times the exposure—that is, the amount of judgment if he does lose. If the cost of continuing litigation is greater than the cost of the settlement, it makes sense for the defendant to settle even if he is absolutely certain that he would prevail in the end; this is likely a strike suit, brought for nuisance value. Even if this condition does not hold, the defendant's willingness to settle does not necessarily reflect belief that the facts do not support him. Especially if the cost of settlement is small in relation to the exposure, the decision to settle may reflect little more than awareness that litigation is an uncertain matter, often yielding inaccurate results.

Therefore, the decision to settle does not necessarily prove that the party believed he was in the wrong. Does this ground justify excluding the evidence? In itself, it probably does not justify a *per se* rule of exclusion. *Sometimes*—depending largely on the numbers—the evidence has relatively little probative value, not enough to warrant admission. But *sometimes* it is highly probative, and even if the jurors will tend to overvalue it (which is by no means certain), it is unlikely that they will overvalue it so much as to make it more prejudicial than probative.

There is another factor weighing in favor of exclusion, however. Suppose you are counsel to the defendant and he is considering making a settlement offer. But he asks you first, "Well, suppose they don't accept it and we go to trial. Is my offer going to be admissible against me? Or what if the plaintiffs' neighbors sue me—will it be admissible then?" Now suppose your answer is, "Well, that depends. If the court thinks your offer was so large in relation to your exposure that it probably reflected your belief in your own liability, and that the jury would be able to discount it for the possibility that it did not reflect that belief, then it will probably be admissible." In that circumstance, the defendant will probably be much warier of making the offer.

In its Note to FRE 408, the Advisory Committee said that this concern, "promotion of the public policy favoring the compromise and settlement of disputes," is a "more consistently impressive ground" for exclusion than is the balance of probative value and prejudice. That is probably so, in the sense that if the Rule is meant to encourage parties to

---

[3]   The Rule clearly applies whether the party who made the settlement offer was a plaintiff or a defendant, whether or not the litigation is the same as the one in which the settlement offer was made, and whether or not it is between the same parties as the one in which the settlement offer was made. *See, e.g.,* McInnis v. A.M.F., Inc., 765 F.2d 240, 247 (1st Cir. 1985).

settle their disputes then it must give them a high degree of confidence that settlements and offers will not be admitted, and this can best be done by a *per se* rule rather than by a balancing test; note the similarity to the instrumental rationale for some privileges, especially attorney-client. At the same time, however, we must recognize the costs of the *per se* rule. In some cases, even if your client knows that a settlement offer is likely to be admitted, in the same litigation or another, his response might be, "Well, that's too bad, but that's just a chance I'll have to take. Even with that risk, making this offer is just too sensible." Sometimes in such a case exclusion is beneficial, because the evidence has little probative value. But in some cases, the *per se* rule of exclusion simply gives the party a windfall, preventing the jury from hearing about settlement conduct that has substantial probative value and in which the party would have engaged even absent the rule.

¶ 17.1: Priestly, a commodities trader, claims that he was damaged because the Devon Trading Company manipulated the futures market for pork bellies. Priestly brings an action against Devon on behalf of himself "and all others similarly situated." Before the action has been certified as a class action, Devon settles Priestly's individual claim for $95,000; Priestly had claimed damages of $100,000. The court approves the settlement. Three months later, Parrish brings a similar action. This one goes to trial. May proof of the settlement with Priestly be admitted?

¶ 17.2: Daddy Bigbucks had an auto collision with a car driven by Polk, in which Pollack was a guest. Polk and Pollack have each sued Bigbucks for $1 million, claiming that he ran into them while they were standing still at a red light. Bigbucks answered that the accident was not his fault, because Polk had driven into the intersection before the light changed. In each of the following cases, consider (i) how great the probative value of the evidence is, (ii) how great the likely prejudicial impact of the evidence is, (iii) what you would do, if you were counsel for the party opposing the evidence and the evidence were admitted, to mitigate its importance, (iv) what policy exclusion is likely to serve, other than the prevention of prejudice, and (v) whether a *per se* rule of exclusion is necessary to serve that policy, or case-by-case decisionmaking is likely to be sufficient.

(a) In Pollack's case, evidence that shortly after the suit was filed Bigbucks offered Pollack $2,000 in settlement.

(b) Same as in (a), but the offer was $300,000.

(c) Same as in (a), but the offer was $900,000.

(d) In Pollack's case, evidence that shortly after the suit was filed Pollack told Bigbucks that he would accept $5,000 in settlement.

(e) In Polk's case, evidence that Bigbucks offered to settle Pollack's claim for $300,000.

(f) In Polk's case, evidence that Bigbucks paid Pollack $600,000 in settlement.

(g) Same as in (f), but the payment was $2,000.

(h) In a criminal case brought against Bigbucks, evidence that he offered to settle Pollack's claim for $900,000.

Settlement conduct includes not only the acts of making an offer and of settling, but also negotiation. And in the course of negotiating, a party often makes statements about the events at issue. Sometimes such a statement is contrary to a position the party takes later in litigation. Under traditional law, such statements are generally admissible as admissions if offered against the party who made them; as with other admissions, they often gain great probative value from the fact that they are contrary to the party's stance in litigation. Nevertheless, the statement might be excluded under traditional law if it were so closely related to the settlement offer that the offer could not be understood without the statement, or if the party making the statement protected himself against later admissibility by accompanying the statement by words such as "Speaking hypothetically," "For settlement purposes only," or "Without prejudice."

FRE 408 reflects a different view. The Advisory Committee believed that the requirement of making some such qualifying statement created undue complexity and "inhibit[ed] free communication with respect to compromise, even among lawyers." The Senate Judiciary Committee added the argument that the requirement "constituted a preference for the sophisticated, and a trap for the unwary." Accordingly, FRE 408(a)(2) brings within the scope of the exclusionary rule evidence of "conduct or a statement made during compromise negotiations about the claim" as well as the compromise or offer itself: Thus, even if a negotiating party making a statement does not accompany it with a mantra like "Speaking hypothetically," the statement cannot be admitted to show that the claim was valid or that it was invalid or how large it was.

This rule does not avoid all complexities. Under it, critical questions sometimes are whether there was a dispute in the first place at the time the statement was made and whether the statement was made as part of an attempt to settle it. Unless the answer to both questions is affirmative, the exclusionary rule never comes into play.

¶ **17.3:** Patsy Partridge is a wholesale paint distributor, and Dan Dandridge, a retailer, was one of her customers. Dandridge fell behind in paying his bills. Patsy called Dandridge on the phone, and they had this conversation:

P: Dan, you're 30 days late. I need payment now on the 50 white drums and the 80 aqua drums.

D: Well, Patsy, you know some of that white stuff was in pretty bad shape by the time I got it. You've got to give me a cut.

P: OK. How about 25%?

D: Sounds fair enough.

P: How about the aqua?

D: What are you talking about? I never ordered any aqua paint from you.

P: Sure you did, Dan. You gave the order to my guy Joe when he was in your shop six weeks ago.

D: Patsy, you're probably confusing me with some other guy. I remember he came by, but I don't remember making any order. Check it out with him again, will you?

P: All right, I will.

D: Meanwhile, I need 40 drums of olive paint.

P: Well, I'm not thrilled about running your tab up any more. When can I get payment on the white?

D: Two weeks.

P: Make it one.

D: Boy, you're going to get blood from a stone before you're through. Give my best to Bill.

P: Bye, Dan.

The next day, Partridge called back to say that she had confirmed with Joe that Dandridge had ordered the aqua. He continued to deny it, and refused to pay on either the white or the aqua. Partridge then sued him. At trial, Dandridge contended not only that he had not ordered the aqua but also that Joe had not in fact visited him, and that the white was so badly damaged that it was essentially valueless. May Partridge introduce evidence of the quoted conversation? If you are Partridge's counsel, how would you argue that Rule 408 does not apply? How would your answer be affected if Partridge taped the conversation?[4]

¶ 17.4: (a) In ¶ 17.2, Bigbucks told Polk shortly after Polk's suit was filed, "Listen, I know it was my fault. I'll even concede that $1 million is a reasonable recovery. But why don't you be sensible? It's going to cost you loads of money to collect, and you won't get anything for a couple of years—and there's always a chance I'd win anyway. I'll give you $500,000 today." Polk rejects the offer and the case goes to trial. May evidence of Bigbucks' acknowledgment of fault be admitted? How about evidence of the offer?

(b)   What if the statement was the same except that instead of the second sentence Bigbucks said, "I'll even concede that you were damaged $800,000 worth"?

(c)   What if the statement was, "Listen, I know it was my fault, though I think your damages claim is way off. I'll give you $100,000 to settle this thing right now"?

Now let's consider whether Congress made the best decision in excluding statements made during compromise negotiations. Consider the following problem.

¶ 17.5:   In   ¶ 17.2,   assume   now   that   Bigbucks   has consistently denied liability. During settlement negotiations, Polk said to him, "Look, I know you weren't going too fast or anything, but the simple fact is that you weren't looking where you were going." At trial, though, Polk presents evidence that Bigbucks was driving too fast. May Bigbucks introduce evidence of Polk's earlier statement to Bigbucks? May Bigbucks introduce evidence that Polk said to a friend, "I know that other guy wasn't going too fast, but he wasn't looking where he was going"?

Is admissibility of Polk's statement likely to hamper negotiations and settlements? If you believe that the prospect of admissibility is likely to make a given negotiator more cautious in what he says, are you assuming that he is likely to be

---

[4]   *See generally* Note, Valerie S. Alabanza, *When are Settlement Communications Protected as "Offers to Compromise Under Rule 408?,"* 40 SANTA CLARA L. REV. 547 (2000)*; cf.* Affiliated Mfrs., Inc. v. Aluminum Co. of America, 56 F.3d 521, 526–27 (3d Cir.1995) (reviewing different cases presenting interpretations of "dispute" and concluding that a "clear difference of opinion" is sufficient, threat of litigation not being necessary); S.A. Healy Co. v. Milwaukee Metropolitan Sewerage Dist., 50 F.3d 476, 480 (7th Cir.1995) (Posner, C.J.) (plaintiff contractor claimed price adjustment under contract's dispute clause; statement by defendant's engineer to contractor that claim probably had merit held to have been made before a dispute arose, and Rule 408 therefore held inapplicable); EEOC v. Gear Petroleum, Inc., 948 F.2d 1542 (10th Cir. 1991); C.J. Duffey Paper Co. v. Reger, 588 N.W.2d 519, 524–25 (Minn. App. 1999); Landise v. Mauro, 725 A.2d 445, 453–54 (D.C. App. 1998).

thinking ahead, in a rational and calculating manner, to the trial? And if he is so rational and calculating, is it unreasonable to expect him, as a precondition to excluding the statement, to flag it as "hypothetical" or "for settlement purposes only"?

As we have seen, the exclusionary rule for statements made during negotiations is based in part on the argument that to require a precaution as a precondition to exclusion would be to create a snare for the unwary. But the questions presented above suggest that this argument may proceed from the wrong end. That is, perhaps the presumption should be that statements like Polk's are admissible, because they are highly probative, and that if a person wants to make a potentially probative and damaging statement in negotiations with a prospective adversary and yet not risk admissibility, she may do so only if she flags it in a prescribed way. In this view, it is only the relatively sophisticated—those who are thinking ahead to evidentiary consequences—who might be inhibited in negotiations by the prospect of admissibility, and those persons can protect themselves by putting up a flag; an exclusionary rule that does not require such a flag gives a windfall to those who make admissions during the course of negotiations without thinking ahead to evidentiary consequences.

¶ 17.6: Of course, even if Polk put up such a flag, Bigbucks might forget it or lie about it. What would Polk have to do to protect herself against such false testimony? If she and Bigbucks testify inconsistently about whether the flag was put up, what should the result be?

Interestingly, the House resisted the extension of the exclusionary rule to statements accompanying offers, but on somewhat different grounds from those presented here. The House Judiciary Committee expressed concern that parties dealing with government agencies might wait until compromise negotiations begin and then provide information in the hopes of immunizing themselves from the use of that information. Such an immunity—preventing use of information, no matter how likely the government would have learned of it otherwise, simply because a party communicated it to the government—would certainly be a silly result. Hence, the Senate, while restoring the exclusionary rule for statements accompanying offers, added to the Rule a sentence expressing the perfectly sensible proposition that a party cannot preclude an adverse party from proving a proposition at trial by the technique of disclosing the proposition to the adversary during negotiations. But a 2006 amendment to the Rule deleted that sentence as superfluous.

¶ 17.7: Suppose that during negotiations a party discloses information that puts the adversary on the trail of other evidence that the adversary probably would not have discovered otherwise. Is that evidence admissible? Put another way, does a sort of "fruit of the poisonous tree" doctrine apply here?

The 2006 amendment also cut back somewhat on the exclusionary rule with respect to statements made during negotiations—and on the rationale that to demand precautions on the part of the individual making the statement would be to create a trap for the unwary. The amendment provides that the rule does not apply when the statement "is offered in a criminal case and the negotiations related to a claim by a public office or agency in the exercise of regulatory, investigative, or enforcement authority." When a statement is made in this circumstance, the Advisory Committee said, "its subsequent admission in a criminal case should not be unexpected." (That can be true, of course, only if the rules allow admissibility, and why it should be true only in this setting is not clear.) But, it added, an individual making the statement and wanting to achieve protection against a subsequent disclosure could seek it "through negotiation and agreement with the civil regulator or an attorney for the government." That appears to assume that the civil regulator or government attorney can effectively bind a subsequent prosecutor; statements made in the course of negotiations over a private claim are still protected by the Rule, the Committee said, because "private ordering" could not protect against subsequent use in a criminal proceeding. At the same time, the Committee reaffirmed that the exclusionary rule does apply to "offer or acceptance of a compromise" of a civil claim even when a prosecutor later tries to use the evidence in a criminal case.

Now, it is important to remember that the exclusion of FRE 408(a) is not a general one, but only for designated uses of the evidence. The core of the exclusion is to prevent the admissibility of the evidence when it is offered "either to prove or disprove the validity or amount of a disputed claim." There may be other purposes for which it is admissible.[5] Rule 408(b) provides a non-exhaustive list of such purposes. Unfortunately, the bold-faced heading to Rule 408(b) is "**Exceptions.**" But that is a mistake. The alternative purposes listed in Rule 408(b) are not exceptions to a broad rule of admissibility stated in Rule 408(a); rather, Rule 408(a) bars admission of the described types of evidence when offered for defined

---

[5] If the evidence is offered for another, valid purpose, there is a possibility that the jury will nevertheless consider it for the forbidden propositions. In some cases, though, the exclusionary rule is enforceable by keeping away from the jury the issue on which FRE 408 bars use of the evidence; this can occur if the proponent of the evidence bears the burden of producing evidence on that issue and has produced insufficient other evidence to support the burden. If the case does go to the jury, limiting instructions could caution the jury against using the evidence for the forbidden purpose. If the court is nonetheless afraid that the jury will use the evidence for the forbidden purpose, it can presumably treat that possibility as a "danger of unfair prejudice" under FRE 403 and consider excluding the evidence altogether.

purposes, and Rule 408(b) illustrates other purposes for which the evidence might be admitted.

¶ 17.8: (a) In ¶ 17.2, assume that Bigbucks has settled with Pollack, who had the weaker claim for damages, for $80,000. At trial of Polk's case, Pollack gives testimony that is primarily favorable to Bigbucks; he says that Polk had begun to edge into the intersection when the collision occurred. May Polk introduce evidence of Bigbucks's settlement with Pollack? If so, on what grounds?

(b) Polk testifies that Bigbucks was going too fast. Now may Bigbucks introduce evidence of Polk's earlier statement, made during compromise negotiations, "Look, I know you weren't going too fast or anything. . . ."?

In considering ¶ 17.8, note that (unlike FRE 407) FRE 408(b) does not mention impeachment among the illustrations of alternative purposes that provide legitimate bases for admissibility. Is this omission significant? FRE 408(b) does mention bias, and bias is an important form of impeachment. So, for example, Bigbucks' payment to Pollack might have biased Pollack's testimony; indeed, Bigbucks might have in effect bought Pollack's testimony. But among the other forms of impeachment are presentation of a prior statement that was made by the witness and that is inconsistent with the witness's current testimony and presentation of other evidence that contradicts the witness's testimony. Before 2006, there was doubt as to whether FRE 408 would allow a statement that was made during compromise negotiations to be admitted on this basis. The 2006 amendment extended the exclusionary rule of Rule 408(a) to prevent the described types of evidence from being used "to impeach by a prior inconsistent statement or a contradiction." The Advisory Committee explained: "Such broad impeachment would tend to swallow the exclusionary rule and would impair the public policy of promoting settlements." There is considerable truth to this assertion, though it is probably somewhat overstated. Often (though not always) the party will be a witness, and often he will testify in a way that is at least *arguably* inconsistent with something he said in compromise negotiations. If that is true, allowing the prior statement in for impeachment would severely undercut the operation of Rule 408. But it is important to recognize that not all states make this judgment. *See, e.g., Hernandez v. State*, 203 Ariz. 196, 52 P.3d 765 (2002).

¶ 17.9: Dailey, a well-known doctor, smashed the windshield of the car of his neighbor, Paley, so he could turn off the car's oversensitive burglar alarm. Dailey has been arraigned for criminal trespass. He has said to Paley, "Listen, if I pay you the cost of fixing the windshield, will you not press charges?" Admissible? What if he offered to pay an extra $3000?

2. APOLOGIES AND PAYMENT OF EXPENSES

Similar in some respects to the rule on compromises, offers, and accompanying statements—but very distinct—is a rule, expressed in FRE 409, excluding "[e]vidence of furnishing or offering or promising to pay medical, hospital, or similar expenses occasioned by an injury." As explained by the Advisory Committee, the latter rule is traditionally justified on grounds rather similar to those used for the former one: The probative value of the evidence may be limited, because it may be attributable to some factor other than consciousness of liability, and rulemakers do not wish to inhibit desirable conduct by attaching adverse evidentiary consequences to it. But these arguments are not all that powerful: Evidence of this sort can be very probative, and probably most often the potential defendant who offers to pay the potential plaintiff's medical expenses has done so spontaneously, with no thought to evidentiary consequences.

There may be another factor at work behind this rule. Perhaps there is some truth to the old quip that "no good deed goes unpunished," but if so that does not represent a happy state of affairs. Arguably, it is not consonant with our sense of fairness to put a defendant in a worse litigation position because he has done a humane thing. Note that this argument applies whether or not the defendant was affected by the evidentiary rule; it is an argument based on fairness and not on incentives. A counter-argument is that one accepts the costs of his conduct. According to this view, a potential defendant offering to pay medical expenses for the potential plaintiff does indeed do a humane thing, but he expects to pay money out of pocket for it, and if he has to pay also by accepting a worse litigation position, so be it.

Interestingly, FRE 409, unlike FRE 408, does not exclude accompanying statements; the Advisory Committee judged that usually these are too incidental to the offer to pay expenses. In recent decades, however, apologies—which may, but need not be, made in conjunction with an offer to pay expenses—have become an increasing subject of focus. Apologies for wrongful conduct clearly serve a beneficial purpose. Indeed, in some cases a potential plaintiff is, or at least professes to be, more interested in receiving an apology than in being awarded tangible compensation. And yet apologies may be highly probative; to the extent they include assertions, they are the quintessence of admissions. Over 35 states have passed legislation making some forms of apology inadmissible. Jennifer K. Robbenholt, *Attorneys, Apologies, and Settlement Negotiation*, 13 Harv. Negot. L. Rev. 349 (2008). Often, these statutes exclude evidence of "statements ... or benevolent gestures expressing sympathy or a general sense of benevolence" relating to the injury of an accident victim and made to the victim or the victim's family. Most of these statutes provide that a statement of fault that is part of, or in addition to, such a statement or gesture is not made inadmissible by the rule. David P. Leonard, *The New Wigmore: Selected Rules of Limited Admissibility* § 4.8.2 (rev. ed. 2002). Thus, under these statutes, "I'm sorry you're hurt" would be excluded, but "I'm sorry I injured you" would not be.[6]

> ¶ **17.10:** (a) After Walker was injured in an accident at work, Eldridge, his employer, came to the hospital and said, "Don't worry about the medical expenses. I'll pay for them all." In a suit by Walker against Eldridge, should evidence of this offer be admitted? Does the statement have substantial probative value? If it were admissible, would offers like Eldridge's be discouraged? Should such discouragement be of concern to the law? Could Eldridge make the offer and still protect himself against admissibility?
>
> (b) Now suppose that Eldridge's first sentence was "I'm sorry about this. It was our fault, and I'll do my best to see that it never happens again." Should Eldridge's utterance be admitted in whole or in part?

3. PLEAS, PLEA BARGAINS, AND ACCOMPANYING STATEMENTS: THE CRIMINAL SIDE

Criminal cases as well as civil ones are most often disposed of by negotiations. Hence, it is necessary to prevent a chill on criminal plea bargaining. FRE 410 is the criminal counterpart of FRE 408.[7] Part of the rule is concerned with withdrawn guilty pleas and pleas of nolo

---

6   Jonathan R. Cohen, *Legislating Apology: The Pros and Cons*, 70 U. Cin. L. Rev. 819, 830–833 (2002). *See also* Aviva Orenstein, *Apology Excepted: Incorporating a Feminist Analysis into Evidence Policy Where You Would Least Expect It*, 28 SW. U. L. REV. 221 (1999) (arguing from a feminist standpoint for a rule excluding apologies in civil litigation); Lee Taft, *Apology Subverted: The Commodification of Apology*, 109 Yale L.J. 1135, 1151–54 (2000) (arguing that the moral nature of apology is subverted when it is "cast into the legal arena"); Hiroshi Wagatsuma & Arthur Rosett, *The Implications of Apology: Law and Culture in Japan and the United States*, 20 LAW & SOC. REV. 461, 492 (1986) (noting that in Japan apology serves the primary purpose of repairing group hierarchy and harmony, putting a premium on acts reflecting submission to that hierarchy, and that "internal ambivalence" in apologizing is more accepted than in the United States). Note by contrast Ontario's Apology Act, 2009, S.O. 2009, c. 3, under which an apology—as broadly defined to mean "an expression of sympathy or regret, a statement that a person is sorry or any other words or actions indicating contrition or commiseration, whether or not the words or actions admit fault or liability or imply an admission of fault or liability in connection with the matter to which the words or actions relate"—cannot be used "in any determination of fault or liability in connection with that matter."

7   For years, FRE 410 and Fed. R. Crim. Pro. 11(e)(6) were kept essentially identical. This complicated the rule-making process—if one changed, the other had to, and the two Rules were under the jurisdiction of different Advisory Committees. The turf question has now been resolved; Fed. R. Crim. Pro. 11(f) simply incorporates FRE 410 by reference.

contendere. We have touched on this topic in Chapter 14, in discussing party admissions, and will not pursue it further here. The rest of the rule is concerned with "statements" made in connection with such pleas and plea discussions. Oddly enough, offers to plead guilty are not explicitly covered by the rule as it now stands, although they were by the rule as it was originally adopted and as it stood until a 1980 amendment; read as a whole, however, the legislative history makes quite clear that such offers are intended to be covered. Note also that the Rule does not apply to guilty pleas that were not withdrawn. Thus, if a criminal defendant pleads guilty to a charge and is later sued civilly with respect to the same incident, the plea will usually be admissible to prove the facts that were necessary to establish his guilt.

¶ **17.11:** Delk and Painter were in an auto accident. The police officer who came to the scene gave Delk a ticket for a traffic violation, refusal to yield. After Delk paid the $200 required to resolve the traffic violation, Painter sued him for $1 million in damages. At trial, Painter sought to prove Delk's conduct in response to the traffic citation. In each of these variations, should evidence of Delk's conduct be admissible?

(a) Delk mailed the ticket in with his payment. The ticket required his signature under a provision asserting that he "did not contest the charge." Delk lives 500 miles away from the courthouse.

(b) Same as (a), except that Delk signed under a provision declaring, "I plead guilty to this charge."

(c) Same as (b), except that Delk lives two miles from the courthouse.

(d) Rather than pay by mail, Delk, who lives two miles from the courthouse, came to court, pled guilty orally, and then paid the $200.[8]

¶ **17.12:** Assume that you favor the old-fashioned rule under which factual statements made in conjunction with negotiation of a civil case may be admitted against the party who made them if they were not phrased hypothetically. Would you apply the same rule to criminal cases?

¶ **17.13:** Dorman is on trial for robbery and unlawful possession of a firearm. Officer Olin is prepared to testify as follows: While he was attempting to arrest Dorman, Dorman

---

[8] See David P. Leonard, *The New Wigmore: Selected Rules of Limited Admissibility* § 5.8.1 (rev. ed. 2002), and sources cited there, for discussions of the various ways in which states handle evidence of pleas and payment of fines in traffic cases.

pulled out a gun and pointed it at him, then dropped the gun and ran. Olin caught up to Dorman, arrested him, and then took him to the stationhouse to book him. There, Dorman asked him, "What are you booking me for?" and Olin replied, "Robbery one, unlawful possession, and attempted murder." Dorman then said, "Hey, man, don't put down attempted murder. I wasn't trying to kill you. Be reasonable and I will, too." Is this admissible? Should it be?[9]

In recent years, some prosecutors have demanded, as a precondition to entering into plea negotiations, that the defendant waive in whole or in part the protection of FRE 410 against use at trial of statements made during those negotiations. The issue of whether such waivers are valid came before the Supreme Court in *United States v. Mezzanatto*, 513 U.S. 196 (1995). Mezzanatto was arrested on drug charges, and he and his attorney asked to meet the prosecutor to discuss the possibility of cooperating with the Government. The prosecutor agreed, but he demanded as a condition to proceeding with the discussion that Mezzanatto agree that, if the negotiations broke down, the case went to trial, and Mezzanatto testified at variance from any statements he made during the meeting, those statements could be used to impeach him. Mezzanatto agreed, but the prosecutor ended the meeting after catching him in a lie. Mezzanatto's case did go to trial, he did testify contrary to statements he had made to the prosecutor, and the prosecutor offered those prior statements to impeach him. The Supreme Court, by a 7–2 vote, held that the waiver was valid and the evidence admissible. Three of the justices in the majority noted that it was unnecessary to decide on the validity of a broader waiver that would allow the use of the defendant's statements in the prosecution's case-in-chief.

¶ 17.14: What do you think of the result in *Mezzanatto*? In a legal system in which defendants may waive many rights, including fundamental ones such as the right to counsel and to trial by jury—and, indeed, the right to trial itself—is there any good reason why they should not be allowed to waive the protection afforded by FRE 410? Should courts be concerned that by demanding waivers prosecutors will be inhibiting plea bargaining? Is this a judgment that should better be left to prosecutors, recognizing that if the demand is too stringent on defendants then defendants will refuse it? Is a waiver a sensible way of giving the prosecutor confidence that the defendant will

---

[9] *Cf.* United States v. Herman, 544 F.2d 791 (5th Cir.1977), noted in the Advisory Committee Note to the 1980 amendment.

speak accurately in plea negotiations and comply with the terms of a plea agreement?[10]

Or does allowing a waiver essentially vitiate the rule? Why would a prosecutor ever *not* demand a waiver? And if the prosecutor does make the demand, will the defendant usually be in a position to refuse, or to secure some compensation for agreeing?

Is there a valid basis for distinguishing between a waiver that, like the one in *Mezzanatto*, allows use of the statements for impeachment and a broader one that allows for use of the statement as part of the case-in-chief?[11] Is there a valid basis for distinguishing between a waiver that, like the one in *Mezzanatto*, is demanded as a precondition for plea negotiations and one that is incorporated into a plea agreement, the waiver to come into force only if the court does not enter judgment on the plea?

B. SUBSEQUENT REMEDIAL MEASURES

FRE 407

Additional Reading: McCormick, Ch. 26, § 267 (*"Subsequent remedial measures"*); Mueller & Kirkpatrick, §§ 4.23–.24

Suppose that after the accident or other incident that is the subject of a civil trial the defendant took measures to minimize the chances of a recurrence. Such subsequent remedial measures may take many forms. Examples include: redesigning a product; manufacturing it with other materials; strengthening a warning label; restricting who may use the product; discharging or reassigning personnel; and altering operating procedures. Should such subsequent measures be admissible to prove that the failure to take such measures beforehand renders the defendant liable? The traditional rule is that they should not, and this rule is expressed in FRE 407.

Subsequent remedial measures appear to show what the defendant, in retrospect, regards as due care or proper behavior; the inference is that

---

[10] *See* Eric Rasmusen, Mezzanatto *and the Economics of Self-Incrimination*, 19 Cardozo L. Rev. 1541 (1998).

[11] *See* United States v. Sylvester, 583 F.3d 285 (5th Cir. 2009), *cert. denied*, 559 U.S. 916 (2010) (extending *Mezzanatto* to statements offered in case-in-chief); United States v. Duffy, 133 F.Supp.2d 213 (E.D.N.Y. 2001) (expressing doubt about extension of *Mezzanatto* to use of statements in case-in-chief). A more modest extension of *Mezzanatto* would allow the prosecutor to use the statement to rebut any evidence presented by the defendant—including but not limited to the defendant's own testimony. *See, e.g.,* United States v. Krilich, 159 F.3d 1020, 1024–26 (7th Cir.1998) (allowing waiver); United States v. Duffy, 133 F.Supp.2d 213 (E.D.N.Y. 2001) (not allowing waiver).

the condition as it existed before must not have been, in the defendant's own view, proper behavior. This inference is not inevitable. Perhaps the defendant's later actions reflect some aim other than safety or represent an abundance of prudence, a standard of care greater than that required by law. Perhaps the accident itself created damage that required the remedial measure. And perhaps, in the words of Baron Bramwell quoted by the Advisory Committee in its Note to FRE 407, the law should reject the notion that "because the world gets wiser as it gets older, therefore it was foolish before."

But, as the Committee suggests, that evidence is not conclusive is not sufficient to render it inadmissible. The Bramwell argument in particular should be treated with care: A negligence plaintiff may have to show not only that the defendant was "foolish" in failing to recognize or minimize a danger beforehand, but also that the condition was in fact dangerous. And the fact that the defendant took a remedial measure afterwards may be highly probative evidence on this point. It suggests that the defendant believes that the condition as it existed before the remedial measure was indeed dangerous. And on a theory akin to that exempting admissions from the rule against hearsay, this is significant evidence in determining whether the condition was in fact dangerous.[12]

The other commonly cited reason for exclusion, emphasized by the Advisory Committee, is one of social policy: Admissibility of the evidence might discourage remedial measures. In some cases that is probably true, and in some it probably isn't. We may well wonder whether this concern is strong enough to justify a *per se* rule of exclusion. It may be that only rarely does the rule cause remedial measures to be taken that would not otherwise have been, and that very frequently it simply gives the defendant a windfall, preventing the factfinder from learning of and relying on probative evidence of a remedial measure that the defendant would almost certainly have taken whatever the evidentiary consequence. On the other hand, if the rule of exclusion is not *per se*, or at least highly predictable, it will not give much comfort to the potential defendant considering remedial behavior, and so will do little good in encouraging such behavior.

Another possible reason for exclusion is that, even apart from discouraging socially beneficial remedial behavior, admissibility effectively punishes such behavior; perhaps, therefore, it is simply unfair to admit the evidence.[13] We have seen this kind of argument in the

---

[12] Again, note the traditional treatment, continued by McCormick, of this topic as a species of "admission by conduct."

[13] Richard O. Lempert & Stephen A. Saltzburg, *A Modern Approach to Evidence* 193 (2d ed. 1982), expressed sympathy for this view. The latest edition of the same work reflects more doubt about it. Richard O. Lempert et al., *A Modern Approach to Evidence* 288 (4th ed. 2011).

context of the rule on payment of medical expenses. It has much the same kind of appeal, and much the same kind of difficulty, in this context. A plaintiff contending for admission of the evidence might argue, "It's all very well that the defendant finally did what it should have done before, but what's unfair about admitting against it the probative evidence it has created? This evidence would help lead the jury to the truth, and so excluding it would be unfair to *me*." Note that in other circumstances we do admit evidence of a party's socially beneficial behavior against the party. Most obviously, it is socially beneficial for people to acknowledge their wrongdoing, and yet we do not exclude admissions of wrongdoing on that ground. Consider also *prior* preventive behavior: Suppose, for example, that a defendant had a standard operating procedure that ordinarily prevented accidents but that was not followed in the particular case. The plaintiff would usually be allowed to prove the standard procedure as well as the conduct on the occasion in question.

Bear these considerations in mind in determining, in each of the following cases, whether evidence of the subsequent remedial measure should be admitted.

¶ 17.15: In 1982, before medicines were routinely sold in tamper-proof packaging, several people died after having taken Tylenol from bottles of the drug that had been laced with acid before being sold. The crime was particularly startling because it was apparently unprecedented, or nearly so. Suppose the widow of one of the decedents sues the manufacturer and wishes to prove that after the killings the manufacturer adopted methods of bottling that would reveal whether bottles had been tampered, and that soon after that the Food and Drug Administration adopted regulations requiring such methods.[14]

¶ 17.16: Dirker, a farmer, owns 160 acres. Much of it is overgrown. Chet, a nine-year-old neighbor, was "exploring" in a remote corner of Dirker's property when he fell into a water-filled ditch that was obscured by the thick growth of weeds. Chet drowned and was found two days later. The next day Dirker cleared the growth away from the ditch and drained it. Chet's parents bring a wrongful death action against Dirker.

¶ 17.17: Pandora slipped and fell on the terrazzo sidewalk outside the Dixon Theater. Three weeks later, Dixon replaced

---

[14] *See Proposed Rules, Tamper-Evident Packaging Requirements for Over-the-Counter Human Drug Products*, 59 FRD 2542, 2543 (Jan. 18, 1994) (recounting history of 21 C.F.R. § 211.132, the regulation for tamper-resistant packaging, first adopted to respond to the emergency created by the Tylenol killings); *Canned Hoax: The Media and the Pepsi Scare*, Chicago Tribune, June 20, 1993, at 1 ("The Tylenol killings hit the public like a bucket of ice water, making it apparent to anyone that . . . products could be contaminated quite easily. The philosophy of product packaging changed after that incident, particularly in the drug industry.").

the sidewalk surface with concrete. Pandora sues Dixon for negligence.

¶ 17.18: Downjohn, Inc. (DI), a multinational corporation, is accused of having engaged in a widespread practice of bribing foreign trade officials to gain access to the markets of those officials' countries. When the president of DI heard rumors that her subordinates were engaging in these practices, she hired a management consultant to investigate the matter, report to her what the situation was, and recommend such further measures as it deemed appropriate. The IRS has brought a civil action against DI, contending that it improperly treated as deductions certain payments that it made to foreign officials.

The report in ¶ 17.18 may be an example of what has been called a "self-critical analysis" (or sometimes a "critical self-analysis"). In itself the report does not fix anything—but it may be the first step in fixing things, by identifying the problem. Whether such self-analyses should be covered by the exclusionary rule, and if so under what conditions, has aroused some controversy in recent years. On the one hand, when an organization is a defendant in a case challenging its performance, statements within the organization critical of its own performance can often—like other admissions—have tremendous probative value. Indeed, because they are meant to communicate, and do so in words, their probative value may be substantially greater than that of noncommunicative conduct such as replacing a slippery tile floor or redesigning an exhaust system. On the other hand, because they may point so explicitly to problems that might come back to haunt the organization in litigation, it may be that one of the concerns underlying the exclusionary rule—the fear that admissibility would inhibit socially beneficial conduct—might apply more powerfully in the case of such reports than in the case of less communicative remedial measures.

The judicial reaction to the "self-critical analysis" theory has been largely, though not entirely, skeptical.[15] Government agencies appear to

---

[15] *See, e.g.,* Dowling v. American Hawaii Cruises, Inc., 971 F.2d 423, 426 (9th Cir.1992) (helpful review, largely but not entirely, hostile to the doctrine); Wimer v. Sealand Service, Inc., 1997 WL 375661 (S.D.N.Y.1997) (same); Reichhold Chemicals, Inc. v. Textron, Inc., 157 F.R.D. 522 (N.D.Fla.1994) (helpful review, sympathetic to doctrine and applying it); Wichita Eagle & Beacon Publishing Co., Inc. v. Simmons, 274 Kan. 194, 50 P.3d 66 (2002) (considering self-critical analysis argument on case-by-case basis, concluding that it was outweighed in the particular case by statutorily expressed public policy favoring openness of records); cf. Note, *The Privilege of Self-Critical Analysis,* 96 Harv. L. Rev. 1083 (1983) (suggesting doctrine and bounds to it); David P. Leonard, *Codifying a Privilege of Self-Critical Analysis,* 25 Harv. J. on Legis. 113 (1988); Eric W. Orts & Paula C. Murray, *Environmental Disclosure and Evidentiary Privilege,* 1997 U. Ill. L. Rev. 1 (proposing a compromise in the environmental area, evidentiary protection in return for disclosure under a system supervised by the EPA, and emphasizing that protection is appropriate only where the statement receives higher level review that might reduce the misconduct); Brad Bacon, Note, *The Privilege of Self-Critical Analysis: Encouraging Recognition of the Misunderstood Privilege,* 8 Kan. J.L. & Pub. Pol'y 221, 236 (1998).

have a better chance than private entities in claiming the protection of the theory, and statements that are evaluative are more likely to be protected than statements that report facts.

¶ **17:19:** In May 2000, at its annual meeting, the Ford Motor Company, under the instigation of its new chairman, William Clay Ford, Jr., issued a Corporate Citizenship Report that expressed concern that sports utility vehicles, including those manufactured by Ford, are not only environmentally unfriendly but pose excessive risks to smaller vehicles in crashes. Suppose the survivors of the driver of a small car killed in a crash with a Ford SUV bring an action against Ford and seek to introduce this report. Should it be admissible?

The traditional arguments offered against admissibility of subsequent remedial measures presuppose a system in which most tort litigation is decided on a negligence standard. When negligence is not necessary to prove liability—and so the case is said to arise in strict liability—the considerations are different. Whether the exclusionary rule should still be applied is a rather complex and highly controversial question.

As you may recall from your Torts course, strict liability applies in various settings, such as when the defendant has engaged in particularly dangerous activities. The setting in which strict liability is most commonly applied—and the setting that most commonly raises the question of whether the exclusionary rule for subsequent remedial measures should be applied to strict liability cases—is that in which the plaintiff is complaining about injury from a defective product. Restatement (Third) of Torts: Products Liability, § 1, which some (but not all) states have followed, states in flat terms: "One engaged in the business of selling or otherwise distributing products who sells or distributes a defective product is subject to liability for harm to persons or property caused by the defect." This simple statement covers a great deal of complexity. A product may be defective, according to § 2 of the Restatement, in manufacture, in design, or because of inadequate warnings—and the definitions of design and warning defects are so dependent on the concepts of reasonableness and foreseeability that at least arguably it is really a negligence standard that applies in these cases.

Many courts have followed California's lead,[16] and held the exclusionary rule inapplicable to manufacturing defect cases, or more generally to strict liability cases. The original language of FRE 407—

---

[16] *See* Ault v. International Harvester Co., 13 Cal.3d 113, 117 Cal.Rptr. 812, 528 P.2d 1148 (1974).

which made the evidence inadmissible only to prove "negligence or culpable conduct"—may give some support to this conclusion, but most of the federal circuits that considered the question held that the Rule does apply when strict liability is the governing standard. So far as the federal courts are concerned, the question was resolved in 1997 by an amendment to Rule 407 providing that evidence of subsequent remedial measures is inadmissible not only to prove negligence and culpable conduct but also to prove "a defect in a product, a defect in a product's design, or a need for a warning or instruction." But be aware that this amendment resolves the issue *only* for the federal courts; the states will continue to go their own ways.[17]

¶ **17.20:** (a) Portnoy, claiming that the accelerator on his 2016 model Derby locked as he went into overdrive, brings a strict liability claim against Derby. Three weeks after the accident Derby redesigned the accelerator system on its models in production and recalled all of its 2016 model cars to examine the accelerators. If Portnoy sues Derby, and the jurisdiction does not have an evidence code, should evidence of the redesign and recall be admissible?

(b) If the evidence in (a) by itself is inadmissible, should it be admitted together with evidence that five other 2016 model Derbies had similar accidents before the recall but none did afterwards?

¶ **17.21:** Arguments (a) through (c) below are sometimes made against applying the exclusionary rule in manufacturing defect cases, or more generally in strict liability cases; arguments (i) through (v) are sometimes made in favor. What do you think of them?

(a) There's no danger of prejudice in a strict liability case: Notice is not an issue, and so there's no danger the jury is going to take later conduct as an indication of what the defendant should have known earlier.

(b) Strict liability often applies, in products liability cases, against mass producers, and they are unlikely to refrain from taking necessary remedial measures that might prevent many accidents because of the evidentiary consequence in one pending action.[18]

---

[17] There is an interesting *Erie* question here: In a federal diversity action in a state that does not apply the exclusionary rule to strict liability actions, should the court follow the state rule? Most federal courts have answered in the negative, *see, e.g.,* Flaminio v. Honda Motor Co., 733 F.2d 463, 470–72 (7th Cir.1984), but the view is not unanimous, *see* Wheeler v. John Deere Co., 862 F.2d 1404, 1410 (10th Cir.1988).

[18] *See, e.g., Ault, supra,* 528 P.2d at 1152.

(c)   A products liability plaintiff must show the product was defective, and a very good way to do that is to show that the defendant itself improved the product.

(i)   Whether the rule of liability is negligence or strict liability is irrelevant to the fact that admitting evidence of remedial measures creates a disincentive to taking those measures.

(ii)   The exclusionary rule is most necessary for mass producers, because they are the ones most likely to be aware of the evidentiary significance of their remedial behavior.

(iii) If the rule excludes evidence offered against a blameworthy defendant, a defendant who has done nothing wrong deserves no less protection.

(iv)   Evidence of a remedial measure has little probative value with respect to whether a product was defective at an earlier time.

(v)   "It is true that the benefits of subsequent remedial measures to the defendant in avoiding future accidents and their associated liability costs are greater, the larger the scale of the defendant's activity; but, by the same token, the costs of those measures to the defendant, in making it more likely that he will be forced to pay damages for accidents that occurred before the measures were adopted, are also greater. The effects are symmetrical."[19]

Another amendment to Rule 407 that became effective in 1997 addressed an ambiguity in the term "subsequent remedial measure"—subsequent to what? The problem arises in this scenario. A manufacturer puts a product on the market and later redesigns it; subsequent copies of the product are made under the new design, but copies of the old design remain in use. Then an accident occurs involving a copy of the product made under the old design, and a person hurt by the accident brings an action against the manufacturer. Should the exclusionary rule apply? The remedial measure was taken after the alleged cause of the accident—the design of the product—but before the accident itself. As it stood before the amendment, the Rule contained the ambiguous phrase "after an event." The 1997 amendment made the exclusionary applicable only if the remedial measures are taken "after an injury or harm allegedly caused by an event"—so in the hypothetical case just described the exclusionary rule would not apply. (The 2011 restyling flips the expression of the Rule, but without changing the substance, by making the exclusion applicable

---

[19]   Flaminio v. Honda Motor Co., 733 F.2d 463, 470 (7th Cir.1984) (Posner, J.).

"[w]hen measures are taken that would have made an earlier injury or harm less likely to occur.") It is far from clear that this is the best rule, and once again many states are likely to differ with the choice made by the federal rulemakers.

¶ **17.22:** Do you think the amendment chose the best resolution of this issue?[20]

¶ **17.23:** Consider whether FRE 407 should be amended by inserting, after "occur," the following clause:

> and the person taking such measures makes a public statement, at the time of taking such measures or within a reasonable time thereafter, that such measures are taken in reliance on this Rule,

Note that FRE 407, like Rule 408, bars use of the evidence for only one type of purpose, basically to prove from a later change that an earlier condition or process was faulty. The Rule does not stand in the way of admitting the evidence for another purpose. The Rule gives as examples of such other purposes "impeachment or—if disputed—proving ownership, control, or the feasibility of precautionary measures." The "if disputed" phrase emphasizes that a plaintiff, trying to get in evidence of subsequent remedial measures, cannot manufacture an issue by trying to prove a point that the defendant does not deny.

The "feasibility of precautionary measures" phrase sits somewhat uncomfortably alongside the prohibition on showing defect. If the device is not defective, that means it is reasonably safe. And if it is reasonably safe, that would seem to mean at least that additional precautionary measures that would have prevented the accident at issue would have been too expensive to implement—or put another way, that they were not feasible economically. So does a party who denies defect therefore automatically deny feasibility of precautionary measures? That would undercut the prohibition on introducing the evidence to show defect. Some courts have attempted to find some open space by holding that a defendant does not deny feasibility of precautionary measures unless it puts itself out on a limb, as by contending that it took all precautions and that no safer design was possible; in this view, the mere contention that the alternative that it actually used was adequate would not in itself be a contravention of feasibility of alternatives.[21] Courts appear to have been

---

[20] *See* David P. Leonard, *The New Wigmore: Selected Rules of Limited Admissibility* § 2.6.4 (rev. ed. 2002)(noting that the 1997 amendment conforms to the majority of federal decisions that had decided the issue under the old rule, but arguing that the amendment is ill-advised).

[21] *See, e.g.,* Grenada Steel Industries, Inc. v. Alabama Oxygen Co., 695 F.2d 883, 888 (5th Cir.1983) (rejecting argument that controversion of feasibility is "inherently" in issue is design defect cases; acknowledging that feasibility may "almost always" be in question, but holding that there are cases, such as this one, in which "the manufacturer does not suggest that another design was impractical but only that it adopted an acceptable one"). See the helpful discussions

more willing to conclude that feasibility has been challenged in products liability cases than in other cases, and this tendency may reflect hesitancy about applying the exclusionary rule in products liability cases altogether.

¶ **17.24:** In ¶ 17.16, Dirker surprises plaintiffs' counsel by denying from the stand that the ditch was on his property. What argument may counsel now use to support admissibility of the repair evidence? Might she have used the same argument before Dirker took the stand, on the ground that plaintiffs have the burden of proof of showing ownership?

¶ **17.25:** In ¶ 17.20, Derby contends that, with the technology available at the time Portnoy's car was made, about one year before the accident, a safer accelerator system was not possible without a fundamental redesign of the Derby. Given this, should the evidence be admissible? What if Derby claims, "We had the technological ability to redesign the accelerator system, but given the safety evidence we had at the time it would been unduly expensive"?

C. LIABILITY INSURANCE

FRE 411

Additional Reading: McCormick, Ch. 19; Mueller & Kirkpatrick, §§ 4.30–.31

It is generally agreed that evidence that the defendant was insured has little bearing either way on liability. There usually is not much substance to the argument that because he is insured he is likely to act recklessly. Nor, especially when insurance is compulsory, as in the case of automobile liability insurance, does the fact that he has taken the precaution of buying insurance point strongly in the other direction by suggesting that he is a prudent person. (Even if it did, the evidence would probably be barred by the general rule barring propensity evidence, which is discussed in the next chapter.) Correspondingly, the argument that the defendant was not insured usually—though perhaps not always—has little probative value.

---

in DAVID P. LEONARD, THE NEW WIGMORE: SELECTED RULES OF LIMITED ADMISSIBILITY § 2.8.3 (rev. ed. 2002), and in Tuer v. McDonald, 347 Md. 507, 701 A.2d 1101 (1997). The discourse in this area can sometimes be confusing because of a tendency to speak of narrow and broad views of feasibility with respect to what are really narrow and broad views, respectfully, of what it means to *controvert* feasibility. Under the narrow view, the defendant controverts feasibility of alternatives if it contends that "the measures were not physically, technologically, or economically possible under the circumstances then pertaining." Under the broader view, feasibility is controverted if the defendant contends that the alternative was not "capable of being utilized successfully." *Tuer*, 701 A.2d at 1109–10.

¶ **17.26:** Price, an entrepreneur, put together a series of real estate limited partnerships. She did some of the legal work herself and relied on Daumier, a lawyer, for the rest. She has had to pay a penalty for failure to file a private placement memorandum with a state agency, and she has sued Daumier for malpractice, claiming that the fault was his. Daumier denies ever being asked to file the form. Daumier's counsel wants to prove that Daumier carried no liability insurance. She argues, "If Daumier knew that he personally, rather than an insurance company, would be ultimately liable, he is far less likely to have made the type of error plaintiff alleges." Persuasive?

While liability insurance generally has little or no probative value in showing the defendant's conduct, there has long been a concern that it may have substantial prejudicial impact, because the jury may well be more willing to "let the insurance company pay" than to hit the defendant with a large judgment that he will have to pay himself. Some research helps clarify the concern. It appears that most modern jurors actually have rather little disposition to play Robin Hood, taking money from a "deep pocket" defendant and giving it to a plaintiff of modest means simply because of the difference in their financial status.[22] The more significant datum to the jury appears to be not the defendant's wealth but whether or not the defendant is insured, and the increasing prevalence of insurance leads the jury to the assumption that the defendant is insured. But if the jurors are already making that assumption, telling them that the defendant is in fact insured may have little impact. "Not exactly a surprise" may be their response. Given this, it may be that "the only parties affected by the rule [excluding mention of liability insurance] are the minority of uninsured defendants who might be hurt by the *absence* of any reference to insurance."[23]

¶ **17.27:** If you are the plaintiff's counsel in a jury trial, by what legitimate means can you let the jurors know that the defendant is insured?

¶ **17.28:** Consider whether the following jury instructions are proper in an auto accident case:

(a) "Now, I know that you all realize that every driver in this state must carry liability insurance, but that has nothing to do with your decision."

---

[22] Valerie P. Hans, *Business on Trial* 219–21 (2000). Hans does find, though, that in some circumstances jurors are tougher on businesses than on individuals. Apparently they believe that because of their greater knowledge, resources, and potential impact, businesses should be held to a higher standard of responsibility than are most individuals.

[23] Samuel R. Gross, *Make-Believe: The Rules Excluding Evidence of Character and Liability Insurance*, 49 Hastings L.J. 843, 855 (1998).

(b) "Now, I know that you all realize that large verdicts for plaintiffs can drive insurance rates up, but that has nothing to do with your decision."[24]

¶ 17.29: In ¶ 17.26, Daumier's counsel argues, "Your honor, it is important that the jurors be informed that my client was not insured, because otherwise they may be unduly generous with what they think is the insurance company's money." Should this argument be accepted?

If there is no good reason to allow mention of insurance, that is sufficient reason not to allow it. And perhaps, in situations in which insurance is not compulsory, the possibility that evidence of being insured would be admissible might have some inhibiting effect on the decisions of potential defendants to take out liability insurance—though we would expect this possibility to be small. In any event, the traditional rule, expressed in FRE 411, prohibits admissibility of evidence of liability insurance or of its absence to show that the defendant did or did not act "negligently or otherwise wrongfully."

As with Rules 407 and 408, however, FRE 411 prohibits only a defined set of uses of the evidence. Sometimes there is good reason to allow mention of insurance—such as when the defendant denies owning a truck that, it turns out, he had insured, or when a witness who testifies favorably to the defense is an investigator for the insurer. The result in cases such as this is straightforward enough. More significant difficulties arise when a statement that is highly probative on liability includes mention of insurance, or when insurance is mentioned before the court can prevent it.

¶ 17.30: In an old case, Owens, a teenager, killed Reid in an auto accident. Reid's widow sued and testified that Owens' father, who was a defendant, said to her, "My boy is careless, and he drives too fast. . . . We have taken out insurance to protect him [and] if you won't prosecute . . . we will do all we can to help you get that $5,000 insurance." Should this statement have been admissible?[25]

¶ 17.31: Plunkel v. Dunkel for auto negligence. Plunkel has testified to his version of the events. On cross, Dunkel's counsel wishes to question Plunkel about a prior inconsistent statement that he has made. She asks, "Mr. Plunkel, do you remember making a statement to somebody about this accident last June

---

[24] *See* Hoover v. Gregory, 253 N.C. 452, 117 S.E.2d 395 (1960).

[25] *See* Reid v. Owens, 98 Utah 50, 93 P.2d 680, 685 (1939) (reference to insurance was "itself freighted with admission").

25?" Plunkel answers, "Yes, to Dunkel's insurance agent." To what relief, if any, is Dunkel entitled?

Note that FRE 411 applies only to liability insurance, not to other forms of insurance. This is ironic, because it appears that when jurors speak about insurance—as they often do—they are most often speaking about health insurance or some other form of first-party insurance that the *plaintiff* might hold and that might have already covered some of plaintiff's medical costs.[26] In most cases, jurors are not supposed to take such payments into account in determining damages—this is the so-called "collateral source" rule—and so courts generally exclude evidence of this insurance on relevance grounds, even without the benefit of an exclusionary rule. But the collateral source rule goes against the instincts of many jurors, who believe they should prevent the plaintiff from "double-dipping," and who may not be aware of the possibility that the insurer will be subrogated to any recovery made by the plaintiff in the litigation. And so they often discuss insurance, though often, too, they constrain these conversations because they understand that they are not supposed to be discussing the matter.

¶ **17.32:** In a personal injury action, *should* the defense be allowed to bring out that the plaintiff has health insurance? If you think so, do you think a ruling excluding such evidence is wrong because the collateral source rule is wrong, or that such a ruling is wrong as a matter of evidence law even given the collateral source rule?

---

[26] *See* Shari Seidman Diamond & Neil Vidmar, *Jury Room Ruminations on a Forbidden Topic,* 87 U. Va. L. Rev.1857, 1889 (2001).

CHAPTER 18

EVIDENCE OF CHARACTER, SIMILAR OCCURRENCES, AND HABIT

■ ■ ■

A. INTRODUCTION

Additional Reading: McCormick, Ch. 17, § 186; Mueller & Kirkpatrick, § 4.11

In ordinary life, when we want to judge how a person will likely act in a given situation, we often rely heavily on an assessment of her character. Indeed, that is a large part of the purpose of job interviews. The same holds true when we are trying to reconstruct what happened in some episode. Did Richard III kill the two little boys in the tower? Surely, in answering this question we would want to know whether it was "in character" for Richard to commit such a vile act; a ruthless, violent, unscrupulous person is more likely to have done so than a conscience-motivated, gentle, law-abiding person.

Although character is often relevant to a material proposition, evidentiary law severely restricts its use. The long-established doctrine, expressed in FRE 404(a)(1), is that, in general, "[e]vidence of a person's character or character trait is not admissible to prove that on a particular occasion the person acted in accordance with the character or trait." And if the fact that the defendant is a bad man cannot be offered to show that he is more likely to have committed murder, it is a corollary that the fact that he has committed previous murders cannot be offered to prove that the defendant is a bad man and therefore more likely to have committed the murder alleged in this case. This corollary is stated in FRE 404(b)(1): "Evidence of a crime, wrong, or other act is not admissible to prove a person's character in order to show that on a particular occasion the person acted in accordance with the character." In this chapter, we shall explore the rationale for the character rule and the limitations to and exceptions from it. We shall also explore how character may be proved when it is an appropriate subject of proof.

At the outset, it is crucial to understand the basic scope of the character rule. The rule does not say that evidence of character, or evidence of other wrongs or acts, is generally inadmissible. It is only the propensity theory—the idea that the person probably acted "in accordance" with his character—that is generally an unacceptable basis

461

for admitting evidence. Section B examines cases in which character itself is in issue; if the character of a person is a material issue in the case, then naturally it is an appropriate subject of proof. We then move beyond the context in which character itself is in issue. Section C analyzes the rationale for the basic exclusion of evidence offered to prove action in conformity with a character trait.

Section D looks at three exceptions to the basic exclusionary rule of propensity evidence. One of these is very controversial: Some states have made past sexual offenses admissible against the defendant in cases involving sexual offenses, and a set of amendments to the Federal Rules of Evidence, adopted by Congress rather than through the usual rule-making procedure, takes this position. The other exceptions are older and more universally established. They apply in certain circumstances to the character of a criminal defendant and of the alleged victim of a crime. Included in this discussion is a limitation on the exception for alleged victims—rape shield laws, such as FRE 412, which bar evidence of the general sexual character of an alleged rape victim and strictly limit the admissibility of information concerning particulars of her past sexual conduct.[1]

Section E then discusses material issues, other than the character of a person, that can be proved in part by acts or transactions of that person other than those that underlie the claim or defense. In this context, admissibility is purportedly based on the relevance that the evidence might have not to a person's character but to some other issue in the case; for example, if the prosecution in an arson case claims that the defendant was attempting to cover up embezzlement, proof of the embezzlement would probably be admissible not because it shows that the defendant is a bad person but because it suggests that he had a motive for the arson.

One other rule must be read in conjunction with the character rules. As expressed in FRE 406, evidence of the habit of a person or the routine practice of an organization is ordinarily admissible "to prove that on a particular occasion the person or organization acted in accordance with the habit or routine practice." Does habit really stand in contrast with character, or does this rule simply indicate that some aspects of character are so probative and consistent that they are acceptable evidence to prove conforming actions? We will address questions such as this in Section F.

Even this brief overview should give you some idea of the complexity and limited nature of the character rule. The exclusionary rule may not

---

[1]   Not included in this chapter is a detailed discussion of the third well-established exception to the basic exclusionary rule, the exception for the character of truthfulness or untruthfulness of a witness. That exception is really part of an entirely separate body of rules, dealing with the impeachment and rehabilitation of witnesses, which we will study separately in Chapter 19.

apply depending upon the proposition for which the evidence is offered; upon the person a trait of whose character is being proven; upon what kind of similar act the evidence involves; and upon whether the trait may appropriately be considered a matter of habit.

B. CHARACTER OR REPUTATION IN ISSUE

FRE 405

Additional Reading: McCormick, Ch. 17, § 187; Mueller & Kirkpatrick, § 4.20

Most often litigation concerns who did what in particular circumstances, not what kind of person each of the parties is. If the defendant really murdered his best friend in a jealous rage, it does not matter, so far as his culpability is concerned, that he is ordinarily a very gentle man. And if he did not in fact commit the murder, it does not alter his innocence that he really is a violent psychopath who might just kill you for looking at him cross-eyed. His character is not an issue in the case. But sometimes the character of a person, or what someone else knew or believed about his character, is an issue—not in the loose sense that if we knew the person's character we would be better able to judge how he likely acted in particular circumstances, but in the more rigorous sense referred to in FRE 405(b), that it is "an essential element of a charge, claim, or defense." More broadly, others' perception of a person's character—the person's reputation—may be an issue.

¶ 18.1: Denver said that Procter, a local banker, is "as corrupt as the day is long." Procter took offense. In Procter's suit for libel, is his character in issue? How about his reputation? If the jury concludes that Procter is in fact as corrupt as the day is long, but that he has an excellent reputation in the community, what should the result be? What if the jury concludes that in fact he is a person of sterling character, but his reputation conforms to Denver's description?[2]

¶ 18.2: Hirst, an Indian serving time in a county prison, was allegedly beaten up by a deputy sheriff, leading to his death. Can Hirst's heirs, in their civil rights action against the county, show that the deputy is a violent bigot with a particular anti-Indian hatred? What foundation must the plaintiffs lay?[3]

---

[2] *Cf.* Guccione v. Hustler Magazine, Inc., 800 F.2d 298 (2d Cir.1986), *cert. denied*, 479 U.S. 1091 (1987); Proper v. Mowry, 90 N.M. 710, 568 P.2d 236 (N.M.App.1977).

[3] *See* Hirst v. Gertzen, 676 F.2d 1252, 1263 (9th Cir.1982); *compare* Estate of Arrington v. Fields, 578 S.W.2d 173 (Tex.Civ.App.1979), *with* Kassman v. Busfield Enterprises, Inc., 131 Ariz. 163, 639 P.2d 353 (Ariz.App.1981); *cf.* Winchester v. Padgett, 167 F.Supp. 444 (N.D.Ga.1952); *see generally* Michael Silver, *Negligent Hiring Claims Take Off*, 73 A.B.A.J., May 1, 1987, at 72.

¶ **18.3:** Paxton, a worker who was trying to organize a union in Dayton's factory, was beaten up severely by Houlihan, the foreman recently hired by Dayton. Houlihan died shortly afterwards. Paxton sues Dayton. On what theory, and by asking what questions of whom, might Paxton's counsel let the jury know that Houlihan was once convicted of armed robbery and charged with attempted murder?

¶ **18.4:** Duncan is accused of distributing heroin. He defends on grounds of entrapment.

(a) Suppose California's test for entrapment applies: "[W]as the conduct of the law enforcement agent likely to induce a normally law-abiding person to commit the offense?" *People v. Barraza*, 23 Cal.3d 675, 689–90, 153 Cal.Rptr. 459, 471, 591 P.2d 947, 955 (1979). May the prosecution introduce evidence that Duncan is a drug addict who has previously sold heroin to the same undercover agent?

(b) Now suppose the jurisdiction applies the federal definition of entrapment, under which "the defendant's predisposition to commit the crime" is ordinarily the critical issue. *United States v. Russell*, 411 U.S. 423, 433 (1973).[4] Does your answer change?

(c) Now suppose the federal definition applies and that the other drug sale, in which Duncan delivered a large quantity of heroin, occurred two months after the one for which he is being tried. Does your answer to part (a) change? Could Duncan be tried simultaneously for the two alleged sales?

¶ **18.5:** Dupuis is accused of murdering an eighty-year-old man. Pathological evidence shows clearly that the victim, a neighbor of Dupuis, was killed by dismemberment. Dupuis denies that he was the criminal. At the guilt phase of the trial, the prosecution offers the testimony of a co-worker of Dupuis that in his opinion Dupuis is a person of violent tendencies, and the testimony of a neighbor that Dupuis is reputed to be a violent person. In arguing for the admissibility of this evidence, the prosecutor declares, "Obviously, the perpetrator was a depraved person. The defendant's character is most certainly in issue." Do you accept this argument? Assuming the evidence is not admissible at the guilt phase, should it be admissible at the sentencing phase?

---

    4 *Cf.* Jacobson v. United States, 503 U.S. 540 (1992) (holding evidence insufficient to show defendant's predisposition to break child pornography laws where defendant did not place illegal mail order for pornographic materials until after receiving many mailings from undercover government agents).

¶ **18.6:** (a) As part of their divorce, Elizabeth Watson and Robert Hudson are litigating custody of their 10-year-old daughter Deborah. Watson claims that Hudson has sexually abused Deborah, and Hudson denies the charge. May Watson introduce evidence that Hudson recently abused Felice, his 13-year-old daughter by a previous marriage?[5]

[handwritten: character for being a good parent is at issue in a custody case]

[handwritten: yes – can use specific instances of conduct if it's an essential element]

(b) Now suppose instead that Hudson is being charged criminally with molesting Deborah. Does your answer change?[6]

[handwritten: still yes because of FRE 414]

If the character of a person, or his reputation, is itself in issue, then it is a fact of the world that must be proven like any other historical fact in the case. Recall the analogy sometimes used to describe the level of probative value necessary to justify admissibility for a single item of evidence: If the fact to be proven is a wall, an individual evidentiary item need be only a single brick. Many such bricks may be used to build the wall; indeed, it may be impossible to build the wall without a large number of bricks. When the fact to be proven is, say, the quality of a tort victim's life, the wall may be built by offering many facts about what she can or cannot do. Similarly, when the fact to be proven is the quality of a person's character or reputation, the wall may require many facts about actions that the person has or has not taken.

¶ **18.7:** In ¶¶ 18.1, .2, and .3, assuming that character is held to be an appropriate subject of proof, how should the party trying to prove it do so? Should proof of the person's reputation, or of the witness' opinion of the person's character, be allowed as proof of the person's character? How about proof of particular acts that the person has committed?

[handwritten: Nope – but can come out on cross]

¶ **18.8:** In ¶ 18.4, in rebutting Duncan's entrapment defense, should the prosecution be allowed to offer

(a) the testimony of Ingle: "Everyone in the neighborhood believes that Burkley is a pusher"?

[handwritten: No! Yes! They can rebut the entrapment defense]

(b) Ingle's testimony: "On March 12, Duncan sold me two tabs of heroin"? [The indictment charges a sale on April 5, but not one on March 12.]

[handwritten: Predisposition to deal drugs is an essential element of the defense so yes specific instances are allowed]

(c) the testimony of Officer Wednesday that Ingle made the statement in (a) to her?

(d) the testimony of Officer Wednesday that Ingle made the statement in (b) to her?[7]

[handwritten: now we have hearsay issues – is being offered for the truth]

---

[5]   *See, e.g.,* M.E.D. v. J.P.M., 3 Va.App. 391, 350 S.E.2d 215 (1986).

[6]   The issue raised by ¶ 18.6(b) is addressed more fully in Section D of this chapter.

[7]   *See generally* United States v. Webster, 649 F.2d 346, 349–50 (5th Cir.1981) (en banc).

C. THE EXCLUSION OF PROPENSITY EVIDENCE

FRE 404(a)(1), (b)(1)

Additional Reading: McCormick, Ch. 17, §§ 188–189; Mueller & Kirkpatrick, § 4.11

Now let's assume that, as is usually the case, character itself is *not* at issue. We will focus for now on the case in which a prosecutor nevertheless seeks to introduce prior bad acts of the defendant.

In the typical criminal case, the *conduct* of the defendant is the principal issue: Did the defendant commit acts that constitute the crime charged? But in determining that question, other acts might be significant. If, for example, the defendant is accused of having robbed a bank, then our assessment of the probability of his guilt will almost certainly rise if we learn that he robbed a bank two years earlier. Most people don't rob banks, and a person who already has robbed a bank is more likely to rob a given bank on another occasion than a person who has never done so or one who we are uncertain has done so. Even if the probability that a given person who has robbed a bank in the past will rob a bank in the future is quite low—and recidivism rates suggest that it is not all that low—it is presumably many times greater than the probability that a given person who has never robbed a bank will do so.

But evidence of other acts is most often not admissible on this basis. This is the basic exclusion of propensity evidence, which is expressed in FRE 404(a)(1) and (b)(1). Subsection (a)(1) provides—subject to some important but limited exceptions—that "[e]vidence of a person's character or character trait is not admissible to prove that on a particular occasion the person acted in accordance with the character or trait." And subsection (b)(1) takes the exclusion a step further by providing: "Evidence of a crime, wrong, or other act is not admissible to prove a person's character in order to show that on a particular occasion the person acted in accordance with the character."

Do not overemphasize the place of this exclusion in the structure of the law. There is not a general exclusion of evidence of character and other acts of a person. Rather, it is only the propensity theory that is specifically barred (with limited exceptions, to be discussed in Section D, and subject also to the "escape valve," discussed in Section F, for propensities sufficiently regular to be considered habits). If evidence of a person's other acts is relevant on other grounds, the propensity rule does not stand in the way. We will address such possible relevance arguments in Section E. For now, we will explore the underpinnings of the rule when the evidence is offered on a propensity theory.

One justification often cited for the exclusionary rule is that the evidence may be overly persuasive to a jury.[8] Note that the Advisory Committee for the Federal Rules quoted with approval a statement by the California Law Revision Commission that "[c]haracter evidence is of slight probative value." Do you buy that? We make predictions of people's conduct all the time based on their past behavior, and we are not irrational in doing so;[9] those who have to predict behavior for a living do the same thing.[10] A jury is not acting irrationally in thinking that the defendant's prior commission of a bank robbery is powerful evidence in the prosecution's favor. On its own, of course, the evidence of the prior crime does not make it likely that the defendant committed the robbery with which he is charged. But psychological and criminological evidence confirms what most of us probably believe intuitively, that although people's behavior varies from situation to situation, commission by a person of a crime on one occasion is evidence that makes it substantially more likely that he will commit a crime, especially a similar crime, on another occasion.[11] We cannot even say with confidence that a jury putting a great deal of weight on evidence of this sort is overvaluing it; in many circumstances the evidence *is* in fact highly probative. And even if

---

[8] *See, e.g.,* Michelson v. United States, 335 U.S. 469, 475–76 (1948).

[9] For a witty encapsulation of this phenomenon, see the short poem *Those Two Boys* by Franklin P. Adams, http://www.bartleby.com/104/89.html.

[10] Some insurers use an "insurance score" to predict future insurance losses. Such a score takes into account various information that has been found to correlate with the probability of an insurance loss, including the number of collections, bankruptcies, outstanding debt, length of credit history, types of credit in use and the number of new applications for credit. Numerous states have limited the ability of insurers to do this—but the objection is based on concerns of differential effects on different demographic groups, not that doing so is irrational from the insurers' point of view. *See generally* Credit-Based Insurance Scores: Impacts on Consumers of Automobile Insurance: A Report to Congress By the Federal Trade Commission (2007), https://www.ftc.gov/reports/credit-based-insurance-scores-impacts-consumers-automobile-insurance-report-congress-federal.

[11] *See, e.g.,* Samuel Yochelson & Stanton Samenow, *The Criminal Personality* (1976); Stanton Samenow, *Inside the Criminal Mind* (1984). The standard reference manual for mental disorders, American Psychiatric Association, *Diagnostic and Statistical Manual of Mental Disorders* (5th ed. 2013)("*DSM-V*"), includes Antisocial Personality Disorder. "The essential feature of antisocial personality disorder," it says, "is a pervasive pattern of disregard for, and violation of, the rights of others that begins in childhood or early adolescence and continues into adulthood." *Id.* at 659. And it lists as one of the diagnostic criteria "[f]ailure to conform to social norms with respect to lawful behaviors, as indicated by repeatedly performing acts that are grounds for arrest." *Id.* Walter Mischel, the pioneer among situationalists—those who contend that behavior is largely a function of environmental or situational factors and "not highly generalized across situations," *Personality and Assessment* 281 (1968)—has cautioned against a caricature of his position that would minimize the importance of personality. *See* Walter Mischel, *The Interaction of Person and Situation,* in *Personality at the Crossroads* 333, 334 (David Magnusson & Norman Edler eds. 1977) ("I know no one who seriously doubts that lives have coherence and that we perceive ourselves and others as relatively stable individuals that have substantial identity and continuity over time, even when our specific actions change.").

For helpful reviews of the psychological literature from a legal perspective, see Susan M. Davies, *Evidence of Character to Prove Conduct: A Reassessment of Relevancy,* 27 Crim. L. Bull. 504 (1991); Roger Park, *Character at the Crossroads,* 49 Hastings L.J. 717 (1998). *See generally* Lee Ross & Richard Nisbett, *The Person and the Situation* (1991).

the jurors do overvalue the evidence somewhat,[12] that may be the lesser evil than keeping the evidence from them, which in effect means that they will give it no weight at all.

Consider, for example, the case of Darwish Hasan Darwish, a leading gynecologist resident in England. One of his patients accused him of raping her while she was in a therapeutic hypnotic trance. The DNA of the woman's daughter indicated strongly that Darwish was the girl's father. Nevertheless, the jury acquitted, apparently because of doubts as to whether the sexual contact was consensual. Consider how likely, and how justifiable, an acquittal would be if the jury had learned that Darwish had been convicted of indecently assaulting nine woman patients over a period of nearly a decade. Arguably, then, the adjudicative system is *under*valuing the evidence by excluding it—though we must take into account that, as in the Darwish case, it is most often a prosecutor who would like to introduce character evidence. Perhaps the small chance of a pro-prosecution error as a result of such evidence outweighs the larger chance of a pro-defendant error as a result of exclusion of the evidence.

There are in any event other justifications for the exclusionary rule. The principal one is that evidence of prior crimes is likely to bias the jury against the defendant, not in the sense that the jury will overvalue the evidence but in the sense that the jury will be overly ready to convict. A juror might be willing to convict the defendant for bad prior conduct, saying, in effect, "I don't particularly care whether he committed the crime with which he's charged in this case. He did the other one, and probably some others we don't even know about, and if he's on the street already he wasn't punished enough for them." Or, in a similar but distinct manner, the juror might implicitly approach the case this way, weakening the standard of persuasion for the present crime: "This guy's such a bad person I won't feel all that bad if we convict him for something he didn't do. So I don't buy this 'beyond a reasonable doubt' stuff. I'm going to apply a lighter burden of proof—I'll vote to convict if there's a pretty good chance he did the crime charged here." These are genuine dangers, and if the jury operates along these lines the use of prior bad acts would seriously undermine the trial process.

Beyond this, there is a danger of distraction and waste of time. Sometimes, it is easy to prove a prior bad act, and there is not much doubt that the defendant committed it. But this is not always so. The defendant might deny that he committed the prior act, as well as the one charged in this case. And then the trial will have multiplied; even though

---

[12] For helpful comments on the psychological literature on this question, see David P. Bryden & Roger C. Park, *"Other Crimes" Evidence in Sex Offense Cases*, 78 Minn. L. Rev. 529, 563–64 (1994).

only one crime is being charged, evidence for and against a whole series of bad acts may become admissible.[13]

However it may be justified, the exclusionary rule is controversial.[14] As we will see, it has been weakened in recent decades, but it still stands, albeit rather shakily.

Thus far, we have concentrated on the exclusionary rule in its most important, and most controversial, application—to prior bad acts of a criminal defendant. But the rule, traditionally and as expressed in FRE 404(a)(1) and (b)(1), is not limited to that context. It applies generally to evidence of character or past acts when offered to make it appear more likely that a person acted in conformity with his character or propensities. Some commentators have argued that the exclusionary rule should not be applied in civil cases. Given that prejudice to a criminal defendant is not at stake in the civil context, there may seem less reason to exclude the evidence, and less reason for a *per se* rule of exclusion. On the other hand, parties in civil cases would rather rarely be able to present character evidence that is as probative as the type of prior-crimes evidence that is routinely excluded in criminal cases. In any event, the exclusionary rule is generally applied to civil as well as criminal cases.

---

[13] This does not exhaust the list of reasons providing some support for the exclusionary rule. One other consideration sometimes mentioned is the fear that if prior bad acts were admissible the authorities would have too great a temptation to secure a conviction by "rounding up the usual suspects." That is, they may charge a person who has committed similar acts in the past, on the basis that even if he did not commit this crime the evidence of his prior conduct will make him easy to convict. In most cases, however, this consideration will not be particularly powerful. Even given inadmissibility of prior bad acts, police do have an incentive, when identity is in issue, to concentrate on those who have committed similar crimes in the past, as by showing mug shots to the victim. (On occasion, therefore, a defendant might actually *want* to prove his prior record: "The reason they got me here was simply that I'd done this before and so they went after me.")

Another argument is that propensity evidence is faulty because we want to try each case on its own, with evidence applicable to that case only. In the criminal context, we might in effect say to the prosecution, "Don't offer generalities. Show us what you have in *this* case." There is a problem with this type of argument, however: All the time, we reason from the general to the specific, using what we know generally about the world ("People like money, and some don't mind how they get it") as *part* of the basis on which to draw inferences about the particular case ("This defendant probably stole the victim's wallet."). So even if the propensity evidence is very general, it would rationally be part of the background in the particular case. (It would be a different matter if the prosecution's case depended totally on propensity evidence, but that is very rare.).

[14] *See, e.g.*, Office of Legal Policy, U.S. Dep't of Justice, *Truth in Criminal Justice Series, Report No. 4, Report to the Attorney General on the Admission of Criminal Histories at Trial* (1986), *reprinted in* 22 U. Mich. J.L. Ref. 707 (1989) (a product of the Reagan Administration's Justice Department, proposing the "uniform admission" of criminal defendants' prior convictions); Kenneth J. Melilli, *The Character Evidence Rule Revisited*, 1998 BYU L. Rev. 1547 (arguing for a simplification that would make the rules more discretionary); David P. Leonard, *In Defense of the Character Evidence Prohibition: Foundations of the Rules Against Trial by Character*, 73 Ind. L. J. 1161 (1998) (defending the exclusionary rules on the basis of "the proposition that people should be tried for their specifically charged acts, not for the flaws of their character").

And note that the rule applies to attempts to prove good character as well as bad character.

In ¶¶ 18.9, .10, and .11, assume that the jurisdiction is a new one without an evidentiary code.

¶ 18.9: In Dupuis' case, ¶ 18.5, the prosecution offers a more straightforward argument for introducing the reputation and opinion evidence of Dupuis' violent tendencies: "It's a simple fact that violent people tend to act in violent ways. Showing that Dupuis is a violent person substantially increases the probability that he committed this vile crime."

(a) Should this argument be accepted? *No – this is a pure propensity argument*

(b) Now suppose the case is tried by a judge. Does this change your answer? *NO*

¶ 18.10: The estate of the old man brings an action against Dupuis. Should the opinion and reputation evidence be excluded? *yes* Now suppose that in this civil action Dupuis wants to introduce the testimony of a neighbor that he is a really sweet, gentle guy, so even-tempered that butter wouldn't melt in his mouth. Should this evidence be excluded? *yes*

¶ 18.11: Dover is on trial for allegedly snatching a gold chain off the neck of a woman who was standing on a subway platform. The prosecution seeks to introduce evidence that on six other occasions Dover has stolen gold chains from women at various places in the same city. *–NO*

(a) Should this evidence be excluded? What argument does the prosecution have in this case that the prosecution in the Dupuis case did not have? *Method / M.O.*

(b) The defense points by analogy to FRE 404(b)(1), and the prosecutor argues, "Even if we were a Federal Rules jurisdiction, Rule 404(b)(1) wouldn't even apply because we are not offering these other acts in order to show character. I have no desire to cast aspersions on Mr. Dover's character. I simply wish to show that he repeatedly stole gold chains. And if the jury finds that he committed such acts on other occasions, it will conclude that he more probably did so on this occasion." Should this argument be accepted?

No – need to stop prosecution to M.O. *this might work under 404 (b)*

nope, sorry, this is still propensity

D. EXCEPTIONS TO THE PROPENSITY RULE

FRE 404(a), 405(a), 412–415

Additional Reading: McCormick, Ch. 17, §§ 191–93; Mueller & Kirkpatrick, §§ 4.12–.14

1. OVERVIEW

In general, as we have seen, the rules exclude evidence of a person's character offered to prove that the person acted in conformity with it. But there are exceptions to this general exclusion, three of which we will consider in this section. This section will not consider the separate question of when evidence of a person's other acts may be offered to prove a material proposition *other than* propensity; that question is treated in Section E.

Subsection 2 discusses a controversial exception, recognized by some jurisdictions, for evidence of prior sexual crimes. Subsection 3 then discusses the exception codified by FRE 404(a)(2)(A), allowing a criminal defendant to present, and the prosecution to rebut, evidence of a relevant trait of his own character. Subsection 4 discusses the exception codified by FRE 404(a)(2)(B), which in some circumstances allows evidence of a relevant trait of the alleged victim of a crime. As part of this topic, we will consider the rape shield laws, the federal version of which is FRE 412. These rules usually, but not uniformly, exclude evidence of the prior sexual conduct of a rape victim, and they operate in part as a limitation on the principle behind Rule 404(a)(2)(B).

Perhaps the most important exception to the rule against propensity evidence is the one allowing any party to attack, and then allowing any other party to support, the character for truthfulness of a witness. The witness-character rules, codified in FRE 607–609 and referred to in FRE 404(a)(3), are distinct from the other character rules. We will deal with the witness-character rules in the next chapter in the context of the general topic of impeachment and support of witnesses, so we will not speak further of them here. But always bear in mind that a separate set of rules applies to witnesses.

Note that the exception for prior sexual misconduct (where it exists) is different in nature from the other exceptions. The other exceptions are procedural and structural, in the sense that they depend principally on whose propensities the evidence concerns; on what party wants to raise the matter; and on what has already occurred at trial. By contrast, the exception for prior sexual misconduct, at least in its federal version, FRE 413–15, simply refuses to apply the rule against propensity evidence to evidence indicating a particular type of propensity. Hence, this rule is best discussed in conjunction with the topic we have just addressed, the considerations for and against the basic exclusion of propensity evidence. And so, though it is far less well established than the other exceptions, we will discuss this one first.

2.   PRIOR SEXUAL MISCONDUCT

Courts have sometimes modified the rule against propensity evidence in cases involving allegations of sexual misconduct. Suppose a defendant is charged with sexual molestation of a small girl, and there is evidence that on another occasion, not charged in the indictment, he molested the same girl. Numerous courts have admitted such evidence to show the defendant's "lewd [or lustful] disposition,"[15] or "depraved sexual instinct."[16] There is no consensus about this practice; some states have never recognized such an exception, or having recognized it have abolished it, in some cases because the language of their codifications, based on the Federal Rules, does not support it.[17] Although some states that apply this exception have limited it to prior conduct with the same victim, the trend has been against this limitation. Most courts that recognize the exception do not apply it to rapes of adult women; at least for the most part, it is a rule applicable to cases of child sexual abuse, including incest.

Note that this ground for admissibility is a propensity theory; hence, it is an exception to the rule against propensity evidence and not merely a way around it. The basic idea seems to be that the propensity revealed by the prior conduct is so unusual, and so relevant to the conduct at issue in the case charged, that the evidence has particularly strong weight and should not be excluded, especially because absent the evidence the jury might believe that the defendant is incapable of committing such an act. Arguably, the need for the evidence on this ground is less than it was in earlier eras; child sexual abuse is no less repugnant today than it was before, but people are far more aware that it does occur and that even respectable-seeming people sometimes commit it.[18]

¶ 18.12: Is there any ground for distinguishing, with respect to the exclusionary rule, between what might be considered particularly aberrant or abnormal sexual behavior—such as the sexual abuse of a child or of an old woman—and the rape of a

---

[15] Burke v. State, 624 P.2d 1240 (Alaska 1980).

[16] Brackens v. State, 480 N.E.2d 536 (Ind.1985).

[17] *See, e.g.,* State v. Kirsch, 139 N.H. 647, 662 A.2d 937 (1995); Getz v. State, 538 A.2d 726 (Del.1988); Edward J. Imwinkelried, Uncharged Misconduct Evidence § 4.18 (1996 & Supp.). Note also Lannan v. State, 600 N.E.2d 1334 (Ind.1992), which has a helpful discussion of the entire field, overruled prior case law, and itself was effectively overruled legislatively. *See* Ind. Code 35–37–4–15, adopted by Pub. L. No. 232–1993, § 2.

[18] This is a point made by *Lannan, supra,* 600 N.E.2d at 1337, in (temporarily) abolishing Indiana's "depraved sexual instinct" exception to the rule against character evidence.

healthy, young adult woman? If you think that the evidence of prior similar conduct should be admitted in the first type of case but not in the second, is it because you believe that "a desire for heterosexual intercourse with an adult, even when forced, is not as unusual or depraved as a desire for sex with a child"? David P. Bryden & Roger C. Park, *"Other Crimes" Evidence in Sex Offense Cases*, 78 Minn. L. Rev. 529, 558–59 (1994) (speculating that this might be the theory motivating some judges).[19] Note in this connection Katharine K. Baker, *Once a Rapist? Motivational Evidence and Relevancy in Rape Law*, 110 Harv L. Rev. 563, 604–06 (1997). Baker contends, "Most men are taught that sexual desire is like hunger: when it is there, you satisfy it. Women are candybars." And this commodified view of sex, Baker argues, makes rape appear unduly like theft. Thus, does the attempt to distinguish between child sexual abuse and rape of an adult reflect a view that rape, like theft, is simply a wrongful taking of what most men want, whereas child molestation reveals an orientation that most men do not have?

On the other hand, if we treat rape of an adult as also reflecting a "depraved sexual instinct," does that reflect an unduly narrow view of who commits rape? Bear in mind that millions of women in the United States have been raped, that millions of men have committed rape, and that most rapes are not committed by strangers to the victim. Also, if we treat prior rapes of an adult as admissible because they reflect a depraved instinct, how does this distinguish rape from other crimes? As Bryden & Park point out, "Murder, after all, is at least arguably more depraved than child abuse, but courts do not routinely admit a murder defendant's prior homicides." 78 Minn. L. Rev. at 559.

Congress made a dramatic entry into this realm in 1994. Recall that most changes to the Federal Rules of Evidence are the product of an extended committee process, at the end of which the proposed amendments are presented to Congress and become effective if Congress does not act. But Rules 413–415 were the products of a more overtly political process. As part of the Violence Against Women Act, which in turn was part of the Violent Crime Control and Law Enforcement Act of 1994, Pub. L. 103–322, 108 Stat. 1796, Congress tentatively added these Rules.[20] Although some Democrats opposed them, they were apparently the price of getting enough Republican votes to secure passage of the

---

[19] *See* Reichard v. State, 510 N.E.2d 163 (Ind.1987) (stating that the rape of an adult woman does not fit the "depraved sexual instinct" exception then recognized by Indiana because the rape of an adult woman is not depraved sexual conduct).

[20] Pub.L.No. 103–322, § 320395, 108 Stat. 1796, 2135–37, 28 U.S.C. App. 1994.

comprehensive bill. Congress provided that these Rules would not become effective immediately, thus giving the United States Judicial Conference time to comment and Congress time to act on the comments. The Judicial Conference, in accordance with the virtually unanimous views of the members of its committees and with most academic commentary, strongly recommended against adoption of the Rules,[21] but Congress did not act on the report and so the Rules became effective in July 1995.

These Rules are much broader than the "lustful disposition" exception applied by many states. Rule 413 provides, subject to a notice provision, that if a criminal defendant "is accused of a sexual assault," then "[t]he court may admit evidence that the defendant committed any other sexual assault," and that this evidence "may be considered on any matter to which it is relevant." Rule 414 contains a similar provision for child molestation.[22] And, for good measure, Rule 415 provides a similar rule for sexual assault or child molestation in civil cases.

It is important to bear in mind that these new Rules govern only the federal courts—and that the federal courts are not a major forum for sexual offenses, except when such offenses are committed on Indian reservations. (A separate set of Military Rules of Evidence, prescribed by the President as Commander-in-Chief, applies to courts-martial, and they have been amended to include Rules 413 and 414 substantially similar to their counterparts in the FRE.) States have not rushed to emulate these Rules—though California, most notably, did so. Cal. Evid. Code § 1108, added by Stats. 1995, c. 439 (A.B. 882), § 2. Two tugs in opposite directions may explain the restrained reaction in the states to the new Rules. First, presumably many state rulemakers, like most of those persons who commented publicly when the new Rules were under consideration, disapprove of the principle of the Rules. Second, the rulemakers may believe that the Rules are unnecessary; as we have seen, many states already cover some of the same ground with a "lustful disposition" exception to the propensity exclusion, and, as we shall see in Section E, courts often make aggressive use of the available end runs around that exclusion.

The draftsmanship of Federal Rules 413–415 has been criticized; for example, are hearsay reports of prior offenses now admissible, and is the evidence of such offenses admissible even if it raises strong concerns of

[21] Report of the Judicial Conference on the Admission of Character Evidence in Certain Sexual Misconduct Cases, 159 F.R.D. 51 (1995).

[22] Rule 414 may seem superfluous in light of Rule 413, but some conduct that is covered by Rule 414 is not covered by Rule 413. In particular, violation of18 U.S.C. § 2252, dealing with child pornography, is within Rule 414's definition of child molestation but not within Rule 413's definition of an offense of sexual assault. Tighter drafting, however, could have resulted in adding only one new Rule instead of three—or better yet, one more exception to Rule 404 and an accompanying amendment to Rule 405. The latter approach was an alternative suggestion made by the Judicial Conference. 159 F.R.D. at 53–57.

the type highlighted by Rule 403?[23] (The California rule is more tightly drafted and avoids these difficulties; it makes clear that it only removes the basic propensity exclusion from this evidence.) Most of the discussion, however, has centered on the substance of the Rules.

Apart from the simple desire to make rape prosecutions easier, to guarantee more convictions, the new Rules were justified by their proponents in significant part by the argument that it is just too coincidental that a person who committed a prior rape would be falsely accused of having committed the one being charged. Unfortunately, that is not always true; in stranger rape cases, police tend to use mug shots, and this can lead to false identifications.[24] Advocates for the new Rules also argued on the basis of their belief that recidivism is high among rapists. The data on this point are unclear. Reported recidivism rates are actually rather low for rape as compared to most crimes.[25] But these data, which depend on subsequent arrest, may not be particularly helpful. For one thing, arguably sexual offenders are far more likely to avoid arrest—in part because of the low reporting rate for rape—than are those who commit other serious crimes.[26] Such evidence as there is suggests that those who are convicted for sexual offenses have, on average, committed multiple offenses of the same type before.[27] This fact does not, however, provide clear support for a crime-specific exception to the propensity exclusion.

Most of the academic commentary, as indicated above, has been hostile to the new Rules, but there are some surprises. Katharine Baker, *Once a Rapist?*, *supra*, argues from a feminist perspective against a

---

[23] *See, e.g.*, United States v. Meacham, 115 F.3d 1488, 1492 (10th Cir. 1997). ("Rule 403 balancing is still applicable, . . . but clearly under Rule 414 the courts are to 'liberally' admit evidence of prior uncharged sex offenses."); James Joseph Duane, *The New Federal Rules of Evidence on Prior Acts of Accused Sex Offenders: A Poorly Drafted Version of a Very Bad Idea*, 157 F.R.D. 95, 115–22 (1995).

[24] *See* Susan Estrich, *Real Rape* 2 (1987) (describing how she nearly made a misidentification based on mug shots presented to her; "being 'really shown' a mug shot means exactly what defense attorneys are afraid it means").

[25] One frequently cited study by the Bureau of Justice Statistics followed 100,000 prisoners for three years after release, and found that only 7.7% of rapists were rearrested for rape—compared to 31.9% of burglars, 24.8% of drug offenders, 19.6% of violent robbers, and 2.8% of murderers who were rearrested for the same crime. Allen J. Beck, *Bureau of Justice Statistics, U.S. Dept. of Justice, Recidivism of Prisoners Released in 1983* at 6 (1989).

[26] *See* A. Nicholas Groth, Robert E. Longo & J. Bradley McFadin, *Undetected Recidivism among Rapists and Child Molesters*, 28 Crime & Delinquency 450 (1998), *quoted in Lannan, supra*, 600 N.E.2d at 1337 n.6.

[27] Furthermore, as Roger Park has pointed out, propensity evidence may be very probative with respect to a particular crime even if recidivism is not particularly high for that crime. What really matters is what might be called the *comparative commission rate*. Suppose the recidivism rate for a given crime is only 1%, but only one in a billion people who have not committed the crime before age 30 do so after. In such a case, evidence that a 35-year-old defendant had committed the crime before turning 30 would be highly probative. *See* Roger Park, *Character at the Crossroads*, 49 Hastings L.J. 717 (1998).

blanket rule permitting admission of acts of prior sexual misconduct.[28] On the other hand, Roger Park, a scholar well within the traditional mainstream, has argued that Congress was right in part, so far as it removed the propensity exclusion from sexual misconduct cases where the defense is based on consent. Roger C. Park, *The Crime Bill of 1994 and the Law of Character Evidence: Congress Was Right About Consent Defense Cases*, 22 Fordham Urban L.J. 271 (1995).[29]

¶ 18.13: (a) Baker argues that Rule 413 maintains a misconception about rape—that rapists are a relatively small class of depraved men—contrary to evidence showing that a very large number of psychologically normal men commit rape. To the extent the Rule was meant to enhance the credibility of rape victims, she argues, it is misconceived: The problem is not that jurors tend to misbelieve complaining witnesses in rape cases, but that they tend not to vindicate women who breach rigid norms of social conduct, such as dressing in certain manners. The Rule, she says, will increase the chances of wrongful convictions, especially of those who have previously been suspects of crime, a group that is disproportionately poor and minority.

Are you persuaded?

(b) Park contends that in rape cases where the defense is consent—typically "date rape" cases—there is no concern about identity and therefore no concern that the authorities have prosecuted the defendant because they have used his prior offense to "round up the usual suspects." In cases of this sort, he argues, evidence of prior acts of a similar nature is especially important because jurors tend to apply too *high* a standard of persuasion, being insufficiently willing to vote for conviction. The evidence also diminishes the ordeal for the victim, providing in effect another voice in the courtroom of someone who claims to have had a similar experience with the defendant.

Are you persuaded?

¶ 18.14: Where would you draw the line? Assume you are the trial judge in a jurisdiction unfettered by codified evidence rules. Would you exclude, in a case charging

(a) child sexual abuse, evidence of prior sexual abuse of

---

[28] *See also* Aviva Orenstein, *No Bad Men! A Feminist Analysis of Character Evidence in Rape Trials*, 49 Hastings L.J. 663 (1998) (arguing against FRE 413 "and other attempts to admit evidence of prior bad acts of the accused," on the ground that they "rest on anti-feminist principles and stereotypes about rapists").

[29] See also the other contributions to the Symposium, *Perspectives on Proposed Federal Rules of Evidence 413–415*, 22 Fordham Urban L.J. 265 (1995).

    (i)   the same child? *no*

    (ii) another child, but in the same manner? *No*

  (b) intercourse with a 7-year-old girl, evidence of a prior incident in which the defendant allegedly fondled the breasts of a 13-year-old girl? *No*

  (c) rape of a 25-year-old woman, evidence

    (i)   of a prior incident in which the defendant allegedly fondled the breasts of a 13-year-old girl? *exclude*

    (ii) that six years earlier the defendant raped the same woman, an acquaintance of his? *in*

    (iii) that six years earlier the defendant raped another woman, then aged 19? *in*

    (iv) that eight years earlier the defendant had murdered another woman? *out*

  (d) murder of a 25-year-old woman, evidence

    (i)   that eight years earlier the defendant had raped a woman, then aged 19? *out*

    (ii) that eight years earlier the defendant had murdered another woman? *in*

    (iii) that eight years earlier the defendant had murdered another man? *in*

One final note: It appears that both the new Federal Rules and the "lustful disposition" doctrine apply only to evidence of specific other acts. The testimony of a witness, "In my opinion, Deak is a person utterly unwilling or unable to control his lewd propensities," would not be allowed.

3. CHARACTER OF A CRIMINAL DEFENDANT

Now we will consider the more traditionally established exceptions. First is an exception, codified in FRE 404(a)(2)(A), that gives a criminal defendant the right to initiate the presentation of evidence of his character. Sometimes this is referred to as "putting his character in issue," but this is a loose form of phrasing; this sense of being "in issue" should not be confused with the narrow sense addressed in Section B of this chapter. If the defendant does present evidence of his good character, the prosecution has the right to "offer evidence to rebut it." This makes perfect sense. If one party presents evidence of a proposition, then fairness demands that the other party have an opportunity to present evidence that the proposition is not true, even if that party would not have been able to introduce the topic into the litigation; the first party has, in the commonly used phrase, "opened the door." But if the defendant does not raise the character issue, then generally the prosecution may not raise it; rules such as FRE 413 and 414 qualify this broad proposition, as does a recent amendment, discussed in the next subsection, allowing the prosecution to present evidence of the defendant's character if the defendant presents evidence of the victim's character.

¶ 18.15: Why do more defendants not take advantage of their right to put a witness on the stand to testify as to their good character?

Why should the defendant, and not the prosecution, have the right to introduce the character issue into the trial? Why should the exception in FRE 404(a)(2)(A) apply only to defendants in criminal actions and not to civil parties?

There are two chief limitations on the defendant's use of character evidence. We will postpone briefly the discussion of one of these, restriction on the method of proof. The second is that the evidence must be "of a pertinent trait of character." For example, the famous pirate Captain Kidd offered to prove in his defense that he had served loyally as a king's officer. "[W]hat would that help in this case of murder?" responded the court.[30]

¶ 18.16: Dimson is on trial for unlawful possession of firearms. May he offer evidence of his character for gentleness, industry, veracity, and lawfulness?[31]

¶ 18.17: Denton is on trial in federal court for securities fraud. May a witness for Denton offer evidence that Denton is

(a) a person of good character?

(b) a law-abiding citizen?

(c) a gentle person?

(d) not the type of person to commit securities fraud?

(e) not the type of person to commit the type of acts alleged in the indictment (which the defense attorney summarizes in questioning the witness)?

¶ 18.18: In defending himself against the charge that he murdered an old man by dismemberment, Dupuis, from ¶ 18.5, offers the opinion of an expert that he does not have the type of

---

[30] Captain Kidd's Trial, 14 How.St.Tr. 123, 146 (Old Bailey 1701), *noted in* 1A John Henry Wigmore, *Evidence* § 59.1 n. 1 (Tillers rev. 1983).

[31] *See, e.g.*, United States v. Hewitt, 634 F.2d 277 (5th Cir.1981).

mental makeup that would incline him to commit the crime charged. Should this be admissible?[32]

yes implicates 704(b) ultimate issue problem

4. CHARACTER OF AN ALLEGED VICTIM

a. Introduction

In some criminal cases the defendant contends that he did not commit a crime, because the alleged victim actually initiated, exacerbated, or participated willingly in the episode. The defendant might contend that a particular trait of the victim's character makes this theory more likely. Thus, if the defendant claims that he killed in self-defense, the victim's propensity for violence would come into play. The traditional principle allowing the defendant to present such evidence is articulated in general terms in FRE 404(a)(2)(B), but almost all its applications have been in two types of cases—involving either the defendant's contention that he acted in self-defense or his defense of consent against charges of sexual misconduct. And in the latter setting, as we shall see, the traditional principle has been very narrowly limited.

¶ **18.19:** Apart from these two types of case, in what other kinds of case might a defense raise a question making relevant a character trait of the asserted victim? Note the title of a W.C. Fields movie: *You Can't Cheat an Honest Man.*

tricked into economic scheme - but maybe evidence they wanted in to track others - didn't defraud - they were greedy? had eyes wide open

Traditionally, and under FRE 404(a)(2)(B), prosecutors may not introduce evidence of a pertinent trait of character of the alleged victim except in rebuttal. Civil litigants are not generally allowed to introduce evidence of the character of an adverse party or complainant.

¶ **18.20:** Why the special treatment for criminal defendants?

try to balance scales - presumption against defendant?

b. Self-Defense Cases

If the defendant is accused of an assault crime, including homicide, he might contend that he acted in self-defense. He may, of course, show what the alleged victim did to justify a violent response. But traditional principles allow the defendant to go further, showing that the victim was a person whose character made it more likely that he would act as the defendant contends he did. If the defendant does introduce evidence of the victim's character, then the prosecutor must naturally be allowed to rebut in kind, just as in the case of evidence of the defendant's own character. These principles are expressed by FRE 404(a)(2)(B)(i).

character - not voir nesses - specific instances

---

[32] *See* 1A John Henry Wigmore, *Evidence* § 56 n. 1, at 1168–69 (Tillers rev. 1983); FRE 704(b); *cf.* State v. Sinnott, 24 N.J. 408, 132 A.2d 298 (1957); People v. Jones, 42 Cal.2d 219, 266 P.2d 38 (1954).

Under the Federal Rules—but not yet under most of the state codifications based on them—the prosecutor now has another option. An amendment added in 2000, creating what is now FRE 404(a)(2)(B)(ii), provides that if the accused introduces evidence of a character trait of the alleged victim, then the prosecution may introduce evidence of "the defendant's same trait." This amendment is not limited in terms to self-defense cases, but plainly its chief anticipated use—and virtually the only one that can be anticipated—is a case in which the accused, trying to support a contention of self-defense, offers evidence that the alleged victim was a violent person and the prosecution wants to prove the same thing about the accused. In supporting the amendment, the Advisory Committee expressed an argument based on evenhandedness—that if the accused presents proof of the hotheadedness of the victim, the prosecution ought to be able to prove the same thing about the accused, so as to afford "a more balanced presentation of character evidence when an accused chooses to attack the character of the alleged victim."

[handwritten: seems to undo any balancing intended by the original rule]

¶ 18.21: Are you persuaded? Can you think of a situation in which, though the hotheadedness of the alleged victim is substantially probative with respect to the accused's contention of self-defense, the hotheadedness of the accused is not? Is it *usually* true that if the victim's hotheadedness is significantly probative, the accused's hotheadedness would be as well?

[handwritten left margin: how does the hotheadedness manifest?]

Thus, as the Federal Rules have been amended, if the accused presents evidence of the victim's character, the prosecution may rebut that evidence or present evidence of the same trait of the accused's character, or both. And in homicide cases, the prosecutor is given some more leeway. Suppose that, although the defendant asserts that he killed in self-defense, and he presents evidence that the alleged victim struck first, he does not present evidence of the alleged victim's character as such. (Recall from Section B that the question of how someone acted on a particular occasion is not considered equivalent to the question of what his character is.) In this case, Rule 404(a)(2)(C) would allow the prosecutor to put the character of the victim in play, even though the defendant has not done so.

¶ 18.22: Is it sensible for this portion of the Rule to:

(a) allow the prosecution to initiate the character issue?

(b) be limited in scope to homicide cases? *[handwritten: i don't think so - shouldn't this apply to assault, too?]*

(c) be limited in scope to rebuttal of evidence that the alleged victim was the first aggressor? *[handwritten: yes, otherwise it's just bolstering victim to make Δ seem worse]*

A schematic summary of the rules on character of the accused and of the victim discussed so far may be helpful. In each case, the prosecutor may not introduce evidence unless the accused opens the door, and the

options the prosecutor has depend on just what door the defense opens.
So:

If the accused	then the prosecutor may
presents evidence of a good character trait of his,	rebut that proof (FRE 404(a)(2)(A)). *w/ specific instances*
presents evidence of a bad character trait (violence) of the alleged victim,	rebut that proof (FRE 404(a)(2)(B)(i)), *or* present evidence that the accused has the same bad character trait (FRE 404(a)(2)(B)(ii)), *or* do both.
presents evidence in a homicide case that the alleged victim was the first aggressor,	present evidence of the alleged victim's trait of peacefulness (FRE 404(a)(2)(C)).

Consider now the question of method of proof—assuming character can be proven, how may it be done?—in connection with the characters of both the defendant and the victim in a crime of violence when the defendant claims self-defense. We have seen that when character is in issue, it may be proven with specific items of conduct or by reputation or opinion evidence. In some circumstances, courts allow the prosecution to prove the prior sexual misconduct of the defendant in a case charging misconduct—but opinion or reputation evidence would almost never be allowed. Note the contrasting attitude reflected in 405. If the defendant raises an issue of his own character or that of the alleged victim, he cannot ask his witnesses about specific acts; if he could, this collateral distraction might dominate the trial. Traditionally, the character witness could testify only to the person's reputation—on the dubious theory that opinions differ but a person only has one reputation. The Federal Rules reasonably allow opinion evidence as well as reputation evidence. Moreover, the adverse party can inquire on cross into specific acts, in an attempt to impeach the character witness.

¶ **18.23:** Deford is on trial for the manslaughter of Vickers. Deford claims self-defense. He wants to prove via the testimony of Nabors both that he is a gentle, law-abiding citizen and that Vickers was a violent, hot-tempered person. The jurisdiction follows FRE 404(a)(1) and (2), so the court holds that these are appropriate subjects of proof.

(a) What considerations weigh for or against allowing Nabors to testify to each of the following? Which of the following testimony would the FRE allow? In each case, what foundation should be required, assuming that the evidence can be admitted at all?

(i) Various gentle, law-abiding acts that Deford has committed. *No* ✓

(ii) Various violent, hot-tempered acts that Vickers has committed. *No*

(iii) Nabors' opinion that Deford is a gentle, law-abiding person and that Vickers is a violent, hot tempered one. *yes*

(iv) Nabors' report that Deford has a reputation as a gentle, law-abiding person, and that Vickers has a reputation as a violent, hot-tempered one. (The traditional rule admitted evidence of this sort but not that in (a)(iii). Given that a report of a person's reputation is hearsay—indeed, there is an exception, FRE 803(21), to remove this problem—is there any sound argument that can be made in favor of this preference?) *yes*

(b) Assume that Nabors has given the testimony in (a)(iii). Peepers, who lived near both Deford and Vickers and knew them both well, has told the prosecutor of violent, hot-tempered acts that Deford has committed and gentle, law-abiding acts that Vickers has committed. On cross-examination, may the prosecutor ask Nabors about these acts? How should she phrase her questions? Should the phrasing differ at all if instead Nabors has given the testimony in (a)(iv)?

both can come out

not sure... does it matter it its opinion v. reputation and you're rebutting w/specific acts?

(c) Assume that on cross-examination, Nabors has denied knowing of, or hearing of, the acts described by Peepers to the prosecutor. May the prosecutor put Peepers on the stand to testify to those acts? If the court excludes such testimony by Peepers, what testimony can he give? *opinion/reputation*   *NO!*

(d) If Peepers testifies for the prosecution, what use can the defense make of the information in (a)(i) and (ii)? *can it come in now as rebuttal? specific acts or opinion* *yes!*

c. Sexual Misconduct Cases: The Rape Shield Laws

Traditionally, the logic behind Rule 404(a)(2)(B) was applied to the complainant in cases alleging rape or other criminal sexual conduct; indeed, the Advisory Committee Notes make clear that the Rule was intended to apply in the ordinary way to the alleged victim of rape. A rape defendant could claim that the alleged victim's "unchaste character" was probative of the proposition that her sexual contact was consensual. This application of the victim-character rules has now been nearly universally abrogated, by FRE 412 and similar "rape shield" statutes and rules that narrowly limit the circumstances in which a defendant may present evidence of the complainant's past sexual conduct.

Excluding evidence of past sexual conduct serves at least five important and valid purposes. First, in the vast majority of cases, the complainant's sexual history has negligible probative value. If the charge is that the defendant overwhelmed his victim with physical force, it is usually hard to see how he can logically support any defense by proving that the victim had extensive sexual experience; consent is not an issue in such a case, and only in rare cases could the victim's past sexual conduct have any relevance at all to any other issue, such as the identity of the assailant. Even if there is a genuine issue in the case that the sexual contact was consensual, proving that the complainant consented to sex even with a variety of partners around the time of the alleged rape will rarely have very much probative value on the question of whether she consented with the defendant on the occasion in question.

Second, evidence of a complainant's past sexual conduct can be highly prejudicial. As in other contexts, there is a concern that the jury may over-value the evidence. Although this book takes the view that the importance of this concern is generally over-played, this is a context in which it may have some significance. Moreover, the evidence may be prejudicial in that it may make the jurors de-value the complainant and so make them less likely to find the defendant guilty even if they believe that he did commit the crime. In short, the evidence may be counterproductive to the truth-determining process.

Third, the exclusionary plays a valuable expressive role. It indicates that the woman's right to be protected against rape is unaffected by her prior sexual history. This is especially so in a case in which the defense is consent; the exclusionary rule helps demonstrate that the woman's right to say no on the occasion in question is not undermined by her prior sexual conduct.

Fourth, examining a complainant in public about her sexual history may be seriously traumatic, as well as a grotesque intrusion into her personal life. Defense counsel will often exercise all the latitude that the rules and the facts of the case allow in exposing the sexual past of the complainant. Often, the defense will attempt to keep the focus on what she has done at other times rather than on what the defendant did at the time in question. (Not always, though; in a given case, counsel may decide that the evidence is unlikely to persuade the jurors, and may only make him look like a bully desperately trying to distract attention from a devastating case.)

Fifth, if evidence of prior sexual conduct were readily admissible, and a rape victim knew that by pressing a complaint she would expose herself to a searching inquiry about her sexual past, she might decide not to pursue the matter. Just how strong a consideration this is may be difficult to determine; it appears that fear of mistreatment by the police, and the fear of retribution by the accused, are far more significant in accounting for the under-reporting of rape than is fear of cross-examination,[33] and empirical studies have found that the shield laws have had far less impact in increasing reports of rape than reformers had anticipated.[34] It is undeniable, though, that rape is not only a very serious and common crime, which often has deep and abiding consequences for its victims, but a vastly under-reported one;[35] removing any disincentive to reporting rape must be counted as an important benefit.

That rape shield laws are necessary is no longer a significant source of controversy; no one today strenuously argues that we should return to the rules that prevailed until well past the middle of the 20th century, under which defense counsel in a rape case was given great latitude in cross-examining the complaining witness about her sexual history. But to say that we ought to have a rape shield law does not remove all difficulty from the area, for countervailing considerations cannot be ignored.

Note that FRE 412 explicitly acknowledges the possibility that admissibility of the evidence may be constitutionally mandated in some circumstances. We must remember that the proponent of the evidence is a criminal defendant, whose liberty is at stake. He is pleading that he did not commit rape. The law presumes that he is indeed innocent, and tolerates his conviction only if his guilt is proven beyond a reasonable doubt. What is more, because he is a criminal defendant we usually accord him more favorable consideration than other types of litigant. Only

---

[33] For an excellent review of the empirical evidence, as well as for an invaluable bibliography on the entire subject, see 23 Charles Alan Wright & Kenneth Graham, Jr., *Federal Practice & Procedure: Evidence* § 5382 (April 2016 update). Other useful sources include Harriett R. Galvin, *Shielding Rape Victims in the State and Federal Courts: A Proposal for the Second Decade*, 70 Minn. L. Rev. 763 (1986), and Cassia Spohn & Julie Horney, *Rape Law Reform: A Grassroots Revolution and Its Impact* (1992).

[34] See notably Spohn & Horney, *Rape Law Reform, supra*, at 100–02.

[35] According to FBI statistics, compiled in the annual Uniform Crime Reports: Crime in the United States, each year there are usually about 80,000 or more forcible rapes (a category that includes attempts but excludes statutory rapes); the number peaked over 109,000 in 1992 and has since receded. But of course no one knows the real number with any degree of certainty. Susan Estrich, *Real Rape* 10–15 (1987), analyzes the reporting problem. She concludes that "aggravated" rapes—involving more than one man, or strangers, or weapons and beatings—are reported to the police more often than most crimes, but that when "simple" cases lacking these features are considered "rape emerges as a far more common, vastly under-reported, and dramatically ignored problem." *Id.* at 10.

with great reluctance should the law prevent him from presenting evidence that may rationally be deemed significantly probative of his case. Indeed, that is the reason for the general principle that criminal defendants are allowed to offer evidence of pertinent character traits of their alleged victims, as well as of themselves.[36]

Recall that the most fundamental question in determining admissibility is not, "Is this evidence *conclusive?*" or even, "Is this evidence *sufficient* to warrant the conclusion that the proponent seeks?" Rather, it is, "Does this evidence *significantly alter the probability* that a factfinder may attach to a material proposition?" Conceding that evidence of the complainant's past sexual conduct *usually* has little or no probative value on any legitimate issue in a rape case, it would be difficult to maintain that this is *always* true. And it is the rare cases in which the evidence may have substantial probative value that are the difficult ones.

A defendant might offer various theories, depending on the facts of the particular case, as to why the complainant's sexual history has substantial probative value. Where consent is an issue, he might present a straight propensity theory: "The fact that she had sex consensually on prior occasions in similar circumstances makes more plausible my contention—which otherwise you might not believe—that she had sex consensually with me on the occasion in question."[37] In some cases, he might claim that the evidence supports his contention that someone else was the rapist. Or he might contend that the past sexual history helps answer a question that a sensible jury will ask itself and that will haunt his defense: "Why would she put herself through this ordeal unless what she has to say is true?" As you consider the problems below, think about the extent to which the defendant is claiming a propensity theory, or some other theory, for admission.

In short, rape shield laws must accommodate conflicting and complex policy concerns, and there is no way of avoiding the need for case-by-case analysis.[38] Because so much is at stake in this area, problems are sometimes difficult to discuss—and even the statement of problems can be controversial.[39] As you consider these problems, bear in mind the

---

[36] As suggested above, however, putting aside the present context of criminal sexual conduct, this doctrine rarely has much application except in crimes of violence, where the defendant claims self-defense.

[37] *Cf.* People v. Hackett, 421 Mich. 338, 365 N.W.2d 120, 135 (1984) (Levin, J., dissenting).

[38] Rape shield laws vary a good deal. For example, if your rulebook includes them, you might notice how different Uniform Rule 412 and California Evidence Code § 1106 are from FRE 412, which was first adopted in 1978, broadened somewhat in 1988, extensively revised in 1994, and restyled in 2011.

[39] Lest readers have a misconception about the basis on which I have selected problems in this section, a word on that matter may be in order.

Some of the problems are meant to reflect the type of evidence that was routinely admitted before the advent of the rape shield laws but would not be admissible given those laws. Others

devastation caused by rape, and the additional pain caused by inquiry into sexual history, and at the same time the judicial system's need to be fair to a criminal defendant.

¶ 18.24: In earlier times, the defense in a rape prosecution could present evidence about the complainant's sexual history, but the prosecution could not use a propensity theory to present evidence about the defendant's prior sexual misconduct. Now the situation has reversed to some degree. In the vast majority of cases, rape shield laws exclude evidence of the complainant's sexual history, and FRE 413—though not yet a typical rule— allows the prosecutor to use a propensity theory to prove prior rapes committed by the defendant. What factors make evidence of the defendant's sexual history more worthy of admission than evidence of the complainant's sexual history? What factors cut the other way? Are the two questions linked—that is, is it persuasive to argue that what is admissible on one side should be admissible on the other?

¶ 18.25: Dabney is accused of raping Cora. She testifies as follows: Dabney approached her and introduced himself in Encounters, a popular singles bar. After a few drinks and about a half-hour's chat, he suggested that they go to another bar. They then went to his car in the parking lot, where he raped her. Dabney admits all this but the last; he admits that they had sexual intercourse, but testifies that it was consensual.

(a) Should Cora, who is 28 years old, be allowed to testify in rebuttal that

(i)   she was a virgin until this encounter?

(ii) she is a lesbian, who had several previous female sexual partners but never a male one?

(b) Suppose instead that it is Dabney who wants to introduce evidence of Cora's past sexual conduct. Consider

---

are meant to test the bounds of the exclusionary rule. Some of these, as indicated by citations, are based on actual reported cases. At least one—the woman who assertedly raised the windowshade to welcome young sexual partners—is based on an actual but unpublished case. A few—in particular the woman who had sex with 25 different partners in a month—are far from typical of reality. Problems of that sort are presented to test such questions as whether, at some extreme, a pattern of prior sexual activity should in itself be sufficient to warrant admissibility of evidence of that activity. These problems are an application of the technique used throughout this book, of varying the facts of hypotheticals slightly to facilitate consideration of how the varying factors weighing for and against admissibility may be balanced.

It is important to underscore that in most actual cases the evidence offered is *not* of extremely extensive or unusual sexual activity, and in most cases a rape shield law excludes without substantial controversy evidence of prior sexual history that, absent the law, the defendant might have introduced. As is the norm in law school courses, the focus here is disproportionately on the unusual cases that present the closer questions.

whether Dabney should be allowed to prove each of the following propositions.

(i) Cora was not a virgin. *no*

(ii) Cora had sex with five different men in the year before her encounter with Dabney. *no*

(iii) Cora had sex with twenty-five different men in the month before her encounter with Dabney. *no*

(iv) Five times in the last month Cora had sex with a man she had met in Encounters the same night. *no*

(v) Five times in the last month Cora had sex in a car in the parking lot at Encounters with a man she had met there that night.[40] *no*

(vi) Earlier in the evening that Cora met Dabney, she told her roommate, "I'm going to Encounters. I want to get me some nookey." The roommate is prepared to testify that she understood Cora to mean that she wanted to find a man with whom to have sexual intercourse.[41] *no* *NOT about prior history — relevant to likelihood of consent*

(vii) Earlier in the evening of her encounter with Dabney she had sex with two different men in their cars in the parking lot at Encounters. *hmm... does this effect identification? N/C physical evidence?*

(c) Suppose now that Dabney is contending that, even if Cora did not consent to sex with him, he believed that she did. He testifies that she acted "invitingly" from the first moment they met, and that she appeared "receptive" to all his advances. Consider whether he should also be allowed to testify as follows: "I wasn't at all surprised that Cora seemed to want to have sex with me. I had heard that she was easy. In particular, I'd heard that she had had sex with a couple of other guys in the parking lot at Encounters." If you do not believe Dabney ought to be *N/C* allowed to testify to this, is your objection to the evidence itself, *Hearsay!* to the underlying defense, or to both? *Ok w/ defense of inviting, but has to be based on her actions*

¶ **18.26:** In ¶ 18.25, the prosecution offers proof that Cora was bruised in the vaginal region and expert evidence that the bruises were of the type that could result from forceful sexual

---

[40] *See* Vivian Berger, *Man's Trial, Woman's Tribulation: Rape Cases in the Courtroom,* 77 Colum. L. Rev. 1, 59–60 (1977); Galvin, *Shielding Rape Victims, supra,* 70 Minn. L. Rev. at 841–47; *cf.* State v. Shoffner, 62 N.C.App. 245, 302 S.E.2d 830 (1983) (holding that defendants claiming that complainant initiated sexual encounter should have been allowed to present evidence that her "*modus operandi* was to accost men at [public places] and make sexual advances by putting her hands 'all over their bodies' ").

[41] *See* Villafranco v. State, 252 Ga. 188, 313 S.E.2d 469 (1984) (holding exclusion in similar circumstances to be reversible error).

contact. May Dabney introduce proof that Cora is a gymnast and had fallen off the balance beam the prior week? May Dabney introduce the testimony of Warren that he had had sex with Cora several times in the five days preceding her encounter with Dabney? *uhh ... is any of it forceful? if that's the allegation, yes*

yes
not related to sexual history

¶ **18.27:** Darrell is accused of raping Colleen, whom he has known for several years, in her apartment. Darrell and Colleen agree that on the evening in question matters began with kissing and necking and proceeded to heavy petting—enough so that they found themselves naked on Colleen's bed. Darrell also admits Colleen's contention that when he attempted to proceed further she said, "No, that's far enough tonight." But Darrell denies Colleen's testimony that he then said, "You can't stop now!" and raped her. He contends instead that they continued petting, with her active and eager participation, and that after several more minutes, when he renewed his advance, she neither said nor did anything to resist.

yes (even if no explicit allegation others forceful) b/c used to show potential for other source

(a) May Darrell testify that once, three years ago, Colleen consensually had sex with him? *no —not probative!*

(b) May Darrell testify that he and Colleen had a previous sexual relationship, lasting for five weeks and ending seven months ago? *no*

(c) May Darrell testify that he and Colleen had sex on an average of once a week for the four months before the night in question? *maybe? yes*

412 (b) (1) (B)

(d) May Darrell testify that he and Colleen were married as of the time in question? (Note that this is an evidentiary, not a substantive, question; an affirmative answer does not suggest that, if Darrell's conduct would otherwise be considered rape, it should be exempted because he and Colleen were married.)

yes, but not as defense (e.g. marital rape laws have changed)

¶ **18.28:** Dewey is accused of raping Charlotte, but denies that they had any sexual contact at all. The police lab tested Dewey's DNA against the DNA of semen taken from Charlotte's vagina after the alleged incident, but the crime scene sample was corrupted, and the most that the lab expert can say is that the profile of the crime scene sample matches Dewey's DNA and that of about 4% of males. May Dewey elicit

(a) Charlotte's testimony on cross-examination that she had intercourse with Wagner the day before the alleged rape, without proof as to Wagner's DNA profile? *no*

(b) the testimony in (a) together with proof that Wagner's DNA profile also matches that of the crime scene sample? *yes* ✓

(c) Charlotte's testimony on cross-examination that she had intercourse with four different men during the two days *n/c* before the alleged rape? *maybe*

(d) the testimony of Iris, formerly a friend of Charlotte, *n/c* that "Charlotte is a person of nondiscriminating tastes, who will sleep with just about anybody"? *no!*

¶ **18.29:** Candace accuses Dobson of raping her, but he denies having had sexual contact at all. May Dobson offer

(a) evidence that one year earlier Candace accused Irving of raping her? *no* *nothing in 412 keeps out prior allegations*

(b) the evidence in (a), together with Irving's testimony that he did not in fact rape her?[42] *yes (?)*

(c) evidence that, at the time of the alleged rape by Dobson, Candace was pregnant by Frederick, her fiancé, and that she and Frederick both came from families that adhered to strict codes prohibiting premarital sex?[43] *uhh no may dude*

¶ **18.30:** Dick, a 15-year-old boy, is accused of raping Cheryl, a woman who lives in his neighborhood, in her bedroom. Dick offers evidence of the following: Cheryl was on intimate terms with numerous boys in the neighborhood. Her custom was to put her 3-year-old boy down for a nap, and then signal, by a raised windowshade, that she was receiving visitors. On this particular occasion, the little boy woke up early from the nap and wandered into his mother's bedroom, to find a scene that surprised him. Is the windowshade evidence admissible? *yes... motive for lying*

¶ **18.31:** Olden is accused of raping Matthews. Matthews testifies that after the rape Olden and his friend Harris dropped her off in the vicinity of the house of Russell, Olden's half- *also, Matthews* brother. Russell testifies that he saw Matthews get out of Harris' *white, Olden Black* car, and that she immediately told him that Harris and Olden *SCOTUS said Olden* had raped her. Olden testifies that he had consensual sex with *had constitutional* Matthews. May Olden introduce evidence that at the time of this *right to show)* episode Matthews was involved in an extramarital relationship with Russell? *See Olden v. Kentucky,* 488 U.S. 227 (1988). *-maybe...motive for lying?*

¶ **18.32:** Diamond is accused of the rape of Charles in prison. Diamond is a black man and Charles, who is married, is a white man. Diamond admits sexual contact but contends that

---

[42] *See, e.g.,* Covington v. State, 703 P.2d 436, 442, *modified on other grounds,* 711 P.2d 1183 (Alaska App.1985); Hughes v. Raines, 641 F.2d 790 (9th Cir.1981).

[43] *Cf.* State v. Jalo, 27 Or.App. 845, 557 P.2d 1359 (1976); State v. Howard, 121 N.H. 53, 426 A.2d 457 (1981).

it was consensual. May he introduce evidence to show that Charles is gay? If so, may he introduce evidence that Charles has had other black male sexual partners?[44] No !.

Note that FRE 412, in common with some of the state laws, contains a provision requiring a party to give advance notice if he wishes to offer evidence of prior sexual conduct under one of the exceptions to the exclusionary rule. (As noted in Chapter 15, notice provisions seem to be a common theme of some modern evidence rules; see also FRE 413–415, 807 and the 1991 amendments to FRE 404(b).) In *Michigan v. Lucas*, 500 U.S. 145 (1991), the Supreme Court upheld the constitutionality in principle of such requirements, without deciding whether the provision there, or its application, was in fact constitutional.

The 1994 amendment to FRE 412 extended the Rule to civil cases "involving alleged sexual misconduct."[45] The extension is rather curious. Recall that the rape shield laws were passed to limit, and protect rape complainants against, the traditional rule codified in FRE 404(a)(2)(B). That rule generally allows the defendant in a criminal case, notwithstanding the rule against propensity evidence, to introduce evidence of a pertinent trait of character of the alleged victim. But there is no comparable exception to the rule against propensity evidence for civil cases, and so a separate shield law should not have been necessary to exclude such evidence in civil cases. Rule 412 does go beyond a prohibition of propensity evidence, of course; it *presumptively* excludes evidence of past sexual behavior and sexual predisposition for whatever reason it may be offered. But it is even more difficult in civil cases than in criminal cases to create categorical rules, and the Advisory Committee expressly disclaimed the attempt, saying, "Greater flexibility is needed to accommodate evolving causes of action such as claims for sexual harassment." Thus, the Rule only states a balancing test for civil cases; unlike the general rule stated by FRE 403, this one puts its thumb on the side of exclusion.

---

[44] *See Hackett, supra; cf.* Kvasnikoff v. State, 674 P.2d 302, 306 (Alaska App.1983).

[45] The 1994 amendment had a curious history. A draft was originally prepared by the Advisory Committee on the Rules of Criminal Procedure, and then substantially revised by the newly appointed Advisory Committee on the Rules of Evidence and the Standing Committee on Practice and Procedure of the Judicial Conference. In a rather rare move, the Supreme Court also altered the proposed Rule before sending it to Congress, deleting the extension to civil cases. Chief Justice Rehnquist explained that the Court had already declared in Meritor Savings Bank v. Vinson, 477 U.S. 57, 69 (1986), that evidence of an alleged victim's "sexually provocative speech or dress" may be relevant in workplace harassment cases, and some members of the Court therefore believed that the amended Rule, by purporting to alter substantive law, might exceed the scope of the Court's rulemaking authority under the Rules Enabling Act. Letter of April 29, 1994, to John F. Gerry, Chair of the Executive Committee of the Judicial Conference, reprinted in 154 F.R.D. 510. The limitations of the Rules Enabling Act do not confine Congress, of course. In the same statute that conditionally promulgated new Rules 413–415, Congress promulgated amended Rule 412 as it had been proposed by the Standing Committee, complete with the extension to civil cases.

¶ 18.33: Pelham brings a sexual harassment action against Dayton, Inc., her employer, claiming that her supervisors at Dayton frequently made lewd looks and suggestive gestures at her and offensive remarks, replete with sexual innuendo, to her. Should Dayton be allowed to introduce evidence that Pelham wore low-cut, fishnet outfits that exposed her breasts quite visibly? (Note that the Advisory Committee Note to FRE 412 indicates that "mode of dress" falls within the definition of evidence relating to "sexual predisposition." Perhaps the best way to understand this statement is that if mode of dress is relevant it is to prove sexual predisposition, andFRE 412 prevents it from being admitted on that basis.)

Wright & Graham, *Federal Practice and Procedure, supra,* § 5382.1 (April 2016 update), argue: "It is preposterous to suppose that a person who wears a tank top and no brassiere is 'asking' to be raped.... But transfer this definition to a civil action for harassment. Is it unreasonable for the defendant to suppose that a woman who dresses to expose her breasts or a man who wears jeans so tight you can count the pimples on his buttocks is 'inviting' others to look at these portions of their anatomy even though others, including the plaintiff, consider such a gaze to be 'sexual harassment'?" Is it?

¶ 18.34: FRE 405(a) allows reputation or opinion evidence whenever "evidence of a person's character or character trait is admissible." Proof of specific instances of conduct is not allowable, except on cross-examination. FRE 412(a) generally overrides Rule 405(a) and prohibits evidence concerning the past sexual behavior or sexual predisposition of an alleged rape victim. Under Rule 412(b), however, proof of "specific instances of a victim's sexual behavior" may be allowed in some circumstances. Similarly, FRE 413–415 allow evidence of past sexual misconduct of a defendant when similar misconduct is charged, but these Rules make no provision for opinion or reputation evidence. Is this apparent flip-flop—giving relatively favorable treatment to proof of specific instances in the context of sexual conduct and relatively disfavorable treatment in other contexts—justified?

E. OTHER PURPOSES FOR PROVING UNCHARGED ACTS, HAPPENINGS, AND TRANSACTIONS

FRE 404(b)(2)

Additional Reading: McCormick, Ch. 17, § 190; Ch. 18; Mueller & Kirkpatrick, §§ 4.15–.18

1. AN OVERVIEW

Up until now, we have concentrated principally on propensity theories—"You should believe that this person acted in this way because that is his character," or " . . . because he acted in that way in the past." But a propensity theory is not the only basis on which evidence of other acts may be relevant.[46]

Some of the non-propensity grounds for introducing other acts of a person are listed in FRE 404(b)(2). It is important to recognize that this list is suggestive, not exhaustive. Furthermore, though courts and commentators often speak of this subsection as providing a list of exceptions to a general rule of exclusion, that is not accurate. Rather, the relationship is the other way around: FRE 404(b)(1) is a rule of very long reach and narrow focus. It applies to evidence of any "other act," not just to a "crime" or "wrong," and it makes the evidence inadmissible only for the specified purpose of proving "a person's character in order to show that on a particular occasion the person acted in accord with the character." Subsection (b)(2) makes clear that this exclusion does not apply to other grounds on which the evidence may be offered.

Suppose, for example, that in a federal prosecution for bank robbery the prosecutor wishes to prove that the defendant Deller parked his car illegally near the bank. Deller objects, "That's an altogether different crime from the one charged. Parking the car illegally is not part of the crime of bank robbery." The prosecutor might well respond,

> That misses the point. I have to be able to tell the story of how Deller committed the crime, and that story doesn't begin and end at the teller's window. Parking the car near the bank is part of the story, because it shows how Deller planned the crime and how he got away. Rule 404(b)(1) prohibits evidence of other crimes or acts only to the extent they're offered on a propensity theory, but that isn't the basis on which I'm offering this evidence. I'm certainly not asking the jurors to conclude that,

---

[46] Indeed, in discussing the rape shield laws we have already considered some of the other ways in which defendants might argue that the complainant's past sexual history is significant for his case.

because Deller parked illegally, he was the type of person who would be more likely than most to rob a bank. Indeed, the fact that the parking place was illegal is secondary; even if he parked it perfectly legally, it would be important for me to show that he parked near the bank.

Sometimes, as we will see, courts are so receptive to non-propensity grounds on which evidence of other acts is offered that the ban on propensity evidence fades in significance.[47] As this hypothetical suggests, non-propensity grounds for offering proof of prior bad acts are particularly useful to prosecutors, and so we will begin with criminal cases.

2.   IN CRIMINAL CASES

The bank robbery hypothetical above represents an everyday situation: A prosecutor is barred from introducing on a propensity theory evidence of some wrongful act committed by the defendant but not charged in the indictment. Nevertheless—in part because she knows the evidence will likely convey a strong propensity suggestion to the jury— she is eager to present the evidence to the jury. Accordingly, she articulates some other ground on which the evidence is admissible, some other material proposition that, she contends, it helps her to prove.

Note the ironic situation that this creates. The prosecutor—naturally eager for the jury to hear evidence suggesting (though the jury isn't supposed to draw the inference) that the defendant is a repeat criminal and a very bad person—scrambles to find some issue that, she says, she just *has* to prove, on which the prior act is helpful. The defendant might say, "You don't have to prove *that*." As you think about the problems below, consider not only the question of whether the evidence tends to prove a material non-propensity proposition in favor of the prosecution, but also the following: Does the prosecution have a genuine need to prove that proposition? Does the probative value of the evidence in proving that proposition outweigh the prejudicial potential that the jury will consider the evidence on the forbidden propensity grounds?

The illustrative list of alternative grounds provided in FRE 404(b)(2) offers a helpful guidepost to prosecutors seeking a non-propensity route to admissibility. But the important thing is not to tie the evidence to one or more of these "pigeonholes"—remember, they are illustrative only!—but rather to show how, in the particular circumstances of the case, the evidence of the other bad act tends to prove a material non-propensity proposition.

---

[47] *See* Kenneth J. Melilli, *The Character Evidence Rule Revisited*, 1998 BYU L. Rev. 1547, 1548 (contending that the exclusionary rule "is more rhetoric than substance," because "character evidence is admitted here, there and everywhere").

Sometimes, as in the bank robbery hypothetical above, evidence of the other bad act helps the prosecution tell the story of the crime charged—why the defendant did it, how he pulled it off, and how the evidence came to be as it is. FRE 404(b)(2)'s references to motive, opportunity, preparation, and plan generally fit this story-telling idea. In some cases, the other bad act is said to be "inextricably intertwined" with the crime charged—it may be impossible, for example, to tell the story of a kidnapping without telling about the battery by which the kidnapping was accomplished—but this context-setting function is not limited to acts so closely related to the one charged.

¶ 18.35: Cunningham, a nurse, is accused of tampering with syringes by removing from them a painkiller, and replacing it with a saline solution. The prosecution wants to introduce evidence that Cunningham is addicted to Demerol; that she had previously pleaded guilty to the theft of Demerol at another hospital; that her license had been suspended as a result of the theft; and that she had falsified results of some of the drug tests that she had to take as a condition of reinstating the license. Should any of this testimony be admitted? *See United States v. Cunningham,* 103 F.3d 553 (7th Cir. 1996).

[handwritten margin note: Hmm this all sounds like pretty good motive for the crime ... but is that an element π has to prove? admissible for motive]

¶ 18.36: H.R. Haldeman and John Ehrlichman were two of President Nixon's former senior advisors accused of participating in a conspiracy to cover up a break-in at the Watergate headquarters of the Democratic National Committee. The prosecution offered, and the defense objected to, evidence that Ehrlichman had authorized an earlier illegal break-in, at the office of the psychiatrist of Daniel Ellsberg, a noted opponent of the Vietnam War. Some of those who participated in the "Ellsberg break-in" were also in the Watergate break-in. How should the court have ruled on the defense objection? *See United States v. Haldeman,* 559 F.2d 31, 88 (D.C.Cir.1976), *cert. denied,* 431 U.S. 933 (1977).

[handwritten margin note: sounds like it would be helpful to show knowledge of how to conduct a break-in / connection to others involved]

¶ 18.37: Jill Coit, sometimes referred to as the "Black Widow," is on trial for the murder of her ninth husband, Gerald Boggs. (It turns out that she has been married a total of eleven times to nine men.) Boggs was murdered just a week before civil litigation between Coit and him was to go to trial. Coit had begun that action to assure her title to a Bed & Breakfast that she owned. Boggs, who had secured annulment of their marriage after learning that marriage no. 8 was not yet terminated, counterclaimed for infliction of emotional distress, in part because of the overlapping marriage situation and in part because Coit had allegedly asserted falsely that she had given birth to a child fathered by Boggs. The prosecution in the murder case wants to introduce evidence of Coit's bigamy, of her false claims of pregnancy, and of fraudulent activities by Coit related to the ownership of the B & B. Should this evidence be allowed?[48]

these don't seem relevant

maybe to show motive — she knew she was going to lose civil action b/c everything was his, so she killed him?

¶ **18.38:** Dalvais is accused of possession of a lethal weapon and assault with intent to kill a police officer. The prosecution will offer the testimony of Officer Alexander that, as the result of a conversation with one Weller, Alexander, who was patrolling in a police car, asked Weller to come into his police car, and made a left turn. As a result of a second conversation, the officer stopped his car when he approached a running man, whom he now identifies as Dalvais, got out of the car, and ordered Dalvais to halt. Instead, Dalvais pulled out a pistol, took a shot at Alexander, and continued to flee. Alexander caught up to Dalvais and arrested him.

sure — just used to show why officer was approaching

At issue is the admissibility of the actual statements made by Weller. The prosecution wants Alexander to testify that in the first conversation Weller said, "Officer, I've been robbed!" and that in the second conversation Weller said, "There's the man!" Can the evidence of these statements be admitted?[49]

or, motive — wants to flee / not get caught

Prior ID if the declarant is testifying

¶ **18.39:** Deller, the alleged bank robber, was arrested the day after the crime, three hundred miles away from the scene. He denies that he was the robber.

(a) Can the prosecution introduce evidence that three days before the robbery Deller stole an automobile?[50]

Yes — opportunity to get 300 miles away from the bank

(b) What if the auto theft was three hours after the bank robbery?

sure — still opportunity to leave

plan / preparation

¶ **18.40:** At Deller's trial, the prosecution alleges that he picked the combination lock on a small safe located adjacent to the banking floor. The prosecutor offers evidence that three years before, at another branch of the same bank in another city, Deller picked a similar lock on a similar safe, also located adjacent to the banking floor. The prosecutor argues that the

---

[48] *Woman Guilty of Murdering Husband No. 9*, N.Y. Times, March 19, 1995, p. 31, col. 1; People v. Coit, 1997 WL 742263 (Colo.App.1997).

[49] For better or worse, a court would probably hold that these statements were made for the primary purpose of addressing an ongoing emergency and so were not testimonial for purposes of the Confrontation Clause. And the statements probably do not pose a hearsay problem because they appear to fit within the excited utterance exception, see FRE 803(2); note the exclamation points.

[50] *See* United States v. Leftwich, 461 F.2d 586 (3d Cir.), *cert. denied*, 409 U.S. 915 (1972); *cf.* Lewis v. United States, 771 F.2d 454, 456 (10th Cir.), *cert. denied*, 474 U.S. 1024 (1985) (theft of cutting torch admissible in case involving post office burglary).

evidence is admissible to show Deller's ability to pick the lock. Is this persuasive? Is it a prerequisite to the admissibility of the evidence on this theory that Deller deny—in his own pleadings, opening statement, or case-in-chief—that he was able to pick combination locks?[51]

¶ 18.41: Dobbins is on trial for robbing a lumber yard. The accusation is that he broke into the yard by cutting the chain-link fence that surrounded the yard. The prosecution introduces evidence that, the week after this theft, Dobbins burglarized a nursery by snipping the slightly thinner chain-link fence that enclosed the nursery. In responding to an objection, the prosecutor argues, "This evidence shows that Dobbins had the ability to cut open a chain-link fence." Is this argument persuasive?

¶ 18.42: DeJohn is charged with cashing forged Treasury checks, the payees of which resided at the same YMCA where DeJohn lived. The prosecution offers testimony of (1) a Y security guard that in another incident he had "arrested" DeJohn for being behind the reception desk, where the mailboxes were, in violation of the rules, and (2) a police officer that in yet another incident DeJohn had acknowledged obtaining a Treasury check from a mailbox behind the reception desk at the Y. Should the testimony be admitted to show DeJohn's access to the boxes?[52] What if DeJohn offers to stipulate that he had access to the boxes? If the court does *not* allow the evidence, how might the prosecution prove access?

As part of the context-setting function, prosecutors often persuade courts that other crimes are admissible to show a "common plan or scheme." Certainly this idea has merit in some circumstances. Suppose the defendant is charged with having defrauded a victim, but the fraud alleged would have been so elaborate—involving printing of brochures and prospectuses, maintenance of offices and telephones, and so forth—that it would have made no sense if it was used only on the victim named in the indictment. In such a case, the prosecution ought to be allowed to prove that in fact the fraud on the victim was part of a larger scheme that gained its profitability from its large

---

[51] *Cf.* United States v. Barrett, 539 F.2d 244, 248 (1st Cir.1976). In *Barrett*, a federal prosecution for transportation of postage stamps stolen from a philatelic museum, and related crimes, the theft—which was not itself part of the charge—had been performed by sophisticated means of bypassing the museum's burglar alarm. The court held that evidence tending to show Barrett's knowledge of alarms, including his possession of certain equipment, was properly admitted.

[52] *See* United States v. DeJohn, 638 F.2d 1048 (7th Cir.1981) (admitting the testimony).

number of victims. Similarly, if a criminal enterprise operated in a smooth manner resulting from extensive experience, the prosecution should probably be allowed to show that.[53] In other words, repeat conduct helps show economy or efficiency of scale. But prosecutors often try, and sometimes successfully, to extend the "common plan or scheme" idea far beyond this type of case. In some cases, the evidence shows little other than that defendant has frequently before committed the same type of crime with which he is charged in this case.[54] This seems basically to be propensity evidence—strong and tempting in some cases, to be sure, but simple propensity evidence nonetheless. Commonality may help the prosecutor prove some other essential point, such as identity or intent, but it should not be taken as an end in itself.[55]

¶ 18.43: Klotter is accused of burglarizing guns from a sporting goods store. One of the key pieces of evidence against him is that, two days after the guns were missing, he sold some of them to another dealer.

(a) May the prosecution prove that, the same day the guns were stolen from the store, guns were also stolen from a house where Klotter had been that day?

(b) May the prosecution prove the theft in (a) together with proof that, at the same time he sold guns that had been taken from the store, he also sold some guns that had been taken from the house?

(c) To what extent are your answers affected by similarities or dissimilarities in the "time, place, and manner" of the two burglaries? See State v. Klotter, 274 Minn. 58, 142 N.W.2d 568 (1966).

---

[53] See, e.g., People v. Ewoldt, 7 Cal.4th 380, 410–11, 27 Cal.Rptr.2d 646, 664–65 , 867 P.2d 757, 775–76 (1994) (Mosk, J., dissenting) (endorsing use of "common scheme or plan" theory when "the evidence is like a jigsaw puzzle, on which the shape of the missing piece can be inferred from examining the pieces around it," and when it tends to show intent or identity, but not otherwise).

[54] See, e.g., the majority opinion in Ewoldt, supra (holding that for admissibility under "common design or plan" theory it is not necessary to show a "single, continuing conception or plot," and that the critical inquiry is whether there are "sufficient common features"; holding admissible under a common plan or scheme theory evidence of sexual molestation years before the act of molestation charged, and on another child); People v. Balcom, 7 Cal.4th 414, 27 Cal.Rptr.2d 666, 867 P.2d 777 (1994) (applying Ewoldt to a rape committed after the one charged, in another state).

[55] This was a point made in the helpful analysis provided by People v. Tassell, 36 Cal.3d 77, 201 Cal.Rptr. 567, 679 P.2d 1 (1984)—but Tassell was later overruled by Ewoldt, supra. Note particularly Tassell's comment: "Absent . . . a 'grand design,' talk of 'common plan or scheme' is really nothing but the bestowing of a respectable label on a disreputable basis for admissibility— the defendant's disposition." 679 P.2d at 5. For another restrained view, in a civil context, see In re Estate of Brandon, 55 N.Y.2d 206, 448 N.Y.S.2d 436, 433 N.E.2d 501 (1982).

¶ **18.44:** Dishy is on trial for possessing two checks that were stolen from the mail, a federal crime. (If the checks were not stolen *from the mail*, there is no federal crime, and Dishy is off the hook in this case.) The prosecution is prepared to offer evidence that the first check was mailed from Chicago to New York on January 4, that it was never recorded in the comptroller's office of its intended recipient, as it ordinarily would have been had it reached that office, and that it was altered by Dishy and deposited in a New York bank account that he controlled on January 8. The prosecution is prepared to present similar evidence with respect to a second check, except that this check was mailed on January 12 from New York to a recipient in Dallas and, after alteration, was deposited in Dishy's New York account on January 15.

Dishy moves to sever the two counts of the indictment, on the grounds that neither one would be admissible at the trial of the other.[56] In response, the prosecutor argues that they show a common plan or scheme. Is this persuasive? Does the prosecutor have any other arguments? Should the counts be severed?[57]

¶ **18.45:** Tassell is accused of raping Anne B. She testifies that she was working as a waitress and that as she left early one morning he asked for a ride home. She agreed because she had seen him at the restaurant, but when they reached his supposed destination he overpowered her, put his hands around her windpipe, demanded oral sex, and then raped her. Tassell contends that they had sex consensually. The prosecution also offers the testimony of two other women. Mrs. G. is prepared to testify that four years earlier, as she was leaving work as a barmaid, Tassell, whom she had seen earlier at the bar, overpowered her at her car, grabbed her in a choke hold, drove her to a secluded spot, attempted to force her to perform oral sex, and then forced anal and vaginal intercourse. Cherie B. is prepared to testify that, three years before the incident with Anne B., Tassell picked her up while she was hitchhiking. He then pulled off the road, grabbed her in a choke hold, demanded oral sex and after a brief time attempted vaginal and anal intercourse.

Assume here, and in the other problems in this Section, that the jurisdiction does *not* have rules comparable to FRE 413–15.

---

[56] *See, e.g.,* Drew v. United States, 331 F.2d 85 (D.C.Cir.1964).

[57] *Cf.* United States v. Graves, 736 F.2d 850 (2d Cir.1984).

Should evidence of either or both of these prior incidents be admitted?[58] yes- M.O.

Often, prior bad acts are offered to show the defendant's state of mind. In addition to motive, a factor we have already considered, questions of state of mind might include such as these: Did the defendant intend to do what he was doing—or could it have been a product of mistake or accident? And, where the law makes it material, what did the defendant intend to do in the future?

¶ 18.46: Hadley, a former elementary school teacher, is accused of having committed aggravated sexual assault—principally anal sexual intercourse—on one of his young students on three separate occasions. Hadley denies that he committed the acts charged. "Sexual contact," an essential element of the charge against Hadley, is defined as "the intentional touching, either directly or through the clothing, of the genitalia, anus, groin, breast, inner thigh, or buttocks of any person with an intent to abuse, humiliate, harass, degrade, or arouse or gratify the sexual desire of any person." The prosecution offers the testimony of another former student of Hadley's that, beginning ten years earlier and for a period of five years, Hadley repeatedly molested him in various ways, including anal intercourse. Hadley objects to this evidence. The prosecution argues that the evidence is admissible on the issue of intent, and Hadley offers not to argue that issue. Should the evidence be admitted?[59] yes

¶ 18.47: Findley is charged with placing his hand on the "private parts" of a young girl. He denies that this occurred. The prosecution offers evidence as part of its case-in-chief that Findley behaved similarly with two adult women nine years earlier. Should this evidence be admissible? Is the case materially different from Hadley's?[60] different proclivities but act shows not "accidental"

¶ 18.48: McGuire is charged with the murder of his 6-month-old daughter Tori. Tori died 45 minutes after McGuire and his wife brought her to a hospital, bluish in color and not breathing. She had a recent bruise on her chest and black and blue marks around her ears. An autopsy indicated many other

---

[58] *See Tassell, supra* (holding that trial court committed harmless error in admitting the testimony), *overruled by Ewoldt, supra.*

[59] *See* United States v. Hadley, 918 F.2d 848 (9th Cir.1990), *cert. granted,* 503 U.S. 905, *and dismissed as improvidently granted,* 506 U.S. 19 (1992) (holding that trial court did not abuse its discretion in admitting evidence).

[60] *See* Findley v. State, 94 Nev. 212, 577 P.2d 867 (1978) (holding the evidence admissible to show intent, or the absence of mistake or accident, and also on a theory of "specific emotional propensity for sexual aberration").

injuries to Tori, including rectal tearing, which was at least six weeks old, and partially healed rib fractures, which were approximately seven weeks old. Questioned by police, McGuire stated his belief that Tori's injuries must have resulted from a fall off the family couch. At trial, however, McGuire does not raise a question of accidental death. The prosecution wishes to offer evidence of the prior injuries, including the rib and rectal injuries, to show that Tori was a battered child. The prosecution does not, however, present evidence closely linking McGuire to the prior injuries.[61]

(a) Should the evidence of the earlier injuries be admitted? *See Estelle v. McGuire*, 502 U.S. 62, 67–70 (1991) (unanimously reversing federal court of appeals, holding no constitutional error in admission).

[handwritten: yes - shows not accident - intent - still an important element it has to prove]

(b) If you are the defense counsel, and you are determined to keep out the evidence of the prior injuries, what tactic might you try? *See id.* at 69–70 ("the prosecution's burden to prove every element of the crime is not relieved by a defendant's tactical decision not to contest an essential element of the offense"; a "simple plea of not guilty . . . puts the prosecution to its proof as to all elements of the crime charged," *quoting Mathews v. United States*, 485 U.S. 58, 64–65 (1988)).

[handwritten margin: well rectal injuries seem unrelated - diff type of abuse / 403 arg / or stipulate that the prior injuries were intentional but maybe someone else inflicted them]

¶ 18.49: (a) Green is accused of murdering his estranged wife. The evidence shows that she was killed by ax blows to her head and midsection. Green contends that she was killed by a robber. Should the prosecution be allowed to prove prior assaults that Green committed against his wife and an attack in which he threw a hatchet at her? If so, on what theory? Do you agree with *State v. Green*, 232 Kan. 116, 652 P.2d 697 (1982), that "where a marital homicide is involved, evidence of a discordant marital relationship, and of the defendant's previous ill treatment of his wife, including his prior threats to kill her, is competent as bearing on the defendant's motive and intent"? *[handwritten: yes]*.

(b) Suppose instead that the victim died of a blunt instrument trauma to the head; Green admits that he struck the blow that caused death, but claims that he hit her lightly, without intent to cause grievous harm, and that she, in recoiling,

---

[61] One cannot say that there was *no* evidence linking McGuire to the prior injuries: There was some evidence linking him to the fatal injury, and the presence of the earlier injuries suggests the plausible possibility that the person who inflicted the fatal injury also inflicted the earlier ones. The Supreme Court said that there was no "direct" evidence linking McGuire to the earlier injuries, 502 U.S. at 69, but in this context, as in many others, "direct" is an amorphous, easily manipulable term. Perhaps it would be more accurate to say there was no *independent* evidence linking him to the injury.

banged her head against an electric wallplate, causing her death.
Does this alter the case? *[handwritten: no - although maybe it helps him? i've hard to harm/o killing her before.]*

¶ **18.50:** Consider the notorious "brides of the bath" case, *R. v. Smith*, 11 Crim. App. 229, 84 L.J.K.B. 2153 (1915). Smith is accused of killing one of his wives, who drowned in a bathtub. He contends that she died of an epileptic seizure. The prosecution offers evidence that two other wives of Smith's also died in the bathtub.[62] Admissible? *[handwritten: yes! M.O.]*

[handwritten margin note: doctrine of chances → lack of accident]

Cases like *Smith* are sometimes addressed under the so-called "doctrine of chances," described by Wigmore as resting on an intuitively appealing "logical process which eliminates the element of innocent intent by multiplying instances of the same result until it is perceived that this element cannot explain them all." 2 Wigmore, *Evidence* § 302.[63] Suppose that it is difficult to choose between two explanations for an incident, that it was accidental and that the defendant intended it. If we then learn that the same type of incident occurred several times in the past, the most plausible explanation is that each of the incidents was intended. Why? Because that explanation is the most economical, in the sense that it rests on the simplest and most easily satisfied set of assumptions. Rather than depending on a series of accidents, or perhaps an accident after a series of intended events, it needs only a single causal factor, a constant or recurring intent on the part of the defendant, to account for all the incidents. But that constant or recurring intent is a propensity. Should this type of evidence therefore be considered propensity evidence and rejected? That is not an appealing result, and it is one courts are unlikely to accept. Or is it simply very good propensity evidence, good enough to overcome the usual rule of exclusion? Or is the use to which the evidence

---

[62] Like Ms. Coit, from ¶ 18.37, Smith did not always avoid simultaneity of marriages. For a transcript of Smith's trial, together with an account of his miserable life, see Eric Watson, ed., *Trial of George Joseph Smith* (1922). Smith is not the only husband who has contended unsuccessfully that successive wives have drowned accidentally. *See* Lisenba v. California, 314 U.S. 219 (1941).

[63] For helpful commentary on the doctrine, see, e.g., Mark Cammack, *Using the Doctrine of Chances to Prove Actus Reus in Child Abuse and Acquaintance Rape:* People v. Ewolt *Reconsidered,* 29 U.C. Davis L. Rev. 355 (1996); Paul F. Rothstein, *Intellectual Coherence in an Evidence Code,* 28 Loyola L. Rev. 1259 (1995); Edward J. Imwinkelried, *The Evolution of the Use of Doctrine of Chances as Theory of Admissibility for Similar Fact Evidence,* 22 Anglo-Am.L.Rev. 73 (1993), *A Small Contribution to the Debate Over the Proposed Legislation Abolishing the Character Evidence Prohibition in Sex Offense Prosecutions,* 44 Syr. L. Rev. 1125 (1993), and *The Dispute Over the Doctrine of Chances,* 7 Crim. Just. 16 (1992); Stephen E. Fienberg & D.H. Kaye, *Legal and Statistical Aspects of Some Mysterious Clusters,* 154 J. R. Statist. Soc. Ser. A 61 (1991). In addition to *Smith,* other frequently discussed cases raising similar issues include Makin v. Atty. Gen. for New South Wales, [1894] App. Cas. 57 (P.C. 1893), and State v. Pankow, 144 Wis.2d 23, 422 N.W.2d 913 (Ct.App.), *review denied,* 430 N.W.2d 351 (1988), both involving repeat deaths of children in the defendants' care, and DPP v. Boardman, [1974] 3 All E.R. 887, [1975] App. Cas. 421 (H.L. 1974), and People v. VanderVliet, 444 Mich. 52, 508 N.W.2d 114 (1993), both involving sex crimes. *VanderVliet* seems to reflect a trend in suggesting that the doctrine of chances may be used to discount the possibility of false accusation. 508 N.W.2d at 128 n.35; *see* Imwinkelried, *Small Contribution, supra,* 44 Syr. L. Rev. at 1134–35.

is put—trying to eliminate the possibility of accident or mistake rather than merely showing that the defendant was likely to engage in an activity because he had done so before—sufficiently different to account for different treatment?

¶ 18.51: Perkins is charged with possession of crack cocaine with intent to distribute. Police were called to his apartment on December 4 as a result of a domestic dispute. While there, the police found several pieces of crack wrapped in torn-off corners of plastic sandwich bags, a razor blade with crack residue, and other evidence suggestive of traffic in drugs, including $5,723 in cash, a pistol and ammunition, and a pager displaying several telephone numbers on its readout, one of which was followed by the numbers 911, a code used by addicts to indicate an urgent need for crack. The prosecution offers to prove that on the prior June 2 Perkins was found in possession of eleven rocks of crack, that as a result he had been charged with possession with intent to deliver, and that he pled guilty to simple possession. Perkins objects, and the prosecution argues that the evidence is admissible to show that Perkins knew that the substance that he possessed in December was crack and to show his intent to distribute it. How should the court rule?[64]

Identity is another issue on which evidence of other wrongs is sometimes offered. If it appears likely that whoever committed the other wrongs also committed the crime charged, and if it also appears likely that the defendant committed the other wrongs, then the other wrongs are probative evidence on the question of identity. In some cases, the link between the crime charged and the other wrongs may be based on the circumstances of the situation: "In all likelihood, the person who burglarized the warehouse is the person who committed the crime charged, killing the guard, and lots of evidence indicates that the defendant is the one who burglarized the warehouse."

Frequently, though, the identity inference is based on similarity between the crimes. In this type of case, the idea generally is that the method by which the two crimes were committed was so distinctive and unusual as practically to constitute a *signature*; sometimes courts also refer to these as *earmark* cases. With this type of case in mind, one court pointed out that "a much greater degree of similarity between the charged crime and the uncharged crime is required when the evidence of the other crime is introduced to prove identity than when it is introduced to prove a

---

[64] *See* United States v. Perkins, 94 F.3d 429 (8th Cir.1996), *cert. denied*, 519 U.S. 1136 (1997).

state of mind."[65] Prosecutors therefore try very hard to find points of similarity between incidents—and defendants try equally hard to find points of difference and to argue that the similarities are not all that telling. Again, we might ask whether this is simply a particularized form of propensity evidence.

¶ 18.52: Myers is on trial for a bank robbery, which was committed by a single gunman in Clearwater, Florida, on June 13. Myers denies that he was the robber. The prosecution seeks to introduce evidence of a robbery committed on July 29 of the same year in Warren, Pennsylvania, committed by Myers and his friend Coffie. (Coffie, who bears a strong resemblance to Myers, says he committed the Florida robbery.) The Government argues these points of similarity: (1) Both crimes were bank robberies, (2) perpetrated between 2 and 3 p.m. In both robberies the bank was (3) located on the outskirts of a town, (4) adjacent to a major highway. In both robberies, the perpetrators (5) used a revolver, (6) furnished their own bag for carrying off the loot, and wore (7) gloves and (8) masks crudely made from nylon stockings. Finally, (9) only women employees were present at both banks, two in one bank and five in the other. (The Government does not mention that the robberies happened on different days of the week and under different Zodiac signs.) Should evidence of the Warren robbery be admitted? *See Myers*, *supra* (holding in the negative).

¶ 18.53: McGahee is on trial for rape. The complainant testifies that while she was sunbathing on a beach McGahee, wearing a white, see-through bikini, approached her, grabbed at her pants, made a suggestive remark, then pushed her back into a sand dune and raped her. The prosecution offers the testimony of another woman that twice during the previous month McGahee, while wearing a red see-through bikini, approached women at the same beach and exposed himself. Should this be admitted?[66]

And now a few procedural points relating to this entire matter of the "end run" purposes by which other acts may be introduced. Bear in mind that in this context we are concerned with *other acts*, not *prior convictions*

---

[65] United States v. Myers, 550 F.2d 1036, 1045 (5th Cir.1977), *cert. denied (after remand and appeal)*, 439 U.S. 847 (1978); see also the useful discussion in Hicks v. State, 690 N.E.2d 215 (Ind. 1997).

[66] *See* McGahee v. Massey, 667 F.2d 1357 (11th Cir.1982), *cert. denied*, 459 U.S. 943 (1982). In *McGahee*, a *habeas corpus* case, the court held that the evidence was admissible to demonstrate "the manner of operation, identity, and type of clothing worn by the defendant," *id.* at 1360. McGahee testified that he was elsewhere at the time of one of the other incidents; he did not testify as to his whereabouts on the day of the rape or the day of the other incident, and cross-examination about those dates was barred.

as such. Such an other act need not have been criminal, and if it was criminal it need not have been prosecuted or have resulted in a conviction; indeed, even if the defendant was acquitted, the prosecution is not foreclosed from proving it.[67] Sometimes, if the other act did result in a conviction, the prosecutor will be allowed to introduce the judgment of conviction, but that is not necessary. Ordinarily the prosecutor will prove the other act just as she would prove most facts at trial, through witnesses who observed it.

¶ **18.54:** Revisit *Huddleston*, discussed in ¶ 8.5: Huddleston is charged with possessing and selling stolen videocassettes, and to show his knowledge that the cassettes were stolen the Government offers evidence that previously he had sold very cheaply 38 TVs that he had obtained from the same source. If Huddleston does not concede that the televisions were stolen, what standard should the trial judge use in determining whether this proposition is sufficiently supported to submit the evidence about the televisions to the jury? Should admissibility of the TV evidence depend on proof that Huddleston knew the TVs were stolen?

In 1991, FRE 404(b) was amended to add a notice provision, applicable to prosecution use of crimes, wrongs, or other acts for purposes other than a propensity theory: upon request by an accused, the prosecution in a criminal case must "provide reasonable notice of the general nature of any such evidence" that it intends to introduce at trial. This proviso was intended to reduce surprise and encourage pretrial resolution of admissibility issues.

The requirement is theoretically perplexing, however. The sentence to which it is attached is simply a reminder that acts other than those actually charged may be proven for purposes other than showing propensity; once again, it is not limited to criminal acts. So does the notice requirement apply to every act of the defendant other than the acts actually constituting the crime charged? In a bank robbery case, for example, walking into the bank is not part of the crime charged; is this an "other" act to which the notice provision applies? Presumably this was not the intention of the Advisory Committee; it said in its Note that the amendment was not intended to "extend to evidence of acts which are 'intrinsic' to the charged offense." Naturally, therefore, we now have litigation over whether a particular act was "intrinsic" to the offense or not.[68]

---

[67] *See* Dowling v. United States, 493 U.S. 342 (1990) (no violation of Double Jeopardy or Due Process Clauses).

[68] The term "intrinsic" does double duty in the context of Rule 404(b). Even before the 1991 amendment, it was sometimes used to describe a test for *admissibility* notwithstanding the

Other issues concerning the notice requirement are how specific the notice must be[69] and, more simply, when notice must be given.[70] However laudable and effective it may prove to be, the notice requirement will likely continue to be a productive source of litigation and a trap for unwary defense counsel and prosecutors, who must respectively make and comply with demands for notice.[71]

3. IN CIVIL CASES

Putting aside the notice provision for prosecution evidence added in1991 to the Federal Rules, the rules in civil cases are the same, and they are implemented in roughly similar fashion: Courts profess adherence to a ban on propensity evidence but tend to be generous in allowing end-runs around it.

---

general prohibition of the Rule, the idea being that the particular evidence is so closely related to the acts being charged. *See* United States v. Williams, 900 F.2d 823, 825 (5th Cir.1990) (stating principle later endorsed by Advisory Committee: " 'Other act' evidence is 'intrinsic' when the evidence of the other act and the evidence of the crime charged are . . . part of a 'single criminal episode' or the other acts were 'necessary preliminaries' to the crime charged."). Some courts have continued to use the term in this sense. *E.g.*, United States v. Cross, 308 F.3d 308, 320 (3d Cir. 2003); United States v. Krout, 66 F.3d 1420, 1421 (5th Cir.1995), *cert. denied*, 516 U.S. 1136 (1996) ("same transactions or series of transactions" test). But now it must also describe a test for whether *notice* is required. *See, e.g.*, United States v. Hemphill, 76 Fed. Appx. 6, 2003 WL 21872509 (6th Cir. 2003); United States v. Barnes, 49 F.3d 1144, 1149 (6th Cir.1995) ("Rule 404(b) is not implicated"—and "the government has no duty to disclose"—"when the other crimes or wrongs evidence is part of a continuing pattern of illegal activity," not occurring "at different times and under different circumstances from the offense charged"; here, no notice necessary for evidence of an earlier drug shipment, because theory of the case was that the shipment in question was to make up for a shortage in the earlier one, and so the earlier one was intrinsic to the one charged).

[69] *See, e.g.*, United States v. Gonzalez, 229 F.3d 1160 (9th Cir. 2000) ("While the government's articulation of the purposes for which it would introduce the prior conviction mirrored the litany of purposes set forth in Rule 404(b), this did not violate the Rule's notice or specificity requirements."); United States v. Long, 814 F.Supp. 72 (D. Kan.1993) (holding notice insufficient where it identified the witness and said he would testify consistent with a prior statement already provided to the defense, but did not describe the nature of the conduct to be proved; notice need not provide precise details regarding date, time, and place of the prior acts prosecution intends to prove, but prosecution should apprise defense of "the kind of prior conduct" it would involve, and "should consider including in its notice the specific purpose, among those listed in the rule, for which the evidence is intended to be introduced at trial"); United States v. Rusin, 889 F.Supp. 1035 (N.D.Ill.1995) (denying demand for extensive information, including dates, places, and persons involved in the specific acts and documents pertaining to them; notice provision is not a tool for open-ended discovery); United States v. Singleton, 922 F.Supp. 1522, 1533 (D.Kan.1996) (in case charging, among other counts, possession of counterfeit checks, holding as too vague and indefinite pretrial notice that the prosecution might offer evidence of other conduct involving manufacture and distribution of counterfeit payroll checks or relating to false statements).

[70] *See, e.g.*, United States v. Nachamie, 91 F.Supp.2d 565, 577 (S.D.N.Y. 2000) (notice of two to three weeks before trial is usual, but longer period may be required where there is not threat to witnesses and evidence is important to action); United States v. Jackson, 850 F.Supp. 1481, 1494 (D. Kan.1994) (granting motion for disclosure at least 30 days before trial); *Rusin*, supra (35 days); *Barnes*, *supra*, 49 F.3d at 1148 (request by defense triggers a continuing obligation to give notice).

[71] *Barnes*, *supra*, 40 F.3d at 1148, emphasizes that "an overly broad and generalized discovery request" by the defendant will not suffice.

¶ **18.55:** Prancer sues Dasher, a used car dealer, claiming that Dasher fraudulently understated the mileage on a car that he sold Prancer. Can Walzer testify for Prancer that Dasher understated the mileage on a car he sold her?[72]

¶ **18.56:** (a) Perez is suing Donnelly, a stockbroker who sold him shares in Slippery Rock Co. Perez claims that Donnelly had bought a large block of shares in the company, and that she was so eager to unload it that she misrepresented its value by suggesting that since Slippery Rock's last SEC filing the company had discovered large oil reserves. Donnelly denies having made the statements. May Perez present the evidence of Wyche that Donnelly made similar statements to him about the value of Slippery Rock stock?

(b) Same problem as (a), but the statements allegedly made to Wyche concerned another company, Slick Stones, Inc.

¶ **18.57:** Pincher owned a munitions factory that has burned down, and he has sued on his policy against his fire insurer.

(a) Can the insurance company introduce evidence that five other munitions factories owned by Pincher have also burned down?

(b) What if the insurance company has evidence that each of those previous fires was caused by arson?[73] Is this case materially distinguishable from ¶ 18.11 (involving the repeated theft of gold chains)?

¶ **18.58:** (a) Portnoy sues the Derby Automobile Company, claiming that he got into an accident because the accelerator on his 2016 model Derby locked as he went into overdrive. Derby denies the claim, and contends that Portnoy was traveling 85 m.p.h. at the time of the accident. (Portnoy says he was only going 55 m.p.h.) Derby offers the evidence of Winkler that Portnoy was speeding—on the same highway as the accident site, twenty miles south of it and heading north—the day before the accident. Is this admissible?

(b) Now change just one fact: It was approximately twenty minutes before the accident that Winkler saw Portnoy. Admissible?

---

[72] *See, e.g.,* Cates v. Darland, 537 P.2d 336, 338 (Okl.1975); Edgar v. Fred Jones Lincoln-Mercury, 524 F.2d 162, 167 (10th Cir.1975).

[73] *Cf.* Smith v. State Farm Fire & Casualty Co., 633 F.2d 401 (5th Cir.1980) (holding trial court did not abuse its discretion in refusing to admit evidence of five prior fires of property owned by claimant, for some of which there was evidence of arson).

¶ **18.59:** Paula sues Bill for sexual harassment. She claims that, when he was the head of the state affiliate of a giant enterprise and she was a low-level employee for the affiliate, he called her up to his hotel room during a convention at which she was working and made unwanted sexual overtures—specifically, asking for oral sex. Paula offers evidence that some time later, when Bill had gone on to head the parent enterprise, he made an uninvited sexual overture to Kathleen, a low-level assistant, and that he had an ongoing sexual relationship (primarily oral sex) with Monica, another low level assistant. Is this evidence admissible?

We have been dealing, in both the criminal and civil contexts, with cases in which the evidence offered is assertedly some prior act of a person, generally a party to the litigation. In many of the cases we have discussed, the basis for admitting evidence of those acts depends on the asserted similarity between them and the alleged acts of the same person that are part of the claim or defense. Now let's look at a closely related context: A party offers evidence of some *other* kind of occurrence—that is, not the act of a person—on the theory that it is similar to the occurrence alleged by that party. Courts still resist allowing one set of events to prove what happened at another time—but note that even in a jurisdiction following the Federal Rules they have to do so under general principles rather than under FRE 404(b), which does not come into play unless the conduct of a person is being proved. The obstacles that often preclude admissibility of "other act" evidence are not as formidable against evidence of other types of occurrence; other kinds of occurrence are less likely to depend on assumptions about the probative value of a person's propensities, and less likely to create prejudice against a party. Generalizations are difficult, however, in part because it is not always easy to determine whether the evidence is more appropriately considered an act of a person or some other type of occurrence.

¶ **18.60:** In ¶ 18.58, Portnoy offers evidence that five other 2016 Derbies had similar accidents, one before his and four afterwards. Is this evidence admissible? Does your answer depend on whether Portnoy's assertion is that the Derby was designed and engineered in an unsatisfactory way or that this particular car was manufactured defectively? In what other respects might your answer depend on the applicable law and on what material issues are in dispute?

¶ **18.61:** Patsy, a 7-year-old child, was injured on a roller coaster operated by Dipster Co. She sues, claiming that Dipster operated the ride at excessive speed. Dipster denies the claim, and contends that Patsy was carelessly leaning out of her seat when she was injured.

(a) Patsy offers proof that three other children have been injured on the same roller coaster, and that all three have contended that the ride was being operated too fast. Can this evidence be admitted? Does the answer depend on whether the other accidents occurred before or after Patsy's, or both? Does it depend on whether Dipster disputes that the actual speed of the roller coaster was as alleged by Patsy, or that the speed Patsy alleges was too great, or both?[74]

(b) Suppose instead that Dipster wants to present evidence that it has had no other accidents. Admissible? Does the answer depend on the nature of Patsy's claim?[75]

¶ 18.62: Same problem as ¶ 18.61, except that now Patsy's claim is that the injury was caused by a tree branch that Dipster allowed to grow too close to the roller coaster. Once again, Dipster defends by contending that Patsy injured herself by leaning out of her seat.

(a) Can Patsy introduce the evidence in ¶ 18.61(a), of three other accidents? Does the answer depend on whether they occurred before or after Patsy's?

(b) Would evidence that there had been no prior accidents be admissible?

F. HABIT AND ROUTINE PRACTICE

FRE 406

Additional Reading: McCormick, Ch. 17, § 195; Mueller & Kirkpatrick, §§ 4.21–.22

By now you are familiar with the general rule that evidence of a person's character trait cannot be introduced to prove that he likely acted in conformity with that trait on a given occasion. Under an associated rule expressed in FRE 404(b)(1), evidence of prior acts of a person is not generally admissible to prove a propensity to act in a certain way and thus the likelihood that he acted in that way on the occasion in question. Existing alongside this rule is another one that looks in the opposite direction. As expressed in FRE 406, "[e]vidence of a person's habit or an organization's routine practice may be admitted to prove that on a particular occasion the person or organization acted in accordance with the habit or routine practice." This rule forces us to ask what the

---

[74] *See generally* McCormick, § 200; Mueller & Kirkpatrick, § 4.5.

[75] *See generally* McCormick, § 200; Mueller & Kirkpatrick, § 4.5; Jay M. Zitter, Annotation, *Admissibility of Evidence of Absence of Other Accidents or Injuries at Place Where Injury or Damage Occurred*, 10 A.L.R.5th 371 (1993) (summarizing authority both ways).

difference is between habit or routine practice, on the one hand, and a character trait or mere repeated pattern of activity, on the other. You may possibly conclude that there really is no difference that can be stated coherently, and that habit is simply the conclusory label that we attach when we have decided, after weighing various considerations, that in the particular case the propensity evidence should be admitted after all.

There are, however, some guideposts for determining whether a particular type of repeated conduct should be considered habit. The *more specific the stimulus*, and the *more regular the response*, the more likely is the practice to be considered a habit. If Wife testifies that Husband usually responded enthusiastically to sports on TV, that probably would not be considered a habit. If Wife testifies that every time the Advocates scored in football, Husband did a number of pushups equal to their score, that probably would be considered a habit. Absolute invariability of response is generally not required. If the tenor of the proponent's argument is, "You should believe that Hannah acted in this way on the occasion in question, because, though you wouldn't infer it without knowing about her, she often acted in this way," a fair amount of variability in response should probably be tolerated. On the other hand, suppose the tenor of the argument is this: "Without knowing about Hannah you might infer that although she often acted in this way she also fairly often failed to do so. But in fact she was very unlikely to fail to do so. Therefore, you should believe that she acted in this way on the occasion in question." Then greater regularity in response should presumably be required.

Assuming that a pattern of behavior constitutes a habit or routine practice, there remains the question of how it should be proved. As presented to Congress, FRE 406 had a subsection (b), which allowed for proof by opinion *or* "by specific instances sufficient in number to warrant a finding that the habit existed or that the practice was routine." But the House Judiciary Committee deleted this provision, saying that the method of proof should be left to the courts on a case-by-case basis. We see here the same choice between generalized assessments and specific instances that we have already seen with respect to Rules 405 (how character may be proved when it is a proper subject of proof) and 412 (the rape shield law). On the one hand, asking a witness for an opinion may be an invitation to a vague and unsubstantiated assessment. On the other hand, asking for specific instances may be an invitation to a long and unilluminating inquiry into other events of only collateral significance to the one at issue. On the whole, it seems courts have been reasonably generous on this matter. Though one prior instance will not be sufficient to prove a habit or routine practice, Rule 406 makes clear that multiple witnesses are not required.[76] And despite the House Judiciary Committee's note that it did not intend that its action "be construed as sanctioning a general authorization of opinion evidence in this area," courts have tolerated evidence of the tenor, "The defendant acted in this way often, though I can't give you exact times and dates."[77]

¶ 18.63: Pell v. Dell for auto negligence. Pell claims that Dell ran through a blinking red light, at the corner of Clark and Forest, without looking. Dell claims that he had the right of way, having arrived at the intersection well before Pell, that he stopped at the light and looked both ways, and that Pell, who was drunk, saw that her light was yellow and accelerated into the intersection.

(a) Consider whether evidence of each of the following propositions should be admissible. Also, if you believe that some evidence of the proposition should be admitted, consider whether that evidence might take the form of an overall evaluation of the person's tendency, or of particular occasions on which he or she had acted in conformity with it, or either.

(i)   Pell is a careless driver.

(ii) Pell is an alcoholic.

(iii) Pell tends to speed into intersections after seeing a yellow light.

(iv) Dell is a careful person.

(v)   Dell is a careful driver.

(vi) Dell usually stops at blinking red lights.

(vii) Dell usually stops at the blinking red light at the corner of Clark and Forest.

(b) Assume that the court is prepared to hold that the tendency in (a)(vii), if sufficiently established, would qualify as habit? Waldron is prepared to testify to that proposition for Dell. How many instances must Waldron have observed for the tendency to be sufficiently made out? What if Waldron is prepared to testify that she was with Dell at that intersection on at least thirty other occasions, and on only one of those did Dell fail to stop at the blinking light?

---

[76] The Rule says that the evidence may be admitted "regardless of whether it was corroborated or whether there was an eyewitness." This is in response to some older cases that had held that habit evidence was a second-best form of proof, to be allowed only if there were not eyewitnesses to the incident at issue.

[77] *See, e.g.,* South v National Railroad Passenger Corp. (AMTRAK), 290 N.W.2d 819, 829 (N.D. 1980) (construing North Dakota Rule 406).

¶ **18.64:** Recall ¶ 18.11, the chain snatching case. Can the evidence be admitted on the theory that Dover had a habit of snatching gold chains from women's necks?[78]

¶ **18.65:** Consider *Levin v. United States*, 338 F.2d 265 (D.C.Cir.1964), *cert. denied*, 379 U.S. 999 (1965). There, the Government claimed that late on a Friday afternoon in February Levin attended a meeting in Washington, D.C., at which he obtained money larcenously. Levin contended that he could not have been at the meeting because he was an observant Jew who spent Sabbath evenings with his family in Queens, New York.

(a) Should the testimony of Levin's rabbi as to Levin's religious practices have been admitted? The *Levin* court held that the evidence was properly excluded; the court said that because of the "volitional basis of the activity" it did not lend itself to a characterization of "invariable regularity."[79] Are you persuaded?

(b) If Levin's rabbi were able to testify, "I distinctly remember that Levin was in synagogue every Friday evening of the winter," would the result change?

(c) What if the testimony were, "I distinctly remember that Levin regularly attended Sabbath services, and because we have a small congregation I would have noticed it if he was ever absent, but I have no recollection of such an absence"?

¶ **18.66:** Durkin is accused of having kidnapped Varla, who has not been found. Among other evidence, the prosecution seeks to introduce the following: Varla was at work on the morning of the alleged kidnapping, a Tuesday, but she did not return after the lunch hour. Walker will testify that he saw Durkin around the corner from Louie's Lunch on that day shortly before noon. Louie himself will testify that Varla ate lunch at his place on noon every Tuesday, but that she did not eat there on the day she disappeared.

Should the evidence be admitted? What if Louie is prepared to testify only that Varla ate at his place "almost every Tuesday at noon"? What if his testimony is that she "often" ate there at noon? What if the kidnapping allegedly occurred, and Durkin was allegedly spotted, not near Louie's but near a synagogue;

---

[78] *Cf.* Perrin v. Anderson, 784 F.2d 1040, 1045–46 (10th Cir.1986) (§ 1983 action against police officers; defendant officers allowed to show, as habit, that decedent "invariably reacted with extreme violence to any contact with a uniformed police officer").

[79] The *Levin* result might have been based in part on the cumulativeness of the testimony, because Levin, corroborated in part by his wife, testified to his religious practice.

would testimony that Varla "often" attended services at that synagogue be admissible?

¶ 18.67: Pechter, an air-conditioning mechanic, was using a can of refrigerant to charge an automobile air-conditioner. It is sometimes necessary, in performing this task, to warm the refrigerant. A warning on the label cautioned against using an immersion coil to heat the water in which the can was placed. The can exploded, and Pechter has sued the manufacturer. In his case-in-chief, Pechter has testified that he used warm water but not an immersion coil; Wachtler, a co-worker, has corroborated this testimony. May the defense introduce the testimony of Wechsler, another co-worker, that Pechter always heated the refrigerant in an immersion coil? What if Wechsler's testimony is that Pechter often used the coil when the refrigerant needed extra heating? What if Wechsler can only say that, on the only two prior occasions that Pechter was having trouble heating the refrigerant, he used a coil?[80]

¶ 18.68: Speedy Couriers, Inc., delivered some documents in an envelope for Parsons, but Parsons has sued Speedy, claiming that Speedy failed to deliver all of the documents and that she therefore lost some valuable business. You are representing Speedy. The agent who received the documents from Parsons has recently died; just before his death, he said that he had no recollection of the episode. Speedy's manual, however, instructs agents that they should always give an empty envelope to the customer and ask the customer to put the documents in the envelope. What use can you make of this information? In particular, whom will you call to the stand, and to testify to what?

---

[80] *Cf.* Halloran v. Virginia Chem. Inc., 41 N.Y.2d 386, 393 N.Y.S.2d 341, 361 N.E.2d 991 (1977).

CHAPTER 19

IMPEACHMENT AND SUPPORT

■ ■ ■

A. AN OVERVIEW

Additional Reading: McCormick, Ch. 5, § 33

It is perhaps surprising how large a portion of evidentiary law is devoted to evidence that is designed to attack or support the credibility of witnesses. Such evidence may be relevant to one of the substantive factual issues in the case, but often it is not. This is one of the distinctive features of the common law of evidence: Our factfinding system depends heavily on witnesses whose sworn testimony the factfinder is asked to accept. It is important for the factfinder, therefore, to assess the truth-telling ability of the witness, both generally and in the particular case; in other words, the factfinder will want to know how good the witness's capacities of perception, memory, sincerity, and articulateness are, and whether her testimony is a product of their proper functioning or of the faulty operation of one or more of them. Accordingly, some forms of evidence may be admitted, notwithstanding the fact that they have nothing to do with the actual facts in dispute, because they bear on a witness's truth-telling ability. All the capacities are properly the subject of inquiry, but often the principal focus is on sincerity.

The body of law governing this area, although probably not as difficult conceptually as some others in evidentiary law, is quite intricate and technical. Summarizing this law accurately and briefly is probably impossible, but the following are some of the general principles that shape it.

A party may impeach a witness by offering evidence to show that the witness's testimonial capacities probably have not functioned properly in this case. For example, the party may prove facts tending to show that the witness has a bias—an extraneous motive tending to break down the capacity of sincerity, and so leading her to give false testimony.

The party may also present certain forms of evidence tending to show that, in general, the witness has a weak testimonial capacity—that, for example, she tends to be a liar. Notice that, at least so far as such evidence concerns the capacity of sincerity, the evidence is character evidence: Its probative value depends on the assumption that, because

513

the witness has a weak character for truthfulness, she is more likely to lie from the witness stand in this case.

Courts sometimes say, speaking rather loosely, that by taking the stand a witness "puts her character in issue."[1] A major question, though, is how a party should be allowed to impeach the witness's character. One way is by presenting an overall evaluation of her capacity for truth-telling. In a jurisdiction following the Federal Rules, a party may offer the testimony of a second witness (a "character witness") that, in her opinion, the first witness (the "primary witness") has a bad character for truthfulness. Alternatively, the character witness may testify that the primary witness has a bad reputation for truthfulness. FRE 608(a), the provision of the Federal Rules authorizing these types of testimony, is the counterpart of FRE 405(a), which, in appropriate cases, allows reputation or opinion evidence to prove the character of a criminal defendant or of an alleged victim. We have already discussed reputation and opinion evidence in Chapter 18, and will return briefly to the subject here.

An impeaching party may want to get more specific than the type of general assessment represented by reputation and opinion evidence. Within discretionary limits, courts will generally allow cross-examination of the primary witness concerning specific instances of conduct tending to undercut her credibility. See FRE 608(b).[2] What kind of conduct might that include? In general, anything that she has done tending to show that she is a dishonest person may, in the discretion of the court, be the subject of inquiry. That might include lies she has told on other occasions, or other acts of deception, even if they were not criminal and even if they have nothing to do with the current case. Furthermore, the testimony just given by the witness might in itself constitute, or help prove, an act of dishonesty. For example, if on cross-examination a witness concedes that testimony she gave on direct as to one point was erroneous, the impact will likely be far greater than merely nullifying her testimony on that point; it may very well cast doubt on her commitment to telling the truth while under oath. Similarly, if on another occasion the witness has made

---

[1] More strictly, a person's character is "in issue" if the character itself is an element of a claim or defense. Recall the discussion in Chapter 18, Section B, of when character is in issue in this strict sense.

[2] Recall that, under the second sentence of FRE 405(a), when one party takes advantage of the rules allowing opinion or reputation evidence to show the character of a criminal defendant or alleged victim, the other party may cross-examine the character witnesses about specific acts of conduct; in that context, the character question must first be put into play by the opinion or reputation evidence. In the FRE 608(b) context, too, inquiry as to specific acts—here, dishonest acts of the witness—is appropriate only on cross. In this context, however, no trigger of opinion or reputation evidence is necessary to make this inquiry valid; by taking the stand, the witness has automatically made her character for truthfulness an appropriate subject of inquiry.

Recall also that when a person's character or reputation as to character is in issue, strictly speaking, as in some libel cases, character may be proven by appropriate means, including direct testimony of prior specific acts. See FRE 405(b).

a statement inconsistent with her current testimony, that may also undermine her credibility, and not only on the particular point that was the subject of the conflicting statements; the conflict may persuade the jury that she must have lied on one occasion or the other.

Notwithstanding its generosity in allowing questions on the ground that they bear on credibility, the law is concerned about the waste of time and distraction that might be created by too great a focus on a secondary issue—secondary in the sense that it is not in itself one of the disputed issues raised by the case, but merely bears on how the factfinder should assess the evidence on those issues. Accordingly, although a party may cross-examine the witness about her dishonest acts, if the only bearing of those acts on the case is that they tend to show that the witness has a poor character for truthfulness, then the impeaching party is limited to cross-examination in proving those acts. If the witness denies committing the bad act, the impeacher must "take the answer" and may not put another witness on the stand to prove the act. This rule is often expressed by saying that if the matter is collateral, then the impeacher cannot prove it by extrinsic evidence.

One important type of extrinsic evidence is allowed on collateral matters, however: If the witness has been convicted of certain types of crimes, the conviction may be proven from the mouth of the witness or, if necessary, by other means.[3] Convictions are obviously powerful evidence in undermining the credibility of the witness, and they may have substantial prejudicial impact. The question of when proof of convictions should be allowed, a subject addressed by FRE 609, is both controversial and very important.

So far we have spoken only about evidence impeaching a witness's credibility. The party who put the witness on the stand, or in some circumstances another party, may want to bolster her credibility. But, perhaps in hopes of avoiding proof on an issue that is not genuinely in contention, the law bars bolstering until the witness's credibility has been

---

[3]   Before 1990, FRE 609 allowed impeachment by proof of convictions only if "elicited from the witness or established by public record during cross-examination." This requirement was widely ignored—especially to allow defendants to lessen the sting of their convictions by acknowledging them on direct—and the 1990 amendments to the rule eliminated it. Nevertheless, in Ohler v. United States, 529 U.S. 753 (2000), discussed in Chapter 22 at the very end of the book, the Supreme Court held that if the defendant does testify to the conviction on direct he cannot appeal on the basis that the conviction ought not to have been admitted. Accordingly, if an accused wants to testify but loses on an *in limine* motion to exclude a prior conviction, he has three choices: (a) decide not to testify, in which case, under the doctrine of Luce v. United States, 469 U.S. 34 (1984) (also discussed in Chapter 22), he may not appeal from the adverse ruling; (b) testify, and admit to the prior conviction on direct, again abandoning any chance of appealing from the adverse ruling; and (c) testify, do not mention the prior conviction on direct, and then, if convicted, appeal on the basis that the prosecution should not have been allowed to introduce the prior. *Ohler* and *Luce*, it must be emphasized, are decisions binding only the federal courts, and many states have declined to follow them.

attacked. The type of rehabilitation then allowed depends on the type of impeaching evidence that has been offered. For example, if a secondary witness has testified to the bad character for truthfulness of the primary witness, then the rehabilitating party may put on his own character witness to testify how truthful the primary witness is. Or if the impeaching party has contended that the witness's testimony is the product of an improper motive, the rehabilitating party may show that the witness said essentially the same thing before the motive arose.

All this is plot summary; it will take some time to spin out the details. Section B of this chapter addresses the question of who may impeach a given witness. Sections C through H examine the various impeachment techniques. Section I explores the extent to which a criminal defendant's right of impeachment is constitutionally protected. Section J then discusses rehabilitation. Finally, Section K discusses the particular problem of polygraphs.

B. WHO MAY IMPEACH AND WHO MAY BE IMPEACHED

FRE 607

Additional Reading: McCormick, Ch. 5, § 38, Ch. 34, § 324.2; Mueller & Kirkpatrick, §§ 6.16–.17

The old-fashioned rule was simple enough: If you put a witness on the stand, you vouched for her credibility, because it would be improper for you to present a witness to the court who you thought was lying. The only trouble with the rule was that it didn't work.

The first breach in the rule in some jurisdictions arose from the recognition that in some cases the witness surprises the party who put her on the stand by giving testimony harmful to the party and at variance with his expectations. At least in that circumstance, it is unfair to hold the party to a voucher rule.

In time, courts recognized that the surprise exception did not remove all the mischief of the voucher rule. Sometimes a party will have to rely on a witness for testimony as to proposition **A**, even though the same witness will give harmful testimony as to proposition **B**. In that case, the party may want to impeach the witness with respect to proposition **B**, such as by showing that the witness's testimony on that point is a product of bias or that she really didn't have a good opportunity to observe the facts. Sometimes, indeed, it may even be necessary to put an adverse party on the stand in hopes that impeachment will break down her story.

¶ **19.1:** Think of a type of case in which the facts might be so peculiarly within your adversary's knowledge that your best chance is to put her on the stand, but because she is likely to lie you may want to impeach her. *maybe elder abuse case where victim can't testify*

FRE 607, reflecting the modern trend, does not rely on exceptions to the voucher rule but does away with it completely—any party, including the calling party, may impeach the witness. But the rule does not answer the question of whether the party has any valid need to impeach.

¶ **19.2:** Recall *California v. Green*, 399 U.S. 149 (1970), discussed (among other places) in ¶ 10.3: Porter identified Green as his drug supplier, but when the prosecution called him as a witness at trial Porter was evasive and said that he didn't remember. Should the prosecution have then been allowed to impeach him by introducing his prior statements implicating Green? *yes*

¶ **19.3:** Morlang is on trial for conspiracy to commit bribery. Wilmoth, a business associate of Morlang, is called as the first prosecution witness. Wilmoth, who has been convicted for his participation in the scheme, testifies to some of the circumstances surrounding the conspiracy. In conversations with the Government, Wilmoth has consistently denied that Morlang was a participant in the bribery attempt. On the stand, Wilmoth again denies that Morlang was a participant. The prosecutor then asks if Wilmoth (made a statement to Crist, a fellow prisoner, in which he implicated Morlang) Wilmoth denies this, too. May the prosecutor call Crist to testify to such a statement?[4]

¶ **19.4:** Consider *Chambers v. Mississippi*, 410 U.S. 284 (1973). Chambers was accused in state court of shooting Officer Liberty to death during a melee that involved several other police officers and 50 to 60 other people. McDonald had admitted on several other occasions, once in a sworn confession, that he killed Liberty, but he later retracted all these statements. At trial, the evidence was conflicting. Chambers called Hardin, who testified that McDonald shot Liberty. Chambers also called McDonald, who again denied having killed Liberty. Chambers was allowed to introduce the prior sworn statement, and the prosecution brought out on cross that McDonald had previously repudiated that statement, which he assertedly made only on the promise of an acquaintance that he would not go to jail and that

---

[4] *See* United States v. Morlang, 531 F.2d 183 (4th Cir.1975) (holding in the negative); *see also* United States v. Webster, 734 F.2d 1191 (7th Cir.1984) (Posner, J.: "[I]t would be an abuse of the rule, in a criminal case, for the prosecution to call a witness that it knew would not give it useful evidence, just so it could introduce hearsay evidence against the defendant in the hope that the jury would miss the subtle distinction between impeachment and substantive evidence—or, if it didn't miss it, would ignore it. . . .").

he would be allowed to share in a tort recovery from the town. Should Chambers have been allowed to impeach McDonald by introducing evidence of the other confessions that McDonald made to various people? Given that the state supreme court held that he could not, was the United States Supreme Court's decision to reverse proper?

C. OPINION AND REPUTATION EVIDENCE OF CHARACTER FOR UNTRUTHFULNESS

FRE 608(a)

Additional Reading: McCormick, Ch. 5, § 43; Mueller & Kirkpatrick, §§ 6.23–.24

When you impeach a witness's credibility you are attempting to show that the witness's testimony is not strongly probative of the propositions to which she has testified. Suppose the witness has testified to proposition **PROP**. In accordance with general principles of probative value, you want to show, to the extent possible, that she was no more likely to give that testimony if **PROP** was true than she was if **PROP** was false. Ordinarily, your principal focus in impeachment will be your attempt to show that she would plausibly testify to **PROP** even if it were not true. Recall from Chapter 4 and from Figure 4.a that a witness might testify inaccurately because of a failure in any of the testimonial incapacities—perception, memory, sincerity, or articulateness. As an impeacher, you would like ideally to show that a failure in each of these capacities might well account for the witness's testimony. For now we will concentrate on failures in sincerity—lying. In Section H we will look at other possible failures.

You might attempt two basic strategies to show that the witness likely lied. One is to try to show that she has a bad character for truthfulness in general, so that she is rather likely to tell lies even when she is under oath. Another is to show that there is particular reason to believe that she has lied in this case. We will first concentrate on the first strategy, the broad-based attack on the witness's character for truthfulness.

Recall from Chapter 18 the basic rule that excludes evidence of a person's propensity offered to show that the person acted in conformity with the propensity. Evidence of a witness's poor character for truthfulness is a form of propensity evidence—"She is a liar, and so she didn't hesitate to lie here"—but it is one of the categories excepted from the general rule of exclusion; see FRE 404(a)(3).

¶ **19.5:** (a) What character trait of a witness is relevant to the trial?

(b) In Chapter 18, we studied extensively the rule expressed in FRE 404(a)(1), which presumptively prevents a party from showing that one of the actors in the story did a bad thing by proving that he has a propensity to do such a thing. Given this rule, is it anomalous to allow a party to show that a witness—who is a step further removed in the sense that she is telling about the story but may not even have participated in it— more likely spoke falsely because she had a propensity to do so? Is the justification that truth-telling runs truer to form than other character traits?

The exception expressed in FRE 404(a)(3) does not mean that you may prove the witness's character however you wish; in fact, the rules are rather tight. The simplest, most general way of proving the witness's bad character for truthfulness is prescribed by FRE 608(a): You may present another witness to testify either that in her opinion the primary witness has a bad character for truthfulness or that the primary witness has a reputation for having such a bad character. This rule is similar to FRE 405(a), which allows reputation or opinion evidence in the limited circumstances when the character of other persons is an appropriate subject of proof. (Recall from the discussion before ¶ 18.23 that traditionally only reputation evidence, not the opinion of the particular witness, was allowed.) But, because truth-telling inclination is the only character trait relevant to the witness's role as witness, FRE 608(a) does not authorize evidence of any other traits; if you want to offer such evidence, you must find another way. Also, the second sentence of Rule 608(a) provides that if an impeaching party attacks the character for truthfulness of a witness, but only then, the proponent may present evidence of the witness's good character for truthfulness. In other words, the impeaching party has the choice of whether to open the door on the inquiry into the witness's character for truthfulness.

¶ 19.6: Dorking is accused of a violent assault. He has available as witnesses Arthur, who would testify that Dorking is a gentle person, and Barbara, who would testify that Dorking has a fine reputation for truthfulness. The prosecution, however, has available Charlie, who would testify that Dorking has a reputation for being violent, and Ernest, who would testify that Dorking is a notorious liar. Under what circumstances, if any, may the testimony of each of these witnesses be presented?

D. OTHER MISCONDUCT AND CRIMINAL CONVICTIONS

FRE 608(b), 609

Additional Reading: McCormick, Ch. 5, §§ 41–42; Mueller & Kirkpatrick, §§ 6.25–.39

1. MISCONDUCT SUGGESTING DISHONESTY

Opinion or reputation evidence gives an overall assessment of the witness's character for truthfulness. It therefore has both the advantages and disadvantages of generality. Its principal drawback is that it does not yield very much information; testimony that "in my opinion she has a very poor character for truthfulness" does not tell us a great deal about why the character witness came to that conclusion. Impeachers are therefore tempted to ask the logical next question: "Can you give us some examples of why you come to that conclusion?" Ordinarily, however, that question will not be allowed. The reason highlights the one large advantage that opinion or reputation evidence has: brevity. That is, by not getting into the grubby details, general assessments of character avoid the spectacle of mini-trials on issues that are collateral to the case being tried; if the case concerns whether Preston or Dunston had the green light, we do not want to get into extended litigation over whether or not Preston's witness Winston plagiarized a paper in law school.

Thus, Dunston may not put witness Carston on the stand to testify to Winston's plagiarism (assuming for now that she was not convicted of any crime in connection with the incident); indeed, even if Dunston puts Carston on to say that Winston has a poor character for truthfulness, Dunston may not ask him to substantiate his opinion by telling about the plagiarism incident. But, at least in jurisdictions following the Federal Rules, evidentiary law has too much of a fixation on the possibility of perjury to forget altogether about prior acts of dishonesty. Thus, FRE 608(b)(1) would allow Dunston—in the discretion of the court—to cross-examine Winston herself about the incident. Or, if Preston put on character witness Hairston to testify, contrary to Carston's testimony, that Winston has a good character for truthfulness, FRE 608(b)(2) would allow Dunston, again in the discretion of the court, to ask Hairston, "Well, did you know about the time she plagiarized a paper in law school?"

¶ 19.7: Why does FRE 608(b) allow inquiry into specific acts on cross-examination but not otherwise? (Note that FRE 608(b) is similar to FRE 405(a) in this respect.) In particular, why may you ask the other side's character witness, but not your own, about specific conduct?

¶ **19.8:** Suppose you are the trial judge in Preston v. Dunston. Winston has just testified for Preston; there have been no character witnesses. Dunston now wants to ask Winston on cross-examination not only about the law school plagiarism episode, which occurred about twenty years ago, but also about an incident three months ago in which Winston, speaking to a local Rotary Club, used without attribution a lengthy passage from a speech given by the late British politician Aneurin Bevan. Should Dunston be allowed to examine Winston on either or both of these?

Now, suppose Dunston is allowed to ask Winston about the plagiarism episode and Winston simply denies it. Dunston has Carston ready to testify to the plagiarism—but the rules will not allow it. Dunston may, within reasonable limits, press Winston for the answer he wants, but then he must "take the witness's answer." Formally expressed, the question of Winston's plagiarism is *collateral*, and Carston's testimony—a type of evidence that does not come out of the mouth of the witness being impeached—would be *extrinsic evidence*. Therefore it runs afoul of a rule that may be expressed in general terms this way: A witness may not be impeached on a collateral matter by extrinsic evidence. Although the Federal Rules do not state this rule in general, Rule 608(b) states it in the present context, for impeachment by specific acts of misconduct of the witness.

The policy behind this rule is plain enough: We do not want mini-trials on issues that are collateral in the sense that they are not material to the dispute. Students sometimes get confused in using the terminology of the rule.

"Extrinsic" refers to how the impeaching evidence is to be offered. Basically, if the impeaching evidence requires the testimony of a witness other than the one being impeached, it is extrinsic.[5] Usually it is easy enough to determine whether evidence is extrinsic, though there is one respect in which the meaning of extrinsic is fuzzy. Suppose the impeaching evidence is a document that can be used to impeach without calling another witness, presumably (though not inevitably) because the witness whose credibility is being questioned is willing to authenticate the document from the stand. Arguably, such evidence should not be

---

[5] Notice again Rule 608(b)(2) allows for cross-examining Hairston, the witness testifying to Winston's good character, as to whether he knew about or heard about the plagiarism incident. This cross, concerning the character for truthfulness or untruthfulness of "another witness whose character the witness being cross-examined has testified about," would not be considered extrinsic, because Hairston is already on the stand, testifying about Winston's good character, and this inquiry impeaches Hairston, challenging the basis of that testimony. But if Hairston denies having known or heard about the episode, Dunston cannot put his own witness on to testify about it.

considered extrinsic, because it does not require calling another witness or opening up a broad inquiry, given that the impeaching information is brought to light through the testimony of the witness herself. But some courts have taken a rigid view that documents, being other than the testimony of the witness being impeached, are extrinsic.[6]

"Collateral" refers to the relationship between the proposition that the impeaching evidence is offered to prove and the rest of the case. It is tricky to get a handle on just what it means to say that a subject is collateral. We will return to the question later, for the rule that impeachment on a collateral matter cannot be made by extrinsic evidence also applies to impeachment by contradiction and prior inconsistent statements. For now, it is enough to say that, if the only reason warranting inquiry into prior misconduct is that it tends to show that the witness has a bad general character for truthfulness, then the misconduct is collateral.[7] In some cases, though, it is not clear whether the misconduct is collateral.

¶ 19.9: Dalton is on trial for selling helicopters illegally to North Korea. He delivered the helicopters to a broker, Borden, in Germany, and he contends in his defense that he thought the ultimate customer of the helicopters was in Germany. Borden, testifying for the prosecution under an immunity grant, says that Dalton knew full well where the copters were going. On cross, the defense asks, "Didn't you tell Anderson [a previous seller] that his helicopters were going to Germany even though they were really headed for North Korea?" Borden denies any such conversation. May the defense bring in Anderson to testify to such a conversation? Is the admissibility of such testimony contingent on proof that Anderson's helicopters actually went to North Korea?

¶ 19.10: Evans has testified for the plaintiff in a medical malpractice case. On cross, she is asked why she left her

---

[6] *See* United States v. Whitehead, 618 F.2d 523, 529 (4th Cir. 1980); In re Gulph Woods Corp., 82 B.R. 373, 375 (Bankruptcy Ct. E.D. Pa. 1988) (orders of state ethics commission inadmissible for impeachment); *cf.* United States v. Jackson, 882 F.2d 1444 (9th Cir. 1989) (holding, over dissent, that limitation on extrinsic evidence was not violated when prosecutor cross-examined defendant with document, securing defendant's admission that he signed document, but never introduced document into evidence).

[7] A 2003 amendment to Rule 608(b) helps make this point. The first sentence of the Rule, as restyled in 2011, now provides: "Except for a criminal conviction under Rule 609, extrinsic evidence is not admissible to prove specific instances of a witness's conduct in order to attack or support the witness's character for truthfulness." Before the 2003 amendment, the Rule referred to the witness's "credibility" rather than to her "character for truthfulness." The problem with that phrasing was that sometimes extrinsic evidence of specific instances of conduct *may* be admissible to attack the witness's credibility, in ways other than by challenging her character for truthfulness; as we will see in Section G, bias, which is not considered an aspect of character, may be proved by extrinsic evidence of specific incidents.

academic position at Slippery Slope State University Medical School. She testifies that she got tired of teaching and preferred practicing on her own. The following exchange ensues:

Q: Isn't it true that you were fired?

A: No, it is not.

Q: Isn't it true that the Dean fired you after a formal hearing in which she concluded that you had lied in your testimony as an expert in another case?

A: No, that isn't true. I just got tired of teaching and bureaucracy.

Plaintiff's counsel now asks for a sidebar. She has noticed that defense counsel has removed a document from his brief case and is apparently about to seek to have it admitted. The document purports to be a transcript of a hearing held by the Dean of Slippery Slope in which, sure enough, the Dean concludes that Evans had lied in testifying as an expert witness, and decides to dismiss her from her position.

(a) Should the defense be allowed to ask Evans to authenticate the transcript and then introduce it into evidence?

(b) Should the defense be allowed to put the Dean on the stand to testify why she fired Evans?

(c) Assume that the court answers both (a) and (b) in the negative. Is there any use that the defense might make of the transcript?

Bear in mind that, for a prior act to be used for impeachment purposes, it generally must relate to the witness's credibility, not to her general character.

¶ 19.11: In ¶ 19.9, the defense wants to prove that Borden, while a lieutenant in the army, sadistically beat up several of the men in his company. How might the defense most likely persuade the court that this evidence should be admissible?

2. PRIOR CONVICTIONS

Subsection 1 assumed that the witness was not criminally convicted for his acts of misconduct. But now suppose that he was. This changes the situation in several respects. For one thing, a criminal conviction suggests that the misconduct was quite serious. In some circumstances, indeed, even if the misconduct did not involve dishonesty, it might suggest that the witness, having failed in another context to recognize his social responsibilities, might similarly fail in his obligation to testify truthfully. Moreover, a criminal conviction is simple to prove; if the witness denies the misconduct, no mini-trial is necessary to prove that he was convicted, because that can be done by an official record that reflects either a plea of guilty or the conclusion of a factfinder—most often a jury—that, beyond a reasonable doubt, he did indeed commit the crime.

On the other hand, informing a jury that a witness has previously been convicted of a crime carries enormous potential for prejudice. One aspect of this prejudice is the possibility that the jury might overvalue the information in judging the credibility of the witness; as usual, though, it is probably best to treat assertions of likely over-valuation with some skepticism. Another aspect, often more troubling, is that the jury will use the information for reasons other than judging credibility. This danger is particularly present when—as is most often the case in use of prior convictions for impeachment—the witness is a criminal defendant. There are two aspects to this danger. First, a jury learning that the defendant, who has taken the stand in his own defense, has been convicted of a crime, is likely to think, "If he committed one crime, he more likely committed this one." As we have discussed in Chapter 18, this is an inferential jump that might have good basis in common sense, but it violates our principle that a defendant should not be convicted on the basis of propensity evidence. Given that our adjudicative system has made the decision not to allow proof of bad conduct to be admitted for the purpose of showing the defendant's propensity to engage in such conduct, the possibility that the jury will draw the propensity inference, no matter how logical it may be, must be counted as a danger rather than as a benefit of the evidence. And this danger is greatest precisely when the prior crime seems to have the most logical bearing on the current one— when the prior crime is similar to the one with which the defendant is now being charged. Second, the jury might think, at least subconsciously, "He's a bad one, this defendant, and even if he didn't commit this crime it wouldn't be so terrible to put him away for some more time; he probably wasn't punished enough last time around. We'll convict him without worrying about that 'beyond a reasonable doubt' stuff."

Courts and rulemakers have reconciled in various ways the competing considerations involved in prior-crime impeachment; FRE 609 was one of the most controversial and debated provisions of the Federal Rules, and even states that have adopted the Rules as a model have not always swallowed Rule 609 whole.[8] Moreover, many of the state adaptations are based on the original Federal Rule, but the Federal Rule itself was substantially amended in 1990 and, less extensively, in 2006, before being thoroughly restyled in 2011. It is nevertheless useful to focus on FRE 609, among other reasons because it presents many of the issues that any decisionmaker must consider.

---

[8]   *E.g.*, People v. Allen, 429 Mich. 558, 420 N.W.2d 499 (1988).

Rule 609(a), in line with traditional law, sets out two types of conviction that may, in appropriate cases, be used for impeachment: (1) for crimes "punish*able* [emphasis added, and please note it: not punish*ed!*] by death or imprisonment in excess of one year under the law under which the witness was convicted," and (2) for crimes that, "regardless of the punishment," involved "dishonesty or false statement." Note that Rule 609(a)(2) provides without qualification—and without depending at all on who the witness being impeached is—that on a proper showing that the crime belongs in the second category the evidence "must be admitted." This is the only context in which the Federal Rules appear to *require* the admission of evidence.[9] Although it also uses the term "must," Rule 609(a)(1) provides less absolute standards for crimes in the first category, felonies. If the witness is not a criminal defendant, then under Rule 609(a)(1)(A) the evidence "must be admitted, subject to Rule 403." And if the witness is a criminal defendant, the evidence "must be admitted . . . if the probative value of the evidence outweighs its prejudicial effect to [should that be "on"?] that defendant." Both of those standards are discretionary, so the use of "must" is not as peremptory as it sounds on its own. What is the difference between the two standards? Recall that FRE 403 effectively puts its thumb on the side of the scale favoring admissibility; with respect to attempts to impeach an accused-witness by showing a prior felony conviction, by contrast, FRE 609(a)(1) puts its thumb on the side favoring exclusion.

We will consider two cross-cutting types of issues related to this Rule. First, does it identify a proper set of prior convictions that may in some circumstances be used for impeachment? Second, does it distinguish properly between an accused-witness and other witnesses?

¶ 19.12: (a) Does the first category (felonies) make sense? In particular, consider these questions: Why should impeachment ever be allowed on the basis of conviction for a crime that did not involve dishonesty or false statement? Does conviction for, say, armed assault have any bearing on a witness's credibility? If conviction should be allowed for some crimes not involving dishonesty or false statement, why should it be limited to crimes with severe penalties?

(b) In opposing a version of FRE 609 that would have allowed impeachment by convictions only for crimes involving dishonesty or false statement, Sen. John McClellan argued as follows:

---

[9] Each of Rules 413, 414, and 415 as originally enacted provided that the type of evidence it covered "is admissible", but that language was open to the interpretation that admissibility in a given case lies in the discretion of the court. The 2011 restyling of those rules implemented that interpretation.

> Surely a person who has committed a serious crime—a
> felony—will just as readily lie under oath as someone who
> has committed a misdemeanor involving lying. Would a
> convicted rapist, cold-blooded murderer or armed robber
> really hesitate to lie under oath any more than a person who
> has previously lied? Would a convicted murderer or robber
> be more truthful than such a person?
>
> Of course not![10]

Are you persuaded?

Sen. McClellan had at least something of a point: There does seem to
be a correlation between serious antisocial behavior and dishonesty.
Persistent lying is one of the diagnostic criteria for Antisocial Personality
Disorder, discussed in the previous chapter.[11]

On the other hand, Sen. McClellan did not draw any distinctions
based on the status in the litigation of the witness being impeached. We
have seen that Rule 609(a), as amended, does distinguish somewhat
between criminal defendants and other witnesses, though not very much;
with respect to impeachment by crimes of dishonesty there is no
distinction at all, and with respect to impeachment by felonies there is a
difference in emphasis. But does it make sense to allow character
impeachment of criminal defendants at all—even by showing prior acts of
dishonesty, and even if they resulted in conviction? Allowing such
impeachment essentially requires the jury to use logic something like
this:

> At first, I thought it was very unlikely that if Defoe committed
> robbery he would then lie about it. But now that I know he was
> committed forgery a year earlier, that seems substantially more
> likely.

For two reasons, though, that logic seems very weak. First, an accused's
testimony is usually self-impeaching. That is, the accused as witness has
an overwhelming and obvious interest in giving self-exculpatory
testimony. If his testimony is persuasive to the jury, it is not likely
because the jury believes that the accused would not be willing to lie in
his self-defense; rather, it is because the jury believes that he could not
bring off a lie so successfully in substance and style. Second, assessing the
probability that the accused would lie *if* he committed the crime charged
requires the hypothetical assumption that he *did* commit the crime; if we

---

[10] 120 Cong.Rec.S. 19909 (daily ed. Nov. 22, 1974), *quoted in* United States v. Smith, 551
F.2d 348, 367 (D.C.Cir.1976).

[11] For a fuller discussion of the various literatures on this correlation, see Richard D.
Friedman, *Character Impeachment Evidence: Psycho-Bayesian [!?] Analysis and a Proposed
Overhaul*, 38 UCLA L.Rev. 637, 652–54 (1991).

are already assuming hypothetically for purposes of this critical question that he committed that crime, there is relatively little value in learning that he committed another crime.[12]

This argument suggests that character impeachment evidence of a criminal defendant has relatively little probative value. Moreover, such evidence may cause substantial harm. As we have seen, if the impeachment is allowed and the defendant takes the stand, there is a substantial danger of prejudice—and such prejudice against a criminal defendant is particularly troublesome. Perhaps more important, the defendant may respond to the anticipated admissibility of character impeachment evidence by declining to take the stand and give his side of the story, but this means forgoing a fundamental right, recall *Rock v. Arkansas*, 483 U.S. 44, 52–53 (1987), presented in ¶ 4.3—as well as denying potentially useful information to the factfinder.

The principal conclusion to which this argument points is that character impeachment evidence of a criminal defendant ought not be allowed; it achieves too little good and too much bad.

That would be a dramatic departure from traditional practice—but Hawaii has a rule that bars use of convictions to impeach a defendant who does not open the door by raising credibility issues.[13] And Montana goes considerably further. Rule of Evidence 609 provides in its entirety: "For the purpose of attacking the credibility of a witness, evidence that the witness has been convicted of a crime is not admissible."

¶ **19.13:** (a) Do you find the above argument persuasive?

(b) Under current law, if a criminal defendant does not testify, the prosecutor is not allowed to comment on this to the jury. *Griffin v. California*, 380 U.S. 609, 614 (1965). Given that many defendants do not take the stand because they are afraid of being burned by their prior convictions, this rule seems appropriate. If the argument presented here were accepted, and character impeachment evidence of criminal defendants were not allowed, should the rule on prosecutorial comment be reversed?

---

[12] For a fuller discussion, see my *Character Impeachment Evidence* article, *supra*, and the later exchange, H. Richard Uviller, *Credence, Character, and the Rules of Evidence: Seeing Through the Liar's Tale*, 42 Duke L.J. 776, 829–30 (1993); Richard D. Friedman, *Character Impeachment Evidence: The Asymmetrical Interaction Between Personality and Situation*, 43 Duke L.J. 816 (1994); H. Richard Uviller, *Unconvinced, Unreconstructed, and Unrepentant: A Reply to Professor Friedman's Response*, 43 Duke L.J. 834 (1994).

[13] Hawaii Rule of Evidence 609(a), implementing the decision in State v. Santiago, 53 H. 254, 492 P.2d 657 (1971), provides that "in a criminal case where the defendant takes the stand, the defendant shall not be questioned or evidence introduced as to whether the defendant has been convicted of a crime, for the sole purpose of attacking credibility, unless the defendant has oneself introduced testimony for the purpose of establishing the defendant's credibility as a witness, in which case the defendant shall be treated as any other witness as provided in this rule."

Cf. Carter v. Kentucky, 450 U.S. 288, 300 & n. 15 (1981) (putting *Griffin* on the basis that there are many reasons for the defendant to decline to testify that the jury might not understand).

Now let's focus on a complexity in Rule 609(a)(2), the portion of the Rule mandating admissibility of evidence that a witness was convicted of a crime that involved dishonesty or false statement. That shorthand form of words—a crime that "involved dishonesty or false statement"—was the actual language used by the Rule before 2006. But it raised an ambiguity. Did that mean that dishonesty or false statement had to be an element of the crime? Or at the other extreme, would it be enough if the witness committed an act of dishonesty in the course of committing the crime— say, lying to get access to a place where he committed theft? An amendment adopted in 2006 was intended to reject both of these views and adopt an intermediate one. The Advisory Committee explained that the Rule is meant to be limited to "those crimes in which the ultimate criminal act was itself an act of deceit." But that could be true "regardless of whether the crime was charged under a section that expressly references deceit." Thus, for example, the federal statute criminalizing obstruction of justice, 18 U.S.C. § 1503, does not require dishonesty or false statement, but such conduct may be an essential part of the prosecution's theory of a given case; that is, it may be that the jury could not find the accused guilty in the particular case without finding that he acted dishonestly. Now note that allowing a conviction in such a case to be used in impeaching the accused should he testify in a subsequent case may require looking beyond the language of the statute or the face of the judgment. The Advisory Committee wanted to avoid "a 'mini-trial' in which the court plumbs the record of the previous proceeding to determine whether the crime was in the nature of crimen falsi." And so the amendment provides that a conviction falls within subsection (a)(2) only if the crime "readily can be determined to have been a crime of dishonesty or false statement." Apart from the statute and the judgment, the Committee noted, "a proponent may offer information such as an indictment, a statement of admitted facts, or jury instructions" to demonstrate that a finding or admission of dishonesty or false statement was essential to the conviction.

¶ **19.14:** Dooling is on trial for murder. The prosecution claims that Vinton beat Dooling up in a barroom brawl, and that in revenge Dooling ambushed Vinton and shot him to death. Dooling admits to the brawl but denies that he shot Vinton. Dooling intends to testify in his own defense and moves to suppress evidence of his one prior conviction. Wallace was a key witness at the trial leading to that conviction. In each of the following alternative hypotheticals, consider whether, and on what showing, Dooling's prior conviction should be admitted, and, if so, what the jury should learn about it.

(a) The prior conviction was for armed robbery. In Dooling's prior case, Wallace testified as follows: She was walking down a dark street one night when Dooling approached her from the other direction, stuck out what appeared to be a gun, said, "This is a stickup. Give me your jewelry." She complied, and he said, "Thanks. Have a nice evening." He then disappeared around a corner.[14]

(b) The prior conviction was for manslaughter. Wallace testified that Dooling got into a barroom brawl with Varnum and that, when Varnum seemed to be having the better of it, Dooling reached for his jacket, which was slung over a chair, pulled out a small pistol, and shot Varnum through the heart.[15]

(c) The prior conviction was for assault, battery, and robbery. Dooling rang her doorbell, and when Wallace answered Dooling said, "Electric company. Got to read your meter." She let him in the house, and he then overpowered her, tied her to a beam in the basement, and ransacked the house, taking many of her valuables.

The context of the criminal defendant as witness has tended to shape the law in this area, and accounts for the tendency of rulemakers to attempt to confine the discretion of trial courts. If there were no need to provide rules for the use of criminal defendants' prior convictions, rulemakers might feel at ease giving trial courts more discretion in dealing with convictions of other witnesses.

¶ 19.15: Green has been convicted of burglary and conspiracy to commit burglary, both felonies. He is now the plaintiff in a products liability action. When he testifies at trial, the defendant manufacturer tries to elicit his acknowledgment of the prior convictions. Should those convictions be admitted?[16]

¶ 19.16: Suppose you are a judge in a jurisdiction that imposes only discretionary limits on use of prior convictions for impeachment in civil cases. You are sitting with a jury in an

---

[14] *Cf.* People v. Beacham, 189 Ill.App.3d 483, 136 Ill.Dec. 868, 875, 545 N.E.2d 392, 399 (1989).

[15] *Cf.* State v. Sheffield, 676 S.W.2d 542, 548–50 (Tenn.1984).

[16] *Cf.* Green v. Bock Laundry Machine Co., 490 U.S. 504 (1989). *Green* held that, in allowing the court to take into account "prejudice to the defendant" in determining whether to admit felonies offered for impeachment, FRE 609(a)(1) as it then stood referred only to a criminal defendant; hence, the judge had no discretion to exclude the convictions. A 1990 amendment, reflecting recognition that any party might suffer prejudice from the use of prior convictions, nullified this holding.

auto negligence case. The plaintiff has presented the testimony of witness Woodling, who was a passenger in the plaintiff's car.

(a) The defendant wants to impeach Woodling with the fact that she had 150 parking tickets in the last year. Admissible? No.

(b) Now assume instead that Woodling had just one parking ticket in the last year. Admissible? Does the possibility of impeachment on such a flimsy basis argue against a liberal discretionary rule in civil cases?[17] No.

E. CONTRADICTION

Additional Reading: McCormick, Ch. 5, §§ 45, 49; Mueller & Kirkpatrick, §§ 6.43–.48

If an adverse witness testifies to a material proposition **PROP,** you are obviously allowed to introduce evidence that **PROP** is not true, not only by cross-examining your adversary's witnesses but also by putting on your own. Introducing such contradicting evidence might accomplish two objectives. First, you may push the jury in the direction of finding **PROP** not to be true. Second, you may undermine the credibility of the adverse witness: If you have persuaded the jurors that her testimony on **PROP** is untrue, or at least dubious, then they may find her unworthy of belief in general, on other propositions as well as on **PROP**.

In such a case, the contradicting evidence is admissible on the merits, and its impeaching effect is an inevitable by-product. Even without prompting, the jury might draw a conclusion as to the witness's credibility, and a court will ordinarily allow you to help it along in argument: "You heard this witness's testimony about **PROP,** and now you know that this wasn't true. Don't think you can trust any other part of her testimony, either."

But now suppose that **PROP,** as to which you have contradictory evidence, is not material to any of the disputed issues in the case. If that is true, how can the witness have been allowed to testify to the proposition, given the fundamental rule of evidence that evidence of immaterial propositions is not admissible? First, it could be that the witness's testimony to **PROP** on direct was not admissible but you failed to object, either intentionally or by inadvertence. Second, it could be that the witness's testimony of **PROP** came out as an incidental part of her testimony of a material proposition: "As I was coming home from the prayer meeting, I saw a green car speeding towards the corner." Third, it could be that you questioned the witness yourself about **PROP,** because

---

[17] *Cf.* N.Y.–McKinney's Veh. & Traf. Law § 155 (providing that a traffic infraction "shall not affect or impair the credibility as a witness or otherwise any person convicted thereof").

you thought that, although it was unrelated to the facts of the case, it might bear on her general truth-telling inclination; most notably, as we have already seen, you might have asked the witness to testify on cross concerning prior dishonest conduct, and **PROP** might be a denial of that conduct.

In each of these cases, **PROP** is characterized as collateral. Hence, the traditional rule is that you may not introduce extrinsic evidence to contradict **PROP**. The Federal Rules do not state this aspect of the collateral-issue rule—though as indicated in Section D, Rule 608(b) states the related rule in the context of misconduct by the witness—but courts operating under them have nevertheless still held it applicable. *E.g.*, *United States v. Beauchamp*, 986 F.2d 1, 3–4 (1st Cir.1993). You cannot put on another witness to testify, for example, "That was no prayer meeting she was coming from." But now we must focus more closely than we have before on the difficult question of how we determine whether a given proposition is in fact collateral. Perhaps a useful approximation is this: If the proponent of the witness elicited the testimony of **PROP**, **PROP** is collateral if a relevance objection, had it been made, would have succeeded. And, as suggested by our discussion of prior misconduct, if the opponent elicited the testimony of **PROP**, then **PROP** is collateral if, putting aside the bearing that the evidence has on the witness's general truth-telling inclination, such an objection would have succeeded.

But perhaps this approach overly rigidifies the concept. Collateralness may be a matter of degree, depending on how much significance contradiction of **PROP** has to the case (though **PROP** itself is not material) beyond what it might indicate about the witness's general truth-telling inclination. In some cases, a juror might reasonably think:

> This witness has testified to **PROP** [for example, that she was coming home from a prayer meeting] and also to material proposition **MAT** [that she saw the green car speeding towards the corner], and now I know that **PROP** is untrue. This makes her testimony on **MAT** more dubious, and not simply because it suggests that she's a liar in general. In this case, **MAT** and the disproof of **PROP** are sufficiently related to each other that proof that **PROP** is untrue, as I now know it is, makes it appear less probable than before that **MAT** is true. And even without assuming a general tendency to fabrication by the witness, she is more likely to have testified inaccurately to **PROP**, as I now know she has, if her testimony about **MAT** was untrue than if it was true.

How strong this logic is in the particular case may help determine whether the proposition is considered collateral. Suppose that the proof that **PROP** is untrue consists of testimony by a friend of the witness that the witness was not at a prayer meeting but at a drunken party. This state of facts makes it more likely that the witness would give inaccurate testimony with respect to **MAT**, because a witness coming home from a drunken party is more likely to misperceive and misremember who went first into an intersection than would a sober one—or at least so the factfinder could conclude. And if the witness did not see the accident clearly because of previous activities that would embarrass her, and therefore made up a story or took a guess as to what happened, she might also fabricate a story to cover up those previous whereabouts. If, on the other hand, the disproof of **PROP** is that the witness was coming home from a bingo party rather than a prayer meeting, it is hard to see how this has much bearing on her testimony as to the accident, apart from suggesting that in general she is not truthful.

Beyond that, bear in mind that the bottom line question is not whether the proposition is collateral; it is whether extrinsic evidence should be allowed. Other factors—such as how inconvenient it would be to allow the extrinsic evidence, and how important the witness's material testimony is to the case—bear on this question. Although the rule is that, if the issue is collateral then extrinsic impeachment is not allowed, the rule may tug in two directions: To a certain extent it may be that if the court is not disposed to allow extrinsic impeachment then it will characterize the issue as collateral.

The following problems illustrate these considerations.

¶ **19.17:** Oswalt is accused of committing a robbery in Seattle on July 14. He presents the testimony of Ardiss, a Portland restaurant owner, that Oswalt was in Ardiss's restaurant on that date at a time that would make it impossible as a practical matter for Oswalt to have participated in the robbery in Seattle. Ardiss testifies that he remembers this occasion in particular because Oswalt arrived with an employee of the restaurant, helped her with her work, and escorted her home. On cross, Ardiss testifies that Oswalt was in his restaurant every day for the last couple of months before July 14. In rebuttal, the prosecution offers the testimony of a police detective that he saw Oswalt in Seattle on June 12, and that Oswalt told him that he had arrived there a couple of days before. Should this testimony be allowed?[18]

¶ **19.18:** Patton is suing Dutton for patent infringement. Widener gives the following testimony for Patton: He had a luncheon meeting with Dutton six months before the suit was filed. Dutton drank a Bloody Mary while they were looking at

---

[18] *See* State v. Oswalt, 62 Wash.2d 118, 381 P.2d 617 (1963).

the menu and three more before the soup arrived. Over the main course, Dutton said, "Confidentially, I hope Patton doesn't find out about us for a while. We've just made a few ornamental changes from his patent for the grimlet wilcher, and we're making zillions of bucks."

(a) Dutton, in contrast, contends as follows: He hates the taste of tomato juice, has never had a Bloody Mary in his life, and was in fact drinking Screwdrivers (which mix orange juice, rather than tomato juice, with vodka). He didn't order his first drink until after he had placed his order, and he only had three drinks before the soup arrived. Which of these assertions, if any, can Dutton try to establish by pressing Widener on cross? To which of them, if any, can Dutton himself testify?

(b) Now suppose instead that Dutton contends that he was a teetotaler at the time, that he asked the waitress on the first round for a Bloody Mary mix without the vodka, and on subsequent rounds simply asked for "Another." Do your answers to the questions in (a) change? What if, in addition, Dutton says that Widener was away from the table when he asked for his first Bloody Mary mix?

¶ **19.19:** In ¶ 19.18, Widener testifies that over lunch "Dutton took out a piece of his personal letterhead stationery and drew a sketch of his grimlet wilcher, and then he carefully shredded the paper." Can Dutton offer his testimony that he had no personal letterhead stationery? Would your answer change if it was on cross, in response to a question by Dutton's counsel, that Widener testified that the paper was Dutton's letterhead?

¶ **19.20:** Wesley was on an autumn hunting trip with three friends, two of whom, Paisley and Dantley, got into a knife fight. In Paisley's suit against Dantley for assault, Wesley testifies that he was about fifteen yards away from the other two, across some fairly dense woods, when he heard Paisley say some harsh words to Dantley. He then looked in their direction and saw Dantley pull out his knife and slash Paisley. Wesley testifies that virtually all the leaves had already fallen from the trees. Can Dantley present the testimony of the fourth hunter, Warren, who did not witness the fight, that there were still many leaves on the trees in that area?[19]

¶ **19.21:** Witness Lofton testifies that he saw a train belonging to the defendant railroad strike and kill the plaintiff's

---

[19] *Cf.* State of Maryland v. Baltimore Transit Co., 329 F.2d 738, 742 (4th Cir.1964), *cert. denied*, 379 U.S. 842 (1964).

mule. He accounts for his presence at the accident by saying that he was on his way home after buying tobacco.

(a) Should the testimony of the storekeeper Copeland, that Lofton was not in the store and did not buy tobacco at that time, be admitted to cast doubt on Lofton's presence at the accident, if the railroad is offering other evidence contesting Lofton's presence at the accident?

(b) What if the railroad does not have any other evidence to cast doubt on Lofton's presence at the accident?[20]

(c) Suppose Copeland acknowledges the Lofton was in the store but testifies that he bought adult magazines rather than tobacco. Does that change your answers?

(d) Suppose it is undisputed that Lofton was at the scene of the accident. Does that change your answers?

¶ **19.22:** In a suit on an insurance policy, a material issue is whether the insured received a particular cancellation notice. He denies that he did, and also denies receiving other notices, which were not material because they did not suspend his policy. Should extrinsic evidence of the mailing of the other notices be allowed?[21]

F. PRIOR INCONSISTENT STATEMENTS

FRE 613

Additional Reading: McCormick, ch. 5, §§ 34–37; Mueller & Kirkpatrick, §§ 6.40–.42

If you introduce evidence that the witness has previously made a statement in conflict with the testimony she has just given in court, you have presented a form of contradiction. In one crucial sense, it is a particularly powerful form: The witness herself, rather than another person, has made a statement contradictory to her current testimony. She may be able to explain the statement away—showing that the statements are not in fact conflicting, or acknowledging that the prior statement was inaccurate, the product of some honest error or of an excusable, or even inexcusable, reason to lie. But the jurors need not accept her explanations, and they may well be left with the belief that she is not a credible witness, either on the subject of the varying statements or, perhaps, on others as well.

---

[20] *See* East Tennessee, Va. & Ga. Ry. Co. v. Daniel, 91 Ga. 768, 18 S.E. 22 (1893) (holding that Copeland's testimony "contradicted the witness as to the train of events which led him to be present, and thus tended to discredit him as to the fact of his presence").

[21] *See* Hartsfield v. Carolina Casualty Ins. Co., 451 P.2d 576 (Alaska 1969).

Courts recognize prior inconsistent statements as a powerful form of impeachment. But note that if a witness has testified to **PROP** and previously said **NOT-PROP,** admitting the prior statement for impeachment does not necessarily mean that it will be admitted as proof of **NOT-PROP**. Traditionally, though not universally, the prior statement is regarded as hearsay, notwithstanding the presence of the declarant on the witness stand, when offered to prove the truth of what it asserts, **NOT-PROP**. As Section C of Chapter 10 has discussed, FRE 801(d)(1)(A) exempts from the definition of hearsay only a narrow category of prior inconsistent statements, those made "under penalty of perjury at a trial, hearing, or other proceeding or in a deposition." Under the Federal Rules' regime, other prior inconsistent statements may not be introduced to prove that they are true (unless, of course, another exception or exemption applies). But this rule does not restrict the use of prior statements to impeach the witness's credibility by showing inconsistency. As offered for that purpose, the statement is not even hearsay. The logic for its admission is not, "The witness previously made this statement. Therefore, it is probably true." Rather, it is, "The witness's own prior statement is in conflict with the testimony he has just given. Therefore, you cannot place any weight on his testimony on this subject [or on any other]."

What does it mean, though, to say that a prior statement of **NOT-PROP** can be used for impeachment but not to prove its truth? In conceptual terms, it means that the jury may use the inconsistency to undermine, or even nullify, the weight it would put on the witness's testimony, including the testimony of **PROP**; the jury may not, however, use the prior statement as affirmative proof of **NOT-PROP**. In other words, if the jury regarded **PROP** as 30% probable before the witness testified to **PROP** and 90% probable afterwards, the prior statement of **NOT-PROP** might return the probability assessment all the way back to 30%, but not lower.

¶ **19.23:** In practical terms, what is the difference between admitting the prior statement for impeachment only and for its truth as well? ~~cant be the only evidence of okay~~

What degree of variance between the present testimony and the prior statement will be regarded as inconsistency? If there is a logical conflict, that will almost inevitably suffice. But requiring a logical conflict would be too restrictive: A prior statement need not be in actual conflict with the current testimony to increase suspicion that the prior statement does not represent a sincere and accurate report of the witness's perceptions. But the "any variance" language that some old-fashioned cases have used, see *O'Neill v. Minneapolis St. Ry. Co.,* 213 Minn. 514, 7 N.W.2d 665 (1942), seems overly generous. McCormick's test seems to come closer to the mark: "Could the jury reasonably find that a witness who believed the truth of the facts testified to at trial would have been unlikely to make a prior statement of this tenor?" § 34.[22]

¶ 19.24: Wolfson witnessed an accident a year ago, and at trial it is now important to fix the exact time that the accident occurred. In each of the following variations, can the prior statement be brought in to impeach Wolfson?

(a) Wolfson testifies that the accident took place "at about 2:10." Shortly after the accident, she said that it occurred "at about 2:05."

(b) Same as (a), but Wolfson's current testimony is that the accident occurred "at about 2 o'clock."

(c) Wolfson testifies that the accident occurred "between 2:10 and 2:20." Shortly after the accident, she said that it occurred "at 2:14."

(d) Variation (c) reversed: Wolfson now testifies that the accident occurred "at 2:14" and earlier said that it occurred "between 2:10 and 2:20."

¶ 19.25: Erickson is seeking worker's compensation for injuries arising out of an auto accident. A friend of his who works nearby and who was a passenger in the car testifies that his auto trip was for two purposes, one personal and the other for the employer. Consider in each of these variations whether the prior statement should be admitted for impeachment. Assuming that it should be, how much impeachment value does it have?

(a) The witness testifies that they were traveling across town to deliver a package for his boss and to visit a mutual friend. Shortly after the accident she said that they were going to visit the friend.

(b) The witness testifies that the trip was to deliver a package for Erickson's boss. Earlier, she said that they had gone to deliver a package for Erickson's boss and to visit a mutual friend.

(c) The witness testifies that she had gone into labor while she was talking with the plaintiff over the phone, and that Erickson said, "I'll take you across town to the hospital. I can

---

[22] We might introduce one significant qualification, however: Admissibility should probably be judged on a relevance-type standard, not a sufficiency-type standard. Therefore, the question probably should be whether the jury could reasonably find that a witness who believed the facts to which she testified would be significantly *less likely* to make the prior statement than one not so believing.

drop a package off for the boss while I'm near there." Shortly after the accident, the witness told a similar story, but did not mention anything about Erickson wanting to drop off a package.[23] *In labor Dub[?]. But, its imped[?] and look dumb* ✓

¶ **19.26:** Gentry is accused of beating his lover's infant daughter. Turner, who was staying with Gentry and the lover at the time, testifies for the prosecution as follows: He had gone to sleep quite drunk, and sometime during the night, only partially awake, he heard a child crying, then footsteps, and a fairly loud thud or slap. May the defense bring out that, in the early hours of morning (after the child's condition was discovered and while Turner was still groggy), Turner failed to provide this information when he was interrogated by a police officer? *See* People v. Gentry, 270 Cal.App.2d 462, 76 Cal.Rptr. 336 (1969). What if the officer did not interrogate Turner but Turner was aware that the officer had visited the house and spoken to the other adult occupants? *No*

It is interesting to note that McCormick, in arguing for generous reception of prior statements that are assertedly inconsistent with current testimony, contends that the prior statements "are often more trustworthy than the testimony." § 34. This argument may be restated, and perhaps extended, in a way that puts the law of evidence into a rather unfavorable light: Hearsay doctrine unwisely excludes most prior statements that are inconsistent with current testimony, even though the prior statement may well be more probative; therefore, we should be lenient in admitting prior statements for impeachment purposes, and hope the jury violates instructions by considering them as well for the truth of what they assert.

Prior inconsistent statements, like contradictions in general, must also face the collateral issue rule. Therefore, if the witness's testimony included an assertion about a collateral matter, and she has previously made a statement inconsistent with that part of her testimony, you may try to get her to acknowledge that she made the prior statement, but you may not introduce extrinsic evidence to prove that she did. The notion of collateralness is, in theory at least, the same in this context as in that of contradiction, or at least quite similar. The test offered by Wigmore seems useful:

> Could the fact as to which the prior self-contradiction is predicated have been shown in evidence for any purpose independently of the self-contradiction?

---

[23] *Cf.* Erickson v. Erickson & Co., 212 Minn. 119, 2 N.W.2d 824 (1942).

3A John Henry Wigmore, *Evidence* § 1020 (Chadbourn rev. 1970).[24]

Assuming the rule is not completely categorical, however, it might be applied less stringently in the context of prior inconsistent statements than in the contradiction context. Often the proposition that the witness made a prior inconsistent statement will be easier to prove, and less likely to generate evidence in disproof, than the proposition that a collateral matter asserted by the witness is untrue.

¶ **19.27:** (a) Recall ¶ 19.18, in which Widener, in the course of testifying for Patton about a lunch with Dutton, said that Dutton had four Bloody Marys before the soup arrived. Suppose that you are representing Dutton. Ingersoll has told you that Widener told her shortly after the lunch, "Dutton had four Screwdrivers before the soup came." (Recall that a Bloody Mary mixes vodka and tomato juice; a Screwdriver mixes vodka and orange juice.) If Widener denies making this statement, can you put Ingersoll on the stand to testify to it?

(b) Now suppose that you believe that Widener made the previous statement in deposition. If Widener denies having given that testimony, may you bring in the court reporter to testify to it? If Widener signed the deposition transcript, may that portion be admitted?

¶ **19.28:** Recall ¶ 19.20, in which Wesley, testifying about a hunting accident, said that virtually all the leaves had fallen. Winchell has told Dantley's counsel that shortly after the accident Wesley told him that there were still many leaves on the trees. Assuming Wesley denies making that statement, may Dantley's counsel put Winchell on the stand to testify to it?

¶ **19.29:** In a prosecution for tax fraud, defense counsel asks a prosecution witness if it is not true that he had previously said that government agents had offered him a bribe to testify for the prosecution. The witness denies having made the statement. The defense does not contend, or present other evidence suggesting, that the witness actually took a bribe. May the defense call a

---

[24] In a passage no longer in the treatise, McCormick (3d ed. 1984), § 36, offered another useful statement:

> [T]o impeach by extrinsic proof of prior inconsistent statements, the statements must have as their subject (1) facts relevant to the issues in the cause, or (2) facts which are themselves provable by extrinsic evidence to discredit the witness.

Although this approach is much different from Wigmore's, the two seem consistent. If evidence of the *fact* asserted by the statement would be admissible—even absent the witness's assertion of the fact—to impeach the witness, then under either approach extrinsic evidence of the witness's prior statement of that fact is also admissible for impeachment. And if evidence of the fact would not be admissible absent the witness's assertion of it, then under either approach such extrinsic evidence is not admissible for impeachment.

second witness to testify that the first had indeed made that statement?[25] No

¶ **19.30:** Ewing is on trial for rape. He denies having had intercourse with the complainant. He presents the testimony of Chamberlin, a mutual friend of the complainant and Ewing who owns the apartment where the rape allegedly took place. Chamberlin's testimony strongly supports Ewing, contradicting various aspects of the complainant's account. On cross, Chamberlin acknowledges that in a conversation with the complainant's mother she (Chamberlin) noted that Ewing was facing the electric chair; however, she denies saying that therefore she must be "on his side." May the prosecution present the testimony of the complainant's mother that Chamberlin said that (1) she believed Ewing to be guilty, but (2) because he was facing the chair she had "got to be on his side"?[26] – motive do bi... yes

The common law, including the famous *Queen Caroline's Case*, 2 Brod. & Bing. 284, 129 Eng.Rep. 976 (1820), discussed in the Advisory Committee's Note to FRE 613(a), prescribed a strict procedure that had to be followed to impeach a witness with a prior inconsistent statement. Think of four steps:

(1) Draw the witness's attention to the time and circumstances of the statement.

(2) Show the statement to the witness, if it is in writing.

(3) Question the witness about the statement.

(4) Offer extrinsic proof of the statement, if it is not on a collateral matter.

Under the common law, an impeaching party had to go through steps (1) and (2) before doing step (3). And, if the party wanted to do step (4), he had to do step (3) first.

One purpose for requiring this procedure was to avoid unfair surprise to the witness. If, for example, the witness was not focusing on the circumstances in which she allegedly made the statement, she might deny having made it, and thus discredit herself more than she would have if she had been alerted. And if the witness didn't have a chance to explain the statement, she might be unfairly impeached: As suggested in the first paragraph of this section, she might, if given the opportunity, explain that the prior statement was not really inconsistent with her current

---

[25] *Cf.* Attorney-General v. Hitchcock, 154 Eng.Rep. 38, 1 Ex. 91, 11 Jur. 478 (1847) (holding in the negative).

[26] *See* Ewing v. United States, 135 F.2d 633 (D.C.Cir.1942), *cert. denied*, 318 U.S. 776 (1943) (holding in the affirmative, 2–1 with respect to statement (1)).

testimony, or she might admit that the prior statement was an honest, or even a dishonest, mistake. But if the witness left after giving her testimony, she might not have this opportunity. Furthermore, if the witness admitted having made the prior inconsistent statement, there was probably no need for the extrinsic evidence. To save time, therefore, the impeaching party first had to ask the witness about the statement.

In recent times, the tendency has been to view this procedure as too restrictive. If the witness is surprised to learn that she previously made an inconsistent statement, or that the impeaching party knows about it, we are less likely to view the surprise as unfair. A conscientious and honest witness would not make inconsistent statements in the first place, or would be aware of them if she did, or at least would not fear inability to explain away any that she couldn't remember, and in any event would not shape her testimony around her belief that the impeaching party didn't know about a prior inconsistent statement that she had made. Giving the witness warning that she is about to be impeached by a prior statement may well allow the dishonest witness to cover her tracks, hedging her story to avoid those inconsistencies that would be revealed by the statement. So the surprise assault, hitting the witness with the prior statement before she has focused on it and sanitized her story, is more likely to be viewed as a good impeachment technique. Thus, FRE 613(a) nullifies the portion of the *Queen's Case* that required a foundation before examining the witness about her prior statement.

There is still merit in the old-fashioned idea that the witness should have an opportunity to explain away the prior inconsistent statement. But that opportunity need not necessarily be at the same time that evidence of the statement is introduced—though that is usually the better procedure. If the prior statement is on a non-collateral matter, so that extrinsic evidence is admissible, and if that evidence is offered after the witness has finished testifying, but the witness is still available, she can presumably be brought back to the stand to give whatever explanation she has. This inverted procedure prevents the impeaching party from being prejudiced if he forgot to ask the witness about the prior statement in the first place, or if he only found out about the prior statement after the witness left the stand. (Of course, the old rule could make an exception for the belated-discovery case, but that would require a messy inquiry into what the party knew and when he knew it.)

But what is lost by the inverted procedure? Some time (assuming that the witness would have admitted making the statement in the first place), but that is likely to be relatively trivial. Perhaps more substantially, if the prior statement is introduced after the witness leaves the stand, it will be more difficult to encourage the jury to consider the prior statement only for impeachment. There is also some extra burden on the witness who may have to be recalled, and the risk that the witness will not be available later. But when the witness does in fact remain available, it seems silly to exclude the evidence because it was not inevitable that she would so remain. Rather than an automatic rule of exclusion, it seems preferable to have a rule imposing on the impeaching party the risk that the witness will become unavailable.

And that is essentially what FRE 613(b) seems to accomplish. The Rule itself specifies only that the witness must have an opportunity to explain or deny the statement, and that the opponent of the impeaching party must have an opportunity to interrogate her on that statement. Even these requirements can be waived, in rare circumstances, if "justice so requires". *Cf. Wammock v. Celotex Corp.*, 793 F.2d 1518 (11th Cir.1986). Also, the requirements do not apply if the statement is a party admission—for then it is admissible independently of its impeachment value. And the Advisory Committee Note makes clear the Committee's understanding that where the Rule does apply it merely requires sufficient opportunity to explain or deny and to examine, "with no specification of any particular time or sequence," thus "relax[ing]" the "traditional insistence that the attention of the witness be directed to the statement on cross-examination." Nevertheless, some courts and commentators[27] continue to prefer the traditional rule; some courts have acted as if the traditional rule stands untouched by FRE 613(b),[28] while others have taken the more moderate position that the Rule leaves the trial judge, as part of her general control over the proceedings, *see* FRE 611, with discretion to impose the traditional requirement in a given case.[29]

¶ **19.31:** Dacre is on trial for robbing an armored truck. Warner, the driver of the truck, identifies Dacre as the robber, and says that he had an "excellent" view of Dacre's face; this is consistent with his testimony at a preliminary hearing.

---

[27] See McCormick, § 37; 3 Stephen A. Saltzburg, Michael M. Martin & Daniel J. Capra, *Federal Rules of Evidence Manual* § 613–.02[5] (11th ed. 2015); *cf.* Mueller & Kirkpatrick, § 6.41 ("the court has authority under FRE 611 to require the attacking party to prove a statement immediately after the witness has testified and might well do so in the interest of minimizing inconvenience to the witness"). The McCormick text, which emphasizes particularly fear that the jury will make improper use of the statement under the loosened procedure, regards FRE 613(b) as the product of a glitch in the drafting process. When the Rule was first drafted, the then-current draft of the Rules called for all prior inconsistent statements to be exempted from the rule against hearsay, meaning that they could be admitted substantively; thus, any concern that the inverted procedure would discourage the jurors from limiting use of the prior statement to the impeachment purpose became moot. The draft hearsay rule was made more rigorous, but Rule 613(b) was not.

[28] *See, e.g.,* United States v. Devine, 934 F.2d 1325, 1344 (5th Cir.1991) (declaring that proof of a prior inconsistent statement offered to impeach a witness "may be elicited by extrinsic evidence only if the witness on cross-examination denies having made the statement," and citing as authority only one case that was decided shortly after passage of the Federal Rules and that appeared not to recognize any changes created by them in this context), *cert. denied,* 502 U.S. 1065 (1992).

[29] *See, e.g.,* United States v. Hudson, 970 F.2d 948, 956 n. 2 (1st Cir.1992).

(a) Warner, who has moved cross-country since the episode, goes home immediately after testifying. A day later, his ex-girlfriend Taylor comes to the office of Dacre's counsel and says that she remembers Warner saying on the day of the robbery, "I was so scared, I didn't get a good look at the guy's face. I'll never be able to make an identification." Should Dacre be able to present Taylor's testimony of this statement?

[handwritten: Yes. 613(b) — if justice so requires!]

(b) Now suppose the same facts as in (a) except that Dacre's counsel knew about the prior statement from Taylor well before trial. The day before trial, Dacre's counsel phones Taylor to tell her to be ready to testify. She learns from Taylor's answering machine that Taylor is away on vacation and will not be back until the following Thursday, the day after Warner's testimony. What should the lawyer do?

[handwritten: Two options: Give notice 1) Confront warner when he testifies 2) Have judge order Warner not to leave the state / extend the subpoena]

(c) Now assume that, as in (b), Dacre's counsel knew about the prior statement from Taylor well before trial. But now assume also that Warner lives twenty-five miles away from the courthouse, and that Taylor is available to testify. Should Dacre's counsel ask Warner on cross about his supposed statement to Taylor—or should she save information about this statement for later?

[handwritten: Ask — hard to recall]

(d) Suppose in (c) that Dacre doesn't ask Warner about a prior statement and then tries to introduce Taylor's testimony, after the prosecution rests. The prosecution objects. The defense points out that the prosecution can recall Warner. The prosecution says this would be inconvenient to Warner. Defense counsel says,

> Well, I'm sorry about that, but I assume the prosecution didn't call Warner as a witness in the first place to do him any favors. True, I could have asked Warner about Taylor's statement when he was on the stand, but I wasn't required to do that and my tactical decision was that the prior statement would make more of an impression on the jury if I presented it through Taylor. Your Honor should respect that decision. If the price of that decision is that the prosecution decides to recall one of their witnesses, that's their business. Preventing inconvenience to the prosecution's witness shouldn't be my burden.

How should the court rule? What if Warner instead lives across the country?

(e) Now switch the facts around: Warner was an alibi witness for the defense, and after the defense rested Taylor testified for the prosecution that Warner told him the alibi was concocted. Dacre did not put Warner back on the stand, and he was convicted. On appeal, he complains about the fact that Warner did not have a chance to explain or deny Taylor's statement and he did not have a chance to examine Warner on it. The prosecution responds that if Dacre wanted Warner to try to respond to Taylor's testimony it could have done so by recalling Warner. How should the court rule?[30] (agree w/ both?)

Finally, note the provision made by FRE 806 for hearsay declarants. If a hearsay statement by an out-of-court declarant is admitted, that Rule allows impeachment of the declarant by any evidence that would be admissible for impeachment were the declarant a live witness. Now suppose the impeaching party wants to introduce a statement inconsistent with the admissible hearsay statement. The proponent of the initial statement might argue, "But the declarant hasn't had a chance to explain the statement away." To which the response would be, "Look, you're the one who wanted to admit this statement notwithstanding that the declarant isn't here. If we're willing to admit that statement without her here, then we should also be willing to admit the inconsistent statement she made." The second sentence of Rule 806 established this principle, providing that an inconsistent statement by the declarant "is not subject to any requirement that the declarant may have been afforded an opportunity to deny or explain."

G. BIAS

Additional Reading: McCormick, ch. 5, § 39; Mueller & Kirkpatrick, §§ 6.19–.20

When you impeach a witness by offering opinion or reputation evidence, or proof of prior misconduct suggesting dishonesty, you are mounting a broad-based attack on her general character for truthfulness. Even when you impeach by contradictory evidence or a prior inconsistent statement on a narrow point, you may be asking the jury to doubt the witness's general truthfulness; if the matter is collateral, that is the only good the evidence would do. Another method of impeachment, more closely focused on the particular case, is to show that the witness has some bias—that is, that some motive or interest, rather than accurate perception and memory of the facts, has led the witness to testify as she has. Sometimes the interest is very obvious—for example, that the witness is a lover or dependent of one of the parties, or that she has a bitter grudge against the party, or that she hates members of the party's race. (Does the name Mark Fuhrman ring a vague bell? He was a

---

[30] *Cf.* United States v. McCall, 85 F.3d 1193, 1196–97 (6th Cir.1996) (holding that, although prosecution should have questioned witness in first instance about prior statement, there was no reversible error because defense had and did not exercise choice to recall him).

detective in the O.J. Simpson case who, it turned out, was blatantly racist.) But the interest need not fit within any prescribed pigeonhole; any interest that might have impelled the witness to testify inaccurately can qualify. Indeed, the bias need not necessarily be for or against a party or a group of which the party is a member; if, for example, a non-party witness with no connection to either party is worried about how her testimony will affect her own reputation, that interest counts as bias.[31]

Although contending that the witness is biased often conveys a charge, express or implied, that the witness has lied, this is not inevitable. In some cases, it could be that the bias has unconsciously caused the witness to testify as she has.

> ¶ **19.32:** Wilkinson was a passenger in the car of her boss, Dumont, when Dumont got into an auto accident with Pinter. Wilkinson testifies that Pinter blindsided Dumont. Pinter seeks to elicit the fact that Wilkinson works for Dumont. Dumont objects, arguing that Wilkinson has no interest in the outcome of the trial. What result? Is the result altered if Dumont can prove that Wilkinson does not have a good personal relationship with Dumont, and that the outcome of this case will not have any substantial impact on the health of Dumont's business?[32]

In some cases, the right to impeach a witness by showing bias is constitutionally protected, as a matter of an accused's confrontation right. The key case is *Davis v. Alaska*, 415 U.S. 308 (1974). Davis was accused of breaking into a bar one morning and stealing its safe. The safe was discovered that afternoon, pried open with its contents removed, on the property of Straight. Green, who was Straight's stepson, testified for the prosecution that he had seen Davis about noon on the day of the theft, standing with another man beside a car parked near his family's home and holding "something like a crowbar." Davis sought on cross-examination to prove that Green, who was 16 at the time the safe was stolen, was then on probation because he had been judged delinquent by juvenile court for burglarizing two cabins. A state rule meant to preserve the confidentiality of juvenile procedures provided, "No adjudication . . . of a juvenile case shall be admissible in a court not acting in the exercise of juvenile jurisdiction except for use in a presentencing procedure." The rule clearly served a valid state purpose. Nevertheless, the Supreme Court, per Chief Justice Burger, held that in this case it was overridden

---

[31] In addition to "bias," McCormick uses the term "partiality," which in some sense may have a broader connotation and therefore be preferable in this context. On the other hand, partiality seems to connote a tilt to one *party* or the other, but the fundamental idea is that the witness has an *interest* deflecting her from the truth. Bias is the more commonly used term, and will be used here.

[32] *Cf.* Majestic v. Louisville & N.R. Co., 147 F.2d 621, 627 (6th Cir. 1945).

as a matter of constitutional law by Davis's need to try to establish bias on the part of Green.

¶ **19.33:** Are you persuaded? How do Green's juvenile adjudication and probation tend to show bias?

¶ **19.34:** Suppose that Davis was not allowed to introduce the impeaching evidence, and that he was convicted. He has now appealed. You are a clerk for one of the judges on the panel that will decide his case. In reviewing the record, you conclude that the evidence overwhelmingly indicates that Davis was guilty. What recommendation should you make to your boss?[33]

¶ **19.35:** Nate Lewis, a university student, is charged with rape of a fellow student. He claims consent. Shortly before trial Lewis receives in the mail an anonymous package containing excerpts from what it turns out is the complainant's diary; assume that authenticity is unchallenged. Lewis offers an excerpt presented below. Citing the state's rape shield law, which you may assume is similar to FRE 412, the prosecution objects to the part printed here in boldface:

> I can't believe the trial's only a week away. I feel guilty (sort of) for trying to get Nate locked up, but his lack of respect for women is terrible. I remember how disrespectful he always was to all of us girls in the courtyard . . . he thinks females are a bunch of sex objects! And he's such a player! He was trying to get with Holly and me, and all the while he had a girlfriend. I think I pounced on Nate because he was the last straw. That, and because I've always seemed to need some drama in my life. Otherwise I get bored. That definitely needs to change. I'm sick of men taking advantage of me . . . **and I'm sick of myself for giving in to them. I'm not a nympho like all those guys think. I'm just not strong enough to say no to them. I'm tired of being a whore. This is where it ends.**

How should the court rule? *See Lewis v. Wilkinson*, 307 F.3d 413 (6th Cir. 2002); *cf. Olden v. Kentucky*, 488 U.S. 227 (1988), presented in ¶ 18.31.

As suggested above, bias represents something other than a defect in the witness's general truth-telling ability. Rather, it reflects a defect in the witness's inclination to tell the truth in this case—or, even more precisely, with respect to this particular matter. For that reason, the facts tending to prove bias are not considered collateral, any more than proof

---

[33] *Cf.* Delaware v. Van Arsdall, 475 U.S. 673 (1986) (holding that the improper exclusion of bias evidence, "like other Confrontation Clause errors," is subject to harmless-error analysis).

that a supposed witness to an auto accident actually had his view obstructed, and so had no opportunity to perceive, would be considered collateral. The consequence of this is that extrinsic evidence—evidence other than from the witness's own mouth—is permissible.

¶ 19.36: Wepner, who has been convicted of drug dealing, is testifying for the prosecution against Diver, a police officer being tried on corruption charges. Diver's counsel wants to portray Wepner as a biased witness eager to get vengeance against Diver.

(a) Which, if any, of the following would be permissible questions to ask of Wepner on cross?

(i) "You hate Diver, don't you?"

(ii) "You have a grudge against Diver because he busted you two years ago, don't you?"

(iii) "You told Tucker that you were going to do whatever you could to get back at Diver, didn't you?"

(b) Suppose that on cross Wepner answered negatively to all three questions in (a). To which, if any, of the following may Tucker testify for Diver?

(i) "In my opinion, Wepner has a grudge against Diver."

(ii) "Diver arrested Wepner two years ago."

(iii) "Wepner told me that he was going to do whatever he could to get back at Diver."

(iv) "Wepner's wife told me Wepner has a grudge against Diver."

(c) Now suppose that in response to the questions in (a), Wepner testified that Diver had indeed arrested him, that he dislikes Diver and "would not shed any tears" if Diver went to jail, but that he doesn't hate Diver, wouldn't lie to help convict Diver, and never suggested to Tucker that he would. Which, if any, of the testimony in (b) may Tucker give for Diver?[34]

(d) Finally, suppose that Diver's counsel did not ask Wepner any of the questions in (a). May Tucker give any of the testimony in (b)?[35]

---

[34] Cf. United States v. Robinson, 530 F.2d 1076, 1079–80 (D.C.Cir.1976) ("Bias may be proved by extrinsic evidence even after a witness's disavowal of partiality," id. at 580).

[35] See, e.g., United States v. DiNapoli, 557 F.2d 962, 964–65 (2d Cir.1977), cert. denied, 434 U.S. 858 (1977) ("The ruling of the trial judge refusing to permit extrinsic evidence of a prior statement showing bias when the witness was not afforded an opportunity to explain or deny the

¶ **19.37:** Abel is being tried for bank robbery. One of his collaborators, Ehle, who has already pleaded guilty, testifies against him. Abel then presents the testimony of Mills, who had spent time with both Ehle and Abel in prison, that Ehle said in a conversation with Mills that he planned to implicate Abel falsely in the robbery. Ehle has told the prosecutor that he, Mills, and Abel were members of a secret prison organization, the Aryan Brotherhood, which required its members to kill, steal, or lie as necessary to protect each other, with stringent penalties for violation of its tenets. Ehle also has told the prosecutor that, in view of how close Abel and Mills were, it would have been "suicide" for him to tell Mills of a plan to implicate Abel falsely. What use, if any, may the prosecutor make of this information?

Notice that impeachment on the ground of bias is nowhere addressed by the Federal Rules of Evidence. This does not mean that such impeachment is impermissible under the Rules. On the contrary, a plausible explanation is that the drafters of this part of the Rules felt that no articulation of the permissibility of, and limitation on, impeachment by bias was necessary.[36] Indeed, you may have noticed that much of the subject matter of this chapter is touched only remotely by the Federal Rules. Even though they supposedly replace the common law of evidence, they are so open-ended in places that the common law must be read in to fill in the gaps.[37]

---

statement is in accord with Fed.R.Evid. 613(b) and is clearly the law of the circuit," *id.* at 965). Note that Rule 613(b) refers only to prior inconsistent statements, not to statements offered to prove bias. Most courts have not discerned any reason to draw a distinction between the two for purposes of this foundational matter—including the question of whether the opportunity to respond must come while the witness to be impeached is still on the stand. Bear in mind, though, that the evidence demonstrating bias need not be a prior statement by the witness, and requiring the impeaching party to summarize this bias-revealing evidence with the witness on the stand may not be convenient. McCormick, § 39, takes the view that usually the impeaching party should be required to ask foundational questions of the witness, but that the court should have discretion to dispense with the requirement.

[36] In United States v. Abel, 469 U.S. 45, 49–52 (1984), the Supreme Court addressed the failure of the Rules to mention bias. The Court began its analysis with a disclaimer:

> Although we are nominally the promulgators of the Rules, and should in theory need only to consult our collective memories to analyze the situation properly, we are in truth merely a conduit when we deal with an undertaking as substantial as preparation of the Federal Rules of Evidence.

In light of the uniformity of pre-Rules law on bias, the breadth of the definition of relevance in Rule 401 and the presumptive admission of relevant evidence provided by Rule 402, references to bias in the Advisory Committee Notes to Rules 608 and 610, and the breadth of the provisions on impeachment and cross-examination in Rules 607 and 611(b), the Court reached the reasonable conclusion that impeachment by bias is permissible under the Rules.

[37] *See id.* at 51–52, *quoting* Edward W. Cleary, *Preliminary Notes on Reading the Rules of Evidence,* 7 Neb. L. Rev. 908, 915 (1978). Prof. Cleary was the Reporter for the Advisory Committee that drafted the original Rules.

H. CHALLENGES TO TESTIMONIAL CAPACITIES OTHER THAN TRUTH-TELLING

Additional Reading: McCormick, ch. 5, § 44; Mueller & Kirkpatrick, §§ 6.21–.22

So far in this chapter, we have concentrated on the testimonial capacity of sincerity. But as we already know, that is not the only capacity involved in giving testimony. Indeed, it may be that a witness who testifies inaccurately is more likely to have erred in perception or memory than to have consciously told a falsehood. The witness may also have sincerely attempted to communicate the truth but been inarticulate in doing so. Thus, courts allow an impeaching party to challenge these other capacities as well as that of truth-telling.

It is tempting to say that the rules applicable to challenging sincerity should be applied in a comparable way when one of the other capacities is in issue. To an extent, this is what courts do. But the law tends to be less settled and more flexible with respect to capacities other than truth-telling.

It is helpful in considering these questions to contrast a general capacity with the specific capacity as applied to the given testimony. We have seen this with respect to sincerity: A witness may have a good general capacity for truthfulness but a specific bias in the particular case that diminishes her ability to provide truthful testimony. Similarly, even if she has excellent eyesight she may have lacked a good opportunity to observe the particular events that are the subject of her testimony.

With respect to the specific capacities, the law is rather clear: The operation of the capacity in the particular case is not deemed collateral, so the impeaching party may not only challenge it by asking questions of the witness herself, but may also present extrinsic evidence. Note how this general statement is an extension of the principle that applies to sincerity. As we already know from Section G, bias, which is a defect of truth-telling ability in the particular case, may be proven by extrinsic evidence.

¶ **19.38:** Bob testifies for the plaintiff in an auto accident case. He says that he was standing on a street corner with his friends Carol and Ted when he saw a red car (the defendant's) roar into the next intersection, about eighty yards away. On cross, he denies that anyone else was standing with the threesome, and says that there was nothing unusual about his own manner or conduct at the time. May the defense present the testimony of Alice that she was standing with the other three?

What if Alice is also prepared to testify that "Bob was acting drunk as a skunk"?[38]

As for challenges to general capacities, the situation becomes somewhat more complicated. Cross-examination to show a defect in one of the capacities is acceptable—you could, for example, ask a witness to admit that she has poor eyesight or a bad memory. A skillful cross may even make such conditions apparent to the jury without the need for questions addressed directly to them.

But how about using extrinsic evidence to prove a general defect in a capacity?[39] As with sincerity, it is helpful to distinguish between a general assessment and specific conduct offered to show the general defect. We know the law with respect to sincerity—you can offer an extrinsic general assessment, in the form of opinion or reputation, but you cannot prove the specific acts, which are deemed collateral. As to the other capacities, the law may tend to follow along similar lines, but it is much iffier.

¶ **19.39:** In ¶ 19.38, to which of the following should Alice be allowed to testify, assuming she is competent?

(a) "Bob has a weak memory."

(b) "Bob is schizophrenic and has trouble distinguishing reality from fantasy."[40]

(c) "Bob is color-blind."

(d) "Bob has poor eyesight."[41]

(e) "Bob is an habitual drunk."

(f) "Bob is a heroin addict."[42]

---

[38] *Cf.* Miles v. Ryan, 484 F.2d 1255, 1257–59 (3d Cir.1973) (evidence of drunkenness admissible only if it establishes that the witness was intoxicated to a degree that affected the witness's capacity to observe).

[39] *Cf.* Gamble v. State, 492 So.2d 1132, 1133–34 (Fla.App.1986) (indicating receptivity to evidence showing "defect" in the witness's "capacity to accurately testify," including evidence "relat[ing] to the witness' memory, eyesight, ability to understand, or observe. . . . A witness' mental state or condition is also a proper basis for this kind of impeachment. There is no requirement for this kind of impeachment that it be material, and, therefore, not 'collateral' to the issues at trial.").

[40] *See* United States v. Lindstrom, 698 F.2d 1154 (11th Cir.1983) (holding trial court committed reversible error in not allowing defense to present full evidence of the schizophrenia of a key witness); *cf.* People v. Borrelli, 624 P.2d 900, 904 (Colo.App.1980) (holding that trial court erred in excluding evidence that a key witness suffered from organic brain syndrome, which could affect his intellectual functioning and memory).

[41] *Cf.* Jones v. State. 833 S.W.2d 634 (Tex. Ct. Apps. 1992) (80-year-old complainant, robbed at night, acknowledges on cross-examination that he has prescription glasses but doesn't wear them because they don't help, that his vision is impaired by cataracts, and that he sees worse at night than during the day; conviction upheld).

[42] *Cf.* Valerio v. State, 542 P.2d 875, 877 (Wyo.1975) (excluding evidence of drug addiction absent evidence that the witness was under the influence at the time of the occurrence in

(g) "I was with Bob the day before the accident and he got roaring drunk."

(h) "I was with Bob the day before the accident and he shot up with heroin."

(i) "I was with Bob the week before the accident and he couldn't remember the phone number of his mother, whom he calls every day."

(j) "I took a walk with Bob on a farm the month before the accident. We came up to a scarecrow, but until we were within forty yards Bob thought it was a man."

¶ 19.40: Andre Young is on trial for the shooting assault of Terry Smith. Young claims mistaken identity. He seeks to have his twin brother Anton sit next to him at counsel table when Smith is asked to identify his assailant. Should this be allowed if

(a) Andre makes no contention as to who the assailant was?

(b) Andre contends that the assailant was his cousin Mark Phillips, and that Phillips resembles him?[43]

¶ 19.41: Is there any justification for according different treatment to impeaching evidence depending on whether it is perception, memory, or sincerity that is being challenged?

¶ 19.42: In a hearing to determine the competency of Longfellow Deeds, two old sisters (testifying together) assert that Deeds is "pixilated." As Deeds' lawyer, you suspect that they have a different, and in general broader, standard for pixilation than most people do. What can you do to prove this? Can you use extrinsic evidence? Cf. Frank Capra's *Mr. Deeds Goes to Town* (starring Gary Cooper and Jean Arthur).

One recurrent issue, which we touched on in Chapter 5, is whether expert witnesses may testify in general to weaknesses of eyewitness testimony. Eyewitness testimony is extremely powerful, but without some expert assistance jurors may not realize the tendency of eyewitnesses to conflate memories of the event with inaccurate information learned soon

---

question or when testifying); People v. West, 156 Ill.App.3d 608, 108 Ill.Dec. 727, 729, 509 N.E.2d 153, 155–56 (1987) (evidence that witness was addicted *at some point* allowed, even absent evidence that witness was *addicted* at time of occurrence or when testifying); McCormick § 44 (noting greater receptivity to evidence of drug addiction, because of greater "social odium," than to evidence of alcoholism).

43 *See* State v. Young, 1998 WL 214610 (Ohio 1998) (asserting that "eyesight or hearing is easy to test by simple experiments in the courtroom," *quoting Weissenberger's Ohio Evidence* (1998), § 607.8, at 232, but holding that trial court did not abuse discretion in refusing to allow this particular experiment).

afterwards, or the lack of a strong correlation between the accuracy of a witness's recall and her confidence in it.

I.   THE CONSTITUTIONAL DIMENSION

Additional Reading: Mueller & Kirkpatrick, §§ 6.2, 8.83

As we already know, an accused has a constitutional right, under the Sixth Amendment's Confrontation Clause, to demand that adverse witnesses testify in his presence, face to face, and if reasonably possible at trial. But what rights does the accused have when the witness is brought in to testify at trial? Wigmore said that the defendant "demands confrontation, not for the idle purpose of gazing upon the witness, or of being gazed upon by him, but for the purpose of cross-examination. . . ." 5 John Henry Wigmore, *Evidence* § 1395, p. 150 (Chadbourn rev. 1974), *quoted in Davis v. Alaska*, 415 U.S. 308, 316 (1974). That is an overstatement—historically, the right to demand that the witness testify face-to-face long predated any right of cross-examination—but it is definitely true that as the confrontation right has developed it includes not only the right to demand that the witness testify in the presence of the accused but also the right to cross-examine. But then this raises a difficult question: To what extent is a jurisdiction constitutionally constrained from imposing limits on that cross-examination? We have already seen in the *Davis* case, presented before ¶ 19.33, that sometimes an accused's right to cross-examination guarantees that he will be allowed to inquire into particular subjects, even if the jurisdiction's evidentiary law would ordinarily prevent him from doing so. But obviously the right must have limits: It would make no sense to hold that the accused had a constitutional right, overriding state law, to ask whatever questions he wanted, no matter how time consuming, intrusive, prejudicial, and irrelevant.

¶ **19.43:** Caicedo testified against Ciro that he and Ciro conspired to distribute cocaine. On cross, Caicedo admitted that he "free based" cocaine about four times a week and that this diminished his ability to recall; that as a result of his agreement to cooperate with the Government he hoped for a light sentence on the count for which he had pled guilty and that he would not be prosecuted for 60 or more other drug deals in which he had been involved; and that he didn't care what happened to Ciro. The trial judge did not, however, allow evidence of a juvenile adjudication against Caicedo several years before involving kidnapping and assault with intent to commit rape. Caicedo was no longer incarcerated or on probation in connection with this adjudication. Did this ruling violate Ciro's rights under FRE 609? Under the Confrontation Clause?[44]

¶ **19.44:** A woman who identified herself as "Jane Jordan" testified in state court that she had bought a bag of heroin from Draiman at a restaurant, with marked money provided by the police. On cross, Draiman's counsel asked if Jane Jordan was her real name. Over a prosecution objection, the court instructed her to answer, and she acknowledged that it was not. The trial court, however, sustained objections to the next two questions, which asked what her real name was and where she lived. Counsel then pursued a full cross-examination about the incident at the restaurant. Draiman was convicted, exhausted all his state remedies, and has now brought a federal habeas corpus petition on the basis of the sustained objections. You are the district judge's clerk.

Why do you suppose the prosecution objected? How should the judge rule? *See Smith v. Illinois*, 390 U.S. 129, 131 (1968) (holding that name and address are "the very starting point in exposing falsehood and bringing out the truth ... open[ing] countless avenues of in-court examination and out-of-court investigation").

¶ **19.45:** Sammons is accused of possessing cocaine with intent to deliver it. At a pretrial hearing to determine whether he was entrapped, the prosecution presents as a witness an informant known to Sammons only as Rick. Because threats were made against Rick, the prosecutor asks that Rick be allowed to testify wearing a mask covering his face and head. How should the judge rule?[45]

We have assumed so far that if a prosecution witness is brought to trial she will in fact testify face-to-face with the accused. And in *Coy v. Iowa*, 487 U.S. 1012 (1988), the Supreme Court held that the defendant in effect has a right in most circumstances to say to his accusers, "Look me in the eye and say that." *Id.* at 1018. Ordinarily, of course, the accused is in the courtroom when the witness testifies, so there is usually no problem. A defendant may be so disruptive that the judge is empowered to remove him from the courtroom, *Illinois v. Allen*, 397 U.S. 337 (1970), but this occurs very rarely.

---

[44] *See* United States v. Ciro, 753 F.2d 248 (2d Cir.1985), *cert. denied*, 471 U.S. 1018, *sub nom.* Sloan v. United States, 471 U.S. 1057 (1985).

[45] *See* People v. Sammons, 191 Mich.App. 351, 478 N.W.2d 901 (Mich.App.1991), *appeal denied*, 439 Mich. 938, 480 N.W.2d 103 (1992), *cert. denied*, 505 U.S. 1213 (1992).

More significantly, in recent decades most states, and Congress as well, have attempted to protect children, especially in cases of alleged sexual abuse, from the usual rigors of testifying in the presence of the accused in open court. We will postpone consideration of these measures to the next chapter, when we consider the array of issues posed by child observers.

J. REHABILITATION

FRE 608(a), 801(d)(1)(B)

Additional Reading: McCormick, ch. 5, § 47; Mueller & Kirkpatrick, §§ 6.49–.52

So far, we have discussed how the credibility of a witness may be attacked. The party putting a witness on the stand is generally not allowed to support the credibility of a witness if it has not yet been attacked. A standard accounting for this rule is that if the witness's credibility is not challenged, such bolstering will consume time, is unlikely to serve any valid interest, and may (when the witness is also an actor in the disputed events) be a play for sympathy. A further reason, which is applicable directly to some cases and may explain some of the force behind the rule, is that if the witness's credibility is supported by a prior statement that she made and that statement is more detailed than her current testimony, then under the guise of supporting credibility the proponent would be trying to introduce information as to which effective cross-examination is difficult or impossible; this is the "overhang" problem that we have already discussed in Chapter 10 in connection with the hearsay aspect of prior consistent statements. But if an opposing party has attacked the credibility of a witness, then the balance swings the other way, and fairness demands that the proponent be allowed to support it.

¶ **19.46:** (a) In ¶ 19.38, the plaintiff wants to elicit from Bob, during her direct examination of him, that the day after the accident he made a statement to a friend to the effect that the red car roared into the intersection at about fifty miles per hour, with its horn blaring. This statement is consistent with, but more elaborate than, the testimony that Bob has just given. Should the court allow testimony of this statement to prove the assertions that Bob made in it? To support Bob's credibility?

(b) Now suppose instead that the plaintiff is seeking to introduce Bob's prior statement on redirect, the defendant having elicited during cross that Bob has a conviction for forgery. Do your answers change?

¶ **19.47:** In a commercial litigation, Jane testifies for the plaintiff to authenticate sales records of which she is the custodian. She describes what the records are, weekly state-by-state and product-by-product tabulations of all the sales of the company, and how they are created and stored. The cross is very gentle, with questions designed for clarification only. Fred, a co-worker, then takes the stand for the plaintiff. In the course of direct, he refers to the sales records, and offers a description of them consistent with Jane's. Defense counsel objects, saying, "He's trying to bolster Jane's testimony but she hasn't even been impeached." What ruling?

Accepting the proposition that credibility may not be supported until it has been attacked, the question remains what type of rehabilitating evidence is permissible. The two principal types of rehabilitating evidence are general assessments of good character for truthfulness and prior statements consistent with the witness's testimony. These are appropriate in different circumstances.

FRE 608(a) expresses the general rule governing opinion or reputation evidence of the witness's character for truthfulness, that it "is admissible only after the character of the witness for truthfulness has been attacked by opinion or reputation evidence or otherwise." Clearly, if the impeaching party has presented a character witness to offer a general assessment that the primary witness has a bad character for truthfulness, the rehabilitating party may respond in kind. But as the "or otherwise" language indicates, the rule is not limited to that circumstance. When else can we say that "the character of the witness for truthfulness has been attacked"? Evidence of misconduct—whether it resulted in a criminal conviction or not—generally would justify that conclusion. Beyond that, it is difficult to speak categorically. As McCormick says, § 47, "a slashing cross-examination can carry strong accusations of misconduct and bad character." But if the impeaching party simply suggested, in essence, that the witness testified inaccurately—even if the suggestion is that she lied—that does not necessarily convey the same accusation. For example, if the impeaching party suggests that the witness lied to protect a family member, that would presumably not be considered an attack on character.

¶ **19.48:** (a) Recall once again *Davis v. Alaska*, presented before ¶ 19.33. Assume that on retrial Davis has presented the impeaching evidence, concerning Green's delinquency record, to which the Supreme Court held he had a right. May the prosecution offer a witness to testify that in her opinion Green has a good character for truthfulness?[46]

(b) Now alter the facts somewhat: Assume that Green was arrested for the prior burglaries, and charges against him were pending at the time he first implicated Davis, but he has since been cleared of the other burglaries and another person has been convicted of them. The theory of impeachment is still essentially the same, that Green was eager to deflect suspicion from himself. Is the opinion evidence as to his good character for truthfulness admissible?[47]

¶ 19.49: Dick, the former president of a large enterprise, is on trial for obstruction of justice. One of the charges is that he destroyed 18 minutes of a tape recording that contained evidence potentially incriminating Dick and some associates in the cover-up of the burglary of a competitor. Rosemary, Dick's secretary, testifies for Dick that she accidentally caused the erasure when she took a phone call while transcribing the tape.

(a) On cross, the prosecutor sets up a portion of the courtroom like Rosemary's office. He then asks her to demonstrate how she could have erased the tape while on the phone. Given the placement of the various instruments, Rosemary has to assume and maintain an extremely uncomfortable, contorted position. She testifies that this is exactly what she did. May Dick offer a witness to testify to Rosemary's good character for truthfulness?[48]

(b) Now assume instead that on cross Rosemary acknowledges that shortly after the tape was erased she said to a friend, "I wonder if Dick erased the tape on purpose. He's clumsy, but he's also tricky." Is the testimony as to Rosemary's good character admissible?

Now consider rehabilitation by use of a prior consistent statement. Bear in mind at the outset that—like most other out-of-court statements, including statements made by someone who is now a witness—prior

---

[46] *Cf.* State v. Johnson, 216 N.J.Super. 588, 524 A.2d 826, 834–35 (App.Div.1987) (holding proper rehabilitation of a state witness by character evidence where the witness's moral character was attacked by a question on cross-examination that tended to suggest that he was not a law-abiding citizen).

[47] *Cf.* State v. Carr, 302 Or. 20, 725 P.2d 1287 (1986) (declaring in light of Oregon Evidence Code Rule 609–1(3)—which explicitly provides that evidence of bias or interest invites only rehabilitation showing lack of bias or interest—that the issue of truthful character of a witness was not raised by testimony suggesting a motive to lie).

[48] *Cf.* Blakely v. Bates, 394 N.W.2d 320, 323 (Iowa 1986) (emphasizing discretion of trial court in determining whether self-contradictory statements in witness's testimony, brought out in cross-examination, warrant rehabilitation).

consistent statements are generally considered hearsay if offered to prove the truth of what they assert. If such a statement is offered for rehabilitation, the question becomes, in essence, "Does the fact that the witness made the statement then substantially increase the probability that he is telling the truth now?"

Sometimes it clearly does not. Suppose, for example, that the defendant in an auto accident case impeaches a witness for the plaintiff by contending that she was in a poor position to observe the accident. It will not help the plaintiff's case to show that immediately after the accident the witness made a statement identical to her later testimony; an erroneous statement is not rendered accurate by virtue of the fact that it has been made before. Similarly (to adapt an illustration already used in Chapter 10), if the defendant claims that the witness is biased because she is the sister-in-law of the plaintiff, it will not help the plaintiff to show that she has consistently spoken in his favor. Or if the defendant claims that the witness is biased because she is his own former sister-in-law, and has had a grudge against him ever since he divorced her sister, it will not help the plaintiff to show that ever since the divorce the witness has spoken consistently with her current testimony; if the alleged bias accounts for the testimony, it probably accounts for the earlier statements as well.

But now suppose that the plaintiff in this case is able to show that, while there was still one big, happy family, the witness made a statement to the same effect as her present testimony. That would certainly help dispel the contention that bias against the defendant accounts for the witness's testimony. In the words of Fed. R. Evid. 801(d)(1)(B)(i), the prior statement is "consistent with the declarant's testimony and is offered . . . to rebut an express or implied charge that the declarant recently fabricated it or acted from a recent improper influence or motive in so testifying."

The word "consistent" in this context should not be taken too literally. Suppose the ex-sister-in-law's testimony is that the defendant was driving 60 miles per hour, in a 30 m.p.h. zone. A prior statement that the defendant was going 65 m.p.h. would not be consistent with this in the strictest sense, nor would a statement that he was going 55 m.p.h. But certainly the 65 m.p.h. statement, and probably the 55 m.p.h. statement, would still have rehabilitative effect in dispelling the contention of improper motive.

Rule 801(d)(1)(B) is something of a textual oddity. Prior consistent statements, like prior inconsistent statements, are not addressed in Article VI of the Federal Rules, which deals with witnesses. Rule 801(d), which does address these statements, provides exemptions from the hearsay rule. We have seen that Rule 801(d)(1)(A), exempting certain prior inconsistent statements from the rule against hearsay, was not meant to state the standard for determining when such statements may be used for impeachment. Before 2014, Rule 801(d)(1)(B) did not include what is now subsection (ii), and it was unclear whether the Rule was intended not only to prescribe when prior consistent statements of a witness are exempt from the rule against hearsay—the proper function for a subsection of Rule 801(d)(1)—but also to state the complete set of circumstances in which such statements may be used for rehabilitation. If it was the latter,[49] it was overly restrictive, because in some circumstances, a prior consistent statement might have significant rehabilitative value even though it would be hard to shoehorn the situation into the "recently fabricated" or "improper influence or motive" categories. For example, a prior consistent statement made shortly after the events it described, while they were fresh in the declarant's mind, may dispel the contention that her current testimony is a product of failed memory; also, impeachment by a prior inconsistent statement does not necessarily suggest that the witness fabricated the current testimony or acted because of an improper influence or motive, and a statement made by the witness that is consistent with the current testimony and made before the prior inconsistent statement may limit the impeachment effect.[50]

The rulemakers eliminated the ambiguity—for the federal courts—by adding Rule 801(d)(1)(B)(ii), which exempts from the rule against hearsay a prior statement that is consistent with the declarant's testimony and is offered "to rehabilitate the declarant's credibility as a witness when attacked on another ground [i.e., a ground other than those specified in Rule 801(d)(1)(B) as it had stood, and in what is now Rule 801(d)(1)(B)(i)]". They probably could have made matters even clearer by eliminating what is now Rule 801(d)(1)(B)(i) and prescribing simply that if a prior consistent statement is admitted to rehabilitate the credibility of the declarant-witness, then it is also exempt from the rule against hearsay.[51]

---

[49] Cryptic language in Tome v. United States, 513 U.S. 150, 167 (1995), suggests this reading (FRE 801(d)(1)(B) "permits the introduction of a declarant's consistent out-of-court statements *to rebut* a charge of recent fabrication . . . only when . . . ") (emphasis added).

[50] *See, e.g., id.*, 513 U.S. at 170 (Breyer, J., dissenting) (noting that, in addition to the circumstance identified in Rule 801(d)(1)(B), a witness may be rehabilitated by prior consistent statements "(a) placing a claimed inconsistent statement in context; (b) showing that an inconsistent statement was not made; [and] (c) indicating that the witness' memory is not as faulty as a cross-examiner has claimed."); United States v. Brennan, 798 F.2d 581 (2d Cir.1986) (satisfying Rule 801(d)(1)(B) not a prerequisite for use in rehabilitation); Richard D. Friedman, *Prior Statements of a Witness: A Nettlesome Corner of the Hearsay Thicket*, 1995 S. Ct. Rev. 277, 304 & n.88.

[51] Note that I say "admitted" rather than "offered," because I believe that the intent of the rule is that the statement has to be admissible for rehabilitation purposes in order to qualify for the hearsay exemption; if the statement does not qualify for rehabilitation, it is not enough that the proponent announce a desire for the statement to be admitted for that purpose.

So the ambiguity is gone, for the federal courts: If a prior consistent statement may be used to rehabilitate the witness, it may be used for the truth of what it asserts.[52] And that avoids the difficulty of having to give an instruction to the jury that would probably be incomprehensible or even incoherent—that it may use a prior statement, in which the witness asserted **PROP**, to rehabilitate the witness's current testimony, in which she testified to **PROP** among other matters, but not for the matter that it asserted. Elimination of ambiguity is all to the good, but that does not necessarily mean that the amendment was net beneficial. Note the comment in an earlier decision, *United States v. Bishop*, 264 F.3d 535, 548 (5th Cir. 2001): "Rule 801(d)(1)(B) cannot be construed to allow the admission of what would otherwise be hearsay every time a law enforcement officer's credibility or memory is challenged; otherwise, cross-examination would always transform hearsay notes into admissible evidence." So now the prospect that the *Bishop* court thought was unacceptable appears to be the rule in federal court: if the memory of a police officer (or any other witness) is challenged, her notes, or another statement that she made shortly after the fact, are admissible to prove that what she said in them is true. Is that a problem? If the prior statement asserted nothing more than the current testimony does, it does not appear troublesome at all. But now recall the "overhang" problem, which we discussed in Chapter 10, in which the prior consistent statement asserts a proposition that the current testimony does not; if, as under traditional law, the statement is admissible for rehabilitation only, it cannot support a finding of that proposition.[53] But if, as Rule 801(d)(1)(B) prescribes, the statement is exempt from the rule against hearsay, it can support a finding of that proposition, even though the witness is not now asserting it. It remains to be seen whether courts will be sensitive to this problem, perhaps by carving up prior consistent

---

[52] Some states do continue, even when the witness has been impeached by the method addressed by what is now FRE 801(d)(1)(B)(i), to adhere explicitly to the traditional rule limiting prior consistent statements to use for rehabilitation. *See, e.g.,* Me. R. Evid. 801(d)(1) ("A prior consistent statement by the declarant, whether or not under oath, is admissible only to rebut an express or implied charge against the declarant of recent fabrication or improper influence or motive"); State v. Brown, 187 Conn. 602, 609 n. 2, 447 A.2d 734, 738 n. 2 (1982) (continuing Connecticut's rejection of FRE 801(d)(1)(B) and adhering to traditional rule); Conn. Code Ev. § 8–5 (counterpart, in Code adopted in 2000, to FRE 801(d)(1), without any a counterpart to FRE 801(d)(1)(B)).

[53] At least one other distinction may be drawn between admissibility for the truth and admissibility only for rehabilitation. Suppose the witness is impeached on a collateral matter and the proponent wishes to rehabilitate her by introducing a prior statement consistent with her testimony on that matter. The court might rule that, if the prior statement is admissible for rehabilitation only, it can be proved by the witness while she is on the stand but not by extrinsic evidence.

statements so that only the substance that is repeated in the current testimony is deemed to be exempt from the hearsay rule.[54]

¶ **19.50:** Bill and Mae Dellinger, who run a gun shop, are on trial with several other defendants for conspiring to smuggle firearms out of the country. A key witness is Werner, a former business associate of the Dellingers, who testifies to a meeting on February 1, 2003 in back of the shop at which the conspiracy was allegedly planned. Werner's testimony presents Bill as having participated actively in the meeting. It is much more ambiguous about Mae; he testifies that she was in and out of the back of the shop, waiting on customers, and does not mention anything she said. Scott, a police officer, is prepared to testify that on July 1, 2003 Werner gave a full description of the meeting, and portrayed both Mae (notwithstanding her intermittent presence) and Bill as having played a leading role in it. In each of the following circumstances, could Scott's testimony be admitted, and if so for what purpose or purposes?

(a) On cross-examination of Werner, the Dellingers bring out that in 2004 Werner had a nasty business dispute with them and did not deal with them afterwards.

(b) On cross-examination of Werner, Mae suggests that Werner has a weak memory and that he is placing her at the meeting not because he remembers her being there but because he knows that she spent most working days at the store.

A useful general approach in determining whether a prior statement is admissible for rehabilitation is this: If the prior consistent statement was made before the alleged failure in testimonial capacity, then it is relevant to show that the testimony could not be the result of that failure. If, however, the statement was made after the alleged failure, then it usually does not have such explanatory power. We have already seen in Chapter 10 that, at least in the context of prior consistent statements offered to rebut charges of recent fabrication or improper influence or motive, the Supreme Court's decision in *Tome* has interpreted FRE 801(d)(1)(B) to make this timing rule absolute: Unless the prior statement was made before the alleged improper influence arose, it cannot be introduced to rebut the charge that the influence led to the testimony.[55]

Sometimes it is relatively easy to time the alleged testimonial failure. If the failure was in perception, it occurred simultaneously with the

---

[54] The problem existed under Rule 801(d)(1)(B) as it stood before 2014, but by extending the hearsay exemption under that Rule to all statements admissible for rehabilitation, the rulemakers also extended the problem, which they appear not to have considered.

[55] In this particular respect, it appears that the *Tome* Court viewed Rule 801(d)(1)(B) as it then stood as limiting the use of prior statements for rehabilitation as well as substantively.

events, and so no later than the prior consistent statement; accordingly, that statement will have no rehabilitative value. A failure in sincerity may also, in certain circumstances, be timed—if, for example, the contention is that the witness is embittered by her sister's marital problems, the failure presumably arose when she first learned of those problems. A corresponding statement could be made about testimony offered by a witness against the employer who fired him.

As the problems presented in ¶ 10.24 have suggested, however, this "premotive" requirement, while certainly a useful guidepost, is unduly rigid, or at least has to be applied carefully: Sometimes motives arise slowly, or in pieces, and the circumstances in which the prior statement was made may occasionally have rehabilitative value even if they were made after the motive arose. The absolutism of *Tome* is not binding on the states; whether it will even continue to bind the federal courts, given the addition of Rule 801(d)(1)(B)(ii), remains to be seen.

With respect to rehabilitation in the face of a contention of failed memory, too, it is difficult to apply any rigid rule. Failure of memory probably cannot be pinpointed in time, because it likely occurred nearly continuously over some period, most of the loss occurring relatively early. A prior consistent statement proves that any memory loss occurring after the statement could not be the cause of the testimony, but the statement does not dispel the significance of memory loss occurring beforehand. Obviously, the earlier the statement, the more powerful it will be in responding to a contention of memory failure.

Now suppose that the impeaching party has offered proof of a prior inconsistent statement. The impeacher is contending, in essence, that the inconsistency shows that the testimony must be the product of some failure of capacity between the prior statement and the testimony. If the rehabilitating party offers proof of a consistent statement made before the inconsistent statement, it may well scuttle this theory, although it still leaves that party with the problem of how to explain away the inconsistent statement. But now assume that the consistent statement was made after the inconsistent statement. In this case, the impeacher is likely to maintain that the consistent statement proves nothing. That the witness may have stated his current version more times than the prior one does not erase the inconsistency, or eliminate the inference that it was caused by a failure in testimonial capacity. Unless there is other proof of when that failure occurred, the impeacher will argue, the timing must be inferred from the statements themselves; if the witness began making statements consistent with his testimony only after making the inconsistent statements, that simply shows that the failure occurred between the last inconsistent statement and the first consistent statement.

¶ **19.51:** Recall the *Gentry* case from ¶ 19.26. The defense proved Turner's failure to make a statement to the first officer about what he had supposedly heard. In response, the prosecution offered proof that later in the morning, when Turner was fully awake, he made a statement to another officer consistent with his testimony. Should this evidence have been admitted? What should the result be if the prior consistent statement was made a week after the first interrogation?

K. POLYGRAPH EVIDENCE

By now you have seen how much of the energy spent at trial, and how much of the law of evidence, is devoted to the matter of determining credibility. It is very tempting, then, to think that litigation would be much improved if we had a reliable, scientific method of determining whether a witness was telling the truth. Considerable effort has been poured into developing such methods. Intelligence and law enforcement agents make extensive use of polygraphs as an investigative tool. For the most part, however, the law of evidence has taken a wary attitude towards evidence of polygraph results.

The most obvious objection to polygraph evidence has been that it is not sufficiently reliable to warrant admissibility, particularly in light of the great weight it is likely to carry, and thus does not satisfy *Frye*, or *Daubert*, or whatever similar standard the jurisdiction maintains. Indeed, recall that *Frye* itself rejected evidence of a purportedly scientific method of lie detection. Over time the force of this objection has diminished, as the quality of polygraphs, when properly administered, has improved— and in the face of empirical studies indicating that jurors are not in fact overawed by polygraph evidence. Some courts, therefore, have drawn back from a hard-and-fast rule against the introduction of such evidence.

If the jurisdiction does *not* have such a categorical rule, the admissibility of polygraph evidence may depend on the context in which it is offered. A few salient aspects of that context are:

• *Who is offering the evidence?* Obviously, admissibility is easier to justify if an accused is offering evidence that a polygraph test indicates that he was telling the truth in relating his exculpatory story than if the prosecution is offering evidence that the accused failed the test. Civil cases lie in between.

• *Did the parties stipulate to admissibility of the results?* Sometimes, before the test is administered, the parties agree that the results—whichever way they come out—will be admissible. Numerous courts now are willing to admit the evidence, at least under some circumstances, given such a stipulation.

• *Has the subject of the test testified?* Most frequently, the subject of a polygraph test that is offered into evidence is the accused in a criminal prosecution. But it may be that the accused does not testify in the case. If he flunked the test, the prosecution wants to prove that, irrespective of whether he testifies—and if he passed it, he wants to prove that, irrespective of whether he testifies. But what is the ground of admissibility in such a case? We cannot say that the polygraph test is being admitted to impeach or rehabilitate a witness, because the person whose credibility at issue in making the statement is not even a witness. What we have is expert testimony about the truthfulness of a person not a witness in making an out-of-court statement about the facts of the case. If the subject does testify, then the situation is closer to the usual case in which a witness is impeached or rehabilitated—but still there is a big difference, because the polygraph evidence concerns the witness's truthfulness not in giving the current testimony but in making a prior statement (which was presumably to similar effect).

¶ **19.52:** (a) Should polygraph evidence be rejected in general on the grounds that, even if it assists in the search for truth, it is an unacceptable usurpation of the factfinding function of the jury?

(b) Assume polygraph evidence develops to the point at which it can be determined with reasonable certainty that it is extremely unlikely in a given case that if the subject is telling the truth a properly qualified polygraph examiner will nevertheless determine that he is lying. Now assume also that Damon, accused by his employer of embezzlement, consents to take a lie detector test, on the understanding that if he does not consent he will be fired. There is no stipulation as to admissibility should the matter be a subject of litigation. The test is administered by a properly qualified examiner, who determines that Damon is lying in denying embezzlement. Damon is prosecuted for embezzlement. Should the prosecutor be allowed to introduce the examiner's testimony about the test,

(i)   as part of her case-in-chief?

(ii)   in rebuttal, if Damon takes the stand and testifies that he did not commit the crime?

¶ **19.53:** Scheffer, a serviceman, was tried in an armed forces court on drug charges, among others. Despite a positive urine sample for methamphetamine, he denied "knowingly" ingesting drugs at any time in the five-week period leading up to the drug test. A polygraph examination conducted by the Air Force's Office of Special Investigations concluded that he was not dissembling in making this statement. Scheffer made a motion to be allowed to lay a foundation for the admissibility of the polygraph, but the judge denied this on the basis of a categorical rule, Military R. Evid. 707, barring the use of lie detector evidence. In closing argument, the prosecuting attorney argued, "He lies. He lies at every opportunity he gets and he has no credibility. Don't believe him." Should Scheffer be entitled to any relief on appeal on constitutional grounds? *See United States v. Scheffer*, 523 U.S. 303 (1998) (holding in the negative, over dissent by Stevens, J.).[56]

---

[56] For useful surveys of the history, law and science regarding polygraph evidence, see, e.g., 5 David L. Faigman et al., *Modern Scientific Evidence: The Law and Science of Expert Testimony* ch. 38 (2015–16 ed.); 1 Paul C. Giannelli et al., *Scientific Evidence* ch. 8 (5th ed. 2012); James R. McCall, *The Personhood Argument Against Polygraph Evidence, or "Even if the Polygraph Really Works, Will Courts Admit the Results?"*, 49 Hastings L.J. 925 (1998); Edward J. Imwinkelried & James R. McCall, *Issues Once Moot: The Other Evidentiary Objections to the Admission of Exculpatory Polygraph Examinations*, 32 Wake Forest L.Rev. 1045, 1064 (1997).

PART IV

FURTHER STRUCTURAL AND PROCEDURAL CONSIDERATIONS
∎ ∎ ∎

CHAPTER 20

THE CHILD OBSERVER

■ ■ ■

Additional Reading: McCormick, ch. 7, § 62; Mueller & Kirkpatrick, §§ 6.3, 8.82

We take up in this chapter a problem that we have postponed til now because it is complex and important and interweaves several issues that we have addressed throughout the book: How should courts treat reports made by children? Such reports, given as testimony at trial or by other means, have gained in importance in recent years. A large part of the reason is the increased recognition of the widespread occurrence of child sexual abuse and increased inclination to prosecute physical as well as sexual abuse of children. Often the child and the accused are the only persons who were present at the scene of the alleged crime. But children, at least very young ones, may be weak and vulnerable witnesses. We focus here on three basic questions. First is the competence question: *May* the child testify at trial? Second is a procedural question: Assuming the child testifies at trial, how should the testimony be given? And finally: Does the child *have to* testify at trial, or are there other means by which her observations may be presented to the jury?

A. COMPETENCE: MAY THE CHILD TESTIFY?

The common law approach to child witnesses was focused largely on the oath requirement. Children of insufficient maturity were considered unable to understand the oath and so unable to give formal testimony. Interestingly, though, it appears to have been common practice until late in the eighteenth century to hear the statements of children too young to take an oath. Such statements could not in themselves support a criminal conviction; they needed corroboration. The law rigidified in one sense as the result of the 1779 decision of *King v. Brasier*, which held that, though there was no given age below which children were incompetent to testify, children's testimony could not be heard without oath.[1] Early in the twentieth century, many states imposed rules of presumptive incompetency—that is, below a given age, such as 12, the child was

---

[1] Leach 199, 168 E.R. 202 (1779). *Brasier*, discussed later in this chapter, is also addressed at length in Thomas D. Lyon & Raymond LaMagna, *The History of Children's Hearsay: From Old Bailey to Post-Davis*, 82 Ind. L.J. 1029 (2007).

presumed incompetent to testify, and could do so only if the court determined that she in fact was of sufficient maturity to understand the obligation of the oath.[2]

Recently the trend has been toward the elimination, or at least the weakening, of any competency requirement for child witnesses. At one extreme are states that, generally on the basis of recent statutes, treat all children as competent to testify, without the need for any inquiry into truth-telling ability.

Interestingly, despite the general rule of competence prescribed by FRE 601, federal law does not quite go to this extreme. A provision of the Crime Control Act of 1990, 18 U.S.C. § 3509(c), creates a presumption of competence and strictly limits to "compelling" cases the circumstances in which a competence hearing may be held; the implication is that such a compelling case is conceivable but rare. Many judges—including federal judges, operating under FRE 603—still inquire into a child's ability to understand the oath or an equivalent assertion. Typically, the judge tries to determine by gentle questions whether the child understands the difference between truth and make-believe and whether she understands that she must now tell the truth—and then almost always admits the testimony, its weight to be assessed by the jury. It appears that in many jurisdictions this inquiry is, as Rule 603 suggests, oriented toward trying to encourage truth-telling more than toward screening out incompetent witnesses.

Finally, some states continue to allow a full inquiry into the child's truth-telling ability, including not only her sense of obligation but also her perceptual ability. But even in these states the inquiry seems to be a light one, with the child usually—but not always!—allowed to testify.[3]

One interesting idea is to try to conduct the inquiry by presenting the child witness with a series of pictures portraying an object and two children describing that object, one accurately and the other inaccurately, in "talk bubbles." If the child witness correctly identifies the accurate description in a series of pictures, this can give us some confidence that she understands what the truth is.[4] The technique also avoids excessive reliance on verbalization, and it can minimize motivational difficulties,

---

[2] 1 John E.B. Myers, *Myers on Evidence in Child, Domestic, and Elder Abuse Cases* § 2.04 (2005).

[3] *See* Lucy S. McGough, *Child Witnesses: Fragile Voices in the American Legal System* 99–105 (1994); 1 Myers, *supra*, § 3.1, at 203–04 nn. 3, 4 (citing cases); *cf.* Thomas D. Lyon, *Child Witnesses and the Oath: Empirical Evidence*, 73 S. Cal. L. Rev.1017 (2000). Lyon indicates that competency of a child witness is frequently an issue in child sex abuse cases, but he does not present evidence supporting the proposition that children are actually frequently held incompetent. An important recent case in which the child was held incompetent to testify at trial is Ohio v. Clark, 135 S.Ct. 2173 (2015), discussed later in this chapter.

[4] Lyon, *supra*.

such as the difficulty of the child identifying herself as a liar, that can arise when "Would you be telling the truth if you said . . . "questions are posed. On the other end, this technique may ask the wrong question, because what we really want to know is not whether the child understands lying in the abstract but to what extent *she* will feel compunction about lying in this particular case.

Much recent research has emphasized that children have the capacities necessary for truth-telling. They perceive, they remember, they understand an obligation to tell the truth (though not necessarily the consequences to others of a lie), and, within their limits, they communicate—not perfectly, of course, but accurately enough, in many cases, to make their statements worth listening to.[5]

On the other hand, children as a group are more susceptible to fading memories and to truth-distorting suggestions than are adults.[6] Moreover, we must remember that it is not only the child's direct testimony that is at stake: Cross-examination, the principal technique on which we rely for ascertaining false testimony by adult witnesses, may be much less effective, and even less acceptable, in the case of child witnesses.[7] Indeed, lawyers often find it excruciatingly difficult and frustrating to cross-examine a child witness.

¶ 20.1: To what extent do you agree with each of the following?

(a) "There shouldn't be any competency requirement for children. Sure, they may be reliability risks, but all evidence poses reliability risks; if admissible evidence were uniformly reliable, we wouldn't have much need for trials. If the child doesn't understand the obligation to tell the truth, that doesn't mean that her statements are worthless, and they should be admitted for what they are worth."[8]

(b) "It's important to retain some sort of competency inquiry. The simple fact is that children are not generally as good witnesses as adults, and it is more difficult in the litigating

---

[5] 1 Myers, *supra*, §§ 1.02[B], 2.06, 2.0, 2.14; John R. Spencer & Rhona H. Flin, *The Evidence of Children: The Law and the Psychology* 54, 285–336 (2d ed. 1993).

[6] 1 Myers, *supra*, §§ 1.02[C], 1.07–13; McGough, *supra*, at 52–74. On the research findings and their applicability to the real world, see the following exchange: Thomas D. Lyon, *The New Wave in Children's Suggestibility Research: A Critique*, 84 Cornell L. Rev. 1004 (1999); Stephen J.Ceci & Richard D. Friedman, *The Suggestibility of Children: Scientific Research and Legal Implications*, 86 Cornell L. Rev. 1 (2000); Thomas D. Lyon, *Applying Suggestibility Research to the Real World: the Case of Repeated Questions*, 65 Law & Contemp. Probs. 97 (2002).

[7] *E.g.*, McGough, *supra*, at 107–08.

[8] Cf. People v. District Court, 791 P.2d 682 (Colo.1990) ("[A] child need not be able to understand what it means to take an oath to tell the truth and need not be able to explain what it means to tell the truth in order to be judged competent to testify. . . .").

context to ascertain their false statements. It's important to
attempt to identify the reliability risks that a child's testimony
poses and, if possible, try to minimize them."[9]

(c) "We shouldn't make very young children trial witnesses
at all. Being a witness requires understanding of the gravity of
the potential consequences of one's statement, and very young
children lack the cognitive development necessary for that
understanding. Moreover, testifying is an ordeal that we impose
as a civic responsibility on members of the community, and
young children should not have to bear that responsibility.
Evidence of the statement of a very young child, if more
probative than prejudicial, should be admitted without the child
having to come to court or go through an oath-like procedure or
face cross-examination. But the adverse party should have an
opportunity to examine the child—not through a lawyer but
through a qualified forensic examiner, operating under a
carefully controlled protocol.[10]

It is important to recognize that vulnerability of a child to suggestive
questioning in court is only the tip of the iceberg. By the time a child has
testified in court, she has almost certainly been interviewed about her
story, probably repeatedly, by people who were previously strangers to
her. In recent years, there has been a great deal of research on the
suggestibility of children in interviews. Much of this research indicates
that suggestiveness on the part of the interviewer, some of it quite subtle
and unconscious, can lead to inaccurate recollections by the child.[11]
Whether this problem is as great in the context of allegations of sexual
abuse as in laboratory experiments may be difficult to know, but it is
nevertheless a serious concern.

The decision of the New Jersey Supreme Court in the notorious case
of Kelly Michaels, a nursery school teacher accused of bizarre acts of

---

[9] Cf. McGough, *supra*, at 107–11 (recommending the retention of a competency
requirement for child witnesses to assess reliability risks).

[10] *See* Richard D. Friedman & Stephen J. Ceci, *The Child Quasi Witness*, 82 U.Chi. L. Rev.
89 (2015); Sherman J. Clark, *An Accuser-Obligation Approach to the Confrontation Clause*, 81
Neb. L. Rev. 1258, 1280–85 (2003).

[11] See, e.g., in addition to the exchange between Lyon and Ceci & Friedman, *supra*,
Gabrielle F. Principe, et al., *Effects of mothers' conversation style and receipt of misinformation
on children's event reports*, 28 Cognitive Devel. 260 (2013); Heather L. Price & Deborah A.
Connolly, *Suggestibility effects persist after one year in children who experienced a single or
repeated event*, 2 J. Appl. Res. Memory & Cognition 89 (2013); Jennifer M. Schaaf, et al.,
Children's false memory and true disclosure in the face of repeated questions, 100 J. Exp. Child
Psych. 157 (2008); Amye R. Warren & Lucy S. McGough, *Research on Children's Suggestibility:
Implications for the Investigative Interview*, in Bette L. Bottoms & Gail S. Goodman, eds.,
International Perspectives on Child Abuse and Children's Testimony (1996), 12; State v.
Michaels, 136 N.J. 299, 307–12, 642 A.2d 1372, 1376–79 (1994) (finding a consensus "that the
use of coercive or highly suggestive interrogation techniques can create a significant risk that the
interrogation itself will distort the child's recollection of events").

sexual abuse, provides a catalogue of interview errors. *State v. Michaels,* 136 N.J. 299, 313–15, 321, 324–35, 642 A.2d 1372, 1379–80, 1383, 1385–92 (1994). The interviewers were investigators with the prosecutor's office and the state's Division of Youth and Family Services who apparently had not been trained in techniques of interviewing very young children. They failed to record or document some of the early interview sessions. They approached the interviews on the premise that Kelly had committed sexual abuse, and made that assumption clear to the children, in part by using extremely leading, suggestive questions. They told the children that other kids had told about the "bad things" Kelly had done, and asked the children to help keep her in jail. They negatively reinforced answers they regarded as unhelpful (ignoring the answer, for example, or telling the child to stop acting like a baby) and positively reinforced answers that seemed helpful. To get the answers they wanted, they used multiple interviews, persistent repetition, mild threats ("I'd hate having to tell your friends that you didn't want to help them"), cajolery, and bribery ("Tell me what Kelly did to your hiney and then you can go.").

After a 9-month trial, centered on the testimony of the children, Michaels was convicted of sexual assault and other crimes, 115 counts in all. But the appellate court unanimously reversed and the state supreme court unanimously affirmed that decision. The defense had offered a basis for believing that the children's statements were the product of coercive or suggestive techniques. Therefore, while recognizing that "assessing reliability as a predicate to the admission of in-court testimony is a somewhat extraordinary step," the court held that a hearing was necessary to determine whether those improprieties "so infected the ability of the children to recall the alleged abusive events that their pretrial statements and in-court testimony based on that recollection are unreliable and should not be admitted into evidence." 299 N.J. at 315–16, 642 A.2d at 1380–81. The prosecutor eventually decided not to make the attempt, and dropped the charges.[12]

¶ **20.2:** Was the decision of the supreme court correct? Empirical research suggests that "[o]nce children have been exposed to and have incorporated misleading information or interpretations from interviewers into their memories, the implanted false portions may be extremely difficult to uproot."[13] But rather than excluding the testimony because of this taint, shouldn't it be left to the jury to evaluate the strengths and weaknesses of the testimony—and if not, why not?

[handwritten margin notes:] No, need to discourage this type of investigation. Keep it out.

Hard, hard to cross-exam kids, hard for jury to weigh evidence

---

[12] For an extensive account of the case, arguing that there was substantial evidence of Michaels' guilt on some charges and that suggestive questioning played less of a role in reaching the verdict than is generally believed, see Ross E. Cheit, *The Witch-Hunt Narrative: Politics, Psychology, and the Sexual Abuse of Children* (2014), at 203–82.

[13] Warren & McGough, *Research on Children's Suggestibility, supra,* at 14.

¶ **20.3:** (a) Rhea is accused of aggravated sexual assault of his daughter, Kay, who was approximately 2½ at the time. The alleged abuse occurred several months before trial. Three weeks after the alleged abuse, Kay was interviewed by a child protection specialist of the Department of Human Resources. During the interview, which was videotaped, she denied several suggestions that her father had acted improperly, but nodded in agreement to the question, "Did daddy make you put his tee-tee in your mouth?" When asked, "What did he tell you to do?" she responded, "I was laying down there [in the bathtub] and sucking it." At a competency hearing at trial seven months after the alleged abuse, Kay has said she doesn't know what the truth is, or a lie or a fib, or what the difference is between telling the truth and telling a story, and has given no indication she understands an obligation to tell the truth. Should Kay be allowed to testify?[14]

(b) Would your response differ if instead the case concerns a bank robbery, in which Kay was not injured, and she is the only witness who says she can identify the robber? What if there are three adult witnesses as well who identify the defendant as the robber? What if it is a civil auto negligence case?

¶ **20.4:** Daniel Webb is accused of molesting his daughter, who was approximately 18 months old at the time, while he had sole custody of her. The prosecution presents medical testimony to the effect that the child suffered anal tears indicative of abuse, but the defense presents contrary medical evidence. Daniel's ex-wife, Cindy, testifies that in the evening when she took the child back from Daniel's custody, she gave her a bath, and that on being lowered into the water the child said, "Ow, bum." After the bath, Cindy says, she examined the girl's anus and found it was red and swollen, as if she had hemorrhoids. During that examination, the child said, "Ow bum daddy." Assume there is no hearsay problem with admissibility of this testimony, should it be excluded as unduly prejudicial? Assuming it is admissible, is there enough evidence to warrant conviction?[15]

[Handwritten margin notes: "just use the video"; "7 months later is an eternity for a 2.5 yo!"; "no, but not bc she's not competent, bc it's unduly traumatic and the video from before is more reliable than testimony now (but, video is prejudicial) (... hearsay)"; "yes, not unwarranted"; "no, not best evidence"; "sure, why not"; "no, jury can hear it"; "no, lots of reasons a kid might say that"]

---

[14] *See* Rhea v. State, 705 S.W.2d 165 (Tex. App. 1985) (holding, over dissent, that trial court erred in determining that the child was competent); *cf.* State v. Hunsaker, 39 Wash. App. 489, 693 P.2d 724 (1984) (allowing admission of testimony, concerning abuse that occurred a year before, given by a 3 1/2-year-old girl who correctly recited her age, birthdate (including year), and address, and sang a stanza of "Three Little Monkeys" to boot).

[15] *See* State v. Webb, 779 P.2d 1108 (Utah 1989) (holding evidence inadmissible and insufficient).

B. PROCEDURES: HOW SHOULD
THE CHILD TESTIFY?

Along with the trend in recent years toward greater receptivity to child witnesses has been a tendency to develop procedures and practices that will enable children to give their testimony and be more comfortable, more likely to testify communicatively, and less likely to be traumatized by the experience.

One approach is to have the child testify formally at trial, but under special procedures that do not put the child in position where she can see the accused. In *Coy v. Iowa*, 487 U.S. 1012 (1988), the trial court placed a large screen between the accused and the witness stand; adjusting the lights allowed him to see the accusing witnesses dimly, but they could not see him at all. By a 6–2 vote, the Supreme Court held that this rather primitive and suggestive procedure was impermissible, at least in the circumstances of that case. Beginning in the 1980s, though, legislatures established far more sophisticated procedures. A substantial majority of states, and Congress also, have adopted a wide variety of procedures allowing the testimony of child witnesses to be presented in some circumstances on videotape or by closed circuit television, or either.[16]

If the only difference from the usual procedure for taking testimony is that the venue and perhaps the timing of the child's testimony have been shifted, but the defendant is allowed to attend and counsel may cross-examine, then the constitutional problems are relatively slight. It may be easier for the child to testify in a comfortable deposition room, with relatively few people around, than in an open courtroom. On the other hand, such a procedure does not relieve the child of what may be the most intimidating aspect of testifying—the need to state her accusations in front of the defendant, of whom she might be terrified.[17]

Thus, often under the new statutes, when the child's testimony is taken in advance of trial on videotape, the defendant is excluded from the deposition room. And when the child testifies during trial but by closed-circuit television from another room, the usual procedure is that the defendant watches from the courtroom, in electronic communication with his lawyer. Some statutes provide for one-way closed circuit television

---

[16] *See* Robert G. Marks, Note, *Should We Believe the People Who Believe the Children? The Need for a New Sexual Abuse Tender Years Hearsay Exception Statute*, 32 Harv. J. on Legis. 207, 220 & nn. 67, 68 (1995) (compiling state statutes). The federal statute, passed as part of the Crime Control Act of 1990 and codified at 18 U.S.C. § 3509(b), authorizes testimony by either videotaped deposition or two-way closed circuit television, with the image of the defendant being transmitted into the room where the child is testifying.

[17] *Cf.* Lucy S. McGough, *Child Witnesses* 196–97 (1994) (saying that to remove the "lesser anxiety about courtroom formality" but to retain cross-examination and lawyers' jargon "would be like finding a child closeted in a room with a bear, a snake and a rabbit and removing the rabbit to protect the child").

(the defendant, along with others in the courtroom, can see the witness but she cannot see them) and others provide for two-way transmission (the witness can see the image of the defendant). That the defendant is not in the room when the child testifies offers some advantages—but is it constitutional?

The Supreme Court addressed that question in *Maryland v. Craig*, 497 U.S. 836 (1990). There, the child testified in a room with only the prosecutor and defense counsel present. The defendant, judge, and jury watched over one-way closed circuit television, the defendant could communicate electronically with her counsel, and both counsel could communicate with the judge. By a 5–4 vote, the Court held that, "if the State makes an adequate showing of necessity, the state interest in protecting child witnesses from the trauma of testifying in a child abuse case is sufficiently important to justify the use of [such] a special procedure," despite the fact that it denies "face-to-face confrontation." *Id.* at 855.[18] But the required finding of necessity, cautioned the Court, must be "case-specific": The trial court must hear evidence and decide whether use of the special procedure is "necessary to protect the welfare of the particular child witness who seeks to testify." *Id.* Also, to justify the "[d]enial of face-to-face confrontation," the state must show that "it is the presence of the defendant that causes the trauma"; more generalized courtroom trauma could be addressed by having the child "testify in less intimidating surroundings, albeit with the defendant present." *Id.* at 856. Without resolving the rather intractable question of just how traumatic the defendant's presence would have to be for the special procedure to be invoked, the Court said that it would have to be "more than *de minimis*." *Id.*

Craig was decided before *Crawford*. The results of the two cases are not incompatible: *Crawford* concerns when a person must be made a trial witness, and *Craig* concerns how that is done. But the weigh-everything-in the-balance approach to the confrontation right of *Craig* is very much at odds with the categorical, bright-line approach of *Crawford*. (Justice O'Connor, a balancer, wrote the majority opinion in *Craig* and was one of

---

[18] The Court's repeated use of the phrase "face-to-face confrontation" is rather curious, for it implicitly assumes that there is some other form of confrontation. Note Justice Scalia's barb in dissent, joined by Justices Brennan, Stevens, and Marshall, that the Maryland procedure "gives the defendant virtually everything the Confrontation Clause guarantees (everything, that is, except confrontation)." *Id.* at 370. Later, a couple of years before *Crawford*, Justice Scalia won a partial victory in the same realm. An amendment to Fed. R. Crim. P. 26 was proposed, relying on *Craig*, that would have allowed witnesses, adults as well as children, to testify from a remote location in unusual circumstances when they could not be brought to trial. In an unusual move, the Court refused to transmit the proposal to Congress. Justice Scalia explained the action in a statement that featured the aphorism, "Virtual confrontation might be sufficient to protect virtual constitutional rights; I doubt whether it is sufficient to protect real ones." Statement, 535 U.S. 1159, 1160 (2002). *See generally* Richard D. Friedman, *Remote Testimony*, 35 U. Mich. J. L. Ref. 695 (2002).

the two justices who did not join in the majority opinion in *Crawford*;
Justice Scalia, a bright-line guy, dissented bitterly in *Craig* and wrote the
majority opinion in *Crawford*.) But so far the Supreme Court has shown
no disposition to disturb *Craig*. It must be emphasized that *Craig* only
sets constitutional outer bounds. A state court is free, as a matter of its
own state constitutional law, to refuse to follow *Craig* and to reject
procedures that allow the child witness to testify without the defendant
being present. At least two state supreme courts have done so—but one of
them has subsequently been effectively overruled by constitutional
amendment.[19]

Let's consider the purposes possibly served by a procedure such as
the one involved in *Craig*. One aim is *to prevent longterm trauma to the
child created by testifying in front of the defendant*. That is clearly a valid
and significant purpose. But it poses several problems as well.

¶ **20.5:** (a) Do you believe longterm trauma to the child from
testifying in front of the defendant—or simply from being asked
to testify in front of him—is likely?[20]

(b) Whether or not children frequently suffer longterm
trauma from testifying face-to-face with the defendant, it is clear

---

[19] Commonwealth v. Ludwig, 527 Pa. 472, 594 A.2d 281 (1991); Commonwealth v. Louden,
536 Pa. 180, 638 A.2d 953 (1994); Brady v. Indiana, 575 N.E.2d 981 (Ind.1991). Interestingly,
both the Pennsylvania and Indiana constitutions guaranteed the defendant the right to be
brought "face to face" with the witnesses against him. But, other courts, despite similar language
in their constitutions, have followed the result in *Craig*. *E.g.*, State v. Foster, 81 Wash. App. 444,
915 P.2d 520 (1996). In 1995, Art. I, § 9 of the Pennsylvania Constitution was amended to
substitute the language of the federal Confrontation Clause—"be confronted with the witnesses
against him"—for the prior language, "meet the witnesses face to face." And for good measure,
the amendment added specific authorization for statutory provision of testimony by child
witnesses in criminal cases through videotaped depositions or closed-circuit television.

[20] The empirical evidence does not yet support this conclusion. An important study of the
effects on children of testifying in court is Gail S. Goodman et al., *Testifying in Criminal Court:
Emotional Effects on Child Sexual Assault Victims*, 57 Monographs of the Society for Research in
Child Development, No. 5, Serial No. 229 (1992). It found that a group of children who testified
and a control group of children who did not showed approximately the same behavioral
adjustment three months after the children testified. By seven months post-testimony, however,
those who did testify showed considerably less improvement than the control group, but this
differential narrowed over time: "[B]y the time the cases were resolved, the behavioral
adjustment of most, but not all, children who testified was similar to that of children who did not
take the stand. The general course for these children, as for the control children, was gradual
improvement." *Id.* at 60–62, 114–15. Testifying in front of the defendant clearly added to the
stress for the child witnesses—but, interestingly, this anxiety added to the child's perceived
credibility. *Id.* at 94–95.

For a useful summary of empirical research on the effects of testifying on child witnesses,
see Myers, *Evidence in Child, Domestic and Elder Abuse Cases*, *supra*, § 3.01. Myers concludes,
"Despite the difficulty, most children are able to testify in the traditional manner, especially
when they are prepared and supported through the process . . . In the final analysis, although
testifying is difficult, children weather the storm." It appears that for some children the effect of
testifying is therapeutic, giving them a sense of empowerment. *See also, e.g.*, Desmond K.
Runyan, *The Emotional Impact of Societal Intervention into Child Abuse*, in Bette L. Bottoms &
Gail S. Goodman, eds., *Child Victims, Child Witnesses: Understanding and Improving Testimony*
(1993), at 263, 270 (suggesting a surprising "salutary effect of juvenile court testimony").

that many find the confrontation extremely stressful.[21] Is the probability of temporary stress enough to justify allowing the child to testify outside the accused's presence?

(c) Assuming that testifying in the defendant's presence would likely cause longterm trauma to the child, should that consideration override the defendant's ordinary constitutional right to be present during the accuser's testimony? Put another way, is there any reason why a child witness should be treated differently, with respect to the presence of the defendant, from an adult witness? In many situations, adults find testifying difficult and even traumatic and intimidating, and so sometimes adult accusers decline to press charges or to testify; consequently, though the prosecution could compel their testimony, many potential charges are not pursued. Should the same principle be followed when the accuser is a child? If (hypothetically) the presence of the defendant during the child's testimony would add significantly to the child's trauma but also to the accuracy of her testimony, should testimony in the defendant's absence be allowed? *Cf.* McGough, *Child Witnesses*, *supra*, at 165 (answering no: "The only 'necessity' that could justify an abridgment of the constitutional right of the accused is that the truth-finding function of a trial cannot otherwise be accomplished."). If the answer is affirmative, should an adult who was allegedly the victim of a rape or violent assault therefore be allowed to testify out of the presence of the defendant?

Another purpose is *to improve the quality of the child's testimony*. Again, this is unquestionably a valid purpose. The principal concern is that the presence of the defendant will impair the child's ability to communicate. Empirical studies seem to show rather clearly that this often happens—and it is just as clear that often it does not.[22] Bear in mind that, as emphasized in *Coy*, inhibition from confrontation cuts both ways: A false accusation as well as a true one may be inhibited, and indeed part of the purpose of the Confrontation Clause may have been to inhibit false accusations.

¶ 20.6: (a) Do you believe the interest in improving the quality of the witness's testimony can validly be weighed against the defendant's ordinary right to be present when his accuser testifies?

---

[21] *E.g.*, Rhona H. Flin, *Hearing and Testing Children's Evidence*, in Goodman & Bottoms, eds., *Child Victims, Child Witnesses, supra*, 279, at 289.

[22] *See, e.g.*, McGough, *supra*, at 165–67.

(b) If the court determines as a threshold matter that the accused abused the child and threatened to harm her if she told anyone about it, and that this explains why the child is intimidated from testifying in his presence, should the defendant be deemed to have forfeited the right to be present when the child testifies?[23] What if the accused made no threats, but the court determines as a threshold matter that the accused abused the child and that the abuse has intimidated the child from testifying in his presence?

(c) In the case of a child witness, do you believe that the presence of an accused is more likely to inhibit a true accusation than a false one? Sufficiently more likely to justify over-riding the defendant's ordinary right to be present?

(d) To the extent the inhibiting effect is the concern, should the trial court first require that the witness be asked to testify in the accused's presence and only then, to the extent she is unable to testify fully with him there, be allowed to testify in his absence?

Craig calls for a case-by-case determination of whether a special procedure is necessary. So far, it appears that if the prosecutor asks for such a procedure—and most try to avoid it—she will usually get it. Some courts hold extended hearings and make careful findings before allowing the child's testimony to be taken without the defendant being face to face, and others are more lax, but the result is usually the same.[24] There have been some rather glaring cases in which courts have allowed a *Craig*-type procedure notwithstanding that there was little or no evidence that the witness would be traumatized by being asked to testify in front of the defendant, but the Supreme Court has not indicated any interest in returning to the area.[25]

---

[23] *Compare* State v. Sheppard, 197 N.J.Super. 411, 435–42, 484 A.2d 1330, 1345–48 (N.J.Super.L.1984) (applying forfeiture theory); State v. Jarzbek, 204 Conn. 683, 699, 529 A.2d 1245, 1253 (1987), *cert. denied*, 484 U.S. 1061 (1988) (declining in dictum to do so).

[24] *Compare, e.g.,* Reutter v. State, 886 P.2d 1298 (Alaska App.1994) (two-day hearing held by trial court), *with* Lively v. State, 940 S.W.2d 380 (Tex. App.1997), and State v. Street, 202 Wis.2d 533, 551, 551 N.W.2d 830, 839 (Ct. Apps. 1996) (both excusing absence of particular findings by trial judge).

[25] Note two cases in which the Supreme Court, over dissent by Justices Scalia and Thomas, denied petitions for *certiorari* from decisions that allowed electronically transmitted testimony despite relatively weak showings of need. Marx v. Texas, 528 U.S. 1034 (1999) (child witness who had been allegedly abused by defendant but who, so far as could be told, was unlikely to be traumatized by giving her testimony, which concerned only abuse of another child; case below, Marx v. State, 987 S.W.2d 577 (1999)); Danner v. Kentucky, 525 U.S. 1010 (1998) (witness, 15 years old, said she was not afraid of the defendant, but "just can't be near him" and did not know whether she would be able to testify if there were breaks in the proceeding; case below, Danner v.Commonwealth, 963 S.W.2d 632 (1998)).

¶ **20.7:** Suppose that you are prosecuting a child sexual abuse case in a jurisdiction that has adopted a procedure identical to the one in *Craig*.

(a) What factors will you consider in determining whether you want to invoke the closed-circuit procedure, as opposed to presenting the live testimony of the child in courtroom?[26]

(b) If you do decide to present the child as a witness in the courtroom, what will you do to try to minimize the possibility that she will suffer trauma, as a result of the presence of the defendant or more generally of the surroundings, and that she will be unable to testify fully?[27]

(c) Assuming you decide to invoke the special procedure, what kind of evidence will you attempt to present to a conscientious judge to demonstrate that use of the procedure in this case is permissible and appropriate? If the court expresses concern that the defendant will be prejudiced by the fact that the jury will see the witness on television and not in person, what standards can you propose to provide the court with some assurance?

If the child, having made an earlier statement describing abuse, testifies at trial but fails to repeat the allegation at trial, the prosecutor will want to present the prior statement. Bear in mind that if a witness testifies at trial, the Confrontation Clause, at least as currently interpreted, poses no obstacle to admission of a prior statement made by the child—but ordinary hearsay law might. Indeed, this was the setting in which the Supreme Court's decision in the *Tome* case, presented before ¶ 10.24, gave a constrained interpretation of Fed. R. Evid. 801(d)(1)(B). *Tome*, of course, is not binding on the states.

¶ **20.8:** Recall Rhea's case, from ¶ 20.3: In a video-recorded interview conducted by a child protection specialist, his daughter Kay, age 2½, made a statement arguably asserting that Rhea

---

[26] *Cf.* Margaret Bull Kovera & Eugene Borgida, *Children on the Witness Stand: The Use of Expert Testimony and Other Procedural Innovations in U.S. Child Sexual Abuse Trials*, in Bette L. Bottoms & Gail S. Goodman, eds., *International Perspectives on Child Abuse and Children's Testimony* (1996) ["International Perspectives"], 201, at 215–16 (summarizing research indicating that juries are more likely to reach guilty verdicts when children testify live rather than on videotape).

[27] *See, e.g.,* Kovera & Borgida, *Children on the Witness Stand, supra,* at 213 (importance of preparing the child witness); John E.B. Myers, *A Decade of International Reform to Accommodate Child Witnesses: Steps Toward a Child Witness Code,* in *International Perspectives, supra,* 221, at 245–56 (proposing various accommodations, including a separate waiting area for children, rearrangement of the courtroom, frequent recesses, and orders prohibiting anybody from entering or leaving the courtroom while the child is testifying); Karen J. Saywitz & Lynn Snyder, *Improving Children's Testimony with Preparation,* Goodman & Bottoms, eds., *Child Victims, Child Witnesses, supra,* at 117.

had abused her several weeks before. Now assume that Kay has been allowed to testify at trial several months later. She has denied that Rhea did anything wrong to her and has said she remembers nothing about the prior interview. Should the videotape be admitted?

C. MUST THE CHILD TESTIFY SUBJECT TO CROSS-EXAMINATION?

Maryland v. Craig allows the child, in some cases, to testify without confronting the accused. But it still anticipates that if the child testifies at trial, or in a deposition taken to preserve her testimony, she will have to be subject to cross-examination. This raises the question of whether the prosecution can introduce evidence of a statement that the child made without having to produce her for testimony, subject to cross-examination, either at trial or in a deposition.

At the outset, note that, even if otherwise the confrontation right or the rule against hearsay would bar introduction of the prior statement without the accused having an opportunity for cross-examination, if the child is deemed unavailable to testify it may be that the accused will be held to have forfeited any objection to use of the prior statement.

¶ 20.9: Suppose William is accused of sexually molesting Silvia, a young girl. Shortly after the incident, Silvia made a statement to a police officer describing sexual abuse by William. But at the time of trial, Silvia says she will not testify, even if William is in another room. The prosecution offers the prior statement into evidence, and William objects on confrontation and hearsay grounds. The prosecution contends that William should be held to have forfeited the objection. Under what circumstances, if any, should this argument prevail?

Forfeiture cannot be presumed, and so prosecutors search for a broader principle that might allow them to introduce a child's prior statement without bringing the child in to testify under cross-examination. Beginning in the 1980s and usually through legislation, many jurisdictions created "tender years" exceptions to the rule against hearsay. These generally provide that in some circumstances an out-of-court statement made by a child under a prescribed age (often ten or twelve) is exempt from the rule against hearsay. Often they require that, if the child does not testify at trial, she be unavailable to do so and that the court determine that the statement is supported by indicia of reliability. These requirements reflect the conception of the pre-*Crawford* era in which they were adopted. Given *Crawford*, presumably some applications of the exceptions are unconstitutional.

¶ **20.10:** Suppose that a state has a "tender years" exception applicable to a statement (1) made by a child twelve years or under, (2) taken by a social worker or other trained professional, (3) avoiding undue use of suggestive questions and (4) recorded on videotape; the exception does not require presence of the defendant or his lawyer.

(a) Should use at trial of a statement made by a 10-year-old child taken in accordance with this exception and made to an interviewer with a child protection agency be considered testimonial for purposes of the Confrontation Clause? What if it were made to a forensic interviewer affiliated with the police department?

(b) Assuming that the statement is not deemed testimonial, should such a statute be limited so that it would allow such a statement to be admitted

(i) only if the child is unable to testify at trial because of a particularized finding that to do so would be too traumatic?

(ii) only if the child is able to testify, so that if the defendant wishes he can call the child as a witness at trial and examine her after the videotape is presented?

(iii) only if the child testifies in court that she remembers making the statement and that it was accurate, with the accused being afforded the opportunity, after the videotape is shown, to cross-examine the child about her honesty and her ability to observe and report accurately the matters described in the videotaped statement? (Note that this procedure is proposed and defended by McGough, *Child Witnesses, supra,* at 197–228, 271–74.)

Presumably some out-of-court statements by children are barred by the Confrontation Clause, but others are not even though they would be if they had been made by an adult or older child under similar circumstances. Let's consider *Ohio v. Clark,* 135 S.Ct. 2173 (2015), the first post-*Crawford* case in which the Supreme Court addressed this problem.

L.P., a boy not quite three and a half, showed up at his Cleveland preschool one day with welts on his face. The staff, suspecting abuse, asked him what happened. L.P. appeared bewildered and at first denied that anything had happened, then he said he fell, and finally he said something on the order of "Dee did it"; Darius Clark, the boyfriend of L.P.'s mother, was known as Dee. Clark was tried on child-abuse charges. The court held L.P. incompetent to testify. But it allowed the preschool teachers to testify about what L.P. had said. Clark was convicted. The state appellate court, and then the state supreme court, held that L.P.'s statements were testimonial and so admitting them violated the Confrontation Clause. But the United States Supreme Court reversed, unanimously. Justice Alito wrote the majority opinion. Justice Scalia, joined by Justice Ginsburg, concurred only in the judgment, because he thought some of the Court's opinion gratuitously undercut *Crawford*. And Justice Thomas also concurred only in the judgment, emphasizing what he regarded as the lack of solemnity in L.P.'s statements.

The majority opinion recognized that statements to persons other than the police could raise confrontation concerns, but it asserted that "such statements are much less likely to be testimonial than statements to law enforcement officers." As for L.P.'s statements, the Court concluded that, "considering all the relevant circumstances," they "were not made with the primary purpose of creating evidence for Clark's prosecution." Rather, they "occurred in the context of an ongoing emergency involving suspected child abuse"; the preschool staff had to know who might be abusing L.P. so they could determine whether other children were at risk and whether it was safe to release him to his guardian at the end of the day. L.P. was not told that his statements might be used to punish Clark, and he gave no indication that he was aware of that possibility. The conversation was "informal and spontaneous." And L.P.'s age "fortifie[d]" this conclusion; "[s]tatements by very young children will rarely, if ever, implicate the Confrontation Clause" because it is "extremely unlikely" that a child as young as L.P. "would intend his statements to be a substitute for trial testimony."

¶ 20.11: (a) Suppose, to take a hypothetical posed by Justice Kagan at argument of the *Clark* case, Transcript at 12, that L.P. had been 13 rather than three, and a teacher at his school, noticing his bruises, had said, "I want to know what happened, but I want to tell you that I'm under a statutory reporting obligation, so everything you tell me, I'm going to tell the police, and I'm going to write down everything you tell me just so I can get the facts straight." If L.P. then said that Dee had hit him, would that statement be testimonial?

(b) Assume the answer to the question in (a) is affirmative. Is the actual case different, so that L.P.'s statement was not testimonial? If L.P.'s statement was not testimonial, why not? Is it that, though L.P. was capable of making a testimonial statement, this one wasn't? Is it because he lacks the cognitive ability to make a testimonial statement for purposes of the Confrontation Clause? *See* Richard D. Friedman & Stephen J. Ceci, *The Child Quasi Witness*, 82 U. Chi. L. Rev. 89 (2015)? Is it that the moral obligation of being a witness should not be imposed on a child so young? *See* Sherman J. Clark, *An Accuser—Obligation Approach to the Confrontation Clause*, 81 Neb. L. Rev. 1258, 1280–85 (2003). Some other factor? Are you persuaded by the *Clark* majority's reasoning as summarized above?

The *Clark* Court cited one other factor in support of its decision: It concluded that historically, at the time of the framing of the Sixth Amendment, statements by children in L.P.'s position would be admitted. The Court's historical discussion was based in large part on its analysis of the classic English case of *King v. Brasier*, 1 Leach 199, 168 E.R. 202 (K.B. 1779), mentioned near the beginning of this chapter. Brasier was charged with an assault with intent to commit a rape on the body of a child under seven years old. According to the report of the case,

> The case against the prisoner was proved by the mother of the child, and by another woman who lodged with her, to whom the child, immediately on her coming home, told all the circumstances of the injury which had been done to her: and there was no fact or circumstance to confirm the information which the child had given, except that the prisoner lodged at the very place which she had described, and that she had received some hurt, and that she, on seeing him the next day, had declared that he was the man; but she was not sworn or produced as a witness on the trial.

Brasier was convicted, but the trial judge held the judgment in abeyance while he referred to the Twelve Judges of King's Bench the question of whether the evidence was proper. The judges

> were unanimously of opinion, That no testimony whatever can be legally received except upon oath; and that an infant, though under the age of seven years, may be sworn in a criminal prosecution, provided such infant appears, on strict examination by the Court, to possess a sufficient knowledge of the nature and consequences of an oath, for there is no precise or fixed rule as to the time within which infants are excluded from giving evidence; but their admissibility depends upon the sense and reason they entertain of the danger and impiety of falsehood, which is to be collected from their answers to questions propounded to them by the Court; but if they are found incompetent to take an oath their testimony cannot be received. The Judges determined, therefore, that the evidence of the information which the infant had, given to her mother and the other witness, ought not to have been received. . . .

¶ **20.12:** Suppose the facts of *Brasier* repeated themselves today in the United States. How should the case be decided?

The *Clark* Court declared that when 18th-century courts like *Brasier* excluded statements of children, "they appeared to do so because the child should have been ruled competent to testify, not because the statements were otherwise inadmissible." But note the consequence of this assertion. L.P. was ruled incompetent to testify at trial; the defense could not have made him a witness even if it had wanted to. The Supreme Court's decision in *Clark* means that there is no Confrontation Clause obstacle to admission of his statement. In one sense, that seems clearly appropriate: L.P.'s statement was certainly probative; it is probably evidence the jury should hear. But what can we say to Clark if he says, "But I'm being convicted on the basis of a statement by a child, and I haven't had a chance to question him at all"?

I have already hinted at my solution in ¶ 20.1(c). Some very young children—I'll leave the term loose for now—should simply not be considered witnesses. The prosecution should not be allowed to present them as witnesses in court, not because what they say lacks value—it doesn't—but because they are incapable, cognitively and perhaps morally, of the act of witnessing. But that doesn't mean that evidence of their statements should be excluded. Ordinarily, it should be admitted, at least if it has not been tainted by unduly suggestive questioning, because it may be highly probative. And the accused cannot complain about a Confrontation Clause violation when this evidence if presented, any more than he can when any other evidence that is not the testimony of a witness is presented. But the accused has a valid argument that as a matter of fundamental fairness he should be allowed to *examine* the source of evidence, in this case the child. That examination should not be cross-examination by a lawyer in court, which is the procedure we use for witnesses. Rather, he should be allowed to have a qualified expert, a forensic interviewer, examine the child out of court, under a prescribed protocol to make sure the child is protected.

> ¶ 20.13: What advantages and disadvantages do you see in this system? If it were implemented, what would the purpose of the interview be? What use would the accused be able to make of it? What conditions should the protocol prescribe?

CHAPTER 21

THE REQUIRED QUANTUM OF EVIDENCE: BURDENS, PRESUMPTIONS, JUDICIAL NOTICE, AND STIPULATIONS

■ ■ ■

FRE 301, 302

Additional Reading (for §§ A–F): McCormick, ch. 36, §§ 336–344, 346–348; Mueller & Kirkpatrick, ch. 3

A. A FIRST LOOK

Most of our focus has been on individual items of evidence. Now we will look at evidence in the aggregate. This chapter asks an interrelated series of questions that might be summarized roughly in one overall inquiry: How much evidence, if any, is required for a party to prevail on a given factual issue? This is a difficult area of evidentiary law, and it has been made more difficult by the confusing statements and ambiguous terminology in many judicial opinions, statutes, and academic commentaries.

It may be impossible to clear up the confusion, but what follows is a simplified model that may offer at least a useful jumping-off point. As before in this book, we will use some symbolic notation, akin to that in probability theory. Even if you consider yourself not mathematically inclined, please try this presentation out; you will find that the concepts are not so strange, and that the notation provides a shorthand that enables us to state propositions with precision and conciseness.

In conventional notation, which we have already used in Chapter 3, $P(\mathbf{X}|\mathbf{Y},\mathbf{Z})$ means the probability of proposition $\mathbf{X}$ given propositions $\mathbf{Y}$ and $\mathbf{Z}$—that is, how probable an observer believes proposition $\mathbf{X}$ is if she assumes that propositions $\mathbf{Y}$ and $\mathbf{Z}$ are true. Recall that probabilities are expressed on a scale from 0 to 1—or, put another way, from 0% to 100%. We have also adopted the convention that $\mathbf{O}$ refers to all the facts that a juror knows about the world before any evidence is presented at trial. Thus, if **LIABLE** is the proposition that the defendant in an auto accident case is liable to the plaintiff, then $P(\mathbf{LIABLE}|\mathbf{O})$ means the juror's assessment that the defendant is liable, as made before any evidence at all is introduced. And if **PLAINTESTIFRED** is the proposition that the plaintiff has testified that the defendant collided with him after running a red light, and **DEFENTESTIFGREEN** the proposition that the defendant has testified the accident occurred the other way around, then $P(\textbf{LIABLE} \mid \textbf{PLAINTESTIFRED},$ **DEFENTESTIFGREEN, O**) represents the juror's assessment of the probability of liability after the testimony of both parties.

Now, one aspect of what we sometimes loosely call the burden of proof is the *burden of persuasion*. This means the degree to which the jury (or other factfinder) must be persuaded of a factual proposition if it is to find for a given party on the issue of whether that proposition is true. As you are probably aware, in most civil cases we ordinarily say that the burden of persuasion is on the plaintiff to prove each element of its claim by a preponderance of the evidence. In Section B of this chapter, we will cast some doubt on this broad statement, but assume for the moment that it is true. Assume also that in our simple auto negligence case the only evidence is the testimony of the two parties. In probabilistic terms, the burden of persuasion may be expressed in this way: If in the jury's view $P(\textbf{LIABLE} \mid \textbf{PLAINTESTIFRED, DEFENTESTIFGREEN, O})$ is less than or equal to 50%, the jury should find for the defendant; if it regards that probability as greater than 50%, it should find for the plaintiff. Thus, although the phrase usually used in the United States is "preponderance of the evidence," a more straightforward term is one sometimes used to explain it, "more likely than not."[1] In Figure 21.a, the burden of persuasion is represented as a simple dividing point midway on the continuum from 0% to 100%.

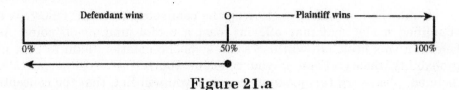

Figure 21.a

Until the jury returns its verdict, however, the judge will not know what the jury's probability assessment is.[2] Moreover, the jury's assessment will not, of course, necessarily be the same as the judge's. The judge must recognize that a reasonable jury might rank the probability either higher or lower than she would herself. But if a reasonable jury could only find one way, there is no reason to submit the case to the jury at all; instead, the judge should simply enter a directed verdict. Thus we have the *burden of production*. With respect to most issues—but not

---

[1] In other common law countries, courts often use the term "balance of probabilities" rather than "preponderance of evidence."

[2] Even then, it will presumably know only whether or not the jury thinks the burden of persuasion has been met.

nearly all, as we shall see—this burden is on the plaintiff. It means, essentially, that the plaintiff must introduce enough evidence that a reasonable jury could find that the burden of persuasion has been met.

This burden can be shown rather easily in our simple graphic representation. Let us assume again that no evidence at all has yet been presented. The judge's assessment of $P(\textbf{LIABLE}\,|\,\textbf{O})$ must be quite low; the probability that one person ran a light and collided with another, given no evidence of that at all, must be regarded as very low.[3] This assessment is represented by the **X** in Figure 21.b. (The graph is not drawn to scale; if it were, **X** would be even closer to 0%.) A reasonable jury's assessment of this probability may be somewhat lower or somewhat higher, but not by very much. What we may call the "reasonableness zone" is represented in this Figure by brackets. Notice that this zone extends from a point very close to 0% to a point only slightly to the right of **X**. The zone does not come even close to reaching the dividing point representing the plaintiff's burden of persuasion. In other words, a reasonable jury could not say that the persuasion burden has been met. And this means that the judge cannot say that the burden of production has been met.

0%   50%   100%

Figure 21.b

But now suppose that the plaintiff testifies and that the judge, while believing that the plaintiff is probably not telling the truth, also recognizes that a reasonable jury might disagree: A jury's assessment of the probability that the defendant ran the light might reasonably still be near zero (if the jury finds the plaintiff not to be a credible witness), or it might be very high (if the jury finds the plaintiff extremely persuasive), or it might be anywhere in between. The situation, in other words, is as represented in Figure 21.c.

---

[3] Of course, we may have a tendency to rate the probability significantly higher, given our knowledge that the plaintiff has brought a lawsuit alleging this to be true, but the allegation is not in itself evidence, and should not be considered in evaluating the probability of liability.

Judge Posner has taken the view that impartiality with respect to a given proposition consists of beginning consideration of the proposition with even odds that it is true. Richard A. Posner, *An Economic Approach to the Law of Evidence*, 51 STAN. L. REV. 1477, 1508, 1514 (1999). I believe that this is quite clearly incorrect, and inconsistent with the presumption of innocence. Just because someone articulates a proposition does not make it as likely to be true as to be not true. In the absence of evidence, a juror must assign very low prior odds to the proposition, "The defendant killed the victim on the date charged in the indictment." *See* Richard D. Friedman, *A Presumption of Innocence, Not of Even Odds*, 52 STAN. L. REV. 873 (2000).

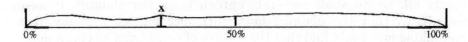

Figure 21.c

Note that if this were a bench trial—that is, if the judge were the factfinder—the judge would not find that the burden of persuasion has been met. But assuming that there is a jury, that is not the question for the judge. Rather, she must ask herself whether the *jury* could find that the plaintiff met the burden of persuasion. And in this case the answer is yes. Thus, the burden of production has been *satisfied*.

In this case, the "reasonableness zone" extends on both sides of the 50% boundary. Thus, the case is for the jurors, because they could reasonably find either way. But that will not always be so. Sometimes even after the plaintiff presents his evidence the rightward edge of the reasonableness zone does not extend beyond the 50% mark. Then the defendant should win a directed verdict motion, because the plaintiff has failed to meet his burden of production. This could happen if the plaintiff has no direct evidence to prove **LIABLE**, and the circumstantial evidence is so weak that the court decides that a juror could not reasonably infer that the element is more probable than not. Correspondingly, sometimes—more rarely—the plaintiff's evidence appears so compelling that after he closes his case even the leftward edge of the reasonableness zone extends beyond the 50% mark. That is, the court concludes that on the basis of the plaintiff's evidence even a highly skeptical but reasonable juror would have to conclude that it is more likely than not that **LIABLE** is true. In that case, the burden of production has *shifted* to the defendant; if the defendant doesn't present sufficient evidence, then it is the plaintiff who is entitled to a directed verdict, because a reasonable jury could not fail to find the plaintiff's case more persuasive.

¶ **21.1:** In a will contest between Plaintiff Powell and Defendant Drake, the only disputed factual question is whether Terrence Thomas died before July 1, 1958. Powell claims that he did. Suppose in each of the following cases that the stated facts are stipulated, and are the only information presented at trial bearing on the issue of whether Thomas was alive on that date. Should the case go to the jury? If not, what should the result be?

(a) Thomas was born on January 1, 1920.

(b) Thomas was born on January 1, 1888.

(c) Thomas was born on January 1, 1868.

(d) Thomas was born on January 1, 1848.

(e) Whitney saw Thomas on June 25, 1958, walking to the Ghosttown train station with a suitcase. Since then, those who would expect to hear from him had no word from him, and after diligent inquiry failed to find him. Thomas was born on January 1, 1920.

(f) Same as in (e), but the encounter was on June 1, 1958.

(g) Same as in (e), but the encounter was on June 1, 1953.

(h) Same as in (e), but the encounter was on June 1, 1946.

(i) Same as in (e), but Whitney asked Thomas where he was going, and he said he was going hiking in the wilderness of Death Mountain; two days later, a vicious blizzard hit the region surrounding Death Mountain.

(j) Same as in (i), but the encounter was on June 1, 1950.

(k) Same as in (j), but with this addition: On December 1, 1938, a person resembling Terrence Thomas, and claiming to be Terrence Thomas, appeared in Ghosttown, and told Drake that he had intended to climb Death Mountain in 1950, but had decided not to when he heard weather reports predicting a blizzard, and instead decided to stay away for a while, because "my family and so-called friends in this place, you all bugged me, and I figured you all thought I was dead anyway, so I might as well leave it that way. But now I hear I have an inheritance coming to me, so I thought maybe it was time to show up again."

In some of the variations in ¶ 21.1, you probably decided the evidence of Thomas's death was sufficient to get to a jury—that is, the burden of production was met. Another way of saying this is that the evidence supports an *inference* that Thomas was dead. But just because that inference is possible does not mean that it is compelled; the jury might also find that Thomas probably was not dead.

In other variations, though, you probably considered that the evidence of Thomas's death was so compelling that Powell should win judgment without the case going to the jury; in other words, the leftward edge of the zone of reasonableness was beyond the 50% line, because even a skeptical but reasonable juror would have to believe it more likely than not that Thomas had died before July 1, 1958. Let's assume that variation (h) is such a case. Now let's reconsider that variation, but without the assumption that all the material facts are stipulated. Instead, assume that, for the propositions that those who would expect to hear from Thomas had no word of him since June 1, 1946, and that diligent efforts were made to find him, we have only the testimony of plaintiff Powell, by now a very old man, and that his testimony has been subjected to as vigorous a cross-examination as his aged heart will stand. Continue to assume that Drake presents no evidence. Even if the judge accepts Powell's testimony as truthful, and concludes that a reasonable juror accepting that testimony would necessarily conclude that Thomas was dead on July 1, 1958, she cannot direct a verdict in Powell's favor, for one simple reason: The jury might disbelieve Powell's testimony, and so not accept the predicate for the conclusion of Thomas's death. But the judge can instruct the jury as follows:

> If you find that since a time before July 1, 1951, those who would expect to hear from Terrence Thomas had no word from him, and after diligent inquiry failed to find him, then you must find that Thomas died before July 1, 1958.

Notice the word "must" in this instruction. The jury is told that if they find certain predicate facts, then they not only may but must find a certain presumed fact. This instruction goes beyond allowing a permissible inference; according to the most commonly accepted terminology, it imposes a *presumption*.[4]

But note that the mandatory aspect of the presumption is limited in two respects. First, the jury is not instructed as to whether the predicate factual propositions are true; if the jury does not accept that those propositions are true, then the presumption never comes into play. Second, the presumption is rebuttable. If Drake presents evidence contradicting the presumed fact—and tending to establish that Thomas has turned up alive and well—the jury is free to accept that evidence; indeed, there would be no need to instruct the jury on the presumption at all. In other words, the presumption conditionally shifts the burden of producing evidence to Drake (the condition being that the jury accept the predicate), but it does not conclusively resolve the issue.

The plan of the rest of this chapter is as follows. Sections B through E address general issues and their implications in civil cases. In Section B, we examine in greater depth the questions of what the burden of persuasion means and where along the continuum to place it. Section C looks at the burden of production, focusing on the issues of which party to place it on and when it should be deemed satisfied—when, in other words, the party with the burden has produced enough evidence to warrant an inference of the proposition for which he contends. Section D then examines the various issues surrounding presumptions—in particular, when they should be created and what their effect should be. Section E considers how the burdens operate in cases in which, though there may be significant generalized information about situations resembling the one in dispute, there is little individualized evidence about that case. Section F turns to issues concerning burdens and presumptions in the

---

[4]   This instruction would be in accordance with the traditional rule that a person who has not been heard from for seven years is presumed dead.

criminal context. Section G examines the apparently distinct question of judicial notice, and contends that, in some respects at least, it may be conceived of as an extension of presumption doctrine. Finally, Section H examines stipulations, which can act as a substitute for evidence.

B. DETERMINING THE BURDEN OF PERSUASION

1. GENERAL ISSUES

According to the simplified model presented in Section A, the burden of persuasion is a simple dividing point on a probability continuum. To the left of that point—that is, if the jury is less persuaded by the plaintiff's or prosecution's case than the level indicated by that point—the jury should find for the defendant. To the right of that point, the jury should find for the plaintiff or prosecution. And what happens if the jury is persuaded exactly to the level indicated by that point? Then, if—as is most often the case—the plaintiff or the prosecution has the burden of persuasion, the plaintiff loses. That is, we say the civil plaintiff must prove its case with "a *preponderance* of the evidence," or demonstrate that it is "*more* likely than not," and that the criminal prosecution must prove its case "*beyond* a reasonable doubt"; ties go to the defendant.

When we place the burden of persuasion on one party, therefore, we select that party as the loser of the tie-breaker. But we not only have to choose who wins when the jury is persuaded exactly to the dividing point; more importantly, we have to decide where that point is. And that decision depends, at least in part, on an assessment of the relative social benefits and losses from correct and incorrect decisions.

Suppose you are fabulously wealthy (just so that risk aversion will not be a factor) and you have been conscripted to play "Let's Make the Best of a Bad Deal." This is the choice you have been given: You must place a chip on one of two portions of a felt cloth, which are marked **G** and **NG,** respectively. A roulette wheel with 100 slots, some marked **G** and the others marked **NG,** will then be spun. The payoffs are then determined this way:

If the ball lands on

		G	NG
and you picked	**G**	you pay $5.	you pay $95.
	NG	you pay $10.	there's no payment either way.

If 99 of the 100 slots are marked **NG**, you should clearly place your chip on **NG**; if, however, 99 of the 100 slots are marked **G**, you should pick **G**. Here is the big question you must answer: What is the least number of slots marked **G** at which it would make sense to place your chip on **G**?

If your algebra is rusty, don't worry—just try to estimate an answer. It's not very tough, though, to derive a simple general rule. Notice that if the ball lands on **G** you are $5 better off if you accurately picked **G** than if you inaccurately picked **NG**. Call this $5 difference **DIFFERENTIAL(G)**. Correspondingly, if the ball lands on **NG** you are $95 better off if you accurately picked **NG** than if you inaccurately picked **G**; this difference is **DIFFERENTIAL(NG)**. Obviously, there is much more to be lost by failing to pick **NG** accurately than by failing to pick **G** accurately. It therefore makes sense to pick **G** only if the odds of G, or $O(G)$, are greater than 95/5, or 19 to 1—or, put in other ways, if $P(G)$, the probability of G, is greater than 95%, or if more than 95 of the slots are marked **G**.[5] In general terms, you should put your chip on **G** if

$$O(G) > \frac{\textbf{DIFFERENTIAL(NG)}}{\textbf{DIFFERENTIAL(G)}}.[6]$$

¶ **21.2:** (a) Sorry—you are no longer fabulously wealthy, and the game you have been conscripted to play is "Decide the Defendant's Destiny." The payoffs will be in the same

---

[5] If exactly 95 of the slots are marked **G**, then the two choices would have equal expected value.

[6] Here is a derivation, in case you are interested. Bear in mind that $P(NG) = 1-P(G)$. The expected value of picking **G** is

$$[P(G) \cdot U_{gg}] + [1-P(G)] \cdot U_{gn}, \qquad (1)$$

where U_{gg} is the payoff (or utility) for picking **G** when the right choice is in fact **G** and U_{gn} is the payoff for picking **G** when the right choice is **NG**. Similarly, the expected value of picking **NG** is

$$[P(G) \cdot U_{ng}] + [1-P(G)] \cdot U_{nn}, \qquad (2)$$

where U_{ng} is the payoff for picking **NG** when the right choice is **G** and U_{nn} is the payoff for picking **NG** when that is the right choice.

To see when **G** is the better choice, determine when Expression (1) minus Expression (2) is greater than 0. This occurs when

$$[P(G) \cdot (U_{gg}-U_{ng})] + [1-P(G)] \cdot (U_{gn}-U_{nn}) > 0. \qquad (3)$$

Rearranging, and recalling that $O(G) = P(G)/[1-P(G)]$, yields

$$O(G) > \frac{U_{nn} - U_{gn}}{U_{gg} - U_{ng}} \qquad (4)$$

which is a somewhat more formal statement of the expression in the text.

proportions as in the table above, but they will be in positive or negative Points of Social Utility (whatever that is) rather than in money, and they will be decided not by the spin of a roulette wheel, but by the Great Omniscience. After you have decided whether the defendant is guilty (**G**) or not guilty (**NG**) of the crime charged, She will make appropriate additions or subtractions to the world's stockpile of Points of Social Utility, depending on which choice you made and on whether you were right or wrong, but the change in the pile will be so imperceptible that you will never know whether you guessed right in a given case or not. How certain do you have to be that the defendant is guilty before selecting **G**?

(b) How do your answers in (a) change if the two different conditions, **G** and **NG**, yield the same results as each other for correct and incorrect results—for example, whether the correct answer is **G** or **NG**, the stockpile gains 100 points if you pick correctly, and loses one point if you pick incorrectly?

¶ **21.3:** Articulate reasons why the ordinary civil plaintiff has a burden of preponderant proof, or showing that his case is "more likely than not," but the criminal prosecution has a burden of proof beyond a reasonable doubt.

2. DETERMINING THE STANDARD OF PERSUASION IN A CIVIL CASE

We have seen that the first question in determining the burden of persuasion is who has the burden, in the sense of who wins when the jury finds itself exactly on the line.

¶ **21.4:** In the ordinary civil case, why should the tie go to the defendant rather than to the plaintiff? And if it should, why shouldn't the defendant win when the plaintiff does only very slightly better than a tie?

It may occur to you that the *who* question is not all that important, because exact equipoise is rare. (Perhaps it is not rare if there is little or no evidence on a point, but then the key question really is not who has the burden of persuasion but who has the burden of producing evidence.) Considerably more important is the question of *how great* the burden is— that is, *where* on the continuum the dividing point is drawn. We shall refer to this as the *standard of persuasion.*

In the ordinary civil case, as we have seen, the usually articulated standard of persuasion is "preponderance of the evidence," which translates into "more likely than not." But confusion arises as to just what must be proven to be more likely than not. In many cases, courts articulate what the plaintiff must prove as a conjunction of separate elements. Thus, in a suit charging slander of a private figure, a court might instruct as follows:

> In this state, there are five elements to a slander claim. First, that the defendant made the alleged statement. Second, that the statement was defamatory—that is, that it was calculated to cause the plaintiff to be held in ridicule or contempt. Third, that the statement was uttered maliciously. Fourth, that the statement was untrue. And finally, that the statement caused actual injury to the reputation of the plaintiff.

In a case like this, courts customarily instruct the jury in terms such as the following:

> The plaintiff bears the burden of proving each of these five elements to a preponderance of the evidence. If you find that he has failed to do so with respect to any of the five elements, then you should return a verdict for the defendant. If, however, you find that the plaintiff has proven each of the five elements to a preponderance, then you should bring in a verdict for the plaintiff.

An instruction like this raises a serious theoretical difficulty, however. Suppose, to take a rather extreme example, the jury thinks the probability of the first element is .6, and that the probability of each of the succeeding elements, given all the elements preceding it, is also .6. Then the jury should conclude that the probability that all five elements are true is .6 x .6 x .6 x .6 x .6 = .07776, which is considerably less than .5. And yet, according to this instruction, the jury should find for the plaintiff, because the probability of *each* element is greater than .5. The solution to the problem is to recognize that the element-by-element approach is incorrect. Instead, an *aggregate* instruction would be more accurate.[7] Assuming the jury is asked only for a general verdict, such an instruction might be something like this:

> You should find for the plaintiff if, and only if, you believe it is more likely than not that all five of these elements are true. It is not enough that you believe, taking the elements one by one, that each individual one is more likely than not true, because

---

    7 *Compare, e.g.,* Richard D. Friedman, *Answering the Bayesioskeptical Challenge*, 1 Int'l J. Evid. & Proof 276 (1997); Dale A. Nance, *A Comment on the Supposed Paradoxes of a Mathematical Interpretation of the Logic of Trials*, 66 B.U.L. Rev. 947 (1986) (contending that the cumulative view is logically correct and that no established law precludes it) *with, e.g.,* L.J. Cohen, *The Probable and the Provable* 58–67 (1977); Ronald J. Allen, *Factual Ambiguity and a Theory of Evidence*, 88 Nw. U. L. Rev. 604, 605–12 (1994) (contending that the "problem of conjunction" creates a serious problem for a probabilistic view of proof). *See generally* David A. Lombardero, *Do Special Verdicts Improve the Structure of Jury Decision-Making?*, 36 Jurimetrics J. 275, 286–87 (1996); Saul Levmore, *Conjunction and Aggregation*, 99 Mich. L. Rev. 723 (2001) (taking group effects into account to explain law's failure to confront problem of conjunction).

you might believe that and still believe that it is not probable that all of the elements are true. For example, if you believed that each element was slightly more likely true than false, you might believe that it is highly improbable that all of them are true. If you find that any one of these elements is more likely false than true, then it cannot be more likely than not that all of the elements are true, and so you should find for the defendant, without the need to consider the other elements.

¶ **21.5:** Assuming that such an instruction is theoretically accurate, should it be given? Suppose a court gave the jury the element-by-element instruction, and the jury believed that the probability of each element, given all the preceding ones, was .6. What do you suppose the jury would do?

We have concentrated on the preponderance, or "more likely than not" standard, which is the one usually articulated in civil cases. In some civil cases, however, an elevated standard of persuasion, usually expressed in such terms as "clear and convincing evidence," is applied. For example, the Supreme Court has held that this elevated standard is constitutionally required for involuntary commitment to a mental hospital,[8] termination of parental rights,[9] deportation,[10] and denaturalization,[11] and it has also applied the standard as a matter of statutory interpretation to patent infringement claims.[12] Apart from this, courts have usually applied such an elevated standard in a wide variety of cases, including "(1) charges of fraud and undue influence, (2) suits on oral contracts to make a will, and suits to establish the terms of a lost will, (3) suits for the specific performance of an oral contract, [and] (4) proceedings to set aside, reform or modify written transactions, or official acts on grounds of fraud, mistake or incompleteness." McCormick § 340 (citations omitted).

¶ **21.6:** Do you think an elevated standard is justified in these types of cases? Why or why not?

Even in civil cases where courts profess to be applying the preponderance standard, we may well doubt whether that truly is the standard used, or at least whether it means the same thing from case to case. For one thing, it is the jurors who actually implement the standard, and it is difficult to know whether, implicitly or explicitly in disregard of instructions, they choose a standard that seems appropriate to them. But, even putting aside the jury, there are often complexities in determining

---

8   Addington v. Texas, 441 U.S. 418 (1979).

9   Santosky v. Kramer, 455 U.S. 745 (1982).

10   Woodby v. INS, 385 U.S. 276 (1966).

11   Schneiderman v. United States, 320 U.S. 118 (1943).

12   Microsoft Corp. v. i4i Limited Partnership, 564 U.S. 91 (2011).

the appropriate standard of persuasion that may not be captured in the simple probability model.

¶ 21.7: Recall § 3.4, in which Smith is suing the Blue Bus Co. (BBC), claiming that one of its buses negligently drove her off the road early one morning. As before, assume that Smith did not get a chance to see the bus; that BBC has conceded that it owned all the buses bearing its logo, and that Smith was hit by a bus, but that BBC has denied that it owned the bus that hit her; and that Ben Blue, the sole owner and busdriver of BBC at the time of the accident, died shortly afterwards, without having spoken about it. Now assume that the only witness other than Smith is Jones, who testified on direct that she saw the bus speed by and believes it more probable than not that it had the BBC logo on it. On cross, there is the following exchange:

Q: How much more likely than not is it that the bus bore the BBC logo?

A: Not very.

Q: Suppose you could bet at even odds on either side of the question. Would you bet for or against the proposition that the bus bore the BBC logo?

A: I'd bet for it.

Q: Now suppose that the side betting on its being a BBC bus would win $49 if it was a BBC bus, but would lose $51 if it was not. Which side would you bet on?

A: Tough to say. It would be a close bet.

Q: Now suppose that if you bet it was a BBC bus you'd get $48 if correct but you would lose $52 if incorrect. Which side of that bet would you want?

A: Well, with those odds I'd bet against it being a BBC bus.

You are the trial judge, trying the case without a jury. Who wins?[13]

If in this problem you are reluctant to grant judgment to Smith, why is that, given that the only evidence suggests that it is more likely than not—albeit only very slightly—that the facts support her? Here are two possibilities.

---

[13] Smith v. Rapid Transit, Inc., 317 Mass. 469, 58 N.E.2d 754 (1945); Daniel Shaviro, *Statistical-Probability Evidence and the Appearance of Justice*, 103 Harv.L.Rev. 530 (1989); Richard D. Friedman, *Generalized Inferences, Individual Merits, and Jury Discretion*, 66 B.U.L.Rev. 509, 515–16 (1986).

First, perhaps we have a sense that, notwithstanding the well-accepted doctrine proclaiming that all that is needed is a very slight "balance of probabilities" tipping in Smith's favor, we really demand something more. A judgment for a plaintiff means that the judicial system will intervene in people's affairs to compel the award of a remedy, and perhaps a healthy sense of inertia suggests that we not do this unless the balance tips more decisively in the plaintiff's favor.

Second, it may be that the most appropriate standard of persuasion differs depending on what the precise issue is. Some errors against a given party, even within a given case, may be worse than others. For example, if a defendant has inaccurately been branded as a tortfeasor and required to suffer a sanction, it may be worse if the inaccuracy is that he is not even the person whose conduct caused the plaintiff harm than if the inaccuracy is that his conduct, while close to the line, actually stayed on the legal side of it. Consider these problems.

¶ **21.8:** As in ¶ 21.7, Smith claims that the Blue Bus ran her off the road. This time, BBC admits that its bus was the one involved in the incident, but it contends that Blue drove perfectly safely, well within his lane and at a slow speed, and that Smith suddenly veered off the road for no apparent reason. As trial judge, how persuaded should you be that Smith's version is correct before you find for her?

¶ **21.9:** Now suppose that Smith is suing Blue for assault. Identity of the assailant is the only disputed issue. Smith testifies, identifying Blue. Blue also testifies, and denies that he was present at the scene; he swears that at the time of the assault he was home asleep in his bed. Again you are the trial judge sitting without a jury, and your personal odds on whether or not Blue was the assailant correspond to Jones' in ¶ 21.7: With a 50–50 payoff, you would bet that Blue was the assailant, at 48–52, you'd bet the other way, and at 49–51 you'd be unsure which side to take. For whom do you find, Smith or Blue?

¶ **21.10:** (a) Pete Popper, 6 years old, is suing Dipster Co. for injuries arising from a fall from a roller coaster. The only disputed issue is whether the roller coaster was being run at "Full Speed" or "Extrafast"; the parties have stipulated that the first would be a safe speed but the second would not. As trial judge, how certain must you be that the coaster was running Extrafast before you can find for Pete?

(b) Same as (a), except now the parties have stipulated that the roller coaster was running Extrafast, and the only dispute is whether this was an unsafe speed. Each side has presented considerable expert and statistical evidence on the point. How convinced do you have to be that Extrafast was unsafe before you can find for Pete?

(c) Now the parties have stipulated both that the roller coaster was running Extrafast and that this was an unsafe speed. Dipster, however, contends that this did not cause the accident. It presents evidence that Pete fell because he stood up and leaned out of his compartment. It contends that because of this conduct Pete would have fallen out even if the car were traveling safely, and that if he had not acted in this way he would have finished the ride safely notwithstanding the excessive speed. How persuaded do you have to be that the excessive speed caused the accident before you find for Pete?

C. ALLOCATING AND SATISFYING THE BURDEN OF PRODUCTION

If we accept the usual idea that the standard of production in an ordinary civil case is "more likely than not," then determining whether it is the plaintiff or the defendant who has the burden of persuasion on a given issue will matter only when the jury is in exact equipoise. Determining the standard of persuasion—in the simplified model, the location of the dividing point on the continuum—may be more significant. But, assuming an issue is submitted to the jurors, it is they who decide whether the standard of persuasion is met on that issue.

The burden of production is altogether different. Allocating that burden determines who loses on a factual issue if—as can often be the case—virtually no helpful evidence is presented on that issue. The judge, rather than the jury, decides whether this burden has been met. In other words, if you have the burden of production on an issue and the judge decides you have not met it, you do not even get to the jury on that issue. And in a civil case, if a loss on that issue is fatal to your claim, that means you are subject to suffering a directed verdict.

What is more, you cannot satisfy the burden of production as to a given proposition merely by presenting any evidence at all on it. You must, in the ordinary case, present enough evidence that a reasonable jury could find in your favor given the appropriate standard of persuasion; it may be that the chief importance of determining the standard of persuasion is that this determination is an essential ingredient in determining whether the burden of production has been met.

Put another way, to satisfy the burden of production you must present sufficient evidence to warrant an inference of the proposition. Often, indeed, it is less difficult to determine who has the initial burden of production than it is to determine whether that party has satisfied the burden, or even shifted the burden to the other party.

Seemingly the handiest guide to determine who has the burden of production in a civil case is the general rule that the plaintiff has the burden on any element of its claim. There is, however, a large component of question-begging in this rule, which you may have discussed in Civil Procedure. What is an element of the claim? Suppose that it is clear under the substantive law that the question of whether proposition **X** is true may be determinative of the outcome of the case; the plaintiff contends that **X** is true, and the defendant contends that **NOT-X** is true. (For example, in an auto accident case **X** may be the proposition that the plaintiff was driving reasonably at the time of the case. If the plaintiff shows that the defendant was negligent, then **X** will be critical, either reducing or eliminating the plaintiff's recovery.) Is **X** an element of the plaintiff's claim, or is **NOT-X** a defense to the claim?[14] If an element is that as to which the plaintiff has the burden, and a defense is that as to which the defendant has the burden, then we are in a circle.

We can break the definitional circle by trying to think functionally about who should have the burden of production on a given issue. Various factors, including the relative access of the parties to evidence bearing on the proposition, will affect the allocation.[15] A useful starting point, though hardly an infallible guide, is to think about the burden in probabilistic terms. Under this approach, a party presumably has the burden of production if, on the state of the evidence, a rational jury applying the appropriate burden of persuasion could not find for that party. Thus, if on the state of the evidence a rational jury must believe that **X** is extremely unlikely, then the plaintiff bears the burden of producing evidence that **X** is true. Before the production of any evidence at all, most of the disputed propositions for which the plaintiff contends must appear highly unlikely to a rational jury, and so will be propositions as to which the plaintiff bears the burden of production. Suppose, for example, that a material proposition in dispute is **SLAM,** Burt's claim that Ernie hit him with a sledgehammer. The rational jury must—acting solely on the basis of the information it is allowed to bring into the courtroom, before any evidence

---

[14] See Fed. R. Civ. P. 8(c) (listing some affirmative defenses).

[15] *See, e.g.,* Bruce L. Hay, *Allocating the Burden of Proof,* 72 Ind. L.J. 651, 663–64 (1997) (analyzing the effect of this and other factors—probable merits, party beliefs as to the probable outcome, the amount at stake for each party, and the social cost of one erroneous outcome or the other); Bruce L. Hay & Kathryn E. Spier, *Burdens of Proof in Civil Litigation: An Economic Perspective,* 26 J. Leg. Studs.1413 (1997) (modeling burden of proof rules as a means of minimizing costs of litigation); Jason R. Bent, *The Telltale Sign of Discrimination: Probabilities, Information Asymmetries, and the Systemic Disparate Treatment Theory,* 44 U. Mich. J. L. Ref. 797 (2011).

at all is introduced—believe that **SLAM** is very unlikely; most people don't go around hitting each other with sledgehammers.[16]

This account would help explain why the plaintiff bears the burden of production on most factual issues. Even if the disputed proposition is **CRASH**, that Burt and Ernie were in a car crash, that, too, must appear highly unlikely in the absence of evidence. But now suppose that Burt's widow, as plaintiff, has provided ample evidence of **CRASH**—photos of the two cars, with Burt and Ernie each dead at his wheel. Whether the plaintiff has a right to recover may depend on the truth of another proposition—**ERNIEFAULT**, that Ernie was at fault. Suppose that there were no eyewitnesses, and that the photos contain no suggestion as to who, if anybody, was at fault. It appears that the plaintiff has the burden of production on **ERNIEFAULT**. But articulating why may be difficult. And attempting to understand why is important in determining whether the burden has been met.

¶ **21.11:** (a) Consider each of the following rationales. Do you find either persuasive?

(i) Burt's widow has the burden of production on **ERNIEFAULT** because this is an element of her claim.

(ii) The plaintiff has the burden of persuading the jury that **ERNIEFAULT** is more likely true than not. But there is no evidence suggesting that Ernie was more probably at fault than Burt, and we must take into consideration the possibility that the accident was the fault of neither, but a fluke or the fault of a third party. Accordingly, a rational juror could only conclude, absent any other evidence, that it was less than 50% probable that the accident was Ernie's fault.

(b) Now suppose that Burt's widow presents the following evidence.

Murphy testifies that ten minutes before the accident, he was in conversation with Ernie, who then looked at his

---

[16] Of course, if the jury knows that Burt contended, both in his opening statement and in his pleadings, that Ernie hit him, then **SLAM** might not appear all that improbable. But neither the pleadings nor the openings are evidence, and so they may not be considered in allocating the production burden or determining whether it has been met; in allocating the burden, we must pose the question—"How probable is **SLAM**?"—to our hypothetical rational jury even before the pleadings are read. But the question is inherently leading: If we ask a hypothetical juror, "How likely is it that Ernie hit Burt with a sledgehammer?" the juror might conclude, from the simple fact that the question has been asked, that the proposition is not all that unlikely. Perhaps the only satisfactory way of running this thought experiment would be to give the hypothetical juror a long questionnaire asking her to assign a probability to a variety of propositions, at least some of which appear very improbable. Faced with such a questionnaire, the hypothetical juror—again acting without any evidence—must believe that **SLAM** is highly improbable. Hence, Burt bears the burden of producing evidence that **SLAM** is true.

watch and said, "Gee, I'm late. I've got to run. Give me a call some time. Let's have lunch."

Farley testifies that she was working in her garden, with her back to the road just at the site where the accident occurred, when she heard a car approach. She then heard another car approach at great speed. She began to turn around to see why the second car was coming so fast, but before she turned far enough to see anything she heard a terrible crash, and she saw the two cars she now knows were Burt's and Ernie's. She has no idea which car was the one traveling so fast, or which direction that car was coming from. She never heard or saw a third car, and she certainly would have seen one if it was involved. It was a pleasant day, with high clouds that blocked the sun but left visibility clear, and the road was in excellent condition; it had not rained for days.

Has the plaintiff met her burden of production on **ERNIEFAULT**? If you do not believe she has, do you find any of the following rationales persuasive?

(i)   A rational juror could still not find that it is more probable than not that Ernie was at fault.

(ii)   A rational juror might find it more probable than not, but not substantially more probable than not, that Ernie was at fault. That is really the burden of persuasion that the court should require, and accordingly a rational juror could not be persuaded that it has been satisfied.

(iii) A rational juror might even guess that it is substantially more probable than not, on the basis of the evidence presented, that Ernie was at fault. There isn't enough evidence to do more than guess, however, and that's not good enough. Much about this incident is totally unknown, and the judicial system should not act against the defendant unless a rational factfinder could have a fair degree of confidence that, if it knew more information, it would still believe the plaintiff had met the burden of persuasion.

¶ 21.12: Now suppose instead that our witness Farley happened to see Ernie's car a few seconds before the crash, and she testifies that it was traveling at very high speed. She did not see the crash, and she has no idea whether Burt was traveling too fast, or in the wrong lane. In its answer, Ernie's estate contended that Burt was contributorily negligent, a proposition that we may label **BURTFAULT.** Do you find any of the following analyses persuasive?

(a) Burt's widow has the burden of proving **NOT-BURTFAULT**, because it is essential to her case and she is the one seeking to alter the status quo.

(b) Ernie's estate has the burden of proving **BURTFAULT**, because asking Burt's widow to prove **NOT-BURTFAULT** would unfairly impose on her the burden of proving a negative. See Kevin W. Saunders, *The Mythic Difficulty in Proving a Negative*, 15 Seton H.L.Rev. 276 (1985).[17]

(c) Ernie's estate has the burden of proving **BURTFAULT**, because the plaintiff's claim was complete without reference to this issue; this is by its nature a defense to that claim.

(d) Ernie's estate has the burden of proving **BURTFAULT**, because absent any evidence that proposition appears improbable.

¶ 21.13: Now suppose that the plaintiff shows both that Ernie was at fault and that Burt was not at fault. But now Burt's widow wants to make Oscar, as well as Ernie, liable. Under the controlling law, Oscar is liable if in driving the car Ernie was acting as Oscar's agent. The plaintiff offers proof that Ernie was an employee of Oscar's and that Oscar owned the car in which Ernie was driving. No other evidence is offered on the agency issue. Do you find any of the following analyses persuasive?

(a) The burden should be put on Oscar of producing evidence against agency, because Oscar has better access to the evidence of whether or not Ernie was driving in the scope of his employment, and so should be given an incentive to produce such evidence.

(b) The burden should be put on Oscar of producing evidence against agency, because it is probable, in the absence of other information, that one who drives his employer's car is doing so in the scope of his employment.

(c) Burt's widow should be held to have satisfied her burden of producing evidence of agency, because a jury could reasonably believe, given the evidence she has produced and

---

[17] Saunders contends that it is not a negative as such that is difficult to prove; a negative can be reworded in affirmative terms. ("Reasonable care," for example, may be the opposite of "absence of negligence.") Rather, it is a universal statement—taking such forms as "There is never . . ." or "It is always true that . . ."—that is generally difficult to prove. An existential statement—in a form such as "There exists an occasion that . . ."—is generally easier to prove.

Oscar's failure to provide any evidence, that Ernie was probably driving in the scope of his employment.

(d) Burt's widow has not satisfied her burden of producing evidence of agency, because she has offered nothing to show that the generalization on which she relies—that an employee who is driving his employer's car is probably on his employer's business—held true in this case.

The last problem may remind you that even absence of evidence is evidence in one sense: The failure of one party to produce evidence may in itself have significance, and so be the equivalent of evidence, in that it alters the probability of a given proposition. This occurs particularly when we would expect a party to have access to, and to produce, evidence of a given type if the facts were favorable to him. The party's failure to produce that type of evidence therefore makes his case appear less probable. In ¶ 2.22 we saw defense counsel argue in this way on the basis of the prosecution's failure to produce evidence that might have been expected had the facts favored the prosecution.

There is one other sense in which we should be reluctant to conclude that there is "no evidence" on a point: Once we know anything at all about a case, we have some basis on which to make a judgment, however preliminary, about a fact at issue. The question is not whether there is literally no evidence of a given proposition, but whether there is too little to support a finding of that proposition.

¶ 21.14: The issue is whether Gordon was continuously insane after 1983. He was continuously, and involuntarily, institutionalized from 1982 to 1986, during which time he was considered insane. He then escaped, and was captured and recommitted, after a hearing in which he was found to be insane, in 1988. He died shortly afterward. How would you respond to the argument, "There is no evidence as to whether he was insane between 1986 and 1988."[18]

¶ 21.15: (a) Packard was chagrined to discover that he had a pair of forceps in his left leg. Should he be able to recover against Dr. Sharp if he proves solely that Sharp operated on that leg one year before Packard discovered the forceps?

(b) Now suppose instead that the surgery on Packard was an appendectomy, and that during the course of it, while he was unconscious, he suffered a traumatic injury, of unknown origin, to a nerve in his shoulder. Packard sues all the doctors and nurses who participated in the operation, claiming negligence.

---

[18] Cf. Galloway v. United States, 319 U.S. 372 (1943).

Should the action be dismissed? What if each of the defendants testifies that he or she saw nothing unusual during the operation that would cause such an injury? *See Ybarra v. Spangard*, 25 Cal.2d 486, 154 P.2d 687 (1945), *on remand*, 93 Cal. App.2d 43, 208 P.2d 445 (1949).

These pages have suggested that probability and access to the evidence are potentially important factors in determining which party bears the burden of producing evidence on a given proposition and whether it has been satisfied. There are other factors as well, however. In some cases, for example, the wording of a contract or statute that governs the case might bear on the burden issue.

¶ **21.16:** Perez is suing the Reliable Insurance Company to recover on a policy that Reliable issued on the life of Perez's late wife, Serena. The policy, which was issued on December 15, 2014, provides that benefits are payable to the beneficiary upon the death of the insured (Serena), "unless death was caused by suicide within two years of the date hereof." In his complaint, Perez alleged that Serena had died "of natural causes on or about January 15, 2015." In its answer, Reliable admitted that the death occurred on or about that date, but denied that it was of natural causes, and instead asserted that it was a suicide.

(a) Who has the burden of production on the issue of cause of death?[19]

(b) Now suppose the only evidence of the cause of Serena's death is the following, to which the parties have stipulated:

> On the afternoon of January 15, 2015, Serena told Perez that she was going in the ocean for a swim. He urged her not to because the water was very rough. She replied, "I know what I'm doing," and walked out of their beach house. When she didn't return after two hours, he went to the water's edge, where he found her clothes neatly piled. He called for help, and the police and Coast Guard searched the water for Serena, but without any luck. He has had no trace of her, either dead or alive.

> Should the case go to the jury? If not, who should win?[20]

(c) Do your answers to (a) or (b) change if instead the insurance policy provided that the benefits would be payable if

---

[19] *See* 1B Appleman, Insurance Law and Practice, § 500, at 386 (1981); Davison v. National Life & Accident Ins. Co., 106 Ga.App. 187, 126 S.E.2d 811 (1962).

[20] Cf. Schelberger v. Eastern Sav. Bank, 93 A.D.2d 188, 461 N.Y.S.2d 785 (1st Dept.), *aff'd*, 60 N.Y.2d 506, 470 N.Y.S.2d 548, 458 N.E.2d 1225 (1983); Wellisch v. John Hancock Mut. Life Ins. Co., 293 N.Y. 178, 56 N.E.2d 540 (1944).

the insured died "by natural or accidental causes, or by homicide," with homicide being defined as "the killing of one person by another"? Does it make sense to make any significant consequence turn on the precise wording in this way? Is it plausible that the parties intended to make any consequence turn on the wording? Is it appropriate for the courts to allow private parties to determine the circumstances in which the courts should grant relief?

(d) Suppose that the policy provides for double indemnity (i.e., double benefits) "in the event of accidental death." Who has the burden of proof on the issue of accidental death? If a stipulation as in (b) is the only information presented, should the case go to the jury? If the case should not go to the jury, who should win on the double indemnity claim?[21]

For the most part, the question of whether one party has satisfied its burden of production is decided on a case-by-case basis, initially by the trial court and sometimes eventually by an appellate court. But sometimes courts feel confident enough about a recurrent situation that they lay down a general rule that a certain accumulation of facts will warrant an inference of another fact. This is as much a matter of substantive law as of evidentiary law. The doctrine of res ipsa loquitur, which you probably recall from torts, is a good illustration. For example, a court might hold,

If there is sufficient evidence that (1) a water main has leaked, (2) at all times the company that installed it had exclusive control of its inspection and maintenance, and (3) mains properly made, installed, inspected, and maintained do not ordinarily leak, then the jury may also conclude that (4) the leakage was caused by the negligence of the installing company.[22]

Occasionally legislatures get into the act as well. Statutes enunciating when a party has borne its burden of proof raise the most significant problems in the criminal context, and so we will postpone discussion of them until Section E.

---

[21] *See* O'Toole v. New York Life Ins. Co., 671 F.2d 913 (5th Cir.1982); Piva v. General Am. Life Ins. Co., 647 S.W.2d 866 (Mo.App.1983).

[22] *Cf.* Hollywood Shop, Inc. v. Pennsylvania Gas & Water Co., 270 Pa.Super. 245, 411 A.2d 509 (1979).

D. PRESUMPTIONS—SHIFTING THE BURDEN OF PROOF

1. THE NATURE OF A PRESUMPTION

In Section C, we have discussed the question of when a given body of evidence is sufficient to warrant an *inference* of a given proposition— sufficient, that is, to *satisfy* the proponent's burden of production. In this section, we will address *presumptions*, which (in the most commonly accepted usage) are evidentiary rules prescribing when that burden is not only satisfied but *shifted* to the other party.

Suppose that the plaintiff Pauling bears the burden of producing evidence of **NOTICE**, the proposition that the defendant Dowling Co. actually received adequate notice of the renewal of a contract. Suppose further that he introduces evidence of **MAIL**, the closely related proposition that he mailed a timely notice to Dowling's correct address. There are at least three possible results: First, the judge might hold that evidence of **MAIL** is insufficient for the jury to conclude **NOTICE**. Second, she might conclude that **MAIL** does support such an inference. In other words, she might hold that Pauling has satisfied his burden of production. Third, the judge might even go a further step, the one on which we will focus in this section: She might hold that the evidence of **MAIL** *conditionally shifts* the burden of production on **NOTICE** to Dowling. Let's see what this means.

Suppose first that Dowling stipulates that **MAIL** is true. The court might hold that, given the truth of **MAIL**, Dowling has the burden of producing evidence to prove that **NO-NOTICE** is true. Thus, if Dowling fails to present sufficient evidence on the point, the judge will simply instruct the jury to take **NOTICE** as true—or, if that proposition is dispositive, the case need not be submitted to the jury at all.

Now suppose that Dowling does not stipulate that **MAIL** is true, and in fact it challenges Pauling's proof of **MAIL**, but apart from doing this it presents no evidence of **NO-NOTICE**. For example, Dowling may undercut Pauling's credibility in general, so that the jury might disbelieve his testimony of **MAIL**. Or it may prove that his address book kept an out-of-date listing for it. In this case, the judge might think, "Well, *if* **MAIL** is true, then **MAIL** still shifts the burden of production to Dowling, and Dowling hasn't met that burden. But Dowling is contesting the truth of **MAIL**." Therefore, the judge might give an instruction such as the following:

> The plaintiff contends that the defendant received timely notice of the renewal of the contract. In connection with this issue, you have heard evidence in favor of and against the proposition that the plaintiff mailed such notice, in a correct and timely manner,

to the defendant at his correct address. I instruct you that if you find that the plaintiff did make such a mailing, then you must find that the defendant received adequate notice. Of course, it is for you to determine whether or not you find the mailing was made.

In this instruction, **MAIL** is the basic or predicate fact, and **NOTICE** the presumed fact. We may say that **NOTICE** is presumed to follow from **MAIL**—or, put another way, that there is a presumption that if **MAIL** is true then **NOTICE** is true as well.

Note that in one sense this instruction is mandatory: The jurors are told that, *if* they find **MAIL** to be true, they *must* find **NOTICE** to be true. Of course, they may disobey the instruction—they may fail to find **NOTICE** even though they believe **MAIL** to be likely. If the jurors do disobey the instruction, then, assuming that they return a general verdict, the court will probably be none the wiser; in this respect, the instruction regarding a presumption is like most other instructions to the jury. In another sense, the instruction is not mandatory at all, because the jurors need not find **MAIL** to be true, and if they do not the presumption never comes into play.

The presumption is limited in another sense as well: It is *rebuttable*. Let's alter the hypothetical slightly, by supposing that Dowling Co. is a one-person operation and that Dowling herself takes the stands and swears that she never received any notice. The jury might believe her, even if it also believes Pauling's evidence that he mailed the notice; the notice might have been lost in transit. In other words, now Dowling has contested the presumed fact (**NOTICE**), as well as the predicate fact (**MAIL**), and has presented enough evidence that the jury could find that the presumed fact is not true even if it finds the predicate to be true. Now the instruction given above would not be appropriate; that instruction was drafted only for the situation in which Dowling challenged **NOTICE** merely by challenging **MAIL**. That is, the presumption was meant to direct the jury to one conclusion absent evidence—or more properly speaking, absent *enough* evidence—pointing to the opposite conclusion. Now that such other evidence has been introduced—that is, now that the presumption has been rebutted—the presumption loses a good deal of its importance, and perhaps even all of it. Just what effect a presumption has once it is rebutted is a significant question that we will discuss in Subsection 3.

We have seen that sometimes the predicate, or conditioning, fact of a presumption is established beyond genuine doubt, as by a stipulation. Sometimes it may even be one of the basic facts that defines the situation. Then a presumption closely resembles an initial allocation of the burden of production—and, indeed, sometimes rules that we might naturally think of as allocations of the burden of production are stated as presumptions. 1 Dan B. Dobbs, et al., *The Law of Torts* 543 (2d ed. 2011). For example, it is sometimes said that there is a presumption that a person was sane at a given time. *E.g., State v. Fleming*, 784 S.E.2d 743 (W.Va. 2016). We might as easily, or more easily, say that the burden of production is on the party who would show that the person was not sane. Similarly, courts occasionally say that a person in possession of his faculties is presumed to have acted with reasonable care for his own safety, *e.g., Ex parte Essary*, 992 So.2d 5, 12 (Ala. 2005)—which is another way of saying that the burden of production is on the party who would show the absence of ordinary care. And of course we say that a criminal defendant is presumed innocent, which is really a way of emphasizing that the burdens of proof are on the prosecution. *See, e.g.,* McCormick § 342. But we needn't be disturbed by this duality of expression, because we should recognize the close relationship between a presumption and the initial allocation of the burden of production. Both types of rule tell a party that she will not reach a jury verdict on an issue unless she presents evidence on that issue. The presumption, unlike the initial allocation, is invoked only if the predicate is established or found to be true. But if the predicate is uncontested, the two types of rule virtually merge.

¶ **21.17:** Recall the issue in ¶ 21.13—whether Oscar was liable to Burt's widow. Assume that you are the judge and that you have decided that, unless Oscar produces evidence that Ernie was not driving in the course of his employment at the time of the accident, Oscar should be held liable for Ernie's torts. Express this ruling as an allocation of the burden and, alternatively, as a presumption.

We have emphasized the rebuttability of presumptions, the fact that they conditionally shift the burden of production but do not (even if the predicate is established) conclusively resolve the truth of the presumed fact. We should note now, however, that not everything that is called a presumption is rebuttable. A *conclusive* or *irrebuttable* presumption is really an awkwardly expressed rule of law. *See, e.g.,* McCormick § 342. Nevertheless, a conclusive presumption has one basic similarity with an ordinary rebuttable presumption: It results in an instruction of the form, "If you find **X**, then you must find **Y**." The difference is that in the case of a conclusive presumption this instruction is proper no matter how much evidence is presented that **Y** is not true. It thus amounts to a rule of law that if **X** is true consequence **Y** must follow.

¶ **21.18:** Examine the following conclusive presumptions. In each case, ask: What policy was this provision meant to serve? Is the provision constitutionally valid? If not, what could the legislature do to achieve the same result in a constitutional manner?

(a) Cal.Bus. & Prof.Code § 6101(a) provides that

Conviction of a felony or misdemeanor, involving moral turpitude, constitutes a cause for disbarment or suspension.

In any proceeding, whether under this article or otherwise, to disbar or suspend an attorney on account of that conviction, the record of conviction shall be conclusive evidence of guilt of the crime of which he or she has been convicted.

(b) Ariz.Rev.Stat.Ann. § 28–4010 addresses the situation in which two or more insurance policies apply to the same vehicle in an incident "out of which a liability loss arises." Subsection (A) provides that if one of the policies insures a person engaged in an automotive-related business, it is "conclusively presumed" that (1) if the person driving that vehicle is the insured or an employee or agent of the insured that policy is primary, but that (2) otherwise it is excess over all other insurance available to the driver. Subsection (B) provides that in all other cases it is "conclusively presumed" that the policy describing or rating the car in question as an owned automobile is primary and all others are excess. Subsection (C) provides that these presumptions may be modified only by a written agreement signed by all insurers who have issued policies applicable to the loss and by all named insureds under these policies.

Now that we have recognized the case of the irrebuttable presumption, let us put it aside for now. We will return to it briefly in the criminal context. The rest of this section will focus on ordinary presumptions.

2. POLICY CONSIDERATIONS SUPPORTING THE CREATION AND INVOCATION OF PRESUMPTIONS

Sometimes the strongest factor explaining the creation of a presumption is a probabilistic relation. Even a simple relation may be an adequate explanation, like, "If **MAIL** is true, then **NOTICE** is probably true." More often, perhaps, we would need a narrower statement to justify a presumption, such as: "If **MAIL** is true, and we have no substantial evidence suggesting **NOT-NOTICE** is true, then **NOTICE** is probably true." A more sophisticated probabilistic statement can take into account other factors concerning the parties' positions and incentives in litigation. For instance, we might say:

If **MAIL** is true, then, given that

(1) there is no substantial evidence suggesting **NOT-NOTICE** is true,

(2) the defendant would probably have easy access to information showing **NOT-NOTICE** is true, if such evidence existed, and

(3) the defendant has an especially strong incentive to produce any evidence of **NOT-NOTICE**, because he knows that he is likely to suffer the consequences of a presumption if he does not,

it follows that **NOTICE** is probably true.

Another approach, yet more sophisticated, would put probabilistic statements in a decision-theoretic context. This approach treats the court as a decision-maker attempting to select the optimal rule for allocating burdens. The court must take into account how probable **NOTICE** is in varied circumstances, but that is not the bottom line. Rather, the bottom-line question is what rule has the highest expected value, and that assessment must also take into account other considerations—such as the incentives for production of evidence one rule or another will create, especially for the party with best access to the evidence, and the costs of errors that a misallocation of the burden will likely yield.[23]

¶ **21.19:** Consider the following illustrative presumptions, drawn from McCormick § 343 and Mueller & Kirkpatrick § 3.5. For each, consider what rationales, if any, justify the presumption. In particular, consider in each case whether the rule should create a presumption or merely establish that a given body of evidence is sufficient to warrant an inference of the fact at issue.

(a) An official action by a public officer is presumed to have been regularly and legally performed.

(b) If a person has not been seen or heard from for seven years by those who would expect to be in touch with him, and diligent efforts have been made to find him, he is presumed dead.

(c) If property has been delivered to a bailee in good condition and returned in a damaged state, the damage is presumed to have been caused by negligence of the bailee.

---

[23] *See, e.g.,* Bruce L. Hay, *Allocating the Burden of Proof,* 72 Ind. L.J. 651, 662–78 (1997) (analyzing costs of allocation of burden in terms of process costs (the expected costs of presenting evidence) and error costs (the costs of erroneous judgments attributable to the allocation)).

(d) The driver of an automobile is presumed to have had permission to drive it.

(e) If an automobile belongs to the employer of the driver, the driver is presumed to be driving it on the employer's business.

(f) A child born to a woman while she is cohabiting with her husband, who is not impotent at the time, is presumed legitimate.

(g) A status or condition once proved to exist is presumed to continue.

As this problem suggests, courts sometimes use the term presumption rather loosely, when all they mean is that the predicate fact supports an inference of another fact; sometimes they speak of "permissive presumptions." For the sake of clarity, it is better to reserve the term presumption for rules having the mandatory nature described here—and because such rules purport to restrict the jury's ability to draw its own conclusions from the evidence before it, courts should probably be rather abstemious in imposing them.

3. REBUTTAL OF PRESUMPTIONS

Now suppose that the party opposing the presumption attempts to rebut it by offering evidence tending to disprove the presumed fact. For example, Dowling Co. might offer evidence that, if believed, would lower the probability of **NOTICE**, even if the jury believed **MAIL**. This evidence is subject to the test of sufficiency; because the presumption has shifted the burden of production to Dowling Co., it must present enough evidence so that a jury could reasonably believe **NO-NOTICE**.

¶ 21.20: Assume that the jurisdiction applies a presumption of delivery from proper mailing. Assume also that Pauling has testified that he made a proper mailing to Dowling Co., at the University of Marlborough Medical School, where Deborah Dowling, the sole proprietor of Dowling Co., was a professor. Assume also that neither the university nor the medical school was a party to the contract, and that delivery to the medical school is not considered personal delivery to Dowling. Dowling died before trial, but in defense her estate presents the testimony of Post, who runs the medical school's mailroom, that she happened to log all mail received on the date two days after Pauling assertedly mailed the check; the log, authenticated by Post, reveals no mail received from Pauling on that date. Is this enough to rebut the presumption?

Now suppose it is clear that Dowling Co.'s evidence, if believed, would plausibly lead to a conclusion of **NO-NOTICE**. Suppose, for example, that Prof. Dowling's former assistant testifies that his practice was to open all mail for Prof. Dowling, that he was familiar with the Pauling contract and would have paid attention to a notice of contract renewal from Pauling, and that he remembers no such notice. Now Dowling Co. has clearly rebutted the presumption. It no longer makes sense to instruct the jurors that if they find **MAIL** they must find **NOTICE**. What should the court do?

For one thing, it should probably still let Pauling get to the jury on the question of whether **NOTICE** is true. There are at least two reasons for this. First, the jury might disbelieve the evidence that Dowling Co. has presented of **NO-NOTICE**; the jury might, for example, think that the former assistant is lying. In that case, the implication of **NOTICE** from **MAIL** would retain its original force. Second, Dowling Co.'s evidence of **NO-NOTICE** may be of the type that, even if believed, is not conclusive on the point. Thus, the jury might believe it possible that the assistant saw the notice of renewal and forgot it, or that for some reason—perhaps because she happened to wander near the mail room— Prof. Dowling received this piece of mail outside the usual routine, without her assistant seeing it. Against these possibilities, the jury must weigh the proof that the notice was mailed; the tendency of **MAIL** to prove **NOTICE** would therefore retain at least some probative significance.

¶ **21.21:** Alter ¶ 21.20 as follows: Post's testimony for the defense is that mail addressed to people or entities at the medical school is first delivered to the main university mail office, and then distributed to the main medical school mail room. From there, it is distributed by department, and the departmental secretary puts the mail in the appropriate recipient's mail box in the departmental office. The boxes are unlocked and are in a room to which faculty, staff, students, and visitors on official business have access.

Is this evidence sufficient to rebut the presumption? Is it sufficient to shift the burden of production back to Pauling? Would a jury be warranted in drawing an inference of notice according to the following logic?

We believe what the defense has shown about the long distribution chain. But that does not compel a conclusion that the notice was not received. In fact, we think it is so likely that a letter properly mailed to the medical school would eventually reach its intended recipient, even given the long internal distribution chain, that on this state of the evidence we think it is probable that Dowling did in fact receive the notice.

If the judge does let the issue go to the jury, she must then decide what instructions to give. Certainly there is no need to tell the jury something like, "There was a rebuttable presumption of **NOTICE** from proof of **MAIL**, but now the defendant has rebutted the presumption." In fact, ordinarily there is no real need to tell the jury anything about the presumption at all. The jurors know that they have to decide whether **NOTICE** is true, they know the evidence that each side has presented, and that is all that they need to know; they can figure out on their own that **MAIL** is strong evidence of **NOTICE**. But in jurisdictions that are comfortable with judicial comment on the evidence, the court might offer an instruction such as:

> In considering whether Dowling received notice, you can, of course, consider the evidence that Pauling mailed a notice. Indeed, this evidence, if you believe it, is sufficient for you to conclude that Dowling received notice. I do not mean to imply that, if you believe the evidence regarding mailing, you must conclude that Dowling actually received the notice, but only that you may so conclude.

The judge might make the reminder even stronger, especially if she believes that the relation between the predicate fact and the inferred fact is not likely to be clear to the jury; she might say something like, "The law regards mailing as strong evidence of actual receipt." But, especially if she gives this latter form of instruction, the judge must be very careful to avoid leaving the implication that if the jurors find the predicate fact they must find the inferred fact as well. That would have been a proper instruction if the presumption had not been rebutted, but given that rebuttal it is not.

And now we come to a question that has engaged many leading evidence writers:[24] Assuming that the presumption has been rebutted, so that the issue is to be presented to the jury (that is, neither party any longer faces a burden of production), does the presumption retain any lingering effect, by altering the burden of persuasion?[25] The initial version of FRE 301, as submitted by the Supreme Court to Congress,

---

[24] *E.g.*, McCormick § 344; Mueller & Kirkpatrick § 3.8; Edmund M. Morgan, *Instructing the Jury on Presumptions and Burden of Proof*, 47 Harv. L. Rev. 59, 77–83 (1933); James Bradley Thayer, *A Preliminary Treatise on Evidence* 336–39 (1898).

[25] The amount of energy spent on this issue suggests that it has some importance. Would all those extraordinary scholars have spent so much time on the question if all that is at stake is the determination of who wins if the evidence leaves the factfinder in perfect equipoise on the presumed fact?

would have answered this question in the affirmative.[26] But Congress amended the Rule to answer in the negative: The burden of persuasion remains on the party on whom it was originally cast.

At least ordinarily, this appears to be the proper result. The burden of persuasion is a reflection of social policy. As the discussion in Section B.1 of this chapter suggests, the burden of persuasion essentially reflects a calculation of how probable the plaintiff's case must be before the expected value of a verdict for the plaintiff exceeds the expected value of a verdict for the defendant. It says nothing about how the factfinder should determine in the specific case whether that probability level has been exceeded. In particular, the burden of persuasion determines who should win at the end of the day, when all the evidence is in and the probabilities of the disputed issues are assessed. The result yielded by the determination of the burden of persuasion is unaffected by the course that the factfinder followed in reaching those final probability assessments. Earlier in the case a presumption may have prescribed that, absent further evidence, a given fact would be deemed so probable that it would not be submitted to the jury. But that says nothing about how probable the jurors must find the fact, if in the end there is enough evidence for it to reach them, before they should find for the plaintiff.

Some presumptions, however, may reflect more than a strong probabilistic relation between the predicate and the presumed fact. In some cases, the courts may be implicitly pursuing logic such as the following:

> If **X** is true, then not only is **Y** probably true, given the defendant's failure to produce contradicting evidence, but the entire situation has changed, because an incorrect verdict for the defendant has far more social disutility if **X** is true than if **X** is not true. Accordingly, if **X** is true then the burden of persuasion on **Y** should be altered, and that is so even if the defendant does present evidence that **Y** is not true.

> ¶ 21.22: Review the presumptions listed in ¶ 21.19. Assume for each that the jurisdiction has adopted the presumption, that the plaintiff has introduced evidence sufficient to establish the predicate of the presumption, and that the defendant has introduced evidence both contradicting the predicate and rebutting the presumed fact. In each case, is any special instruction to the jury appropriate? Should the burden of persuasion be altered? Why or why not?

---

[26] *See* 56 F.R.D. 183, 208 (1972) (Rule 301 as submitted by the Court: "In all cases not otherwise provided . . . a presumption imposes on the party against whom it is directed the burden of proving that the nonexistence of the presumed fact is more probable than its existence").

Courts tend to use the term presumption so freely that sometimes the rebuttal of a presumption comes in the form of evidence supporting another presumption. Courts have often tried to create doctrines to resolve such battles of presumptions, but what is primarily needed is a healthy dose of common sense.

¶ 21.23: S, the son of W, claims that W was the widow of H, and therefore that W, who also has died, was entitled to half his property on his death. The critical question is whether H and W were validly married. S proves that W and H married on July 1, 1985, and cites the presumption that a marriage was valid. D, the defendant, proves that on July 1, 1982, W married another man, and cites the often stated doctrine that a status or condition once proved to exist is presumed to have continued. What result? What if the prior marriage were June 20, 1985? What if it were July 1, 1965? *See* McCormick § 344(A); Mueller & Kirkpatrick § 3.9.

E. BURDENS AND GENERALIZED EVIDENCE

We have been using a probabilistic model in analyzing the standard of persuasion. But, as the discussion of relevance and particularly of statistical evidence in Chapter 3 may have suggested to you, the validity of such a model has been a much contested academic issue. One aspect of the controversy has been the question of what to do when the evidence, though supporting a conclusion that the facts probably are in the plaintiff's favor, is quite meager. That can occur when relatively little is known about the case at hand, but generalized knowledge—including information such as statistics about similar situations or about a group of situations that includes the present case—seems to support the plaintiff. Many people have a resistance in such a case to allowing judgment for the plaintiff without individualized evidence in the plaintiff's favor. Some scholars take this resistance as a basis for resisting a probabilistic account of the standard of persuasion. Some rigorous probabilists take the view that the resistance is shortsighted; skimpiness of the evidence can be taken into account in determining how probable the factfinder believes it to be that the defendant is liable, they argue, but if the factfinder reaches the assessment that the defendant is probably liable it would be wrong to deny judgment to the plaintiff simply because the information base is less complete than we would like. An intermediate position might be that probability is an essential aspect of the standard of persuasion, in accordance with the model presented here, but not the full story. In this view, the standard would demand not only that liability be probable but also that the evidence satisfy some measure of completeness or resilience.[27]

¶ 21.24: (a) Assume again that Ms. Smith is suing the Blue Bus Company. Assume, as in ¶ 3.4, that Smith is able to present no eyewitnesses to the accident, other than herself. She was not able to see any marks identifying the bus. She does, however, present evidence that the Blue Bus Company is the only company that has bus service scheduled on Main Street, where the accident occurred. Assuming there is no jury, who should win the case? If there is a jury, what should happen?

(b) Now suppose that, as in ¶ 3.4, Ms. Smith presents, instead of the schedule evidence, results of a month-long observation that 72 of the 90 buses passing the point of the accident between 12:30 and 1:30 A.M. belong to RTI. The accident occurred about 1:08 a.m. Assuming there is no jury, who should win the case? If there is a jury, what should happen? What if the observation is that 4608 of 5760 buses passing the point at any time during the month belong to RTI?

¶ 21.25: Mrs. Kaminsky was injured by ice falling off a truck, behind which she had driven for several miles. The truck bore the Hertz logo. A stipulation provides that 90% of the trucks bearing that logo are owned by Hertz; the rest are owned by licensees or franchisees, or are vehicles that Hertz has sold but from which the logo has not been removed. No other proof indicates who owned the truck in question. Assume that under the controlling law Hertz would be liable if it owned the truck, but not otherwise. Under this proof, who should win the case, assuming there is no jury? If there is a jury, what should happen? *See* Kaminsky v. Hertz Corp., 94 Mich.App. 356, 288 N.W.2d 426 (1979); Galvin v. Eli Lilly and Co., 488 F.3d 1026 (D.C. Cir. 2007); Kramer v. Weedhopper of Utah, Inc., 490 N.E.2d 104 (Ill.App. 1986).

¶ 21.26: (a) A rodeo promoter sues Abel's estate, claiming that Abel did not pay for entrance to the rodeo. The promoter introduces a videotape clearly showing that Abel and 999 other fans attended the rodeo. The promoter also introduces her

---

[27] *See, e.g.*, Richard D. Friedman, *Answering the Bayesioskeptical Challenge*, 1 Int'l J. Evid. & Proof 276 (1997); D.H. Kaye, *Do We Need a Calculus of Weight to Understand Proof Beyond a Reasonable Doubt?*, 66 BU.L. Rev. 657, 667 n.20 (1986). Professor Nance, in line with his emphasis on the best-evidence principle, contends that "the burden of proof should reflect the need to avoid rendering a judgment on the basis of an evidentiary package that is unreasonably incomplete, completeness being measured relative to the total package of evidence that is (or should have been) reasonably available to the tribunal." Dale A. Nance, *Evidential Completeness and the Burden of Proof*, 49 Hastings L.J. 621, 621 (1998).

receipts, showing that only 499 of the 1000 paid. There is no other evidence as to who paid and who did not; Abel died shortly after the suit was commenced. Assuming there is no jury, who should win the case? If there is a jury, what should happen?

(b) Assume instead that Abel is still alive but does not take the stand in his own defense. Does that change your conclusion?

(c) Reconsider (a) and (b) on the hypothesis that only 300 of the 1000 spectators paid. What results?

(d) Reconsider (a) and (b) on these varied facts: An entire section of the grandstand had been closed, but a crowd of 1200 fans—of whom 1000, including Abel, were men—took advantage of the ticket-taker, who was blind, and crashed the gate. The ticket-taker testifies that after the rodeo one man came to the gate and paid the admission price, saying he had crashed and felt badly about it. The ticket-taker has no memory at all of what the man sounded like, how old he was, or any other identifying characteristic.

Variations of the blue bus and gatecrasher cases have generated enormous scholarly literature.[28] But these problems raise issues that are not simply of academic interest. If, following Prof. Margaret Berger, we speak of the Blue Pharmaceutical Company, or the Blue Asbestos Company, we can see how these issues become of great importance in mass tort cases.

¶ 21.27: DES was a drug intended to prevent miscarriage. The makers of the drug knew or should have known that it created a grave risk of long-delayed cancer in the daughters of women who took it during pregnancy, but they did not warn of its danger. As a result of DES taken by her mother, Judith Sindell has developed a form of cancer. Approximately 200 companies marketed DES at the time her mother was pregnant, and she is unable to identify which one, or ones, manufactured the doses actually taken by her mother. She sues five of the companies, which in the aggregate appear to have made most of the DES. What should the court do? *See Sindell v. Abbott*

---

[28] These hypotheticals are discussed *passim* in the symposium *Probability and Inference in the Law of Evidence*, 66 B.U. L. Rev. 377 et seq. (1986). *See also, e.g.,* James Franklin, *The Objective Bayesian Conceptualisation of Proof and Reference Class Problems*, 33 Sydney L. Rev. 545 (2011); Tung Yin, *The Probative Values and Pitfalls of Drug Courier Profiles as Probabilistic Evidence*, 5 Tex. F. On C.L. & C.R. 141 (2000); David H.Kaye, David H., *The Paradox of the Gatecrasher and Other Stories*, 1979 Ariz.St.L.J. 101; James L. Brook, *The Use of Statistical Evidence of Identification in Civil Litigation: Well-Worn Hypotheticals, Real Cases, and Controversy*, 29 St. Louis U.L.J. 293 (1985); Mark L. Huffman, Comment, *When the Blue Bus Crashes into the Gate: The Problem with* People v. Collins *in the Probabilistic Evidence Debate*, 46 U. Miami L. Rev. 975 (1992).

Laboratories, 26 Cal.3d 588, 163 Cal.Rptr. 132, 607 P.2d 924, *cert. denied*, 449 U.S. 912 (1980).[29]

¶ **21.28:** (a) Vary the *Sindell* case as follows: Eli Lilly & Co. is clearly established as the manufacturer of the DES taken by Sindell's mother. It is not clear, however, that the DES caused her cancer. The best epidemiological proof available shows that, among women in Sindell's age group, the chance of contracting this type of cancer is 1 in 10,000 for a woman not exposed before birth to DES, and 2.8 in 10,000 for a woman who was exposed. The case is tried to the court. What should the court do? What if the odds for an exposed woman are only 1.4 in 10,000? What if they are 15.6 in 10,000?[30]

(b) Should the outcome change if Sindell brought her suit as a class action on behalf of all women who contracted her form of cancer and whose mothers took Eli Lilly DES? *Cf. In re "Agent Orange" Prod. Liab. Lit.*, 597 F.Supp. 740, 833–43 (E.D.N.Y.1984), *modified on other grounds*, 818 F.2d 145 (2d Cir.1987), *cert. denied*, 484 U.S. 1004 (1988).

F. BURDENS AND PRESUMPTIONS IN CRIMINAL CASES

Now we turn to criminal cases, where the concepts of burdens and presumptions apply differently. At the outset, we may identify three principles that account for much of the difference:

a. Constitutionally, the prosecution must bear the burden of proving any element of the crime—whatever that is—beyond a reasonable doubt.[31]

---

[29] *See also, e.g.*, Ariel Porat, *Misalignments in Tort Law*, 121 Yale L.J. 82, 110 (2011) (arguing that market-share liabiity is necessary to preserve proper alignment between standard of care and risk of liability); Steve Gold, Note, *Causation in Toxic Torts: Burdens of Proof, Standards of Persuasion, and Statistical Evidence*, 96 Yale L.J. 376 (1986).

[30] *See* Daubert v. Merrell Dow Pharmaceuticals, Inc., 43 F.3d 1311, 1320 (9th Cir. 1995) (on remand) (to show that Bendectin more likely than not caused plaintiffs' birth defects, "plaintiffs must establish not just that their mothers' ingestion of Bendectin increased somewhat the likelihood of birth defects, but that it more than doubled it"). Sander Greenland & James M. Robins, *Epidemiology, Justice, and the Problem of Causation*, 40 Jurimetrics J. 321 (2000), contends that the approach reflected by the *Daubert* opinion on remand understates the probability of causation in some cases. If the tortious exposure accelerates an illness, they argue, it could be that the probability that a given individual's illness was caused by the exposure is greater than 50% even though the exposure did not come close to doubling the expected incidence of illness within a given time.

[31] This discussion will not address the doctrine of Apprendi v. New Jersey, 530 U.S. 466 (2000), which held that the Constitution requires that any fact that increases the penalty for a crime beyond what would otherwise be the prescribed statutory maximum, other than the fact of a prior conviction, must be charged in an indictment (if in federal court), submitted to a jury and proved beyond a reasonable doubt. Although in one subsequent case, the Court indicated that

b. No matter how overwhelming the prosecution's evidence is, the accused has a right not to be determined guilty except by jury verdict; a verdict may not be directed against him.

c. The accused has a constitutional right to decline to testify.

1. THE LEVEL OF THE BURDENS IN A CRIMINAL CASE

In *In re Winship*, 397 U.S. 358, 364 (1970), the Supreme Court held that the "beyond a reasonable doubt" standard is constitutionally mandated in criminal cases. If you doubt the wisdom of this decision, think about this. We all know that guilty people often escape criminal punishment. A criminal might not be apprehended; if apprehended, he might not be tried; if tried, he might be acquitted. We are not happy about this situation, but it is an everyday matter that we tolerate. But consider how troubling—and how noteworthy—we find it on those relatively rare occasions when we punish somebody for a crime that, it turns out later, he did not commit. (Such occasions are less rare than was previously supposed; see the National Registry of Exonerations, http://www.law.umich.edu/special/exoneration/Pages/about.aspx.)

Section B.2 suggested that the standard of persuasion in a civil case may be highly variable, depending on the nature of the precise issue at stake. In a criminal case, however, whatever proof "beyond a reasonable doubt" may mean, it means proof to a very high probability. The phrase itself is highly cryptic, and courts have sometimes tried to explain what it means.[32] Sometimes, though, their attempts have just made more of a muddle.

¶ 21.29: (a) Consider whether each of the following instructions should be considered constitutional, and whether the trial court should give it.

(i) "Beyond a reasonable doubt" means more than 95% certain.

(ii) reasonable doubt is defined as follows: It is not a mere possible doubt; because everything relating to human

---

Apprendi applies only to elements of the crime and not "sentencing factors," Harris v. United States, 536 U.S. 545 (2002), the Court has not adhered to that distinction. *See, e.g.,* Ring v. Arizona, 536 U.S. 584 (2002) (determination of facts necessary for death penalty; decided the same day as *Harris*); Blakely v. Washington, 542 U.S. 296 (2004) (sentencing above maximum range that would apply solely on basis of facts admitted in plea bargain, enhancement based on judicially determined facts, held within *Apprendi*); Hurst v. Florida, 136 S.Ct. (2016) (advisory jury verdict not sufficient to avoid rule of *Ring*).

[32] In England, the courts no longer use this expression. Instead, they usually tell the jury that it may find the defendant guilty only if it is "satisfied so as to be sure" of his guilt.

affairs, and depending on moral evidence, is open to some possible or imaginary doubt. It is the state of the case which, after the entire comparison and consideration of all the evidence, leaves the minds of the jurors in that condition that they cannot say they feel an abiding conviction, to a moral certainty, of the truth of the charge.[33]

(iii) "Beyond a reasonable doubt" means that you must be virtually certain. The law does not demand that, for you to find the defendant guilty, you be absolutely certain of his guilt, because there are few, if any, things in life we can be absolutely certain about. But often in life we refrain from taking certain action in the face of uncertainty because the cost if we are wrong is so much greater than the benefit if we are right that it does not make sense to take that action unless we are very sure it is right. You would not, for example, run across a street while a car is approaching at high speed unless you were very sure you could reach the other side safely. The cost if you are wrong—serious injury or death—is so much greater than the benefit if you are right that you almost certainly will stand and wait, even if doing so means that you will be late for an engagement. Similarly, the law regards the cost of finding the defendant guilty when in fact he is innocent as many times worse than the cost of finding him innocent when in fact he is guilty.

(b) Does the meaning of the reasonable doubt standard differ between a petty larceny case and a murder case?

Alongside the high standard of persuasion in a criminal case runs the doctrine that the credibility of witnesses is a matter for the jury. Empirical studies have shown that eyewitness testimony is often much more problematic than most people recognize.[34] Nevertheless, courts

---

[33] This is the key part of the charge given, and upheld against constitutional attack, in *Victor v. Nebraska*, 511 U.S. 1 (1994). Everything after the colon was lifted verbatim from the famous charge given by Chief Justice Lemuel Shaw in *Commonwealth v. Webster*, 59 Mass. 295, 320 (1850). The mysterious phrases "moral evidence" and "moral certainty" have their origins in the philosophical writings of the 17th and 18th centuries. *See Victor, supra,* at 19–12. In upholding the constitutionality of the charge, the Court distinguished it from the charge held constitutionally invalid in *Cage v. Louisiana*, 498 U.S. 39 (1990). The key language of the charge in *Cage* instructed the jury that a reasonable doubt "must be such doubt as would give rise to a grave uncertainty. . . . It is an actual substantial doubt. . . . What is required is not an absolute or mathematical certainty, but a moral certainty." Although the *Cage* Court had put some emphasis on the "moral certainty" phrase, the *Victor* Court emphasized, as had *Cage*, that it is important to look at the charge as a whole, not simply phrase by phrase. *Cage* noted that federal courts have often criticized attempts to define "reasonable doubt."

[34] *See generally* Elizabeth Loftus, et al., *Eyewitness Testimony: Civil and Criminal* (5th ed. 2013); Michael P. Toglia, et al., eds., *Handbook of Eyewitness Psychology* (2 vols. 2007); Christian Sheehan, *Making the Jury the "Experts": The Case for Eyewitness Identification Jury Instructions*, 52 B.C. L. Rev. 651 (2011) (proposing cautionary instructions, before eyewitness

generally hold that the testimony of one witness to a matter that the witness purports to have observed personally is sufficient to establish her description of the event beyond a reasonable doubt. In a few settings courts continue to apply corroboration requirements—as they did, until relatively recently, in rape cases—but for the most part these are things of the past, in part because of the recognition that some crimes have no witnesses but the perpetrator and the victim.[35] Even if evidentiary requirements do not confine them, however, prosecutors often decline to pursue cases absent corroboration—in part because absent corroboration juries are often loath to convict.[36]

Just as the standard of persuasion is heavier in a criminal case, so is the burden of production; in general, the prosecution bears the burden of producing sufficient evidence for a jury to find reasonably that the standard of persuasion has been met. Thus, the Supreme Court has held that a criminal case should not go to the jury unless the prosecution has presented sufficient evidence for a rational jury to find guilt beyond a reasonable doubt. *Jackson v. Virginia*, 443 U.S. 307 (1979). But, as we shall soon see, on some issues the prosecution may have the burden of persuasion but not of production.

2.   THE SPECIFICITY OF THE BURDEN

Granting that the prosecution has the burden of proving the elements of the crime beyond a reasonable doubt, there is a perplexing problem of just what propositions must be proven with that confidence in a given case. Pretty much any proposition can be expressed as a disjunction of multiple propositions. Thus, the proposition "Defendant stabbed the victim with a knife between 10 and 11 pm on July 2" may be divided into "Defendant stabbed the victim with a knife between 10:00 and 10:01 pm on July 2, or . . . between 10:00 and 10:01 pm on July 2, or . . . between 10:59 and 11:00 pm on July 2." And plainly this is just a first cut: We could divide time almost infinitely, and we haven't even started working on the knife.

Now, plainly it suffices for conviction if the jury is persuaded beyond a reasonable doubt that defendant stabbed the victim with a knife between 10 and 11 pm on July 2; the jury does not have to be satisfied

testifies, as a better remedy than expert testimony). For judicial discussions of weaknesses of eyewitness testimony, with references to empirical studies, see, e.g., Arizona v. Youngblood, 488 U.S. 51, 72 n. 8 (1988) (Blackmun, J., dissenting); United States v. Cook, 102 F.3d 249, 252 (7th Cir.1996) (Easterbrook, J.). *See also, e.g.*, Sheri Lynn Johnson, *Cross-Racial Identification Errors in Criminal Cases*, 69 Corn. L. Rev. 934 (1984) (collecting studies).

[35] For a brief discussion of corroboration rules, see Richard D. Friedman, *Anchors and Flotsam: Is Evidence Law "Adrift"?*, 107 Yale L.J. 1921, 1929–30 & nn. 45, 46 (1998).

[36] *See, e.g.*, Susan Estrich, *Rape*, 95 Yale L.J. 1087, 1091 (1986) ("Corroboration requirements unique to rape may have been repealed, but they continue to be enforced as a matter of practice in many jurisdictions.").

beyond a reasonable doubt that any more particularistic proposition is true. But how far can the prosecution take this? The prosecution cannot charge the defendant with having "committed either crime **X** or crime **Y**, we're not really sure which." But what if the state's definition of a crime **Z** is broad enough to include either **X** or **Y** as modes of having committed it?

In *Schad v. Arizona*, 501 U.S. 624 (1991), the defendant was convicted of first degree murder. But the trial court instructed the jury, in accordance with state law, that first degree murder includes both premeditated murder and felony murder; the jurors were not required to agree on one theory or the other, and so far as it appears an individual juror might have voted for conviction even though undecided between the two theories. The *Schad* plurality emphasized that jurors in returning a general verdict are not "required to agree upon a single means of commission." *Id.* at 631. At the same time, the plurality declined to accept the view

> that the Due Process Clause places no limits on a State's capacity to define different courses of conduct, or states of mind, as merely alternative means of committing a single offense, thereby permitting a defendant's conviction without jury agreement as to which course or state actually occurred.

Id. at 632. The plurality also declined "to lay down any single analytical model for determining when two means are so disparate as to exemplify two inherently separate offenses." *Id.* at 643. It did, however, put weight on the question of whether the mental state of the defendant under the two theories of the case could reasonably be considered "moral equivalent[s]." *Id.* at 643–44. *Schad* upheld the defendant's conviction, by a 5–4 vote, but Justice Scalia, who provided the fifth vote for affirmance, did not accept the plurality's analysis; he would have decided the case on the basis that submitting felony murder and premeditated murder to the jury on a single charge is a practice with a long history of acceptance.[37]

The Court's majority pointed in the other direction in *Richardson v. United States*, 526 U.S. 813 (1999). Richardson was tried for engaging in a continuing criminal enterprise, in violation of 21 U.S.C. § 848. The charge required that he have committed a crime that was "a part of a continuing series of violations" of the federal drug laws, and the question was whether the jury had to agree on what violations constituted part of that series. Six members of the Court, per Justice Breyer, posed the question "whether the statute's phrase 'series of violations' refers to one element, namely a 'series,' in respect to which the 'violations' constitute the underlying brute facts or means, or whether those words create

---

[37] *Cf.* Thatcher v. The Queen, 39 D.L.R. (4th) 276 (Sup. Ct. Canada 1987) (holding that it was proper to present a case to the jury on the alternative theories that the accused murdered his wife himself and that he aided and abetted in the murder.).

several elements, namely the several 'violations,' in respect to each of which the jury must agree unanimously and separately." The majority adopted the latter construction. Justice Kennedy, joined by Justices O'Connor and Ginsburg, dissented.

¶ 21.30: In the cases presented below, the prosecution presents evidence to support each of the alternative theories described. Should the jury be allowed to convict without specifying which theory it accepts? In thinking about each of these cases, consider whether the following analysis helps, and how it would apply.

> In all cases in which a defendant is alleged to have committed an offense by one or another, or all, of multiple means, judges must decide if there is sufficient evidence by which individual jurors can find beyond a reasonable doubt that, if the defendant did not commit the alleged offense by one of the alleged means, he must have committed it by another of the alleged means. If such evidence is lacking, judges must instruct jurors that they cannot convict without agreeing on which means the defendant used. If such evidence is present, jurors may convict if, as among the various alleged means, one particular means exists that each juror believes beyond a reasonable doubt is either the very means the defendant used or the means (or among the means) he must have used if he did not use any of the other alleged means.

Peter Westen & Eric Ow, *Reaching Agreement on When Jurors Must Agree*, 10 New Crim. L. Rev. 153, 154 (2007).

(a) Charge: Murder. Prosecution theories: Andersen murdered Saunders, *either* by shooting him or by drowning him. *Cf. Andersen v. United States*, 170 U.S. 481 (1898).

(b) Charge: Assault. Prosecution theories: Able assaulted *either* Baker or Charlie. *See Schad, supra*, 501 U.S. at 651 (Scalia, J., concurring).

(c) Charge: "Crime," defined by statute to include, inter alia, embezzlement, reckless driving, murder, burglary, tax evasion, or littering. Prosecution theories: Acker *either* drove recklessly or embezzled from Evans. *Cf. Schad, supra*, 501 U.S. at 633; *id.* at 656 (White, J., dissenting).

(d) Charge: Theft. Prosecution theories: Asher stole jewels from the victim's house *either* on Friday night or on Saturday night.

(e) Charge: Theft. Prosecution theories: Two jewels were sitting in a bag in the victim's dresser. Asher stole *either* the one on the left or the one on the right.

(f) Charge: Engaging in a "continuing criminal enterprise," under 18 U.S.C. § 848, which requires a "continuing series of violations" of the drug laws, a continuing series being deemed to involve at least three violations. Prosecution theories: Richardson committed at least three of a long series of drug offenses. *See Richardson v. United States*, 526 U.S. 813 (1999).

3. ALLOCATING THE BURDENS ON PARTICULAR ISSUES

In *Winship*, the Court held that constitutional due process requires the "beyond a reasonable doubt standard" to apply to "every fact necessary to constitute the crime with which [the defendant] is charged." 397 U.S. at 364. But sometimes it is not entirely clear what facts those are. That a factual issue may determine the outcome of a criminal trial does not necessarily mean that the prosecution must bear the burden of persuasion. On some issues, labeled as defenses, a jurisdiction may impose on the defendant the burden of persuasion. Furthermore, even if the prosecution bears the burden of persuasion on an issue, that does not necessarily mean that it must also bear the burden of production. In other words, on a given issue it may be that the defendant bears the burden of putting the issue into play, but once he has done so the prosecution must prove its side of the issue beyond a reasonable doubt.

In this subsection, we shall address the prudential standards that guide jurisdictions in allocating the burdens, and also constitutional limitations on ordinary inferences. In Subsection 3, we shall address the constitutional standards that limit the attempts of a jurisdiction to shift the burdens to defendants.

¶ **21.31:** In each of the following criminal prosecutions, who should have the burden of persuasion on the stated issue? If the defendant, what should the measure of that burden be? With respect to each of these issues, who should have the burden of production? If in any of these cases you think the defendant should have the burden of production but not of persuasion, how do you justify the split?

(a) Charge: Carrying a weapon without a license. Issue: Whether defendant was licensed.[38]

---

[38] *See* 29 Am.Jur.2d, *Evidence* § 193 (rev. 2008) (common rule to impose burden of production, but not burden of persuasion, on defendant).

(b) Charge: Robbery. Issue: Whether the defendant, who had previously been kidnapped by her co-conspirators, was acting under duress in committing the robbery.[39]

(c) Charge: Sale of drugs. Issue: Entrapment.[40]

(d) Charge: Possession of morphine without a prescription. Issue: Possession of a prescription.[41]

(e) Charge: Murder. Issue: Self-defense.[42]

(f) Charge: Murder. Issue: Sanity of defendant at the time of the crime.[43]

(g) Charge: Murder. Issue: Whether defendant intended to kill the victim when he struck the fatal blow.[44]

(h) Charge: Murder. Issue: Competence of the accused to stand trial.[45]

(i) Charge: Possession of stolen mail. Issue: Defendant's knowledge that the material had been stolen.[46]

(j) Charge: Conspiracy to distribute narcotics. Issue: Whether defendant withdrew from the conspiracy outside the statute-of-limitations period.[47]

¶ 21.32: A directed verdict cannot be entered against a criminal defendant. Given this, what consequence, if any, would follow from a holding that the defendant has the burden of production on, say, the issue of whether he was entrapped but has not satisfied that burden?

---

[39] *Cf.* Dixon v. United States, 548 U.S. 1 (2006) (involving charges of receiving a firearm while under indictment and of making false statements in connection with the acquisition of a firearm); United States v. Hearst, 563 F.2d 1331, 1336 & n. 2 (9th Cir.1977), cert. denied, 435 U.S. 1000 (1978) (duress claimed by kidnap victim of revolutionary organization who later participated with it in robbery).

[40] *See* United States v. Rivera, 855 F.2d 420, 423–24 (7th Cir.1988).

[41] *See* Casey v. United States, 276 U.S. 413, 418 (1928); Burgin v. State, 431 N.E.2d 864, 866 (Ind.App.1982).

[42] *Cf.* Martin v. Ohio, 480 U.S. 228 (1987) (upholding constitutionality of state law imposing burden of persuasion on defendant).

[43] *See* State v. Box, 109 Wash.2d 320, 745 P.2d 23 (1987); Leland v. Oregon, 343 U.S. 790 (1952), discussed below in ¶ 21.36.

[44] *See* Francis v. Franklin, 471 U.S. 307 (1985), discussed below in Subsection 4.

[45] *See* Medina v. California, 505 U.S. 437 (1992) (upholding against constitutional attack a state statute, Cal. Penal Code § 1367, presuming the defendant to be mentally competent and imposing on him the burden of proving by a preponderance that he is incompetent as a result of mental disorder or developmental disability); Cooper v. Oklahoma, 517 U.S. 348 (1996) (holding unconstitutional state law imposing on defendant burden of proving incompetence by clear and convincing evidence).

[46] *See* Barnes v. United States, 412 U.S. 837 (1973).

[47] *See* Smith v. United States, 133 S.Ct. 714 (2013).

Even assuming the prosecution has the burden of production on an issue, that does not necessarily mean that the prosecution must introduce evidence in addition to that which it has offered on other issues. Like a civil party, the prosecution can ordinarily rely on inferences "that reason and common sense justify in light of the proven facts before the jury." *Francis v. Franklin*, 471 U.S. 307, 314–15 (1985). For example, suppose that in a murder case the prosecution offers a witness's testimony that the defendant fatally wounded the victim by stabbing him three times in the heart, but no additional evidence on the element of intent. A motion by the defendant that the prosecution has failed to prove the element of intent would be rejected out of hand. Clearly, if the jury accepts the prosecution evidence that the defendant stabbed the victim three times in the heart, it can further infer that in doing so the defendant intended to kill the victim; after all, what's the point of stabbing someone multiple times in the heart if not to kill him?[48]

¶ **21.33:** Tombs is on trial in federal court for the crime of possessing material stolen from the mail; if the material was not stolen from the mail, Tombs committed no federal offense. Chenery testifies for the prosecution that she mailed Phelan a check at Marlborough Medical school, and Phelan testifies that she never received it. On cross-examination, Phelan testifies about the delivery and distribution of mail at the medical school, giving a description similar to that in ¶ 21.21. The prosecution offers other evidence proving that the check wound up in the hands of Tombs, who altered it (by the replacement of his name for Phelan's) and cashed it. Both sides then rest. Should the case go to the jury, and if so with what instructions?

¶ **21.34:** Boozer is on trial for violating two statutes, one for the possession of an illegal still and the other for participating in the conduct of an illegal distilling business. There is strong evidence that the still in question was illegal, and was used illegally for the manufacture of liquor. The still is located in a remote, wooded area of public land, accessible only by a badly maintained dirt road (and in the last forty yards only by a footpath). The only evidence linking Boozer to the crimes is that he was found by federal agents sleeping right by the still, which was covered by an unenclosed shed. Should the case go to the jury on either count?[49]

---

[48] *Cf.* United States v. Aluminum Co. of America, 148 F.2d 416, 432 (2d Cir.1945) (L. Hand, J.) (holding that § 2 of the Sherman Act does not require specific intent because "no monopolist monopolizes unconscious of what he is doing").

[49] As we will see in conjunction with ¶ 21.42, there are statutory presumptions that bear on this problem. But for now, consider the problem in the absence of those statutes.

One of the ordinary inferences that a prosecutor might ask a jury to draw is the one that might appear to follow from the absence of evidence. Recall the *Walker* case, ¶ 2.22, in which defense counsel based an argument on the failure of the prosecution to produce a given piece of evidence. Now turn the case around: Suppose that the prosecution has offered proof that Walker's fingerprint was found at the scene of the burglary, and that Walker has not taken the stand to explain how. The prosecutor might be very tempted to say to the jury, "Of course he hasn't testified, because he doesn't have a good explanation of how his fingerprint wound up at the crime scene." But in *Griffin v. California*, 380 U.S. 609, 614 (1965), the Supreme Court held that this type of argument would impose intolerably on the defendant's right to remain silent. The *Griffin* rule is not inevitable; one might hold that the defendant has a right to remain silent but then must bear the ordinary consequences of doing so, one of which is an adverse inference that follows reasonably from the silence.[50] But given that a primary reason why many criminal defendants decline to testify is that doing so would expose them to character impeachment evidence, it seems intolerable to allow a prosecutor to argue that the reason the defendant has not testified is that he has nothing to say helpful to his side. If the rules allowing character impeachment of a criminal defendant were abolished, it might well be worthwhile thinking about whether to alter the *Griffin* rule. Meanwhile, however, the Supreme Court has held that not only is the prosecutor prohibited from asking for an adverse inference from refusal to testify, but the defendant, on request, has a right to have the jury instructed not to draw an adverse interest. *Carter v. Kentucky*, 450 U.S. 288 (1981).[51]

Griffin and *Carter* do not remove all difficulty from the area. One problem is that it is very difficult for a jury to do what *Griffin* says it must, ignore the fact of the defendant's failure to testify. In deciding whether or not there is reasonable doubt about the defendant's guilt, the jury must ask itself whether there is a plausible story consistent with innocence that is also consistent with all the information that the jury has. One piece of information the jury has is that the defendant has not

---

[50] The Court may have moved somewhat in this direction in United States v. Robinson, 485 U.S. 25 (1988). There, the defense contended in its closing argument that Government investigators had not given the defendant a chance to explain his side of the story. The Court treated these comments as opening the door to comments by the prosecutor on the defendant's failure to testify. Writing for the majority, Chief Justice Rehnquist characterized as "broad dicta" *Griffin*'s statement that the Fifth Amendment "forbids . . . comment by the prosecution on the accused's silence." 485 U.S. at 33. The Court went on to say: "There may be some 'cost' to the defendant in having remained silent in each situation [that is, in *Griffin* and in the case before it], but we decline to expand *Griffin* to preclude a fair response by the prosecutor in situations such as the present one." Justice Marshall's dissent complained that the majority was being faithless to the bright-line rule of *Griffin*. *Id.* at 37–38 (Marshall, J., dissenting).

[51] *Carter* emphasized other reasons, besides the threat of character impeachment, why an innocent defendant might not take the stand, including excessive timidity, fear of being a bad witness, and reluctance to incriminate others. 450 U.S. at 300 & n.15.

testified. Telling the jurors not to take this piece of information into account is essentially like telling them to assume that if the defendant were innocent he would be no more likely to testify than if he were guilty. Such an instruction is logically coherent, but it is so far contrary to intuition that compliance with it is very difficult.

Further, *Griffin* does not clearly prohibit prosecutors from seeking an adverse inference from *any* failure of the defendant to present evidence. Some courts have held that the impropriety is only when the inference is sought from the defendant's failure to testify. Of course, if the prosecution evidence is the testimony of a witness as to a conversation she says she held alone with the witness, the inference is obviously addressed to the defendant's failure to testify, for no one else but the defendant could have contradicted the witness's testimony. It is a different matter, however, if, for example, the defense fails to present evidence contradicting a statement on DNA evidence made by a prosecution expert.[52]

¶ 21.35: (a) Walker's fingerprint is at the scene of the burglary, the interior of an apartment. He was found with some of the stolen items, and he has not testified. Should the defense ask for an instruction that the jury is to draw no adverse inferences from Walker's failure to testify? If the defense does not ask for such an instruction, should the court give one anyway?[53]

(b) Now put yourself in a juror's shoes. The court has given a "no adverse instruction" inference. Juror no. 1 says that it is possible that Walker painted the apartment and left his fingerprint there then, and that he was framed by a colleague who put some of the stolen items in his bag. Juror no. 2 points out that there is no evidence to support this story, and says that if there was such evidence Walker would be expected to present it. You are Juror no. 3, and your colleagues are looking for guidance. What response do you have to the comments of Jurors nos. 1 and 2?

---

[52] *See, e.g.*, Mahla v. State, 496 N.E.2d 568, 571–72 (Ind.1986). *Mahla* discussed the distinction "between prosecutorial remarks directed to a defendant's specific decision to remain silent and argument to the effect the defense has presented no evidence to refute the State's case." It also endorsed the condemnation in United States v. Flannery, 451 F.2d 880, 882 (1st Cir.1971), of comments seeking an adverse inference "when it is apparent on the record that there was no one other than himself whom the defendant could have called to contradict the testimony." *See also, e.g.*, United States v. Moore, 917 F.2d 215, 225 (6th Cir.1990), *cert. denied*, 499 U.S. 963 (1991); United States v. Butler, 71 F.3d 243, 255 (7th Cir.1995).

[53] In Lakeside v. Oregon, 435 U.S. 333 (1978), the Court held that it does not violate the Constitution to give a "no adverse inference" instruction over defense objection.

4. CONSTITUTIONAL LIMITATIONS ON ATTEMPTS TO ALLOCATE THE BURDENS

Legislatures often attempt to ease the burdens on the prosecution in a criminal case. Courts may do this as well, either explicitly by announcing a rule of general application or effectively in a particular case through the instructions to the jury. In this subsection, we will discuss the constitutional hurdles that such attempts must clear.

Oddly enough, the most powerful way in which a jurisdiction can ease the prosecution's burden is also the one least vulnerable to constitutional attack: It may simply alter the definition of the crime. For example, the statute prohibiting knowing possession of stolen mail, 18 U.S.C. § 1708, used to include as an element the defendant's knowledge that the material was stolen from the United States mail. Proving this element turned out to be an "impossible burden" on the prosecution, *Smith v. United States*, 343 F.2d 539, 543 (5th Cir.1965), and so Congress simply amended the statute; the statute no longer requires that the defendant knew that the material was stolen from the mails. *Barnes v. United States*, 412 U.S. 837, 847 (1973). Presto! The Government must still prove that the material was stolen from the mails and that the defendant knew it was stolen, but it doesn't have the burden on the issue of whether the defendant knew it was stolen from the mails because there is no such issue any more.[54]

Apart from amending the substantive criminal standards, jurisdictions often try to ease the prosecution's burdens in two basic ways. First, they may try to do so directly, providing that on a particular issue the defendant has the burdens. Second, they may provide that certain types of evidence are to be given certain types of effect; in particular, they may create a statutory inference or presumption.

We will first consider direct allocations of the burdens.

¶ 21.36: Consider *Leland v. Oregon*, 343 U.S. 790 (1952). There, the Supreme Court upheld against constitutional attack a provision of state law imposing on the defendant the burden of proving beyond a reasonable doubt that he was insane at the time of the charged crime. Do you think this is the proper outcome? If you think it was not, would your opinion change if only a preponderance burden was placed on the defendant? Would *Leland* be decided the same way after *Winship*? Assuming *Leland* was decided correctly, could a state nevertheless impose

---

[54] Where the legislature does not clearly express an intention to remove an element from the definition of a crime, it may expect the courts to construe the statute as adhering to the traditional definition. *See, e.g.*, Morissette v. United States, 342 U.S. 246 (1952) (reading element of criminal intent into a federal theft statute).

on the prosecution the burden of persuasion on the insanity issue?

Consider *Mullaney v. Wilbur*, 421 U.S. 684 (1975), and *Patterson v. New York*, 432 U.S. 197 (1977), both state murder cases. In *Mullaney*, the judge told the jurors that malice aforethought was an essential element for the crime of murder. But he also told them that if the prosecution proved that the homicide was both intentional and unlawful, malice aforethought should be presumed, unless the defendant proved "by a fair preponderance of the evidence that . . . he killed in the heat of passion upon sudden provocation."[55] Such a showing would reduce the charge to manslaughter. The Court held that this charge violated *Winship*. Maine was not providing that even if the defendant acted with malice aforethought the crime could be reduced to manslaughter if he also acted in the heat of passion on sudden provocation; rather, as the trial judge explained the terms, they were "two inconsistent things." Thus, the instruction provided in substance that, given an intentional and unlawful killing, an essential element of the crime should be presumed, with the defendant having the opportunity to prove by a preponderance that the element did not hold. 421 U.S. at 686–87, 700–01.

In *Patterson*, by contrast, the state defined murder in the second degree to be intentional killing of another person and provided for reduction to manslaughter if the defendant proved by a preponderance of the evidence that he had acted under the influence of "extreme emotional disturbance." The Court upheld this provision. New York's statute did not require malice aforethought as an element of murder; it only required death, causation, and intent. To prove "extreme emotional disturbance," therefore, the defendant would not be required to disprove an element of the crime as New York had defined it. Thus, by including less in the definition of the crime, New York was able to put a greater burden on the defendant.

¶ 21.37: (a) Do you agree with either *Mullaney* or *Patterson* or both? Do you find persuasive the distinction drawn by the Court? Is there any substance to it? Does it give a perverse incentive to the legislature?

(b) Suppose a state defines criminal assault in the first degree and an affirmative defense to it as follows:

> Criminal assault in the first degree is an act that causes, and is intended to cause, harmful contact with another person, done without the consent of the other person. It is an

---

[55] For quotations from the charge, see the opinions of the Court of Appeals in 473 F.2d 943, 944 (1st Cir.1973), and 496 F.2d 1303, 1304 (1st Cir.1974). *Mullaney* was in the federal courts on the defendant's petition for habeas corpus relief.

affirmative defense to criminal assault in the first degree
that the other person did not die as a result of the contact.
The defendant shall bear the burden of proof as to this
defense. If, but for this defense, the defendant would be
guilty of criminal assault in the first degree, he or she is
guilty of criminal assault in the second degree.

Would this statute be constitutional? Practical?[56]

Now let us consider the effect of statutes and other rules that
prescribe the effect that a given body of evidence is to have. The language
of such rules is often confusing, leaving it unclear just what effect the
evidence is supposed to have.[57] And trial courts frequently compound the
difficulty, because it is often difficult to tell just what they intended their
jury instructions to mean—or, more significantly, just what a jury likely
inferred the instructions to mean.[58]

Thus, such a rule might have any of several different meanings.
First, and most drastically, it might be intended to create a conclusive
presumption—that is, to provide that, if the jurors find a given
proposition to be true, then they must find an element of the crime to be
proven. *Second*, it might be construed to be a rebuttable presumption, but
one that shifts the burden of persuasion on an element of the crime as
well as the burden of production. *Sandstrom v. Montana*, 442 U.S. 510
(1979), addressed the constitutionality of such provisions.

Sandstrom was another state murder case. The defendant
acknowledged having committed the homicide but contended that,
because of a personality order aggravated by alcohol, he did not do so
"purposely or knowingly," as required by Montana's definition of
"deliberate homicide." The trial court instructed the jury that "the law
presumes that a person intends the ordinary consequences of his
voluntary acts." The Supreme Court held that the jury might have
construed this instruction as establishing a conclusive presumption or as

---

[56] *Cf.* Schad v. Arizona, 501 U.S. 624, 633 ("there are limits on a State's authority to decide
what facts are indispensable to proof of a given offense"), 640 ("a freakish definition of the
elements of a crime that finds no analogue in history or in the criminal law of other jurisdictions"
is vulnerable to condemnation as invalid burden-shifting).

[57] Consider, for example, the statute involved in Tot v. United States, 319 U.S. 463 (1943),
providing that possession of a firearm is "presumptive evidence" that the possession is illegal. It
seems doubtful that this statute was intended to create a true presumption, so that in the
absence of any further evidence on legality the jury would be violating its instructions if it
acquitted; most likely it was intended to express a legislative judgment that possession was
sufficient to get the case to the jury.

[58] The Supreme Court has declared that in determining the validity of a jury instruction
the critical question is "whether there is a reasonable likelihood that the jury has applied the
challenged instruction in a way that violates the Constitution." Estelle v. McGuire, 502 U.S. 62,
72 (1991) (citation and internal quotation marks omitted). In doing so, it disapproved of language
that had inquired into how a "reasonable juror" would have understood the instruction. *Id.* at
n.4.

shifting the burden of persuasion on the "purposely or knowingly" issue to the defendant. Neither type of presumption would be valid under *Winship*, the Court held.

¶ **21.38:** Suppose the state legislature had expressly provided, "In the determination of whether a defendant who has committed homicide acted purposely or knowingly, it shall be conclusively presumed that the defendant intended the ordinary consequences of his or her voluntary acts." That clearly would be invalid under *Sandstrom*. But now suppose that the legislature, instead of defining "deliberate homicide," defined "predictable homicide" as follows: "Homicide is predictable homicide if the defendant acted purposely or knowingly, or if homicide was the ordinary consequence of the defendant's voluntary acts." Would this be valid?

¶ **21.39:** (a) Does the holding in *Sandstrom* regarding presumptions that shift the burden of persuasion conflict with the holding of *Leland v. Oregon*, discussed in ¶ 21.36, that a state may impose the burden of persuasion on the defendant on an affirmative defense? If the two are reconcilable, how do you distinguish between an element and an affirmative defense? The following hypothetical statutes press this issue.

(b) First, suppose the Montana legislature revamps its homicide statute in the following way. Section 1 provides that a person commits criminal homicide in the first degree if he or she "causes the death of another being without justification." Section 2 provides that, "in a homicide prosecution, if the elements of criminal homicide in the first degree are proved beyond a reasonable doubt by the prosecution but the defendant proves to a preponderance of the evidence that he or she did not act purposely or knowingly, then he or she shall be guilty of criminal homicide in the second degree, and not of criminal homicide in the first degree." Section 3 provides penalties, the penalties for the first-degree crime being the same as those previously provided for deliberate homicide, and the penalties for the second-degree crime being comparable to those previously provided for lower-level homicides. Is this statute valid?

(c) Similarly, consider whether the following statute would be constitutional:

It shall be a misdemeanor for any person to operate a motor vehicle while his or her blood alcohol level is 0.10% or greater; provided that, it shall be an affirmative defense, as to which the defendant shall bear the burden of persuasion, that at the time the defendant was not under the influence of alcohol to the extent that his or her normal faculties were impaired.

¶ **21.40:** *Montana v. Egelhoff,* 518 U.S. 37, 116 S.Ct. 2013 (1996), concerned a state statute providing that voluntary intoxication "may not be taken into consideration in determining the existence of a mental state which is an element of [a criminal] offense." The state supreme court, viewing the statute as one that improperly excludes probative evidence of mental state, unanimously held that the statute violated the accused's constitutional right to present a defense. By a 5–4 vote, with no majority opinion, the United States Supreme Court reversed. The plurality emphasized that the Montana statute restored what had been the dominant rule at common law in an earlier period. Justice Ginsburg in concurrence characterized the statute as a redefinition of the mental-state element of the offense. The dissenters, acknowledging that the state could redefine that element, concluded that it had not done so. Does the result in *Egelhoff* amount to a cut-back on *Sandstrom,* in that the statute presumes conclusively that voluntary intoxication has no bearing on the existence of a culpable mental state?

Third, and as an intermediate possibility, a statute or rule prescribing the effect of a given body of evidence might be construed to impose a true, ordinary, rebuttable presumption—that is, simply to shift the burden of production to the defendant. The Supreme Court has made various pronouncements on the validity of such presumptions against a criminal defendant. *County Court of Ulster County v. Allen,* 442 U.S. 140, 167 (1979), indicated that a mandatory presumption (what we have been calling an ordinary rebuttable presumption) may be valid if "the fact proved is sufficient to support the inference of guilt beyond a reasonable doubt." But the same term the Court decided *Sandstrom,* with its condemnation of presumptions that shift the burden of persuasion. The Court later confirmed that condemnation, in *Francis v. Franklin,* 471 U.S. 307 (1985).[59] It is not clear why, if presumptions that shift the burden of persuasion on an element of the crime are not allowed, a presumption ought to be allowed to shift the burden of production. Given that a proposition is an element of the crime as defined by governing law, it seems that the jury should never be told that some lesser proposition

---

[59] In *Francis,* the Court stated squarely: "Mandatory presumptions . . . violate the Due Process Clause if they relieve the State of the burden of persuasion on an element of the offense." *Id.* at 314. The Court divided 5–4, but not over the issue of whether presumptions that shift the burden of persuasion are invalid; the dissent, by Justice Powell, assumed that such instructions are invalid but contended that in context the instruction involved in that case could not reasonably be viewed as shifting that burden. *Id.* at 327–28 (Powell, J., dissenting).

requires a finding against the defendant. If the legislature wants to redefine the crime, it may, but presumptions should not fill in for lack of legislative will.

Francis seemed to take a step in the direction of this argument, including a footnote seemingly inconsistent with *Allen*: "We are not required to decide in this case whether a mandatory presumption that shifts only a burden of production to the defendant is consistent with the Due Process Clause, and we express no opinion on that question." 471 U.S. at 314 n.3. The Court went further in this direction in *Carella v. California*, 491 U.S. 263, 265 (1989), in which the Court seemed to suggest that any "mandatory" presumption is unconstitutional, such a presumption being defined as one that would "require [the jury] to find the presumed fact if the State proves certain predicate facts." Note that the Court did not distinguish between presumptions that shift the burden of persuasion and those that do not. Carella's jury was told that a person is "presumed to have embezzled" a rented vehicle if it is not returned within five days of the expiration of the rental agreement, and that "intent to commit theft by fraud is presumed" from failure to return rented property within twenty days of demand. "These mandatory directions," declared the Court,

> directly foreclosed independent jury consideration of whether the facts proved established certain elements of the offenses with which Carella was charged. The instructions also relieved the State of its burden of proof articulated in *Winship*, namely, proving by evidence every essential element of Carella's crime beyond a reasonable doubt.

Id. at 266. Hence, the Court held the instructions unconstitutional. And in *Yates v. Evatt*, 500 U.S. 391, 401–02 & nn.6, 7 (1991), the Court apparently assumed implicitly that any "mandatory presumption" against a criminal defendant—including one that, like the presumption involved in that case, did not shift the burden of persuasion—would be unconstitutional.[60]

¶ 21.41: To examine more closely what's at stake here, let's use a simple shorthand. **DUI** stands for the proposition that the defendant was driving under the influence of alcohol to the extent that his normal faculties were impaired, and **BAL10** for the proposition that his blood alcohol level was 0.10% or greater. Suppose the state's criminal law provides that the defendant has

---

[60] *Yates* held that the error in giving two instructions creating such presumptions was not harmless. The trial judge in that case instructed the jury that malice, an element of the crime, "is implied or presumed by the law from the willful, deliberate, and intentional doing of an unlawful act without any just cause or excuse" and also from the use of a deadly weapon, but that these presumption are rebuttable.

committed a misdemeanor if **DUI** is true, and that its evidentiary law provides that if **BAL10** is true then the defendant bears the burden of producing evidence that **DUI** is not true.

(a) Suppose that the judge in a particular case holds that the defendant has not met that burden by offering sufficient evidence contrary to **DUI**. Then it would seem that an instruction of this sort would be called for by the statute:

> If you find that the defendant's blood alcohol level was 0.10% or greater, then you must find that he was driving under the influence of alcohol.

Do you think that is a valid instruction under the Supreme Court cases? Should it be? What, if anything, does it achieve?

(b) If the judge holds that the defendant *has* met the burden of producing evidence contrary to **DUI,** is any instruction regarding the burden of production proper?

(c) You are clerking for a judge who is contemplating the following instruction. Advise her as to whether you think it is valid, and how she might alter it if she wishes to minimize her chances of being reversed on appeal.

> If you find from the evidence that the defendant had a blood alcohol level of 0.10% or more, that evidence would be sufficient by itself to establish that the defendant was under the influence of alcohol to the extent that his normal faculties were impaired. However, such evidence may be contradicted or rebutted by other evidence.[61]

Finally, and at the opposite end of the spectrum, a statute prescribing the effect of a given body of evidence might be more modestly interpreted as merely a declaration that the body of evidence is sufficient to warrant a given inference. The constitutional problems posed by such a statute—if it clearly has only this effect—are less urgent than those posed by a statute that purports to bind the jury. We might well wonder, though, why legislation is needed for cases in which the evidence does reasonably support the inference, and whether the statutory provision

---

[61] *See* State v. Rolle, 560 So.2d 1154 (Fla.), *cert. denied*, 498 U.S. 867 (1990) (holding instruction valid, reversing decision of intermediate appellate court); *cf.* Wilhelm v. State, 568 So.2d 1 (Fla. 1990) (holding unconstitutional an instruction that evidence of a blood alcohol level of .10% "is a prima facie case that the defendant was under the influence . . ."; *Rolle* distinguished on the basis that " '[p]rima facie' is a technical legal term without a common meaning for the lay person"); Miller v. Norvell, 775 F.2d 1572, 1574 (11th Cir.1985) (holding invalid an instruction that failure to spend funds properly "shall constitute prima facie evidence of intent to defraud"; instruction might have been understood to require finding of intent to defraud absent rebuttal evidence), *cert. denied*, 476 U.S. 1126 (1986).

should be honored in cases in which the evidence does *not* support the inference.

¶ **21.42:** (a) Reconsider ¶ 21.34, Boozer's case, in light of the statutes that were at issue in *United States v. Gainey*, 380 U.S. 63 (1965), and *United States v. Romano*, 382 U.S. 136 (1965). *Gainey* involved a statute that made presence at the site of a still sufficient to convict the defendant of carrying on the business of distilling—a broad offense that covered almost any act connected with the operation of a still—"unless the defendant explain[ed] such presence to the satisfaction of the jury." *Romano* involved a similar statute that allowed unexplained presence at the still to support an inference of possession of the still. Should these statutes change the outcomes on either count of Boozer's indictment? The Court held the statute in *Gainey* valid but not the statute in *Romano*. Can you see why? Does this make sense?

(b) Alter ¶ 21.34 in this way: Boozer is a farmer, and the still at which he was found was about one hundred yards off his property, in thick woods. Boozer was not asleep but was kneeling, loading a shotgun, when he was arrested. What results now, in light of the statutes?

G. JUDICIAL NOTICE

FRE 201

Additional Reading: McCormick, ch. 35; Mueller & Kirkpatrick, ch. 2

Speaking generally, the term judicial notice refers to circumstances in which the judicial system assumes a factual proposition to be true even without proof of that proposition. The term is used casually, however, to cover several different meanings.

First is what is sometimes called "jury notice" but should more properly be called *factfinder notice*.[62] This refers to the idea that sometimes a factfinder, whether judge or jury, may act on the belief that a given proposition is true, even without proof of that proposition. For example, we have seen that in a murder case the prosecution can satisfy its burden of producing evidence on intent to kill by showing that the defendant stabbed the victim multiple times in the heart. The unspoken premise here is that a person who stabs another multiple times in the heart probably intends to kill the victim. We would not demand that the prosecution introduce evidence of that premise; this is something jurors could bring with them into the courthouse from their knowledge of the

---

[62] *Cf.* John Mansfield, *Jury Notice*, 74 Geo.L.J. 395 (1985).

world. Or, in a bench trial, so could the judge, who might say that she is taking "judicial notice" of that proposition.

¶ 21.43: "The factfinder may operate on the basis of a proposition only if (i) evidence has been introduced as to that proposition, or (ii) the proposition is not reasonably subject to dispute." Do you agree with this assertion? In thinking about this, consider whether the following propositions are beyond reasonable dispute, and whether evidence of them should be required before the factfinder can act on them:

(a) "Eating a sandwich with one hand while driving substantially raises one's chances of getting into an accident."

(b) "A letter addressed to an employee of a medical school and delivered to the school's mailroom will probably be delivered to the addressee reasonably timely."

The second sense in which the term judicial notice is used is really the classic case, and the one addressed by FRE 201, what is known as judicial notice of an *adjudicative fact*. Roughly speaking, an adjudicative fact is one that, given the governing law, is significant to the present case. Judicial notice in this sense consists of an instruction by the judge mandating that the jury accept a certain fact as true: "Members of the jury, the ferry from Boomville to Bustville runs in a southerly direction." It may seem strange at first that the judge is doing some of the factfinding, but recall that in the case of presumptions in a civil case the judge also gives an instruction that mandates a finding. Of course, the presumption is conditional, in that it only takes effect if the jury finds the predicate fact to be true. But most judicial notice instructions could also be expressed in this conditional way, such as: "If you find that this boat was a ferry and that it was going from the Boomville docks to the Bustville docks, then you must find that it was moving in a southerly direction."

Of course, in the ferry example it is unlikely that there is any serious dispute as to whether the boat was a ferry and the direction in which it was moving, whereas in the presumption case the predicate may be hotly in dispute. But recall that this is not always true about presumptions, either; the court may pronounce a presumption that if the car driven by Ernie was Oscar's (when nobody doubts that it was), then Ernie is presumed to have been acting as Oscar's agent.

The principal difference between an invocation of judicial notice and an ordinary presumption is that—at least usually, and in a civil case—the court will not allow evidence controverting the proposition covered by the judicial notice instruction. *See* FRE 201(f) and Advisory Committee Note to original FRE 201(g). In this sense, judicial notice resembles an irrebuttable presumption. But notice the two qualifications.

¶ **21.44:** It is sometimes said that judicial notice should only be allowed in cases that are beyond reasonable dispute, and therefore that if judicial notice is proper, contradicting evidence is inappropriate. This appears to be the logic behind the portion of FRE 201 applicable to civil cases. What argument could you make that, at least in a class of cases, judicial notice should be invoked but the opposing side should have the option of introducing contrary evidence?

¶ **21.45:** FRE 201(f) makes clear that a criminal jury is not required to accept as conclusive any fact judicially noticed. Why does the rule include this provision? Is it broader than necessary? Does it mean that the opponent has the right to introduce evidence contrary to a fact judicially noticed?

The basis for invoking judicial notice seems to be that, even absent the formal introduction of evidence, the proposition in question appears overwhelmingly probable. As FRE 201(b) indicates, there are two basic ways of reaching that conclusion: The proposition may be "generally known within the trial court's territorial jurisdiction," or it may be capable of being "accurately and readily determined from sources whose accuracy cannot reasonably be questioned." The first, or "common knowledge," branch sometimes poses problems, because it may be tempting for the judge to instruct the jury on matters that she knows (or believes she knows!) to be true, even though they are not generally known.

¶ **21.46:** In an auto negligence case, which of the following may the judge properly tell the jury?

(a) "Jurors, lest there be any confusion, Elm Street is one way running west, and Pine Street is one way running south."

(b) "Jurors, on April 27, the sun set at 7:42 in the evening."

(c) "Jurors, at the time of evening when this accident occurred, the sun is very difficult for a driver on Elm Street."

(d) "Jurors, a standard shift car is most efficiently driven between 2,000 and 3,000 rpm."

¶ **21.47:** (a) If a proposition is really generally known within the jurisdiction, what need is there for the court to take judicial notice of it? Think about this in two circumstances: Suppose that the plaintiff's argument that the court should take judicial notice of a proposition is made (i) during his presentation of his evidence, or (ii) at the close of the case, when he is responding to a motion for directed verdict. *See generally* Leonard M. Niehoff, *Judicial Notice: The* Deus Ex Machina *of Evidence*, 27 Litigation No. 1, p. 31 (Fall 2000).

> (b) Can a proposition be so well known within the jurisdiction that a judicial notice instruction is not even needed? Think of an example or two.

A third sense of the term judicial notice refers to notice of what are called *legislative facts*. The Advisory Committee's Note to FRE 201 is helpful in explaining legislative facts; you should read it carefully. Basically, the idea is that often (perhaps always) in deciding what the law is a court must act at least implicitly on its perception of some general facts of how the world works.[63] The Committee offered a useful example. In *Hawkins v. United States*, 358 U.S. 74 (1958), the Supreme Court adhered to the old rule that a criminal defendant has a privilege to preclude his spouse from testifying against him. The opinion included this passage:

> [N]ot all marital flare-ups in which one spouse wants to hurt the other are permanent. The widespread success achieved by courts throughout the country in conciliating family differences is a real indication that some apparently broken homes can be saved provided no unforgivable act is done by either party. Adverse testimony given in criminal proceedings would, we think, be likely to destroy almost any marriage.

Id. at 77–78. In *Trammel v. United States*, 445 U.S. 40 (1980), the Court limited Hawkins by holding that only the witness-spouse has the privilege; she "may be neither compelled to testify nor foreclosed from testifying." *Id.* at 53. *Trammel* included this sentence:

> When one spouse is willing to testify against the other in a criminal proceeding—whatever the motivation—their relationship is almost certainly in disrepair; there is probably little in the way of marital harmony for the privilege to preserve.

Id. at 52. Note how the two decisions came to fundamentally different conclusions as to what the law should be, based on different perceptions about the facts of the world.

The court can act on its perception of legislative facts even if those facts are not established beyond genuine dispute; indeed, sometimes it *has* to do this. Thus, in deciding the *Hawkins-Trammel* issue of whether the defendant-spouse has the privilege, the Court did not have the luxury of operating on the basis of universally acknowledged facts concerning the dynamics of marriage; rather, the Court had to take one view or another

---

[63] Note the implicit legal realism here; we are assuming that at least sometimes courts make law and not only discern it. Judicial notice of legislative facts may actually be considered a species of factfinder notice because, even where there is a jury, it is the court that decides these facts.

of those dynamics, and the persuasiveness of its decision depends largely on the persuasiveness of its perception on that score.

Nor, in deciding legislative facts, is a court limited to the presentations made by the parties. If the judicial system reaches a poor result because a party does a terrible job in presenting the adjudicative facts of its case, then (for the most part) it is only that party who is hurt; the factual findings in the case do not bind parties who were not represented. But the same is not true of questions of law. When a court adopts a principle of law, it means for the principle to be applied in other cases presenting materially similar circumstances; that is a large part of what law is all about. It would not be acceptable for a court to adopt a poor principle of law because the advocacy in the first case presenting the issue was inferior—"Sorry, we know this is bad law that we're applying against you, and we knew it was bad even when we enunciated it the first time, but our hands were tied because the lawyering in that case was so weak." The court is permitted to do, and should do, its own thinking and its own research on questions of law. And the same holds true for issues of legislative fact, because these issues have the same breadth of application as issues of law. If the parties do not present the court with the materials it feels it needs to ascertain a matter of legislative fact, the court can do its own research.

What limitations are there? Basically, the thickness of the court's own skin. Suppose the Supreme Court had said in *Hawkins* or in *Trammel*,

> We really don't know very much about the likely effects on marriages of allowing the witness spouse to testify over the defendant spouse's objection. We're not confident that we can rely on whatever we learn in our own library research. And we sure don't like the idea of trying to decide this by having our own conversations with social psychologists.

Given that perspective, the Court might decide that the issue is one on which open advocacy at the trial level would help, perhaps with an evidentiary hearing at which the parties, and even the court, could call expert witnesses. But eventually, the court of last resort would have to determine its own view of the legislative facts.

Do not assume that there is always a clear line between legislative and adjudicative facts. Sometimes that depends on how the court sets up an issue. If the court says, "If fact **A** is true, then proposition **B** is the law," then **A** appears to be a legislative fact. On the other hand, if the court says, "The law is that if fact **A** is true then consequence **B** follows," then **A** appears to be an adjudicative fact. Which form is better will depend in part on whether the truth of **A** appears to be constant from one case to another; if so, on whether the court wishes to determine the facts rather than leave them, say, to a jury in a class action; and on whether the court wishes to enunciate a broad rule of law.

For example, it makes perfect sense to say, "The law governing cases in which a stillbirth was caused by asphyxiation is that if the obstetrician delayed unduly in performing a Caesarian, then the obstetrician was negligent." It does not make sense to say, "Obstetricians delay unduly in performing Caesarians. Therefore, the law governing cases in which a stillbirth was caused by asphyxiation is that the obstetrician was negligent." On the other hand, if the court sees a given medical technique recurring from case to case, it may be tempted to create a flat rule— "Chorionic villus sampling in the seventh week of pregnancy does not accord with acceptable standards of medical practice"—to avoid inconsistent results and the necessity for repeat determination of the same facts.

¶ **21.48:** Consider *Brown v. Board of Education*, 347 U.S. 483 (1954). The Court's decision was based in significant part on this conclusion regarding children in grade and high schools: "To separate them from others of similar age and qualifications solely because of their race generates a feeling of inferiority as to their status in the community that may affect their hearts and minds in a way unlikely ever to be undone." *Id.* at 494. Suppose a trial court in a desegregation case after *Brown* holds an evidentiary hearing and concludes, "Whatever the effect may be elsewhere, the evidence is clear that in this school district separating children on the basis of race avoids generating feelings of inferiority on the part of one group or another and enables children of both races to perform better in and out of school." The court therefore declines to order desegregation of the school district. What should an appellate court do?[64]

¶ **21.49:** In *Rusk v. State*,[65] the defendant was accused of raping the complaining witness. He admitted having had sex with her, but claimed that it was consensual. The evidence of coercion included various circumstances—such as the facts that the defendant had taken her car keys, and that she was in a bad neighborhood that she did not know well. Also, the complainant testified that at one point the defendant "lightly choked" her, though at oral argument it appeared that this might have been a

[64] A few trial courts tried this tack, *e.g.*, Stell v. Savannah-Chatham Cty. Bd. of Educ., 220 F.Supp. 667, 676–78 (S.D.Ga.1963), and got promptly slapped down. *See* Stell v. Savannah-Chatham County Bd. of Ed., 333 F.2d 55, 61 (5th Cir.), *cert. denied*, 379 U.S. 933 (1964); Jackson Municipal Separate School Dist. Jackson Municipal Separate School Dist. v. Evers, 357 F.2d 653 (5th Cir.), *cert. denied*, 384 U.S. 961 (1966).

[65] 43 Md.App. 476, 406 A.2d 624 (1979) (en banc), *reversed*, 289 Md. 230, 424 A.2d 720 (1981), *discussed in* Susan Estrich, *Rape*, 95 Yale L.J. 1087, 1112–15 (1986).

"heavy caress." The majority of the Court of Special Appeals (which was later reversed) wrote:

> We do not believe that "lightly choking" along with all the facts and circumstances in the case [was] sufficient to cause a reasonable fear which overcame her ability to resist.

43 Md.App. at 499, 406 A.2d at 628. Is this an assertion of law, of fact, or of both? To the extent it is an assertion of fact, is it of legislative or adjudicative fact? Who should decide whether it is true? With what information, and on what authority?

Professors Laurens Walker and John Monahan have contended that in some cases social research findings may be neither adjudicative nor legislative facts in themselves but may incorporate aspects of both these uses. In this use, which Walker and Monahan call "social frameworks," "general research results are used to construct a frame of reference or background context for deciding factual issues crucial to the resolution of a specific case."[66] They argue that the court should instruct the jury on such frameworks in much the way that it does on matters of law, or when it takes judicial notice of an adjudicative fact, with similar binding effect.[67]

¶ 21.50: Davis, age 27, has pleaded guilty to murder. A trial is now being held in front of a jury to determine whether he should be executed or serve a mandatory minimum thirty-year sentence. The defendant has a sociologist who is prepared to testify or argue that numerous studies show that murderers have a low recidivism rate, that males aged 55–59 are highly unlikely to commit homicide, and that after age 29 crime rates decrease with age, so that it is very unlikely Davis, if sentenced to the thirty-year term, would ever again commit a serious crime. What use, if any, should the court make or allow of the sociologist's data?[68]

---

[66] Laurens Walker & John Monahan, *Social Frameworks: A New Use of Social Science in Law*, 73 Va.L.Rev. 559, 559 (1987).

[67] *Id.* at 594. In Laurens Walker & John Monahan, *Social Facts: Scientific Methodology as Legal Precedent*, 76 Cal.L.Rev. 877 (1988), they contend that social science methodologies, but not applications, should have precedential force. The Supreme Court's decision in *General Electric Co. v. Joiner*, discussed in Chapter 5, suggests that courts are likely to be hesitant to draw this distinction.

[68] See State v. Davis, 96 N.J. 611, 477 A.2d 308 (1984) (holding that evidence of this type is admissible because it may "encapsulate ordinary human experience and provide an appropriate frame of reference for a jury's consideration of a defendant's character"), *discussed in* Walker & Monahan, *Social Frameworks*, *supra*, at 565–70, 596 & n.123 (suggesting communicating information of this sort by instruction)

H. STIPULATIONS

When a court takes judicial notice of an adjudicative fact, it determines that no evidence of the fact is necessary—and, in a civil case under FRE 201(f), no other evidence is even allowed. There is another way in which evidence of a material proposition may be rendered unnecessary and even inadmissible: The parties, or a party, may stipulate to it.

Stipulations are a type of what is sometimes called *judicial admissions*. This distinguishes them from *evidentiary admissions*, the ordinary type of admissions we studied in Chapter 14. Recall that the making of an evidentiary admission must be proven like any other out-of-court event, and proof of it does not foreclose litigation of an issue; the party who made the admission may contend, for a variety of reasons, that the admission was not true. Judicial admissions are very different. They are formal acknowledgments of the truth of a proposition, made as part of the litigation, through the lawyer in the case of a represented party, and they are sought and made for the purpose of establishing the proposition as true in the litigation without the need for evidence. A judicial admission may be made in the course of an answer to the complaint in civil litigation, as under Fed. R. Civ. P. 8(b). Or it may be made in response to a formal request to admit, as under Fed. R. Civ. P. 36. Or it may be made in writing, or even orally in open court, by the lawyer formally stipulating to the truth of a proposition.

Once you make a judicial admission, you are precluded from contesting the admitted fact, unless the court or governing rules grant you relief. Though amendment of pleadings early in the litigation is relatively easy, getting relief from a judicial admission later on can be very difficult. Some courts say that relief should be granted only to prevent "manifest injustice" or where the stipulation was entered through inadvertence or because of an erroneous view of the facts or law. *E.g. Southworth v. Board of Regents*, 307 F.3d 566, 571 (7th Cir. 2002). Assuming the stipulation remains binding, there is sometimes disagreement over just how much the party admitted; the stipulation, like any other text, may be subject to varying interpretations.

If a proposition is provable and not in genuine dispute, a lawyer ought generally be willing to stipulate to it, as a matter of professional responsibility and courtesy—and, if nothing else, to save the lawyer's own time. But lawyers are often hesitant to give away something for nothing. Stipulations are typically made as part of a lawyers' deal. For example, the court may encourage the lawyers, in preparing a pretrial order, to stipulate to as many issues as possible so that the issues requiring trial can be narrowed. The lawyers may therefore trade stipulations, each giving away little issues that they did not seriously plan to contest anyway.

Another situation in which stipulations are made as part of a deal often arises when one party offers evidence that has some probative value on a material issue but that might also be prejudicial in its favor on another issue. Typically, it is a prosecutor who is the offering party, seeking to gain admittance of a prior bad act of the defendant. Suppose the defendant is charged with theft from a bank, allegedly committed by picking the lock on the bank's sophisticated safe. The prosecution offers evidence that once, twenty years before, the defendant picked the lock on the door to the pantry of his high school. The defendant makes the predictable objection. The prosecutor might respond, "I'm not offering this on a propensity basis. I'm offering it because it shows that the defendant had the ability to pick the lock on the bank's safe. If the defendant will stipulate that he had that ability, I will withdraw the proffer." Thus, the prosecutor might use the threat of offering the evidence as a wedge to try to gain a stipulation.

More often, the shoe is on the other foot—the defense is eager to stipulate, if only the evidence will be excluded. This occurs especially where there is no substantial doubt about the proposition that the evidence is purportedly offered to prove but the evidence has great potential prejudicial impact. In such a case, the prosecutor might argue that she should be allowed to prove her case the way she prefers.

The Supreme Court considered the problem in *Old Chief v. United States*, 519 U.S. 172 (1997). Old Chief was arrested after an incident that involved the use of a firearm and charged with assault with a deadly weapon, using a firearm in relation to a crime of violence, and violation of 18 U.S.C. § 922(g)(1). That statute generally prohibits possession of a firearm by anyone with a prior felony conviction—more precisely, by anyone who has been convicted of "a crime punishable by imprisonment for a term exceeding one year." Old Chief had been convicted of assault causing serious bodily injury, a felony. Given the felon-in-possession charge against him, he could not prevent the jury from learning that he had a felony conviction—but naturally, especially given the other charges against him, he was eager to prevent the jury from learning *which* felony. Apart from its bearing on the felon-in-possession charge, the prior crime would have been inadmissible. Accordingly, Old Chief asked the trial court to tell the jury that he had been convicted of a crime punishable by imprisonment exceeding one year—and to bar any other mention of the prior felony. But the prosecutor and the trial judge refused to go along, and the jury learned what felony Old Chief had been convicted of committing.

The Supreme Court declined to hold flatly that a stipulation to the proposition that a piece of evidence is offered to prove deprives the evidence of all probative value. Instead, the decision must be made on the basis of the usual case-by-case weighing of probative value and prejudice. The Court declared that the prosecutor was entitled to tell "a colorful story with descriptive richness" rather than simply accept a stipulation to "an abstract premise." 519 U.S. at 187. "When a juror's duty does seem hard," Justice Souter wrote,

> the evidentiary account of what a defendant has thought and done can accomplish what no set of abstract statements ever could, not just to prove a fact but to establish its human significance, and so to implicate the law's moral underpinnings and a juror's obligation to sit in judgment. Thus, the prosecution may fairly seek to place its evidence before the jurors, as much to tell a story of guiltiness as to support an inference of guilt, to convince the jurors that a guilty verdict would be morally reasonable as much as to point to the discrete elements of a defendant's legal fault.

Id. at 187–88. Furthermore, the prosecutor had to "satisfy the jurors' expectations about what proper proof should be." *Id.* at 188.

But here, the Court held, the prosecution did not need "to tell a continuous story." All that was at stake was the defendant's "legal status," not a part of the narrative of what he did to commit the current offense. The felon-in-possession statute itself made clear that fine distinctions based on the nature of the prior felony did not matter to whether the defendant should be guilty of the present crime. *Id.* at 190–91. Thus, the Court held that when proof of convict status is at issue the nature of the prior conviction generally should be inadmissible. By contrast, "when a defendant seeks to force the substitution of an admission for evidence creating a coherent narrative of his thoughts and actions in perpetrating the offense for which he is being tried," the prosecutor's choice to prove the case her way should "generally survive a Rule 403 analysis." *Id.* at 191–92.

Four justices dissented. They noted that § 922(g) does draw some distinctions among crimes punishable by more than one year's imprisonment—it excludes certain business crimes and state crimes that, while classified as misdemeanors, are subject to punishment of up to two years in prison. Any firearm would do for the felon-in-possession statute, but surely the prosecution, needing evidentiary depth to satisfy the heavy standard of persuasion, was entitled to show what kind of a firearm Old Chief possessed; the same should go for the prior felony, the dissenters argued. Any incremental prejudice resulting from proof of the name or basic nature of the prior felony could be mitigated by limiting instructions. The dissent also argued more broadly that a defendant's strategic decision to agree that the Government need not prove an element of the crime cannot relieve the Government of its burden to prove that element. *Id.* at 192–201 (O'Connor, J., dissenting).[69]

¶ **21.51:** (a) How should *Old Chief* have been decided? Did the Court go too far in allowing defendants to stipulate to a proposition and thereby bar prosecution proof of that proposition? Not far enough? Assuming the court does allow the stipulation, does that remove the element of convict status completely from the jury's consideration? Which party do you think would argue that it does?[70]

(b) Suppose New Chief is accused of having committed theft by picking the lock of a grocery store. The prosecution offers proof that on four other occasions New Chief has committed theft by picking store locks. New Chief objects to the evidence, and the prosecutor contends that she needs the evidence to prove that New Chief has the ability to pick locks. New Chief asks the court to exclude the evidence and instruct the jury that New Chief had the ability to pick locks of the type involved in this case. The prosecutor opposes the request, saying she should be allowed to prove the point her way. How should the court rule? *Cf., e.g., United States v. Crowder,* 141 F.3d 1202 (D.C. Cir. 1998).

---

[69] For comments on *Old Chief,* see, e.g., Todd E. Pettys, Evidentiary Relevance, Morally Reasonable Verdicts, and Jury Nullification, 86 Iowa L. Rev. 467 (2001); James Joseph Duane, *Litigating Felon-with-a-Firearm Cases After* Old Chief, 20 Crim. Justice 18 (1997) (noting that courts differ as to whether stipulation allows court to remove an element of the crime altogether from the jury's consideration); *Screw Your Courage to the Sticking-Place: The Role of Evidence, Stipulations, and Jury Instructions in Criminal Cases,* 49 Hastings L.J. 463 (1998); D. Michael Risinger, *John Henry Wigmore, Johnny Lynn Old Chief, and "Legitimate Moral Force"—Keeping the Courtroom Safe for Heartstrings and Gore,* 49 Hastings L.J. 403(1998).

[70] *See* Duane, *Litigating Felon-with-a-Firearm Cases After* Old Chief, *supra* note 66 (noting varied results in lower courts).

CHAPTER 22

LITIGATING ADMISSIBILITY AND PRESERVING THE RECORD

■ ■ ■

FRE 103, 105

Additional Reading: McCormick, ch. 6, §§ 51–52, 57, 59–60; Mueller & Kirkpatrick, §§ 1.3–.8

If you lose on an evidentiary issue at trial, you may yet win on appeal, though it is difficult to persuade a court to reverse for evidentiary error. Your chances will be much worse if you have not properly preserved the record. Section A of this chapter discusses what the litigant who has unsuccessfully tried to exclude evidence must do. Much the same goes for the litigant who has unsuccessfully attempted to introduce evidence, but that situation also raises some additional issues, which are addressed in Section B. Section C examines particular problems relating to preservation of issues by a criminal defendant who wants to (a) preserve the ability to appeal on the basis of a ruling by the trial court holding evidence impeaching him admissible, but (c) minimize the damage done at trial by such evidence, and yet (c) testify.

A. OBJECTIONS, MOTIONS TO STRIKE, AND MOTIONS TO SUPPRESS

Sometimes, when proffered evidence is of dubious admissibility, or just plain inadmissible, the judge will realize this herself and make a ruling. But you never want to rely on the judge to do your work. If you are against admission of the evidence, you must call the judge's attention to the problem by objecting. If possible, you should make the objection even before the evidence is offered; this is what pretrial suppression motions are all about. A pretrial motion not only ensures that the objection is timely but also helps in trial preparation. For example, in representing a defendant with a criminal record, you will want to know beforehand which, if any, of his prior convictions will be admissible to impeach him if he takes the stand in his own defense. If the judge's answer is "Every last one of them, including the kidnaps and murders," you may decide that the defendant will be wiser not to testify. And it will be helpful to know this before the opening statements.

Sometimes a pretrial motion is not possible, for any of several reasons; most significantly, you may not know that your opponent will ask a particular question until he has done so. In that case, it is important to make the objection before the witness's answer, or other evidence, comes in. If you do not, you may succeed on a motion to strike, and get an instruction to the jurors to disregard what they have just heard, but these are likely to be cold comfort. There is an unfortunate grain of truth in the lawyer's quip that the most significant exception to the rule against hearsay is the quick answer. This puts a premium on your listening ability when your adversary is conducting an examination.

Apart from your desire to win the evidentiary point at trial, there is another, very important reason to make prompt, crisp objections: preservation of the record for appeal. Read FRE 103(a)(1) carefully; it has real teeth in it. The rule provides, in substance, that you cannot win reversal on appeal on the basis that the judge improperly admitted evidence unless the evidence caused some prejudice to your client and you made a timely objection or motion to strike, on the record; what is more, you must state the ground of the objection unless it is clear from the context.

Why is Rule 103(a)(1) so restrictive? This is a "fix it now" rule, similar to the rule on stating objections to questions at deposition, discussed in Section D of Chapter 6. An appellant who is demanding reversal because evidence was improperly admitted is contending in essence that the evidence denied her a fair trial. It is wasteful to reverse for that reason if the appellant could have obviated the problem in the first instance. Thus, the burden is put on him to show that he did everything that could be expected of him to prevent the need for reversal. And this means that he must ensure that the trial judge had a fair chance to understand the issue and rule on it, so that she could fix the problem, if there was one, then and there.

¶ **22.1:** Consider this exchange reported by Professor Frederick Moss:

> Plaintiff's Attorney: The bus ran the red light, didn't it?
>
> Defendant's Attorney: Objection. He's leading the witness, your honor.
>
> Plaintiff's Attorney: The judge is asleep.
>
> Defendant's Attorney: Well, wake him up.
>
> Plaintiff's Attorney: You wake him up. It's your objection!

Was the plaintiff's attorney correct?

No doubt the requirement of a prompt objection or motion to strike sometimes causes unfortunate results—when the failure to make an objection, which was sound but would not have persuaded the trial judge, means that the issue is not considered on appeal—but it gives lawyers a very important incentive to raise objections promptly. Indeed, if the rule were otherwise, lawyers might have an incentive to allow errors to go unnoticed at trial, thus creating opportunities for reversal.

There is an escape valve to Rule 103(a)(1): FRE 103(e) allows the appellate court to take notice of plain errors even though they were not brought to the attention of the court. But this is not a rule on which you want to have to rely. Litigants who have lost at trial often invoke Rule 103(e), but rarely successfully. Appellate courts tend to be eager to affirm trial courts when they can. If they can do so without even considering the merits of an evidentiary dispute because the issue was not properly preserved, they usually will seize the opportunity.

¶ **22.2:** Fendley was tried for tax evasion. One of the prosecution's exhibits was an account record of the insurance company for which Fendley worked. Fendley objected to this document as hearsay. It plainly was hearsay, but the objection was overruled. The document might well have qualified under the business records exception to the hearsay rule if the authenticating witness had testified about the source of the data. No questions on that subject were asked, however, and no mention of the business records doctrine was made at trial. On appeal, should the court consider the question of whether the document was admissible? *See United States v. Fendley*, 522 F.2d 181 (5th Cir.1975) (holding in the negative).

The "timely objects" language of Rule 103(a)(1) contains an interesting ambiguity. Can an objection be too *early* to preserve an issue? The situation may arise this way: The opponent makes a motion, perhaps pretrial, to exclude evidence, and the court denies the motion. When the proponent offers the evidence at trial, the opponent does not object further. The proponent wins at trial, the opponent appeals on the basis of the evidentiary ruling, the proponent contends that the opponent did not preserve the issue for appeal, and the opponent responds, "The judge slapped me down once. Why did I have to get slapped down again?"

Federal courts resolved this situation in different ways, and in 1995 the Advisory Committee for the Federal Rules proposed adding the following subsection to Rule 103:

Effect of Pretrial Ruling. A pretrial objection to or proffer of evidence must be timely renewed at trial unless the court states on the record, or the context clearly demonstrates, that a ruling on the objection or proffer is final.

163 F.R.D. 153. In response to public commentary, the Committee deferred action on the proposal in 1996. The Committee noted that a majority of its members "agreed that a uniform default rule ought to be codified as to whether a pretrial objection to, or proffer of, evidence must be renewed at trial," but there was no consensus as to whether the proposed rule or its opposite—providing that renewal is *not* ordinarily required—is better. 171 F.R.D. 713. When the whole process was done in 2000, the virtually opposite rule was adopted. Rule 103(b) now provides:

> Once the court rules definitively on the record—either before or at trial—a party need not renew an objection or offer of proof to preserve a claim of error for appeal.

¶ 22.3: Assuming the desirability of "a uniform default rule," what do you think the best solution is: The prior proposal? The one that was eventually adopted? Something else? If the court has just ruled against you on an *in limine* objection, and you want to make certain that you have preserved a claim of error for appeal, but you don't want to raise the matter at trial gratuitously (or are afraid you might forget), what might you do now?

When you make an objection, the judge may sustain it, overrule it, or sustain it in part. She may, for example, hold that evidence is admissible for one purpose but not for another.

¶ 22.4: Paley was killed in an auto accident with Daley, and his widow is suing Daley for wrongful death. Apart from Paley and Daley, the only person present at the scene was Whaley. The plaintiff puts Whaley on the stand, and the following exchange occurs.

Q: Who had the green light when Paley drove into the intersection?

A: Daley did.

Q: She did? Didn't you tell me three days after the accident that—

Defense counsel: Objection. Hearsay.

Plaintiff's counsel: Well, we'd better approach. [At sidebar.] Prior inconsistent statement, Your Honor. He told me that Paley had the light.

The Court: OK, you can ask it for impeachment, but not for the truth of the prior statement.

What consequences does the limitation on admissibility have? Do these consequences have any significance?

B. OFFERS OF PROOF

Corresponding to an objection by the opponent of the evidence is the "offer of proof" by the proponent. The offer of proof can have two parts—one to make clear what the evidence would be if it is admitted, and the other to state the grounds as to why it should be admitted. Note that FRE 103(a)(2), the offer of proof's counterpart to Rule 103(a)(1), explicitly refers only to the first part. As with an objection, one purpose for the offer of proof is to try to win the point at trial, and a second is to preserve the record for appeal. The offer is particularly important for the latter purpose. As with an objection, if the offer of proof is not made at trial, the appellate court may believe that the evidentiary point could have been correctly resolved below if counsel had been diligent; accordingly, the appeals judges will be exceedingly reluctant to reverse. More than that, however: If the offer of proof is not made, the appellate court might not even know what the evidence would have been.

¶ 22.5: Penny has sued Denny for failure to pay for merchandise; Denny pleads payment. At trial, Winny, another supplier of Denny, takes the stand for Penny. Her testimony includes the following passage:

Q: Did you have a conversation with Sonny [Denny's buyer] on October 3?

A: Yes, I did.

Q: What did he say in that conversation?

Defense counsel: Objection. Hearsay.

The Court: Sustained.

Plaintiff's counsel: Well, then, I have no further questions of this witness.

Denny wins a verdict, and Penny appeals.

On appeal, Penny contends, "The hearsay ruling was improper because Sonny was Denny's agent, so Sonny's statement was a party admission by an agent under FRE 801(d)(2)(D). The error was critical, because Winny would have testified that Sonny said, 'We can't pay you now, because we owe Penny $10,000.' "

What should the appellate court do? What should Penny's trial counsel have done when Denny's counsel made the objection?

Even if it is clear, from an offer of proof or otherwise, what the evidence would have been, appellate courts may, as in the objection context, be very sticky if at trial the proponent does not assert the proper grounds for admitting the evidence.

¶ 22.6: Huff was driving a White truck-tractor that caught fire after a collision. Huff died of burns nine days later, and his wife sued White for wrongful death, claiming that the fire was the result of defective design of the fuel tank. At trial, White offered Myles' testimony that Huff said, while in the hospital, that just before the collision his pants leg had caught fire, causing him to lose control of the truck. The evidence was hearsay, but White contended that it was admissible as a party admission under FRE 801(d)(2) or under a residual exception to the hearsay rule, FRE 804(b)(5). The trial judge excluded the evidence.

On appeal, White seeks to justify admissibility of Myles' testimony on the additional ground that Huff's assertion was a statement against interest within another hearsay exception, FRE 804(b)(3). Should the appellate court consider this ground?

Note the Seventh Circuit's reasoning on this point:

When an objection identifies the rule of evidence on which admission or exclusion depends, the proponent ordinarily need not do more to preserve error than offer the evidence. But when the objection, hearsay in this case, does not focus on the specific issue presented on review, here the applicability of the statement-against-interest exception, error is not preserved unless the proponent alerts the trial court to that issue. This is in accord with the general principle that to preserve error in a ruling on evidence a party must notify the trial court of his position and the specific rule of evidence on which he relies.

Huff v. White Motor Corp., 609 F.2d 286, 290 n. 2 (7th Cir.1979).

Is this reasoning consistent with that of *Fendley*, in ¶ 22.2? Does it effectively put the opponent of the evidence in a stronger position by making a less precise objection?[1] Or is the governing principle that if you can win by being vague, all to the good, but if you lose you had better be precise?

Often, it will suffice for the lawyer to make an offer of proof by telling the court, at sidebar or during a recess in trial, what the evidence would

---

[1] The Seventh Circuit rejected the argument under FRE 801(d)(2) because Huff's wife, not he, was the party, and the rule does not speak of "privity-based admissions." *See* ¶ 14.47. It held, however, that the evidence was admissible under the residual exception. A cynic might conclude that the court avoided an easy result—a holding under the statement-against-interest exception—because it wanted to write a far-reaching opinion on the residual exception.

be or would have been and why it should be admitted. Sometimes, however, it is advisable to make the offer in question-and-answer form, in which the witness answers the questions for the record, just as if the judge had decided to admit his testimony. For obvious reasons, the offer, in whichever form, must be made out of the hearing of the jury; *see* FRE 103(d).

¶ **22.7:** Same situation as ¶ 22.5, but Winny has not testified; instead, Sonny is testifying for Denny, and has stated that the debt was paid. On cross, Penny's counsel asks, "Did you ever tell anybody that your company owed Penny $10,000?" A hearsay objection is made and sustained. What kind of offer of proof should Penny's counsel make? Why?

Note that FRE 103(b) applies to the unsuccessful proponent of evidence as well as to the unsuccessful opponent: If Rule 103(b) is satisfied, and the court has made a definitive ruling excluding the evidence before trial or otherwise before the time the proponent would actually attempt to introduce it, the proponent need not make a new offer of proof at trial to preserve the issue for appeal.

C. THE *LUCE* PROBLEM

One frequently recurring situation arises this way: A criminal defendant has some prior convictions that will not be admissible if he does not testify but that *might* be admissible, to impeach him, if he does. He therefore makes a pretrial, or *in limine*, motion to suppress the priors. At this point, there are three possible outcomes, to be determined by decisions made, respectively, by the court and the defendant:

(1) The priors are inadmissible, and the defendant testifies.

(2) The priors are admissible to impeach the defendant, but he testifies nevertheless.

(3) The defendant does not testify.

The court denies the motion, so that the defendant is now facing a choice between options (2) and (3). If the priors have significant persuasive value, option (2) might be disastrous for the defendant. But if he takes option (3), declining to testify, can he preserve for appeal the issue of whether he should have had option (1)—that is, whether the priors should have been suppressed?

In *Luce v. United States*, 469 U.S. 38 (1984), interpreting the Federal Rules of Evidence, the Supreme Court held unanimously in the negative. The Court noted that Rule 609(a)(1) requires the trial judge to balance the probative value of prior convictions against their prejudicial impact, and a reviewing appellate court to assess whether the trial judge did that balancing reasonably. Thus, the defendant's decision not to testify deprives the appeals court of the information needed—"the precise nature of the defendant's testimony"—to assess both the correctness of the trial court's evidentiary ruling, and, if it was erroneous, the harmfulness of the error. *Id.* at 41.

¶ 22.8: (a) Are you persuaded by this argument? The argument is based on the perception that, absent the defendant's testimony, it is too difficult to evaluate the admissibility of the priors. But does this fly in the face of the fact that, by hypothesis, it *has* made a ruling on the defendant's motion? Is it significant that such a preliminary ruling by the trial judge is by its nature tentative only, and that if the defendant did actually testify the trial judge could rule that the priors were not admissible after all (though presumably she could not switch the other way), but the appellate court must make a final ruling?

(b) There is an obvious possible solution to the concern about lack of information. If there is really doubt about what the defendant's testimony would have been, the defendant can be required, as a prerequisite for preserving appellate consideration of the issue of the priors, to make an offer of proof of his testimony.[2] But the Court noted that the actual testimony "could, for any number of reasons, differ from the proffer." *Id.* at 41 n.5. What responses might you make to this argument?

The Court also concluded that the harm to the defendant from the Court's *in limine* ruling was "wholly speculative." If the defendant had testified, the trial judge might in the end decide not to allow impeachment by the prior convictions, and the prosecutor might even decide not to use them.

¶ 22.9: Are you persuaded? If you learn of a case in which a prosecutor, having fought and beaten an *in limine* motion to preclude priors, decides after the defendant testifies not to bother using them after all, please send the particulars to the author of this book. A similar request in the second and third editions of this book did not receive any responses. Nor did a similar one made by Professor Duane before an audience of prosecutors.[3] Why do you suppose that is?

The Court further expressed concern about game-playing by defendants. It might be that the defendant would choose not to testify even if the priors were inadmissible; that is, he might prefer option (3) to

---

[2] People v. Finley, 431 Mich. 506, 431 N.W.2d 19, 35 (1988) (opinion of Levin, J.) (concurring in part and dissenting in part).

[3] James Duane, *The Supreme Court Opens a Pandora's Box for Opening the Door in Opening Statements: You Heard it Here First!* (2000), available at https://www.regent.edu/acad/schlaw/faculty_staff/docs/PandorasBox.pdf.

option (1) as well as to option (2). If so, he would be making the motion to suppress for tactical reasons only, in hopes that it would be denied; if it was denied, he would then tell the court that, in light of that ruling, he would not testify, and then he would have a viable issue for appeal. And what if he were cursed by being granted what he asked for—suppression of the convictions? Then the defendant might mumble something to the court about changed trial strategies, thanking Your Honor and sorry to have troubled you, but the defendant has decided not to testify after all.

¶ 22.10: How serious do you find this concern? Perhaps this situation could be avoided if the defendant, before the ruling on the motion to suppress, made a commitment to testify if the motion were granted. In other words, the judge would tell the defendant, in effect, "If you want to preserve the issue for appeal, then you must make a commitment before I rule that if I rule in your favor you will testify." The *Luce* Court dismissed this possibility out of hand, saying that "such a commitment is virtually risk free because of the difficulty of enforcing it." *Id.* at 42. Are you persuaded?

If you are inclined to set up such a commitment procedure, how would you handle the situation in which the court suppresses most, but not all, of the defendant's priors?

Luce was a decision construing the Federal Rules of Evidence. Hence, it is binding in the federal courts only. Several states, and individual judges in some jurisdictions, reject *Luce*, contending that it unnecessarily forces defendants to elect between preserving an important issue for appeal and making the best possible case before the jury in light of the trial judge's ruling.[4] At least one state has an evidentiary rule that is inconsistent with the *Luce* rule.[5] And at least one appears to provide that it is sufficient to preserve the issue if the accused makes an offer of what his testimony would be and makes it clear that his decision to testify

---

[4] *See, e.g.,* Butler v. United States, 688 A.2d 381, 389 (D.C.1996) (Ferren, J., concurring); Commonwealth v. Crouse, 855 N.E.2d 391, 397 (Mass. 2006); State v. Whitehead, 104 N.J. 353, 517 A.2d 373, 376 (N.J. 1986).

[5] Tennessee Rule of Evidence 609(a)(3) provides:

If the witness to be impeached is the accused in a criminal prosecution, the State must give the accused reasonable written notice of the impeaching conviction before trial, and the court upon request must determine that the conviction's probative value on credibility outweighs its unfair prejudicial effect on the substantive issues. The court may rule on the admissibility of such proof prior to the trial but in any event shall rule prior to the testimony of the accused. If the court makes a final determination that such proof is admissible for impeachment purposes, the accused need not actually testify at the trial to later challenge the propriety of the determination.

depends on the court's resolution of the evidentiary issue.[6] But many states have simply gone along with *Luce*.[7]

A further question, assuming the jurisdiction applies *Luce*, is how far its principle should extend. Courts that follow *Luce* have not found troubling the broad idea that it can be applied to impeachment or rebuttal evidence other than evidence of prior convictions.[8] Some courts, however, have imposed limitations on the principle. Chief Justice Burger's opinion for the Court in *Luce* itself suggested in a backhanded way that it might not be applicable to the situation in which the grounds for resisting the rebuttal or impeachment evidence are constitutionally based.[9] It is somewhat mysterious, though, what difference that factor should make. Justice Brennan, while joining the Court's opinion, added a brief concurrence, joined by Justice Marshall, that attempted to justify the distinction and perhaps suggested a broader limiting principle. Where "the determinative question turns on legal and not factual considerations," he wrote, "a requirement that the defendant actually testify at trial to preserve the admissibility issue for appeal might not necessarily be appropriate." He suggested that when the defendant raises a constitutional objection "the appellate court's need to frame the question in a concrete factual context would be less acute" than in the context of Rule 609, 469 U.S. at 44—presumably because broad questions of principle and not merely case-specific balancing would likely be determinative.

---

[6]   Warren v. State, 124 P.3d 522, 527–28 (Nev. 2005). *Warren* relied on the decision of the intermediate appellate court in Wickham v. State, 770 P.2d 757 (Alaska Ct. App. 1989), but that decision was reversed, State v. Wickham, 796 P.d 1354 (Alaska 1990).

[7]   Note the collection of cases going both ways in Warren v. State, 124 P.3d 522, 527 (Nev. 2005). *See also, e.g.,* Wagner v. State, 347 P.3d 109 (Alaska 2015); State v. Duran, 312 P.3d 109 (Ariz. 2013); *cert. denied*, 134 S.Ct. 2679 (2014); Bailey v. United States, 699 A.2d 392 (D.C. Ct. Apps. 1997); Morgan v. State, 891 S.W.2d 733, 735 (Tex.App.1994); People v. Sims, 5 Cal.4th 405, 454–57, 20 Cal.Rptr.2d 537, 567–69, 853 P.2d 992, 1022–24 (Cal. 1993), *cert. denied*, 512 U.S. 1253 (1994).

[8]   *See, e.g.,* Wagner v. State, 347 P.3d 109 (Alaska 2015); State v. Duran, 312 P.3d 109 (Ariz. 2013); *cert. denied*, 134 S.Ct. 2679 (2014); United States v. Sanderson, 966 F.2d 184, 189–90 (6th Cir.1992) (agreeing with four other circuits that "an appeal of a Rule 608(b) ruling is precluded where the defendant did not testify at trial"). In one case, the trial court ruled that testimony by the defendants would allow the Government to introduce evidence of past misconduct, apparently to disprove defense theories of entrapment and lack of knowledge and intent; this evidence would have been admitted during cross-examination and in rebuttal under FRE 404(b) rather than under FRE 608 or 609, because it addressed the defendants' substantive theories rather than their credibility. The defendants did not testify and this evidence was not offered; the appellate court applied *Luce* and held that the propriety of the trial court's ruling was not preserved for appeal. United States v. Johnson, 767 F.2d 1259, 1269–70 (8th Cir.1985).

[9]   *Luce* distinguished cases in which the Court had considered the merits of Fifth Amendment rulings by state courts that had assertedly dissuaded defendants from testifying; there, state procedure had allowed the issue to be preserved without the defendant's testifying. Those cases, said the *Luce* Court, "did not hold that a federal court's preliminary ruling on a question not reaching constitutional dimensions—such as a decision under Rule 609(a)—is reviewable on appeal." 469 U.S. at 42–43.

¶ **22.11:** Amidon is accused of sexual assault. At one point, he reached a plea agreement with the prosecution, and in conjunction with a presentence investigation (PSI) he made a statement to the effect that he and the complainant, with whom he had had an intermittent consensual sexual relationship, had begun necking but then she said she did not want to have sex with him and he "didn't take no for an answer." After reviewing the PSI report, the trial court refused to accept the sentencing recommendation, and Amidon was allowed to withdraw his plea. He made an *in limine* objection to any use at trial of his PSI statement, but the court held that the statement would be admissible for impeachment if he testified contrary to the statement. He did not testify, and the jury found him guilty. He has now appealed, arguing that the trial court's decision about use of the PSI statement violated the state's counterpart to Fed. R. Crim. P. 11 and Fed. R. Evid. 410. The state contends that Amidon failed to preserve the issue because he did not testify. *Amidon* argues that, even if the jurisdiction follows *Luce*, it should not apply, because his argument that the statement was inadmissible depends on a "purely legal question" rather than on "review . . . of a trial court's discretionary decision on a subtle evidentiary question requiring the careful fact-specific weighing of probative value versus prejudicial effect." Is that argument persuasive?[10]

The Supreme Court has extended *Luce* in another dimension, but by a 5–4 vote, in *Ohler v. United States*, 529 U.S. 753 (2000). Suppose a criminal defendant makes an *in limine* motion to exclude evidence of his prior convictions if he testifies, but the court rules that the convictions would be admissible and the defendant decides that it is nevertheless better for him to testify. In this circumstance, it is common practice for the defendant to raise the convictions himself, perhaps in his lawyer's opening statement, perhaps in his own testimony. Doing this, it is often said, can "remove the sting" of the impeachment. Before 1990, it was not clear that the Federal Rules allowed this practice, because Rule 609(a) spoke of certain prior crimes being admissible to impeach a witness "if elicited from the witness or established by public record during cross-examination." Most courts, however, refused to hold that the defendant-witness must ignore the conviction and wait to be impeached with it on cross-examination. In 1990, Rule 609(a) was amended to make clear that the defendant can acknowledge the convictions while he is testifying on

---

[10] State v. Amidon, 967 A.2d 1126 (Vt. 2008) (answering in the affirmative); *see also, e.g.,* People v. Brown, 42 Cal.App.4th 461, 468–71 (Cal.App.4th Dist.1996) (holding in the affirmative and citing cases going both ways in similar situations), *review denied* (Cal. Apr. 25, 1996); *but see, e.g.,* State v. Duran, 312 P.3d 109 (Ariz. 2013); *cert. denied,* 134 S.Ct. 2679 (2014).

direct. But now suppose that the defendant does so, is then convicted, and wants to appeal on the basis that the priors should not have been admissible. The prosecutor contends, "You can't appeal because of that— *you* introduced the evidence." The defendant responds, "But only because you won on the *in limine* motion and you would have introduced it if I hadn't." To which the prosecutor replies, "Who says I would have? Just as in *Luce*, maybe in the end I would have decided not to, because if I thought our case looked strong I wouldn't have wanted to take a chance of introducing reversible error, and maybe the court would have decided not to let me." A bare majority of the Supreme Court took the prosecutor's position.

¶ **22.12:** (a) Do you think the majority reached the right result?

(i) Consider Chief Justice Rehnquist's argument for the majority that to allow the defendant to introduce the conviction and then appeal on that basis would deny the prosecution "its usual right to decide, after she testifies, whether or not to use her prior conviction against her." 529 U.S. at 758. Are you persuaded?

(ii) Consider the argument made by Justice Souter in dissent: "The jury may feel that in testifying without saying anything about the convictions the defendant has meant to conceal them." *Id.* at 764. Given that the defendant is fighting tooth and nail to exclude the convictions from evidence, isn't it very true that the defendant has meant to conceal them?

(b) Would a rule along these lines be a plausible compromise? When a witness has otherwise concluded giving direct testimony, the party that called her to the stand may ask the opposing party out of the hearing of the jury to state a "final answer" as to whether that party wishes to introduce character impeachment evidence, and may ask the court for a final ruling as to whether such evidence would be admissible. If the answer to both questions is in the affirmative, then before concluding direct testimony the witness may acknowledge the prior convictions or other impeaching facts.

Reaction to *Ohler* in the state courts has been predominantly hostile, unusually so for a decision of the United States Supreme Court.[11]

---

[11] Cases declining to follow *Ohler* include Cure v. State, 26 A.3d 899 (Md. 2011) (noting, *id.* at 908, that "[t]he majority of state appellate courts to consider the issue, after *Ohler*, rejected the reasoning of the *Ohler* Majority"); State v. Swanson, 707 N.W.2d 645 (Minn. 2006); State v. Thang, 41 P.3d 1159 (Wash. 2002); State v. Keiser 807 A.2d 378 (Vt. 2002); *State v. Daly*, 623 N.W.2d 799 (Iowa 2001).

For a comprehensive (and critical) analysis of the case, see L. Timothy Perrin, *Pricking Boils, Preserving Error: On the Horns of a Dilemma After Ohler v. United States*, 34 U.C. Davis L.Rev. 615, 617 (2001).

INDEX

References are to Pages